The BROWN SCAPULAR *of* OUR LADY *of* MOUNT CARMEL
Authenticity and Definitive Proof

The Validity of the Visions of the Mother of God to St. Simon Stock and Pope John XXII

Rosalia Vitale Kehrig

A STUDY OF THE
BROWN SCAPULAR DEVOTION
OF OUR LADY OF MOUNT CARMEL

THE VALIDITY OF THE VISIONS
OF THE MOTHER OF GOD TO ST. SIMON STOCK
AND TO POPE JOHN XXII

By Rosalia Vitale Kehrig

Library of Congress Number 2017954109

Published by:
    Queenship Publishing
    P.O. Box 220
    Goleta, CA 93116
    (800) 647-9882 • (805) 692-0043 • Fax: (805) 967-5133
    www.queenship.org

Printed in the United States of America

ISBN: 978-1-57918-456-1

DEDICATION

The gift of a mother is a great blessing from the hand of God. A mother is friend, a companion, a protector and nurturer – one who guides you all through your earthly life and prepares you for the life to come. So it was with my earthly mother. It was from her hand that I received the Rosary as a small child, learned to wear the Scapular and was taught the simplest rules to get to Heaven. It was from the heart of my earthly mother that I learned to love the Mother of God, the ultimate Mother whose love for us knows no bounds.

Mom, you have now passed into eternity, thank you for what you have taught me in my life, for your great gift of faith and for entrusting me to my heavenly Mother Mary, my friend, my constant companion in life, my protector and nurturer and my heavenly guide — the one who prepares me for the life to come and to whom I am dedicating this book.

Thank you for being my mother, Mary, for placing me under your mantle of protection, for coming to my aid in the midst of my trials and for loving me with an unconditional love that only a true mother can provide.

With your Scapular, Mother Mary, I know I will see you someday and be with you forever. Thank you for the love you have given me, the graces you have accorded me throughout my life and the abundant blessings that have come to me through your powerful intercession

Our Lady of Mount Carmel, Mother of the Brown Scapular and Queen of the Most Holy Rosary, pray for us now and at the hour of our death.

TABLE OF CONTENTS

FOREWORD

In reciting the Hail Mary, we ask the Blessed Mother to pray for us now and at the hour of our death. Mary is "our Mother in the order of grace" as Vatican II so beautifully puts it (Lumen Gentium, 61). As a true Mother, our Lady constantly intercedes for us not only at the moment of death but even after death if we need purification for our sins. In his 2002 Apostolic Letter, St. John Paul II writes that Mary "is 'all-powerful by grace', to use the bold expression, which needs to be properly understood, of Blessed Bartolo Longo in his Supplication to Our Lady. This is a conviction which, beginning with the Gospel, has grown ever more firm in the experience of the Christian people" (n. 16). Mary's power of intercession is, of course, dependent on the power of God, but as "our Mother in the order of grace" she has been given the special privilege of helping lead souls out of purgatory into the divine light of Heaven.

The Brown Scapular of Our Lady of Mount Carmel is a special sign of Mary's maternal protection for the faithful as they face death and prepare for God's judgment. The Sabbatine Privilege, which is intimately associated with the Brown Scapular, affirms Mary's special intercessory power for those who have died in the state of grace but still need purification before entering into heaven. If Mary is "our Mother in the order of grace" it only makes sense that she would care for her children who need to undergo post-mortem purification. When Our Lord was dying on the Cross of Calvary, He gave Mary as "mother" to the beloved disciple and to all the faithful (Jn 19:26-27). At this sacred moment, the Mother of Christ was "given as mother to every single individual and to all mankind" (John Paul II, Redemptoris Mater, 23). The brown scapular is a concrete sign of trust in the Mother of Christ who is our mother.

Unfortunately many Catholic sources today—some by otherwise reliable scholars—have tried to dismiss the historicity of the traditions that establish devotion to the Brown Scapular and the Sabbatine Privilege. Our Lady of Mt. Carmel, though, appeared to St. Simon Stock in 1251 holding the scapular and saying: "This is a privilege for you and your order: whoever dies wearing this Scapular will be saved." Some 71 years later our Lady of Mt. Carmel appeared to Pope John XXII, who issued a Bull in 1322 establishing the "Sabbatine Privilege." This Privilege affirms that the Virgin will deliver from Purgatory—especially on the first Saturday (Sabbatum) after death—the souls of those who observed chastity according to their state, recited certain prayers, and wore the habit [or scapular] of Carmel. Between 1530 and 1664 eight different popes affirmed the authenticity of the 1322 Sabbatine Bull. Over the last 100 years, numerous popes—including Benedict XV, Pius XI, Pius XII, St. John XXIII, Blessed Paul VI, and St. John Paul II—have encouraged the faithful to wear the brown scapular.

This book, *The Brown Scapular of Our Lady of Mount Carmel, Authenticity and Definitive Proof*, by Mrs. Kehrig, is a beautiful witness to the spiritual fruitfulness of the Brown Scapular. It is a testimony of love for Our Lady of Mount Carmel and her Scapular. As we move toward the 100th anniversary of the apparitions of Fatima, it's important to recall that Our Lady of Fatima was seen as Our Lady of Mount Carmel. There is a clear unity between the Rosary and the Scapular. Both are signs of Mary's maternal protection for her beloved children. In these days of doubt and darkness, the Brown Scapular is a sure sign that our heavenly Mother will never abandon us in this life or the next.

Robert L. Fastiggi, Ph.D.
Professor of Systematic Theology
Sacred Heart Major Seminary
Detroit, Michigan USA

PREFACE

There is no fruit of grace in the history of salvation that does not have as its necessary instrument, the mediation of Our Lady.

(Homily of Pope Benedict XVI at the Canonization Mass of Fr. Antonio de Sant'Ana Galvão, O.F.M., Brazil, May 11, 2007)

Oh Beautiful Flower of Carmel, most Fruitful Vine,
Splendor of Heaven, holy and singular, who
Brought forth the Son of God, still ever remaining
A Pure Virgin, assist me in this necessity.

Oh Star of the Sea, help and protect me!
Show me that thou art my Mother.
(Prayer of St. Simon Stock to Our Lady)

Mary, Queen of Heaven, Mother of the Divine Savior is the most breathtaking flower of all creation. She is the highest of all of God's creatures: the Mother of Mankind, Queen of the Universe, of Angels and of Men and Mother of Mercy. Above all, she is the Mother of God: *Theotokos* (Council of Ephesus, 431 AD). Exalted by Him from all Eternity, she became the Tabernacle of the Most High, carrying the Lamb of God in her most pure and virginal womb. *She is called "Full of Grace" as to herself, for she had an immense grace, one which was sufficient, and corresponded with her immense dignity, so much so that it fitted her to be the "Mother of God"* (The Glories of Mary, St. Alphonsus Liguori, 1977, p. 290)

At the Marriage Feast of Cana, with a whisper in the ear of her Divine Son, she obtained for the guests, His miraculous powers, of which they were so much in need. It was at that moment that she became *Mediatrix* and *Intercessor* for all humanity and gently gave the command: *Do whatever He tells you.* (John 2:5) *For She being obedient, became a cause of salvation for herself and the whole human race.* (St. Irenaeus, *Vatican II Marian Council*, Fr. William Most, p. 10) Mary gave up her mother's rights over her Son to procure the salvation of mankind. *One can truly affirm that together with Christ, She has redeemed the human race.* (Pope Benedict XV, *Inter Sodalicia*,

May 22, 1918, AAS 10,182; Ibid, p. 18)

Whoever considers the height of dignity to which God has raised the most August Virgin Mary, will easily perceive how important it is both for the public and private good, that devotion to her should be assiduously practiced and daily promoted more and more. (Pope Leo XIII Encycl. *Augustissimae,* September 12, 1897)

From the numerous approved apparitions of Our Blessed Lady after her Assumption into Heaven sprang many beautiful titles under which she is invoked and many popular devotions under which she is honored. *In the first rank of the most favored of these devotions, that of the Holy Carmelite Scapular must be placed.* Pope Pius XII, Letter: *For the occasion of the Seventh Centenery of the Brown Scapular,* February 11, 1950. The apparition of Our Lady to St. Simon Stock on July 16, 1251 gave birth to the Scapular Devotion of Our Lady of Mt. Carmel. Holding the habit of the Order in her hands, she gave a pledge and a promise that *Whosoever dies wearing this (Scapular) shall not suffer eternal fire.* (*Your Brown Scapular,* Most Rev. E.K. Lynch, O.Carm., 1950, p. 10)

The Scapular is a visible sign of our consecration to her Immaculate Heart. It is a sign of her love, protection and powerful intercession for the salvation of souls: a badge that identifies us as her special adopted children, a symbol of the pact of love between a mother and child.

Many of the Blessed Saints in Heaven, many Popes and even members of the households of royal families deeply embraced the devotion and wore the Scapular affectionately and faithfully over their hearts. God has confirmed this Devotion through the approbation and confirmation of many Solemn Pontiffs over the centuries including Pope John Paul II as well as the authoritative confirmation of the Church; many countless documented miracles have been attributed to this visible sign of our consecration and our protection.

Therefore, brethren, stand fast and uphold the traditions which you have learned, whether by word or by our epistle. (2 Thess. 2:15, D.R. *Douay Rheims*).

The tradition of the Church is full of various titles under which the intercessory power of the Blessed Virgin Mary may be invoked. This book is concerned with one of these titles and according to Church tradition is one of the most glorious of all: *Our Lady of Mt. Carmel.*

The Brown Scapular of Our Lady of Mount Carmel, Authenticity and Definitive Proof, is a timely, concise and balanced presentation of the Origins of the Scapular Devotion, its basis and its foundation. It consists of a compilation of historical documentation, Papal approbation and eye-witness accounts of the authenticity and historicity of the Scapular Devotion of Our Lady of Mount Carmel, from the formation of the Order on Mount Carmel in Palestine 900 years before the birth of Christ continuing to the present day.

During my years as President of the Holy See's Pontifical Council for the Family, I was privileged to work with the Eternal Life Apostolate in Bardstown, Kentucky co-founded by Fr. John A. Hardon and Mr. William J. Smith. Through Mr. Smith, I was introduced to the Marian Catechist and author of this Study, Rosalia Kehrig and soon after became her Spiritual Director for this endeavor.

It is with great joy and thanksgiving to Almighty God and to Our Blessed Mother, that I bestow my blessings upon this book: *The Brown Scapular of Our Lady of Mount Carmel, Authenticity and Definitive Proof.* As a child, I was attentive to the words of the parish priest on the importance of wearing the livery of Our Lady, which carries the promise of eternal salvation. I was privileged to be enrolled in the Scapular Confraternity during my school years. I now carry close to my heart the Scapular I obtained at Mount Carmel in Palestine during a trip to the Holy Land over ten years ago.

It is my humble prayer that those who are inspired to read this scholarly work on the Brown Scapular will be moved to heed the words of Our Lady of Mt. Carmel. May you always remain close to the heart of her Divine Son and grow deeper in love with the one who is the joy of my heart, Mary, the Mother of God.

July 16, 2007
Feast of Our Lady of Mount Carmel

+ Edouard Cardinal Gagnon p. p.s.

+ Edouard Cardinal Gagnon, P. S. S

ACKNOWLEDGMENTS

The Late **Father John A. Hardon, S. J.**, Master Teacher, Theologian, Catechist and Author of numerous publications and Assistant to the Holy See for 33 years, for initiating this research in 1999 and for his direction, encouragement, his sufferings and for his undying love and fidelity to Christ, His Church and His most Beloved Mother Mary.

With eternal gratitude to His Eminence, **Emeritus Francis Cardinal Arinze**, who, then Prefect of the Congregation for Divine Worship and the Discipline of Sacraments (in the year 2005) appointed his assistant and collaborator, Monsignor Gerard Njen to supervise, guide and sustain this research on the Study of the Brown Scapular of Our Lady of Mount Carmel.

His Eminence, the late **Edouard Cardinal Gagnon, P.S.S.**, the first Spiritual Director of this Scapular Study, for all of his guidance, Spiritual Direction and support of this Scapular Research, for his Preface to the book and for all of his prayers and sacrifices which have helped to make this work a reality.

His Eminence, **The Most Rev. Raymond Leo Cardinal Burke**, Patron of the Sovereign Militatry Order of Malta and International Director of the Marian Catechist Apostolate, for his direction and guidance, his fidelity to the Church and the Magisterium and for his gracious assistance and support of "A Study of the Scapular Devotion of Our Lady of Mount Carmel."

My Spiritual Father and current Spiritual Director of *The Brown Scapular of Our Lady of Mount Carmel, Authenticity and Definitive Proof*, **Archbishop Emeritus Dom Vitorio Pavanello**, formerly of the Archdiocese of Campo Grande, Brazil, (with his story of the Drums and the Bells) for his direction, guidance, assistance, his compassion and prayers and for his video-taped interview on Devotion to Our Blessed Mother.

My Spiritual Mother, **Mother Lodovica Pellegrini**, Foundress of the Oblate Sisters of the Immaculate Heart of Mary in Rome, Italy, (*Suore Oblate del Cuore Immacolato di Maria*) and all of the Sisters, who so generously and graciously and in humble charity, opened their arms and their hearts to us and heroically assisted both physically and spiritually with all aspects of this Scapular Study. Without the Sisters, this book could not have come to fruition.

Fr. Douglas Terrien, Pastor of Immaculate Conception Church, Lapeer, Michigan (the author's Parish) for his great generosity, his continual support and encouragement of this research project, and for his zealous devotion to the Mother of God especially under the title of Our Lady of Mount Carmel.

Mother Mary John Hennessey, my dear friend and Spiritual Sister in Christ, for her valuable insights into the mind of the Scapular Devotion, for her true devotion to the Mother of God and for her courage and deep commitment to spreading the Scapular Devotion in the world.

Fr. Ladis Cizik, who with great love and devotion to the most Holy Mother of God, opened his heart and his home to the work of *The Brown Scapular of Our Lady of Mount Carmel, Authenticity and Definitive Proof* and assisted with materials, information and continual prayers.

Don Massimo Consolaro, former Chaplain of the *Suore Oblate* in Rome, now Pastor of the Church of St. Louis Gonzaga, Focene, Fiumicino, Italy, for video-taped interviews on Devotion to the Mother of God and other extremely helpful assistance to the Author while in Rome.

Fr. Richard Souilliere for his kindness and charity his prayers and sacrifices and his life long efforts to help spread deep devotion to Our Blessed Mother under the title of Our Lady of Mount Carmel.

Fr. John Simoneau, for his courage and fortitude in accessing pivotal information on the Brown Scapular in Europe, not accessible to the laity and for his willingness to patiently assist with the difficult aspects of the research, in interpreting, and translating and in providing transportation in Europe.

Professor Robert Fastiggi, Ph.D, Professor of Systematic Theology, Sacred Heart Seminary, Detroit, Michigan, for his kindness and charity in arriving with outstretched arms in service to Our Lady, for the countless hours of translations of the Latin, Spanish, Italian and French portions of the research and for his love and dedication to Our Blessed Mother, most especially to Our Lady of Mt. Carmel and her Holy Scapular.

Anne Simoneau, artist and traveling companion, my family, friend and my Spiritual Sister in Christ, for all of her beautiful and creative art illustrations in this book, which graciously adorn the majesty of Our Lady of Mt. Carmel and her Devotion, but most of all for her patient assistance, advice, her encouragement and her colossal faith.

Aileen O'Sullivan, my dear friend, who traveled several times from Ireland and England to Rome and to the United States, to assist in providing diverse publications and informational pamphlets used in this Study of the Brown Scapular Devotion. Aileen was privileged to work for 20 years with the Carmelite Prior General Kilian Lynch and his brothers at the Scapular Shrine in Aylesford, England. One of the tasks that she was given was that of attending to the relics of St Simon Stock that had, at that time been recently returned to England from the place of his burial in Bordeaux, France, in 1951.

John Mathias Haffert, for the wonderful contribution of his book in 1942: *Mary in Her Scapular Promise* and for resurrecting and reviving the love, knowledge and devotion to the Brown Scapular of Our Lady of Mount Carmel as the voice of the Scapular world-wide in the 20th Century.

Pat Haffert, spouse of John Mathias Haffert, whom the author had the privilege of meeting in New Jersey, several years ago; for her genuine kindness, charity and continual prayers in assisting this author to continue the important work of spreading the Scapular Devotion through this Study, for the glory of God and for the salvation of souls.

Julia Ceravalo, my dear friend and Sister in Christ, Italian interpreter on the first trip to Rome, without whose expertise, the greatest resources regarding this work would not have been obtained in Rome and for her continual prayers.

Elias Arnaout, Computer Engineer for the tireless hours of dedication to editing, organizing, digitizing, scanning and preparing for publication into disc form the research of the Devotion to the Brown Scapular of Our Lady of Mt. Carmel and for his continual patient computer assistance in Europe and in the U.S. with the development and conclusion of this book.

Lon Rinn, owner of Zip Nerdz and Biz Card Group, a genius of a young man, who assisted the author with technical support, for his continual patience and kindness in helping with the preparation of this book and for his great faith in God and love for Our Dear Mother Mary.

Denis Duggan, Technical Engineer, for his kind and untiring patient assistance with the resolution and editing of the electronic files of the book, and for his tremendous faith and love for Our Blessed Mother and for Holy Mother Church.

In memory of **John Marzolf** and with sincere and tremendous gratitude to his wife, Donna for her generous and charitable contribution for the publication of the book and her undying love for Our Lady of Mt. Carmel and her Brown Scapular.

To my precious daughter, **Jacinta** who is named after the little seer of Fatima, for her love and support, her wisdom and tremendous insights, for her continued love and dedication to Our Blessed Mother and Holy Mother Church, and to all my wonderful children, Michael, Maria, Anthony, Genevieve, Rosalie, Jacinta and their families, I love you very much.

Finally, in memory of my beloved husband **Michael Kehrig** who passed away on November 2, 2015. A faithful member of the Men of the Sacred Hearts, whose love for Our Blessed Mother, the Holy Rosary and the Brown Scapular knew no bounds, had waited so patiently for the publication of this book before his death. His enduring love and patient assistance from Heaven continue still and has made this book a reality. I love you and thank you with all of my heart, until we meet again in Heaven.

WITH ETERNAL GRATITUDE TO:

His Eminence, Emeritus Francis Cardinal Arinze, who, then Prefect of the Congregation for Divine Worship and the Discipline of Sacraments (in the year 2005) appointed his assistant and collaborator, Monsignor Gerard Njen to supervise, direct and sustain this research on the *The Brown Scapular of Our Lady of Mount Carmel, Authenticity and Definitive Proof.*

His Eminence, the late Edouard Cardinal Gagnon, P.S.S., the first Spiritual Director of this Scapular Study, for all of his guidance, Spiritual Direction and support of this Scapular Research, for his Preface to the book and for all of his prayers and sacrifices which have helped to make this work a reality.

His Eminence, The Most Rev. Raymond Leo Cardinal Burke, Patron of the Sovereign Military Order of Malta and International Director of the Marian Catechist Apostolate, for his direction and guidance, his fidelity to the Church and the Magisterium and for his gracious assistance and support of *The Brown Scapular of Our Lady of Mount Carmel, Authenticity and Definitive Proof.*

WITH GENUINE LOVE AND HEARTFELT APPRECIATION TO:

LE SUORE OBLATE DEL CUORE IMMACOLATO DI MARIA, ROME, ITALY

(THE OBLATE SISTERS OF THE IMMACULATE HEART OF MARY)

The Oblate Sisters of the Immaculate Heart of Mary, in Rome, Italy, is a Community of Sisters whose Charism is Perpetual Adoration, Pastoral work, Catechesis and the diffusion of the Fatima Message throughout the world. The author was truly privileged and blessed to have been received by the Sisters in Rome, thirteen years ago, and to have returned there for several years afterward to continue the research for this book: *The Brown Scapular of Our Lady of Mount Carmel, Authenticity and Definitive Proof.* It is because of their support, assistance, overwhelming kindness and the loving shelter they provided that this book was brought into existence.

To my wonderful Spiritual Mother and Foundress of the Oblate Sisters of the Immaculate Heart of Mary, Mother Lodovica Pellegrini, to the benevolent new Mother of the Community, Mother Deo Gratias, to Sister Gemma, Sister Lourdes, Sister Benedetta, Sister Rosaria and to all of the wonderful Sisters in Rome and in Turin who assisted the author and her companions both physically and spiritually in the formation and the completion of this Scapular research project, thank you for all you have done. May God Bless you, and May Our Dear Mother of Mount Carmel reward you abundantly for your tremendous love, your extraordinary charity, and your undying devotion to the Immaculate Heart of Mary and her Son, Jesus. You are always in my prayers and forever in my heart.

Pope Pius XII wrote: *May the Scapular be a sign to them (all who wear it) of their consecration to the Most Pure Heart of the Immaculate Virgin, which in recent times We have so strongly recommended.* Pius XII, Letter *Neminem profecto latet* [11 February 1950: *AAS* 42, 1950, pp. 390-391]

Translator:
Professor Robert L. Fastiggi

Robert Fastiggi Ph.D. is Professor of Systematic Theology at Sacred Heart Major Seminary in Detroit, MI. USA where he's been since 1999. From 1985–1999, he taught at St. Edward's University in Austin, Texas. He holds an A.B. from Dartmouth College and an M.A. and Ph.D. in Theology from Fordham University. In addition to his own publications, he is the co-editor of the English translation of the 43rd edition of the Denzinger-Hünermann *Enchirdion symbolorum* (Ignatius Press, 2012) and the executive editor of the 2009–2013 supplements to the *New Catholic Encyclopedia* (Gale Cengage Learning in cooperation with the Catholic University of America). Dr. Fastiggi was elected president of the Mariological Society of America in 2014 for a two year term (2014–2016). He and his wife, Kathleen, have been married since 1984 and are parents of three children: Mary, Anthony and Clare.

With deepest and sincere appreciation to Professor Fastiggi for the countless hours of translations of the French, Latin, Spanish and Italian excerpts of the book, for his tremendous patience and gracious support of this research, but most importantly for his deep love and devotion to the Mother of God and his dedication to the education of the Catholic faith. May God Bless you for your fidelity to Holy Mother the Church and May our Dear Mother of Mount Carmel guide and protect you and the future priests that you instruct for the salvation of souls.

Artist:
Anne Marie Simoneau

Anne Marie Simoneau is a free-lance artist of "Religious Themes." Her education in the field of Art was initiated at Cass Tech, Detroit, Michigan, after which she received a scholarship at Columbus College of Art and Design in Columbus Ohio to continue her training there. She is the designer of major billboards found along the roadways across the State of Michigan and served in the area of advertising for a local distributer. The inspiration for her artwork was drawn from the heart of family life. She is the creator of "Rosebuds," an art strip for the *Detroit Free Press* Newspaper and for a dozen other newspaper and magazine publications throughout the country. She is the artistic designer of magnificent murals found in Holy Family Church in downtown Detroit, and in Sts. Cyril and Methodius Church in Sterling Heights, Michigan. Anne is the Illustrator of several Byzantine clip art books for the Religious Order, the Brazilians, located in Detroit. She was the artist for the 2007 Calendar edition for the Eternal Life Apostolate based in Bardstown, Kentucky and illustrated the cover of "Meditations on the Angels," by Fr. John A. Hardon. Her artistic designs have adorned the pages of Catholic Church Bulletins through Parish Publications not only locally, but throughout the country as well. One of her greatest artistic accomplishments is the illustration of two Byzantine-Ukrainian and English Prayer Missals, with over 500 illustrations contained in each book. At present, she is the Illustrator of many Catholic books and Periodicals and is the central artist for the current book, *The Brown Scapular of Our Lady of Mount Carmel, Authenticity and Definitive Proof.*

She and her husband Gerald have been married for 45 years, and are the proud parents of six children: Therese, Marie, John, Margaret, Katie and Joe, and the proud grandparents of 30 grandchildren. With sincere gratitude to my family member, my friend, and my dearest "Sister in Christ," Anne Simoneau whose love and devotion for Our Blessed Mother resounds powerfully through the artistic strokes of her brush seen throughout the deeply inspiring works of art in this book. Thank you for your patience, for your selfless assistance, for your majestic works of art, but most of all for your love of Our Lady and Her Son, reflected in the beautiful images so graciously designed as a powerful means of the inspiration and transmission of the Faith.

My Dear Brothers and Sisters in Christ,

In the "Dogmatic Constitution on the Church," *Lumen Gentium,*" The Sacred Synod exhorted that the Liturgical Cult of the Blessed Virgin be generously promoted, and in a special way, the practices and devotions recommended by the Magesterium of the Church. Afterwards, during the Marian Congress in 1965, held at Santo Domingo, Pope Paul VI had confirmed the words of the Sacred Synod saying:

"It is our conviction that the Rosary of Mary and the Scapular of Mount Carmel are among the recommended practices."

This letter refers to the Scapular of Mount Carmel. The Scapular has been, for centuries, one of the most acclaimed devotions in the Church, and has been richly endowed with numerous indulgences. When I was in Rome, I examined a scholarly work. It is a presentation, greatly detailed on the origin and history of the Scapular Devotion, which is rooted in the Old Testament entitled:

"A Study of Scapular Devotion of Our Lady of Mount Carmel: The Validity of the Visions of the Mother of God to St. Simon Stock and to Pope John XXII."

I met the author of this work, Mrs. Rosalia Kehrig, nine years ago in Rome; she is a Marian Catechist, dedicated and committed to inspiring and educating others with a profound knowledge of true devotion to Jesus through His Holy Mother Mary. The Scapular of Mount Carmel is a sacramental of the Church, and an external sign of our consecration to the Mother of God.

"Devotion to the Blessed Virgin is a privileged means of finding Jesus Christ perfectly, of loving Him tenderly and of serving Him faithfully." (Letter, Pope John Paul II, *"True Devotion to Mary Leads us closer to Jesus,"* December 8, 2003, to the Montfort religious family on the occasion of the 160th anniversary of the publication on the *"Treatise on True Devotion to the Blessed Virgin Mary,"* written by St. Louis Marie Grignon de Montfort, n. 62.)

As Spiritual Director of Mrs. Rosalia Kehrig's work entitled: "A Study of the Devotion of Our Lady of Mount Carmel," I completely support and confirm the validity and authenticity of this timely presentation.

I recommend wholeheartedly the practice of the devotion to the Brown Scapular of Our Lady of Mount Carmel as a means of obtaining the intercession of Our Blessed Mother for our eternal salvation.

Devotedly yours in the Hearts of Jesus and Mary,

The Most Reverend Dom Vitorio' Pavanello,
Archbishop Emeritus of the Archdiocese of Campo Grande, Brazil

Above is an ancient depiction of the Carmelite Symbol, or Ensignia, originally discovered in a book about the life of St. Albert, Carmelite in 1499. A mountain painted in brown, with rounded sides, its tip reaching to the sky refers to Mount Carmel, the place of origin of the Carmelites. Three stars each with six points, one colored silver at the center of the mountain and the other two colored gold are placed symmetrically in the heavens, colored white on either side of the mountain. The lower star represents Carmelites still on the way to the top of Mount Carmel, while the other two stars higher up represent Carmelites who have ended their journey "by reaching the top of the holy Mountain." (Carmelite Missal, 1980, Opening Prayer on the Solemnity of the Bl. Virgin Mary of Mount Carmel.) The crown of gold represents the Kingdom of God. {Carmelites} see their vocation as calling to "implant and strengthen the Kingdom of Christ in souls and to spread it to the four corners of the earth." (Carmelite Constitutions no. 5) In offering this service to God, Carmelites take their inspiration from Elijah the Prophet and Mary the Virgin. (cf. Carmelite Constitutions no. 25) (http://ocarm.org/en/content/ocarm/shield.)

INTRODUCTION

The Brown Scapular of Our Lady of Mount Carmel, Authenticity and Definitive Proof, is an historic overview of the origins and promises that became the basis of the Devotion. Through this research, the author acquired a basic understanding of the origin of the Brown Scapular Devotion of Our Lady of Mt. Carmel, as well as its oppositions and defenses throughout the centuries, from numerous publications and Pontifical Bulls discovered in the libraries in Rome, Italy.

Besides gathering information for the Study, the author traveled extensively to different locations in Italy and Sicily in search of the historicity of the Devotion and the documented miracles attached to the Scapular promises. Ancient paintings depicting authentic Pontifical Bulls issued in the early Centuries regarding the Scapular Devotion and its Privileges were also discovered in the cities of Palermo and Corleone, Sicily.

Libraries accessed to gather information on the Brown Scapular Devotion, its origin and history, were:

1. The Vatican Library, Vatican City

2. The Teresianum Library, Rome, Italy

3. The Pontifical North American College, Rome, Italy

4. The Pontifical Gregorian University, Rome, Italy

5. The College of Saint Albert, Rome, Italy

6. The Marian Library at University of Dayton, Dayton, Ohio, USA

Also accessed was the "Osservatore Romano" Office in Vatican City.

Cities visited to gather information on Incorrupt Scapular Miracles and information on the Scapular Devotion were:

1. Turin, Italy for the Incorrupt Scapular of St. John Bosco

2. Marianella, Naples, for the Incorrupt Scapular of St. Alphonsus di Liguori

3. Arezzo, Italy, Museum for the Incorrupt Scapular of Pope Gregory X

4   Palermo, Sicily for the famous painting depicting the Brown Scapular Devotion by Thomas De Vigilia, based on the Pontifical Bulls issued at the time

5   Corleone, Sicily, for the authentic painting by the same author

A number of telephone conversations was conducted to England, Ireland and Italy, with written communication to Spain, as well as videotaped interviews on Marian Devotion with the following:

1   Archbishop Emeritus, Dom Vitorio Pavanello, former Metropolitan Archbishop of Campo Grande, Brazil and current Spiritual Director for "A Study of the Brown Scapular Devotion of Our Lady of Mount Carmel."

2   Don Massimo Consolaro, former Chaplain of the *Suore Oblate del Cuore Immacolato di Maria,* in Rome, now Pastor of Parrochia San Luigi Gonzaga, of the Diocesi Suburbicaria di Porto-Santa Rufina, located in Focene, Fiumicino.

3   Professor William Giordano, Wayne State University, MI, U.S.A.

4   Aileen O'Sullivan, originally from Ireland. She is the last surviving Third Order Carmelite to have worked in Aylesford, England during the Restoration of the Carmelite Monastery in 1949. She worked with Fathers Kilian, Malachi, and Elias Lynch and had the care of the relics of St. Simon Stock which were returned to Ayelsford in 1951.

5   Fr. John Wadell, from (Mallorca), Spain, who helped to procure documentation in the pursuit of the authenticity of the Scapular Visions with his written assistance.

This Study was initially begun for the sole purpose of producing an updated version of the videotape: "Stories of the Brown Scapular," originally produced by Fr. Howard Rafferty, O. Carm., in the 20th century. This videotape is no longer in production or available to the public. It was Fr. Howard Rafferty who in 1950, had the privilege of interviewing Sr. Lucia, the surviving visionary of the Fatima Apparitions in 1917 and questioned her regarding the apparition of Our Lady of Mt. Carmel, holding in her hand the Brown Scapular during the Miracle of the Sun, October 13, 1917.

This study of the Scapular Devotion presents a balanced overview of the objections and the defense of the Devotion, as well as a variety of references, resources, historical evidence, documented miracles, eye-witness testimony and authentic Pontifical Documents, authorizing the erection of Scapular Confraternities throughout the world and promulgating this Devotion. These Pontifical Documents officially affirm, confirm and verify the authenticity of the Scapular Visions of Our Lady to both St. Simon Stock and to Pope John XXII.

It is my hope that this Study may help to revitalize an ancient Devotion, once revered and practiced all over the world and that this research may humbly assist in the universal springtime of Marian Devotion. It is my hope as well, that all those who read this work may come to see what has been clearly revealed in the unspoken words of this text: that Our Lady, through the power given to her by Almighty God, is one of the keys to our Eternal Salvation and the Scapular is one of the vehicles of her "Suppliant Omnipotence." (Pope Benedict XV, *Epistle, Decessorem Nostrum,* April 19, 1915)

Rosalia Vitale Kehrig

WHO IS THE MOTHER OF GOD?

Chapter 1

Who is the Mother of God?

From whom can we expect the salvation of the Christian people today if not from her of whom it is written that whosoever shall find her shall find life and shall have salvation from the Lord?

Letter, Cum valde, to Cardinal Esteban, February 20, 1929.
(Salvation of Christianity) Pope Pius XI

The children of man shall put their trust under the cover of thy wings.
(Ps. 35:8)

Mary is the Mother of God and Our Mother. (1) She is the woman of the Old Testament and the New, (2) the New Eve, whose complete obedience, brought about the redemption of mankind.

The first document in this Chapter has an explanation of Mary's role in Salvation History. Her cooperation with God was the instrument through which the gates of Heaven were opened up for a sinful mankind. In studying the Brown Scapular Devotion of Our Lady of Mt. Carmel in the proceeding chapters, one might ask:

How is it possible that the Mother of God can make a promise of eternal salvation, as she did when she gave the Scapular to the world through St. Simon Stock, on July 16, 1251? (*Whosoever shall die wearing this (Scapular) shall not suffer eternal fire.*) How is she a channel of grace? What is meant by her Spiritual Motherhood and her role as Mediatrix of all Graces?

How can we believe that a piece of cloth worn around the neck can save a man from Hell? The Brown Scapular is the badge of the Blessed Virgin. The Scapular Promise is fulfilled through the intercession of Our Blessed Mother. She has promised to save from Hell by her intercession anyone who dies clothed in it and she is

1

empowered to keep her Promise, first, because she is the Mother of God, what incalculable power, therefore, must be in her intercession, second, because she is the Mother of each of us, announced from the cross by the Son of Man, that His Mother was to be the Mother of all men, third, because she is the Mother of all who wear her Scapular, because as Foundress of the Carmelite Order, Mary has entered into a relationship with Carmel and has intervened, many times, on its behalf. *(Take This Scapular,* Carmelite Fathers and Tertiaries, Chicago, 1949, pp. 26, 27, 28 paraphrased)

Mary was called by Pope Benedict XV, *Suppliant Omnipotence* meaning she can obtain by her intercession, anything that the all-powerful God can do by His own inherent power. (3)

"The Titles of Our Lady, Our Blessed Mother,"(4) is a compilation of on-line scriptural quotes and Papal documents, taken from various Church teachings, verifying Our Lady's role in the economy of our salvation and referencing the Church's continual teaching, that Mary is always interceding for us. Pope St. John Paul II stated so clearly: "The sign of the Scapular points to an effective 'Synthesis of Marian Spirituality.'"(5) Therefore Our Lady does, truly indeed, have the power to intercede for our eternal salvation through her Brown Scapular Promise.

The Brown Scapular:
A Reflection of Church Teaching on
the Power of the Mother of God

By a Woman the Whole World was saved.

(St. Jerome, cf. Tertullian, De carne Christi 17) (a)

Who was this woman by whom the whole world would be saved? She is a woman whose coming was foretold in numerous references throughout the Old Testament: a woman whose seed would bring about the eternal salvation of all mankind, lost to us through the sin contracted by the first parents of the human race—Adam and Eve.

In the Book of Genesis, Adam and Eve fell slave to the manipulations of the serpent and lost the gifts of supernatural grace and innocence. Almighty God in His mercy and compassion, promised a Redeemer who would bring about the redemption of man through the seed of a woman:

> *I will put enmity between thee and the woman, and thy seed and her seed: she shall crush thy head and thou shalt lie in wait of her heel.* (1)

Enmity means complete and total opposition. She would be in total opposition with the serpent. It would be by her seed, Jesus Christ that the woman will crush the serpent's head (2) and salvation would be restored once again.

The woman is Mary, Mother of God (3) and our Mother, a woman who was chosen by God from all eternity, immaculately conceived as tradition tells us in the womb of St. Anne her mother, and preserved from the stain of all sin to become the pure and stainless vessel of the most High God.

Among the numerous examples in the Old Testament of the foreshadowing of Mary, we find the prophecy of Isaiah 7:14, which speaks of the Virgin-Mother of Emmanuel: *Therefore the Lord himself will give you a sign. Behold a virgin shall conceive and bear a son, and his name shall be called Emmanuel.* Later in Isaiah, Emmanuel is referred to as the future Savior of His people. (4) The prophecy

3

of Micah 5:2-3 foretells the birth of the Savior in Bethlehem from a woman who will "bring forth the ruler of Israel."(5) The "Temple of God" in 1 Kings 8 represented a sanctified house of God which foreshadowed Mary as the future tabernacle of Jesus. (6)

Nine hundred centuries before the birth of Christ, the Virgin appeared to the Prophet Elijah on Mt. Carmel in a little cloud rising from the Sea, showing him the Religious Institution that he was to consecrate to the Mother of the future Redeemer. (7)

The ancient Historian of the Order of Carmel, John XLIV and Patriarch of Jerusalem, also recalled the constant tradition of the Order on the symbolism of the cloud of Carmel that appeared over the Sea to the Holy Prophet Elijas. It was seen as the prefigurement of the Immaculate Virgin who would rise pure out of a sea of sinful mankind. Many mysteries were revealed to the Prophet Elijah in a vision, at that moment: the Immaculate Conception of the Virgin, her perpetual Virginity, the Incarnation of her Divine Son in her pure womb and the time in which these mysteries would be realized. From that moment on, Elijah became known as the "Prophet of the Immaculate Conception." (8)

The Second Vatican Council confirmed:

> *She is already prophetically foreshadowed in the promise of victory over the serpent which was given to our first parents after their fall into sin* (9). *After a long period of waiting, the times are fulfilled in her, the exalted Daughter of Sion and the new plan of salvation is established, when the Son of God has taken human nature from her, that He might in the mysteries of His flesh, free man from sin.* (10)

The New Testament manifests several revealed truths about the Blessed Virgin that are both centrally positioned and theologically profound. The citations of Mary in the New Testament surround the central Christian mysteries revealed in the Gospel: "The Annunciation" (Lk 1:26-38), "The Visitation" (Lk 1:39-56), "The Nativity" (Lk 2:4-20), "The Presentation" (Lk 2:22-38), "The Finding of the Child Jesus in the Temple" (Lk 2:41-52), "The Wedding at Cana" (Jn 2:1-11), "Mary at the Foot of the Cross" (Jn 19:25-27), "The presence of Mary in the Upper Room" (Acts 1:13-2:4), Marian reference of Revelation 12:1 where Mary is seen as a type of the Church, etc. (11)

The first symbol of Mary, Mother of the Church, seen in a very significant fresco found in the Catacombs of St. Agnes, depicts Mary situated between Sts. Peter and Paul, with her arms outstretched to both. This fresco is the earliest symbol of Mary as "Mother of the Church." Mary's prominent position between Sts. Peter and Paul illustrates the recognition by the Apostolic Church of the maternal centrality (Spiritual Motherhood) of the Savior's Mother in His prevailing Church. It is also clear from the number of representations of the Blessed Virgin and their locations in the catacombs, that Mary was seen not only as a historical person but also as a sign of protection and defense and of intercession. Her image was present on the tombs, as well as on the large central vaults of the catacombs. Clearly the early Christians dwelling in the catacombs prayed to Mary as intercessor to her Son for special protection and for motherly assistance. So we see clearly from the First Century to the first half of the Second Century that Mary's role as Spiritual Mother and Intercessor was recognized and invoked. (12)

Mary became our Spiritual Mother initially at the Annunciation, but her Motherhood was perfected on Calvary, participating in the spiritual regeneration or rebirth of the human family. (13)

Following tradition, the Council (Vatican II), does not hesitate to call Mary "The Mother of Christ and Mother of Mankind." (14) Mary's unique role cannot be ignored as she continues to cooperate in bringing us to her Son. St. Bernard of Clairvaux defined Mary's role by the statement that the Virgin Mary is 'the neck of the Body of Christ.' She is without a doubt an important link between Christ and His Church as both model Christian and Spiritual Mother. (15)

The Church Fathers called Mary the "Go-between" (Mediatrix). Logically, since Mary gave the source of all Grace to men, it is to be expected that she would also cooperate in the distribution of all Grace. Thus, there is a mediation: *Mary places herself between her Son and mankind in the reality of their wants, needs and sufferings;* (16) *she also has that specifically maternal role of Mediatrix of Mercy at His final coming.* (17) *From that great treasure of all graces, which the Lord has brought, nothing, according to the Will of God, comes to us except through Mary, so that as nobody can approach the Supreme Father except through the Son, similarly nobody can approach Christ except through His Mother.* (18)

Mary, as the first human being to kiss the face of God and the first to believe in Jesus as her Savior, took her place in Salvation History as the first Christian. It is Mary who bridges the Old and New Testaments. Mary's continuing role in Salvation History is that of the Mother of the King of Kings, (Queen Mother). In that role, she continues to intercede for us, her Spiritual Children, as she did at the Wedding Feast in Cana: "Do Whatever He tells you." (19)

God is the only efficient cause of Grace...and Christ is the Channel. Mary, in her way is the indirect cause (of the Dispensary of Grace) by her powerful intercessory prayer. She asks her Divine Son to dispense the life and the impulse of Grace, and it is at her bidding that He chooses to do so. Hence, we can say that all Grace flows through Mary because in His exaltation of His Holy Mother, God has deigned to make her Prayer an indirect cause of Grace. Jesus had made her by participation, what He is by nature. In a dependent way, Mary is all powerful. (20)

Pope Benedict XV declared: *All gifts which the Author of all good (God) has deigned to communicate to the unhappy posterity of Adam, are, according to the loving resolve of His Divine Providence, dispensed by the hands of the Most Holy Virgin.* (21) In the words of Pope Benedict XV, Mary is *Suppliant Omnipotence.* Whatever God does through His own inherent power (salvation), Our Lady can obtain by her intercession. (22) *Thus, does she continually cooperate with her Divine Son in His eternal Mission. In this Office, she is called Mediatrix of all Grace.* (23)

In the past 2000 years, we have witnessed the power of the intercessory prayers of Our Lady, manifested through her approved apparitions in the Church, such as in Fatima, in 1917. Out of love for her Spiritual Children and through her cooperation with her Son in procuring the salvation of souls, Our Lady has intervened time and time again, with a plea for prayer, penance and daily sacrifice to warn the world of impending calamities if people do not stop offending God. As a gentle and loving Mother, she nourishes guides and protects us, helping us to grow everyday in the life of *Supernatural Grace.* In her last apparition at Fatima, on October 13, 1917, Mary revealed herself as "Our Lady of the Rosary," asking for the recitation of the Rosary each day.

On October 16, 2002, Pope St. John Paul II issued an Apostolic Letter on the "Most Holy Rosary," *Rosarium Virginis Mariae,* regarding the insertions of the *Mysteries of Light* into the Rosary, which, itself, has within it, "all the depth of the Gospel Message in its entirety." The Luminous Mysteries refer to the initiation of the public ministry of Our Lord and Savior Jesus Christ, beginning with the first Mystery of Light: the Baptism of Our Lord Jesus in the Jordan River. The Jordan River is not only the location of the Baptism of Our Lord and countless other repentive penitents, but it is also marked as a place of transition and enlightenment, marked by the bestowal of the Holy Spirit and the opening of Heaven. It signifies the end of one prophetic mission and the beginning of the other, for it was at the Jordan that Joshua entered into the Promised Land and it was at the Jordan that Elijah exited the Promised Land and was taken up to Heaven in a fiery chariot. (23a) These remarkable heavenly events imbued the Jordan River with a supernatural spirit of enlightenment and it became a "place of refuge," the first "Sanctuary of Christianity," the first Sanctuary of the Universal Church. It is here where Our Beloved Lord returned, to the place of his Baptism of Water, as a Pilgrim, to the place in which he was publicly anointed for his Royal Mission, a place that beheld the revelation of the Trinity, to withdraw from His enemies, so that He would draw strength and courage to prepare Himself for His anticipated Baptism of Blood. The Gospel Reading on the Fifth Friday in Lent tells us that there were those that wanted to stone Him, so Jesus returned to the place of His Baptism to prepare Himself, because it was a place of illumination: *The Jews then took up stones to stone him...And he went again beyond the Jordan, into that place where John was baptizing first; and there he abode...* (23b)

Through the Sacrament of Baptism we have been marked with the indelible character and identity of Christ on our soul and have become the adopted sons and daughters of our Heavenly Father. *For whosoever are led by the Spirit of God, they are the sons of God, for you have not received the spirit of bondage again in fear, but you have received the spirit of adoption of sons, whereby we cry: Abba, (Father), for the Spirit himself giveth testimony to our spirit, that we are the sons of God.* (23c) We are anointed with God's Holy Spirit at Baptism so that we can be empowered by the Grace of the Holy Spirit to "return to the place of our Baptism," to pick up our cross and follow Jesus...especially throughout the most difficult trials and tribulations of our every day life.

In the words of Pope St. John Paul II we read: *Consequently for the Rosary to become more fully a compendium of the Gospel, it is fitting to add... a meditation on certain particular significant moments in His public ministry; this addition of the new Mysteries (The Mysteries of Light) is meant to give it a fresh life and to enkindle renewed interest in the Rosary's place in Christian Spirituality as a true doorway to the depths of the Heart of Christ, ocean of joy and light, of suffering and glory.* (23d)

The revelation made directly by the Father at the Baptism in the Jordan and echoed by John the Baptist, is placed upon Mary's lips at Cana and it becomes the great maternal counsel which Mary addresses to the Church of every age: *Do whatever He tells you.* (Jn 2:5) This counsel is a fitting introduction to the words and signs of Christ's public ministry, and it forms the Marian foundation of all the Mysteries of Light. (23e)

As Our Lady of the Rosary, Our Beloved Mother Mary continually beseeches us to meditate daily on the recitation of the Mysteries of the Rosary, to return with Him spiritually to the place of our illumination, our Baptism, to help us grow in deeper union with Her Son Jesus. To continue her powerful assistance for her beloved children here on earth, she appeared at Fatima, Portugal, on the 13th of May, 1917 for six successive months. During the phenomenon of the Miracle of the Sun, on October 13, 1917, the children (Lucia, Jacinta and Francisco) beheld, among others, the Vision of Our Heavenly Mother, dressed in the Habit of Carmel, signifying the Glorious Mysteries, as she held down the Brown Scapular to the world as a final plea, silently beseeching us to clothe ourselves in her garment of protection as a sign of love and consecration to her Immaculate Heart.

The Rosary is the weapon for our defense, and the Scapular is the armour of her love...for Lucia later proclaimed...*the Rosary and the Scapular are inseparable.* (24)

According to a venerable tradition, Our Lady bestowed upon St. Simon Stock, the Brown Scapular of Carmel on July 16, 1251. She gave the Promise that: *Whosoever dies clothed in this shall not suffer eternal fire.* Her Promise conveyed to the world, that she is directly involved in the work of our eternal salvation.

In the last Marian Congress of Belgium, held in the year 1922, one of the Theologians read a paper in which he explained the influence of devotion to the Holy Scapular on the strong and universal belief of the Church in the Doctrine of "Mary Mediatrix of Graces." (25)

During its (more than) seven centuries of existence, the Scapular has explained Our Lady's position in the Divine Plan of Salvation. One of the theologians speaking at the Marian Congress of Belgium, in 1922 mentioned this fact when he declared that if the doctrine of Mary, Mediatrix of all Grace, is ever declared a Dogma of Faith it will be due in large part to the Scapular Devotion. (25a)

The Doctrine of Mary's Universal Mediation of Grace is based on her cooperation in the Incarnation. Her position as Mediatrix of all Grace is organically associated with Mary's Spiritual Motherhood which is in turn based on Scripture and with her intimate participation in the work of her Divine Son. (26)

Pope Emeritus Benedict XVI, beginning a new cycle of catechesis on the Christian School of prayer, at a General Audience in Rome, March 14, 2012, referred to Our Lady, in these words: *If there is no Church without Pentecost, there is no Pentecost without the Mother of Jesus, because she lived in a unique way that which the Church experiences each day under the action of the Holy Spirit... it is therefore the Church gathered in the upper room with Mary, the Mother of Jesus, and with her, her brothers...one cannot therefore speak of the Church unless Mary, Mother of God is present. Mother of God and Mother of the Church, Mary exercises this Motherhood until the end of history.* (26a)

Mary continued the work of Her Son Jesus, after His Death and Resurrection, who Himself, descended to the dead on the First Saturday after His death. "An Ancient Homily for Holy Saturday, printed in the Catechism in no. 635, speaks of Holy Saturday as the day in which Christ went into Hell and sought out all the righteous, declaring salvation to them..." (26ab) Traditionally the Church has dedicated Saturday to the Mother of God, *....we sanctify Saturday in honor of the glorious Virgin Mary who remained unshaken in faith all day Saturday after the death of her Divine Son.* (26b) As Our Lady's faith remained unshaken on the "First Saturday" after His death, so, according to a venerable tradition, she promised to Pope John XXII, in the 14th Century, to free from Purgatory, on the "First Saturday" after their death, all those who wore the Scapular and faithfully followed the conditions prescribed, in what is known as the "Sabbatine Privilege"' and later in 1917 Our Heavenly Mother appeared in Fatima, Portugal, to ask, among other requests, for the Communions of Reparation to Her Immaculate Heart, on five consecutive "First Saturdays" of the month, confirming the tradition of the Church's veneration of Mary on Saturdays.

Continuing with the Devotion of the Brown Scapular of Our Lady of Mount Carmel, visible proof of Our Lady's intercessory position in the Divine Plan of Salvation, "the theological foundation for the Scapular Devotion is similar to that of Marian consecration, namely the Spiritual Motherhood of Mary in her ability to intercede for her children, for what Vatican II refers to as the 'Gifts of Eternal Salvation.'"(27)

As Mediatrix of all Graces, Mary can grant the Graces necessary for salvation to those who *faithfully* wear the Scapular as an external symbol of their internal devotion and dependence on the Mother of

Jesus. (28) It is because of her love for us that she made the Scapular Promise and it is by her prayer-power that she keeps it. (29)

Pope Pius XII spoke of the powerful spiritual effects of wearing the Scapular in the following discourse:

> *How many souls even in circumstances which, humanly speaking, were beyond hope have owed their final conversion and their eternal salvation to the Scapular which they were wearing! How many more, thanks to it, have experienced the motherly protection of Mary in dangers of body and soul?* (30)

She made the Scapular the *Sign of her Intercession*. It is a visible sign of Mary's invisible mediation. (31) It is an invitation to come within the folds of her mantle where we cannot be lost in uniting ourselves to her. It is a symbol of the loving contract between Mother and child.

Because of the filial devotion of her spiritual children in so eagerly accepting the Scapular after the vision to St. Simon Stock, Our Blessed Mother, so full of love and generosity, granted a second promise even more astounding to those who wear her Scapular faithfully. It is a promise that extends into Purgatory *because Mary, through her intercession, has complete dominion over Purgatory.* (32)

Following a vision of Our Blessed Mother granting a special Privilege in Purgatory, to those who die wearing the Scapular, Pope John XXII issued a Bull on March 3, 1322, in which he recorded the words of Our Lady: *I, the Mother of Grace, shall descend into Purgatory on the Saturday after their death, and whosoever I shall find in Purgatory, I shall free.* This was the Sabbatine Privilege granted by the Universal Church to the devotees of the Scapular, provided that certain conditions are followed.

As Mary, through her Spiritual Motherhood in the Order of Grace, has the ability to intercede for us, so as Mediatrix of all Graces, she has the ability to obtain for us the gift of our eternal salvation and as ["Coredemptrix" (32a)] in the Redemptive work of her Son, she has the power to guarantee us that, if we wear her Scapular with true love and devotion, we will receive from her, at the hour of our death, either the Grace of Final Perseverance, or the Grace of Final Contrition. Mary, through the unspeakable bond of love in her Scapular, has provided for our spiritual nourishment, soul to soul, to nurse us in the growth of the Divine Life. She is a true Mother in every way, for only a true Mother desires to be united with her children for all Eternity.

According to a pious tradition, Our Lady revealed, that one day, through the Rosary and the Scapular, she would save the world. (33)

Standing at the right hand of her only begotten Son, Our Lord Jesus Christ, she pleads strongly for us with a Mother's prayers, and what she seeks, she finds, nor can she ask in vain. Therefore, let all the faithful rejoice to be subject to the authority of the Virgin Mother of God, whose power is a Queen's, and whose love is a Mothers. (34)

Titles of Our Lady, Our Blessed Mother

Many are devoted to Our Lady because She always leads us to Jesus Christ and is the most perfect way to achieve holiness. The titles of Our Lady to which Our Lady's Warriors cling to are those very important titles that She has; Mother of God, Our Mother, Co-Redemptrix, Mediatrix of Grace, and Advocate. The titles represent the responsibilities (i.e., roles) of Our Lady. Church doctrinal and dogmatic references are shown below regarding the basis for belief in these titles, which have been known for centuries. They have been stated (long) before, during and after Vatican II, and cannot therefore be argued as a recent phenomenon of Pope John Paul II (in spite of various Modernist claims) or as an inhibitor to ecumenism. As to the latter point, this Catholic doctrine was known centuries before there even existed a Protestant set of religions which, after their creation by various men, introduced the need for ecumenism which, in the true sense of the term, is to bring the stray flocks back into the One Holy Catholic and Apostolic Faith—not to deny Catholic doctrine in a false compromise. One will also note the intricate linking of all Our Lady's roles, so much so that these roles are inseparable and inter-dependent. Information was obtained from *Fundamentals of Catholic Dogma* by Dr. Ludwig Ott, the Vatican II document Dogmatic Constitution of the Church, and other Church teachings as referenced.

Mother of God

The reality and integrity of Christ's human nature is especially guaranteed by the fact that Christ was truly generated and born of a human mother. Through His descent from a daughter of Adam, He was, as to His humanity, incorporated into the posterity of Adam. He had identity of essence with man and community of race; Christ became our Brother.

The Church, in her Symbols of Faith, teaches that Christ was generated and born of the Virgin Mary, that is, out of the substance of the Virgin Mary. Reference the Apostles Creed "conceived by the Holy Ghost and born of the Virgin Mary." In both the Old and New Testaments the Messiah is designated as the posterity of Abraham and David (Genesis 22:18, Matthew 1:1, 9:27, 12:23, 22:42, Romans 1:2, 2 Timothy 2:8). The New Testament explicitly stresses the motherhood of Mary; Matthew 1:16 Mary "of whom Jesus was born;" Luke 1:31 "Behold thou shalt conceive in thy womb and shalt bring forth a son;" Galatians 4:4 "made of a woman;" Luke 1:43 "Mother of the Lord;" John 2:1 "Mother of Jesus;" and still others in the Gospel according to Matthew.

The Council of Ephesus in 431 with St. Cyril of Alexandria declared "If anyone does not confess that the Emmanuel (Christ) in truth is God and that on this account the Holy Virgin if the Mother of God (*Theotokos*)—since according to the flesh She brought forth the Word of God made flesh—let him be *anathema*."

From Chapter VIII of the **Dogmatic Constitution of the Church** 52. Wishing in his supreme goodness and wisdom to effect the redemption of the world, "when the fullness of time came, God sent his Son, born of a woman . . . that we might receive the adoption of sons" (Gal. 4:4). "He for us men, and for our salvation, came down from heaven, and was incarnated by the Holy Spirit from the Virgin Mary." This divine mystery of salvation is revealed to us and continued in the Church, which the Lord established as his body. Joined to Christ the head and in communion with all his saints, the faithful must in the first place reverence the memory "of the glorious ever Virgin Mary, *Mother of God and of our Lord Jesus Christ*."

Our Mother

In the Bible, Jesus tells us as He is dying on the Cross that the Blessed Virgin Mary is our Mother, as indicated by the disciple in the verse. After all, doesn't following Jesus make us His disciple? Notice that the disciple listened to Our Lord and took her to his own. We must also obey Our Savior. What a wonderful gift from God.

John 19:26-27 - *When Jesus therefore had seen his mother and the disciple standing whom he loved, he saith to his mother:* <u>*Woman, behold thy son.*</u> *After that, he saith to the disciple:* <u>*Behold thy mother.*</u> *And from that hour,* <u>the disciple took her to his own.</u>

Encyclical Mother of the Redeemer (Redemptoris Mater) of March 25, 1987 47. At the [Second Vatican] Council *Paul VI* solemnly proclaimed that Mary is the Mother of the Church, "that is, <u>Mother of the entire Christian people</u>, both faithful and pastors." Later, in 1968, in the Profession of faith known as the "Credo of the People of God," he restated this truth in an even more forceful way in these words: "We believe that the Most Holy Mother of God, the new Eve, the Mother of the Church, carries on in heaven her maternal role with regard to the members of Christ, cooperating in the birth and development of divine life in the souls of the redeemed."

The Council's teaching emphasized that the truth concerning the Blessed Virgin, Mother of Christ, is an effective aid in exploring more deeply the truth concerning the Church. When speaking of the *Constitution Lumen Gentium*, which had just been approved by the Council, Paul VI said: "Knowledge of the true Catholic doctrine regarding the Blessed Virgin Mary will always be a key to the exact understanding of the mystery of Christ and of the Church." Mary is present in the Church as the Mother of Christ, and at the same time as that Mother whom Christ, in the mystery of the Redemption, gave to humanity in the person of the Apostle John. Thus, in her new motherhood in the Spirit, Mary embraces each and every one in the Church, and embraces each and every one through the Church. In this sense Mary, Mother of the Church, is also the Church's model. Indeed, as Paul VI hopes and asks, the Church must draw "from the Virgin Mother of God the most authentic form of perfect imitation of Christ."

The idea of the Spiritual Motherhood of Mary, that is our Mother, is part of the ancient Christian tradition, independent of the Scriptural support. According to Origen the perfect Christ has Mary as Mother: "Every perfect person no longer lives (of himself) but Christ lives in Him; and because Christ lives in him, it is said to him of Mary: Behold thy Son Christ" (Com. in Ioan I 4, 23). St. Epiphanius derives Mary's Spiritual Motherhood from the Eve-Mary parallel: "She (Mary) is she of whom Eve is the prototype, who, as such received the appellation 'mother of the living' ... as to externals the whole human race stemmed from that Eve.. Thus in truth, through Mary, the very life of the world was born, so that She bore the Living One, and became Mother of the Living" (Haer 78, 18). St. Augustine bases Mary's Spiritual Motherhood on the "mystical unity of the faithful with Christ. As the bodily Mother of God, she is, in a spiritual fashion, also the Mother of those who are articulated with Christ" (cf. De s. virginitate 6, 6).

Co-Redemptrix

The title Co-Redemptrix (sometimes also said as Co-redemptress), has been current since the 15th century, and also appears in some current Church documents under St. Pope Pius X (cf. D 1978 a). This must not be conceived in the sense of an equation of the efficacy of Mary with the redemptive activity of Christ, the sole Redeemer of humanity (1Timothy 2:5). As She Herself required redemption and was in fact redeemed by Christ, she could not of Herself merit the Grace of the redemption of humanity in accordance with the principle: *Principium meriti non cadit sub eodum merito* (The author of an act of merit cannot be a recipient of the same act of merit). Her cooperation in the objective redemption is an indirect, remote cooperation, and derives from this that She voluntarily devoted Her whole life to the service of the Redeemer, and, under the Cross, suffered and sacrificed with Him.

The Church Fathers contrast Mary's obedience at the Annunciation with Eve's disobedience. Mary by Her obedience became the cause of the Salvation, while Eve by her disobedience became the cause of death. St. Irenaeus teaches "As she (Eve) who had Adam as her husband, but was nevertheless a virgin, was disobedient, and thereby became the cause of death to herself and to the whole of mankind, so also Mary, who has a pre-ordained husband, and was still a virgin, by Her obedience became a cause of Her own salvation and the salvation of the whole human race" (Adv. Haer. III 22, 4; cf. V 19, 1). St. Jerome says "By a woman the whole world was saved" (cf. Tertullian, De carne Christi 17).

As Pope Pius XII says in the *Encyclical Mystici Coporis* in 1943, She "offered Him on Golgotha to the Eternal Father together with the holocaust of Her maternal rights and Her motherly love like a new Eve for all children of Adam." (D 2291). As "the New Eve," She is, as the same Pope declares, in the Apostolic Constitution *Munificentissimus Deus* in 1950 "the sublime associate of our Redeemer" (cf. D. 3031).

Pope John Paul II on March 31, 1985 as part of the Angelus prayer: "May Mary our Protectress, the Co-Redemptrix, to whom we offer our prayer with great outpouring, make our desire generously correspond to the desire of the Redeemer."

Pope John Paul II on October 6, 1991 after Mass to honor the canonization of St. Birgitta: "Birgitta looked to Mary as her model and support in the various moments of her life. She spoke energetically about the divine privilege of Mary's Immaculate Conception. She contemplated her astonishing mission as Mother of the Savior. She invoked her as the Immaculate Conception, Our Lady of Sorrows, and Co-Redemptrix, exalting Mary's singular role in the history of salvation and the life of Christian people."

Pope John Paul II on November 4, 1984 while visiting Arona to honor St. Charles Borromeo: "To Our Lady"—the Co-Redemptrix— Charles turned with singularly revealing accents."

Mediatrix of All Grace and Advocate

The Church Fathers called Mary the "Go-between" (Mediatrix). A prayer by St. Ephrem says of Her: "After the Mediator thou art the Mediatrix of the whole world" (Oratio IV ad Deiparam. 4th Lesson of the Office of the Feast). The title Mediatrix is attached to Mary in official Church documents such as the Bull "Ineffabilis" of Pope Pius IX in 1854, in the Rosary Encyclicals "Adiuricem" and "Fidentem" of Pope Leo XIII in 1895 and 1896 and in the Encyclical "Ad Diem Illum" by Pope St. Pius X in 1904. More references are shown in detail below. The doctrine of Mary's universal Mediation of Grace is based on Her cooperation in the Incarnation which is definitely manifest in the sources of Faith. Her position as Mediatrix of All Grace is organically associated with Mary's Spiritual Motherhood which is in turn based on Scripture and with Her intimate participation in the work of Her Divine Son. Logically, since Mary gave the source of all Grace to men, it is to be expected that She would also cooperate in the distribution of all Grace. And since Mary became the Spiritual Mother of all the redeemed, it is fitting that She, by Her constant Motherly intercession should care for the supernatural life of all Her children (i.e., including advocacy). What remains is to formalize the constant doctrine of Her position into dogma.

Vatican II Dogmatic Constitution on the Church (Lumen Gentium) 62. This maternity of Mary in the order of grace began with the consent which she gave in faith at the Annunciation and which she sustained without wavering beneath the cross, and lasts until the eternal fulfillment of all the elect. Taken up to heaven she did not lay aside this salvific duty, but by her constant intercession continued to bring us the gifts of eternal salvation. By her maternal charity, she cares for the brethren of her Son, who still journey on earth surrounded by dangers and cultics, until they are led into the happiness of their true home. Therefore the Blessed Virgin is invoked by the Church under the titles of Advocate, Auxiliatrix, Adjutrix, and Mediatrix. This, however, is to be so understood that it neither takes away from nor adds anything to the dignity and efficaciousness of Christ the one Mediator.

For no creature could ever be counted as equal with the Incarnate Word and Redeemer. Just as the priesthood of Christ is shared in various ways both by the ministers and by the faithful, and as the one goodness of God is really communicated in different ways to His creatures, so also the unique mediation of the Redeemer does not exclude but rather gives rise to a manifold cooperation which is but a sharing in this one source.

The Church does not hesitate to profess this subordinate role of Mary. It knows it through unfailing experience of it and commends it to the hearts of the faithful, so that encouraged by this maternal help they may the more intimately adhere to the Mediator and Redeemer.

Pope John Paul II Encyclical **Mother of the Redeemer (Redemptoris Mater)** of March 25, 1987 40. After the events of the Resurrection and Ascension Mary entered the Upper Room together with the Apostles to await Pentecost, and was present there as the Mother of the glorified Lord. She was not only the one who "advanced in her pilgrimage of faith" and loyally persevered in her union with her Son "unto the Cross," but she was also the "handmaid of the Lord," left by her Son as Mother in the midst of the infant Church: "Behold your mother." Thus there began to develop a special bond between this Mother and the Church. For the infant Church was the fruit of the Cross and Resurrection of her Son. Mary, who from the beginning had given herself without reserve to the person and work of her Son, could not but pour out upon the Church, from the very beginning, her maternal self-giving. After her Son's departure, her motherhood remains in the Church as maternal mediation: interceding for all her children, the Mother cooperates in the saving work of her Son, the Redeemer of the world. In fact the Council teaches that the "motherhood of Mary in the order of grace will last without interruption until the eternal fulfillment of all the elect." With the redeeming death of her Son, the maternal mediation of the handmaid of the Lord took on a universal dimension, for the work of redemption embraces the whole of humanity. Thus there is manifested in a singular way the efficacy of the one and universal mediation of Christ "between God and men" Mary's cooperation shares, in its subordinate character, in the universality of the mediation of the Redeemer, the one Mediator. This is clearly indicated by the Council in the words quoted above.

"For," the text goes on, "taken up to heaven, she did not lay aside this saving role, but by her manifold acts of intercession continues to win for us gifts of eternal salvation." With this character of "intercession," first manifested at Cana in Galilee, Mary's mediation continues in the history of the Church and the world. We read that Mary "by her maternal charity, cares for the brethren of her Son who still journey on earth surrounded by dangers and difficulties, until they are led to their happy homeland." In this way Mary's motherhood continues unceasingly in the Church as the mediation which intercedes, and the Church expresses her faith in this truth by invoking Mary "under the titles of Advocate, Auxiliatrix, Adjutrix and Mediatrix."

Pope John Paul II Encyclical **Mother of the Redeemer (Redemptoris Mater)** of March 25, 1987 41. By the mystery of the Assumption into heaven there were definitively accomplished in Mary all the effects of the one mediation of Christ the Redeemer of the world and Risen Lord: "In Christ shall all be made alive. But each in his own order: Christ the first fruits, then at his coming those who belong to Christ" (1 Cor. 15:22-23). In the mystery of the Assumption is expressed the faith of the Church, according to which Mary is "united by a close and indissoluble bond" to Christ, for, if as Virgin and Mother she was singularly united with him in his first coming, so through her continued collaboration with him she will also be united with him in expectation of the second; "redeemed in an especially sublime manner by reason of the merits of her Son," (109) she also has that specifically maternal role of Mediatrix of mercy at his final coming, when all those who belong to Christ "shall be made alive," when "the last enemy to be destroyed is death" (1 Cor. 15:26)." ... Pope John Paul II Encyclical **Mother of the Redeemer (Redemptoris Mater)** of March 25, 1987 21. What deep understanding existed between Jesus and his mother? How can we probe the mystery of their intimate spiritual union? But the fact speaks for itself. It is certain that that event already quite clearly outlines the new dimension, the new meaning of Mary's motherhood. Her motherhood has a significance which is not exclusively contained in the words of Jesus and in the various episodes reported by the Synoptics (Lk. 11:27-28 and Lk. 8:19-21; Mt. 12:46-50; Mk. 3:31-35). In these texts Jesus means above all to contrast the motherhood resulting from the fact of birth with what this "motherhood" (and also "brotherhood") is to be in the dimension of the Kingdom of God, in the salvific radius of God's fatherhood. In John's text on the other hand, the description of the Cana event outlines what is actually manifested as a new kind of motherhood according to the spirit and not just according to the flesh, that is to say Mary's solicitude for human beings, her coming to them in the wide variety of their wants and needs. At Cana in Galilee there is shown only one concrete aspect of human need, apparently a small one of little importance ("They have no wine"). But it has a symbolic value: this coming to the aid of human needs means, at the same time, bringing those needs within the radius of Christ's messianic mission and salvific power. Thus there is a mediation: Mary places herself between her Son and mankind in the reality of their wants, needs and sufferings. She puts herself "in the middle," that is to say she acts as a Mediatrix not as an outsider, but in her position as mother. She knows that as such she can point out to her Son the needs of mankind, and in fact, she "has the right" to do so. Her mediation is thus in the nature of intercession: Mary "intercedes" for mankind. And that is not all. As a mother she also wishes the messianic power of her Son to be manifested, that salvific power of his which is meant to help man in his misfortunes, to free him from the evil which in various forms and degrees weighs heavily upon his life. Precisely as the Prophet Isaiah had foretold about the Messiah in the famous passage which Jesus quoted before his fellow townsfolk in Nazareth: "To preach good news to the poor. . . to proclaim release to the captives and recovering of sight to the blind ..." (cf. Lk. 4:18).

Pope Leo XIII Encyclical on the Rosary (Octobri Mense) of 1891 "From that great treasure of all graces, which the Lord has bought, nothing, according to the Will of God, comes to us except through Mary, so that, as nobody can approach the Supreme Father except through the Son, similarly nobody can approach Christ except through His Mother."

Pope Pius X calls Mary "the Dispenser of all gifts, which Jesus has acquired for us through His death and His Blood" (D 1978 A).

Pope Benedict XV declared "All gifts which the Author of all good (God) has deigned to communicate to the unhappy posterity of Adam, are, according to the loving resolve of His Divine Providence, dispensed by the hands of the Most Holy Virgin" (AAS 9, 1917, 266).

Pope Pius XI in the Encyclical "Ingravescentibus Malis" in 1937 quotes with approval St. Bernard: "Thus it is His (God's) Will that we should have everything through Mary" (AAS 29, 1937, 373). Similarly, Pope Pius XII said the same in his Encyclical "Mediator Dei" of 1947.

Explicit testimonies to Mary's position as Mediatrix of Grace are found since the eighth century. They became more numerous during the peak period of the middle ages. St. Germanus of Constantinople († 733) says "Nobody can achieve salvation except through thee ... O Most Holy One ... Nobody can receive a gift of Grace except through thee ... O Most Chaste One" (Or. 9, 5. Lesson of the Office of the Feast). St. Bernard of Clairvaux († 1153) says of Mary: "God wished that we had nothing, except by the hands of Mary." (In Vig. Nativit. Domini serm. 3, 10). Albert the Great calls Mary: "The universal dispenser of all riches" (omnium bonitatum universaliter distributiva; Super Missus est q. 29). Other saintly advocates include St. Peter Canisius (Doctor of the Church) and St. Alphonsus Ligouri. (Information taken from: *http://www.ourladyswarriors.org/articles/mother.htm*)

Titles and Attributes of Our Lady by the Popes

From, *Papal Teachings, Our Lady,*
The Benedictine Monks of Solesmes, Boston, 1961

- "Mother of God" (Pope Benedict XIV) p. 25
- "Mother of Mercy," "Mother of Pity and of Grace" (Pope Pius VIII) p. 47
- "Immaculate Conception" (Pope Pius IX) p. 61
- "Mediatrix of Divine Grace," "Mediatrix to the Mediator," (Pope Leo XIII) pp. 125-148
- "Mediatrix and Advocate" (Pope Pius X) p. 173
- "Mother of the Prince of Peace," "Mediatrix with God" (Pope Benedict XV) p. 191
- "Coredemptrix" (Pope Pius XI) p. 191
- "Divine Mother of Mount Carmel" (Pope Pius XII) p. 289
- "Seat of Wisdom," "Mother of the God of all Knowledge," "Queen of the Apostles" (Pope Pius XII) p. 427
- "Queen of Peace" (Pope John XXIII) p. 470
- "Mother of the Redeemer," "Advocate," "Auxiliatrix," "Mediatrix" (Pope Paul VI) *Lumen Gentium:* Chapters: 55, 62
- "Star of the New Evangelization," "Flower of Carmel," "Star of the Sea," "Coredemptrix" (John Paul II) *Letter of John Paul II to the Carmelites,* March 25, 2001, Pope John Paul II: *Address on World Youth Day,* March 11, 1985
- "Mother of the Eucharist" "Queen of Mount Carmel," Queen of Peace (Pope Benedict XVI) *Osservatore Romano,* May 29-31, 2005; July 16, 2006, Benedict XVI
- "Blessed Virgin Mary Immaculate, Mediatrix of all Graces" (Pope Benedict XVI) *Letter of Pope Benedict XVI, Designating Archbishop Zygmunt Simowski, President of the Pontifical Council for Health,* Pastoral Care, January 10, 2013

CHAPTER 1 ENDNOTES

WHO IS THE MOTHER OF GOD?

1   *Council of Ephesus.* 431 AD; John 19: 26-27

2   *Genesis.* 3:15; *Revelation* 5, 12: 1-2

3   Pope Benedict XV: Epistle, *Decessorem Nostrum,*
     April 19, 1915

4   http://www.ourladyswarriors.org/articles/mother.htm

5   *Message of John Paul II to the Carmelite Family on the*
     750th anniversary of the bestowal of the Scapular, March 25, 2001

A REFLECTION OF CHURCH TEACHING ON THE POWER OF THE MOTHER OF GOD

a   St. Jerome-cf Tertullian, De carne Christi 17;
     www.ourladyswarriors.org/abtmary.htm

1   *Genesis,* 3:15 Douay Rheims Bible, Latin Vulgate

2   *Ibid,* www.drbo.org/chapter/01003.htm

3   *Council of Ephesus,* 431 A.D.

4   Isaiah 8:8-9: *Introduction to Mary,* Mark Miravalle, S.T.D, California,
     1993, p. 18

5   *Ibid,* p. 18, paraphrased

6   *Ibid,* p.19; Cf. Pius IX, *Ineffabilis Deus,* December 8, 1854

7   *Le Scapulaire de Notre Dame du Mont-Carmel est authentique,*
     P. Marie Joseph du Sacre Coeur, "Avant Propos," translated

8   Translated from: *Enciclopedia del Escapulario del Carmen,* P. Simon
     M. Besalduch, p.41; *De Institutione Primorum Monach* 1. VI, c. I in
     Spec. Carm., t. I. pag.54

9   *Lumen Gentium, No. 55; Introduction to Mary,* Dr. Mark Miravalle, p.19

10   *Lumen Gentium,* No. 55; *Ibid,* p. 19

11   *Introduction to Mary,* Dr. Mark Miravalle, pp. 20-23

12   *Ibid,* p. 24; cf.Murphy *Origin and Nature of Marian Cult* in Carol,
     ed. "Mariology," Vol.III, (Milwaukee: Bruce, 1961), pp. 1-20,
     (footnote #5 on p. 31 *Introduction to Mary,* Dr. Mark Miravalle)

13   *Introduction to Mary,* p. 64

14   John Paul II. *Redemptoris Mater,* No. 23,45; *Introduction to Mary,* p. 60

15   *The Virgin Mary's Role in Salvation History* :
      www.agapebiblestudy.com/documents/TheVirginMarys
      RoleinSalvationHistory-Mediatrix of All Graces and Advocate

16   John Paul II Ency. *Mother of the Redeemer,* (*Redemptoris Mater*)
      March 25, 1987, #21

17   *Ibid,* #41

18   Pope Leo XIII Ency. *On the Rosary* (Octobri Mense), 1891;
      Titles of Our Lady. Our Blessed Mother:
      www.ourladvswarriors.org/articles/mother.htm

19   John 2:5; *The Virgin Mary's Role in Salvation History:*
      www.agapebiblestudy.com/documents/
      TheVirginMarysRoleinSalvationHistory

20   *Mary in Her Scapular Promise.* John Mathias Haffert. 1942.
      pp. 43, 44, paraphrased

21   AAS 9, 1917, 266; *Titles of Our Lady. Our Blessed Mother*
      http://www.ourladyswarriors.org/articles/mother.htm

22   Pope Benedict XV: *Decessorem nostrum,* April 19, 1915; The
      MOST Theological Collection: A Basic Catholic Catechism Part XVII:
      Prayer: Prayer in general: The Our Father and the Hail Mary

23   *Mary in Her Scapular Promise,* John Mathias Haffert, 1942, p.44

23a   *The Luminous Mysteries,* Biblical Reflections on the Life of Christ,
      Tim Gray, Ohio, 2004, pp. 5-6, paraphrased

23b   John 10: 31, 40 (Douay Rheims)

23c   Romans 8: 14-16 (Douay Rheims)

23d   Apostolic Letter, Pope John Paul II, *Rosarium Virginis Mariae,*
      October 16, 2002, #19

23e   *Ibid,* #21

24   *Fatima and the Scapular,* Carmelite Third Order Press, Chicago, 1950,
      p. 14, taken from *Our Lady of Fatima and the Brown Scapular,*
      Rev., Kilian Lynch, O. Carm., Aylesford, 1956, p. 14

25   Maria-Congres, B. 11, bl. 66. from: *Take This Scapular,* Carmelite
      Fathers and Tertiaries, Chicago, 1949, p. 110

25a *Consecration,* Fr. Howard Rafferty, O.Carm, Chicago, 1953, p. 4

26 *Titles of Our Lady. Our Blessed Mother;* Mediatrix of All Grace
and Advocate www.ourladyswarriors.org/articles/mother.htm

26a   Pope Benedict XVI, General Audience, March 14, 2012,Vatican
Radio: "New Cycle of Catechesis on the Christian School of
Prayer," www.oecumene.radiovaticana.org/EN1/
articolo.asp?c=571235

26ab *Our Sunday Visitor, Descended into Hell?* Monsignor
M. Francis Mannion, October 30, 2011, www.osv.com
/tabid/7621/itemid/8567/Msgr-M-Francis-Mannion

26b *Our Lady of Fatima in the Light of History,*
Fr. John A. Hardon, S.J., The Real Presence Association
http://www.therealpresence.org/archives/Mariology/
Mariology_030.htm

27 *Introduction to Mary,* by Dr. Mark Miravalle, 1993,
p. 125; Lumen Gentium, No. 62

28 *Ibid,* p. 125

29 *Mary in Her Scapular Promise,* John Mathias Haffert, 1942, p. 46

30 *Introduction to Mary,* p. 126; Pope Pius XII, *Discourses
and Radio Broadcasts,* Vol. 12 (1950-51) p. 165

31 *Mary in Her Scapular Promise,* John Mathias Haffert, 1942,
p. 50, paraphrased

32 *Ibid,* p. 77; St. Bernardine: Serm. 3, de Nom. Mar. a. 2, c. 3,
paraphrased

32a Pope Pius XI: *Allocution* to pilgrims of Vicenza, November 30, 1933,
The Coredemptrix

33 *Fatima, The Great Sign,* Francis Johnston, Illinois, 1980,
p. 111, footnote #1

34 Pope Pius XII, Encycl. *Ad coeli Reginam,* October 11,
1954, *Papal Teachings, Our Lady,* The Benedictine Monks of
Solesmes, Boston, 1961, pp. 395-396

CHAPTER 2

SYNTHESIS OF THE BROWN SCAPULAR DEVOTION OF OUR LADY OF MOUNT CARMEL

Chapter 2

Synthesis of the Brown Scapular Devotion
What is the Brown Scapular?

In Heaven as Queen at the right hand of her only Son, clothed in golden raiment and all manner of jewels, there is nothing she cannot obtain from Him.
Pope Pius IX, Encyclical: *Quanta Cura*, December 8, 1864, on modern errors (Queen and Mother)

And I passed by thee and saw thee: and behold thy time was the time of lovers: and I spread my garment over thee and covered thy ignominy. And I swore to thee, and I entered into a covenant with thee...and thou becamest mine. (Ez:16:8)

The Brown Scapular is a highly indulgenced sacramental of the Holy Roman Catholic Church. It is a reduced form of the religious habit of the Order of the Friars of the Blessed Virgin of Mount Carmel (1). Worn around the neck, over the scapula bone, it comprises two small pieces of brown wool cloth, connected by string. It is an external, visible sign of the love Our Heavenly Mother Mary has for her children.

According to a pious tradition in the Church, Our Blessed Mother appeared to St. Simon Stock, in Cambridge, England, on July 16, 1251. St. Simon Stock had begged the Mother of God to bring an end to the opposition, division and persecution of the Order both within and outside of the Carmelite Community at the time. (2)

She appeared to him holding the habit of the Order in her hands and said: *Receive my beloved son this habit of thy Order: This shall be to thee and to all Carmelites a privilege, that whosoever dies clothed in this shall not suffer eternal fire.* (3) Just as God had chosen to send salvation from sin to the fallen race through His Mother, so again He sent

25

deliverance to the beloved of Carmel through His Mother Mary. (*Take This Scapular,* Carmelite Fathers and Tertiaries, Chicago, 1949, p. 5)

The Scapular is a pledge of love, a promise of protection and the assurance of the Grace of Final Contrition before death, so that no soul will be lost.

According to tradition, Our Lady extended an added privilege to the wearing of her Scapular, known as the Sabbatine Privilege, a special indulgence of the Church. She appeared to Pope John XXII, (which he revealed in his Bull: *Sacratissimo uti culmine* March 3, 1322) saying: *I, the Mother of Grace, shall descend on the Saturday after their death and whoso I shall find in Purgatory, I shall free so that I may lead them unto the Holy Mountain of life everlasing."* (4)

Enrollment in the Confraternity of Our Lady of Mt. Carmel is a necessary requirement to receive the spiritual benefits associated with the Promises of our Blessed Mother.

This chapter will introduce the reader to the research. It will also explain the elements of the Devotion itself, the Synthesis and contains a description of the Sabbatine Bull of Pope John XXII, documents of the Sabbatine Privilege, exerpts from current Church Teaching regarding the Scapular Devotion and the affection and love the great Pope St. John Paul II had for the Brown Scapular of Our Lady of Mount Carmel.

A Synthesis of the
Brown Scapular Devotion

My son, hear the instruction of thy father and forsake not the law of thy Mother that grace may be added to thy head and a chain of gold to thy neck. (1)

God has committed to her (Mary) the treasury of all good things in order that everyone may know that through her are obtained every hope, every grace and all salvation. For this is His Will, that we obtain everything through Mary. (2)

The Basis of the Scapular Devotion is:

1   The Visions of Our Lady to St. Simon Stock and to Pope John XXII

2   The Promises made by Our Blessed Mother

The Theological Foundation of the Scapular Devotion is Church Teaching, namely:

1   The *Spiritual Motherhood* of Mary in her ability to intercede for her children for what Vatican II refers to as: the "Gifts of Eternal Salvation";

2   Mary as *Mediatrix of all Graces* in granting the graces necessary for salvation (through her intercessory role for us in Heaven). (3)

The content of private revelations in devotions must be considered to be based on the teachings of the Faith, suggested historically by the revelation.

Devotions or Feasts connected with private revelations are to be considered as based primarily on the teachings of the Catholic Faith accordingly as they are suggested by the revelation. In the light of these considerations, the doctrinal outline of the Scapular Devotion may be proposed in the following manner:

1   It is a cult of the Blessed Mother of God,

2   Under the particular aspect of her special protection at the hour of death and in Purgatory, after death for those particularly devoted to her,

3   Which cult is founded on her prerogatives of Spiritual Maternity and Mediation of Grace, as taught by the Catholic Faith,

4   The cult is motivated by belief in her promises. (4)

Thus, the major consideration in the Scapular Devotion is that it begets a devotion to the Blessed Mother which is a confident reliance on her aid for eternal salvation and assistance after death in Purgatory on the plane of Catholic Faith. (4) cont.

As the Second Vatican Council profoundly summarizes:

This maternity of Mary in the Order of Grace began with the consent which she gave in faith at the Annunciation and which she sustained without wavering beneath the cross and lasts until the eternal fulfillment of all the elect. Taken up to Heaven she did not lay aside this salvific duty, but by her constant intercession continued to bring us the gifts of eternal salvation. By her maternal charity, she cares for the brethren of her Son, who still journey on earth surrounded by dangers and cultics, until they are led into the happiness of their true home... (5)

Therefore, two truths are evoked by the sign of the Scapular: on the one hand, the constant protection of the Blessed Virgin, not only on life's journey, but also at the moment of passing into the fullness of eternal glory, on the other, the awareness that devotion to her cannot be limited to prayers and tributes in her honor on certain occasions, but must become a 'habit' that is a permanent orientation of one's own Christian conduct. In this way, the Scapular becomes a sign of the "covenant" and reciprocal communion between Mary and the faithful; indeed, it concretely translates the gift of His Mother which Jesus gave on the Cross to John and through Him to all of us and the entrustment of the beloved Apostle and of us to her who became our Spiritual Mother. (6)

For this reason, Pope Pius XII delivered a powerful warning regarding the wearing of the Scapular, in the following discourse:

However, let not those who wear it think that they can in sloth and indolence of spirit, attain eternal life, for the Apostle thus openly admonishes: "Work out your salvation in fear and trembling." (7)

The Scapular Promises prove the power of Our Blessed Mother to intercede for our eternal salvation. The Scapular itself is the masterpiece of love of the Virgin Mary and the tangible Sign of the mystery of her powerful intercession for our salvation. It is a constant teaching of the Church that Mary, Our Mother, continually intercedes for us with her prayer at the throne of her Divine Son.

900 years before the birth of Christ, the Prophet Elias founded the Carmelite Order on Mt. Carmel in Palestine. He instructed his many disciples to venerate, in the little cloud that appeared to him over the sea, the Holy Virgin who had not yet been born and from whom would come the Son of God. According to tradition, the mysteries of the Immaculate Conception, Our Lady's Perpetual Virginity, and the Incarnation, were revealed to Elias in the symbolic little cloud and were transmitted by the Prophet to his disciples from generation to generation, accompanied by his testimony of the vision with sublime teachings of this great mystery. From that time on, the principle Feast of the Order was the Immaculate Conception and was celebrated in all Convents with great solemnity. (8)

Thus the components of the Scapular Devotion incorporate a) the historical origins on Mount Carmel, starting with the Prophet Elias, Founder of the Carmelites, b) the bestowal of the Scapular by Our Lady to the Successor of Elias, St. Simon Stock, c) the confirmation of the Sabbatine Privilege granted by Heaven to the members of the Scapular Confraternity, promulgated by Pope John XXII, d) the doctrinal and theological teachings of the Church on the "Spiritual Motherhood of Mary" and her title as "Mediatrix of all Graces," on which the Devotion is founded.

THE BASIS AND SOURCE
OF THE SCAPULAR DEVOTION

The Visions and the Promises

The terrible persecutions of the Monks at the hands of the Saracens on Mount Carmel soon prompted the exodus of the Carmelites from the East to the West. St. Simon Stock became the sixth Prior General of the Order of Carmel in the year 1245. It was to him that the Mother of God appeared on July 16, 1251 holding the Scapular of the Order, she said: *This will be for you and for all Carmelites, a privilege; he who dies in this will not suffer fire for eternity, that is, he who dies in this will be saved.* (9)

The Vision and the Promise given by the Mother of God to Pope John XXII, to all those wearing the Scapular, recorded in the Sabbatine Bull dated March 3, 1322 is: *I, the Mother of Grace, shall descend on the Saturday after their death and whoso I shall find in Purgatory, I shall free so that I may lead them unto the holy mountain of life everlasting.* (10)

By the middle of the seventeenth century, the Scapular had undergone the examination of Church authorities, had passed this test successfully and had been widely propagated. (10a)

Regarding traditions of apparitions or revelations, St. Pius X also cited the decision of the Congregation of the Councils in 1877: *Such apparitions or revelations have been neither approved nor condemned by the Apostolic See, but only permitted as piously to be believed by human faith alone, according to the tradition which they bear, confirmed by suitable testimonies and witnesses.* (11)

In passing judgement on pious traditions this must be borne in mind: that the Church acts so prudently in this matter that it does not allow such traditions to be narrated in books unless great caution has been employed. (11a)

All those things which could create difficulty both in the vision of (St. Simon) Stock and in the Sabbatine Bull have been removed both by the wise observations of learned men and the decree of the Roman Pontiff, (Paul V, 1613).(12)

THE FOUNDATION
OF THE SCAPULAR DEVOTION

The Scapular Devotion has been approved by the Church because it is founded on Catholic teaching, namely, the *Spiritual Motherhood of Mary,* and *Mary as Mediatrix of All Graces* and is an undeniable source of grace for the soul.

The Privilege, commonly called the Sabbatine, of John XXII, approved and confirmed by Clement VII (in *Ex clemente* 12 Aug., 1530) by (Saint) Pius V (in *Superna dispositione* 18 Feb., 1566) by Gregory XIII (in *Ut laudes* 18 Sept., 1577) and by others as also by the Holy Roman and Universal Inquisition under Paul V on the 20th Jan. 1613, is by a Decree of the following tenor:

It is lawful for the Carmelite Fathers to preach that Christians may piously believe in the help promised to the souls of the brethren and the members of the Confraternity of the Blessed Virgin Mary of Mount Carmel, namely, that the Blessed Virgin will assist by her continual intercession, suffrages and merits and also by her special protection, particularly on the Saturday after death (which day has been consecrated to her by the Church), the souls of the brothers and the members of the Confraternity departing this life in charity who shall have worn the habit and shall have observed chastity according to their particular state of life and also have recited the Little Office (of the Blessed Virgin or if unable to read, have kept the fasts of the Church and have abstained from the use of meat on Wednesdays and Saturdays, unless the Feast of the Nativity of Our Divine Lord should fall on one of those days.) (13)

Pope St. Pius X: S. Congregatio S. Officii, December 16th, 1910: (The substitution of the Scapular Medal for the Cloth Scapular under certain conditions)

*For the future all the faithful already inscribed or who shall be inscribed in one or other of the real Scapulars approved by the Holy See...shall be enabled to share in and gain all the spiritual favors (**not excepting what is known as the Sabbatine Privilege of the Scapular of our Lady of Mount Carmel**) and all the privileges attached to each. The right side of this medal must show the image of Our Most Holy Redeemer, Jesus Christ, showing His Sacred Heart and the obverse that of the Most Blessed Virgin Mary. I desire most vehemently that the cloth Scapulars be worn as heretofore.* (14)

Three things principally are enunciated in this Decree:

1 **Recognition of the Scapular Devotion as a universal Devotion;**

2 **The earnest wish of the Holy Father, Pope Pius X that the faithful continue to wear the cloth Scapular as before;**

3 **The extension of the Scapular Indulgences and spiritual favors to the medal).** (14a)

Pope Pius XII Letter: *Neminem profecto*, to the Superior General of the Carmelites, February 11, 1950:

*For this reason We have been glad to hear that as the Seventh Centenary of the Institution of this Scapular of the divine Mother of Mount Carmel approaches the Carmelite Brethren have decided to hold solemn celebrations in honor of the Blessed Virgin Mary. As a Marian Vestment, the Sacred Scapular is certainly a sign and guarantee of the protection of the Mother of God. ...On her part, the most holy Mother will not fail to intercede with God that her children who in purgatory are expiating their sins, may, at the earliest possible moment, reach the Eternal Fatherland in accordance with the so-called **Sabbatine Privilege.** (15)*

Pope John Paul II General Audience: *Mary has Universal Spiritual Motherhood*, Wednesday, 24 September, 1997:

Mary is Mother of humanity in the order of grace. The Second Vatican Council highlights this role of Mary, linking it to her co-operation in Christ's Redemption...With these statements the constitution "Lumen Gentium"wishes to give proper emphasis to the fact that the Blessed Virgin was intimately associated with Christ's redemptive work, becoming the Savior's "generous associate" in a singular way.

Mary exercises her role as "Advocate" by co-operating both with the Spirit the Paraclete and with the One who interceded on the Cross for his persecutors (cf. Lk 23:34) whom John calls our 'advocate with the Father' (1 Jn 2:1). As a mother, she defends her children and protects them from the harm caused by their own sins. As maternal Mediatrix, Mary presents our desires and petitions to Christ and transmits the divine gifts to us, interceding continually on our behalf. (16)

Pope John Paul II General Audience: *We can count on Mary's intercession,* Wednesday, 5 November, 1997:

Having received salvation and grace from Christ, the Blessed Virgin is called to play an important role in humanity's redemption. Through Marian devotion Christians acknowledge the value of Mary's presence on their journey to salvation, having recourse to her for every kind of grace. They especially know that they can count on her motherly intercession to receive from the Lord everything necessary for growing in the divine life and for attaining eternal salvation. As the many titles attributed to the Blessed Virgin and the continual pilgrimage to Marian shrines attest, the trust of the faithful in Jesus' Mother spurs them to call upon her for their daily needs. They are certain that her maternal heart cannot remain indifferent to the material and spiritual distress of her children. (17)

We owe the Scapular to the direct intervention of the holy Mother of God, who in this new proof of her love for man chose St. Simon Stock as her instrument. The Scapular was revealed to him in a celebrated vision with which the Mother of God favored him on the 16th of July, 1251 at Cambridge with a promise to St. Simon Stock that: *He who dies clothed with this Scapular shall not suffer eternal fire.* This is what is called the **Privilege of Preservation,** meaning that the Blessed Virgin, by her powerful intercession, will draw from the divine treasury in favor of the associates, special graces to help the good to persevere to the end and to move sinners to avail themselves of favorable opportunities of conversion before death seizes them. The Sabbatine Privilege is known as the **Privilege of Delivery,** which refers to and is grounded on the promise of the Blessed Virgin, made to Pope John XXII, embodied in his famous Bull, *Sacratissimo uti culmine,* more commonly known as the Sabbatine Bull in which Our Lady promised to withdraw promptly from Purgatory and especially on the first Saturday after death, the associates of the Scapular of Carmel. In the Second Nocturn of the Office of the Feast of Our Lady of Mount Carmel, given in the Roman Breviary, we read: *It is piously believed since her power and mercy have everywhere great efficacy, that the Most Blessed Virgin consoles with special maternal affection the associates of this Scapular, when detained in the fire of Purgatory, who have practiced certain light abstinences, repeated certain prescribed prayers, and observed chastity according to their state in life, and that she will endeavor to bring them to Heaven sooner than would otherwise happen.* (18)

THE THEOLOGY
OF THE SCAPULAR DEVOTION

For the grace of God, which is a healing for the human race, descends to us through her as if through an aqueduct, since the dispensing of grace is attributed to the Virgin not as to its beginning, but because of her position through merit. (18a)

The source of life in the Church is the Sacred Heart of Jesus; this life is communicated to us by the shedding of His Precious Blood; and these merits and graces flow from His Sacred Heart through an Immaculate medium which distributes them to each soul; this is the Blessed Virgin Mary (19)

God made His Mother the great missionary at the foot of the Cross on Calvary. From the Cross Our Beloved Lord said to her: *Woman, behold thy son.* (John 19:27, D.R.) One is standing there who is achieving the mission of co-Redemptrix and receiving that of Universal Mediatrix. (19a)

Now it is God's will that man, by the Merits of the Precious Blood, enter through the Immaculate Virgin Mary into the Sacred Heart of Jesus and not only is this God's will, but He has also given us a way of thus coming to Him...(19aa) *For she is the neck of our Head, by which all spiritual gifts are communicated to His Mystical Body.* (19ab) The conduit through which the merits of the Precious Blood flow to us is the Blessed Virgin Mary. That conduit stands for four phases of Mary's relation to God and man; first, it shows Our Lady's union with the Sacred Heart; second, her union with man; third, her applying of the Precious Blood to our souls, and finally the medium through which we will enter into Our Lord's Heart. (19b) *For from her, as in a most abundant conduit, the drafts of heavenly graces are given: "... in her hands are the treasures of the mercies of the Lord"; "for God wills that she be the principle of all good things."* (19bb)

The Precious Blood signifies Salvation, and the Scapular, being Our Lady's assurance of Salvation, is really the Badge of the Precious Blood. It is a pledge that the Blood of Christ will not have been shed in vain; a pledge that Our Lady will apply the Merits of the Precious Blood to our souls. (19c)

In no other devotion has Mary unconditionally promised Salvation, or made us special children *brought forth by Her and nourished at Her breasts* (Greg. X III Ut Laudes, Sept. 18, 1577) or given such a Sign of perpetual homage that it even makes us members of her first and most dear family. A unique and glorious character of this childlike, simple devotion (is): that it is wordless. The wearing of the Scapular gives rise to a mystical union between the soul and Mary where not a word is spoken. Anyone who actually thinks of Mary with love, confidence and homage, is morally united to her and, by the Scapular, this union is continual. (20)

Therefore, the alliance is two-sided: Mary on her part offers to be our Mother, we offer to be her children; moral union is the result. It is the Sign of a bi-lateral contract and, on her side, Mary assures us of her intercession. Therefore, the Scapular is a bond of union between Mary and the soul. The one who wears the Scapular enjoys Mary's presence by her contract and his. The Scapular is the symbol of that contract and since Satan can do nothing against Mary, the Immaculate Conception, he can do nothing against us when she protects us. That is why one who practices true devotion to her and more particularly one who wears the Scapular cannot be lost. (20a)

So may the most powerful Virgin Mother who once cooperated in love that the faithful might be born in the Church, be even now the means and mediatrix of our salvation. (20aa)

The Sabbatine Bull and
The Sabbatine Privilege

What is the *Sabbatine Bull*? The word *Bull* is the name given to certain important decrees issued by the Holy Father; "it is a most solemn and weighty form of papal letter; the name is derived from the Latin 'Bulla' (seal) since a leaden seal is attached to such a document."(1) (With the promulgation of the new Code of Canon Law in 1918, the use of the term "Bull" has been restricted, and is now applied to documents in which the Pope officially appoints a bishop.) (1a) The *Sabbatine Bull* is a formal decree issued by Pope John XXII, dated March 3, 1322, in which he recorded Our Heavenly Mother's appearance to the Vicar of Christ making an extraordinary promise (to those who wear her Scapular): *I, the Mother of Grace, shall descend on the Saturday after their death and whoso I shall find in Purgatory, I shall free so that I may lead them unto the holy mountain of life everlasting.*(2). This promise is known as: "The Sabbatine Privilege," a particular privilege of the Scapular Confraternity, granted by Jesus Christ, through the intercession of His Most Blessed Mother Mary, confirmed and promulgated by Pope John XXII and indulgenced by the Church; it is contained in the Sabbatine Bull of Pope John XXII and was confirmed in a Decree under His Holiness, Pope Paul V and by the Roman and Universal Inquisition on January 20, 1613.

The Decree of Paul V, issued January 20, 1613 is as follows: *It is lawful for the Carmelite Fathers to preach that Christians may piously believe in the help promised to the souls of the brethren and members of the Confraternity of the Blessed Virgin of Mount Carmel, namely, that the Blessed Virgin will assist by her continual intercession, suffrages and merits, and also by her special protection, particularly on the Saturday after death (which day has been consecrated to her by the Church) the souls of the brothers and the members of the Confraternity departing this life in charity who shall have worn the habit, and shall have observed chastity according to their particular state of life, and also have recited the Little Office (or, if unable to read, have kept the fasts of the Church, and have abstained from the use of meat on Wednesdays and Saturdays, unless the Feast of the Nativity of Our Divine Lord should fall on one of those days.)* (3)

The Brown Scapular of Our Lady of Mount Carmel

In order to gain the Sabbatine Privilege one must have:

1. Departed this life in Charity (the state of Sanctifying Grace or love of God);

2. During life have been a member of the Scapular Confraternity (by being invested with the Brown Scapular by a Priest);

3. Faithfully worn the Scapular (particularly at the time of death);

4. Daily recited the Little Office of the Blessed Virgin, or (a) observed the fasts of the Church and abstained from the use of meat on Wednesdays and Saturdays, or (b) done some other pious work with the permission of one's confessor;

5. Observed chastity according to his (or her) state of life (avoid every sin of thought, word and deed against the Sixth and Ninth Commandments). (3a)

The Summary of Indulgences for the Confratres of the Holy Scapular, confirmed on April 8, 1908, by the Sacred Congregation of Indulgences, distinctly points out that the Sabbatine Privilege of the Supreme Pontiff, John XXII, had been approved and confirmed by Clement VII (August 12, 1530), Pius V (February 18, 1566), Gregory XIII (September 18, 1577), and others and by the Holy Roman Inquisition under Paul V. (3b) That 16th Century Popes had known of the Sabbatine Bull, was evident by the fact they had confirmed it. (4) According to a history of the decisions rendered concerning the Sabbatine Privilege by the Holy See, written by Eliseus Monsignani, Procurator General of the Order in 1718, the originals of these Bulls were submitted to the Holy Office in 1611. There is no question of the authenticity of these Bulls. (5)

St. Robert Bellarmine, who was the most influential of the Cardinals deciding the question of the Sabbatine Privilege by the Decree of 1613, laid down the principle of the authority of the Church. He said: "It cannot be denied to the Carmelite Fathers to preach according to the tenor of the Bulls."(6) It was, in fact, the statements of (Saint) Cardinal Bellarmine which were incorporated into the Decree of 1613. (6a)

The Bull of Pope Clement VII...stipulated the conditions of the Sabbatine Privilege for the members of the "Confraternity of Mount Carmel," one of which was to "wear the habit." (Scapular) (7)

The Carmelite Confraternity includes all those who living in the world and wearing piously the Holy Scapular, have their names entered on the Roll of this Society and observe its rules faithfully. The Confraternity is grounded on the words of Our Lady to St. Simon Stock and the declarations of several Popes who in their Bulls have joined persons of all stations and of both sexes, into a spiritual community, declaring them partakers in all the ... good works which are performed in the Carmelite Order. (8)

This Vision (to St. Simon Stock), was vouchsafed by saintly General at the Carmelite convent of Cambridge. Some authorities are satisfied that St. Simon instituted at Cambridge a Confraternity of the Scapular in organic dependence on the Carmelite Order to unite the devout clients of Mary in certain regular exercises of religion and piety. The Rev. R. Masters believes that this Cambridge Confraternity existed as early as the year 1272 (only 21 years after the Scapular vision). (9)

After receiving the Scapular from the hands of Our Heavenly Mother, St. Simon Stock immediately instituted the first Confraternity of the Scapular and several sick persons were cured on receiving the habit (Scapular) from his hands. These included King Edward I of England, (King) St. Louis of France and nearly all the sovereigns of Europe with their subjects to be invested in the Scapular. This is the famous Confraternity of Our Lady of Mt. Carmel, which all the popes for the last six centuries have approved, confirmed and endowed with privileges and the most abundant graces. This Confraternity, one of the most ancient in the Church as well as the most favored by God, the Blessed Virgin and the Holy See, received a new glory by the gift of the Scapular, after which it is now called. This gift from Heaven, this distinctive mark of the Confraternity and the instrument of so many graces is, as we have seen, the fruit of the prayers of St. Simon Stock. (10)

The Sabbatine Bull, therefore, contained the second Promise, known as the Sabbatine Privilege, made by the Blessed Virgin Mary in favor of the Carmelites and members of the Scapular Confraternity. The first Promise made by Our Lady was to St. Simon Stock on the evening of July 16, 1251:

Receive my dearest son, the Scapular of your Order, the sign of my Confraternity, a Privilege for yourself and all Carmelites. Anyone dying in this (habit) shall not suffer eternal flames. It is a sign of Salvation, a safeguard in dangers and a pledge of peace and of an everlasting alliance.(11)

Consequently, the (Sabbatine) Privilege, as a particular Privilege of the Scapular Confraternity cannot be denied. As such, it may be revoked only by the authority of the Church. It is not, therefore, sufficient to say that the Sabbatine Privilege rests merely on the general theological principle assuring its spiritual value, but on the authority of the Church as a particular benefit of the Scapular Confraternity, which no other Confraternity or Sodality or Society as such enjoys. (12)

Regarding the Papal Bull of Pope John XXII, March 3, 1322, issuing the Sabbatine Privilege granted by Heaven, the Bull itself is prefaced in the Decree of the Holy Office, January 20, 1613, (found in the Indulgentiarum, December 1, 1866, following this document) which confirms the Privilege granting the Indulgence to the Scapular Confraternity. Later, in the Acta Sanctae Sedis, July 4, 1908, the preface of the Bull of Pope John XXII (granting the Sabbatine Privilege), is removed. However, the name of Pope John XXII is retained as those of Pope Clement VII, Pope Pius V and Pope Gregory XIII all of whom confirmed the Bull of Pope John XXII: The "Sabbatine Bull."

The Decree supposed the fact of the revelation as it was traditionally handed down, particularly through the 16th century Papal Bulls. The King of Portugal had petitioned Pope Paul V not to reject the Privilege of the Sabbatine Bull (13) in a letter from His Catholic Majesty, the King, praying that the Holy Father (Paul V) and the Congregation would not alter the Privilege (Sabbatine) nor diminish the graces which the Holy Father had already given to the Bull, which had been called the Sabbatine. He expressed a desire that the Holy Father would confirm the (Sabbatine) Bull in the terms of Gregory XIII. (13a) Cardinal Bellarmine said the petition could not be denied. Consequently, the Holy Office in its decision expressed no doubt or suspicion of the fact of the revelation in spite of all the historical difficulties, of which it possessed a full knowledge. (14)

Therefore, the decision of the Holy Office, which Pope Benedict XIV termed: "the wise Decree of Pope Paul V," supposing the revelation and approving it as credible, stands. (15)

We have already pointed out the consistency between the revelation of the great Promise of the Scapular attributed to St. Simon Stock and the revelation of the Sabbatine Privilege. The former speaks in terms of eternal salvation...the latter, addressed immediately to the faithful through a pope, makes conditions explicit and speaks in terms of Purgatory. The conditions themselves constitute a suitable devotion to the Blessed Virgin. One revelation, in fact, seems to be a corollary of the other. (16)

The revelations themselves and what has followed from centuries of their acceptance in the Church is nothing more than a concrete expression of the Spiritual Maternity and Mediation of the Blessed Virgin. (17)

As the Faith teaches, she is our Mother in life, our Mother in death, our Mother even beyond death. This aspect of Mariology has been realized concretely in the Devotion. (18)

Concerning the Sabbatine Privilege, therefore, the Decree of the Holy Office of 1613 must be admitted to regulate the entire question, including the historical aspect. No one may gainsay the Decree unless he wishes to place himself above the authority of the Church. (19)

Pope Clement VII, Pope Paul III, Pope Paul IV, Pope Julius III, Pope Pius V, Pope Gregory XIII, all confirm the concessions of their predecessors, mentioning the names of Pope John XXII and Pope Alexander V approving and ratifying the contents of their Bulls. These Popes would not surely quote these two Bulls (the Sabbatine Bull of Pope John XXII and that of Pope Alexander V confirming it) and make them the foundation of their own if there were any doubt of their authenticity. To these authorities we may add that of the Sacred Congregation of Rites, which has approved the Lessons of the Second Nocturn of the Breviary for the feast of the Solemn Commemoration of the Blessed Virgin of Mount Carmel, and the Decree of the Congregation of the Inquisition, under Pope Paul V, February 15th, 1613; both confirm of the privileges of the Sabbatine Bull. (20)

The very impressive *Letter* addressed by Pope Pius XI, in loving memory of the Most Reverend Elias Magennis, then Prior General of the Carmelites, on the occasion of the Sixth Centenary of the Sabbatine Bull, is but another in the long list of Papal Documents that might be quoted. It begins (in this manner): *Almost six hundred years have passed since the Sabbatine Privilege was first preached in the Church.* In the course of the *Letter,* His Holiness urges all the members of the Scapular Confraternity to gain the indulgences to which they are entitled, and *particularly that indulgence which is the principal and the greatest of them all, namely, the Sabbatine.* (20a)

Be it noted in passing that as early as 1913 the Sacred Congregation of Rites approved three proper Masses in honor of the Virgin of Carmel, and that on March 26, 1919, it granted to the Carmelite Order a proper preface: in both these liturgical documents the Sabbatine Privilege is very evidently referred to. The proper office for the Scapular Feast on July 16th with the same Sabbatine teaching (had) been in use for three hundred years; it too was approved by the Sacred Congregation. More proof, not only from papal documents, but also from other sources could indeed be offered. But enough has been given, certainly, to reassure any who doubted regarding the firm foundations of the Sabbatine Devotion. (20a)

The Decree of the Sabbatine Privilege is granted by Heaven, and indulgenced by the Church, on behalf of those who have worn the Scapular with love and devotion to the Mother of God and to her Son, throughout their lives.

This great Privilege is in possession of the Confraternity of Mount Carmel, and only one power on earth could deprive the members of it, and that is the power that gave it at the suggestion of God's own Mother (Mary). (21)

Both those who preach the Devotion to the faithful and those who practice it will perhaps best comprehend it and the ideals it strives to inculcate from the words of the Church, in the special Preface for the Feast of Our Lady of Mount Carmel: *For these the Blessed Virgin has taken to herself by means of the Holy Scapular as children of her special love.* (22)

Introduction to Published Decrees on the Sabbatine Privilege: "Authentic Rescript;" "Summary of the Acts of the Holy See"

Acta Apostolicae Sedis is Latin for "Acts of the Apostolic See." It is the official journal of the Vatican that serves as the standard record of the Holy See. It was established by Pope Pius X in the decree, *Promulgandi Pontificios Constitutionis*, promulgated on September 29, 1908. The first issue was published on January 1, 1909. The Acta Apostolicae Sedis (abbreviated AAS), contains the texts of encyclicals, apostolic constitutions, papal and curial audiences and releases from the various dicasteries of the Roman Curia. Its other major function is to issue canon law, as decreed by Canon 8 such new decrees becoming effective three months from the date of their promulgation.

Acta Sanctae Sedis is Latin for "Acts of the Holy See." It is the "predecessor publication" to the *Acta Apostolicae Sedis* and it served as the principal source of the published public documents of the Holy See. Begun in 1895, it had previously been an unofficial journal and was made official on May 23, 1904. It was superseded in 1909 by the *AAS*. Both of these journals, the *A.S.S.*, and the *A.A.S.* may be found on the Vatican website. *OSVs Encyclopedia of Catholic History.* Matthew Bunson, D. Min., Indiana, 1995, 2004, pp. 38, 39.

In Appendix 1 is a document from the *Rescripta Authentica of the Sacred Congregation of Indulgences—Sacred Relics*, the Summary of Indulgences, dated December 1, 1866. On page 475 of that document, the Decree of January 20, 1613 is prefaced not only by the name of Pope John XXII but also by the words of the Sabbatine Bull of Pope John XXII, March 3, 1322: *Sic mihi,* in which is recorded that Our Blessed Lady appeared to His Holiness, granting the Privilege from Heaven in favor of all those who die wearing the Scapular.

Following the *Rescripta* is a document taken from the *Acta Sanctae Sedis*, Volume XLI, p. 609 given on the 4th of July, 1908. It is the published Decree of the Sabbatine Privilege that was granted by Pope Paul V, on January 20, 1613. The Decree itself is prefaced by the name of Pope John XXII, (to whom Our Blessed Mother appeared in the second of the Scapular Visions, asking him to ratify on earth the Privilege that had been granted in Heaven to all those who died wearing the Scapular) followed by the names of Pope Clement VII, Pope (Saint) Pius V and Pope Gregory XIII, all of whom confirmed the Sabbatine Bull of Pope John XXII. Note: See Appendix 1, for *The Rescripta and the Summarium.*

Pope St. John Paul II and the Brown Scapular

In the year 2001, the Carmelite Order celebrated the 750th Anniversary of the bestowal of the Brown Scapular of Our Lady of Mount Carmel. The Anniversary was noted by a special letter of Pope St. John Paul II, dated March 25, 2001, in which he states: *In this regard, I cannot fail to stress a happy coincidence, the celebration of this Marian year for the whole Carmel is taking place, according to a venerable tradition of the Order itself on the 750th Anniversary of the bestowal of the Scapular.* (1)

Throughout his Pontificacy, His Holiness never failed to express to the faithful, his love for Our Lady and especially for the Brown Scapular, which he testified to wearing from his childhood to throughout his Papacy, as seen in the following pictures.

The Scapular Devotion has been a Universal Devotion in the Church for Centuries. The Scapular is a Marian habit or garment. It is both a sign and pledge, a sign of belonging to Mary, a pledge of her motherly protection, not only in this life, but after death, it is a sign of devotion to and trust in her Immaculate Heart, an incitement to become like Mary, by imitating her virtues, above all her humility, chastity and spirit of prayer (2) and a participation in the spiritual benefits and good works of the Carmelite Community.

According to a venerable Carmelite tradition, Our Lady appeared to the Prior General of the Carmelite Order, St. Simon Stock, on July 16, 1251, holding the Scapular of the Order in her hands. She said:

Whosoever dies clothed in this Scapular shall not suffer the fires of hell. (3) This is known as the Scapular Promise. A second promise was made by Our Blessed Mother, in favor of those who wear her Scapular, to Pope John XXII, which was written in a Bull issued by this same Pope dated March 3, 1322: *I the Mother of Grace, shall descend on the Saturday after their death and whoso I shall find in Purgatory, I shall free, so that I may lead them unto the holy mountain of life everlasing.* (4) In 1613, The Holy Office of the Inquisition, under Pope Paul V, issued the Decree, the Indulgence of the Scapular Confraternity known as the *Sabbatine Privilege.*

This Devotion began to flourish immediately among the people from the time of St. Simon Stock. Chapter 3, "The Chronology of Events" will help the reader to understand the importance and magnitude of this ancient and great Devotion to the Mother of God, rooted in the Old Testament.

Message of Pope St. John Paul II to the Carmelite Family, On the 750th Anniversary of the Bestowal of the Scapular, Vatican City, March 25, 2001

...The celebration of this Marian year for the whole of Carmel is taking place, according to a venerable tradition of the Order itself, on the 750th anniversary of the bestowal of the Scapular...This intense Marian life, which is expressed in trusting prayer, enthusiastic praise and diligent imitation, enables us to understand how the most genuine form of devotion to the Blessed Virgin, expressed by the humble sign of the Scapular, is consecration to her Immaculate Heart. (cf. Pius XII, Letter Neminem profecto latet [11 February 1950: AAS 42, 1950, pp. 390-391]; Dogmatic Constitution on the Church Lumen gentium, n. 67). In this way, the heart grows in communion and familiarity with the Blessed Virgin, as a new way of living for God and of continuing here on earth the love of Jesus the Son for His Mother Mary. (cf. Angelus Address, in Insegnamenti XI/3, 1988, p. 173) (5)

Karol Wojtyla, as a young factory worker,
wearing his Brown Scapular.

What is Pope John Paul II's affiliation with the Carmelites?

In a letter to Cardinal Ballestrero OCD dated 14 September 1981, the Holy Father had said: "From Childhood we have been so closely linked with the sons of the admirable St. Teresa that we became a Carmelite tertiary." (A souvenir of JPII's visit to Britain, 1981. Printed by the Nuns of the Darlington Carmel, p. 15.)

Carmelites are very happy to count among our numbers our Holy Father, Pope John Paul II. The vocation of a Carmelite is a vocation for all Christians, to live in intimacy with the Holy Trinity, with devotion to His Holy Mother Mary, and to grow in charity and grace, striving to live His perfect Will.

"The Marian patrimony of Carmel has become, over time, through the spread of the devotion of the Holy Scapular, a treasure for the whole Church. For its simplicity, for its anthropological value and for the relationship with Mary as regards the Church and humanity, this devotion has been profoundly and widely grasped by the people of God, so much so as to find expression in the commemoration of July 16th, which is present in the Liturgical Calendar of the Universal Church". As far as the Scapular is concerned in a specific way, John Paul II emphasized that it is worn by many simple faithful, as a devotion to Mary, which in this way find themselves associated with the great Carmelite families, and inserted a memory and a personal testimony. "I too have worn on my heart, and have for a long time, the Carmelite Scapular."

From "The confiding of the pontiff in a letter to the Superior Generals of the Carmelite Order and to the Discalced Carmelites Vatican City, March 27th (VID)"

VIA Inside the Vatican Newsflash: John Paul II and the Brown Scapular by John Drogin

Pope John Paul II insisted doctors not remove his brown scapular during surgery on him following the assassination attempt in May 1981. Father Mariano Cera, a Carmelite priest, told Inside the Vatican: "Just before the Holy Father was operated on, he told the doctors 'Don't take off the scapular.' And the surgeons left it on." Father Cera made the comments at the beginning of celebrations for the 750th anniversary of the Carmelite scapular, now underway in Rome. Some 750 years ago monks were banished from Mount Carmel in Palestine by Muslims. Nearly eight centuries later, Pope John Paul is convinced that Our Lady of Mount Carmel, along with Our Lady of Fatima, saved him from the bullets of Mehmet Ali Agca. [See Inside the Vatican, July 2001, page 44] The Virgin Mary appeared at the final apparition of Fatima (Portugal) and at Lourdes (France) wearing the brown scapular. The pontiff, a Third Order Carmelite, has worn the scapular of Our Lady of Mount Carmel since he was a young boy. He frequently asks Our Lady of Mount Carmel to help him make important decisions.

In observation of the 750th anniversary, to be celebrated on July 16, Pope John Paul II has written a special letter to the Carmelites, saying: "I also carry the scapular on my heart...for the love that it nurtures toward the common Heavenly mother, whose protection is continually springing forth."

Currently more than half a million people around the world wear the brown scapular. On Sunday evening, July 8, in the overflowing Carmelite church of Santa Maria in Transpontina, 30 laymen became a part of that expanding number. Father Cera, the chief celebrant, invested these men of faith with the scapular. The scapular of Our Lady of Mount Carmel is inseparable with the events of the past century: Fatima, Russia, the Pope's shooting and especially the hope of reuniting East and West. The Carmelites are the only Order founded in the East that that has settled in the West. Pope Paul VI said the devotion of the brown scapular and the Holy Rosary are the two most recommended devotions by the magisterium of the Church.
www.ourgardenofcarmel.org/carmspecial.html

The Scapular Devotion of Pope John Paul II

✝ www.catholiccompany.com /getfed/the-scapular-devotion-of-pope-john-paul-ii/

Gretchen Filz

Pope John Paul II had a great devotion to the Blessed Virgin Mary, and as such faithfully wore a scapular (notice him wearing his scapular in the above photo).

He is reported to have worn a brown scapular since he was a boy, and he insisted that doctors not remove it during surgery following the assassination attempt on his life in May of 1981.

Father Mariano Cera, a Carmelite priest, told Inside the Vatican magazine: *"Just before the Holy Father was operated on, he told the doctors, 'Don't take off the scapular.' And the surgeons left it on."* The Holy Father credited the miraculous preservation of this life to the protection of the Blessed Virgin Mary.

The Brown Scapular of Our Lady of Mount Carmel

In his message to the Carmelites at the 750th anniversary of the bestowal of the scapular, Pope John Paul II said those who wear the scapular — or habit, as he called it — dedicate themselves to the service of Our Lady for the good of the whole Church.

"The sign of the Scapular points to an effective synthesis of Marian spirituality, which nourishes the devotion of believers and makes them sensitive to the Virgin Mother's loving presence in their lives. The Scapular is essentially a "habit". Those who receive it are associated more or less closely with the Order of Carmel and dedicate themselves to the service of Our Lady for the good of the whole Church."

. . .

"Two truths are evoked by the sign of the Scapular: on the one hand, the constant protection of the Blessed Virgin, not only on life's journey, but also at the moment of passing into the fullness of eternal glory; on the other, the awareness that devotion to her cannot be limited to prayers and tributes in her honour on certain occasions, but must become a "habit", that is, a permanent orientation of one's own Christian conduct, woven of prayer and interior life, through frequent reception of the sacraments and the concrete practice of the spiritual and corporal works of mercy. In this way the Scapular becomes a sign of the "covenant" and reciprocal communion between Mary and the faithful: indeed, it concretely translates the gift of his Mother, which Jesus gave on the Cross to John and, through him, to all of us, and the entrustment of the beloved Apostle and of us to her, who became our spiritual Mother."

The original scapular is the brown scapular associated with the Carmelite order, presented by Our Lady to St. Simon Stock in the year 1251. The Virgin Mary appeared to him surrounded by angels and holding in her hands the brown scapular of the Carmelite habit. She said to him, *"This shall be a privilege for you and for all Carmelites: whoever dies clothed in this shall not suffer eternal fire, rather, he shall be saved."*

The Brown Scapular is a sacramental of the Catholic Church, a devotion as old as the Holy Rosary. A sacramental is, by definition, *"a sacred sign which bears resemblance to the sacraments, and by means of which spiritual effects are signified and obtained through the prayers of the Church"* (CCC 1667). Today there are many different kinds of scapulars associated with various devotions and religious orders with various attached promises. Learn more about them here.

John Paul II:
Remove the Bullet—Not My Scapular!

by Taylor Marshall

As everyone knows, His Holiness John Paul II was shot in Saint Peter's Square on 13 May, 1981—the anniversary of Our Lady's first apparition at Fatima.

Just before doctors were about to begin surgery in order to remove the embedded bullet, the Holy Father regained consciousness and instructed the doctors "do not remove my scapular" during the operation. John Paul II was, after all, Totus Tuus in his devotion to the Mother of God.

Beautiful story.
If you don't wear the Scapular, why not be enrolled this Lent?

John Paul II: Remove the Bullet - Not My Scapular!
http://www.taylormarshall.com/2010/02/john-paul-ii-remove-bullet-not-my.html

Pope Saint John Paul II and His Connection to Carmel

Citoc Online

Millions came to Rome for the canonization of two Popes, John XXIII and John Paul II. Especially with Pope John Paul II so many people had stories of personal encounters with him. Sometimes those encounters actually took place in crowds but for the individuals it was a very personal moment between them and the Pope John Paul II.

Carmelites, too, have many stories of personal encounters to tell. In 26 years, Pope John Paul II visited many churches and almost daily hosted groups at his residences. Among these were some Carmelites. He penned a library of documents some of which were directed to the Carmelites themselves.

As has been well documented, this pope had a deep devotion to Mary and particularly to Our Lady of Mount Carmel. He himself had a deep devotion to the Carmelite scapular (see accompanying story). He often used examples from the lives and writings of the Carmelite saints to make a point in his speeches and writings.

The Pope also showed he was aware of the Carmelites of today and our ministry to the Church worldwide. He reached into the Order to find bishops to serve in several dioceses around the world. Some 18 monasteries of enclosed nuns were erected during his pontificate.

In a letter to the Prior General, Joseph Chalmers, on the occasion of the 2001 General Chapter, Pope John Paul recalled that 2001 was the 750th anniversary of the giving of the scapular, the 7th centenary of the birth of the Carmelite bishop and saint Andrew Corsini, as well as the beginning of the Third Millennium which the Pope felt called to lead the Church into. He wrote about Elijah and Mary as the symbols of the Order and talked about "the journey" that the Order has embarked on.

He continued "You are called to re-read your rich spiritual inheritance in the light of today's challenges so that the 'joys, the hopes, the sadnesses and the anguish of humanity today, of the poor, and above all of those who suffer' are 'the joys and the hope, the sadnesses and the anguish of Christ's disciples' (Gaudium et Spes, n.1) and, in a special way, of every Carmelite."

Carmelite Holy Figures

One occasionally found the pope using quotes from a Carmelite to reinforce his teaching. He himself was very familiar with the life of the 16th century Carmelite mystic John of the Cross. The Carmelite was the subject of his doctoral thesis *Doctrina de fide apud Sanctum Ioannem a Cruce*.

Speaking to young pilgrims at the general audience on November 6, 1985, John Paul called Titus Brandsma "the example...to show us that love is stronger than hate and is destined, even after some moments of failure, to triumph." This was a theme the pope would repeat time after time in his own life. For newly weds, the pope again used Brandsma to teach that even those so involved in the problems of daily life can attain spiritual heights. At the Sunday Angelus on the 50th anniversary John Paul referred to Brandsma's martyrdom as "the highest expression of service to the Gospel and solidly rooted in the spirituality of Carmel.

The Pope appreciated what La Madonna "la Bruna" means to Naples. Venerated by the Neapolitans since the 13th century, the tradition says that the icon was brought to the city by the Carmelites who fled the Holy Land. During a visit to that Italian city in 1990, the pope said that La Bruna "so loved by all the Neapolitans...kept their faith firm and intact."

The Carmelite Scapular

Particularly around the time of the Feast of Our Lady of Mount Carmel in July, the Pope often spoke of the Carmelite scapular, usually in the context of its value for today's Christian. In an audience on July 16, 1988, with a group of the Alpini, a branch of the Italian military, John Paul II quoted his predecessor Pius XII to single out the scapular from among the many expressions of devotion to Mary.

Some days later at the summer residence in Castelgandolfo, the Pope called the scapular "a particular grace" of Mary. In this way, the heart grows in communion and familiarity with the Blessed Virgin Mary. He spoke of this as "a new way of living for God and of continuing here on earth the love of Jesus the Son for his Mother Mary."

In a talk with the youth of the Carmelite parish of St. Mary in Transpontina in 1989, the pope said he owed much in his youth to the Carmelite scapular. Then he compared Mary's clothing us in the scapular to a mother who sees that her children are properly clothed. "Our Lady of Mount Carmel dresses us in a spiritual sense. She dresses us with the grace of God and helps us always ..."

Mary - Our Lady of Mt. Carmel

The deep devotion of Pope John Paul II to Our Lady under her various titles was well documented during his 26-year pontificate. He began his pontificate by saying to the crowd gathered in St. Peter's for his first *Urbi et Orbi* blessing that he accepted the election "in the spirit of obedience to Our Lord and with total trust in his Mother, the Most Holy Madonna." He attributed his survival of the attempted assassination on May 13, 1981 to Our Lady of Fatima whose feast was celebrated the day of the attempt.

His devotion to Mary as Our Lady of Mount Carmel was also manifest during his years as pope. In a general audience on July 13, 1988 the Pope challenged the young people to examine their own devotion to Mary and then suggested they think about devotion to Our Lady of Mount Carmel.

At the same audience, he told the sick that "Our Lady of Mount Carmel sheds light on the beauty of the mystery of suffering." He asked the newlyweds in the piazza to "put your love under the protection of Our Lady of Mount Carmel" reminding them that "it is her prayer and intercession that will protect your love from danger and will cause your love to always be faithful and rich."

During the Angelus celebrated at Castelgandolfo on July 24, 1988, the Pope recalled that Carmelite mystics experienced God in their lives as "the way of perfection" and "ascending Mount Carmel" —always in the presence of Mary as Mother, Patroness, and Sister. He said that for those in Carmel and in every soul which is deeply Carmelite, a life of intense communion and closeness to the Virgin Mary grows.

At the Carmelite parish of Traspontina in January 1989, the Pope admitted to the young people who came to meet him that Our Lady of Mount Carmel had been of great help to him as a youngster. "I can not say exactly to what extent but I think she helped me greatly. She assisted me in finding the grace of my vocation."

During the Sunday Angelus on July 16, 2000, while on vacation in Aosta, the Pope spoke again of the Carmelites as the mountains around him made him think of Mount Carmel in Palestine. Recalling that Carmel is a symbol of total adhesion to the divine will and of our eternal salvation, he said "We are called to climb this spiritual mountain courageously and without pausing. Walking together with the Virgin, model of total fidelity to the Lord, we will not fear obstacles or difficulties. Sustained by her maternal intercession, like Elijah, we will be able to fulfill our vocation to be authentic "prophets" of the Gospel in our time.

He prayed that "the Blessed Virgin of Mount Carmel help us to rise tirelessly toward the top of the mountain of sanctity, and to hold nothing more dear than Christ, who reveals the mystery of divine love and humanity's true dignity to the world."

May his prayer become a reality in our lives.

http://ocarm.org/en/content/ocarm/saint-pope-john-paul-ii-and-his-connection-carmel

CHAPTER 2 ENDNOTES

WHAT IS THE BROWN SCAPULAR?

1   *The Directory on Popular Piety and the Liturgy, Principles and Guidelines,* Congregation for Divine Worship and the Discipline of Sacraments, *Veneration of the Holy Mother of God,* #205, Vatican City, December 2001

2   *Mary in Her Scapular Promise,* John Haffert, New Jersey, 1942 p.8, paraphrased.

3   *Ibid*, p. 10 Cf. from *Viridarium Ordinis B. Virginis Mariae de Monte Carmelo* per Johannem Grossi, reproduced in the Analecta Ordinis Carmelitarum VIII (1932, Rome) from the Spec., t. I. by Danielis a V.M; See footnote # 10, p. 233 in "Mary in Her Scapular Promise"

4   The Sabbatine Privilege of the Scapular, 1322-1922 A.D., P. E. Magennis, New York, 1923, p. 18

A SYNTHESIS OF THE DEVOTION

1   Prov 1: 8, 9 Douay Rheims

2   Pope Pius IX, 1846-1878, Encyclical: *Ubi Primum,* February 2, 1849, *Papal Teachings Out Lady,* The Benedictine Monks of Solesmes, Boston, 1961, p. 57

3   *Introduction to Mary,* Dr. Mark Miravalle, S.T.D, 1993, p. 125 *Lumen Gentium* No. 62, (paraphrased)

4   *The Credibility of the Scapular Promises,* Rev Christian P. Ceroke, O.Carm., Rome, 1950, pp.38,41,43

5   Dogmatic Constitution on the Church, *Lumen Gentium,* No. 62; Pope Paul VI, November 21, 1964

6   Message of John Paul II Carmelite Family on the 750th Anniversary of the bestowal of the Scapular, Vatican, 25 March, 2001

7   Letter, Pope Pius XII, *Neminem profecto,* to the Superior General of the Carmelites, February 11,1950; *Papal Teachings on Our Lady,* Benedictine Monk of Solesmes, 1961, p. 289

8   Paraphrased and translated from: *Enciclopedia del Escapulario del Carmen,* por el P. Simon M. Besalduch, Barcelona, 1931, pp. 41-45); De Institutione Primorum Monach., 1. VI, c. I, in Spec. Carm., t. I, p. 54

9   Viridarium, (John) Grossi, 2 ms. Vat. lat. 3813, ff. 12v-13r: *The Credibility* of the Scapular Promises, Christian P. Ceroke, O. Carm., 1950, Appendix I, p. 79

10   *Ibid*, Appendix II, p. 90

10a *Take This Scapular,* Carmelite Fathers and Tertiaries, Chicago, 1949, p. 216

11   A A S. 2, (1910) 665, Pope Pius X,

11a *The Scapular and Some Critics,* P. E. Magennis, O.C.C., Rome, 1914, p. 10

12   *De Festes,* Chapter 78, Pope Benedict XIV, cf: *The Irish Ecclesiastical Record,* John E. Bartley, O.C.C., Vol. VIII, Dublin. 1887, p. 807, parce

13 *The Sabbatine Privilege of the Scapular. 1322-1922*, P. E. Magennis, Ord. Carm., New York, 1923, p. 78

14 S. Congregatio S. Officii, December 16th 1910; cf. Analecta O. Carm, vol. II, pp. 3 and 4

14a *Take This Scapular,* Carmelite Fathers and Tertiaries, Chicago, 1949, p. 49

15 *Papal Teachings, Our Lady,* Benedictine Monks of Solesmes, Boston, 1961, pp. 288-290

16 Pope John Paul II, General Audience, *Mary has Universal Spiritual Motherhood,* Wednesday, 24 September 1997

17 Pope John Paul II, General Audience, *We can count on Mary's intercession,* Wednesday, 5 November 1997

18 *The Sacramentals of the Holy Catholic Church*, by Rev. A. A. Lambing, LL.D., Benzinger Brothers (Printers to the Holy Apostolic See), New York, Cincinnati, Chicago, 1892, (from the Library of Congress, Washington) pp. 166, 173, 174, 175, 176, paraphrased

18a "Bonaventure: The Grace of God, Healing for the human race descends to us through Mary," Wednesday, June 1, 2011, Bonaventure of Bagnorea (1221-1274): Homily, from Mattins of the Feast of the Blessed Virgin Mary, Queen, in the Old Breviary @ http://lzkiss.net/cgi-bin/horas/ brevi.pl)

19 Authentic Manuscript of John Mathias Haffert, *Maria,* 1940, p. 7

19a *Mary in Her Scapular Promise*, John Mathias Haffert, 1942, pp. 106, 108, paraphrased

19aa Authentic Manuscript of John Mathias Haffert, *Maria,* 1940, p. 7

19ab [St. Bernardine of Siena, *Quadrag. De Evangelio aeterno, Sermo X,* a. 3. C. 3.] St. Pius X Encyclical *Ad diem illum,* Feb. 2, 1904, *AAS* 36, 1904. 453-54

19b Authentic Manuscript of John Mathias Haffert, 1940, *Maria,* p. 8

19bb [Internal quotes are from St. John Damascene, *Series I De Nativitate Virginis* and St. Irenaeus, *Against Valentinus* III. 33.]. Leo XIII, Encyclical, *Diuturni temporis spatium,* Sept 5,1898, *ASS* 31, 1898, 146

19c Authentic Manuscript of John Mathias Haffert, *Maria,* 1940, p. 10

20 *Mary in Her Scapular Promise*, John Mathias Haffert, New Jersey, 1942, p. 48, paraphrased

20a *Ibid,* pp. 50, 52, paraphrased

20aa Citing St. Augustine, De sancta Virginitate 6.] Leo XIII, *Parta humano generi*, Apostolic Letter, Sept. 8, 1901, *ASS* 34, 1901, 195

THE SABBATINE BULL AND
THE SABBATINE PRIVILEGE

1   www.catholicculture.org/culture/library/dictionary CatholicCulture. org (under B: bull, papal) paraphrased

1a *Take This Scapular*, Carmelite Fathers and Tertiaries, Chicago, 1949, p. 53

2   *The Sabbatine Privilege of the Scapular*, P. E. Magennis, O. Carm., New York, 1923, p. 18

3   *Take this Scapular,* Carmelite Fathers and Tertiaries, Chicago, 1949, p. 55

3a *Ibid*, p. 56

3b *Ibid*, p. 54

4   *The Credibility of the Scapular Promises,* 1950, pp. 31, 32

5   *Ibid*, p. 32. Notes to Chapter Two, footnote #2, p. 14; also see Analecta Ord. Carm. Vol. IV, (Romae, 1917), pp. 246-247; 251ff.

6   *Ibid*, pp. 163-164;

6a *Ibid*, p. 164, footnote #6, See notes to Chapter Five, footnote #6, p. 49

7   *Ibid*, pp. 161-162

8   *The White Friars,* Rev. P.R. McCaffrey, Ord. Carm., Dublin, 1926, p. 66

9   *Ibid*, p. 55

10 *The Carmelites and the Brown Scapular,* A.E. Farrington, D.D., O.C.C., Dublin, 1891, pp. 104-105 paraphrased; also p. 108

11 *Ibid*, p. 104

12 *The Credibility of the Scapular Promises,* p, 167

13 *Ibid*, p. 171; Cf. "Ralazione di Tutti" in Archives of the Order; **(13a):** *The Sabbatine Privilege of the Scapular,* P. E. Magennis, Ord. Carm., New York, 1923, p. 86

14 *Ibid*, p. 172

15 *Ibid*, pp. 172-173

16 *Ibid*, p. 173

17 *Ibid*, p. 173

18 *Ibid*, p. 173; *Decretum de Scapulari B.M.V. de Monte Carmelo a simultanea traditione excipienda*, 27 April 1887, Ex. S. Congreg. Indulgentiarum, A.S.S., Vol. XIX, 1886, (sic) pp. 554-555 (footnote #34, Chapter V, *"The Credibility of the Scapular Promises,"* p. 56 under "Chapter Notes.")

19 *Ibid*, p. 173-174

20 *The Irish Ecclesiastical Record*, Vol. VIII, No. 1, Dublin, January, 1887, pp. 802, 803; V. Spec. Carm., T. 1, p. 491 par.

20a *The American Ecclesiastical Review, The Sabbatine Privilege*, Fr. Gabriel Pausback, Vol. CIX, July, 1943, pp. 68-71

21 *The Sabbatine Privilege of the Scapular*, 1322AD – 1922AD., P. E. Magennis, Ord. Carm., New York, 1923, p. 11

22 *The Credibility of the Scapular Promises*, ev. Christian P. Ceroke, 1950, p. 200, paraphrased

POPE ST. JOHN PAUL II AND THE BROWN SCAPULAR

1 *Letter of John Paul II to the Carmelites on the Occasion of the 750th Anniversary of the Scapular*, March 25, 2001

2 ZENIT-Brown Scapular, A Silent Devotion, Carmelite Recounts Mary's Promise to St. Simon Stock, July 16, 2008

3 *Mary in Her Scapular Promise*, John Mathias Haffert, NJ 1942, p. 22

4 *The Sabbatine Privilege of the Scapular*, P. E. Magennis, New York, 1923, p. 18

5 *Letter of John Paul II to the Carmelites on the Occasion of the 750th Anniversary of the Scapular*, March 25, 2001

CHAPTER 3
THE CHRONOLOGY OF EVENTS

Chapter 3

The Chronology of Events

When did the Devotion Begin?

...Blessed be the God and Father of Our Lord Jesus Christ, the Father of mercies and the God of all comfort, who comforteth us in all tribulation and with our Lord may She be blessed whom He constituted Mother of Mercy, Queen and our most loving Advocate, Mediatrix of His Graces, Dispenser of His treasures!

...As the first-born daughter of the Father, the perfect Mother of the Word, the beloved Spouse of the Holy Spirit, she is related in virtue of the Hypostatic Union to the Most Holy Trinity...

> R.M. on the occasion of the coronation of the
> statue of Our Lady of Fatima, May 13, 1946
> (Mary's Universal Queenship), Pope Pius XII

The Glory of the Lord appeared in the cloud.
(Ex. 16: 10)

"It is a tradition well received and very ancient, that the Order of Carmel originated at the time of the Prophets and especially from the Institute of Elias and that it holds a hereditary succession commenced on Mount Carmel, from which it has borrowed its name. This tradition may be regarded as venerable, all the more as seven Sovereign Pontiffs, in the Bulls accorded to the Order, speak in the following terms of the Religious who are its members: *They shine in charity as a mirror and a model holding an hereditary succession from the holy Prophets Elias and Eliseus, and the other Fathers, who have inhabited the holy mountain of Carmel near the fountain of Elias.* (1)

The great Prophet Elias has always been regarded by the Carmelites as the Founder and Patriarch of their Order. This ancient and cherished tradition has been sanctioned by the Church, for the statue of the Prophet stands in the Vatican (In the Basilica of St. Peters), among the Founders of the Religious Orders, bearing the following inscription: *Universus Ordo Carmelitarum Fundatori Suo Sancto Ellae Prophetae Erexit.* (The Order of Carmel has erected this statue to the Holy Prophet Elias, its Founder). The rescript which accorded this privilege was granted by Benedict XIII, written with his own hand, and addressed to the Carmelite Fathers, June 26, 1725. (2)

In regard to the antiquity of Carmel, the authority of the Doctors, of history, ancient and modern, the old monuments of the Order of Carmel and the added testimony of the Sovereign Pontiffs assure us that the Order owes its origin to the discipline and institute of Elias. (3)

In the subsequent pages under, "The Chronology of Events," the origin of the Carmelite Order and the Scapular Devotion is traced from the Prophet Elias on Mount Carmel in the Old Testament to its present state in the 21st century. According to the Historian John XLIV, Patriarch of Jerusalem: to Elias were revealed the mysteries of the Incarnation, among them, that of the Immaculate Conception of Our Blessed Lady (as he beheld the vision in the little cloud in the shape of a foot, found in the Book of Kings I, 18:44.) From that moment, he was called Elias, the Prophet of the Immaculate. (4)

The Virgin symbolized in the cloud was the final cause in the foundation of the Order. (5) From the Institution of Elias on Mt. Carmel, centuries later came a saintly Carmelite, a successor of Elias, gifted from childhood with heavenly visions and immensely devoted to the Mother of God, who was elected Prior General of the whole Order in 1245, St. Simon Stock. Chosen by the Queen of Heaven, it was through him that she bestowed the heavenly gift of the Scapular to the world.

The Chronology of Events will be a journey through time and will trace the confirmation and approbation of numerous Solemn Pontiffs, of the Visions of Our Lady to St. Simon Stock and to Pope John XXII. Faithful Carmelite historians throughout the centuries have attested, through eyewitness testimony, to the fact of the authenticity of the Visions. To this day, the Scapular and its meaning and purpose were confirmed by Holy Father Emeritus, Benedict XVI.

THE GREAT PROPHET ELIAS

FOUNDER AND PATRIARCH
OF THE CARMELITE ORDER

Elias was born at Thesbe on the border of Arabia of the tribe of Aaron the Levite, but he lived in Galaa. St. Epiphanius in his "Lives of the Prophets," tells us that when his mother gave birth to Elias, his father Sobac had a vision: Men, carrying a white garment before them, were paying homage to a little boy whom they tore from his mother's breast and cast into the fire. They even fed him with flames of fire instead of food; and the prophecy was made: His speech shall be interpretation and wisdom; he shall judge Israel with fire and with a two-edged sword.

The name "Elias" means the "Lord God" according to the interpretation of St. Isidore, who calls him a man full of faith and lofty devotion, strong under hardship, fruitful in resources, endowed with a powerful intellect, rigid in austere virtue, unwearied in holy meditation, fearless in the face of death.

His virtues are praised by Saints and Doctors of the Church, who call him the chief of the Prophets and the Father of the monastic life. All the Fathers agree in saying that he was a virgin. St. Gregory of Nyssa proposes him, with St. John the Baptist, as an example and model of virginity; and St. Ephrem teaches that virginity will serve as a chariot, lifting heavenward all those who guard it, as Elias did.

St. Bernardine of Siena speaks of his wonderful obedience, and St. Augustine proposes him to us as a figure of Jesus Christ. He fasted forty days and forty nights like Our Lord; he stood up as a fire burning with zeal for the glory of God, preaching and recalling sinners, announcing to them the ways of justice and sanctity. He raised the dead to life like the Son of God, and he was the chosen symbol of His Ascension, being raised aloft in a triumphal chariot.

The Father and Founder of Carmel is, then, one of the most illustrious Saints of the Church of God and he truly is indeed the Father and Founder of the Carmel today, may be shown by abundant testimony. St. Jerome, writing to St. Paulinus says that if the source of the monastic life is sought for in Scripture it will be found that Elias is its Founder. (1)

61

{1}*And Elias the prophet stood up, as a fire, and his word burnt like a torch.* [2] *He brought a famine upon them, and they that provoked him in their envy, were reduced to a small number, for they could not endure the commandments of the Lord.* [3] *By the word of the Lord he shut up the heaven, and he brought down fire from heaven thrice.* [4] *Thus was Elias magnified in his wondrous works. And who can glory like to thee?* [5] *Who raised up a dead man from below, from the lot of death, by the word of the Lord God.* [6] *Who broughtest down kings to destruction, and brokest easily their power in pieces, and the glorious from their bed.* [7] *Who heardest judgment in Sina, and in Horeb the judgments of vengeance.* [8] *Who anointedst kings to penance, and madest prophets successors after thee.* [9] *Who wast taken up in a whirlwind of fire, in a chariot of fiery horses.* [10] *Who art registered in the judgments of times to appease the wrath of the Lord, to reconcile the heart of the father to the son, and to restore the tribes of Jacob.* [11] *Blessed are they that saw thee, and were honoured with thy friendship.* [12] *For we live only in our life, but after death our name shall not be such.* [13] *Elias was indeed covered with the whirlwind, and his spirit was filled up in Eliseus: in his days he feared not the prince, and no man was more powerful than he.* [14] *No word could overcome him, and after death his body prophesied.* [15] *In his life he did great wonders, and his death he wrought miracles.*(2)

And Elias went up to the top of Mount Carmel, and casting himself down upon the earth put his face between his knees. And he said to his servant: *Go up, and look toward the sea.* And he went up, and looked and said: *There is nothing.* And again he said to him: *Return seven times.* And at the seventh time: Behold a little cloud arose out of the sea like a man's footstep. And he said: *Go up, and say to Achab: Prepare thy chariot, and go down, lest the rain prevent thee.* (I Kings)

And while he turned himself this way and that way, behold the heavens grew dark, with clouds and wind, and there fell a great rain. (I Kings, 18:43-45)

This expectation of Elias for the rain—the Redemption that would save the earth from the drought—and his idea that the little cloud was a symbol of the Virgin Mary were the reasons why Elias' followers began to come and pray at Mount Carmel for the advent of Our Lady and Our Lord. Those hermits of Mount Carmel were considered the beginning of the Carmelite Order, which is the firstborn of the Religious Orders and also the first dedicated to Our Lady. Because of this particular episode, Elias is considered the first devotee of the

Virgin Mary in History.

The following texts taken from the book *Élie le Prophète selon les Écritures et les Traditions Chrétiennes* [Elias, the Prophet according to Scriptures and Christian Traditions] from the Carmelite Studies collection (Desclée de Brower, 1956, 2 volumes), confirm this tradition:

- From the top of Carmel Mount, "I could gaze long on that point in the horizon where the servant of Elias saw the small cloud rising from the sea, the symbol of the fecund grace which the Immaculate Virgin would attract to earth." (Fr. Paul Marie de la Croix, O.C.D., *ibid*, vol. 1, p. 23).

- "Carmelite writers interpret the small cloud as a figure of the Virgin Mary" (Fr. De Vaux, O.P., *ibid*, vol. 1, p. 64.)

- "God revealed to Elias under the symbol of the small cloud a young woman, the Blessed Virgin Mary" (Fr. Daniel de la Vierge, O.C.D., *ibid*, vol. 2, p. 31).

- "There is a relation between the Madonna as contemplated by Elias and the same figure seen by St. John—*Signum magnum apparuit in caelo* [A great sign appeared in the heavens]. Elias also considered Mary as a *signum*. Elias saw her as a small cloud rising from the sea; St. John saw her standing, her feet on the crescent moon, which is [like the sea] an image of changeability" (Fr. Bruno Borchert, O.C.D., *ibid*, vol. 2, p. 31).

- "The symbolism of the small cloud whereby the Prophet acknowledged the Virginity of Mary and her fecund Maternity was already spotlighted in the sixth book of the *Institutions of the First Monks* [*Speculum Carmelitanum*, 1680, n. 22, p. 56]" (Fr. Elisée de la Nativité, O.C.D., *ibid*, vol. 2, p. 97).

The author of the *Institutions of the First Monks* considered that God revealed four secrets to Elias regarding the virginity of Mary:

1   **Her Immaculate Conception.** Like the cloud, the Virgin rose up from the salty water of a guilty humanity, being of the same nature as the sea water but without its bitterness;

2   **The voluntary virginity of Mary would be similar to that of Elias.** The small cloud moved toward the Mount Carmel like a man's footsteps, indicating that Mary's vow of virginity followed the footsteps of Elias, first who climbed Carmel to the heights of voluntary virginity.

3   **The time of the Virgin's birth.** The disciples of Elias would see the Virgin Mary only after seven epochs, just as his servant returned seven times to see the small cloud.

4   **Her maternal virginity.** God came down into the small cloud as a sweet rain, without any mark of human collaboration, that is, without breaking her purity" (Fr. Bruno Borchert, O.C.D., *ibid*, vol. 2, p. 97)

http://www.traditioninaction.org/Questions/F024_EliasCloud.htm;

An ancient Carmelite interpretation of the cloud of pure rain that Elijah saw rising from the salty sea (1 Kings 18:44) is that it prefigured Mary who was born immaculate. This painting of the episode, depicting Elijah in the Carmelite habit, is in Saint Albert's International Centre in Rome. http://www.carmelite.org/index.php?nuc=content&id=341

MAGNI PROPHETÆ
ELIÆ
Sacri Ordinis Carmelitarum Fundatoris
VISIO
De Immaculatâ Deiparæ Virginis Conceptione

A Carmelitis omnium primò culta ac propugnata,

ET AB ECCLESIA JAM PROXIME DEFINIBILI

Insertis proindè Resolutionibus variis Apologeticis de necessitate Pacti ad peccatum originale : veræ & perfectæ, quoad substantiam, Monasticæ Religionis Primatu in Elia; Summi Pontificis per se, & extra Concilium Generale, etiam in Quæstionibus facti fidem & mores salutares concernentis, infallibilitate : & Joannis-44. Patriarchæ Jerosolymitani ab Hæreticorum erroribus libera fide. Quorum finiente prælô

Accessit Appendix Apologetica pro eodem JOANNE 44. *adversùs* P.M. CHRISTIANUM LUPUM *Ord. Erem. S.Augustini.*

Authore R. P. F. FRANCISCO BONÆ SPEI ejusdem Ordinis Provinciæ Flandro-Belgicæ Exprovinciali, & in florentissimâ Universitate Lovan. S. Theologiæ ac Scripturæ Professore.

Dum fluet unda maris, curretque per æthera phœbus:
Vivet Carmeli candidus Ordo mihi.

ANTVERPIÆ, Sumpt. ENGELBERTI GYMNICI, M.DC.LXV.

Translation:

(An excerpt from the Book on the Vision of Elias in the cloud)

THE GREAT PROPHET

ELIAS

FOUNDER OF THE
HOLY ORDER OF CARMELITES

VISION

OF THE IMMACULATE CONCEPTION

OF THE VIRGIN MOTHER OF GOD

A FIRST DEFENSE OF THE CARMELITES

SOLEMNLY DEFINED BY THE CHURCH

BY

R.P. Francisco Bonae Spei
Provincial of the Order, Fleming, Belgium
University of Lovan, Professor of Sacred Theology
and Sacred Scripture
1665

FACVLTAS

REVERENDI ADMODUM

PATRIS PROVINCIALIS.

EX *commiſſione Reverendi Patris noſtri Generalis legi, & examinavi librum, cui titulus eſt,* Magni Prophetæ Eliæ ſacri Ordinis Carmelitarum Fundatoris Viſio de Immaculata Deiparæ Virginis Conceptione, à Carmelitis omnium primò culta, & propugnata; inſertis proindè Reſolutionibus variis Apologeticis de neceſſitate paſti ad peccatum originale.: veræ & perfeſtæ quoad ſubſtantiam Monaſticæ Religionis Primatu in Elia: Summi Pontificis per ſe, & extra Concilium, etiam in Quæſtionibus faſti fidem, & mores ſalutares concernentis, infallibilitate: & Joannis 44. Patriarchæ Jeroſolymitani ab Hæreticorum erroribus libera fide: *conſcriptum à Reverendo Patre Franciſco Bonæ Spei Ordinis noſtri, Provinciæ Flandro-Belgicæ Exprovinciali, ſacræ Theologiæ & Scripturæ Lectore in generali ſtudio Lovanienſi: in quo nedùm nihil fidei, boniſve moribus contrarium deprehendi; ſed doctrinam ſolidam, quâ Conceptio ſacræ Virginis Deiparæ ab omni prorsùs labe immunis, ex antiquiſſima, per bina millenaria, & quinque ferè ſæcula, in Ordine noſtro traditione, à ſancto Noſtro Elia (cui in typo Nubeculæ, ex amaro, & ponderoſo mari, dulcis & levis aſcendentis, præmonſtratus fuit puriſſimæ Virginis Deum paritura ortus, & aſcenſus tanquam nubis levis, ex corrupta maſſa humanæ naturæ, ſine tamen amaritudine culpæ originalis & abſque pondere peccatorum actualium) atque aliis graviſſimis authoritatibus, & firmiſſimis rationibus erudité, & graviter demonſtratur; eapropter libri iſtius editionem, ad ejuſdem Virginis Dei Matris honorem, & legentium utilitatem futurum cenſeo. Datum Bruxellis die trigeſimâ Octobris ann.* 1664.

FR. DANIEL à VIRGINE MARIA, quòndam ſacræ
Theologiæ Lector, Provincialis Provinciæ
Flandro-Belgicæ Ordinis Fratrum Beatæ Virginis Mariæ de Monte Carmelo.

***

A P-

Translation:

Faculty of the
Very Reverend Provincial Father:

The Commission of Reverend Father Generals have read and examined this book entitled "The Great Prohpet Elias, Founder of the Holy Order of Carmelites, on the Vision of the Conception of the Immaculate Virgin" first cultivated and propagated by the Carmelities, inserted accordingly for the necessary resolution of various apologetices regarding original sin. The true and perfect substance of the Primacy of the Monastic Religious life in Elias; Questions concerning faith and salutary morals regarding infallibility by the Pope and the Council.

This book entitled *The Great Prophet Elias, Founder of the Holy Order of Carmelites on the Vision of the Conception of the Immaculate Virgin Mother of God,* has been examined by the Commission of the Reverend Fathers of our General delegate...and by John, the 44th Patriarch of Jerusalem, and is judged as free from heretical errors to the faith. It was written by the Reverend Father Francisco Bona Spei of our Order, Former Provincial of the Flemish-Belgian Province, General Professor of Sacred Theology and Sacred Scripture from the University of Louvain.

There is found nothing in it contrary to faith and good morals; but rather a solid doctrine by which the Conception of the Holy Virgin Mother of God is entirely free from the stain of sin according to the most ancient tradition of our Order through two thousand years and nearly five centuries from our holy Elias (to whom in the figure of a cloud, rising from a bitter and heavy sea was foreshadowed the rising up of the most pure Virgin Mother of God ascending sweetly and softly like a light cloud from the corrupt mass of human nature yet free from the bitterness of original sin and the weight of actual sin) and it is thoroughly approved by other dignified authorities for the most solid and learned reasons and therefore this book may be published in honor of the Virgin Mother of God and I believe it will be profitable for future reading. Given in Brussels on the 30th of October, 1664.

Fr. Daniel of the Virgin Mary, Lecturer of Sacred Theology, Provincial of the Province of Flanders-Belgium, Order of the Brothers of the Blessed Virgin Mary of Mount Carmel.

66 F.Francifci Bonæ Spei *de Eliæ Vifione Imm.Concept.D.V.*

DISPVTATIO TERTIA
ET CAPITALIS
IN QVA
MAGNI PROPHETÆ ELIÆ
SACRI ORDINIS CARMELITARUM
FVNDATORIS
VISIO
DE IMMACVLATA
DEIPARÆ VIRGINIS
CONCEPTIONE
A CARMELITIS
OMNIUM PRIMO CULTA ET PROPUGNATA
VERIFICATUR.

1   Ifputatio hæc hujus libri finis & fcopus eft: eaque magis hiftorica, quàm fcholaftica; ideóque de Carmelitarum fundatione ab Elia, hujufque veræ & perfectæ, quoad fubftan- tiam, monafticæ Religionis Primatu, ab eo Conceptionis Immaculatæ Deiparæ Virginis Vifione ab Annis 2590. five à tempore vifionis Magni Prophetæ Eliæ; & hinc à Carmelitis antiquiffimo ejufdem cultu, Hiftoriæ per fex ad difputationem de Immaculata Conceptione præfuppofita agemus, & cùm ifta maximè pendeant

ab

Translation:

THIRD CAPITAL DEBATE

IN

THE GREAT PROPHET ELIAS

FOUNDER OF THE HOLY CARMELITE ORDER
ON THE

VISION

OF THE IMMACULATE CONCEPTION
OF
THE VIRGIN MOTHER OF GOD
FIRST CULTIVATED AND PROPAGATED BY THE
CARMELITES

VERIFIED

70 F.Francisci Bonæ Spei *de Eliæ Visione Imm.Concept.D.V.*

litarum Pallium puriſſimæ, & candidiſſimæ Virginis immunitati ſignificandæ fuiſſe tributum. Nec longè abeſt Trithemius Abbas, acerrimus Carmeliticæ antiquitatis vindex, qui libro 1. de Ordine Carmelitarum cap. 7. ſcribit, candorem hujus Pallii exprimere munditiam, ac puritatem Deiparæ, quam amantiſſimam Patronam clientes Carmelitæ & moribus, & habitu referre geſtiunt.

6 Adſtipulatur Philippus Abbas Jeropolitanus in Joan.1. apud Palæonydor.lib.2.cap.1. ſic dicens: O Carmelitarum Religio! quàm magna faɛta es in domo Domini. Nunquid olim à modico fonte Eliæ, Dei Prophetæ, principium habuiſti? Et ecce, nunc in magnum fluvium creviſti. Tu olim plantata in eremo, nunc faɛta es Civitas plena populo. Tu fundatorem habes adhuc in Paradiſo viventem, & glorioſam Virginem Mariam Reginam Cœli, Dominam mundi, in patronam ſingularem. Sicut enim olim de te proceſſerunt Patriarchæ & Prophetæ, ſic nunc de te procedunt Sacerdotes & Levitæ, Doɛtores & Evangeliſtæ, qui Patres, & Patroni omnium Religioſorum faɛti ſunt.

7 Maximè favet Summus Pontifex Joannes XXII. qui anno 1322. in Bulla, Sacratiſſimo, quam confirmavit Alexander V. poſteà ſui Pontificatus annô primô, refert, quandam revelationem B. Virginis, in qua dicitur, hunc ordinem per Eliam & Eliſæum fuiſſe in Monte Carmelo inchoatum. De hac porrò Bulla, data ipſius, eaq; revelatione, & aliis concernentibus, circà id tempus dicemus.

8 Favet & alia ejuſdem B.Virginis revelatio B.Petro Thomæ Patriarchæ Conſtantinopolitano, poſt aliquot annos ab hoc tempore, faɛta, prout ſuô locô referemus, quà conſtat, eandèm beatiſſimam Virginem illi dixiſſe, Religionem Carmelitarum in finem uſque mundi duraturam; quia Elias, ejus Inſtitutor, id à Domino impetraverat. Habetur hoc ex Joanne de Hildensheim Saxone lib.contrà detraɛtor. Ordin. cap. 5. & ex aliis hiſtoricis domeſticis, ac exteris, & quod magis eſt, ex approbatione Sacræ Congregationis Rituum in officio ejuſdem Beati ſub Urbano Oɛtavo, ſub anno 1628. de quo aliàs.

9 Temporis etiam ordo poſtulat, ut Cantabrigienſis Academiæ in Anglia celeberrimæ, & Doɛtorum ipſius egregium teſtimonium, deciſio, ac ſententia pro parte, quam tuemur, in medium producatur. Accidit enim circa ann. Dom. 1374. ut nonnulli Univerſitatis prædiɛtæ ſcholaſtici, juvenili forſan levitate duɛti, & ab aliquibus ex majoribus excitati inſtitutionem, intitulationem, & confirmationem Ordinis adeò præſumptuosè cavillarent, ut cùm quidam alii veritatis propugnatores in medium proſilirent, rixæ & diſcordiæ inter ipſos ſuſcitarentur. Erat eo tempore quidam Ordinis noſtri Profeſſor, ac Regens in ea Univerſitate, Joannes Hornebius, vir doɛtus ac pius, qui pro Religionis honore ſugillantium ora obtrudere cupiens, rem ad Univerſitatis Cancellarium juridicè diſcutiendam detulit. Hic convocatis Aſſiſtentibus, & aliis Academiæ Collegiis ſub die 23. Februarii anni prædiɛti ſequens promulgavit decretum, prout in ſpeculo Ordinis fol. 81. & aliis Ordinis monumentis apparet: Univerſis Sanɛtæ Matris Eccleſiæ filiis præſentes litteras inſpeɛturis, Joannes de Donelhico, Cancellarius Univerſitatis Cantabrigiæ, ſalutem in Domino ſempiternam. Cùm nuper à nonnullis Univerſitatis prædiɛtæ ſtudentibus Inſtitutio, intitulatio, & confirmatio Ordinis Fratrum B. Mariæ de Monte Carmeli nimis præſumptuosè revocabantur in dubium: undè diſcordiæ ac rixæ quamplurimæ inter ſcholares ejuſdem Univerſitatis fuerant ſuſci-

Translation:

#7 on Page 70 of Fr. Francis Bonae Spei
on

Elias' Vision of the
Immaculate Conception of the Virgin

#7:

The Supreme Pontiff, John XXII, especially promotes [the Privilege] in the year 1322 by his Bull *Sacratissimo* which was confirmed by Alexander V, who after the first year of his Pontificate, refers also to the revelation of the Blessed Virgin in which it is said that this Order was founded on Mount Carmel by Elias and Elisha. From this we will say that the Bull itself was revealed to other concerned parties around this time.

Blessed Titus Brandsma

February 23, 1881 - July 26, 1942

From the circumstances in which the Prophet, after his sevenfold prayer, saw the cloud rise above the sea, we may conclude that to see in it a prototype of the Mother of God—a type of the mystery of the Incarnation would be in entire agreement with the prototypal character of the Old Testament. Blessed Titus Brandsma, O. Carm.

The following is an excerpt from the writings of Titus Brandsma, O. Carm. on the Vision of Elias on Mt. Carmel taken from "Carmelite Mysticism Historical Sketches" by Titus Brandsma, O.Carm. , the Carmelite Press, Darien, Illinois 1986. "Vision of the Mother of God Governing Carmel's Life of Prayer." Special attention must be called to the vision of Elias on Carmel. This vision is the foundation of the Marian character of Carmelite spirituality:

It was on Carmel's summit that the Prophet after sevenfold prayer saw a little cloud—bearer of the rain which would deliver the parched earth. It is not necessary to give an authentic explanation of this vision. Still I may say that many commentators of the Holy Scriptures have seen in this cloud a prototype of the Holy Virgin, who bore in her womb the Redeemer of the world. It is not the first time that a cloud was used as a symbol. In the wilderness a cloud covering the Ark of the Covenant was the sign of the presence of God. Numerous circumstances in which this type of cloud is mentioned are applied to God's descent on earth and His dwelling among the sons of men. From the circumstances in which the Prophet, after his sevenfold prayer, saw the cloud rise above the sea, we may conclude that to see in it a prototype of the Mother of God—a type of the mystery of the Incarnation—would be in entire agreement with the prototypal character of the Old Testament; the more so, since Holy Scripture expressly mentions this vision in the life of a prophet who would be raised to such a high degree of contemplation. At all events this much is sure—and this settles the question for the definition of the guiding principles of the Carmelite life of prayer that in the Order this vision of Elias has always been seen as a prototype of the Mystery of the Incarnation and a distant veneration of the Mother of God. And it was because of this belief, according to the tradition of Carmel, that the old sanctuary dedicated to the Holy Maid was built on the mountain in the midst of the hermits' caves. In the devotion of the Order, in the school of Carmel, this vision has its own place, and it has been looked upon for ages as the favourite image by which the Order looks to her. We need only read the Canonical Hours of the Feast of Our Lady of Mount Carmel to see the importance of this vision for the spiritual life of Carmel. In a special lecture we will say more about the Marian character of Carmelite spirituality. (http://www.carmelnet.org/brandsma/Carmelite%20Mysticism%20Historical%20Sketches.pdf)

Titus Brandsma is honored as a martyr within the Roman Catholic Church. He was beatified on 3 November 3, 1985 by Pope St. John Paul II. His canonizing is pending. In 2005, Titus Brandsma was chosen by the inhabitants of Nijmegen as the greatest citizen to have lived there. He is the Patron Saint of Catholic Journalists. (http://www.marypages.com/TitusBrandsmaEng.htm)

Chronology of Events

*She became a cause of salvation for herself
and the whole human race.*(1)

930 years BC: Elias, the Thesbite, of the inhabitants of Galaad is first mentioned in Sacred Scripture. (S. Jerome, S. Augustine, the Patriarch John of Jerusalem and S. Peter Damian, defend the opinion that Elias was sanctified in his mother's womb like John the Baptist, to whom he was similar in all things.) It is in this year, 930 BC that Elias appeared before Achab, the King of Israel. (As the Fathers of the Church find in him (Elias) the figure and precursor of the Messiah, it appears probable that at the time of his public appearance, he was about 30 years of age.) (2) During the days of Elias, Achab, the King of Israel, *did evil in the sight of God above all that were before him...and he went and served Baal and adored him.* Since punishment from above was the only thing that would bring King and people to their senses, the Prophet (Elias) closed the heavens. (3) He addressed to Achab these words: *As the Lord, the God of Israel liveth, before whose face I stand, "There shall be in these years neither dew nor rain, but according to the words of my mouth."* (4) The result was that after a drought of three years and six months the scourge of famine fell upon Samaria, and Achab was worried. (5)

929 years BC: Elias was hidden in the caves near the brook of Carith, since when everything dried up for lack of rain, his life was no longer safe, as Achab would have attempted to force him by tortures to speak the word that would bring the desired rain. It was then, that Elias formed the resolution to leave after him, successors to the monastic eremitical life which he had commenced as the first of all...so this Elianic community was to be the germ and nucleus of the Christian monastic communities. (6)

928 years BC: As a consequence of the continued drought, the brook Carith dried up, Elias was sent to the widow of Sarepta near Sidon. Here he multiplied miraculously the flour and oil and the same year raised the son of the widow from the dead, the first miracle of the kind on record. This son, according to the traditions of the Hebrews, was Jonas, the prophet, whom his mother confided to the

76

care and education of Elias, so that he became one of the first Religious on Mount Carmel. Both S. Jerome and Patriarch John mention this tradition. (7)

927 years BC: Three years and six months had passed without rain. Then, by order of God, Elias presented himself and asked to have the people and the priests of Baal assembled on Mount Carmel: *Gather unto me all Israel, unto Mt. Carmel and the prophets of Baal four hundred and fifty, and the prophets of the groves four hundred, who eat at Jezebel's table.* (7a) He called fire from Heaven upon his holocaust... the prophets of Baal were killed in order to exterminate idolatry and (he) had the vision of the little cloud rising from the Mediterranean in the shape of a man's foot. By prophetic inspiration, he herein saw the figure of the Immaculate Conception of the Blessed Virgin, and later on explaining this mystery to his disciples, he bid them to venerate the future Mother of the Messiah. (7b) After he (Elias) had brought down a miraculous fire and proved that "God is God" and after he had seen the whole nation fall to its knees with the cry *The Lord is God! The Lord is God!* the mysterious prophet turns to the King and says:...*now it will rain.* (7c)

"(Elias) is not only about to present a material salvation to them but is also about to behold a prophetic vision of the spiritual Salvation of all mankind through an Immaculate Virgin."(8)

...[a]nd he said to his servant: *Go up, and look toward the sea.* And he went up, and looked, and said: *There is nothing.* And again he said to him: *Return seven times.* And at the seventh time, behold a little cloud arose out of the sea like a man's foot. (Kings III, 18: 43-44) "The Heavens grew dark with clouds and wind and there fell a great rain." (9)

In the near tomorrows, sainted Doctors of the true Church will explain to the world how this little cloud, rising pure out its bitter sea and leaving all impurities behind, is a figure of an Immaculate Virgin who will rise pure out of the sea of humankind, free of its universal impurity of original sin. (9a)

The Virgin appeared to the Prophet Elias on Mt. Carmel in a little cloud rising from the sea, showing him the religious institution that he was to consecrate to the Mother of the future Redeemer. (9b)

"...[T]he holy Father (Elias) was given the task of manifesting to his followers the mysteries of the cloud he had seen. He told them that in this cloud, which he saw come from the sea, there was represented a Hebrew Virgin named Mary who, many centuries later, by the will of Heaven, was to be born to the world near the city of Nazareth in order to be the Mother of the anticipated Messiah." (10)

The ancient Historian of the Order, John XLIV, Patriarch of Jerusalem, picks up the constant tradition of the Order on the symbolism of the thundercloud of Carmel, and says that in a vision there were revealed to the Prophet Elijah, (Elias) among other mysteries: the Immaculate Conception of the Virgin, her vow of virginity, the Incarnation of the Divine Word in her most pure womb, and the time in which this mystery would be realized. Thus, Elijah came to be called *The Prophet of the Immaculate*. (10a)

The mystery of the pure Conception of Mary, which Elijah beheld in the symbolic vision of the thundercloud, was transmitted by the Prophet to his descendents, accompanied by the account of the sublime teachings of such a great mystery. The very words of the Church in the preface to the Mass of July 16 (the epistle is taken from the third book of Kings [1 Kings] chapter 18) say that the devotion of Carmel to the mystery of the Immaculate Conception, which was revealed to Elijah, was passed on from generation to generation to his whole glorious posterity, with the reality following the figure and reaching up to the successors of the "Sons of the Prophets" of the New Law, who are the Carmelite religious of our day. (11)

926 years BC: Elias anointed Eliseus as Prophet (and his successor) and threw his mantle over him, making him thereby an associated monk. He settled with Eliseus and his other disciples on Mount Carmel and in this year, 926 BC, the Order of Mount Carmel had its beginning. (12) By the end of 926 BC, the Holy Prophet Elijah founded the Carmelite family on Mt. Carmel; he had numerous disciples whom he instructed to venerate in the thundercloud that appeared to him, the Most Holy Virgin who must bring forth Jesus; in this way the Madonna came to be known and venerated ahead of time before she was generated by St. Joachim and St. Anne. (12a)

925 years BC: The Patriarch John tells us that Elias taught his followers to gather three times a day, morning, noon and evening in the Seunion, the house of worhip he had built in order to offer up praise to God. Their Oratory was the center around which the disciples of the Holy Prophets gathered even after, so that the Popes, Sixtus IV, Julius II and Gregory XIII, speak in their Bulls of the Carmelites as holding the hereditary succession of Elias, Eliseus and the other Fathers who inhabited the holy Mount Carmel near the Fountain of

Elias. Thus the constant tradition of the Order has received papal sanction and though it is far from us to conclude that in consequence, the uninterrupted succession of the Order has become an Article of Faith, yet the sovereign Pontiffs do not use words which they have not carefully weighed and hence their dicta constitute a very strong human evidence. (12b)

914 years BC: Elias was taken away in a fiery chariot, and his spirit and the government of the Order descended upon Eliseus. In rising, Elias dropped his cloak, which Eliseus took as a token of his succession and the same day he miraculously divides the waters of the Jordan with it. (13) Elias being taken away in a fiery chariot, Eliseus succeeded him, not only in the double spirit of prophecy and miracles, but also in the government of the Order as may be seen in the fourth book of Kings. (13a)

849 years BC: Eliseus died at about the age of 105 years old. According to Roman Martyrology, he died on June 14th. The year after the death of Eliseus, a dead man, coming in contact with the Prophet's bones, was restored to life. (13b)

739 years BC: The King of Assyria captured the whole country (Israel) and led the people into the Assyrian captivity. Patriarch John relates that by the special providence of God the inhabitants of Mount Carmel were left in undisturbed possession. This was the reward for their faithful observance of the law and their fervent labors in the vineyard of God. (13c)

538 years BC: In this year falls the visit of Pythagoras to Mount Carmel. The Order had then a flourishing school for young men who were not members of the Order, and many of the principles which Pythagoras inculcated to his followers were learned during his stay on Carmel. (13d)

337-300 BC: In this time, the Elianic Order (Order of Elias) suffered greatly by the war of Alexander the Great against the Persians and the wars of his successors amongst themselves...the times were certainly not propitious for a religious life as it was nothing but wars, rebellions, treason, religious quarrels... which history records. (13dd)

78 years BC: Emerentiana, a chaste virgin, with the consent of her parents, visited certain devout brothers living on Mount Carmel and began to speak with them about the coming of the Messiah and the prophecies referring to it. She was married and gave birth to a daughter, "Ann," (St. Ann, the future mother of the Blessed Virgin Mary.) She also gave birth to another girl, Esmeria (Sobe), who was the mother of St. Elizabeth, of whom was born John the Baptist. (13e)

38 years BC: This year was significant for the Jews, for Herod became King. According to Josephus Flavius and Palaeonydorus, he (Herod) treated the family of Carmel with honor "during his life, though to others he was a bloodthirsty tyrant."(13f)

16-15 years BC: In these years, the Immaculate Conception and nativity of the Blessed Virgin, the Mother of God, took place. We can easily understand with what attention the inhabitants of Mount Carmel watched the family of Emerentiana...for nine hundred years they had venerated the future Mother of God. During that length of time they had preserved sacredly the traditions about her Immaculate Conception; they had sighed for the redemption of Israel and now they beheld the Mother of the Redeemer with their own eyes. Such ecstatic joy had never before filled their hearts. (14)

13 years BC: The Blessed Virgin presented herself in the temple, where she was educated for 12 years and where she made a vow of perpetual chastity. (14a)

2-1 years BC: The espousals of the Blessed Virgin with S. Joseph took place by Divine Command. (14b)

1-34 years AD: During the lifetime of Our Lord, the Blessed Virgin repeatedly honored Mount Carmel with her presence, bringing untold joy to the hearts of the community there. She instructed them in many things that concerned Our Savior, she comforted them in their adversities; she exhorted them to perseverence and assured them of her assistance, protection and prayers. Those heremetical fathers, knowing assuredly that this was the Virgin whom the holy patriarchs and Prophet Elias had foreseen more than 900 years before she was born...dedicated themselves wholly to her as her perpetual servants, children, devotees, considering her as the only refuge, advocate and mother of their Congregation. Josephus of Antioch who lived in the year 130 and wrote the annals of the primitive Church says: "As helpers of the perfect soldiers of Christ, the Apostles, there arose very strong men, solitaires, given to meditation, the followers of the Holy Prophets, Elias and Eliseus." They descended from Mount Carmel and spread the faith of Christ constantly through Galilee, Samaria and Palestine. They also erected on the slopes of Mount Carmel an oratory in honor of the Virgin Mary, where they specially served the Mother of the Savior. (14c)

A little after the birth of Our Savior, St. Elizabeth, fearing the tyranny of Herod who had killed many thousands of infants, fled with her son, St. John the Baptist into the desert where he joined himself to the successors of Elias and embraced the Institute as St. Ambrose expressly says. (Epist. Ad Varcel. Ap.14). (14cc)

35 years AD: The outbreak of the first persecutions against the Christians took place. Among them were a number of Carmelites, some of whom went to Spain with the Holy Apostle James. One of them, Elpidius by name, became the first Bishop of Toledo and dedicated the first chapel in Spain in honor of the Blessed Virgin. S. Elpidius was a Carmelite monk, and converted to the Faith by the first sermon of S. Peter and came to Spain with many companions. (14d)

36 years AD: In this year, the inhabitants of Mount Carmel commenced to be called the "Brothers of the Blessed Virgin of Mount Carmel." Their Superior at the time was Enoch of Amathion who converted the Seunion, or Oratory of S. Elias into the Oratory of the Blessed Virgin. Among them was also Agabus, the Prophet mentioned in the Acts of the Apostles. (14e)

39 years AD: Eusebius says of Antioch, where St. Peter had his Chair at the time that, owing to the persecution raised in Jerusalem after the death of St. Stephen, many came to Antioch and gathered there a most flourishing congregation, amongst whom there were a great many men of the Prophetic Order (the Order of Elias). In this same year the spot in which the Blessed Virgin was conceived was occupied and converted into a chapel by the Carmelites, after they, the year before, in 38 AD, had built a chapel in Mary's honor on the slope of Mount Carmel. (14f)

48 AD: This is the year of the Assumption of the Blessed Virgin. At her death and burial there were present Enoch and Agabus of

Mount Carmel who, according to our (Carmelite) chronicles, had been invited by Mary herself. (14ff)

60 AD: During the persecution of the Church under (Emperor) Nero, St. Elpidus, the Bishop of Toledo attended with other bishops a council held in (now Pensicola), near Valencia in Spain. There all were imprisoned and suffered martyrdom under Judge Alotus. Elpidus, not long before his death, had visited St. Paul then a prisoner in Rome, bringing him alms collected among the Spanish Christians. (14fff)

67 AD: This is the year of the martyrdom of Sts. Peter and Paul. We mention it because in the Church of S. Maria Traspontina, which is the Mother-house of the Carmelite Order in Rome, there are preserved parts of two columns to which the holy Apostles were tied during their flagellation. (14fg)

83 AD: These first Carmelites of the New Testament could not certainly detach from the cult of Jesus, that which was due to His Great Mother already honored for many centuries before her birth, so in the year 83 of Christ, they built the first temple in the world in honor of Our Lady on Mount Carmel. (14g)

It was close to this spot ("Grotto of the Prophet Elias"), that the first Christian Church was built in honor of Our Blessed Lady in the year 83 as the chapel dedicated to the Blessed Virgin, near the fountain of Elias on Mount Carmel, which had existed since the year 38 AD, was crumbling...Hence the Carmelites raised a new Church on top of the mountain on the spot where Elias had seen the little cloud rising from the sea (15) and over the Grotto itself there stands today the magnificent Basilica of Our Lady of Mount Carmel which is considered as the most ancient of all the shrines of Our Blessed Mother. (15a)

Near the grotto, which is still venerated today, not only by Christians, but also by Turks, Moors and Arabs, there a chapel was built which is considered as the most ancient of all built in honor of the Most Holy Virgin having the name of Our Lady of Carmel and it dates back to 83 A.D. Mary frequently visited the Carmel. (16)

130 AD: Josephus of Antioch, writing about the year 130 on the state of the primitive Church, states that the pious Solitaries of Mount Carmel, followers of Elias and Eliseus were very efficient helpers of the Apostles in spreading the Faith throughout Palestine, Samaria and Galilee. (17)

In the Acts of the Apostles, reference is made to the coming of the Prophets from Jerusalem to Antioch. (18)

139 AD: (Pope) St. Telesphorus, (Bishop of Rome) a Greek, was called from the desert to the Chair of St. Peter. He is said to have been a monk before becoming a bishop; some sources depict Telesphorus as previously being a hermit living on Mount Carmel and the Carmelites thus venerate him as a patron saint of the Order. He established the Fast of Lent on a firm basis, decreed the celebration of the three Masses for Christmas Day (the *Liber Pontificalis* credits him with initiating the tradition of Christmas Midnight Masses). He is the first of the Roman Bishops to be martyred after Saint Peter, according to Irenaeus of Lyons. He suffered martyrdom in the year 139 and was buried near the body of St. Peter in the Vatican (Breviary of the Carmelites, February 3). (19)

259 AD: (Pope) St. Dionysius lived on Mount Carmel and followed the examples of the leaders of the religious life…and led in very truth, the life of a Prophet. He was raised to the Chair of Peter. He reigned eleven years (as Pope) and was buried in the Catacombs of Callistus on the Appian Way. (20)

326 AD: A second Temple was built also on Mount Carmel of the Great Prophet Elijah, (Elias) in the year 326 through the initiative of the Empress, St. Helena, Mother of Constantine, who found herself on Carmel enthusiastically moved by the spirit of these hermits. (21)

371 AD: In this year, John, the later (44th) Patriarch of Jerusalem and Historian of the (Carmelite) Order, joined the Order on Mount Carmel. About the same time Cyril was born, who, as Patriarch of Jerusalem was such a shining light in the Church and champion against heresy. (21a)

379 AD: About this time, John, who afterwards became the 44th Patriarch of Jerusalem and the Historian of the Order, had for his disciple Palladius, who in the year 422, was sent by Pope Celestine to Great Britain as its first apostle. (21aa)

386 AD: It was probably in this year that after the death of Cyril, John ascended the Patriarchal See of Jerusalem...he was called, by the Bishop of Cyra, "a man worthy of admiration." The monk John is famous for the purity of his life and the gift of prophecy which he received from the Lord...he induced by word and example, his companions, the monks on Mount Carmel to acquire perfection according to the discipline of monastic life, introduced by the Prophet Elias. He finally for his sanctity was elected to the Episcopal Chair of the Church of Jerusalem, the 44th successor of James the Apostle. (21b)

412 AD: About this time, Patriarch John of Jerusalem wrote his book *De ortu Monachorum* to a certain Caprasius, a hermit on Mount Carmel and very probably John's successor as the supreme moderator of the hermits of the Elianic institute. The book contains the mystical explanation of the origin of the Order, its habits and its principal obligations. This book was treated by the Carmelites as their first written rule, as S. Cyril of Constantinople testifies in his letter to the hermit Eusebius on Mount Nervi and it was translated by Patriarch Aymera of Antioch. (21c) (It was John, Patriarch of Jerusalem, who recorded the vision of Our Lady to Elias in a little cloud over the sea.)

413-414 AD: St. Cyril occupied the patriarchal throne of Alexandria. He professes himself a hermit of Mount Carmel, fought the heresies of his time and built a convent for women to which he gave the Carmelite rule. St. Cyril, as the Legate of Pope Celestine, presided at the Council of Ephesus, where the heresy of Nestorius was condemned and the title "Mother of God" was bestowed upon the Blessed Virgin. (21cc)

416 AD: The year 416 saw the death of Patriarch John. He was called Blessed or Saint by many writers, both at and after his time, but was never canonized by the Church. (21d)

444 AD: This year is notable for the death of St. Cyril, the Patriarch of Alexandria. Before his death he saw the fruit of his labors, in behalf of orthodoxy: Nestorius was deposed and banished, the dignity of the Mother of God solemnly vindicated and Cyril succeeded in bringing back to the Faith many who for a time had favored Nestorianism. (21dd)

504-513 AD: The Carmelites in Palestine were hard pressed and persecuted by the Saracens, under the Sultan, Alamundaz. Some suffered martyrdom; others fled into a new monastery. The hermits of Mount Carmel assisted Patriarch Flavian of Antioch against heretics who made him suffer much. (21e)

612 AD: Chrosroes, Emperor of Persia, led his army into Palestine and began a cruel persecution of the Christians. All the sacred places were desecrated. This persecution was carried on without interruption by the Persians and Mohammedans for over four centuries. (22)

614 AD: In 614 with the decapitation of St. Anastasius, a Persian soldier of Chrosroes II, who had converted to Christianity, there was the initiation of the first Carmelite martyrs due to the Persian invasion of Carmel. (23)

847 AD: Pope Leo IV (elected in the year 847) proved himself the protector (of the Carmelites) and granted special indulgences to all who would assist by their alms, the persecuted Solitaires of Mount Carmel; (thus) they were able to continue their existence on the holy mountain. (24)

1099 AD: At the end of the early era and the beginning of the Latin era in the history of the Order, with the advent of the first Crusade to Palestine, there was in its army the noble and valiant soldier Berthold of Malafaida who took the Carmelite habit and became its first Latin General. (25)

1165 AD: St. Simon Stock was born in Canzia or Kent in the southern region of England in 1165. (26) When he was twelve years of age he withdrew himself into the woods where he lived in the trunk of a hollow oak tree for twenty years; prayer was his great occupation and his soul acquired purity so great that he became like the very angels of God. As a raven brought food to the great prophet Elias in like manner a little dog supplied food sometimes to this servant of God. In this solitude, Simon received many supernatural graces from the Almighty God and especially, he enjoyed the familiar conversation of the Blessed Virgin, who one day appearing to him, told him that shortly some religious men who were under her protection were to come from Palestine to England and that he should embrace their Institute. This prediction of the sacred Virgin was verified in the year 1212. (26a)

1188 AD: St. Brocard, a native of Jerusalem, was elected second Prior-General of the Order. Under his administration the Carmelites spread throughout Palestine. He petitioned St. Albert, Patriarch of Jerusalem to arrange for them a Rule that would embrace every constitution of the Order. (27)

1209 AD: A primitive Rule of the Hermits of Carmel had been given by the hermit, John, Patriarch of Jerusalem, written in the Greek language but the definitive rule was given in 1209 by St. Albert, also the Patriarch of Jerusalem called the legislator, which was written in Latin by the hands of St. Brocard who then was the General of the Order. Constituted in this way, the Carmelite Order was already founded in earlier centuries by the Prophet Elijah (Elias). (28)

1212 AD: Some Englishmen, who had lived amongst the hermits on Mt.Carmel returned to their native land and taking up hermitages close by where Simon was yet in his tree-cell, formed an acquaintance with him. Simon asked to be admitted to membership of their Order and the hermits already aware of the sanctity of his life, his fame was known in all the neighborhood, gladly received the holy man (St. Simon) into their number (verifying the prophecy of the Blessed Virgin to Simon years earlier). (28a)

1215 AD: In the year 1215, St. Brocard, Prior of Mount Carmel and General of the Order appointed our Saint (Simon Stock) Vicar-General over all the western provinces. (28b)

1224 AD: Taking note of the terrible Muslim persecutions in Palestine, the Madonna appeared on Mount Carmel in 1224 to make known her desire that the Carmelites move *en masse* to the West, where some Convents had already been opened. (29)

1226 AD: The Carmelites asked Pope Honorius III to approve the rule, but he at first declined. But during the night the Blessed Virgin appeared to him commanding him to take the Order under his protection and announcing that the two officials who were most opposed to the Order, would be found dead in the morning. Hence Honorius, on Jan 30th, 1226, by a solemn Bull confirmed the Order. The following year Gregory IX confirmed this approbation. (29a)

With the approval of the Rule, Honorius III, by means of a proper

Bull, established—beginning in 1226—July 16 as the Feast of the Madonna of Carmel and the Blessed Virgin herself confirmed this feast a few years later with the great gift of the Holy Scapular to St. Simon Stock specifically on July 16, giving the clearest proof of her maternal protection for her Order and for the Christian people. (30)

1238 AD: The "Saracens" fell upon the religious who had gathered there from the other convents in Palestine because of the persecutions and consequently were very numerous and there put them all to death. Not content with their death, the infidels dragged the corpses to this valley, throwing several into the Fountain of Elias. This Fountain is said to have sprung from the rock at the touch of the Prophet thus miraculously supplying the needs of his disciples. (31)

1241 AD: In 1241 refugees from Mount Carmel arrived in Aylesford fleeing the persecutions of the Saracens in the East. (32)

1242 AD: The Aylesford Priory, or in its traditional name: "The Friars," was founded in 1242 after the first Carmelites arrived from the Holy Land. They came under the patronage of Richard de Grey, a Crusader who gave them a small piece of land at his manor of Aylesford. (33)

1244 AD: Pope John XXII, whose secular name was James d'Euse, was born at Cahors in or about the year 1244. (According to a venerable tradition, he is the author of the Sabbatine Bull dated March 3, 1322). (34)

1244 AD: (Also): Blessed Alan of Brittainy, the Fifth Latin General moved his residence to England because of the violent invasion of the Khorosans (Persian Muslims) into Palestine. (35)

1245 AD: The Superior General was St. Simon of Quercia (which is the translation of the name Stock, by which the saint is ordinarily known) elected in 1245 in the Capital of Ayelsford in England. (36) (St. Simon Stock had been elected Prior General of the Friars of Our Lady of Mount Carmel in the Chapter held at Aylesford...1245.) (36a)

1245 AD: At the General Chapter held at Aylesford in 1245, the venerable Peter Swaynton of the Order of Carmel, secretary, companion and confessor of the Saint (Simon Stock) was sent to

Pope Innocent IV to have portions of the Rule explained and to obtain some mitigations. Peter Swaynton (or sometimes written as Swaynington) was a native of Norfolk, England and was a great and profound scholar and Professor in the University of Oxford. He was the first Carmelite made a Doctor of Divinity by the world-wide and renowned school of learning. He was unanimously chosen to defend the Religious Orders against the attacks of their enemies. He lived to a great age which he spent in the service of God and His Church. He was most zealous in spreading devotion to the Blessed Virgin by means of the Holy Scapular. He died at Bordeaux about five years after the precious death of St. Simon Stock. He wrote many learned works, also an account of the giving of the Scapular to St. Simon by the Blessed Virgin. (36b)

1247 AD: (October 1): Innocent IV confirmed the Rule of the Carmelites with a Bull, which was given in Lyon, France in the fifth year of his Pontificate. (37)

1249 AD: St. Simon Stock founded the Convent of Cambridge (England), which attained much recognition in a brief time. (38)

1251 AD: The persecution of the Order, on the part of the Parish clergy, became more and more fierce. According to the official report of Fr. Swanington, the Secretary of St. Simon Stock: "St. Simon Stock, now old, exhausted by penance and oppressed by grief at the persecutions which his Order suffered in the East and in the West, addressed himself to the Blessed Virgin…reminding her that it was the Order of her brethren that sought help. He repeated the invocation: *Flower of Carmel…etc.* After she appeared, she commanded him to approach the Vicar of her Son (Pope Innocent IV) who would put an end to all grievances." (38a)

To this holy religious, (St. Simon Stock) in 1251, the Virgin Mary gave the great sign of her favor for all the sons of Carmel (July 16, 1251.) To St. Simon Stock, one of the most holy among the Carmelite saints—who prayed and offered his entire self in order to obtain a sensible sign for his Order from the sweet benevolence of Mary— from the night of July 15th to the 16th, the Virgin appeared with a great retinue, holding in her hand the Habit of the Order and said to him: *This will be the sign of privilege which I have obtained for thee and your sons of Carmel. Whoever will die piously clothed with this habit will be preserved from the infernal fire.* (And to this privilege the Virgin Most

Holy attached the other of liberation from Purgatory, which came to be promulgated by John XXII with the Bull of March 3, 1322, the principal object of this great commemorative feast.) (39)

Words cannot describe the joy of St. Simon on receiving the Scapular. He immediately published everywhere the graces which he had received from the Holy Virgin and showed in proof of the Vision, the Scapular that she had left him. He immediately commenced the "Confraternity of the Scapular" and several sick persons were cured on receiving the habit from his hands. (39a)

There are few who do not know that before the apparition of the Virgin to St. Simon Stock and the handing over of the Scapular in 1251, the Immaculate Conception was the principal feast of the Order, which was celebrated in all the Carmelite convents with the highest solemnity. (40)

1252 AD: The Carmelites, obedient to the command of the Blessed Virgin to approach the Vicar of Christ to end all grievances, appealed to Pope Innocent IV, who sent encyclical letters to all the Bishops commanding them to receive the brethren of the Order kindly, to protect them in their rights and against imposition and under censure to compel their clergy to do likewise. This put a stop to petty persecutions and the number of monasteries increased, spreading the Order all over Europe. The Bull of Pope Innocent IV, (January 13, 1252), issued less than six months after the Vision of St. Simon, clearly exhibits the protection for the Carmelites in an efficacious manner by the Pope. An almost radical change had taken place in the attitude of the ecclesiastical authorities (towards the Carmelites, after the Vision). (40a)

1253 AD: St. Louis IX, King of France had spent four years crusading in the East. When he learned of the death of his mother, Blanche of Castile, he immediately set about making his preparations for his departure for France; a violent tempest arose. St. Louis gave himself up to prayer to the Queen of Carmel promising to make a foundation of her Order in France should she save him from the death that seemed inevitable. Instantly they were carried in safety to the Harbour of St. Louis...in testimony of his gratitude, he asked for and obtained six religious whom he brought to France in the year 1253. (41)

1262 AD: Bull of Pope Urban IV issued on May 8, 1262 mentions permission to hear confessions of *Confrates* (Confraternity Members) thereby providing evidence for the existence of the Carmelite Confraternities at an earlier date while at that time, there were no Confraternities in other Orders. (41a)

1265 AD: St. Simon Stock had served the Carmelite Community for 50 years. In 1245, he (St. Simon Stock) was elected General of the entire Carmelite Order, a responsibility he held for some 20 years up to his death which occurred in 1265 at the age of 100 years. (42)

1276 AD: Pope Gregory X was laid to rest at Arezzo, Italy, January 10, 1276. In 1830 his remains were disinterred to be newly placed in a silver reliquary. There in the old tomb, a small Scapular was lying over the Pontiff's shoulders, incorrupt. It is now in perfect preservation, one of the great treasures of the celebrated Arezzo museum. This is the first small Scapular in history. A record of those times tells us that Gregory X became affiliated to the Carmelite Order before ascending the papal throne and that he wore the Carmelite Habit as a sign of affiliation. (43)

1276 AD: Around the year 1276, the authority of the Holy See confirmed the cult of devotion to St. Simon Stock. Pope Nicholas III was elected in 1277, twelve years after the death of the Saint; after juridical information regarding his life and miracles, his feast day was established as May 16, the day of his death; this feast came to be celebrated each year in the Carmelite Church of Bordeaux with the Mass and Office of Confessors. (44)

1287 AD: The General Chapter held at Montpellier in July, 1287, officially designated the Scapular as the habit. According to two early editions of the Constitutions in the years, 1357 and 1369, a description is given of the Chapter of 1287 regarding the Scapular. (44a) The cloak or mantle was changed by the permission of the Holy See. It was enacted that the mantle or cloak was in future to be so shaped that the Scapular and Habit might be clearly distinguished...we must remember that this Chapter was held about twenty years after the death of St. Simon. (44b)

1289 AD: (July 1) Pope Nicholas IV, by means of a Brief on this date, confirmed the erection of the Carmelite Province of Spain which had been decreed in the General Chapter, which took place in Montpellier in 1287. (45)

1290 AD: William of Sanvico wrote, (from the province of the Holy Land; work written about 1290) *Chronica de multiplicatione religionis Carmelitarum* ...Ch. 7 (Cf. *Analecta 111*, 302-315; VII. 186); the text is taken from Daniel's Speculum, I, 103: ... "And so the Virgin Mary revealed to their Prior that they should fearlessly approach the Supreme Pontiff, Innocent, because they would obtain from him a salutary remedy for their troubles." (46) In the seventh chapter of this work, William de Sanvico informs us that the devil envied the rapid progress of the Order at its first appearance in Europe and obstacles arose. (46a)

1291 AD: The savage Saracen persecution erupted, which set the illustrious monastery of Mount Carmel on fire. The Carmelites sang the Salve [Regina] while they were being martyred. At this period of time the Carmelite Order was extinguished in the Holy Land. (47)

1314 AD: After the death of Clement V the Sacred College of Cardinals met, first at Carpentea, then at Lyons, in France, in order to elect a Successor. But it was prolonged more than two years, partly by dissension among the Cardinals and by the wars in Germany, England, France and Italy, which was the cause of the great schism in the Church...one of the Cardinals, James Arnald (James Cardinal Ossa), a Frenchman of the Province of Aquitain, a great devotee of the Blessed Virgin Mary, prayed to the Mother of Mercies, beseeching that she would, by her intercession, obtain from her Son, a worthy pastor for the Church and one who would remedy the disorder. (47a) On the night before his election, Cardinal Ossa, who would become Pope John XXII, beheld the Mother of God in the habit of Carmel. (47b) The Blessed Virgin appeared to him at night, clad in the Carmelite habit and said to him: *I shall take thee out of the hands of thy adversaries and make thee Pope and Vicar of my Son. Therefore, see that you confirm my Order, commenced by Elias and Eliseus on Mount Carmel, and ordered by my servant, the Patriarch Albert. And as Honorius and Innocent, my sons and your predecessors have enjoined this rule into the remission of sins, so in my name and the name of my Son, thou shalt give my Order this Privilege* (known as the 'Sabbatine Privilege') *that whosoever enters it, devoutly obeying it, shall be saved and freed from punishment and guilt, etc.* (47c)

The Blessed Virgin appeared to him and promised to place him in the Chair of St. Peter and also to assist and deliver him from all his enemies on this condition, that being made Sovereign Prelate of the Church, he should be favorable to her Religious, the successors of Elias and that he should publish and confirm on earth, what Jesus Christ her beloved Son, at her request, had confirmed in Heaven: that those who should make themselves religious of her Order of Mount Carmel or should, out of devotion, enter into the Confraternity of the Blessed Virgin and wear her Habit (the Scapular) should be absolved from part of their sins; and if after death they should go to Purgatory, that the most sacred Virgin would deliver them, supposing that during their lifetime they had fulfilled certain conditions... (47d) (This Promise became known as The Sabbatine Privilege.)

1316 AD: The above Promise and prediction of the Mother of God was fulfilled; first, when James D'Euse was elected Pope John XXII and was crowned in the city of Lyons on the 5th of September, 1316; second, when in the following year he was delivered from a conspiracy of some Cardinals against him and from being poisoned; third, when the Antipope, Corburious ended the schism. (47e) We (also) find him tutor to the son of the King, who himself afterwards became King under the name of Charles II. He was likewise the tutor of Louis of (Toulouse) whom he afterward raised to the Altar of the Church. It has been noted by more than one of his biographers that on the removal of his body (Pope John XXII) to another part of the Cathedral in the year 1759, that his body was found intact. (48)

Moreover, we have from him two Canonization Bulls expressed in the style of the Sabbatine Bull—the one on St. Thomas Aquinas and the other on St. Louis of Toulouse—the style of the time often used in the Bulls of the Thirteenth and Fourteenth Centuries. (49)

1318 AD: On July 8, 1318, Pope John XXII granted indulgences to the Church of the monastery of monks of Blessed Mary of Mount Carmel of Messina. (50)

1320 AD: In the Bull of Pope John XXII, *Pia Mater Ecclesia* of 1320, special indulgences are similarly given to all the Christian faithful, who approach the Church of the Brothers of the Order of the Blessed Mary of Mount Carmel of Bononia during each and every feast of the Blessed and Glorious and Ever-Virgin Mary...and on each and every Saturday assist at a Mass which is solemnly celebrated in honor of the Blessed Virgin Mary for the sake of devotions, pilgrimages or prayers. (51)

1322 AD: Jacques d'Euse, born in Cahors (France), Pope from 1316 to 1334: It is to this Pope (John XXII) that the "Sabbatine Bull" (*Sacratissimo uti culmine*) dated March 3, 1322—containing the Sabbatine Privilege, many times confirmed by successive Supreme Pontiffs—is attributed. (52) The Bull was issued by John XXII as a result of the apparition of Our Blessed Mother to the Holy Father, (to accomplish on his behalf, what the Blessed Virgin required of him before his ascent to the Papal Throne) granting the *Privilege* to all who die wearing the Scapular. "It is the second great Scapular Promise of delivery from Purgatory on the Saturday after death, and was first announced in a Papal Document, the 'Sabbatine Bull.' The announcement was made in 1322 by Pope John XXII." (53)

1323 AD: St. Thomas Aquinas died in the year 1274 and was canonized (July 18) by Pope John XXII in 1323, less than 50 years after his death. (54)

1324 AD: The obligation to wear the Scapular, night and day, and unceasingly with the greatest diligence and care, is imposed by the Constitutions in the year 1324...the Brothers are commanded to sleep in tunic and Scapular...it is exactly this option that clearly shows that it was the Promise (of Our Lady) which had occasioned this legislation. (54a)

1348 AD: William of Coventry was an English Carmelite of the 14th Century, equally notable for his virtues as for his erudition and elegant Latin. In 1348, he composed a work entitled *Scutum Carmelitarum* (The Shield of the Carmelites). In this text, William of Coventry reproduces the account of Swanington in the first of the foundational documents on the devotion of the holy Scapular; he confirms it entirely. Here then, is a great testimony brought to bear on the Vision of St. Simon Stock, less than one century after the event by a Carmelite whom historians are pleased to proclaim with high esteem. (55)

1351 AD: She (the Virgin) wished to appear again in 1351 to her devout servant, St. Peter-Thomas and assure him of the perpetuity of the Carmelite Order, a grace that the Prophet Elijah obtained from Jesus transfigured on Mt. Tabor. (56)

1355 AD: In the Bull of the Pontiff, Innocent VI *Splendor paternae gloriae* of September 22, 1355, indulgences are similarly granted to those who "during the four major feasts of the same Blessed Virgin Mary devoutly attend the Mass of the members of the Confraternity of the Church of the Blessed Virgin in Donza, as it is commonly called (according to its celebrated name) in the Diocese of Tournai, in a church of the Brothers of the Order of Blessed Mary of Mt. Carmel in the above mentioned city of Bruges." (57)

1374 AD: The miracle of the city of Chester (England) is verified. An image of the Virgin pointing with a finger to the Carmelites said in a loud voice, "These are my Brothers." (58)

1389 AD: In 1389, the General of the Carmelite Order John Grossi (Johannes) wrote the book known as "The Viridarium," a Catalogue of the Carmelite Saints. It gives an integral account of the Scapular Vision. He was scholarly as well as holy. John Grossi's word is (considered) sacred; he consulted the very companions of those who had lived with and had talked to Saint Simon. He had access to all the libraries in the Order. (59)

1409 AD: Pope Alexander V certifies the Sabbatine Bull of Pope John XXII. Alexander V completely inserts the Sabbatine Bull of John XXII *Sacratissimo uti culmine*, into the Bull *Tenorem cujusdam privilegi*, of December 7, 1409, in order to give the first one certitude even more ample and undeniable for the future. Alexander V gives assurance that he saw and diligently examined the original Sabbatine Bull. (60)

1409 AD: By a Bull dated October 2 of the year 1409, Pope Alexander V nominated John Grossi Professor and Master of Theology, to be Superior-General of the whole Order although he had been General of other parts. Thus the union of the Carmelites occurred under Alexander V and the General nominated by Alexander was the same who was subsequently elected by the vocales of the whole Order in the Chapter of 1411 (John Grossi). (60a)

1421 AD: The Carmelites hold a General Chapter at Montpellier in 1420. There it is decided that the original of the Bull, *Tenorem cujusdam privilegi* of Alexander V, would go to rejoin the Sabbatine Bull of John XXII *Sacratissimo uti culmine*, in the General Archives of the convent in London. But previously, they had received an authentic copy from a notary of Mallorca on January 2, 1421. (61)

1421 AD: In Mallorca in 1421 an authentic copy of the Sabbatine Bull was made with all the formalities of the law. From the aforementioned important document many copies were soon made, many examples of which are found in the Vatican Archives. (62)

1430 AD: Another authentic copy of the original was taken, nine years after the preceding one to be deposited in the Archives of the Carmelite convent of Genoa. (63)

Visual testimony of the existence of this Act, among others, is that of Fr. Philip of the Most Holy Trinity, General of the Scalced Carmelites who speaks of it in his "Carmelite Theology" with these words: *I saw that (authentic transcript) in the Archive of our Carmelite Fathers of the Genoan Observance and I faithfully described it. And this I set forth word for word.* (64)

1443 AD: Before the original of the aforesaid Bull of Alexander V had been carried to London, a new authentic copy was made in Messina on August 5, 1443 by Mathieu Pagliarino, Apostolic Notary. The two authentic copies of 1430, conserved in the Carmelite convent of Genoa and that of the 1433 copy of Messina, are considered the most ancient and most certain of those possessed by the Carmelites. (See "The Magnificent Beauty of Christian Art," under Chapter 7, of this book for a copy of the Sabbatine Bull made in Messina) (65)

1450 AD: Thomas Bradley Scrope (made Bishop of Dromor, Ireland in 1450) wrote a full account of the Scapular Vision. There are two texts (of the Scapular Vision) one at Cambridge University Library ms. FF. 6. 11. ff. 42-43, the other in "Tractatus de fundatione:" "The Blessed Virgin Mary appeared to him with a multitude of angels, holding in her blessed hands the Scapular of the ancient Order of Carmelites and saying, *This will be for you and for all Carmelites a Privilege that he who dies in this will not suffer eternal fire, that is he who dies in this will be saved."* (66)

1452 AD: Blessed John Soreth, Prior General, approached Pope Nicholas V to offer cloistered nuns and lay people the opportunity to live Carmelite spirituality in the world. So on October 7, 1452, Pope Nicholas V granted the Bull *Cum nulla* granting canonical status for the addition of the cloistered nuns and the establishment of the Third

Order of the Laity to the Carmelite Order. (66a)

1461 AD: Nicholas Calciuri (from the Province of Sicily, work written in 1461): *Vita de Sancti e Romiti del Monte Carmelo.* The author was from the convent of Messina in the province of Sicily. He recorded, "And the most glorious Virgin Mary appeared to the blessed Simon with a great multitude of angels and held in her hand the Scapular of the Order and said these words, *This will be for you and for all Carmelites a Privilege and he who dies with this Scapular will not suffer the pain of fire for eternity and he who dies with this will be saved.*" (67)

1480 AD: Arnoldus Bostius, Carmelite, relates in his great *Speculum historiale,* the apparition of the Virgin to Pope John XXII in the year 1316, at the time of his elevation to the pontifical throne and narrates once again, the Privilege of the Sabbatine Bull. He also says that the Bull of this Pope is conserved in England and that the convent of the Carmelites of Genoa possesses one of the authentic copies. (68)

1483 AD: Baldwin Leersies (Arras, around 1483) Leersies, Sub-Prior of the convent of the ancient observance of Arras devoted his life to bringing together the marks of the special protection given by the Most Holy Virgin to his beloved Order. He died of the plague in 1483, leaving behind a precious book entitled, *Collectaneum Exemplorem et Miraculorum* [Collection of Examples and Miracles]. This collection of the deeds and miracles accomplished by the Most Holy Mother of God on behalf of his Order relates in chapter IV (p. 367 of the *Speculum*) the apparition of the Virgin to St. Simon Stock, with the same appearance and holding the Scapular, she says, *This will be the mark of the Privilege that I obtained for you and the children of Carmel. Whoever dies wearing this habit [Scapular] will be saved.* (69)

1492 AD: A Document on the Sabbatine Bull: An icon, depicting the Scapular Vision and Our Lady granting the Sabbatine Privilege to Pope John XXII, is venerated in the Church of Carmine Maggiore in Palermo, Sicily. This ancient painting has the value of a perfectly authentic document. The tableau was painted by the disciples of Thomas de Vigilia in 1492. (70) (A similar painting is also found in the Church of San Martino in Corleone, Sicily, painted in 1492 by Thomas de Vigilia. The author personally photographed these two paintings. See Chapter 7, under "The Magnificent Beauty of Christian Art," in this book.)

1499 AD: Arnold Bostius (Ghent) ob. 1499. He described the (Scapular) Vision several times, both in *De patronatu B.V.Mariae* written in 1479 and in *Speculum historiale* written about 1490. (71)

1517 AD: On October 31, 1517 (Martin) Luther (an Augustinian friar) published his 95 thesis in Wittenberg, Germany. October 31st is the day Protestants mark as Reformation Day. Luther considered the assurances (indulgences) false and feared for the salvation of his parishioners. He preached against indulgences and questioned them in his thesis. He was excommunicated by the Church of Rome. Declared an outlaw by the Holy Roman Empire, he became the "Father of the Reformation." (72)

1517 AD: In the Acts of the General Chapter of the Order in 1517 there is mention of the Sabbatine Bull. It is in agreement with an authentic copy made from the original; "Likewise, they entrusted to the Most Reverend Father General what will be required of the religious community for promoting the Sabbatine Bull for Saturdays." (73)

1528 AD: Clement VII (Card. Medici) in his Bull of May 15, 1528 says: "On the Saturday following the death of the Religious and the members of the Confraternity of Carmel, the Glorious Virgin Mother of God, Mary, visiting them in Purgatory will liberate them from their sufferings." (74)

1530 AD: In his Bull *Ex clementi* of August 12, 1530, Clement VII cites almost word for word the Sabbatine Bull of John XXII, renewed and confirmed by Alexander V. He approves and confirms it again in the same manner which the content in those Bulls expressed and inserted in what is published by Apostolic Authority. (75)

1534 AD: Paul III in his Bull *Provisionis nostrae* of November 3, 1534, recalls the text of Clement VII, his predecessor, by declaring that he wishes to accord to the tenor of this (Sabbatine) Bull, thus inserted, the same faith and vigor that was given to the original Bull as if one had it before his eyes. (76)

1534 AD: The Pope (Clement VII) excommunicates the King (Henry VIII), who then unleashes a terrible bloody persecution against Catholics and religious communities. The library of their [the

Carmelites'] convent in London, which was looked upon as one of the most outstanding of the Kingdom by the number and quality of its manuscripts and books, was pillaged. The Sabbatine Bull of Pope John XXII was lost in the devastation of the General Archives of the Order which followed the schism of Henry VIII, King of England. One should not be shocked that the original Sabbatine Bull disappeared in such a torment. (77)

1545 AD: The Council of Trent opened in Northern Italy. By the time the third and last phase concluded in 1563, the Church of Rome had committed to rid itself of gross abuses, clarified and reaffirmed Catholic Dogma, made provision for a new catechism and stamped Reformation teachings as heresy. (78)

1549 AD: Paul III in his Bull *Dum a nobis* of April 27, 1549, confirms the privileges conceded to the Order of Our Lady of Mount Carmel and especially he says the graces, concessions and indults contained in the Bull of Clement VII of August 12, 1530. (79)

1559 AD: John Bale, originally an English Carmelite, converts to Protestantism under Henry VIII. He had inspected the majority of the libraries of his day and in particular, those of the Order. Thus his testimony carries great authority. The most esteemed of his works has the title, *Scriptorum illustrium majoris Britanniae Catalogus* (Bale, 1559). Bale afterwards adds in the appendix to the Fifteeenth Century, "This apparition (of Our Lady to Pope John XXII) with its exceptional indulgences and deliverance of souls from purgatory, WHICH I have read both in England as in Hainaut [Belgium], in a certain Bull, was reissued in Rome in 1530 under Clement VII." The Bull *Sacratissimo uti culmine*, of John XXII and that of Alexander V, *Tenorem cujusdam privilegi* were placed in the General Archives of London where one witness, John Bale, affirms as having seen and read. This witness of John Bale is confirmed by his contemporary, Charles Drelincourt (1595-1669), a French Protestant Pastor and prodigious writer who says in his book on the honor of the Holy Virgin, that the Bull of John XXII was authentically confirmed by Alexander V. (80)

1561 AD: Pius IV by his Bull *Cum a nobis* of May 30, 1561 addressed to the provincials, priors and other brothers of the Carmel in Portugal, confirms all the liberties, faculties, graces, concessions and immunities accorded to them, whether as privileges or otherwise by John XXII, Alexander V, Clement VII, Paul III and by other Roman pontiffs. (81)

1562 AD: (August 24), Santa Teresa de Jesus, Carmelite [St. Teresa of Avila] inaugurates her Reform with the foundation of the Convent of the religious of St. John of Avila. (82)

1566 AD: St. Pius V with the Bull *Superna dispositione* of Feb. 18, 1566 approves all the privileges, indulgences and graces conceded to the Carmelite Order, including the Sabbatine Privilege. (83) (Of the nine popes who have sanctioned the Sabbatine Privilege, note these words of St. Pius V (*Superna dispositione*): *With apostolic authority and by tenor of the present, we approve each of the privileges (of the Carmelite Order) and also the Sabbatine.* (83a)

1566 AD: St. Pius V in the Bull *Superna dispositione* of Feb. 18, 1566, concedes to the church, the new Convent, built in Rome in replacement of that of Santa Maria della Transpontina—destroyed because of its' proximity to the St. Agnes castle—all the privileges, indulgences and other graces as well as the Sabbatine, otherwise accorded to the ancient church by John XXII and Clement VII. (84)

1567 AD: Saint Pius V promulgated in his motu proprio *Etsi dominici,* the abrogation of all the indulgences for which alms were required or manus adiutrices. Also in 1567, Rev. Father Rossi, Prior General of the Carmelite Order visited Spain, Lisbon, Seville and Salamanca. There he issued letters of Brotherhood into the (Carmelite) Order, granting indulgences to the faithful, especially in order to enjoy the grace of the Sabbatine Bull expressed in the noted letters of brotherhood. The mention of the Sabbatine Privilege is very explicit. The Bishop, Don Pedro Gonzalez de Mondoza, intervened and ordered the letters to be gathered up, mandating him to suspend the graces until the truth and certainty of this Sabbatine Privilege could be determined.

(See below personal letter to the author with attached translation of P. Balbino Velasco, Madrid, Spain on the following pages). (85)

Madrid 20 de marzo de 2005
Rev. John A. Wadell
Muro (Mallorca).
Contesto por encargo de unos compañeros a su cuenta del 15 de febrero de 2005 le envio unos datos que estimo pueden esclarecer a la Sra. Que V. conoce y esta interesado por el tema del Escapulario del Carmen.

"Como en otros lugares por donde habia pasado el Rmo. P. Rubeo en 1567, la estancia del general del Carmen suscitó tambien en Andalucia, y particularmente en Sevilla, gran afluencia de gente, a causa de la facultad extraordinaria que del papa traia para conceder divers as indulgencias a los fieles, y mas aun por la facultad ordinaria de su oficio para conceder cartas de hermandad. "Abriendo, pues mana franca y liberal - refiere el cronista andaluz- fue innumerable el concurso de uno y otro sexo de los devotos y piadosos sevillanos a pedir bendiciones para sus rosarios y cartas de herrnand, de las que se repartieron muchisimas, por lo que se acrecento indeciblemente el fervor y la devocion del santo Escapulario de Nuestra Madre Santisima". No solo los seglares, sino tambien personas eclesiasticas, muchos religiosos y religiosas de otras ordenes, se hicieron hermanos de'la Orden carmelitana, tomando el escapulario y haciendose inscribir en el libro de los cofrades, especialmente para gozar de la gracia de la bula sabatina, expresada en dichas partas de hermandad. El tenor de estas cartas, otorgadas por el padre Rubeo en su visita a España, nos ha sido conservado por el padre Miguel de la Fuente en su *Compendio historial*. La mencion del privilegio sabatino es muy explicita. Entre otras gracias de que gozan los cofrades del Carmen, se menciona claramente esta: "Que se les conceden los privilegios contenidos en la bula sabatina, a saber, que la Madre de Dios y siempre Virgen Maria, verdadera Madre de misericordia y piedad, por su intercesion continua y ayuda especial -segun las cartas apostolicas de Juan XXII, Alejandro V y Clemente VII, les socorrera en el purgatorio el primer sabado despues de su muerte". Por su parte, los cofrades tendran que vivir cristianamente segun su estado y guardar abstinencia de carne todos los miercoles y sabados del año a no ser que en tales dias cayere la fiesta de Navidad, 0 si la enfermedad, flaqueza 0 necesidad les obligare a tomarla. Como en Sevilla y Lisboa tambien en Salamanca otorga el padre Rubeo muchas cartas de hermandad a los devotos de la Orden. No ha pasado mucho tiempo cuando interviene el obispo, don Pedro Gonzalez de Mendoza, dando ordenes a su provisor, Juan de Zufiiga, para que se recojan esas cartas, mandando suspender las gracias hasta que se averiguase la verdad y certeca deste privilegio de la-bula sabatina. La intervencion es mas bien de orden disciplinar y juridico; debe inspirarse en los decretos tridentinos que prescriben la derogacion de muchas indulgencias. El mismo afio de 1567 San Pio V promulga en su motu proprio, *Etsi dominici,* la abrogacion de todas las indulgencias para las cuales se exige limosnas, o *manus adiutrices.* Se plantea ahora la cuestion: primero, si las indulgencias del privilegio sabatino estan fundadas en documentos pontificios autenticos; y, en segundo lugar, si caen bajo la prohibicion del Concilio 0 del motu proprio de San Pio V. El examen de la causa, llevada por el obispado de salamanca ante el tribunal de la Universidad, se encomienda a una comision de excelentes teologos, formada por el doctor fray Mancio de Corpus Christi, sucesor de Vitoria; el maestro Rodriguez, el maestro fray Bartolome de Medina y el doctor sancho. Por lo visto, las autoridades de Sevilla han consultado tambien con la Universidad de salamanca.

Dos afios mas tarde se terminara este litigio despues de que los teologos emitieran sus pareceres favorables a la bula sabatina, declarando que es autentica y que las gracias contenidas en ella no ofrecen punto censurable ni incurren en los terminos de los decretos tridentino 0 del motu proprio de San Pio V.

Estos datos pueden V. encontrarlos en la obra del P. Otger Steggink, *la reforma del Carmelo espanol,* Roma, 1965, p. 268 ss.

Me permito tambien afiadir una indicacion, *La bula Sabatina,* a que se hace referencia en estos documentos se considera falsa por los historiadores modemos. Vease: Ludovico Saggi, O. Carm., *La bolla Sabatina,* en *Carmelus,* 13 (1966) 24-302; 14 (1967) 63-89. Si desea alguna aclaracion sobre e1 tema puede V. consultarme directamente a la siguiente direcci6n:

P. Balbino Velasco
c/ Pintor Ribera. 9 28016 MADRID
Affmo. en Cristo Balbino Velasco

The Brown Scapular of Our Lady of Mount Carmel

Translation:

Madrid March 20, 2005 Rev. John Wadell Muro (Mallorca)

I am answering, through the requests of some companions your report which you sent to them on February 15, 2005, some facts which I believe are able to offer some clarification to the Senora whom you know and is interested in the Scapular of Carmel. "As in other places where the Reverend Father Rubeo had visited in 1567, the stay of the General of Carmel provoked in Andalucia, and particularly in Seville, a great crowd of people because of the extraordinary power which the Pope had given to grant diverse indulgences to the faithful and even more through the ordinary power of his office to grant letters of brotherhood." Upon opening, with certainly a generous and free hand-reports an Andalucian reporter - there was an innumerable gathering of both sexes of the devotees and the pious Sevillians to request blessings for their rosaries and letters of brotherhood; of these many were distributed, through which was promoted unutterably the fervor and devotion of the "Holy Scapular of Our Most Holy Mother." Not only laymen, but also ecclesiastical persons, many religious and religious of other orders became brothers of the Carmelite Order, taking the Scapular and inscribing themselves in the book of members especially in order to enjoy the grace of the Sabbatine Bull expressed in the noted letters of brotherhood. The tenor of these letters, granted by Father Rubeo in his visit to Spain has been preserved for us by Father Miguel of the Fuente in his Historical Compendium. The mention of the Sabbatine Privilege is very explicit. Among other graces of which the members of Carmel enjoy, this is clearly mentioned: "That they are granted the privileges contained in the Sabbatine Bull, namely, that the Mother of God and Ever Virgin Mary, true Mother of Mercy and Piety, through her continual and special help - according to the apostolic letters of John XXII, Alexander V and Clement VII will aid them in Purgatory the First Saturday after their death." For their part, the members will have to live in a Christian way according to their state in life and keep abstinence from meat every Wednesday and Saturday of the year unless such days fall on the Feast of Christmas or if sickness, weakness or necessity obliges them to take something. As in Seville and Lisbon also in Salamanca Father Rubeo granted many letters of brotherhood to the devotees of the Order. Not much time passed when the Bishop intervened, Don Pedro Gonzalez de Mondoza, giving orders to his provisor, Juan de Zuniga, in order that these letters be gathered up, mandating him to suspend the graces until the truth and certainty of this Sabbatine Privilege could be determined. The intervention is more of a disciplinary and juridic order; it ought to be in harmony with the Tridentine decrees which proscribe the derogation of many indulgencias. In the same year of 1567 Saint Pius V promulgated in his motu proprio, *Etsi dominici,* the abrogation of all the indulgencias for which alms were required, or *menus adiutrioes.* Now is posed this question: First, whether the indulgencias of the Sabbatine Privilege are founded in authentic pontifical documents and in the second place, if they fall under the prohibition of the Council or of the motu proprio of St. Pius V. The examination of the case, carried out by the Bishop of Salamanca before the Tribunal of the University, was committed to a commission of excellent theologians, formed by Doctor Fray Mancio de Corpus Christi, successor of Vitoria, Professor Rodriguez, Professor Fray Bartolome de Medina and Doctor Sancho. Apparently the authorities of Seville had consulted also with the University of Salamanca. Two years later this dispsute was ended, after which the theologians issued its favorable opinions of the Sabbatine Bull, declaring that it is authentic and that the graces contained in it do not offer nor do they incur any censurable element according to the norms of the Tridentine decrees or the motu proprio of Saint Pius V.

These facts are able to be found in the work of P. Otger Stegginnk, *The Reform of Spanish Carmel,* Rome, 1965, pages 268ff.

Permit me also to add an indication. The Sabbatine Bull, to which reference is made in these documents, is considered false by modern historians. See: Ludovico Saggi, O. Carm., *The Sabbatine Bull,* in Carmel, 13 (1966) 24-302; 14 (1967) 63-89.If one desires some clarification on this theme, please consult me directly at the following address:

P. Balbino Velasco
c/Pintor Ribera, 9
28016 MADRID (85)
Sincerely in Christ, Balbino Velasco

1568 AD: The first Carmelite Convent of the religious of the Reform of Santa Teresa de Jesus and San Juan de la Cruz was opened in Duruelo, in Old Castile. (86)

1569 AD: When the Prior General (Giovanni Battista Rossi) visited Spain and freely distributed such letters of affiliation (the letters also make mention of the assistance of the Madonna to the Souls in Purgatory), he provoked the suspicion of the Inquisition. Therefore the official called "Secular Justice of Degrees" of Seville and the Bishop of Salamanca took these letters they had received and deferred the case to the University of Salamanca. In a definitive manner it undertook the task of examining whether the indulgences mentioned in these letters were authentic and whether they were in any way in contradiction to the Decrees of Trent. Four doctors, namely, the professors Mancio and Bartolomeo of Medina, both Dominicans, Francisco Sanchez, canon of Salamanca and Rodriquez, professor of Moral Theology discussed for a long time (two years) the question. In the end they pronounced in favor of the aforementioned letters and in favor of the authenticity of the Bull of John XXII, that is, the Sabbatine Bull. (87)

The University of Salamanca, the most illustrious of all of Spain, in the year 1569 deputed four of its principal professors to study the matter, namely: the Father Master Mancio, Dominican and professor of theology, Francisco Sanchez, canon of Salamanca, the Father Master Rodriguez and the Father Master Bartolomeo de Medina, Dominican, recognized as one of the most learned theologians of his time. "All of them concluded in favor of the authenticity of the privileges of the Scapular and of the Sabbatine Bull, affirmed by the successive Bulls of John XXII, Alexander V and Clement VII, with nothing in the decisions of the Council of Trent standing in opposition. Their unanimous conclusion, received by the Bishop and confirmed by him was solemnly published." (88)

1577 AD: Gregory XIII in his Bull *Ut laudes*, of September 18, 1577, gives a summary account and confirms all the privileges and indulgences accorded by his predecessors to the associates of Our Lady of Mt. Carmel, among others the privileges of the Bull of John XXII from which he cites the words, in favor of those who having worn the Habit [Scapular] or taken part in the Confraternity and who, finding themselves still in Purgatory, will receive the Saturday after their death, a help wholly special from the Holy Virgin. (89)

1598 AD: Gregory XIV, Pope from December 5, 1590 to October 15, 1591: *Hence, it seems noteworthy that many members of the faithful from ancient times have sought to belong to this Confraternity ... And in the same way in modern times when the Most Reverend General*

Giovanni Battista Rossi, of happy memory, visited Spain, he found that the King of Portugal wore the Carmelite Habit [Scapular] with particular devotion along with innumerable people of his kingdom. Niccolò Sfrondato later said that Gregory XIII, the Supreme Pontiff of happy memory, along with many Cardinals, Bishops and other Prelates of the Church of God, were adorned and continued to be adorned by this Sign so noble and salutary in reverence and honor of our most glorious Patroness. (90)

1603 AD: Didacus de Coria Maldonado – Carmelite of Córdoba, Doctor of Theology, a man of an excellent nature, esteemed for his various writings, around 1603 related in a work called *Dilucidario* (book 10, chap.9) how, by means of an apparition of the Blessed Virgin Mary to Pope Honorius, she spoke to the communities and confirmed the rule of the Carmelites and he added the following: "The words of the Virgin are these: 'Do not have any indications contrary to the things I have offered to thee, nor any expression opposed to the things I have promoted.'" (91)

1604 AD: Clement VIII issued a Bull: *Dominici Gregis Cura,* July 14, 1604 by which he accords ample privileges to the Discalced Carmelites of Italy saying: *Distinguished as you are by humility, poverty, abnegation, abstinence, fasts and austerities of life, you show that you are the disciples of your Father, St. Elias, the Founder of your Institute.* (92)

1609 AD: The Sacred Congregation of Rites approved and confirmed an Office of Nine Lessons for the Feast of the Solemn Commemoration (of Our Lady of Mt. Carmel). The Lessons were, if not the work of the great Cardinal Bellarmine, at least submitted to his judgment and supervision as a member of the Congregation. Benedict XIV evidently believed that some prestige is added to the Lessons, or at least to their historical value because of the connection they have with the Cardinal (Bellarmine) whom he calls Venerable. (93)

1609 AD: The University of Bologna, in Italy, in 1609 took hold of the same question. The Dean, Fr. Master Paul Faxinelle, Augustinian, declared the Bull of John XXII, not only was not annulled but had been confirmed by several popes in such a way that it retained all its canonical value. This was upheld successively by all the learned professors of this celebrated university. (94)

1613 AD: **The Decree of the Sabbatine Privilege:** *The Privilege,* commonly called the *Sabbatine,* of John XXII, approved and confirmed by Clement VII, (in *Ex Clemente* 12 Aug., 1530) by Saint Pius V (in *Superna dispositione* 18 Feb., 1566) by Gregory XIII (in *Ut laudes* 18 Sept., 1577) and by others as also by the Holy Roman and Universal Inquisition under Paul V on the 20th of January, 1613, by a Decree of the following tenor (reads):

It is lawful for the Carmelite Fathers to preach that Christians may piously believe in the help promised to the souls of the brethren and the members of the Confraternity of the Blessed Virgin Mary of Mount Carmel, namely, that the Blessed Virgin will assist by her continual intercession, suffrages and merits and also by her special protection, particularly on the Saturday after death (which day has been consecrated to her by the Church), the souls of the brothers and the members of the Confraternity departing this life in charity who shall have worn the habit, and shall have observed chastity according to their particular state of life, and also have recited the Little Office (or if unable to read, have kept the fasts of the Church, and have abstained from the use of meat on Wednesdays and Saturdays, unless the Feast of the Nativity of Our Divine Lord should fall on one of those days. (95)

John Launoy considered this Decree to condemn both the Sabbatine Bull of John XXII and the apparition. This opinion has been shown to be false by the simple fact that the Church, when conceding the Sabbatine Privilege to the Scapular Confraternity by the above decree of Pope Paul V, has premised it by citing first the Bull of John XXII: **Sic mihi, 3 Mart. 1322.** [See: *Rescripta Authentica* (*Authentic Rescript of the Sacred Congregation presiding over Indulgences and Sacred Rellics as well as the Summary of Indulgences*) found in this book in Chapter 2, "What is the Brown Scapular?" and Appendix 1 "The Summarium," dated December 1, 1866, p. 475] (96)

1635 AD: Manuscript 3813 of the Vatican Library confirms the testimony of Grossi on the authenticity of the Holy Scapular (The Viridarium of John Grossi). You should also carefully consider the important fact that the sacred tribunal of the Inquisition, by an act of August 23, 1635 recognized the existence of this manuscript 3813 in the Vatican Library at the request of the Discalced Carmelites. (97)

1642 AD: THE ERRONEOUS TEACHINGS OF LAUNOY: Four hundred years after St. Simon Stock had received the Scapular from Our Blessed Lady, John de Launoy, or Launoy, made a fierce attack on the Scapular. In 1642, John Launoy, a Doctor of the Paris schools put an end to this unchallenged spread of the (Scapular) devotion. Launoy wrote two books on the Scapular revelations. The occasion for his attack was Father Mark Anthony Alegre de Casanate's work: *Carmelitici decoris Paradisus*, which had already been placed on the Index by the Holy See and was condemned also by the University of Paris and *L'Adoptions des Enfants de la Vierge dans l'Ordre et la Confrerie de Notre Dame de Mont Carmel*, (by Gregorius Nazienzenus of St. Basil). Launoy's avowed purpose as he stated in the prefaces to both works, consisted in "determining the origin of the so-called privileged Scapular."

THE BOOKS OF JOHN LAUNOY:

1. Dissertatio Duplex 1642
2. De Simonis Stocchi Viso, De Sabbatinae Bullae Privilegio
Et de Scapularis Carmelitarum Sodalitate Dissertationes V, 1653

His chief weapon was the "negative argument." The negative argument of Launoy is based on the absence of any mention of the Vision of St. Simon by several Carmelite writers. In his negative arguments, he betrays an ignorance of the Scapular history that a diligent student of the subject never could betray. He rejected both the apparition to St. Simon (the Scapular Vision) and that attributed to John XXII (The Sabbatine Bull) and declared both unpreachable due to a lack of documentary evidence. Finally, about thirty of the works of this 17th century Jansenist were banned by the ecclesiastical authorities and the present work: *Dissertationes V. de Simonis Stochii Viso etc.* was condemned 18th April, 1689 AD. The *Index Librorum Prohibitorum*, published by authority of Pius X (1907) with *Praefatio* by Secretary of S. Ind. Congr., contains 27 works of Launoy. Many of them have been condemned more than once.

The fact remains that Launoy was engaged in a work of destruction and he had an eye only for defects. The labor of a destructive critic must be immense if his work is ever to be considered reliable. The modern debate (in the 20th and 21st Centuries) is in general outline, nothing but a modification of the position of Launoy. (Refering to Launoy's theological arguments against the Scapular Vision): *they have no direct reference in any way to the Scapular Vision; in reality, they strike at the root of all private revelations.* (98)

Who was Launoy? Priest and Doctor of the Sorbonne, he was *novitatis magis quam vertitatis studiosus*: more a friend of novelty than the truth. He was a hypercritic, an enemy of papal authority and of Religious Orders. Hostile to saints, he was a man of crude and muddled erudition who discarded documents and more certain facts if they did not harmonize with his pre-established opinions. A most worthless writer, whose hand like that of the other Ishmael, waged war against everyone and the hands of all were against him. Another author dedicated the following lines to the Jansenist, Launoy: "It was not only with the Carmelites that his satirical nature had quarrels but also with the Jesuits, the Dominicans and others; he was called the Discreditor of Saints." (99)

1642 AD: Fr. John Cheron, a Carmelite of Bordeaux (was the first who) attempted to refute Launoy's arguments in his *Privilegiati Scapularis et visionis S. Simonis Stockii vindicaiae* (Bordeaux, apud Ducoq, 192 pp.). Before his death, the Jesuit Fathers made out a number of questions relative to the life of St. Simon Stock and the questions were answered by the Carmelites from documents preserved by Cheron under the seal of the Province. The accuracy of the answers, as well as the source of information, is attested to by the Provincial of the Province of Aquitania and the Prior of the Bordeaux Convent under the official seal of the Province. (100)

1645 AD: Fr. Philibert Fesayus, O. Carm, wrote against the "Dissertatio Duplex" of John Launoy in his: *Duplex privilegium sacri Scapularis Ordinis et Confraternitatis gloriosae Virginis Mariae de Monte Carmelo, seu Responsio ad Ioannis Launoy dissertations* (Aix, 1645); thus summed up his argument against Launoy's denial of the fact of the Vision of St. Simon: *That it is contrary to common opinion, to the opinion of the theologians, to a very ancient tradition, to the declaration of the Cardinals of the Sacred Congregation of Rites, to reason and to propriety.* (101)

1648 AD: Fr. Thomas Aquinas of St. Joseph, O.C.D, wrote against the "Dissertatio Duplex" entitled: *Pro sodalitio sacri Scapularis adversus duplicem dissertationem I. Launoy.* (Tutelae, 1648) To Launoy's claim that the Vision was "fidei inexploratae," (of uninvestigated faith) Thomas Aquinas responded that the fact of universal belief which included Popes, Cardinals, Bishops and Theologians was sufficient examination. It may and must be considered to be examined in the list of those things confirmed by the consent of the Church. (102)

1648 AD: In France, the priests of the city of Rouen opposed any of the Discalced Carmelites enrolling the faithful in the Confraternity of the Scapular, or publishing the indulgences notably that of the Sabbatine Bull. The religious published the Bulls which they authorized. The Archbishop of Rouen, not wishing to involve himself in the debate, submitted the matter to the University of Paris. Eight of the principal Doctors of this renowned faculty of Theology were delegated to examine it. After taking several months, on August 19, 1648, they rendered a verdict which declared licit the erection of the above-mentioned Confraternity of the Scapular as well as the preaching of the Sabbatine Privilege in the forms prescribed by the Decree of Paul V of February 15, 1613. (103)

1654 AD: Fr. Theophilus Raynaud, S. J., joined forces with the Carmelites supporting the Scapular Tradition. The fact that this was written by one not of the (Carmelite) Order gave it greater prestige and value. He wrote: *Scapulare Parthenico-Marianum illustratum et defensum,* (in Defense of the Scapular Visions) Paris, 1654. (104)

1673 AD: Giovan Battista Emilio Altieri: Pope Clement X, with the Bull *Commissae nobis* of May 8, 1673, confirms the Bull of his predecessors on the Sabbatine Privilege. (105)

1680 AD: Finally, in the year 1680, Pope Innocent XI, in order to reinvigorate the zeal of the faithful for the cult of our Saint (Simon Stock), unjustly discredited by the bold criticism of Mr. Launoy, with two Bulls given in Rome, the first on May 21st and the second on May 27th of the same month, confirmed the Briefs of his predecessors on this matter. Various Martyrologies make mention of St. Simon Stock and celebrate his virtues and his miracles, among others, the *English Martyrology* of Gregory Wilson in the 14th century, that of John Molan in his additions to the Martyrology, M. Dussausay in his Martyrology of the Saints of France. (106)

1725 AD: The Great Prophet Elias has always been regarded by the Carmelites as the Founder and Patriarch of their Order. This ancient and cherished tradition has been sanctioned by the Church, for the statue of the Prophet stands in the Vatican among the founders of the Religious Orders bearing the following inscription: *Universus Ordo Carmelitarum Fundatori Suo Sancto Ellae Prophetae Erexit.* (The Order of Carmel has erected this statue to the Holy Prophet Elias its Founder). The rescript which accorded this privilege was granted by

Pope Benedict XIII, written with his own hand and addressed to the Carmelite Fathers, June 26, 1725. (107)

1726 AD: Pope Benedict XIII, by his Decree, *Urbi et Orbi*, of September 24, 1726, approves the Office for the Feast of Our Lady of Mount Carmel and directs that it be recited as a double major rite by all the faithful of both sexes who are bound to it. (108)

1740 AD: Cardinal Lambertini, later Pope Benedict XIV, in fact accepts the Vision of St. Simon Stock, the gift of the Scapular by the Blessed Virgin and the Privilege attached to it. Here are his words: *We believe the vision is truthful and we think all should hold it as such. It is, in fact, reported exactly by Suvaningron (Swanyngton) who was the friend and secretary of Blessed Simon and who told us that he heard the story from the very mouth of the saint: "This vision I have written under the dictation of the man of God, unworthy though it is." The original of this writing was formerly placed for safe keeping and hidden far away in the archives of the convent of Bordeaux. It was brought to light at the height of the controversy on the Scapular; then it was published by Fr. Jean Cheron, the Prior of the monastery of Bordeaux in the Vindiciae Scapularis, pp. 165 and following.* (109)

Also, after having exposed with impartiality the opinions for and against the Bull of John XXII, he [Pope Benedict XIV] pronounced formally in favor of the authenticity of this pontifical document, recognizing as peremptory the demonstration made by Fr. Theophile Raynaud. Here is the text of Benedict XIV: "The truth both of the Sabbatine Bull and the things it relates are vindicated before Theophile Raynaud." (110)

1751 AD: May 11, 1751, Pope Benedict XIV granted a plenary indulgence which was extended for that year through the whole Octave of the Solemn Commemoration of Our Lady of Mt. Carmel. It was requested "in memoriam tanti benefici," that is to say, the giving of the Scapular to St. Simon Stock. (111)

1759 AD: It has been noted by more than one of his biographers that (upon the removal of his body (the body of Pope John XXII,) to another part of the Cathedral in the year 1759 that his body was found intact. (112)

1760 AD: Pope Clement XIII (Rescript of September 20, 1760) confirms the Privilege of the Order which he reserved, the erection of

Confraternities of the Holy Scapular. (113)

1829 AD: Pope Pius VIII (Indult of July 7, 1829) declares the octave of the feast of Our Lady of Mount Carmel up to July 16, a *privileged octave*. (114)

1834-1844 AD: Pope Gregory XVI, by two rescripts—one of June 9, 1834, the other of April 16, 1844, grants a plenary indulgence plus one of 300 days for all those who assist, during the above-mentioned octave of the Feast of Our Lady of Mount Carmel at Matins and Lauds said before dusk in churches of the Discalced Carmelites. (115)

1858 AD: Our Lady chose July 16, 1858, (the anniversary of the bestowal of the Scapular of Our Lady to St. Simon Stock) to make her final appearance at Lourdes, (to Bernadette Soubirous.) (At Lourdes, Our Lady proclaimed *I am the Immaculate Conception,*—the embodiment of the revelation of the Immaculate Conception in the cloud to the Prophet Elias on Mount Carmel.) Bernadette always wore her Scapular. (115a) The apparitions of Our Lady to Bernadette in Lourdes, France, were officially approved by the Church on January 18, 1862 by Bertrand Severe Laurence, Bishop of Tarbes. (115b)

1865 AD: Pope Pius IX (Rescript of June 22, 1865) accords for perpetuity that the Masses, which are said in the Confraternity of Our Lady of Mount Carmel, at whatever altar, for the solace of the souls of the Confraternity of the Holy Scapular, enjoying the benefit of a privileged altar. (116)

1869 AD: Pope Pius IX, in his *Brief,* dated October 23, 1869, to author Alfred Monbrun, in recognition of his book: "The Life of Saint Simon Stock," affirmed the sanctity and admirable virtues of this great saint. (116a)

1887 AD: Pope Leo XIII said: *In fact the Carmelite Scapular was given by the Most Blessed Virgin to Blessed Simon Stock as something distinctive of his Order* singling out the Scapular of the Blessed Virgin of Mount Carmel from the tradition of many other Scapulars. April 27, 1887 *Acta Sanctae Sedis* XIX, 554-556. (117)

1892 AD: One of the most magnificent of the indulgences heaped upon the Scapular was granted by a modern Pope, Leo XIII: *To* *increase more and more among the faithful the devotion and piety towards the Most Blessed Virgin of Mount Carmel, whence flow the richest and most wholesome fruits for the soul,* on May 16, 1892 (Pope Leo XIII) granted a plenary indulgence, applicable to the Souls in Purgatory, to all who visit a Carmelite Church on the Scapular Feast, as often as they repeat the visit. (118)

1896 AD: September 20, 1896, Pope Leo XIII issued the Encyclical: *Fidentem Piumque* ("Close to the Mediator"): *She is from whom Jesus is born; she is therefore, truly His Mother and for this reason, a worthy and acceptable "Mediatrix to the Mediator."*(119)

1907 AD: Toward the end of his Encyclical on Modernism (*Pascendi Dominici Gregis,* September 8, 1907) the Holy Father (Pope St. Pius X) decrees that a council be formed, which he terms a "Council of Vigilance,"... he then proceeds to detail the duty of those members: *They shall watch most carefully for the traces and signs of Modernism both in books and teaching. Let them guard against novelties of words, remembering the admonition of Leo XIII. That manner of speaking cannot be approved of in the writings of Catholics which, striving after a vicious novelty, seems to deride the piety of the faithful, and speaks of a new order of Christian life, new directions of the Church, new wants of the modern soul.*

They must not neglect books which treat of the pious traditions of certain places or of sacred relics. They must not permit questions of this kind to be discussed in newspapers or periodicals intended to foster piety; neither must they allow them to be spoken of with expressions savoring of mockery or contempt, nor with dogmatic pronouncements especially if, as usually happens, the affirmations do not pass the bounds of probability or are merely based on prejudiced opinions.

In passing judgement on pious traditions this must be borne in mind: that the Church acts so prudently in this matter that it does not allow such traditions to be narrated in books unless great caution has been employed and the narrative is premised by the declaration imposed by Urban VIII... The Sacred Congregation of Rites, thirty years ago, decreed that these apparitions or revelations have neither been approved nor condemned by the Apostolic See, but have been merely permitted as things to be piously believed by merely human faith according as the tradition which they bear has been confirmed by suitable testimonies and documents. Anyone who follows this rule shall have no ground for fear. <u>For the devotion based on any apparition, in as far as it regards the fact itself and is called relative, always implies as a condition the truth of the fact; but in so far as it is absolute, it is always based on the</u>

truth, for it is offered to the very persons of the Saints who are honored. (120)

1910 AD: Pope St. Pius X: *All the faithful already inscribed or to be inscribed in the future with the rule as it is said, of inscription, to one or more of the Scapulars approved by the Holy See can, after the inscription, wear in place of these same cloth Scapulars, whether with one or many on their person — on the neck or otherwise, but in a decent manner — a unique medal made of metal, by which, observing the laws proper to each of these, can share in all the spiritual favors (not excluding the so-called Sabbatine Privilege of the Scapular of the Blessed Virgin Mary of Mount Carmel) and gain all the indulgences attached to each.* (Decree of the Holy Office of December 16, 1910. A.A.S., III, p. 23). (121)

1916 AD: Pope Benedict XV, the celebrated "World War (I) Pontiff," granted 500 days indulgence for the kissing of the Scapular, every time it is kissed. (122)

1917 AD: Following continual rejection of his peace proposals by world leaders (to end World War I), on May 5, 1917, Pope Benedict XV called upon Mary, the Mother of Mercy, to end the War. Eight days later (May 13, 1917), the Virgin Mary appeared at Fatima and said: "Pray the Rosary every day for peace in the world and an end to the War." (122a)

On July 16, 1917, Pope Benedict XV, addressing the Seminarians of Rome said: *Let all of you have a common language and a common armor: the language, the sentences of the Gospel; the common armor, the Scapular of the Virgin of Carmel, which you all ought to wear and which enjoys the singular privilege of protection even after death.* (122b)

On October 13, 1917, the Miracle of the Sun took place in Fatima, Portugal, at the final apparition of Our Lady of the Rosary, to Lucia, Jacinta, and Francisco. During the miracle, the children were privileged to see visions of the Holy Family, then Our Lady of Sorrows with Our Lord and finally Our Lady of Mount Carmel, holding the Scapular in her hand. (122c) The Fatima apparitions were officially approved on October 13, 1930, by Dom Jose Alves Correia da Silva, Bishop of the Diocese of Leiria-Fatima, and declared worthy of belief; devotion to Our Lady of Fatima was officially permitted. (122d)

1922 AD: *Letter* of Pope Pius XI: *Petis tu quidem,* to Father Elias Magennis, Superior General of the Carmelites, March 18, 1922, on the Anniversary of the *Sixth Centenary of the Sabbatine Privilege: You ask*

Us to recommend - at the closing of the Sixth Centennial commemorating the universal diffusion in the Church of the "Sabbatine Privilege"- to the faithful throughout the Catholic world, the devotion to Our Lady of Mount Carmel, and the sodalities for lay people, which take their name from the Virgin herself. We willingly do so with this letter. (123)

1922 AD: In the last Marian Congress of Belgium held in the year 1922, one of the theologians read a paper in which he explained the influence of devotion to the Holy Scapular on the strong and universal belief of the Church in the Doctrine of "Mary, Mediatrix of Graces." Many think that this Doctrine will soon become a dogma of the Church. (124)

"One of the theologians speaking at the Marian Congress of Belgium in 1922 mentioned this fact when he declared that if the doctrine of Mary, Mediatrix of all Grace, is ever declared a dogma of the Faith it will be due in large part to the Scapular Devotion." (125)

1923 AD: (April 29): Beatification of St. Thérèse of the Child Jesus by Pope Pius XI. She was born January 2, 1873, entered into the Carmel of Lisieux (France) April 9, 1888, and on the night that she died, September 30, 1897, in the Convent of Carmel in Lisieux, they took off her Scapular. Today, it is still there in a reliquary on her bed. (126)

1925 AD: (May 17): Canonization of St. Thérèse of the Child Jesus by the Supreme Pontiff, Pope Pius XI. (127)

1929 AD: (the 11th of February): The Order of Calced Carmelites was reinstated in the Holy Land with the foundation of a Convent in the city of Naplus (ancient Schechem or Sychar), three kilometers from the Well of Jacob separated from Mount Carmel by the Valley of Esdrelon. (128)

1933 AD: Pope Pius XI, November 30, 1933 *All. To pilgrims from Vicenza, November 30, 1933 (The Coredemptrix): From the nature of His work, the Redeemer ought to have associated His Mother with His work. For this reason we invoke her under the title of Coredemptrix. She gave us the Savior, she accompanied Him in the work of Redemption as far as the Cross itself, sharing with Him the sorrows of the agony and of the death in which Jesus consummated the Redemption of Mankind.* (129)

1942 AD: With the book: *Mary in Her Scapular Promise,* written in

1942 by world renowned author, John Mathias Haffert and through his efforts to defend the authenticity of the divine origins of the Devotion and repair the damage incurred through the interminable objections by the Historians throughout the years on the validity of the promises of Our Lady, the Devotion to the Brown Scapular of Our Lady of Mount Carmel was once again restored to its rightful place of honor and dignity in the devotional life of the Church in the 20th Century. Mr. Haffert's life was dedicated to promoting the Message of Our Lady of Fatima and the Brown Scapular Devotion. He died while wearing his Brown Scapular, a sign of his consecration to the Immaculate Heart of Mary. (129a)

1950 AD: Venerable Pope Pius XII, Letter, *Neminem profecto* to the Superior General of the Carmelites, February 11, 1950 (on the Seventh Centenary of the Scapular of Mount Carmel): *For this reason we have been glad to hear that as of the Seventh Centenary of the institution of this Scapular of the divine Mother of Mount Camel approaches, the Carmelite brethren have decided to hold solemn celebrations in honor of the Blessed Virgin Mary. On her part, the most holy Mother will not fail to intercede with God that her children who in Purgatory are expiating their sins, may at the earliest possible moment reach the Eternal Fatherland in accordance with the so-called Sabbatine Privilege."*(130)

1950 AD: The renowned Carmelite, Venerable Fr. Bartholomew F.M. Xiberta, O. Carm., wrote a monumental work on the authenticity and historical foundations of the Scapular Visions in his book: *De Visione Sancti Simonis Stock,* Rome, 1950. "There are no grounds in historical criticism for doubting any of the facts it relates about the life of St. Simon Stock." He (Fr. Xiberta) was noted for living his Carmelite vocation in a very profound way and for his devotion to Mary. He accepted election as an Assistant General of the Order and distinguished himself in the Church as a theologian, researcher, historian, and as a teacher. He was a consulter for the Second Vatican Council and was a Consulter for the Spanish Bishops. He was declared "Venerable" on September 26, 2003. (130a)

1951 AD: From the Reliquaries, there venerated over the centuries, was taken the skull of the Saint (Simon Stock) and on July 16, 1951 on the occasion of the worldwide celebrations of the Seventh Centenary of the great gift of the little Habit of Carmel, it [the skull] was carried solemnly in procession in England in order to be then given to the most ancient Carmel of Ayelsford, within whose walls St. Simon Stock lived many years before. (131)

1951 AD: *Letter* of Venerable Pope Pius XII to Killian Lynch, Prior General of the Carmelite Order on the occasion of the Seventh Centenary of the Institution of the Scapular and the transfer of the mortal remains of Saint Simon Stock from France to Ayelsford, England, June 30, 1951:

...It is your happy privilege, beloved son, to close the cycle of these centenary celebrations with a function of historic import, namely, the transfer of the mortal remains of Saint Simon Stock from their sheltered exile on the hospitable shores of France to their rightful place in the Dowry of Mary, to the home of his earthly sojourn at Aylesford.

Seven hundred years have passed since, according to the sacred traditions of the Carmelite family, Simon Stock was vouchsafed the vision of Our Lady of Mount Carmel, yet in the light of that vision, countless thousands throughout the world sustain the warfare of life and walk through the darkness and shadow of death to the mount of God. What more fitting close therefore, could there be to the Sept-centenary celebrations of the Scapular than the hallowed remains of him who sang the praises of the Flower of Carmel should have come to rest again in Aylesford for the festival of promise which he opened to the world – the feast of Our Lady of Mount Carmel...(132)

1959 AD: The Supreme Pontiff Pope St. John XXIII in the *Osservatore Romano*, February 20, 1959 said: *The name of John, eminently holy and apostolic, unites us to the person of Jesus, the Divine Founder and the Head of the Holy Church, but he [John] was not foreign to our thought. It was likewise agreeable for us to feel united, across six centuries to the last of the numerous Pontiffs with this name: John XXII, Jacques d'Euse de Cahors, the Bishop of Avignon who governed the Church for 18 years and died more than ninety years of age in 1334. This was a great Pontiff. His life was full of tribulations, but rich in works and merits, a true servant of the servants of God. He had, among other things, the honor of canonizing St. Thomas Aquinas. Above all, he was very devoted to Mary. It is to him that history attributes the happy idea of reciting one Our Father and one Hail Mary at the ringing of the evening bells; to him also belongs the fatherhood of the Sabbatine Privilege, so precious and dear to the those who wear the Scapular.* (133)

1961 AD: Sunday, July 15, Pope St. John XXIII in his General Audience Discourse exhorted: *Tomorrow July 16 is the commemoration* *of the Madonna of Carmel. The piety of the faithful in various centuries has always wished to honor the glorious Mother of God with various titles and with acts of more heartfelt homage. It should be remembered that it was the Pontiff John XXII, in the 14th Century who promoted devotion to Mary under this title and certainly from its history we should draw upon all that can render more clear and distinct this form of prayer and homage.* (134)

1964 AD: Pope St. John XXIII [published the year after his death]: *The Mother of the Divine Savior is justly hailed as the Beauty of Mount Carmel from which the prophet Elijah enthusiastically contemplated the storm cloud which rose from the sea, symbol of the most chosen graces.* (135)

1964 AD: Blessed Pope Paul VI: Dogmatic Constitution on the Church: *Lumen Gentium: This most Holy Synod deliberately teaches this Catholic Doctrine and at the same time admonishes all the sons of the Church that the cult, especially the liturgical cult, of the Blessed Virgin, be generously fostered and the practices and exercises of piety recommended by the Magisterium of the Church toward her in the course of centuries be made of great moment and those decrees which have been given in the early days regarding the cult of Images of Christ, the Blessed Virgin and the Saints be religiously observed.* (136)

1965 AD: Blessed Pope Paul VI: *In Dominica Republicana:*
It is our conviction that the Rosary of Mary and the Scapular of Carmel are among these recommended practices. This Scapular was worn by the Heroes of Latin America. The Scapular is a practice of piety, "which by its very simplicity is suited to everyone, and has spread widely among the faithful to their spiritual profit." In instructing the Christian people let it be pointed out repeatedly and emphatically that when the Mother is honored, then the Son is rightly known, loved and praised – the Son through whom all things have their being and in whom it has pleased the Eternal Father that all fullness should dwell. (137)

1973 AD: *A Pastoral Letter on the Blessed Virgin Mary,*
November 21, 1973: *We view with great sympathy the distress our people feel over the loss of devotion to Our Lady and we share their concern that the young be taught a deep and true love for the Mother of God. We Bishops of the United States wish to affirm with all our strength the lucid statements of the Second Vatican Council on the permanent importance of authentic devotion to the Blessed Virgin, not only in the liturgy, where the Church accords her a most special place under Jesus, her Son, but also in the beloved*

devotions that have been repeatedly approved and encouraged by the Church and that are still filled with meaning for Catholics. As Pope Paul has reminded us, the Rosary and the Scapular are among these testesd forms of devotion that bring us closer to Christ through the example and protection of His Holy Mother. (138)

1974 AD: Blessed Pope Paul VI, *Marialis Cultis*, February 2, 1974: *Mary, the New Woman, stands at the side of Christ, the New Man, within whose mystery the mystery of man alone finds true light; She is given to it as a pledge and guarantee that God's plan in Christ for the salvation of the whole man has already achieved realization in a creature: in Her.* (139)

1981 AD: A secular journal of Rome with a large circulation affirms that the Carmelite Scapular was distinctly observed on the chest of the Holy Father (Pope St. John Paul II) on the occasion of his surgery at the Gemelli Hospital on May 13, 1981, following the attempt on his life. "We are trying, with the help of those present, to reconstruct the condition of the Pope before the long surgery." Shortly before six in the afternoon, when the Pontiff entered the operating room, he no longer had the white Habit. He only was wearing an undergarment and on his skin, the two piece Scapular of brown cloth [was] on his chest and back bound by a cord with the image of the Madonna of Carmel. Next to him was his personal secretary Msgr. Stanislaw Dziwisz, wearing a violet stole and having in his hand little viles of the oil of the infirmed. (140)

1988 AD: July 21: In the recitation of the Sunday Angelus – Pilgrims with the Pope (St. John Paul II) through the "Geography of the Faith and Marian piety, said:

...*One particular grace of the Madonna toward the Carmelites, recorded in a venerable tradition associated with St. Simon Stock, has radiated in the Christian people with so many spiritual fruits. It is the Carmelite Scapular, the means of affiliation to the Order of Carmel by sharing the spiritual benefits and the vehicle for tender and filial Marian devotion (cf .Pope Pius XII "Neminem Profecto Latet"). Through the Scapular the devotees of the Madonna of Carmel express the wish to mold their existence under the example of Mary the Mother, the Patroness, the Sister, the most pure Virgin* ... (141)

1991 AD: "Our Sunday Visitor," February 24, 1991: "Unfortunately, this Sacramental (The Brown Scapular) seems to have gone the way of other pious practices such as Benediction of the Blessed Sacrament and the Nine First Friday Devotions. Today rarely is the Scapular explained from the pulpit or teacher's desk. Even more unusual is the enrolling in the Brown Scapular of the faithful. Some say the Scapular has seen its better days, and that the faithful should no longer be governed by silly superstition. The Rosary and the Brown Scapular are much needed Marian Devotions in the modern world. Both promote purity, a virtue noticeably at a premium." (142)

1992 AD: Pope St. John Paul II did not need to recuperate in the hospital only one time. Also in 1992 it again proved necessary. The journal already cited, reports another episode which confirms once again the devotion of the Pope to the (Brown) Scapular: *Your Holiness, you know that today is the Feast of Our Lady of Carmel? Yes, I know and I also know that today begins the feast in Trastevere.* John Paul II, yesterday morning, 24 hours after leaving the operating room, was already seated in an armchair in his room in the Gemelli Hospital. From his gown could be seen the Scapular of the Virgin of Carmel, which he never removes. (143)

2000 AD: On September 3, 2000, Pope St. John XXIII (Angelo Giuseppe Roncalli), Pope from October 28, 1958 to June 3, 1963, was beatified by Pope John Paul II. Referring to the day of his election and how Cardinal Tisserant of France came to ask him what name he would take, the Holy Father, Pope John XXIII, reflects on the name of John saying of his predecessor, Pope John XXII...*He had the honor of canonizing St. Thomas Aquinas; to him also, the paternity of the "Saturday Privilege* (The Sabbatine Privilege), *so precious and so dear to those who wear the Scapular of Our Lady of Mt. Carmel.* (143a)

2001 AD: March 25, 2001: *Message of John Paul II to the Carmelite Family* On the 750th Anniversary of the Bestowal of the Scapular:
    In this regard, I cannot fail to stress a happy coincidence; the celebration of this Marian year for the whole of Carmel is taking place, according to a venerable tradition of the Order itself on the 750th Anniversary of the bestowal of the Scapular. (144)

2002 AD: Pope St. John Paul II (Here, the Holy Father refers to private revelation in his Apostolic Letter), *Rosarium Virginis Mariae: Well-known are the occasions in the Nineteenth and the Twentieth Centuries on which the Mother of Christ made her presence felt and her voice heard,* *in order to exhort the People of God (to this form of) contemplative prayer. I would mention in particular, on account of their great influence on the lives of Christians and the authoritative recognition they have received from the Church, the apparitions of Lourdes and of Fatima.* (145)

2005 AD: *Osservatore Romano, 2005:* Monday-Tuesday, November 7-8: (Following the death of Pope John Paul II on April 2, 2005), the first session of the tribunal of the requested process for the cause for the beatification and canonization of the Servant of God, John Paul II took place. Some of the practices of piety by which the Servant of God expressed his love for Christ and Mary are counted among those of popular piety. He, a man of great intellect and artistic soul, was not embarrassed by the Scapular of Our Lady of Mount Carmel and these simple forms of piety. (146)

2006 AD: Pope Benedict XVI, *Angelus: Dear Brothers and Sisters, through a happy coincidence, this Sunday falls on 16 July, the day when the liturgy commemorates Our Lady of Mt. Carmel. The slopes of Carmel, a high ridge that runs down the eastern coast of the Mediterranean Sea at the altitude of Galilee, are dotted with numerous natural caves beloved by hermits. The most famous of these men of God was the great Prophet Elijah, (Elias) who in the ninth century before Christ, strenuously defended the purity of faith in the one true God from contamination by idolatrous cults. Inspired by the figure of Elijah, the contemplative Order of Carmelites arose... The Carmelites have spread among the Christian people devotion to Our Lady of Mount Carmel, holding her up as a model of prayer, contemplation and dedication to God. Today, I would like to entrust to the Queen of Mount Carmel all contemplatiave life communities scattered throughout the world, especially those of the Carmelite Order...* (147)

2008 AD: *Cardinal Urges Devotion to Rosary and Scapular,* Lima, Peru, July 17, 2008. Peruvian Cardinal Juan Luis Cipriani invited Lima's faithful to take the Rosary and the Carmelite Scapular to all homes in the context of the city's Great Mission. The Archdiocese of Lima launched the Great Mission...in keeping with the Continental Mission convoked by Benedict XVI in May 2006 at the shrine of Aparecida, Brazil...He urged the faithful to *take on one hand, the holy Rosary, and on the other, the Scapular of the Virgin of Carmel,"*and to spread the Devotion to others. Cardinal Cipriani also encouraged the faithful to approach Mary, Our Lady of Mount Carmel, with confidence, and to undertake with her the Way of the Cross. *She, Our Lady of Carmel, will give you the strength...* (147a)

2009 AD: Pope Pius XII (Eugenio Pacelli), Pope from 1939 to 1958 was declared "Venerable" on December 19, 2009 by Pope Benedict XVI. It was Pope Pius XII who spoke these words: *The Scapular is the Sign of Consecration to the Immaculate Heart of Mary – which (consecration) in recent times we have so strongly recommended.* (*Apostolic Letter* on the 7th Centenary of the Scapular Vision, Feast of the Apparition at Lourdes, February 11, 1950) The Documents of Pope Pius XII on the (Brown) Scapular Devotion are some of the most significant ever to come from the Holy See. Along with his tribute to the Scapular Devotion, he often sung the praises of Our Lady of Mount Carmel. Besides many references to Carmel's Queen in Scapular Documents, he dedicated cities, dioceses and whole nations to her name. Through what he called his "own devotion to Our Blessed Lady of Mount Carmel," he immensely increased respect and love for her throughout the world. (147b)

2010 AD: *Pope Benedict XVI will present a new statue of Our Lady of Mt. Carmel to Chile during this week's Wednesday General Audience. The statue will travel throughout the country bringing consolation to those suffering from the devastating February 27th earthquake....* (148)

2011 AD: On May, 1st, 2011, Divine Mercy Sunday, Pope John Paul II (Karol Jozef Wojtyla), Third Order Carmelite and Pope from October 16, 1978 to April 2, 2005, was beatified by Pope Benedict XVI. Blessed Pope John Paul II, by his own admission, wore the Brown Scapular. Among the promises of the Scapular is that those who wear it will avoid Hell and be delivered to Heaven on the First Saturday of the month following their deaths (The Sabbatine Privilege). The Pope died on the First Saturday itself, April 2... *I too have worn the Scapular of Carmel over my heart for a long time!* he said in 2001. (148a)

2011 AD: Pope Benedict XVI, July 17, 2011: today, noted that the Scapular is a *particular sign of union with Jesus and Mary.* Saturday was the feast of Our Lady of Mt. Carmel, the feast to which the Scapular is linked. Simon Stock, General Superior of the Carmelite Order, received the Scapular in 1251, during an apparition of the Virgin when she promised special assistance in life and death to all those who wear it with devotion. *For those who wear it, it is a sign of filial abandonment to the protection of the Immaculate Virgin* he said. (149)

2012 AD: On December 20, 2012, Pope Paul VI (Giovanni Battista Enrico Antonio Maria Montini) Pope from June 21, 1963 to August 6, 1978, was declared "Venerable" by Pope Benedict XVI. Pope Paul VI said the Devotion of the Brown Scapular and the Holy Rosary are the two most recommended Devotions by the Magisterium of the Church. He said: *Let the faithful hold in high esteem the practices and devotions to the Blessed Virgin…the Rosary and the Scapular of Carmel… so highly recommended by our illustrious predecessors.* (149a)

2013 AD: Pope Benedict XVI, *Angelus,* January 20, 2013: *…Dear friends, once more to the prayer for Christian unity I would like to add a prayer for peace…for both of these intentions, let us invoke the intercession of Mary Most Holy, the Mediatrix of Grace.* (150) (See the year 1922 AD**)**

CHAPTER 3 ENDNOTES

WHEN DID THE DEVOTION BEGIN?

1   *Mount Carmel,* Carmelites, Abridgement of: Carmel, Its History and Spirit, London, 1923, p. 32

2   *Ibid,* p. 25, "Bullarium Carmelitarum", Tom. III, p. 348

3   *Ibid,* p. 32, paraphrased; Tom. X., pp. 1073, 1074

4   *Enciclopedia Del Escapulario Del Carmen,* P. Simon Besalduch, Barcelona, 1931, p. 41, translated and paraphrased

5   *Ibid,* p. 43, translated and paraphrased

THE GREAT PROPHET ELIAS

1   *Mount Carmel,* Carmelites, Abridgement of Carmel: Its History and Spirit, Burns, Oates and Washbourne, London, 1923, pp. 25-27, paraphr.

2   *Douay Rheims,* Book of Ecclesiasticus 48: 1-15

CHRONOLOGY OF EVENTS

1   *Vatican II On the Church.* 56, Vatican II Marian Council, William G. Most, Ireland, 1972, p. 14

2   *The Carmelite Review,* A Monthly Catholic Journal Devoted to Our Blessed Lady of Mount Carmel, published by the Carmelite Fathers of North America, Vol. X, Welland, Ont., March, 1902, N. 3 p. 92

3   *Your Brown Scapular,* Rev. E.K. Lynch O.Carm., Maryland, 1950, pp. 1, 2

4   *The Carmelite Review,* Vol. X, March, 1902, No. 3, p. 92, Excerpted from the *Annals of the Order*

5   *Your Brown Scapular,* Rev. E. K. Lynch, O. Carm, 1950, p. 2

6   *The Carmelite Review,* Vol. X, March, 1902, No. 3, pp. 92, 93, paraphrased, *Annals of the Order*

7   *Ibid,* p. 93, Exercepted from the *Annals of the Order*

7a   *Your Brown Scapular,* Rev. E. K. Lynch, O. Carm., 1950, p. 2; 3 Kings 18: 18, 19

7b   *The Carmelite Review,* Vol. X, March 1902, No. 3, p. 93, *Annals of the Order*

7c   *Mary in Her Scapular Promise,* John Mathias Haffert, New Jersey, 1942, p. 3

8   *Ibid,* p. 4, paraphrased

9   Kings III, ch. 18, *Mary in Her Scapular Promise,* John Mathias Haffert, 1942, p. 4

9a   S. Antoninus in Summa, pg. 4 tit. 15, c. 4; St. Albertus Magnus in *Super Missus est;* St. Augustine in his Sermon, XXVII, *in Natali Domini,* xix; St. Ambrose, *"De Institutione Virginis,"* xiii; etc. *Ibid,* p. 4 see also footnote #2, p. 233 in *Mary in Her Scapular Promise,* John Mathias Haffert, 1942

9b   *Le Scapulaire de Notre Dame du Mont-Carmel est authentique,* P. Marie Joseph du Sacre Coeur, Avignon, 1928, AVANT-PROPOS; translated

10   *Sacre Instruttioni Per beneficio de Divoti del S. Scapolare Della Gloriosissima sempre Vergine Maria Nostra Signora del Carmine,* R.P.F. Gabrielle Ferri da Bologna, 1656, pp. 5-6, translated

10a *Enciclopedia del Escapulario del Carmen,* P. Simon Besalduch, Barcelona, 1931, p. 41, translated

11   *Enciclopedia del Escapulario del Carmen,,* P. Simon M. Besalduch, Barcelona, 1931 p. 44, translated

12   *The Carmelite Review,* Vol. X, March, 1902, No. 3, pp. 93, 94; *Annals of the Order*

12a *Alla Madre di Dio Regina Dell'Universo Gloria Letizia,* Raffaele Improta dello Scapolare Del Carmine, Napoli, 1956, p. 5, translated

12b   *The Carmelite Review,* Vol. X, March, 1902, No. 3, p. 94, *Annals of the Order*

13   *Ibid,* p. 95

13a   *The Carmelites and the Brown Scapular,* A. E. Farrington, D.D., O.C.C., Dublin, 1891, p. 3

13b   *The Carmelite Review,* Vol. X, May, 1902, No. 5, p. 144, *Annals of the Order*

13c   *Ibid,* p. 145; *Annals of the Order*

13d   *Ibid,* p. 146; *Annals of the Order*

13dd *Ibid,* p. 146; *Annals of the Order*

13e   *Ibid,* p. 147; *Annals of the Order*

13f   *Ibid,* p. 147; *Annals of the Order,* paraphrased

14   *Ibid,* pp. 147, 148; *Annals of the Order*

14a   *Ibid,* p. 148; *Annals of the Order*

14b   *Ibid,* p. 148; *Annals of the Order*

14c   *Ibid,* p. 148; *Annals of the Order,* also: *A Short Treatise on the Antiquity, Institution, Excellency, Indulgences, privileges, etc., of the ancient Confraternity of Our Blessed Lady of Mount Carmel, Called the Scapular...* Rev. R. J. Colgan, D.D., S.M.T., Perpetual Procurator-General of the Grand Carmelite Order, Philadelphia, the 1850's, pp., 22, 23

14cc *A Short Treatise on the Antiquity, Institution, Excellency, etc., ibid,* p. 23

14d   *The Carmelite Review,* Vol. X, May, 1902, No. 5, p. 149, *Annals of the Order,* paraphrased

14e   *Ibid,* p. 149, *Annals of the Order*

14f   *Ibid,* p. 149, *Annals of the Order*

14ff *Ibid,* p. 149, *Annals of the Order*

14fff *Ibid,* p. 149, *Annals of the Order*

14fg *Ibid,* p. 149, *Annals of the Order*

14g   *Alla Madre Di Dio, Regina Dell'Universo Gloria Letizia,* Raffaele Improta dello Scapolare Del Carmine, Napoli, 1956, p. 6, translated

15   *The Carmelite Review,* Vol. X, May, 1901, No. 5, p. 150, *Annals of the Order,* paraphrased

15a   *Mount Carmel,* Author: Carmelites, London, 1923, p. 21

16   *Escapulario de N.S. Del Carmen,* Coleccion De Instrucciones, R.P.Brocardo de Sta. Teresa, Vitoria, 1895, p. 13

17   *Mount Carmel,* p. 34; also in "Speculum perfectae Ecclesiae primitivae," cap. xii.)

18   *Ibid,* p. 34, also: Acts xi, 27

19   *Ibid,* p. 40; also http://www.newworldencyclopedia.org/entry/Pope Telesphorus

20   *Mount Carmel,* Author: Carmelites, London, 1923, p. 40, paraphrased

21   *Alla Madre Di Dio, Regina Dell'Universo Gloria Letizia,* Raffaele Improta dello Scapolare Del Carmine, Napoli, 1956, p. 6

21a   *The Carmelite Review,* Vol. X, June, 1902, No. 6, p. 200, *Annals of the Order*

21aa *Ibid,* p. 200, *Annals of the Order*

21b   *Ibid,* p. 200, *Annals of the Order,* paraphrased

21c   *Ibid,* p. 201, *Annals of the Order*

21cc *Ibid,* p. 201, *Annals of the Order*

21d   *Ibid,* p. 201, *Annals of the Order*

21dd *Ibid,* p. 201, 202, *Annals of the Order*

21e   *Ibid,* p. 202, *Annals of the Order*

22   *Mount Carmel.* Author: Carmelites, London, 1923, pp. 44-45

23   *Alla Madre Di Dio,* Raffaele Improta dello Scapolare Del Carmine, Napoli, 1956, p. 6

24   *Mount Carmel,* Author: Carmelites, London, 1923, pp. 45-46, paraphrased

25   *Enciclopedia del Scapulario del Carmen,* P. Simon M. Besalduch, Barcelona, 1931, p. 85

26   *Alla Madre di Dio.* Raffaele Improta dello Scapolare Del Carmine, Napoli, 1956, p. 7

26a   *The Carmelites and the Brown Scapular, A. E. Farrington, D.D.,O.C.C., Dublin, 1891, p. 92, also A Short Treatise on the Antiquity, Institution, Excellency, Indulgences, Privileges, etc., of the Ancient Confraternity of Our Blessed Lady of Mount Carmel, called the Scapular,* Rev. R. J. Colgan D.D.,D.M.T.,Perpetual Procurator General of the Grand Carmelite Order, Philadelphia, 1850s, p. 30

27   *Mount Carmel,* Author: Carmelites, London, 1923, p. 50

28   *Alla Madre di Dio,* Raffaele Improta dello Scapolare Del Carmine, Napoli, 1956, p. 6

28a   *The Scapular and Some Critics,* P. E. Magennis, O.C.C., Rome, 1914, p. 15

28b   *The Carmelite Review,* A Catholic Monthly Magazine devoted to *Our Blessed Lady of Mount Carmel,* published by the Carmelite Fathers of the United States and Canada, Vol. X., No. 1, Jan. Canada, 1902, p. 156

29   *Alla Madre di Dio,* Raffaele Improta, 1956, p. 6

29a   *The Carmelite Review,* Vol. X, August, 1902, No. 8, p. 256, *Annals of the Order*

30   *Alla Madre di Dio,* Raffaele Improta, 1956, p. 7

31   *The White Friars,* Rev. P. R. McCaffrey, Ord. Carm., Dublin, 1926, p. 22

32   *Alla Madre di Dio,* Raffaele Improta, 1956, p. 7

33   *A Brief History of the Friars,* The Friars-Aylesford; www.thefriars.org.uk/history.htm

34   *The Sabbatine Privilege of the Scapular,* P. E. Magennis, Ord. Carm, New York, 1923, p. 25

35   *Enciclopedia del Scapulario del Carmen,* P. Simon M. Besalduch, Barcelona, 1931, p. 85

36   *Spighe Del Carmelo,* Ricordo del VI Centenario del Privilegio Sabatino, Palermo, Carmine Maggiore, 1923, p. 11

36a   *The Scapular and Some Critics,* P. E. Magennis, O.C.C., Rome, 1914, p. 28

36b   *The Carmelites and the Brown Scapular,* A. E. Farrington, D.D., O.C.C., Dublin 1891, pp. 108, 109, paraphrased

37   *Enciclopledia del Scapulario del Carmen,* p. 85

38   *Ibid,* p. 85

38a   *The Carmelite Review,* Vol. X, August, 1902, No. 8, pp. 257-258

39   *Spighe del Carmelo,,* pp. 11 and 35

39a   *The Carmelites and the Brown Scapular,* A.E. Farrington, D.D.,O.C.C., Dublin, 1891, pp. 104, 105

40   *Enciclopedia del Scapulario del Carmen,* p. 45

40a   *The Scapular and Some Critics,* P. E. Magennis, Rome, 1914, p. 31, paraphrased; also, *The Carmelite Review,* Vol. X, August, 1902, No. 8, p. 258, *Annals of the Order*

41   *The White Friars.,* Rev. P. R. McCaffrey, Ord. Carm., Dublin, 1926, p. 27, paraphrased

41a   *The Most Theological Collection, Mary in Our Life,* Appendix VI, The Brown Scapular; *Analecta Ord. Carm.* II, 612

42   *Alla Madre di Dio,* p. 7

43   *Mary in Her Scapular Promise,* pp. 31-32; MS. Harley 3, 383 Bale's *Heliades*

44   *Vita di San Simone de Stock.* Alfred Mombrum, Siena, 1884, pp. 104-105

44   *The Most Theological Collection, Mary in Our Life,* Appendix VI, The Brown Scapular

44b *The Scapular and Some Critics,* P. E. Magennis, O. C. C. , Rome, 1914, p. 52

45   *Enciclopedia del Scapulario Del Carmen* P. Simon M. Besalduch, Barcelona, 1931, p. 85

46   *Take this Scapular.* Carmelite Fathers and Tertiaries, Chicago, 1949, p. 222

46a *The Scapular and Some Critics,* P. E. Magennis, O. C. C., Rome, 1914, p. 29

47   *Enciclopedia de Scapulario Del Carmen.* pp. 85-86

47a *A Short Treatise on the Antiquity, Institution, Excellency, Indulgences, Privileges, etc., of the Ancient Confraternity of Our Blessed Lady of Mount Carmel, called the Scapular...*Rev. R. J. Colgan, D.D., S.M.T., Perpetual Procurator-General of the Grand Carmelite Order, Philadelphia, 1850s, pp. 33, 34

47b *The Carmelite Review,* Vol. II, Falls View, Ont., July 1894, No. 7, p. 158, *Annals of the Order*

47c *The Carmelite Review, V*ol. X, Welland, Ont., October 1902, No. 10, p. 330, *Annals of the Order*

47d *A Short Treatise on the Antiquity, Institution, Excellency, Indulgences, Privileges, etc., of the Ancient Confraternity of Our Blessed Lady of Mount Carmel, called the Scapular...* Rev. R. J. Colgan, D.D., S.M.T., Perpetual Procurator-General of the Grand Carmelite Order, Philadelphia, 1850s, p. 34

47e *Ibid*, p. 35

48   *The Sabbatine Privilege of the Scapular,* P. E. Magennis, New York, 1923 pp. 26, 27, 37

49   *Le Scapulaire de Notre Dame du Mont-Carmel est authentique,* pp. 58, 59

50   *Enciclopedia del Escapulario Del Carmen,* p. 72

51   *Commemoratio Solemnis Beatae Mariae Virginis De Monte Carmelo.* Historia et Liturgia, Augustinus M. Forcadell, 1951, Romae, p. 14

52   *Nella Famiglia di Maria,* I Papi e lo Scapolare del Carmine, Roma, 1996, p. 9

53   *Take This Scaplular,* Carmelite Fathers and Tertiaries, 1949, p. 84, paraphrased

54   *Rome Reports,*T. V. News Agency: Who was St. Thomas Aquinas? Benedict XVI Explains, 1/28/2011

54a   *The Scapular and Some Critics,* P. E. Magennis, O.C.C., Rome, 1914, p. 54

55   *Le Scapulaire,* pp. 32, 33

56   *Ibid,* Avant-Propos; Le fait est rapportè par l'office du saint, au Breviaire romain, Vme lecon; - Parraud, "Vie de Saint Pierre-Thomas," 1895, Avignon, p. 70

57   Bullarium carmelitanum III, p. 84 also in *Commemoratio Solemnis Beatae Mariae Virginis de Monte Carmelo,* p. 15

58   *Enciclopedia del Scapulario Del Carmen,* p. 86

59   *Viridarium Ordinis B. Virginis Mariae de Monte Carmelo per Joannem Grossi; Analecta Ord. Carm VIII,* p. 124; *Mary in Her Scapular Promise,* pp. 28, 29 paraphrased

60   *Le Scapulaire,* p. 61

60a   *The Sabbatine Privilege of the Scapular,* P. E. Magennis, Ord. Carm., New York, 1923, p. 43

61   *Le Scapulaire,* pp. 64, 65

62   *Enciclopedia del Scapulario Del Carmen,* p. 143

63   *Le Scapulaire,* p. 65

64   apud P. Daniel. T. I. p. 2 pag. 544; *Ristretto Della Vita Di S. Simone Stock.* P. S. Mattei, 1873, p. 85

65   *Le Scapulaire,* p. 65

66   Extant Document of the Scapular Vision recorded by Thomas Bradley Scrope, Bishop of Dromor: *Take This Scapular,* Carmelite Fathers and Tertiaries, pp. 225, 226

66a   *Message of John Paul II for the 550th Anniversary of the Addition of the Cloistered Nuns and the Third Order of the Laity to the Carmelite Order,* October 7, 2002

67   *Take This Scapular,* Carmelite Fathersand Tertiaries, p. 227

68   *Le Scapulaire.* p. 66 ; "Speculum historiale," libr. VII, c. 36

69   *Le Scapulaire,* p. 46

70   *Le Scapulaire.* p. 68

71   *Take This Scapular,* p. 230

72   *National Geographic,* October, 1983, pp. 426, 431

73   *Enciclopedia del Scapulario Del Carmen,* P. Simon Besalduch, Barcelona, 1931, p. 139

74   *Ibid,* p. 177

75   *Le Scapulaire de Notre-Dame du Mont-Carmel est authentique,* P. Marie Joseph du Sacre-Coeur, Avignon, 1928, p. 73

76   *Ibid,* p. 73

77   *Ibid,* pp. 105, 106

78   *The National Geographic,* October, 1983, pp. 457

79   *Le Scapulaire.* P. Marie Joseph du Sacre Coeur, Avignon, 1928, p. 74

80   *Le Scapulaire,* P. Marie Joseph du Sacre Coeur, Avignon, 1928, pp. 62, 63

81   *Ibid,* p. 74

82   *Enciclopedia del Scapulario del Carmen,* P. Simon Besalduch, Barcelona, 1931, p. 86

83   B. C., II, 141, *Lo Scapolare,* 2, VII Centenario Dello Scapolare, Roma, p. 62

83a   *Mary in Her Scapular Promise,* John Mathias Haffert, 1942, footnote #17, p. 240

84   *Le Scapulaire,* P. Marie Joseph du Sacre Coeur, Avignon, 1928, p. 74

85   Taken from a personal letter to the author, dated March 20, 2005. Added information was provided by P. Balbino Velasco, Madrid, Spain

86   *Enciclopedia del Escapulario del Carmen,* P. Simon Besalduch, Barcelona, 1931, p, 86

87   *Lo Scapolare,* 2, VII Centenario Dello Scapolare, Roma, pp. 73, 74

88   *Le Scapulaire.* P. Marie Joseph du Sacre Coeur, Avignon, 1928, p. 80

89   *Le Scapulaire,* P. Marie Joseph du Sacre Coeur, Avignon, 1928, p. 75

90   *Lo Scapolare.* 2, VII Centenario Dello Scapolare, Roma, p. 63

91   *Commemoratio Solemnis Beatae Mariae Virginis de Monte Carmelo.* p. 45

92   *Mt. Carmel,* Carmelites, London, 1923, pp. 32-33 "Bullarium Carmelitarum," Tom. III., p. 348

93   *The Sabbatine Privilege of the Scapular,* P. E. Magennis, New York, 1923, p. 69

94   *Le Scapulaire,* P. Marie Joseph du Sacre Coeur, Avignon, 1928, p. 80

95   *The Sabbatine Privilege of the Scapular,* P.E.Magennis, New York, 1923, p. 78

96   *The Credibility of the Scapular Promises,* Rev. Christian P. Ceroke, Rome, 1950, p.50, also see the *Rescripta Authentica* (Authentic Rescript of the Sacred Congregation presiding over Indulgences and Sacred Relics as well as the Summary of Indulgences) found in this Book, in Appendix 1, "The Summarium," p. 475, dated Dec. 1, 1866

97   *Le Scapulaire,* P. Marie Joseph du Sacre Coeur, Avignon, 1928, p. 38

98   *Take This Scapular,* Carmelite Fathers and Tertiaries, Chicago, 1949, p. 216; *The Credibility of the Scapular Promises,* Rev. Christian P. Ceroke, O. Carm, Rome, 1950, pp. 1, 2, 4; *The Scapular and Some Critics.*P. E. Magennis. O.C.C., Rome, 1914, pp. 122, 123,125, 129, 130, 131, 132, paraphrased.

99   *Enciclopedia del Escapulario Del Carmen.,* P. Simon Besalduch, Barcelona, 1931, p. 295

100   *Take This Scapular,* pp. 217, 260; *The Scapular and Some Critics,* p. 137

101   *Take This Scapular,* p. 260; *The Credibility of the Scapular Promises,* p. l8

102   *The Credibility of the Scapular Promises,* 1950, pp. 17, 18; *Take This Scapular,* p. 260

103   *Le Scapulaire de Notre-Dame du Mont-Carmel est authentique,* P. Marie Joseph du Sacre-Coeur, Avignon, 1928, pp. 80 – 81

104   *Take This Scapular,* Carmelite Fathers and Tertiaries, Chicago, 1949, pp. 217, 261

105   B.C. II, 596. *Lo Scapolare,* 2, VII Centenario Dello Scapolare, Roma, p. 64

106   *Vita di San Simone De Stock,,* Alfredo Mombrun, Sienna, 1884, pp. 105, 106

107   *Mount Carmel,* Carmelites, London, 1923, p. 25

108   *Le Scapulaire de Notre-Dame du Mont-Carmel est authentique,* P. Marie Joseph du Sacre Coeur, Avignon, 1929, p. 79

109   *Ibid,* p. 86

110   *Ibid,* p. 87

111   *The Scapular and Some Critics.* P. E. Magennis, O.C.C., Rome, 1914, p. 150

112   *The Sabbatine Privilege of the Scapular,* P.E. Magennnis, O. Carm., New York, 1923, p. 37

113   *Le Scapulaire.de Notre -Dame du Mont-Carmel est authentique,* P. Marie-Joseph du Sacre Coeur, Avignon, 1928, p. 117; Bullarium Carmelitanum, t. IV, p. 440

114   *Ibid,* p. 117

115   *Ibid,* p. 117

115a   *National Catholic Register: The Brown Scapular Still Sanctifies Souls,* Joseph Pronechen, July 13-19, 2008 Issue

115b   *The Miracle Hunter-* Vatican Approved Apparitions

116 *Le Scapulaire de Notre-Dame du Mont-Carmel est authentique*, P. Marie-Joseph du Sacre Coeur, p. 117

116a Pope Pius IX, *Brief*, dated October 23, 1869, written to Alfred Monbrun, author of *The Life of Saint Simon Stock*, recalling the admirable virtues and sanctity of this great saint.

117 *De Scapulari B. Mariae Virg. De Monte Carmelo excipiendo a simultanea plurium Scapularium traditione.* 27 aprile, 1887. *Acta S. Sedis, XIX, 554-556 Lo Scapolare*, 2. Roma, p. 66

118 *Mary in Her Scapular Promise*, John Mathias Haffert, New Jersey, 1942, p. 85; *Enciclopedia*, Chapter XXIX: El Jubileo del Carmen, pp. 444-459

119 *Papal Teachings: Our Lady*, The Benedictine Monks of Solesmes, Boston, 1961, pp. 145 – 150, Pope Leo XIII, Ency. *Fidentem piumque*, September 20, 1896

120 *The Scapular and Some Critics*, P. E. Magennis, Rome, 1914, pp. 8-10; *Pascendi Dominici Gregis*, Pope Pius X, September 8, 1907, #55

121 *Lo Scapolare*, 2, VII Centenario Dello Scapolare, Roma, p. 67

122 *Mary in Her Scapular Promise*, John Mathias Haffert, New Jersey, 1942, p. 65

122a *Soul Magazine, Why the Blessed Virgin Mary Came to Fatima*, by Warren H. Carroll, Ph.D., May-June, 1995, pp. 4, 5; *The Five Unique Aspects of Fatima*, by Timothy Tindal-Robertson

122b Pope Benedict XV: *Osservatore Romano*, July 16, 1917

122c See Chapter 7, *Private Revelation in the Church*, in this book

122d October 13, 1930, *The Approval of Fatima: A Pastoral Letter*-Fatima Approval Letter by Ed Tarkowski; *The Miracle Hunter* – Vatican approved apparitions

123 Pope Pius XI, Letter, *Petis tu Quidem*, March 18, 1922, (*Sixth centenary of the Sabbatine Privilege – The Confraternities of Our Lady of Mt. Carmel*), *Papal Teachings on Our Lady*, p. 204

124 *Take This Scapular*, p. 110; *Maria-Congres*, B., 11, bl. 66

125 *Consecration.*, with study club outline, Scapular Consecration to Mary, Rev. Howard Rafferty, O. Carm., Provincial Director of the Third Order, Chicago, 1953, p. 4

126 *Enciclopedia del Escapulario Del Carmen,*, P. Simon Besalduch, Barcelona, 1931, p. 86; *Leaflets*, by Fr. Howard Rafferty, O. Carm, www.catholictradition.org/Mary/purgatory3.htm

127 *Ibid*, p. 87

128   *Ibid*, p. 87

129   Pope Pius XI, All. To Pilgrims from Vicenza, November 30, 1933,
      Papal Teachings on Our Lady, p. 224

129a www.twoheartsdesign.com/jmh_obit.html

130   *Papal Teachings on Our Lady*, pp. 288-289: Pope Pius XII, Letter:
      Neminem profecto, to the Superior General of the Carmelites, February
      11, 1950, (Papal Teachings on Our Lady)

130a CITOC, No. 4, October-December, 2003; www.scribd.com/...
      Bartolome-Xiberta-Datos-Biografi

131   *Alla Madre Di Dio*, p. 9

132   Pius XII, Letter to Fr. Killian Lynch, Superior General of the Orders
      of the Friars of the Blessed Virgin Mary of Mt. Carmel on the Seventh
      Centenary of the Institution of the Sacred Carmelite Scapular (June
      30, 1951) *Acta Apostolicae Sedis*, ANNUS XXXXIII, Series II, Vol. XVIII,
      (1951); 589-590

133   *Osservatore Romano*, February 20, 1959, "Il Sommo Pontefice
      Giovanni XXIII visita la Chiesa e le Istitutioni di S. Luigi dei Francesi

134   *Nella Famiglia di Maria, I Papi e Lo Scapolare*. Provincia Italiana dei
      Carmelitani, Roma, 1996, p. 31

135   *Ibid*, p. 30 *(Acta Apostolicae Sedis*, LVI [31, giugno, 1964], p. 77)

136   *Dogmatic Constitution on the Church: Lumen Gentium.*, Paul VI,
      November 21, 1964, #67

137   From the Letter, *In Dominica Republicana*. dated February 2, 1965,
      appointing Cardinal Silva of Santiago, Chile, papal legate to the
      Mariological and Marian Congress held in Santo Domingo, March,
      1965. (translated by Rev. Eamon Carroll, O. Carm); *Mary*. Vol. 26, n. 3,
      July, August, September, 1965, pp. 10, 11

138   National Catholic Conference of Bishops, *Behold Your Mother*.
      November 21, 1973, p. 35, #93

139   Apostolic Exhortation of His Holiness Paul VI, *Marialus Cultis*, #57,
      February 2, 1974

140   *Nella Famiglia Di Maria. I Papi e lo Scapolare del Carmine*, p. 34-35;
      Silvano Mazzocchi in *La Repubblica*, 15 maggio, 1981

141   *Ibid*, pp. 36-37; Pope John Paul II: L'Osservatore Romano, 25-26
      luglio 1988, 1

142   *Our Sunday Visitor*, "Unearthing a Buried Treasure of the Church," Fr.
      Charles Mangan, February 24, 1991

143   *La Repubblica,* venerdi 17 luglio, 1992, 12) -- *Nella Famiglia di Maria, I Papi e lo Scapolare del Carmine,* pp. 37-38

143a From a Sermon of Pope John XXIII-opening words: *La voix du pape* preached at St. Louis of France Church, Rome, February 18, 1959, for the closing of the Lourdes centenary year

144   *Message of John Paul II to the Carmelite Family,* on the Anniversary of the Bestowal of the Scapular, March 25, 2001

145   Apostolic Letter: *Rosarium Virginis Mariae,* Pope John Paul II, October 16, 2002, Behold Your Mother, #7

146   *Osservatore Romano,* Lunedi-Martedi 7-8, Novembre, 2005, p.7, La Prima sessione del Tribunale del processo rogatorio per la Causa di beatificazione e canonizzazione del servo di Dio Giovanni Paolo II

147   *Angelus Message on Our Lady of Mount Carmel,* Benedict XVI, July 16, 2006; www.zenit.org

147a Zenit.org: *Cardinal Urges Devotion to Rosary and Scapular,* July 17, 2008

147b *Apostolic Letter,* Pope Pius XII, *Letter of His Holiness for the Occasion of the Seventh Centenary of the Brown Scapular,* Feb. 11, 1950; *Pius XII and His Heritage to Carmel, MARY,* Vol. 20, No. 4, July-August, 1959, p. 51

148   Article: "Benedict XVI to send Our Lady of Mt. Carmel Statue to Earthquake-stricken Chile." *Catholic News Agency,* March 22, 2010

148a *Spirit Daily, John Paul tied to Scapular Promise and to St. Gregory-Another "Great" Pope who shortened a Great Chastisement,* by Michael Brown; www.spiritdaily.net/popescapular.htm

149   *Pontiff Praises Wearing the Scapular* July 17, 2011, www.zenit.org

149a *Letter,* Pope Paul VI: *In Dominica Republicana,* dated February 2, 1965, appointing Cardinal Silva of Santiago, Chile, Papal Legate to the Mariological and Marian congresses held in Santo Domingo, March, 1965

150   Pope Benedict XVI, *Letter* designating Archbishop Zygmunt Simowski, President of the Pontifical Council for Health Pastoral Care, January 10, 2013

Chapter 4

The Controversies of the Visions Explained

Why must it be defended?

The Virgin of Carmel (is) the patroness of seafaring people who entrust their lives daily to the fluctuation of wind and wave!

From our post, as helmsman of St. Peter's bark, when we hear the storm raging and see spuming before our eyes the furious surge that would fain submerge our vessel, calmly and confidently we look up to the Virgin of Mount Carmel, "Respice Stellam, voca Mariam" and beseech her not to desert us. Although hell unceasingly renews its attacks, and the violence, audacity and fury of evil forces are ever increasing as long as we rely on her powerful patronage we never may doubt the victory. R. M. to the National Marian Congress of Columbia, July 19, 1946 (The Safety of Society) Pope Pius XII

> **For if this council or this work be of men it will come to nought but if it be of God you cannot overthrow it...** (Acts 5: 38, 39)

As was previously stated in the very beginning of this book in "The Introduction," the very purpose of this research was for the production of an updated version of the film: *Miracles of the Brown Scapular* previously produced by Fr. Howard Rafferty O. Carm., in the mid 20th century, as the videotape was no longer found to be available for distribution.

Enthusiastically, this student of the Scapular embarked on a journey to begin the research phase in preparation for this film. Upon immediate investigation into the history of the Scapular Devotion, it was surprisingly noted that certain 20th and 21st century publications indicate that the Sabbatine Bull of John XXII is now considered spurious and can no longer be accepted as historically credible. To add to this, certain publications maintain the solid stand that the very existence of St. Simon Stock, now considered to be an "elusive" character is questionable, that the apparition of Our Blessed Mother to St. Simon Stock is considered a legend and that the Sabbatine Bull of Pope John XXII is considered to be false as well.

How could this be? For years we had been taught that the Brown Scapular, a Universal Devotion in the Church for over 750 years, was truly the vehicle through which Our Heavenly Mother chose to clothe and protect us, giving us the promise of eternal salvation when worn with true love and devotion to her and in complete obedience to the Commandments of her Son.

Could it be true, that the origin of the Brown Scapular Devotion grounded in the solid tradition of the Church for centuries and evidenced by an enormous number of authenticated miracles through the wearing of the Brown Scapular, the solemn confirmation and approbation by numerous Holy Fathers since the 13th century, the promise of deliverance from the pains of purgatory the First Saturday after *our* death and the enrollment of the First Communicants in the Habit of Our Lady on their First Holy Communion day was nothing more than an exaggerated fable devised by the Carmelite Community to satisfy the needs of the laity?

Further research began to reveal the turbulent and wounded state of the Devotion. It was as if it had been delivered a crushing blow to the very heart of it. But who is at the heart of this Devotion and who is the real victim of this crushing blow? Our Blessed Mother herself; a Mother so full of love and compassion, given to us by Christ Himself at the foot of the cross, who out of an everlasting love for her spiritual children, wove us a garment for the salvation of our souls.

Needless to say, this student of the Scapular abandoned the theatrical pursuit and began an exhausting and continuous fifteen-year investigation into the allegations of falsehood against the Scapular Visions of Our Lady to St. Simon Stock and Pope John XXII.

This Chapter contains is an exposé of the assailants involved in the injurious assault inflicted upon this beloved Devotion beginning in the 17th century. It continues in Appendix 2 with a compilation of resources, explicitly exposing both ancient and modern day objections to the authenticity of the Scapular Visions and it contains the authenticated responses of those who immediately rose to its defense. The Publications in Opposition are many. The Publications in Defense are overwhelming. See Appendix 2 and Appendix 3.

They became vain in their thoughts... professing themselves to be wise, they became fools.

(Romans I: 21, 22; DR)

THE ERRONEOUS TEACHINGS OF JOHN LAUNOY

By the middle of the 17th century, the Brown Scapular Devotion had undergone the examination of the Church Authorities, had passed this test successfully and had been widely propagated. (1)

However in 1642, John Launoy, a Doctor of the Paris schools put an end to this unchallenged spread of the Devotion (2) through his critical and erroneous Dissertations on this holy and revered Sacramental of the Holy Roman Catholic Church.

Since the 17th century, two major controversies have fueled the fires of doubt over the authenticity of the Visions of Our Blessed Mother to St. Simon Stock and Pope John XXII. These controversies ruptured the unbroken waves of worldwide zealous devotion to the Brown Scapular of Our Lady of Mt. Carmel after hundreds of years of successive confirmation and papal approbation, casting a great shadow of doubt and seriously wounding the credibility and authenticity of the origins of the Devotion by derogating the traditional teachings on this most holy and highly indulgenced Sacramental of the Church.

The most damaging assault on the Scapular began in 1642 (with John Launoy or Jean de Launoy), reached its height in 1653 and thereafter seems to have gradually subsided. The second debate occurred between the years of 1904-1911 when the principal writings appeared. It has continued to this day; it has not yet terminated. (3)

John Launoy was a Doctor at the Sorbonne University in Paris. He was a theologian and studied philosophy and Theology at the College of Navarre in Paris, of which he became a historian. Receiving a Licentiate and Doctorate in 1634, he was ordained a priest in 1636. As an historian he developed an extreme form of criticism, pointing out the false attributions of works and the unchecked assertion of the Martyrologium. (4). He is described as anti-papal and anti-authority. In papal politics he was a Gallican, in theology, a Jansenist. (5)

He wrote two books on the Scapular revelations in which he maliciously assailed the credibility of the Scapular Visions.

The first, published in 1642 was entitled:

1) *Dissertatio Duplex: Una de Origine et Confirmatione Privilegiati*

138

Scapularis Carmelitarum; Altera de Visione Simonis Stochii Prioris ac Magistri Generalis Carmelitarum, 1642.

His second work was entitled:

2) *De Simonis Stocchi Viso, De Sabbatinae Bullae Privilegio et de Scapularis Carmelitarum Sodalitate Dissertationes V., Lutetiae Parisiorum, 1653* (6)

Several Carmelite writers then immediately responded with rebuttals to his assault on the Scapular Visions such as: Fr. John Cheron in 1642, Fr. Thomas Aquinas of St. Joseph, Carm. Disc., in 1648 and Fr. Philibert Fesayus, O. Carm., in 1645. The quarrel raged on and public opposition to the Scapular continued inspite of the valiant efforts of these courageous and dedicated writers in defense of the Scapular. (7)

For two centuries the Devotion remained practically in the same state in which it was left by the 17th century controversies. Even during the 19th century, its adversaries appealed to the arguments of Launoy and were quickly defended by others who offered the same arguments as their predecessors. (8)

In 1884 "The Catholic Dictionary" (Addis and Arnold), a product of lay converts, rejected both the Vision of St. Simon Stock and the Sabbatine Privilege on the grounds of lack of documentation. The authority (of this rejection) was John Launoy whose dissertations, in the opinion of the writers, were (described by the authors of "The Catholic Dictionary" as a work of "wonderful learning." The articles in the "Dictionary" were criticized and rejected by Joseph Clark, S.J. (9) (An excellent defense of the Scapular Devotion against the attack by the "Catholic Dictionary," (Addis and Arnold) may be found in *The Month* in Appendix 3 of this book.

In 1901 Fr. Benedict of the Cross Zimmerman Ord. Carm. Disc., discounted the traditions of the Order and favored the opponents (against the origin of the Visions). In 1904 he treated the question of the Sabbatine Bull, agreeing with the other authorities as to its falsity but concluding that some document in all probability was given by Pope John XXII testifying to the apparition and the Promise. (10)

Around the same time, Fr. Herbert Thurston, S. J. seriously questioned the authenticity of the Fragment (written testimony) of Peter Swanyngton, (Secretary to St. Simon Stock who recorded the Vision from the mouth of St. Simon and whose writings were used as a defense by Fr. John Cheron in 1642 against Launoy's *Dissertatio*). Fr. Thurston suggested a "legendary" origin of the story of the Vision due to others frequent in religious orders. (11)

In 1942 John Mathias Haffert renowned author and devotee of Our Lady of Mount Carmel and her Brown Scapular, restored the Scapular Devotion to its rightful place of honor in the 20th century once again through his book, *Mary in Her Scapular Promise*, 1942 and through his immense research, writings, lectures, and instruction of the laity on the importance and authenticity of this most holy and revered Sacramental.

However in 1967 the Carmelite, Ludovico Saggi wrote his thesis: "La Bolla Sabbatina" in which he cited the originator of the assault on the Scapular, John Launoy and reverberated his 17th century objections as a foundation for his claim that the Sabbatine Bull of John XXII was a *forgery*, questioning the Visions and relying heavily on the identical objections of John Launoy.

The battle continues until today, with the haunting erroneous teachings of John Launoy and the insidious legendary suggestions of the Visions that have crept into certain 20th and 21st century Carmelite publications, as the reader will see in the following chapters, striking an injurious blow not only to the Scapular Devotion which has enjoyed over 760 years of papal approbation and confirmations and has been richly indulgenced by the Church but striking also at the heel of all devotions based on private revelation. As the reader will note in the upcoming chapter, "the modern debate is in general, nothing but a modification of the position of Launoy." (12)

John Launoy versus John Grossi

The author of this research would like now to introduce you to two very important men in the history of the Scapular Devotion of Our Lady of Mt. Carmel: John Launoy and John Grossi; one, a French priest and scholar at the Sorbonne in Paris, the other a Carmelite Prior-General from the Province of Toulouse, France. Both men were marked with the indelible character of eternal priesthood in the service of Christ and His Holy Church, both men were committed and dedicated to the advancement of a cause but both choosing very opposite directions in the execution of their powerful vocation, produced lasting astounding effects in the spiritual and material world for hundreds of years to come, for one had malice in his heart and the other one had love. Both priests hold a significant place in the history of the Scapular Devotion, one was the Defender, the other was the Assailant.

We begin with the Carmelite Prior General Fr. John Grossi who was born about 80 years after the death of St. Simon Stock and began his religious life at the Monastery of Pamiers, one of the Monasteries that formed the Carmelite Province of Toulouse. The Province of Toulouse is within close proximity of the Province of Aquitaine, the principal Monastery of which is Bordeaux; it was here that St. Simon Stock died on the 16th of May, 1265. (1) John Grossi (a Doctor of Theology,) was a great and holy man, famous in the whole Church because of his activity to end the Western Schism. Holy as well as scholarly, John Grossi's word was sacred. No one has ever attempted to deny the intellectual ability of Grossi. (2) He was a man of "integrity of character, both trustworthy and reliable." (3)

"Destined to render services of incalculable worth to all of Christendom," his successful efforts helped to bring about the end of one of the most trying crises in the history of the Church: "The Great Western Schism." (4) The Western Schism, also called Great Schism or Great Western Schism in the history of the Roman Catholic Church (was) the period from 1378 to 1417 when there were two and later three rival popes, each with his own following, his own Sacred College of Cardinals and his own Administrative Offices. (5) The Great Western Schism caused division in the Church and also in Religious Orders depending on which Pope one's personal loyalty was given to (The Carmelite Order) was divided then, some for the Roman Pope and some for the French Pope. When the Papacy was restored to order, Fr. John Grossi reunited the Order in 1411. It was mainly through Fr. Grossi's instrumentality that the blessings of peace and union had been restored to the Order. (6). He became famous throughout the entire Church.

A great devotee of the Brown Scapular, he was elected Superior-General of one of the two sections of the Carmelite Community in the year 1389 A.D. But because of his great efforts to attain peace and unity and his reputation for integrity and holiness, he was unanimously elected, although he was quite advanced in age, Prior-General of all the Carmelites (when order to the Papacy had been restored) in a Chapter specially convened in 1411 A.D. (7) It is interesting to note that it was Pope Alexander V (who confirmed the Sabbatine Bull of Pope John XXII in his Bull: *Tenorem cujusdam privilegii* December 7, 1409) who nominated John Grossi, Professor and Master of Theology to be Superior General of the whole Order by a Bull, dated October 2 in the year 1409, thus the union of the Carmelites occurred under Pope Alexander V and General John Grossi. (7a)

However Fr. John Grossi did have an agenda and a purpose in mind. His agenda was to increase the fervor and zeal for the faith of those in his own religious community and to edify, instruct and to help his Religious to grow in holiness through his writings. So strong was his desire to insure that the devotion and piety of the monastic life would be permanently revived in his own Order, that he wrote a well-known compilation of the lives of Carmelite Saints called: "The Catalogue of Saints" known as the *Viridarium* (1389). (8) His main object was to illustrate the ideal of the true Carmelite's life by the examples of certain saints of the Order who had reached holiness, simply by observing (and obeying) a Rule that contained a compendium of the traditions handed down to them from the days of the Prophet Elias. Amongst others was St. Simon Stock who obtained for them so great a Privilege at the hands of the Blessed Virgin in virtue of those selfsame traditions, appealing to her on behalf of his brethren then sorely tried throughout Europe. (9)

Fr. Grossi related the entire traditional account of the Scapular Vision (of Our Lady to St. Simon Stock) in his writings, even referring to the popularity of the Scapular Devotion in England. He consulted the very companions of those who had lived with and talked to St. Simon Stock (we have positive evidence to show that certain Carmelites who had been professed in the Order before the death of St. Simon Stock were still living in 1338, many of these religious had reached their 90th year.) Consequently, had there ever been the slightest misgiving about the exact interpretation of the Scapular Promise, many of John Grossi's own contemporaries could testify to what they themselves had heard from the lips of those venerable men concerning so remarkable an event in the history of the Order. (10)

He was living at a time when the life and works of St. Simon Stock were still alive in the memories of many men. He had opportunities of speaking with Religious who had spoken with the later contemporaries of St. Simon. He had every opportunity of gaining reliable information, having access to the Convent of London (the largest and the most valuable Library in London) in which were kept from the time of St. Simon Stock the archives of the Order: important documents, treasures, apostolic diplomas and Bulls granted to the Order. (11) In writing the *Viridarium*, he knew he could advance the purpose he had in mind by speaking of his own recent experience in England, where he had witnessed some of the marvelous results of Our Lady's Promise. And in doing so he has left a reliable account of the actual sense in which the Scapular Devotion was understood by the faithful generally within Grossi's own memory, which brings us very close to the time of St. Simon Stock. (12) He was a capable writer and from his position in the Order and before the ecclesiastical world, he was worthy of the highest credence. (13)

What is the historical value of all these facts? Fr. Grossi gives us the answer; he tells us he has not depended on himself in the writing of the *Viridarium*, he has had recourse to ancient documents. (14) Would he record the Scapular Vision without verifying it?

So we are assured, on the reliable authority of Fr. Grossi in his *Viridarium* that:

A St. Simon Stock had occasion to implore Our Lady's miraculous intervention during some crisis in the history of the Carmelite Order.

B The Blessed Virgin appeared to him and gave him the Scapular of his Order as a sign of her special protection, attaching a promise to the wearing of the same.

C That all the faithful might participate in this Promise and many began to wear the Scapular of the Carmelites secretly.

D That it was in virtue of this Promise benefactors became so devoted to the Order, particularly in England.(15)

Undoubtedly the testimony of Fr. John Grossi in his *Viridarium* will have a high place in the history of the Scapular Devotion for all time.

But it was not only Prior-General John Grossi who researched and related the Scapular Vision and recorded the miracles he witnessed from those who wore the Scapular with faith and devotion in his time, he was one of many devoted and trustworthy historians, Carmelites as well, who had access to ancient documents and evidence of the supernatural apparition of the Mother of God to St. Simon Stock. The list of historians is endless, all attesting to the authenticity of the Vision of the Mother of God bestowing the Scapular of the Order to St. Simon Stock with the promise of eternal salvation and also to the added Privilege from Our Lady, revealed in an apparition to Pope John XXII in which Our Lady promised to release from Purgatory on the First Saturday after their death, all souls devoted to her Brown Scapular recorded in: "The Sabbatine Bull" of John XXII.

The Vision was recorded by St. Simon Stock himself, in a circular addressed to all the members of his Order in which he made known this extraordinary Vision and at the same time said: *Brethren, make your elections sure by good works and never faint. Watch and offer thanksgiving to God for so much mercy, pray without ceasing so that the words spoken by the Blessed Virgin to me may be glorified, to the praise of the most Holy Trinity, Father, Son, and Holy Ghost and of the ever Blessed Virgin Mary.* (a) The Scapular vision was also recorded by Peter Swaynton (secretary, confessor and companion to St. Simon Stock), William of Sanvico, 1290, Pope John XXII, 1322 (in his Bull: *Sacratissimo uti culmine*) William of Coventry, 1348, John Wilson, 1360, John of Hildesheim, 1370, John Grossi, 1426, Thomas Bradley Scrope (made Bishop of Dromor, Ireland), 1430, Nicholas Calciuri, 1461, Peter Bruyne, 1474, Baldwin Leersius, 1483, Arnold Bostius, 1494, John Palaeonydor, 1497, Giles Fabri, Prior of Brusels, 1506, Menaldus of the Rosary, 1510, John Bale, 1563, John Cheron, 1642 just to name a few. (16)

Sadly despite the impressive list of Papal Approbations and confirmations of these Visions by several Holy Fathers, by many dignified university scholars worldwide and by holy men in the service of God and His Church, the malice that lies in the hearts of men, perpetrated by the enemy never ceases to undermine the sacred truths revealed to us by the power of God, through His Holy Mother Mary. *She shall crush thy head and thou shalt lie in wait of her heel.* (17)

The character of John Grossi was impeccable, unquestionable and beyond reproach; he was faithful, loyal, trustworthy, reliable, honest, courageous a peacemaker and a true leader of the Faith and of his religious community.

He kept up a correspondence with the leading religious of each Province, and could have corrected any defects he perceived in the traditions taught him in the earlier days of his religious life. And this applies in a special manner to England, the home of St. Simon and the Scapular Vision; he not only corresponded with the prominent theologian Thomas of Walden, but he actually visited that country in 1413 AD. (17a)

John Grossi entered the Carmelite Order at a very early age; he found, as all those do who enter such Orders, certain traditions. As the trend of his mind was directed to historical affairs, he interested himself in the things he heard and wished to confirm them by facts and documents. We have every reason to say John Grossi merely reduced to historical form what he heard from his superiors and companions and what he was afterwards to find verified in writing. We stand assured, with the testimony of John Grossi that we have here a sufficient reason for saying the traditional account of the Scapular Devotion is worthy of a place in history and to deny it such a place would be to speak with prejudice or of a lack of sufficient study. (17b)

But in the year 1642, an ugly dragon reared its head in the form of a heretical priest who rejected and taunted the authentic evidence presented in defense of the Scapular Visions; his malicious character, his accusations and his unfounded objections have found their way into the 21st century. His name: John Launoy!

Animated by a spirit of bitter hostility to the Holy See, to the canonized saints, Religious Orders and Catholic devotional practices, he viciously attacked the insurmountable evidence to the validity and authenticity of the Visions, especially as related by the numerous historians of the Order. His facts were often groundless, his arguments unsound, his conclusions false and we may add too that his works have, nearly all, been condemned by the Holy See. (18)

His attack on the Scapular Vision was destined to become famous, not indeed because of the intrinsic worth of Launoy's first contribution (against the Scapular vision) *De Viso Simonis Stochii,* but because of the <u>character</u> of the assailant! The ideas of Launoy were revolutionary not only in reference to the Scapular but also in relation to the pious beliefs of his time. Launoy's knowledge of the history of the Scapular when he began his attack on this Devotion was not only deficient, but certainly erroneous and he seemed to rely more on his popularity as an *assailant* of pious beliefs than upon diligent or even careful research. His chief weapon was the "negative argument." (19)

So critical and arrogant was his attitude and his desire for pivotal destruction that he approached the convincing testimony of John Grossi on the Scapular Vision, in the only logical way possible in order to destroy its force: he declared that John Grossi was not a reliable author! (20)

His attempt however to prove the unreliability of Grossi was a failure. The value of the testimony of John Grossi is not to be questioned. To imagine that John Grossi could consent to retail a story of little historical value, much less to invent one is for us outside the limits of possibility. (21)

These two men of God were both intellectual, scholarly and famous for their works but the similarities end there for their characters were as opposite as the forces of nature, easily reflected in their works and accomplishments; the character of John Grossi was one of benevolence and good will and John Launoy, one of deception and destruction.

Character overpowers what may try to be convincing in words and must be carefully scrutinized before determining the weight of the evidence presented. The continuing analysis of John Launoy on the following page is a revelation of what lies within the heart of this man and the lasting negative effect he has sadly produced in the world of the Scapular Devotion, for he himself, appears to be the unreliable one.

The Weight of the evidence will very much depend on the character of the witnesses.

"By their fruits you shall know them."
(Matthew 7:20)

The character of a person is a revelation of what lies in the heart and soul of a man; the fruits of his actions define his very nature, the words from his tongue the tablet of truth or deception.

The zeitgeist at the height of 17th century France was known as the "Age of Absolutism and Unbelief." France, a country that had always been a zealous defender of the Church and of the Holy See was unfortunatly influenced by the errors of the Protestant Reformation in the 16th century. The attacks of Luther against the Papacy and his rejection of all religious authority and the Authority of the Church gave way to rebellion and religious and political unrest. A caustic struggle was born against the central authority of Rome (the Papacy), giving way to the infamous ideology and movement in France called: Gallicanism. The Gallicans, (comprised mostly of the French Clergy and the laity) began their struggle to yield obedience to the King of France rather than to the Pope and to obtain and preserve an administrative independence from Rome. (1)

Simultaneously, the insidious smoke of religious rebellion reared its evil head in a new heresy and rooted itself in the heart of 17th century France. This heresy, (a total denial of Catholic Doctrine), essentially taught that God's saving grace is irresistible though not given to everyone. According to (Cornelius) Jansen, (Bishop of Ypres in the early 17th century), a person could neither accept nor reject this grace due to his fallen nature, although persons who received it were sure of salvation. Unfortunately not everyone received this saving grace. God decreed who was saved and who was lost. Cornelius Jansen, (Jansenism), denied human free will and God's desire to save everyone. (2)

The rising and corruptive influence of the Jansenist Party helped to spread the defiant and revolutionary Gallican teaching among the French Clergy and the Laity to whom many priests fall victim.

Out of this "Age of Absolutism and Unbelief" arose one such

147

victim: the infamous revolutionary by the name of John Launoy, or sometimes referred to as Jean de Launoy (1603 – 1678). John Launoy studied philosophy and theology at the College of Navarre in Paris and became an historian. He received a Licenciate and Doctorate in 1634 and was ordained a priest in 1636. (2a)

An extreme critic, he was a follower of Jansenism and a Gallican. His (first) attack (against the Scapular) was destined to become famous, not because of the intrinsic worth of Launoy's first contribution but because of the character of the assailant. (3) "No doubt Launoy was a man of great learning but he turned it to bad account."(4)

He used his intellectual knowledge and capabilities to fuel the Catholic resistance to Papal and all religious authority, from the Reformation to the French Revolution. Gallicanism had a strong hold upon France and the influence of writers like John Launoy and of Dupin helped to spread Gallicanism among the clergy and laymen of the rising generation. (5)

But the title he so earnestly and proudly gained for himself will be mostly remembered in the history of the Church for generations to come as: "The Denicheur of Saints." It was proudly said of him that he had dethroned more Saints than any ten Popes had added to the Calendar of the Church. (6) It is said that he was very severe regarding the Roman Saints, which he excluded three of them from Heaven altogether and either purified or tore to pieces the legends of others. (7)

Popularly known as the "assailant of pious beliefs," the destructive criticisms of John Launoy eventually won him a place in history forever as the most notorious assailant of the Brown Scapular Devotion of Our Lady of Mt. Carmel.

Almost four hundred peaceful years had passed since the world received the blessed Scapular from Our Lady through the hands of her humble servant and Successor of Elias, St. Simon Stock on July 16, 1251. But in 1642 the era of peace would come to an end as the determined and unrelenting John Launoy took it upon himself to launch the most notorious assault on the historicity and authenticity of the Scapular Visions in his publications: *Dissertatio Duplex*, Paris and *De Simonis Stokii Viso, de Sabbatinae Bullae Privilegio et de Scapularis Carmelitarum Sodalitate Dissertationes quinque.*

Fr. P.E. Magennis, O.C.C. in his book *The Scapular and Some Critics* boldly stated that when he (John Launoy) launched his attack on the authenticity of the Visions of Our Blessed Mother to St. Simon Stock and Pope John XXII, that "he did so without sufficient knowledge of the devotion; he was not only deficient, but certainly erroneous. He had no knowledge of the subject except what he could gather from two authors, neither of whom can be considered an authority on the history of the Scapular." (8)

It is a well known fact that his works are distinguished by their skeptical and erroneous teachings. Nearly all of them have been proscribed by the Sacred Congregation of the Index. (9) His work: *Dissertationes V. de Simonis Stochii Viso, etc.* was condemned on April 18th, 1689 A.D. The *Index Librorum Prohibitorum* published by the authority of Pope Pius X in 1907 contains twenty-seven works of Launoy; many of them have been condemned more than once. (10)

(The Index Librorum Prohibitorum [Index of Prohibited Books] was a list of books that the Catholic Church considered immoral or theologically erroneous, [heretical or anti-clerical] or in any way posed a threat to the power of the Roman Catholic hierarchy [and of which all Roman Catholics were prohibited from reading or even owning under pain of excommunication]. Several of John Launoy's books were on this list. Originally created by Paul IV in 1559 and lasting until 1948, twenty editions of the Index were prepared. On June 14, 1966, Blessed Pope Paul VI officially abolished the Index.) (10a)

(Although the Index was abolished, the Decree of the Sacred Congregation of the Index, [later renamed the Congregation for the Doctrine of the Faith], on December 5, 1881, declared that: *Books denounced before the Sacred Congregation of the Index and dismissed or not prohibited by the same (Congregation) must not be considered free from all error against faith and morals, and may also be criticized philosophically as well as theologically without the charge of rashness.*) (10b)

But what can we say of the character of this assailant? "He held weekly conferences at his residence in Paris at which opinions were taught so subversive of society and the authority of the Church that the King was obliged to interdict them in 1636. He next made war on religious orders, canonized saints and some of the most cherished devotions of the Church, "employing his acrimonious pen in endeavoring to discredit them by false objections and unfounded imputations."(11)

He wrote against the "Formulary of Alexander VII" who was the condemnatory of Jansenism; he is accused of altering with incredible audacity, texts which he quoted in proof of his theory. He published a work on the force of negative arguments entitled: *De Auctoritate Negantis Argumenti,* (this was his chief argument against the authenticity of the Scapular Visions). Launoy's negative argument against the Scapular is based on the silence or absence of any mention of the Vision (of Our Lady) to St. Simon Stock by many Carmelite writers for several years after the Vision. (12) In other words according to John Launoy, if it was not mentioned, then it did not exist.

Launoy demanded contemporaneous documentation (documents originating from the same time period) as proof of the authenticity of the Visions (as a device by which he hoped to achieve his destructive purpose). But when faced with the documents suited to his desire, he rejected them. (13)

Numerous other objections of John Launoy (regarding the Scapular Vision and the Vision of John XXII and his Sabbatine Bull) are listed in the present Chapter, "all which have been refuted over and over again by various learned writers," (as you will see by the evidence provided throughout this text and in the "Irish Ecclesiastical Record," Appendix 3, and "Responses to the Objections," Appendix 2. (14)

However Launoy in his *De Viso*, did not concede any historical value whatever to any account of the Vision his opponents offered him. The reason is obvious! He had no intention of accepting the Scapular Promise in spite of all evidence given him; he indicated it plainly at the close of the book. His last comment on the Vision of St. Simon was this: "The Church is not ruled by private revelation and neither are the faithful to be ruled by it." His aim was nothing else than to eject the Scapular Promise from the Church. The reason? He did not think it should be there! (15)

This cynical and unscrupulous critic attacked, to use the words of Benedict XIV, with inexpressible fury, the Vision to St. Simon Stock and the Bull of John XXII. (16) In his work on the "Canonization of Saints," he (John Launoy) is called by Benedict XIV, "a most pronounced enemy of the Roman Pontiffs and the Apostolic See."(17)

He has been greatly praised by Protestants and his works have been reproduced by them, no doubt because of his anti-Catholic and anti-Papal tendencies. (18)

The Council of Trent was the 19th ecumenical Council of the Roman Catholic Church. It was held at Trent in northern Italy and opened on December 13, 1545 closing on December 4, 1563. Its main object was the definitive determination of the doctrines of the Church in order to correct the heresies of the Protestant Reformation and the numerous abuses which had developed in the Church at the time.

Some theologians (today) claim that the Council of Trent lends support to the idea that the Catholic Church, (which has always proclaimed the absolute indissolubility of the sacrament of marriage), could accept divorce and remarriage. Careful scholarship reveals that this is not true. The story actually goes back to the Seventeenth Century and John Launoy.

Following in the examples of his repeated open rebellion to the Chair of Peter, the Jansenist, Launoy (along with another anti-Roman theologian) was one such person who wrote against the Church's Teaching on the Indissolubility of Marriage. In his *De regia in matrimonium potestate* (1674), he argued that the Council (of Trent) meant to leave open the question of whether remarriage after divorce was sometimes legitimate. This work along with numerous others of his erroneous writings confirm the anti-Catholic and anti-Papal tendencies of the 17th century Jansenist, John Launoy. (18a)

"In 1617, Pope Paul V decreed that no one should dare to teach publicly that Mary was conceived in original sin." Although the Bull, *Sanctissimus*, (September 12, 1617) of Pope Paul V forbade public action agains the doctrine (of the Immaculate Conception), **(18a)** sadly years later in his continued attack on the Mother of God, John Launoy wrote a dissertation in 1676 against the doctrine of the Immaculate Conception of the Blessed Virgin Mary. His work was entitled: *Praescriptiones de Conceptu B.M.V.* In it he brought 13 citations against this doctrine, from the theological writings of seven popes to show that Jesus Christ alone, as having been miraculously conceived is Immaculate in His conception. Can we imagine any of the real and undoubted articles of the Catholic Faith being treated by an opponent, as Launoy treats this? (19)

The following matter is related in a work by Benedict XIV himself, in *Benedict XIV De Festis, T. 2, p.330 Loavanii 1761:*

To show the lengths to which the man's morbid desire for attacking admitted facts carried him and the kind of arguments he used, we may mention that he stoutly maintained that St. Thomas was not the author of the Summa Theologica. The matter is thus related by Benedict XIV and we give it here because it is much to our present purpose. (This book by Launoy, on St. Thomas Aquinas is on the Index.) (20)

As well as discrediting the work of St. Thomas Aquinas, "John Launoy was the first writer to deny openly the actual existence of St. Patrick."(21) To add to his list of assassinations, he completed the discrediting of Saint Catherine's legend (as well). "The Life of

Saint Catherine, Virgin and Martyr" is fabulous throughout from beginning to end. (22)

"M. de Launoy, Doctor of Theology had cut Saint Catherine, Virgin and Martyr out of his calendar. He said that her life was a myth and to show that he placed no faith in it, every year when the feast of the saint came around, he said a Requiem Mass. This curious circumstance I learned from his own telling." (23)

The venerable tradition of the final resting place of St. Mary Magdalene was not to escape the wrath of John Launoy as well. Maintained throughout the centuries is the belief that St. Mary Magdelene, under the guidance and accompaniment of St. Maximinus, confessor and Pontiff traveled by vessel to Marseilles, France (after the Resurrection of Christ), settled in the county of Aix and brought the knowledge and worship of God to the local people, through their prayers, preaching and fasts. At the end of her life, St. Maximinus erected a Basilica over her remains and requested that upon his death, his remains be placed next to her body. Many miracles were obtained through the intercession of both of these Holy Saints and as a result, the place of their burial became noteworthy.

However when Protestantism appeared in the 16th century, this beautiful tradition was called into question. In the next (17th) century, the Jansenist Jean de Launoy (John Launoy) disputed the authenticity of this tradition and in 1641, published a work entitled: *Dissertation sur la Mensongere Venue en Provence de Lazare, Maximin, Madeleine et Marthe*. In it he maintained that this tradition was recent because it had only appeared in Provence in the 11th century. His actions provoked a general outcry of the people from Provence, against the Sorbonne Doctor. (24)

The destructive criticism which began with John Launoy in the 17th century, has been supported, developed and disseminated throughout the world by some of the most highly renowned Catholic scholars.

Lamentably, the above statement not only remains true for St. Mary Magdalene, St. Thomas Aquinas, St. Patrick, St. Catherine, Virgin and Martyr, many other Saints, traditions, pious beliefs and beloved and venerated Devotions in the Church, but it remains most explicitly true regarding the calamnous assault of John Launoy in the sacred domain of the Brown Scapular Devotion of Our Lady of Mt. Carmel.

Catholic Scholars of the highest name throughout the world have developed and supported the erroneous opinions, condemned books, rebellious teachings and criticisms regarding the Scapular Devotion of John Launoy well into the 21st century.

In: "The Irish Ecclesiastical Record," Volume VIII, John E. Bartley, O.C.C., 1887, John Launoy has been described as:

The enemy of the Holy See, the contemner of Papal Bulls, the calumniator of saints and religious orders, the sneerer at and reviler of religious practices whose works have nearly all been condemned by the Sacred Congregation of the Index. (25)

In an article written by Isaac D'Israeli speaking of the renowned and once celebrated Jesuit priest, Fr. Theophilus Raynaud, S.J. (who wrote *Scapulare Parthenico-Marianum illustratum et defensum*; Paris, 1654 "In Defense of the Scapular Visions") he quotes Fr. Raynaud as saying:

"When the learned de Launoy had successfully attacked the legends of saints, every parish priest trembled for his favorite." Fr. Raynaud entitled a libel on this new Iconoclast:

Hercules Commodianus Joannes Launoius

He (Fr. Raynaud) compared Launoy to the Emperor Commodes, who though he was the most cowardly of men, conceived himself formidable when he dressed himself as Hercules. (26)

The author would like to ask the reader some questions at this point: "Would you believe the opinions, writings, teachings and actions of a man of this character? Would you embrace, uphold and place value upon the historical criticisms of a heretic? Would you disseminate the published conclusions of a man who is insubordinate to authority? Would you entrust your life to him? Would you entrust to him your immortal soul?

The disputes, arguments and denials of John Launoy regarding the authenticity of the origins of the Brown Scapular Devotion: (the Visions of Our Lady to St. Simon Stock and to Pope John XXII) are still to this day, believed, quoted, upheld, sustained and cited by many religious scholars and can be found in various religious and scholarly documents, declarations and publications throughout the world. As the saying goes, "a man is known by the company he keeps."

Regrettably as the reader will discover in the forthwith chapter, many of the objections against the authenticity of the Brown Scapular Devotion from the 20th and 21st centuries progressives, are strikingly similar to those of John Launoy whose certain objections in English are found at the beginning of this chapter and in Appendix 2.

The errors perpetrated by this 17th century Gallican and Jansenist,

John Launoy have permeated the walls of Universities and Religious Communities worldwide and have resulted in seriously wounding the celebrated position the revered Brown Scapular Devotion of Our Lady of Mt. Carmel once held in the Church and throughout the world.

Due to the erroneous teachings of John Launoy that have trickled down into the 21st century, the Visions of Our Lady to St. Simon Stock and to Pope John XXII regarding the Scapular and the Sabbatine Privilege are now under suspicion as legend; the Contemporary Objectors and Opposers of the traditional origins of the Scapular Devotion are ignoring the ancient documentations, confirmations, indulgences, miracles and approbations of the Successors of Peter; they have cited and embraced the objections and works of this "enemy of the Church," they have directly and indirectly quoted John Launoy in official documentation, and have rewritten the origins of the Devotion, detouring the Brown Scapular to a Contemporary approach.

Because of this mentality, all devotions in the Church based on private revelation, are vulnerable to attack and may become in danger of extinction.

In the "Catholic Dictionary," Addis and Arnold, 1884, the information given regarding the Scapular is based on the condemned writings of a disloyal and bitter enemy of the Holy See (John Launoy). According to the tenor of the article in the Catholic Dictionary, the Scapular is no longer a gift from Mary's own hands, giving him who carries it a *claim* to her protection; it is no longer supernatural in its origin. The Promise that one who wears it faithfully and dies with it upon him, will not be allowed to fall into the flames of Hell, is ridiculed as a bit of superstition or at least unreliable under the light of modern criticism. Any attack on the Scapular is indirectly an attack on the power and privileges of the Holy Mother of God. (27)

"How many historical facts could stand if methods employed by Launoy would prevail? Even the most sacred and fundamental truths of religion have been attacked in the same way by unbelieving and heretical writers who have furnished in their *own* opinion and the opinion of those who believe with them, a superabundance of reasons against doctrines which they do not wish to admit but which are held by all Catholics." (28)

"Launoy's theological arguments against the Scapular Vision have no direct reference in any way to the Scapular Vision; in reality they strike at the root of all private revelations." (29)

"The weight of the evidence will very much depend on the character of the witnesses." (30)

Note: See Appendix 2 for Ancient and Modern Day Objections, and Responses to Objections. Also see Appendix 3.

CHAPTER 4 ENDNOTES

THE ERRONEOUS TEACHINGS OF JOHN LAUNOY

1   *Take This Scapular,* by the Carmelite Fathers and Tertiaries, Chicago, 1949, p. 216

2   *Ibid,* p. 216

3   *The Credibility of the Scapular Promises,* Rev. Christian P. Ceroke, O. Carm, Rome, 1950, p. 1

4   New Catholic Encyclopedia/HighBeam Research-Jean de Launoy

5   Nation Master Encyclopedia>Jean Launoy; www.nationmaster.com/ encyclopedia/Jean-Launoy

6   *The Credibility of the Scapular Promises,* 1950, pp. 1, 2

7   *Take This Scapular,* p. 217, paraphrased

8   *Ibid,* p. 218, paraphrased

9   *The Credibility of the Scapular Promises,* 1950, p. 23

10 *Ibid,* p. 24, paraphrased

11 *Ibid,* p. 25

12 *Ibid,* p. 1

JOHN LAUNOY VERSUS JOHN GROSSI

1   *The Scapular and Some Critics,* P. E. Magennis, 1914, p. 42-43, paraphrased

2   *Ibid,* p. 43, paraphrased; *Mary in Her Scapular Promise,* John Mathias Haffert, 1942, p. 29

3   *Mary in Her Scapular Promise,* John Mathias Haffert, 1942, p. 29, paraphrased.

4   *The Irish Ecclesiastical Record,* James P. Rushe, O.D.C., Vol. XXIX, January-June, 1911, p. 274; paraphrased. www.archive.org/stream/ irishecclesiasti29dubloft/irishecclesiasti

5   www.britannica.com/EBchecked/topic/640848/Western-Schism

6   *Irish Ecclesiastical. Record,* James P. Rushe, O.D.C., Vol. XXIX, Jan.-June, 1911, p. 274

7   *Ibid,* p. 274, paraphrased

7a *The Sabbatine Privilege of the Scapular,* P.E. Magennis, New York, 1923, p. 43

8   *Irish Ecclesiastical Record,* James P. Rushe, O.D.C., Vol. XXIX, Jan-June, 1911, pp. 274-275, paraphrased

9   *Ibid,* p. 275, paraphrased

10 *Ibid,* pp. 275-276, paraphrased

11 *Irish Eccesiastical Record.* John E. Bartley, O.C.C., Vol. VIII ,1887, p. 801; and *The Scapular and Some Critics,* P. E. Magennis, O.C.C., Rome, 1914, p. 47, paraphrased

12 *The Irish Eccesiastical Record,* James P. Rushe, O.D.C., Vol. XXIX, 1911, p. 275

13 *The Scapular and Some Critics,* P. E. Magennis, Rome, 1914, p. 47

14 *Ibid,* p. 48

15 *The Irish Eccl. Record,* James P. Rushe, O.D.C., Vol. XXIX Jan-June, 1911, pp. 277-278

15a *The Meaning and the Use of the Scapular of Our Lady of Mount Carmel,* The Bishop of Salford, Salford, 1893, p. 9

16 *The Irish Ecclesiastical Record,* John E. Bartley, O.C.C., Vol.VIII, Jan. 1887; 1009-1014; *Take this Scapular,* Carmelite Fathers and Tertiaries, 1949, pp 221-237

17 Genesis 3-15, Douay Rheims version

17a *The Scapular and Some Critics,* The Vision, P. E. Magennis, O.C.C., Rome, 1914, p. 46, paraphrased

17b *Ibid,* pp. 46, 47, paraphrased

18 *The Irish Ecclesiastical Record,* John E. Bartley, O.C.C., Vol. VIII, Jan. 1887, p. l004, paraphrased

19 *The Scapular and Some Critics,* P. E. Magennis, O.C.C., Rome, 1914, pp. 122-124

20 *Ibid,* p. 40; *De Viso Simonis Stochii,* Joanne De Launoy, Paris 1642, pp. 39, 40

21 *The Scapular and Some Critics,* P. E. Magennis, Rome, 1914; *ibid,* pp. 40, 44

THE WEIGHT OF THE EVIDENCE WILL VERY MUCH DEPEND ON THE CHARACTER OF THE WITNESSES.

1   *History of the Catholic Church from the Renaissance to the French Revolution,* Rev. James MacCaffrey, S. J., 1914, Vol I, Chapter VI: Theological Controversies; Chapter VII, the Age of Absolutism and Unbelief; Gallicanism, paraphrased. http://catholicity.elcore.net/ MacCaffrey/HCCRFRTOC.html, paraphrased

2   http://www.catholicnewsagency.com/resource.php?n=977, paraphrased

2a   Catholic Encyclopedia/High Beam Research-Jean de Launoy, paraphrased

3   *The Scapular and Some Critics,* P. E. Magennis, O.C.C., Rome, 1914, p. 122

4   *The Irish Ecclesiastical Record,* Volume VIII, 1887, John E. Bartley, O.C.C., pp. 796

5   *History of the Catholic Church from the Renaissance to the French Revolution,* Rev. James MacCaffrey, Vol. I, Chap. VII, "The Age of Absolutism and Unbelief." (Gallicanism) paraphrased

6   *The Scapular and Some Critics,* P. E. Magennis, O.C.C., 1914, p.123, paraphrased

7   *The Romish Doctrine of the Immaculate Conception,* Dr. Edward Preuss, Edinburgh, 1867, p. 164, paraphrased

8   *The Scapular and Some Critics,* P. E. Magennis, Rome, 1914, pp. 123, 131

9   *The Irish Ecclesiastical Record,* John E. Bartley, 1887, p. 795

10   *The Scapular and Some Critics,* P. E. Magennis, Rome, 1914, p. 132

10a *The Catholic Gene,* Saturday, September 24, 2011; *About Agnosticism/ Atheism: Index of Forbidden Books,* paraphrased

10b Denzinger,Heinrich and Peter Hunermann, EDS: *Compendium of Creeds, Definitions, and Declarations on Matters of Faith and Morals.* Edited by Robert Fastiggi and Anne Englund Nash, 43rd Edition, Ignatius Press, San Francisco, 2012: *Decree of the Sacred Congregation of the Index, December 5, 1881: The Freedom to Criticize Works Whose Proceedings Have Been Dismissed by the Sacred Congregation of the Index*: #3154-3155, pp. 630 to 631, paraphrased

11   *The Irish Ecclesiastical Record,* John E. Bartley, O.C.C. Volume VIII, 1887, p. 796

12 *Ibid*, p. 796; and *The Scapular and Some Critics*, p. 125, paraphrased

13 *The Credibility of the Scapular Promises*, Rev. Christian P. Ceroke, A Dissertation, 1950 p. 116, paraphrased

14 *The Irish Ecclesiastical Record*, John E. Bartley, O.C.C., 1887, pp. 794-808 found in Appendix 3 in this book

15 *The Credibility of the Scapular Promises*, Rev. Christian P. Ceroke, A Dissertation, 1950, p. 116

16 *Irish Ecclesiastical Record*, John E. Bartley, O.C.C., Volume VIII, No. 1, 1887, p. 796

17 1 Act de Canon Ser. Dei. Lib. I., c. 44., n. 18; *Ibid*, p. 795

18 *The Irish Ecclesiastical Record*, John E. Bartley, O.C.C., Volume VIII, No. 1, 1887, p. 796.

18a Catholic Encyclopedia: Council of Trent, paraphrased. http://catholicism.academic.ru/13670/Council_of_Trent; *Damnatio Memoria:* The Council of Trent and Catholic Teaching on Divorce, by E. Christian Brugger, October 17, 2014, Footnote #12: _ Jean de Launoy (1603–1678); see *De regia in matrimonium potestate* (1674), par. III, art. I, cap. 5, no. 78; in *Opera* (Cologne/Geneva, 1731), tom. 1, cap. I, p. 855

18b Fr. Paul Haffner, "The Mystery of Mary" (Herefordshire, United Kingdom: Gracewing, 2004, p. 87; Fr. Michael O'Carroll, C. S. Sp., "Theotokos: A Theological Encyclopedia of the Blessed Virgin Mary" Eugene, OR: Wipf and Stock, 2000, p. 181. The 1617 Bull of Paul V *Sanctissimus* is cited by Blessed Pope Pius IX in footnote 9 of his 1854 Bull *Ineffabilis Deus* defining the Immaculate Conception.

19 *The Christian Remembrancer*, Volume 23, January – June, William Scott, Francis Garden, James Bowling Mozley, 1852, London, pp. 413, 414, 417. See also Creeds of Christendom with a History of Critical Notes: The Papal Definition of the Immaculate Conception of the Virgin Mary 1854

20 *Irish Ecclesiastical Record*, Volume VIII, No. 1, January 1887, p. 796

21 *Studies in Hiberno-Latin Literature*, Google Books, Mario Esposito, 2006, XXI, p. 138, index p. 8-Jean de Launoy, or "*Irish Historical Studies:* Vol. 10, 1957, books.google.com, "The Patrician Problem and A Possible Solution"

22 *The Life of Joan of Arc*, by Anatole France, 1909, Footnote #114

23 *The Life of Joan of Arc*, by Anatole France, 1909, Footnote # 114

24 "Did St. Mary Magdelene come to Provence," by Brother Thomas of Our Lady of Perpetual Help: #81 – June, 2009

25 *Irish Ecclesiastical Record*, John E. Bartley, O.C.C., 1887, p. 806

26 *Curiosities of Literature;* First series, Isaac D'Israeli, 1766-1848, New York "Secret History of Authors Who Have Ruined their Booksellers"

27 *The Month,* A Catholic Magazine and Review, Vol. LVIII, September-December, London, 1886, pp. 306-307, paraphrased

28 *The Irish Ecclesiastical Record,* John E. Bartley, O.C.C., pp. 797; Volume VIII, No. 1, Third Series, 1887

29 *The Scapular and Some Critics,* P. E. Magennis, Rome, 1914 pp. 130, 131

30 *The Irish Ecclesiastical Record,* John E. Bartley, O.C.C., Vol. VIII, 1887, p. 795

CHAPTER 5

TESTIMONIALS OF THE SAINTS ON THE SCAPULAR THROUGHOUT THE CENTURIES

Chapter 5

Testimonials of the Saints on the Scapular throughout the Centuries

How is it proven authentic?

She, in fact, is the most loving and most powerful Mother of God and of us all and never was it heard that anyone has had suppliant recourse to her and has not experienced her most efficacious protection.

Continue, therefore, as you have been doing, to venerate her with fervent piety and to love her ardently and to invoke her with these words which you have been accustomed to address her: "To you alone has it been given, O most holy and most pure Mother of God, unfailingly to have your petitions ever answered. Apost. Letter *Sacro vergente anno,* to the people of Russia, July 7, 1952 Pope Pius XII

> *I have brought you into the land of Carmel to eat the fruit of thereof and the best things thereof.* (Jer. 2:7)

The Brown Scapular of Our Lady of Mount Carmel has drawn down upon itself the riches and treasures of the Church, attracting some of the most illustrious and holy people in the world. The Saints, the Blessed, Princes of the Church and the Heads of State and their households have all received the spiritual benefits of being clothed with the mantle of her protection as a Sign of Love, Dedication and Consecration to the Mother of the Redeemer.

The Princes of the Church and of the State were enrolled in the Confraternity of the Holy Scapular. The Sovereign Pontiffs and the Crowned Heads honored the Scapular and wore it with respect. Among the first ranks of the distinguished who have worn the Scapular with love and devotion, the Confraternity first counts the Holy Fathers: **Urban VII, Alexander VII, Clement X, Alexander V,**

Clement VII, Paul III, Paul IV Pius V, Gregory XII, Paul V, Gregory X, Edward, King of England, The Emperors: Ferdinand II, Ferdinand III, Sebastien, King of Portugal; and especially our Monarchs who have much accredited it by their examples : Saint Louis, Louis XIII, Louis XIV, received the Scapular in 1653; Louis XV in 1717; Monseigneur le Dauphin, in 1740; the Queen and Ladies of France received it similarly. (1)

A personal observation to note: A question may be asked at this point. If the Scapular of Our Lady of Mount Carmel did not owe its origins to a heavenly visit from the Mother of God, if it was not the vehicle of astounding miraculous intervention, if it was not revered and confirmed by the Holy Fathers and highly indulgenced by Holy Mother Church, if it did not carry the Promise of eternal salvation, would the numerous members of the Royal Households, those mentioned above and those throughout the centuries, have elected to wear, sometimes in secret, the badge of the Confraternity of Our Lady Mount Carmel as part of their royal attire if there were no promise attached? If it was the earthly invention of a Religious Community, intended only to extend a share of the spirituality of their Order through a visible symbol, without the promise of eternal salvation, would the Royalty of the past decades or the millions of faithful today elect to wear a simple, ordinary article of brown wool, not consistent with the fashion of the day?

This chapter contains a compilation of testimonials of Saints and Blessed in the Church and authenticated documents confirming the authenticity of the Scapular Visions from saintly men, Solemn Pontiffs and men of unquestionable character. The documented miracles of the Scapular recorded in this book are hardly a fraction of the abounding miracles that have existed throughout the centuries, including miracles that are still are occuring to this very day.

It has been discovered that with this Devotion, it is impossible to hold a middle ground. The Scapular Devotion has been proven to be indisputably authentic by the Heirarchy of the Church and promulgated from its inception without any cessation in a spirit of peace until before 1642, in the latter 19th century, the early 20th century and up into the 21st century. Either it is the celestial vehicle of Our Lady that holds the Promise of eternal salvation proven by numerous documented miracles and confirmed and indulgenced by the Holy Fathers or it isn't. We leave that decision to the Church. *For those who believe, no explanation is necessary, for those who do not believe, no explanation is possible.* (2)

TESTIMONIALS OF SAINTS

1) **Saint Peter Damian** (1007-1073): had written that on the Feasts of the Assumption, Christmas and Easter: *Our Lady descends into Purgatory and takes many souls from it.* (1)

2) **King St. Louis IX of France** (1214-1270): Greatly devoted to Our Lady St. Louis was responsible for bringing the Carmelite Order to France. While on a Crusade in the Holy Land, King Louis' ship ran into a violent storm within view of Mt. Carmel. The sound of the bells from the chapel of Our Lady of Mt. Carmel pierced the roar of the wind and the waves. The King, kneeling in prayer, begged Our Lady to save his ship, promising in return a pilgrimage to Carmel. The ship was saved. King Louis climbed the slopes of Carmel to visit the holy hermits who lived near the chapel. Greatly edified by their life of prayer and solitude, he asked several of them to come to France where he established a monastery for them. This was a great help to the Carmelites who were finding life in Palestine very difficult, due to the hostility of the Moslems.(2)

3) **St. Bridget of Sweden** (1303-1373): The Divine Mother once addressed these words to Saint Bridget: *I am the Mother of all souls in Purgatory for all the pains that they have deserved for their sins are every hour, as long as they remain there, in some way mitigated by my prayers.* (3)

4) **St. Nuno of Saint Mary Alvares Pereira, O. Carm.** (1360-1431): He was the last great medieval knight. He became the Constable of Portugal and the head of the army. On August 13, 1385, Nuno had asked God for a sign that his outnumbered army would be victorious through the intercession of Our Lady, Queen of Portugal. As the troops crossed the Mount of Saint Michael overlooking the Cova da Iria, the horses began to kneel as Nuno was led to the spot where six hundred years later, Our Lady would appear to the three children of Fatima, in 1917. On the vigil of the Feast of the Assumption, Nuno miraculously won the victory and freed Portugal. He became a Brother in the Carmelite Monastery in 1423. Nuno lived out the last years of his life dedicated to the Rosary and the Scapular, his two favorite Devotions which he propagated in Portugal. He said: *Before all else, I kiss the Holy Scapular, the precious gift which the Mother of God brought down from Heaven in defense of her Friars.* He is the National

Hero of Portugal. He was beatified by Pope Benedict XV in 1918 and canonized by Pope Benedict XVI in 2009. (4)

5) St. Bernadine of Siena (1380-1444): He positively asserts that the Blessed Virgin has the power of delivering souls from Purgatory, but particularly those of her clients, by her prayers and by applying her merits for them. (5)

6) St. Dennis the Carthusian (1492-1608): He, as well as St. Peter Damian, had written that on the feasts of the Assumption, Christmas and Easter: *Our Lady descends into Purgatory and takes many souls from it.* (6)

7) Pope Saint Pius V (1504-572): The Sabbatine Privilege, first granted by Pope John XXII was approved and confirmed (by several Pontiffs); of the nine Popes who have sanctioned the Sabbatine Privilege, note these words of Pope St. Pius V in (his Bull confirming the Sabbatine Privilege of John XXII called): *Superna dispositione*…(dated February 18, 1566): *With Apostolic Authority and by tenor of the present, we approve each of the Privileges (of the Carmelite Order) and also the Sabbatine.* (7)

8) St. Teresa of Avila (1515-1582): When St. Teresa was astonished at seeing a certain Carmelite carried straight to Heaven *without even going to Purgatory,* she was given to understand that he had been faithful to his Rule and avoided Purgatory because of Bulls granted to the Carmelite Order. *I was amazed that he had not gone to Purgatory. I understood that having become a friar and carefully kept the Rule, the Bulls of the Order had been of use to him, so that he did not pass into Purgatory.* (8)

9) St. Teresa of Avila (1515-1582): *Once in prayer, with much recollection, sweetness and repose, I saw myself, as it seemed to me, surrounded with angels and was close to God. I began to intercede with His Majesty on behalf of the Church, and I was given to understand the great services which the Scapular family would render in the latter days.* (9)

10) St. John of the Cross (1542-1591): (He spoke these words as he lay dying in 1591): *The Mother of God and of Carmel hastens to Purgatory with Grace on Saturday and delivers those souls who have worn her Scapular. Blessed be such a Lady who wills that on this day of Saturday I shall depart from this life.* (10)

11) **St. Robert Bellarmine** (1542-1621): He was the most influential of the Cardinals deciding the question of the Sabbatine Privilege by the Decree of 1613, laid down the principle of the authority of the Church. He said: *It cannot be denied to the Carmelite Fathers to preach according to the tenors of the Bulls.* (It was in fact the statements of Cardinal Bellarmine which were incorporated into the Decree of 1613.) (11)

12) **St. Robert Bellarmine** (1542-1621): *On this day (July 16th) Mary took to herself by means of the Holy Scapular, sons of love. Who would ever dare to snatch these children from the bosom of Mary when they have taken refuge there? What power of hell, what temptation can overcome them if they place their confidence in this great Mother, the Mother of God and of them?* (12)

13) **St. Peter Claver** (1581-1654): He considered the Scapular of Our Lady the special instrument given by Divine Providence to aid in the salvation of souls. During his lifetime in New Granada (South America) he converted and baptised over three hundred thousand slaves. He sent each one to Our Lady by enrolling him in her Scapular, confident that Mary would watch over and bring safely to eternity every soul entrusted to her care. (13)

14) **St. Claude de la Columbiere** (1641-1682): *I wanted to know if Mary really and truly interested herself in me. And in the Scapular, she has given me the most tangible assurance; I have only to open my eyes. She has attached her protection to this Scapular: "Whosoever dies clothed in this shall not suffer eternal fire.* (14)

15) **St. Claude de la Columbiere** (1641-1682): From him the world received Our Lord's revelations to the saintly Visitation Sister (St. Margaret Mary) about Consecration to the Sacred Heart: *Because all forms of our love for the Blessed Virgin cannot be equally agreeable to her, I aver without a moment's hesitation that the Scapular is most favored of all. Because of the alliance which Mary contracts with us and which we contract with her, no other devotion renders our salvation so certain. Here is the Queen herself who in that celebrated revelation, reveals all the tenderness of her heart to Saint Simon Stock ... I have but to glance at my Scapular, tangible proof before my eyes and recall the Promise attached to its devout wearing: "Whosoever shall die clothed in this (Scapular) shall not suffer eternal fire.* (15)

16) **St. Alphonsus Liguori** (1696-1787): *The Promise made by our Blessed Lady to Pope John XXII is well known. She appeared to him and ordered him to make known to all that on the Saturday after their death, she would deliver from Purgatory all who wore the Carmelite Scapular.* (16)

17) **St. John Vianney, Cure of Ars** (1786-1859): He was outstanding for his devotion to Our Lady under the title of Our Lady of Mt. Carmel. He had great faith in Our Lady's promise, always speaking of the Scapular as "one's safeguard against temptation." In his own life he suffered many physical attacks from the devil. From experience therefore he told his people that the Scapular would protect them from every onslaught of the devil. (17)

18) **St. John Don Bosco** (1815-1888): From his childhood Don Bosco had a particular devotion to the Scapular. When he was buried in 1888, he held the Scapular and the Crucifix in his hands. Years later in 1929, when his tomb was opened for the official examination before his beatification, Crucifix and Scapular were found to be intact beneath the rotted garments. This great apostle and educator of youth knew the treasures hidden in Mary's Garment. (18)

19) **St. Conrad of Altotten** (1818-1894): Canonized by Pope Pius XI during his more than forty years as porter (in the Capuchin Order), he influenced thousands through his love for Our Lady and the practice of giving the Scapular to as many visitors as possible. (19)

20) **St. Bernadette Soubirous** (1844-1879): On July 16th, 1251, (Our Lady) had given us the Scapular, and on the same day, in 1858, St. Bernadette (who faithfully wore the Brown Scapular all the days of her life), felt within her the summons to the Grotto at Lourdes. Just as the evening Angelus was about to sound from the parish belfry on the feast of Our Lady of Mt. Carmel, she started to cry: *There she is! There she is! She had never been so beautiful!* After the apparitions, Bernadette wished to become a Carmelite. (20)

21) **Pope Saint Pius X** (1858-1914): In 1910, Pope Pius X made an astounding legislation. He declared that the cloth Scapular, after the enrollment, could be replaced by a medal which bore on one side an image of the Sacred Heart and on the other an image of Our Lady. It would posess the same Promises and Indulgences as the Brown Scapular. St. Pius added explicitly to his consent that for ordinary

circumstances: *"I desire most vehemently that the cloth Scapular is to be worn as heretofore."* Prior, he stated: *"I believe in the Scapular Vision!"* (21)

22) **St. Therese of Liseux** (1873-1897): (The Little Flower) in a letter to Celine dated July 1894: *I had asked for you, dear Celine, from Our Lady of Mount Carmel the grace you have obtained at Lourdes. How happy I am that you are clothed in the Holy Scapular! It is a sure Sign of predestination and besides, are you not more intimately united by means of it to your little sisters in Carmel?* (22)

23) **Pope Saint John XXIII** (1881-1965): Referring to the day of his election and how Cardinal Tisserant of France came to ask him what name he would take), the Holy Father reflects on the name of John saying of his predecessor John XXII: *He had the honor of canonizing St. Thomas Aquinas; to him also is assigned the paternity of the "Saturday Privilege" so precious and so dear to those who wear the Scapular of Our Lady of Mt. Carmel.* Pope John XXIII spoke of the Mother of God, who is honored in this Church of Our Lady of Mt. Carmel. (23)

24) **Pope Saint John Paul II** (1920-2005): VIA Inside the Vatican Newsflash: John Paul II and the Brown Scapular: Pope John Paul II insisted doctors not remove his Brown Scapular during surgery on him following the assassination attempt in May 1981. Fr. Mariano Cera, a Carmelite Priest, told *Inside the Vatican: Just before the Holy Father was operated on, he told the doctors "Don't take off the Scapular" and the surgeon left it on.* Fr. Cera made the comments at the beginning of celebrations for the 750th anniversary of the Carmelite Scapular. Pope Saint John Paul II was convinced that Our Lady of Mt. Carmel along with Our Lady of Fatima saved him from the bullets of Mehmet Ali Agca. The Virgin Mary appeared at the final apparition of Fatima (Portugal) and at Lourdes (France) wearing the Brown Scapular. The Pontiff, a Third Order Carmelite, had worn the Scapular of Our Lady of Mt. Carmel since he was a young boy. He frequently asked Our Lady of Mt. Carmel to help him make important decisions. (24)

Pope Saint John Paul II died after a long fight against Parkinson's disease, among other illnesses, at the age of 84 on April 2 at 21:37, 2005. It was the First Saturday, before the Sunday of Divine Mercy. (25)

Letters

OF ST. THERESE OF LISIEUX

volume II
1890–1897

General Correspondence
Translated from the Original Manuscripts by
John Clarke, O.C.D.

(as the world believes), it raises them up and renders them capable of *loving*, or *loving* with a love *almost infinite* since this love must continue after this mortal life which is given to us only for meriting the homeland of heaven where we shall find again the dear ones whom we have loved on earth!

I had asked for you, dear Céline, from Our Lady of Mount Carmel the grace you have obtained at Lourdes. How happy I am that you are clothed in the holy scapular![2] It is a sure sign of predestination and besides are you not more intimately united by means of it to your little sisters in Carmel?...

You ask, dear little cousin, that I pray for your dear husband; do you think, then, I could fail in this?... No, I could not separate you in my weak prayers. I am asking Our Lord to be as generous in your regard as he was formerly to the spouses at the wedding of Cana. May He always change water into wine![3]... That is to say, may He continue to make you happy and to soften as much as possible the trials that you encounter in life.

Trials, how could I place this word in my letter, when I know everything is happiness for you?...

Pardon me, dear little friend; enjoy in peace the joy God is giving you, without disturbing yourself regarding the future. He is reserving for you, I am sure, new graces and many consolations.

Our good Mother Marie de Gonzague is very appreciative of your kind remembrance of her, and she herself is not forgetting her dear little Céline. Our Mother and Sister Marie of the Sacred Heart are also very happy because of your joy, and they ask me to assure you of their affection.

I dare, dear little *cousin*,[4] to beg you to offer my respectful regards to *Monsieur* Pottier, whom I cannot refrain from considering also as my *cousin*.

I leave you, dear Céline, remaining always united to you in my heart, and I shall, throughout my life, be happy to call myself,

Your little sister in Jesus,
Thérèse of the Child Jesus
rel. carm. ind.

LT 166/*LC 159*   July 1894   867

Autograph.

1. See the last message of Thérèse to Mme. Pottier, sent by Sister Marie
of the Eucharist (Marie Guérin): "God is calling her to be a real saint
in the world, and He has plans and a very special love for her" (DE,
p. 718, letter of July 20, 1898).

2. "Wear the scapular of Mount Carmel; it will be a great joy for me,
and we shall be united by still greater spiritual bonds" (Marie Guérin
to Céline Maudelonde, undated letter, a little before June 19, date
of her marriage).

3. See John 2:7-9.

4. See LT 159, note 2.

LC 159   From Céline to Thérèse.

July 17, 1894

LT 165

                                                July 17, 1894

Dear Thérèse,

I am going to write you in haste, for these days I do not have time
to turn around. Joseph de Cornière[1] is here, and we are busy doing
photography. We dress up and are making a whole story of travellers
in living pictures;[2] it will be very amusing. In the meanwhile,
however, I am beginning to get enough of it. My days seem insipid
to me, no more reading, no time to write, hardly any time to make
meditation; we are always on the go.[3]
Dear Thérèse, oh! I would be unable to tell you how this life weighs
on me.... When I received your letter, I was again recollected, I
enjoyed and relished your letter...but at present I am like a piece
of wood, there is no longer anything to draw on from within me.
When I received your letter, dear Thérèse, my soul was not sad but
filled with fervor to be good and practice virtue, and it is again to
you that I owed this feeling. Your book by P. Surin[4] is extraordinary,
and certainly I shall buy a copy of it. It is really this type of language
that I need to sustain myself.... I say the same thing for each book
that you lend me, but I believe I have never found any that may
do me as much good as the evangelical counsels. Thérèse!... Oh!

BLESSED IN THE CHURCH

1   **Blessed Pope Gregory X** (1210-1276): He was a holy Tertiary Pope of the Thirteenth Century and friend of St. Bonaventure, he was a true son of St. Francis and distinguished himself by his love for the holy places in Palestine. He was buried wearing the Scapular, only 25 years after the Vision (of Our Lady to St. Simon Stock). When his tomb was opened years later, (in 1830), the Wool Scapular remained perfectly intact and had not degraded in the least. (1)

2   **Blessed Joan of Toulouse** (1220-1271): She became truly great because of the Scapular. The great joy and delight of her life, she tells us, was to be clothed in Our Lady's Scapular, wearing it day and night. Through zeal and love for her Scapular she succeeded in bringing thousands to know and love Our Lady. (2)

3   **Blessed Frank of Siena** (Born in the 1200's-1291): In the life of another Carmelite Brother, Blessed Frank of Siena, we find the great value of the Scapular as a Sign of Victory over Satan. After the death of his parents, he gave himself to a life of sin. When God struck him blind, he repented and his sight was returned, but Satan continued to tempt him fiercely against holy purity. Then Our Lady appeared to him, urging him to put on the Carmelite Habit. He went to the Carmel of Siena where an angel from Heaven invested him in the presence of the whole Community. Ever afterwards he made extraordinary progress in virtue and was often visited by the Blessed Virgin Mary. (3)

4   **Blessed John Soreth** (1394-1471): Blessed John Soreth gave the Third Order Secular its canonical status. He carried out what Blessed Joan of Toulouse had begun. She (Blessed Joan of Toulouse) had received the habit of the Tertiary from St. Simon Stock himself and had persuaded thousands to be enrolled in the Brown Scapular. Animated by her zeal, Blessed John preached and taught love for the Scapular and led thousands to follow the footsteps of Blessed Joan. (4)

5   **Blessed Baptist of Mantua** (1447-1516): Early in his life, he was filled with a consuming love for God and His Mother Mary and joined the Carmelites. As a Carmelite he became a great and shining light

through his love for the Scapular. IT WAS HE WHO PERSONALLY RECEIVED THE SABBATINE BULL FROM POPE CLEMENT VII WITH THE AUTHORITY TO PROMULGATE AND PREACH IT. (5)

6   **Blessed Anne of St. Bartholomew** (1549-1626): This humble and dedicated soul was born Anne Garcia in Almendral, Spain. She was graced with mystical experiences throughout her life. Anne was a poor shepherdess who felt a call to enter the first monastery of Discalced Carmelites (the Carmel of St. Joseph in Avila, Spain). Sister Anne was very dearly loved by Our Holy Mother St. Teresa of Jesus, the foundress of the Order, becoming Mother's travel companion and eventually her secretary as well after St. Teresa ordered her to learn to read and write. She was also St. Teresa's nurse, and it was in Sister Anne's arms that St. Teresa drew her last breath on October 4, 1582, the Feast of St. Francis of Assisi, as the Saint had wished. Pope Benedict XV declared Anne "Blessed" in 1917. *I will lead you into my family of Carmel where you will wear MY HABIT.* (Our Lady to Blessed Anne of St. Bartholomew) (6)

7   **Blessed Catherine Anne Emmerich** (1774-1824):
The vision of the Blessed Catherine Emmerick casts some light upon the mysterious connection between the prophetic vision on Carmel and the speaking vision at Lourdes. Long before Bernadette saw Mary on that mountain in the Pyrenees, Catherine had the following vision: *I then saw another vision. I saw, after the hermits began to live in community, a monk on his knees in his cell. The Mother of God appeared to him with the Infant Jesus on her arm. She looked exactly like the statue that I had seen by the spring to the mountain. She gave him an article of dress in which was a square opening for the head to pass through. It fell in front over the breast. It was shining with light, the colors brown and white intermingling, as in the vestment of the High-Priest Zacharias showed to Saint Joseph. On the straps that went over the shoulders were letters inscribed. Mary spoke long to the monk. When she vanished and he returned to himself, he was filled with emotion on seeing himself clothed with the Scapular. I saw him assemble his brethren and show it to them.*

Then I had a vision of a Church festival on Mount Carmel. I saw in the choirs of the Church Triumphant as the first of the ancient hermits, and yet separated from them, Elias. Over the spring where once stood Mary's statue, now arose a convent and its church…above the altar was the Mother of God with the Infant Jesus just as she appeared to the hermit… the holy Virgin was surrounded by the angelic choirs and at her feet, above the tabernacle

172

wherein reposed the Blessed Sacrament, hung the large Scapular she had given the hermit in a Vision. (7)

8   **Blessed Pope Pius IX** (1792-1878): *This most extraordinary gift of the Scapular from the Mother of God to St. Simon Stock...brings its great usefulness not only to the Carmelite Family of Mary, but also to all the rest of the faithful who wish, affiliated to that Family, to follow Mary with a very special devotion.* (8)

9   **Venerable Pope Pius XII** (1876-1958): In *Addresses* and *Letters*, the late Holy Father touched upon many phases of Carmelite life. His documents on the Scapular Devotion are some of the most significant ever to come from the Holy See. In placing the Scapular *in the first rank of the most favored of these (private) devotions,* and pointing out that *the Habit or Garment of Mary is a Sign and Pledge of the Protection of the Mother of God,* he revived Scapular Devotion and clarified its theology for the 20th century man.

Seven hundred years have passed since according to the sacred traditions of the Carmelite family, Simon Stock was vouchsafed the Vision of Our Lady of Mount Carmel... (9)

Certainly this most gentle mother will not delay to open, as soon as possible, through her intercession with God, the Gates of Heaven for her children who are expiating their faults in Purgatory, a trust based on that Promise know as the Sabbatine Privilege. (10)

10 **Blessed Isidore Bakanja** (1887-1909): (Declared Blessed April 24, 1994): Less than a century ago, an African teenager, Isidore Bakanja, withstood a severe beating with spiked leather straps from a cruel plantation master provoked by his praying the Rosary and his refusal to remove his Scapular of Mount Carmel. Isidore was asked why the white man beat him: Isidore's reply: *The white man did not like Christians...he did not want me to wear the Scapular.* Isidore's body was wholly infected, Isidore's very bones were exposed; he died on either the 8th or the 15th in August of 1909, Rosary in hand and Scapular around his neck. (11)

11 **Venerable Archbishop Fulton J. Sheen, Third Order Carmelite** (1895-1979): (Declared Venerable, June 28, 2012) Starting in 1930, Bishop Fulton Sheen began and hosted a weekly Sunday night radio broadcast called *The Catholic Hour.* In 1951 Sheen hosted a Catholic television program entitled *Life is Worth Living.* In 1952, he won an

Emmy Award for "Most Outstanding Television Personality." Fulton Sheen credited the Gospel writers: Matthew, Mark, Luke and John for their valuable contribution to his success: (12)

One sees in the Scapular, which is a miniature clothing a reversal of the penalties and effects of Original Sin. Before Adam sinned, he was naked but not ashamed. That was because of the integrity of his human nature by which senses were subject to reason and reason to God. His union with God was, as it were, the clothing of his whole being. But once that union was disrupted, he was naked and ashamed. He now had need of clothing.

There must be something of this symbolism in Mary's gift of the Scapular which was originally a habit, "The beauty of the King's daughter is from within." Mary's gift of clothing is just a simple Garment, sufficient to cover the traces of Original Sin in us, but its very simplicity is also a witness to the fact that her own beautiful mantle covers our souls. The Scapular bears therefore a double witness: to Mary's protection against the ravages of the flesh occasioned by the Fall and to Mary's influence as Mediatrix of Graces, who covers our souls with the richness of her Son's Redemption. (13)

12 Servant of God Fr. Bartholomew F.M. Xiberta, O. Carm (1897-1967): (Declared Servant of God, September 26, 2003) It was the Servant of God, Fr. Bartholomew F. M. Xiberta, O. Carm., who established a solid and accurate historical foundation for the earliest recording of the Scapular Vision, in his monumental work: *De Visione Sancti Simonis Stock*, Rome, 1950. From his article, *Annotations on the Status of the Scapular Question* is taken the following quote from Fr. Xiberta:

In consideration of these conclusions I am compelled to affirm that the Vision of St. Simon Stock, which occupies so dominant a place in the Scapular Devotion, is as solidly founded on historical evidence as could be expected. Let anyone who is so minded belittle faith in the Vision; lest, however, he make himself ridiculous, let him do so before the bar of history. (14)

13 Blessed Pope Paul VI (1897-1978): (Declared Venerable December 20, 2012): *It is Our conviction that the Rosary of Mary and the Scapular of Carmel are among these recommended practices. The Scapular was worn by the heroes of Latin America. The Scapular is a practice of piety, which by its very simplicity is suited to everyone, and has spread widely among the faithful to their spiritual profit. In instructing the Christian people let it be pointed out repeatedly and emphatically that when the Mother is honored, then the Son is rightly known, loved and praised...* (15)

14 Venerable Sister Maria Lucia of Jesus of the Immaculate Heart (Sister Lucia of Fatima): (1907-2005) (Declared Servant of God, February 13, 2008): Sister Lucia, was one of the three children of Fatima who saw Our Lady in 1917, along with her two cousins, Blessed Jacinta and Blessed Francisco Marto. In a series of apparitions to the children, from May 13 to October 13, Our Lady revealed herself as Our Lady of the Rosary and asked the children to pray the Rosary daily, to do penance, to practice the Five First Saturday Devotions and asked for the Consecration of Russia to her Immaculate Heart. In the final apparition during the Miracle of the Sun, on October 13, 1917, Our Lady appeared to the three children dressed as Our Lady of Mount Carmel, holding down to the world, the Scapular in her hand.

In a 1949 interview of Sr. Lucia by the Very Rev. Fr. Donald O'Callaghan, O. Carm., Sr. Lucia was asked what her interpretation was of Our Lady coming as Our Lady of Mount Carmel. She said that Our Lady had told her that she would come as Our Lady of Mount Carmel and that her interpretation was that the Scapular Devotion was pleasing to Our Lady, that she desired it to be propogated. When asked if she thought the Scapular was part of the Fatima Message, she answered: *Most definitely, the Rosary and the Scapular are inseparable. The Scapular is a Sign of Consecration to Our Lady.* (16)

NEW SAINT GIVES JOY TO THE POPE

by John M. Haffert

Pope John Paul II at Beatification of Blessed Isidore Bakanja, April 24, 1994. From *Voice of the Sacred Heart.*

APPROBATIONS
OF THE HOLY FATHERS

From: *Nella Famiglia di Maria*: "I Papi e lo Scapolare del Carmine" Provincia Italiana dei Carmelitani, Roma, 1996 Papal Approbations of the Scapular Devotion and the Sabbatine Privilege from 1322 - 2013

See *Catholic Dictionary*, pp. 191-193 for Glossary of Terms.

1   **Pope John XXII:** James of Euse, born in Cahors (France), Pope from 1316 to 1334. The Sabbatine Bull, March 3, 1322, is attributed to this Pope, containing the Sabbatine Privilege, many times confirmed by successive Supreme Pontiffs. (1)

2   **Pope Alexander V:** Pietro Filargo, elected June 26, 1409, died May 3, 1410. The second Constitution of Alexander V as found in the Carmelite Bullarium is the one in reference to the Sabbatine Bull. A note mentions that the Constitution is taken from an authentic copy, which is in the archives of the Order in Rome. The introduction to this copy is addressed to the Prior General and all the brothers and sisters as well as the members of the Confraternity and it testifies that an authentic copy of the said Bull of John XXII of happy memory has been seen and examined, the copy of which is then reproduced. (The Bull of Alexander V, *Tenorem cujusdam privilegii,* which contains the Bull of John XXII, is dated December 7, 1409.) Many years afterwards a pious Carmelite writer recalled a fact which others, too, must have noticed, namely that he who had confirmed the Privilege granted by John XXII to the members of the Carmelite Confraternity, died on a Saturday. (2)

3   **Pope Clement VII:** Giulio de Medici, born in Florence May 26, 1478; Pope from November 19, 1523 to September 25, 1534. By the Bull *Ex clementi Sedis Apostolicae* of August 12, 1530, he approves the Sabbatine Bull. (3)

4   **Pope Paul III**: Alessandro Farnese, born in Canino (Rome) in February 1478; Pope from October 13, 1534 to November 10, 1549. By the Bull *Provisionis nostrae* of November 3, 1534, he confirms the Sabbatine Privilege. (4)

5 **Pope St. Pius V:** Antonio Ghislieri, born in Bosco Marengo (Alessandria) on January 17, 1504; Pope from January 7, 1566 to May 1, 1572. By the Bull *Superna dispositione* of February 18, 1566, he approves all the Privileges, Indulgences, and Graces granted to the Carmelite Order, contained within the Sabbatine Privilege. (5)

6 **Pope Gregory XIII:** Ugo Boncompagni, born in Bologna, February 7, 1502; Pope from May 13, 1572 to April 10, 1585. By the Bull, *Ut laudes*, of September 18, 1577, he confirms once again, among the other Graces of the Carmelite Order, the Sabbatine Privilege (B.C., II, 194); Ibid., 10). Gregory XIII ordered that the brothers of this religious congregation (the Carmelites) neither by day nor by night should be without the Scapular, in order to gain the infinite Graces and Indulgences of the Devotion, which, as much as possible, those wearing it in death will have for salvation. (6)

7 **Pope Gregory XIV:** Nicolo Sfrondati, born in Cremona, Feb. 11, 1535; Pope from December 5, 1590 to October 15, 1591: *During ancient times many of the faithful were inscribed into this Confraternity …When the Prior General Giovanni Battista Rossi visited Spain, he realized that even the King of Portugal, by his particular devotion, wore the Carmelite habit, and so many other people of these two kingdoms. We have seen that Niccolo Sfrondati (who became Pope Gregory XIV), many cardinals, bishops, and other prelates of the Church of God have worn and continue to adorn themselves with such a noble and healthy Sign through their devotion and honor of our most glorious Patroness.* (7)

8 **Pope Leo XI:** Allesandro d'Ottaviano de Medici, born in Florence June 11, 1535: Pope from April 1, 1605 to April 27, 1605. When Leo XI was elected pope, he came without his cardinal garments on in order to be dressed in papal attire. The prelate who dressed him wished, together with the other clothes, to take away the Carmelite Scapular, which the same Leo had worn since infancy, saying that the papal attire was superior to any other Habit. The Pontiff prevented him with these words: *Leave Mary for me, because Mary does not leave me,* which is to say: *Do not take Mary from me, because Mary never ceases to protect me.* (8)

9 **Pope Paul V:** Camillo Borghese, born in Rome September 17, 1522; Pope from May 16, 1605 to January 28, 1621: *The Carmelite fathers are permitted to preach that the Christian people can piously believe*

all that pertains to the help given to the souls of the brothers and sisters of the sodality of the most blessed Virgin Mary of Mt. Carmel: namely that the most blessed Virgin will help the souls of the brothers and sisters who die in charity who during their lifetimes have worn her scapular ... by her continuous intercessions, her pious suffrages and merits, and with special protection after their death, especially on the day of Saturday (the day that is dedicated by the Church to the same most Blessed Virgin). However, images, which are designed or painted by the faithful on this subject, should in no way represent the descent of the most blessed Virgin into purgatory to liberate souls, but instead show these, by the intercession of the Blessed Virgin, being transported from this great punishment into Heaven by the hand of angels. (9)

10 **Pope Alexander VII:** Fabio Chigi, born in Siena Feb. 13, 1599; Pope from April 7, 1655 to May 22, 1667. In the year 1655, the same day in which he entered into conclave, Alexander VII, from Siena, originally called Fabio Chigi, went to the Convent of the Carmelites of Santa Maria in Traspontina: there, after having prayed, he received from Rev. Father Mario Venturino, the Prior General of the entire Order (and its affiliates), the Marian Scapular, and was inscribed into its Confraternity; fortified by this distinction of the patronage of the Mother of God he went to the Vatican and was elevated to the supreme Pontificate with the patronage, as one can believe, of the Mother of God, on Wednesday, a day dedicated to the honor of the Virgin Mother of God by abstinence on the part of the confreres which Cardinal Fabio Chigi then scrupulously observed. His confessor, Fr. Battista Cancellati, S.J., praises the devotion of this Pope to the Mother of Carmel: *On the day of Wednesday you have celebrated the nuptial joy of the light by the customary abstinence of the Carmelites, the pious throng of the faithful who profess a particular devotion to the Virgin by the sacred Scapular worn around the chest and the back, almost as a sign of servitude.* (10)

11 **Pope Clement X:** Giovan Battista Emilio Altieri, born in Rome, July 13, 1590; Pope from April 29 1670 to July 22, 1676. By the Bull: *Commissae nobis,* of May 8 1673, he confirms the Bulls of his predecessors on the Sabbatine Privilege. (11)

12 **Pope Clement XI:** Giovanni Francesco Albani, born in Urbino July 23, 1649; Pope from November 23, 1700 to March 19, 1721. During the pontificate of Clement XI there is made, even better known, one Devotion (of the Carmelites) that is so great that God had preserved

it for many long years for the good of the Church. With heroic virtue and singular admiration he vested a niece of his in the Habit of the Virgin. This Devotion was so essential to the Albani household that all were glorified as children of Mary of Carmel and wore the sacred Scapular. … Because of this, the Virgin …never ceased to bestow upon the Holy Father every special assistance with her most Divine Son, and especially during the times of greatest need when the world is completely chaotic and the bark of the Church is agitated; because the Divine Goodness has established her as a most Skilled Navigator. (12)

13 **Pope Benedict XIV:** Prospero Lambertini, born in Bologna March 31, 1675; Pope from August 17, 1740 to May 3, 1758. *In the course of the 13th century Simon Stock, General of the Carmelite order died. He was a man of eminent sanctity, to whom much earlier the Blessed Virgin appeared and she gave him the Scapular as a Sign of recognition of the Carmelite Order as a particular guarantee of her special protection; then 50 years later the Blessed Virgin appeared also to the Supreme Pontiff John XXII and disclosed to him many indulgences that she had petitioned from Jesus Christ, her Son, for the brothers and sisters of the Carmelite Order, indulgences that the same Pontiff then promulgated on March 3, 1322. And this is the one called the Sabbatine Privilege for the reason I will afterwards explain; and the same one said to have been confirmed successively by the Supreme Pontiffs Clement VII, Pius V, and Gregory XIII. It is reported that when the Blessed Virgin gave the Scapular to Blessed Simon, she said: "This will be for you and all the Carmelites a Privilege: whoever will die with this will not endure the eternal fire." And we believe that the Vision is true, and that all should hold it as true.* This Vision is mentioned in the Roman breviary. (13)

14 **Pope Pius VI:** Giovanni Angelo Braschi, born in Cesena on December 27, 1717: Pope from February 15, 1775 to August 29, 1799. To the Carmelites housed in Rome in the Convent of S. Maria in Traspontina for the General Chapter, he recalled: *Almost every day in Cesena, We visited the Church of the Carmelites, very close to our paternal house and often we lingered with the religious of this community.* And he added: *We were distinguished by the honor of the Supreme Papacy on a Wednesday of this past month of February, a day dedicated by special devotion to the most holy Virgin of Carmel, which is why we attribute the supreme authority that we carry to her patronage.* (14)

15 Blessed Pope Pius IX: Giovan Maria Mastai-Ferrenti (Beatified Sept. 3, 2000) born in Senigallia (Ancona) March 13, 1792; Pope from June 16, 1846 to Feb. 7, 1878:

The life of St. Simon Stock became so much more agreeable to us from what you wrote, because the admirable virtue of this man and his zeal not only can inspire a devout following for such a great man but can also stimulate and promote devotion and reverence toward the most blessed Virgin by means of the stupendous witness given by him toward the Mother of God and especially by the esteemed benefit of the Holy Scapular, given to him for the good not only of the Carmelite family, but for the good also of those other faithful, who wish to honor her by particular veneration with this Religious Order. (15)

Among so many devout followers of the Scapular who were then elevated to the altar [of sainthood], it's good to remember at least three who were friends of Pope Pius IX: St. Anthony Maria Claret, St. John Bosco, and St. Vincent Palotti, who was their extraordinary confessor. St. Vincenzo Maria Strambi, moreover, assisted the first years of the new priest, Giammaria Mastai Ferranti. (15a)

16 Pope Leo XIII: Gioacchino Pecci, born in Carpineto Romano (Rome) on March 2, 1810; Pope from Feb. 20, 1878 to July 20, 1903;
Indeed, with the Carmelite Scapular, and the same nobility of its origins, its widespread propagation over many centuries of the Christian people, the salutary effects of piety derived by its use and the miraculous signs attested to that have occurred, recommended in a special way, it seems necessary to request a distinction of honor with its own rite of concession in a manner that does not impose unity or confusion among the other Scapulars as one of any of them but which impresses itself upon the faithful distinctively as they say because in its initial institution the most Blessed Virgin gave it to Blessed Simon Stock as something distinctive of his Order since, as they say, the most pious Virgin had given assurance of conferring Special Favors, Graces, and Privileges to those who devoutly wear her Sign of Predilection. (16)

A Pope Leo XIII: Gioacchino Pecci, born in Carpineto Romano (Rome) on March 2, 1810; Pope from Feb. 20, 1878 to July 20, 1903.
Therefore, basing ourselves on the omnipotent mercy of God and on the authority of his Blessed Apostles, Peter and Paul to each and everyone of the faithful of both sexes who truly repentant and nourished by Holy Communion—as well as how many monks and nuns, whether calced or discalced of the entire Carmelite Order, in whatever place they dwell— devoutly visit any Church or public oratory on the day July 16 of each year,

the day in which the feast of the Madonna of Mt. Carmel is celebrated from first vespers to the fall of the sun on the day itself and they lift up pious prayers to God for harmony among Christian princes for the elimination of heresies, for the conversion of sinners and for the exaltation of Holy Mother Church, we mercifully grant in the Lord that every time they do this, they acquire each time the Indulgence and full remission of all their sins, which they can also apply by way of suffrage to the souls of faithful who have passed from this life in the Grace of God. (16a)

His Holiness Pope Leo XIII, regarding the social matter, was a member of the Confraternity of Our Lady of Mount Carmel. During his final illness, he comforted himself by kissing repeatedly the Scapular and exorted a family member saying: *Let us now make a novena to Our Lady of Mount Carmel and then I will die!* His serene transition to eternal life took place on July 20, 1903, while in the Church of Santa Maria in Traspontina, so close to the Vatican, as the solemn octave in honor of the Queen of Carmel was unfolding. (16b)

17 **Pope St. Pius X**: Giuseppe Sarto, born at Riese (Treviso) on the 2nd of June, 1835; Pope from the 4th of August 1903 to the 20th of August, 1914. *All of the faithful already or who will enroll in the future in one or more of the Scapulars approved by the Holy See, may, after the enrollment, wear instead of the same Scapular of cloth a medal made from metal. With this, observing all of the laws proper for each Scapular, they participate in all of the spiritual favors (including the so called Sabbatine Privilege of the Scapular of the Blessed Virgin Mary of Mount Carmel), and obtain all of the indulgences connected to each Scapular.* (17)

A   **Pope St. Pius X**: Giuseppe Sarto, born at Riese (Treviso) on the 2nd of June, 1835; On the occasion of the canonization of of Pius the X, his nieces and nephews affirmed that the holy Pope was very devoted to the Madonna of Mount Carmel, very much venerated in his native Riese. When he was parish priest at Salzano, he was the director of the Confraternity, which had started in 1578. In the archives of the seminary at Treviso there is a copy of a Panegyric to our Lady of Carmel. In fact, many times he kept this Panegyric to the Queen of Carmel in the Convent of the Discalced Carmelites in Venice and Treviso. (With admiration, the Carmelites of Rome also remember the assiduousness of the Pope towards their church of St. Mary in Traspontina, so as to honor the Queen of Carmel: this Devotion was profoundly rooted in the Sarto home).(17a)

18 **Pope Benedict XV**: Benedict XV: Giacomo Della Chiesa, born at Genoa on the 21st of November, 1854; Pope from the 3rd of September, 1914 to the 22nd of January, 1922. He exhorted the youth of the Roman Seminary, even though they were divided into major and minor seminarians, to be united in one spirit. For this reason he said, *Let all of you have a common language and a common armor: the language, the sentences of the Gospel, which we have just proclaimed to you, and the common armor, the Brown Scapular of the Virgin of Carmel, which you ought to wear, and which enjoys the singular Privilege and protection after death.* […Next he imparted his apostolic blessing…] (18)

A **Pope Benedict XV:** During a brief address, the Holy Father (in his *Allocution* to the Third Order Carmelites, July 28, 1917) responded that their presence was an echo of the devout prayers and praises that elevated in the nearby church, Transpontina, during those days of the octave of the Virgin of Carmel, allowing every one to have a taste of the mystical fragrance from the afore mentioned beloved feast. Then, taking inspiration from the words of the Prophet Isaiah *Clothe me with the clothes of salvation,* he stayed a good while, speaking of the admirable efficaciousness of the Little Holy Habit of Carmel, physical and moral. Above all he recollected the powerful help that the Virgin extended beyond the tomb, into the prison of Purgatory, to all who in life carried the celestial livery with the proper dispositions. Finally, after exhorting everyone with ardent words, especially the Christian mothers, to fall in love with the Little Holy Habit and to infuse this love in their children's hearts, he imparted his Apostolic Blessing. (18a)

Pope Benedict XV also manifested his preference for the Scapular made of material. He granted a 500 day indulgence for all those who kissed it. He specified, *The medal will not confer this Grace.* (18b)

19 **Pope Pius XI:** Achille Ratti, born at Desio (Milan) on the 30th of May, 1857; Pope from the 6th of February, 1922 to the 10 of February, 1939. *We ask in the recurrence of the 6th Century by when you began to disclose in the Church, the Sabbatine Privilege, to recommend to the Catholics throughout the world the Devotion to the Blessed Virgin of Mount Carmel, as well as to the lay sodalities that bear the title of the same Virgin. With this letter, we express this support. We are happy to be able to render this pious witness to the Mother of God, whom we have loved from our infancy with all our heart and under whose protection we place the commencement of our pontificacy. It is not necessary to prolong ourselves in recommending these sodalities, which the very same Virgin freely recommends, that our*

predecessors have enriched with many graces, and the diligent charity of the Carmelites have long propagated with much fruit throughout the world. It seems sufficient to exhort all those who have given their names to such sodalities, that they continue to make an effort to do all that is prescribed in order to gain the indulgences granted, especially the extraordinary Indulgence known as the Sabbatine [Privilege]. (19)

20 **Venerable Pope Pius XII:** Eugenio Pacelli, born at Rome on the 2nd of March, 1876; Pope from the 2nd of March, 1939 to the 9th of October, 1958. The Pontiff, who proclaimed the Dogma of the Assumption, spoke, wrote and recommended the Devotion to our Lady of Carmel on many occasions, for which reason he is rightly known as *The Cantor of the Scapular. (20)*

No one can certainly ignore how much love for the Mother of God has invigorated the Christian Faith, especially by means of those express devotions which, preferred beyond others, seem to enrich minds with supernatural doctrine and motivate souls to practice the Christian virtues. Among these we remember firstly the Devotion to the Holy Scapular of the Carmelites, as being the one that has adapted itself best to the character of each person for its simplicity and its fertile spiritual fruits, extensively diffused among the Faithful. (20a)

21 **Pope St. John XXIII:** Angelo Giuseppe Roncalli, (Beatified the 3rd of September, 2000) born at Sotto il Monte (Bergamo) on the 25th of November, 1881; Pope from the 28th of October, 1958 to the 3rd of June, 1963. *The Mother of the Divine Savior is justly hailed as the beauty of Mount Carmel from which the Prophet Elijah enthusiastically contemplated the storm cloud which rose from the sea, symbol of the most chosen Graces.* The blessed image of the Virgin that the Scapular offers is an inspiration to religious fervor, meekness, chastity and encouragement to trust and to peace. (Acta Apostolicae Sedis, LVI [June 31st, 1964], 77) (21)

A **Pope St. John XXIII:** *It was likewise pleasing to us (in choosing the name of John) to feel united across six centuries of history, to the last of the numerous Pontiffs of this name, John XXII...The Bishop of Avignon, who governed the Church for 18 years and died more than ninety years of age in 1334. This was a great Pontiff. His life was full of tribulations, but rich in works and merits in every way; a true servant of the Servants of God. He was very devoted to Mary; to him, history attributes the Fatherhood of the Sabbatine Privilege, so precious and so dear to those who wear the Scapular of Our Lady of Mount Carmel. (21a)*

22 **Blessed Pope Paul VI:** Giovanni Battista Montini, born at Concesio (Brescia) on the 26th of September, 1897; Pope from the 21st of June, 1963 to the 6th of August, 1978. *Letter*, Paul VI, to Our Beloved Son, Kilian Healy, Prior General of the Carmelite Order of the Ancient Observance, dated May 29th, 1965: *In sending you Our cordial felicitations, We pray that the material rebuilding of this sanctuary of the Blessed Virgin may be a pledge and a herald of the rebuilding of the Catholic Faith in England. To play their part in this work, so dear to Us, the Brothers of the Blessed Virgin Mary of Mount Carmel must bear living witness to the Marian spirit of their Order, and encourage among other devotions that of the Scapular, so highly praised and recommended by Our illustrious Predecessors. (22)*

A **Blessed Pope Paul VI:** *Let the faithful hold in high esteem the practices and devotions to the Blessed Virgin approved by the teaching authority of the Church in the course of the centuries.* (no. 67 - from the Constitution "On the Church", published November 21,1964). *It is our conviction that the Rosary of Mary and the Scapular of Carmel are among these recommended practices. (22a)*

23 **Pope St. John Paul II:** Karol Josef Woityla, born in Wadovice (Poland) May 18, 1920; Pope from October 16th 1978 to April 2, 2005. When the Holy Father entered into the operating room, he was no longer wearing his white Habit. He was wearing only a Tee shirt and on him was the Scapular, two pieces of brown cloth on his his chest and on his back connected with two cords, with the image of Our Lady of Mount Carmel. (23)

A **Pope St. John Paul II:** *The rich Marian heritage which Carmel possesses has become over time a treasure for the whole Church through the spread of the Devotion of the Brown Scapular. By means of its simplicity, its relatedness to ordinary human life and its connection with the role of Mary in the Church and the whole of humanity, this Devotion has been profoundly and whole heartedly received by the people of God, so much so as to be remembered in the memorial of 16th July, which is in the liturgical calendar of the Universal Church. The Scapular represents a synthesis of Marian spirituality. It nourishes the devotion of believers, making them sensitive to the loving presence of the Virgin Mother in their lives. There are two truths which the Sign of the Scapular brings out: on the one hand, there is the continuous protection of the Blessed Virgin, not only along the pathways of this life but also at the moment of passing into the fullness of eternal glory; on the other hand there is the awareness that devotion toward Our Lady cannot be limited to the occasional prayer in her honor but must* become a "habit" that is a permanent way of Christian living, made up of prayer and the interior life, frequent recourse to the Sacraments and the concrete exercise of the corporal and spiritual works of mercy. For a very long time, I too have worn the Carmelite Scapular! (23a)

24 **Pope Benedict XVI:** Joseph Alois Ratzinger born April 16, 1927 in Marktl am Inn, Bavaria, Germany. Pope from April 2005 to February 28, 2013. *Through a happy coincidence, this Sunday falls on 16 July, the day when the liturgy commemorates Our Lady of Mount Carmel. The most famous of these men (hermits) of God was the great Prophet Elijah, who in the Ninth Century before Christ strenuously defended the purity of the faith in the one true God from contamination by idolatrous cults. Inspired by the figure of Elijah, the contemplative order of Carmelites arose.*

The Carmelites have spread among the Christian people Devotion to Our Lady of Mount Carmel, holding her up as a model of prayer, contemplation and dedication to God. Today, I would like to entrust to the Queen of Mount Carmel all contemplative life communities scattered throughout the world, especially those of the Carmelite Order, among which I recall the Monastery of Quart, not far from here that I have had the opportunity to visit in these days. May Mary help every Christian to find God in the silence of prayer. (24)

A **Pope Benedict XVI:** Pontiff Praises Wearing the Scapular: Benedict XVI today noted that the Scapular is a *particular sign of union with Jesus and Mary.* Saturday was the feast of Our Lady of Mount Carmel, the feast to which the Scapular is linked. Simon Stock, general Superior of the Carmelite Order, received the Scapular in 1251, during an apparition of the Virgin, when she promised special assistance in life and in death to all those who wear it with devotion. *"For those who wear it, it is a sign of filial abandonment to the protection of the Immaculate Virgin"* he said, *"In our battle against evil, may Mary our Mother wrap us in her mantle."* (24a)

Note: See Appendix 4 "Papal Documents Confirming the Scapular Visions" for further details on the Popes.

CHAPTER 5 ENDNOTES

HOW IS IT PROVEN AUTHENTIC?

1   *Instruction sur L'Adoration perpetuelle du Tres Saint Sacrement de L'Autel:,* "Instructions sur Les Devotions du Saint Rosaire et du Saint Scapulaire," J. J. L. Ancelle, MDCCCX, (1810) p. 57, translated and paraphrased

2   Franz Werfel, *Song of Bernadette*, 1941; original quote from St. Thomas Aquinas: *To one who has faith, no explanation is necessary. To one without faith, no explanation is possible.* Summa Theologica

TESTIMONIALS OF THE SAINTS

1   *Mary in Her Scapular Promise,* John Mathias Haffert, New Jersey, 1942, p. 78; St. Dionysius, Cart. Serm 2 de Ass N.B.; note that the Saint says that Mary *descends* and that *on a certain day.*

2   Fountain of Elias: "God, France, and Marguerite," August 25, 2012;fountainofelias.blogspot.com/2009/08/god-france-and-marguerite.html

3   *The Glories of Mary,* St. Alphonsus Liguori, Illinois, 1852, 1868, 1977, p. 206

4   Take This Scapular, Carmelite Fathers and Tertiaries, Carmelite Third Order Press, Chicago, 1949, p.76; *First Miracle of Fatima*-1385 AD.: www.unitypublishing.com/Apparitions/NunoCanon.htm

5   *The Glories of Mary,* St. Alphonsus Liguori, p. 207

6   *Mary in Her Scapular Promise,* John Mathias Haffert, 1942, p. 78

7   *Lo Scapolare,* 2 Dedicato a Sua Santita, Pio XII, A cura Del comitato Italiano VII Centenario Dello Scapolare, Roma, Via Della Conciliazione, 14b, p. 62; www.catholictradition.org/mary/scapular7.htm

8   *Autobiography,* Ch.xxxviii (near end), from *Mary in Her Scapular Promise,* John Mathias Haffert, 1942, p. 78 (footnote #11, p. 240)

9   *Ibid,* p. 201; *Autobiography* cf. Analecta Ord. Carm. V, 411: *De Revelatione S. Theresiae quoad futura Ordinis Nostri; Speculum Carmelitanum,* IX, p. 790, N.B.

10 Deposition of a witness present at the last moments of Saint John: Barthelemy de Saint Basile: cf. *St. Jean de la Croix,* by R.P. Bruno de Jesus-Marie (Plon. 1929), pp. 360, 461 from: Mary in Her Scapular Promise, p. 82

11 *The Credibility of the Scapular Promises,* Rev. Christian P. Ceroke, O.Carm., 1950, pp. 163, 164

12 *Mary in Her Scapular Promise,* John Mathias Haffert, 1942, p. 132

13 *Take This Scapular,* Carmelite Fathers and Tertiaries, 1949, pp. 66, 67

14 *Mary in Her Scapular Promise,* John Mathias Haffert, 1942, p. 62

15 *Take This Scapular,* Carmelite Fathers and Tertiaries, 1949, pp. 68, 69

16   *The Glories of Mary*, St. Alphonsus Liguori, Illinois, 1852, 1868, 1977, p. 208

17   *Take This Scapular*, Carmelite Fathers and Tertiaries, 1949, p. 67

18   *Ibid*, p. 67

19   *Ibid*, pp. 67, 68

20   *Les Chroniques du Carmel, III*, pp. 208, 394; cf. *Mary in Her Scapular Promise*, J. Haffert, 1942, p. 180

21   S. Congregatio S. Officii, December 16, 1910 cf. Analecta O. Carm., Vol. II, pg. 3, 4; www.saintisidore.org/religious-info/brown-scapular.htm

22   *Letter of St. Therese to Celine*, July, 1894, From the Centre de Documentation, Lisieux, Theresienne

23   From a sermon of Pope John XXIII. Opening words: *La Voix du Pape* preached at St. Louis of France Church, Rome, February 18, 1959, for the closing of the Lourdes centenary year. Pope John XXIII: spoke of the Mother of God, who is honored in this Church of Our Lady of Mt. Carmel

24   www.ourgardenofcarmel.org/carmspecial.html (See *Inside the Vatican*, July 2001, p. 44)

25   www.marypages.com/paus.htm

BLESSED IN THE CHURCH

1   *A Catholic Life: Our Lady of Mt. Carmel and the Brown Scapular*, http://www.roman-catholic-saints.com/blessed-gregory-x.html; Blessed (Pope) Gregory X-Britannica Online Encyclopedia;

2   *Take This Scapular*, Carmelite Fathers and Tertiaries, 1949, p. 77

3   *Ibid*, pp. 76, 77

4   *Ibid*, pp. 72, 73

5   *Ibid*, p. 73

6   *Autobiography of the Blessed Mother Anne of Saint Bartholomew, inseparable companion of Saint Teresa and Foundress of the Carmels of Pontoise*, Tours and Antwerp, 1917, Preface, paraphrased; *Les Chroniques du Carmel*, Vol. I, pg. 114 from Mary in Her Scapular Promise, John Mathias Haffert, 1942, p. 123

7   *Les Chroniques du Carmel: II, pg. 210;* Mary in Her Scapular Promise, 1942, pp. 181, 182

8   *La Vie de St. Simon Stock*, Alfred Monbrun, in Preface by Pius IX, *ibid*, p. 11

9   *The Manifold Manifestations, Letter,* Pope Pius XII, On the Occasion of the transference of the remains of St. Simon Stock from France to Aylesford, England; *Letter* dated June 30th, 1951

10 Pope Pius XII: *Letter, Neminem profecto latet,* to Kilian Lynch, Prior General of the Order of the Most Blessed Virgin Mary of Mount Carmel, February 11, 1950. "It is one of the most important documents ever to come from the Holy See." (Footnotes 9 and 10 are taken from *Pius XII and His Heritage to Carmel,* compiled by Brendan Hill, O. Carm., cf. Mary, Illinois, Vol. 20, No. 4, July-August, 1959, pp. 51-64)

11 *Isidore Bakanja, Africa's Scapular Martyr,* Rev. Redemptus Maria Valabek, O. Carm., 1990, pp. 3, 16, 17, *The Annals of St. Anne de Beaupre,* July-August 1998, p. 206

12 *Bishop Fulton J. Sheen: Life is Worth Living - About Archbishop Fulton J. Sheen* www.bishopsheen.com/about-sheen.aspx

13 *Preface,* by Archbishop Fulton J. Sheen, Feast of St. Simon Stock, May 16, 1940, found in: Mary in Her Scapular Promise, by John Mathias Haffert, 1942, pp. viii, ix

14 *Annotations on the Status of the Scapular Question,* Fr. Bartholomew F.M. Xiberta, found in: *Take This Scapular,* Carmelite Fathers and Tertiaries, Chicago, 1949, pp. 242-243

15 *Pope Paul VI Speaks about the Scapular and the Rosary,* From the Letter, *In Dominica Republicana,* dated February 2, 1965, appoing Cardinal Silva of Santiago, Chile, Papal Legate to the Mariological and Marian Congresses held in Santo Domingo, March, 1965, translated by Rev. Eamon Carroll, O. Carm., found in MARY, Vol. 26, No. 3, July-August-September, 1965, pp. 10, 11

16 *Our Lady of Fatima and the Brown Scapular,* The Most Reverend Father Kilian Lynch, O. Carm. Prior General, Dublin, 1959, pp. 12-13, paraphrased

APPROBATIONS OF THE HOLY FATHERS

1   Nella Famiglia di Maria, *I Papi e lo Scapolare del Carmine,* Provincia Italiana dei Carmelitani, Roma, 1996, p. 9

2   *The Sabbatine Privilege of the Scapular. 1322-1922 AD.,* P. E. Magennis, Ord. Carm., New York, 1923, pp. 41-42

3   *I Papi e Lo Scapolare del Carmine,* Provincia Italiana dei Carmelitani, 1996, p. 9; Bull Carm, II, 47

4   Bull Carm., II, 68; *ibid,* p. 9

5   Bull Carm., II, 141; *ibid*, p. 10

6   Bull Carm., II, 194; *ibid*, p. 10; Didaco Martinez di Coria Maldonado, *Dilucidario y Demonstracion de las Cronicas etc.*, Cordoba 1598. T., p. 465

7   Pietro Lucius, *Compendio historico dell'ordine etc.* Firenze 1598, p. 167 (*ibid*, pp. 10-11)

8   *Segerus Pauli in vita Simonis Angli.* Spec. Carm. II, p. 433, n. 1523; *ibid*, pp. 11-12

9   *Decreto della S. Inquisizione [S. Uffizio]* del 20 gennaio 1613. B. C. I, 62 e II, 601, where an ancient Italian translation is found; it was this Pope who beatified S. Teresa d'Avila; *ibid*, p. 12

10 P. Raffaele di S. Giuseppe, O.C.D. *Signum salutis*, Linz 1718, p. 626; *ibid*, p. 13

11 B.C., II, 596; *ibid*; p. 14

12 F. Arsenio Di S. Antonio, *Impulsi di pieta*, Roma, 1704, pp. 98-99; *ibid*, p. 14

13 Benedetto XIV *De festis D. N. I. C. et B Mariae Virg.*, lib. II, cap. VI, nn. 4, 6, 8, e 10; *ibid*, pp. 15, 16

14 *Allocuzione* del 3 giugno 1775 ai Gremiali del Capitolo generale, A.C.G. II, 434-437; *ibid*, pp. 16, 17

15 (Pio IX), {*Breve* del 23 ottobre 1869 per la *Vita di S. Simone Stock* di Alfredo Mombrun, Bordeaux, 1870}, *ibid*, p.17

15a *Ibid*, p. 19

16 {*De Scapulari B. Mariae Virg. De Monte Carmelo excipiendo a simultanea plurium Scapularium traditione.* 27 aprile 1887.} *Acta S. Sedis*, XIX, 554-556; (Leone XIII); *ibid*, p. 20

16a Leo XIII, {Breve del 16 maggio 1892. Acta Leonis XIII, vol. XII, p.128}; *ibid*, p. 21

16b *Ibid*, pp. 21, 22

17 *Decreto del S. Uffizio del 16 dicembre 1910. A.A.S., III, p.* 23; *ibid*, p. 22

17a *Ibid*, pp. 22, 23

18 Benedetto XV: (*Allocuzione* agli alunni del pontificio Seminario romano, 18, 1uglio, 1917, dall' Osservatore Romano; *ibid*, p. 24

18a *Allocuzione* ai Terziari Carmelitani, 28 luglio 1917 dall' Osservatore Romano; *ibid*, pp. 24, 25

18b *Ibid*, p. 23

19 Pio XI: (*Autografo* per il VI Centenario del Privilegio Sabatino, 18 marzo, 1922, *A. A. S., XIV,* 274); *ibid*, pp. 25-26

20 Pope Pius XII, *Radiomessaggio* alla Colombia, 19 luglio, 1946, *A. A. S.,* *XXXVII,* 34; *ibid,* p. 27 28

20a Dall' *autografo* in occasione del settimo Centenario dello Scapolare; *ibid,* pp. 28, 29

21 *Acta Apostolicae Sedis,* LVI [31 giugno 1964], 77; *ibid,* p. 30, 31;

21a (Pope John XXIII at the closing of the Jubilee of Lourdes, February 18, 1959, *Osservatore Romano,* Friday, Feb. 20, 1959), *Histoire Des Miracles du Saint Scapulaire,* Doctor J. Biroat, prieur de Cluny, 1963 (found in Appendix 4)

22 Pope Paul VI: *Letter* to our beloved son Kilian Healy, Prior General of the Carmelite Order of the Ancient Observance, May 29th, 1965 found in *MARY,* Vol. 26, No. 4, October-December, 1965, p. 48

22a *Letter, In Dominica Republicana,* dated February 2, 1965, appointing Cardinal Silva of Santiago, Chile, papal legate to the Mariological and Marian Congresses held in Santo Domingo, March, 1965

23 Silvano Mazzocchi in *La Repubblica,* 15 maggio,1981 found in *I Papi e Lo Scapolare del Carmine,* pp. 34, 35

23a *Letter,* Pope John Paul II *to the General of the Order of Carmelites on the 750th Anniversary of the Bestowal of the Scapular to St. Simon Stock, given on March 25, 2001*

24 *Queen of Carmel, Queen of Peace,* Sunday July 16, 2006; *L'Osservatore Romano,* 19 July 2006

24a Zenit.org, July 17, 2011, Castel Gandolfo, Italy: *Pontiff Praises Wearing the Scapular*

CATHOLIC DICTIONARY

Bull, Apostolic or Papal is common but unofficial name given to certain important decrees issued by the Holy Father. The term "Bull" comes from the Latin Bulla (seal), since a lead or waxen seal is affixed to the decrees

Reverend Peter M.J. Stravinskas, Ph.D., S.T.L. Our Sunday Visitor's Catholic Dictionary. Copyright © 1994, Our Sunday Visitor.

Brief, Apostolic (also **Breve**)
A papal letter of less solemnity than a bull, a brief is authenticated with a stamped representation of the Seal of the Fisherman. Most often, the brief is signed by the Cardinal Secretary of State or his representative.

Allocution is a formal address given by the Pope from the throne to the College of Cardinals during a secret consistory. If relevant to the faithful, the allocution is later published. It comes from the Latin *ad loqui*, "to speak to," the term allocution or allocutio refers to a form of address made to a group of persons.

Encyclical: The highest form of papal teaching document, generally addressed to all the bishops and/or to all the faithful.

Encyclical
A letter written by the Pope and usually addressed to all Ordinaries in the world, although sometimes encyclicals are addressed to all the faithful, or to the Church in specific regions. Technically, there are two types of encyclicals, namely encyclical letters and encyclical epistles, of which encyclical letters are the more frequent and formal. The distinction, however, is of minor importance.

Papal Letters: A generic term for any kind of official letter or document signed by the Pope.
Papal Letters
Generic term for any kind of official but not necessarily public letter issued by the Pope. They are signed either by the Pope himself or issued with his approval under the signatures of the prefect and secretary of a Roman Congregation or other agency. There are various kinds of papal letters, some concerning legal matters and others of a doctrinal or teaching nature. The most important form of papal pronouncement is the Apostolic Constitution, which is usually a statement of definitive legal or doctrinal nature. Second to it is the encyclical, always a teaching document. Other forms of papal letters are the motu proprio, papal epistle, exhortation and decree.

Apostolic Constitution: The highest form of ecclesiastical legal, or legislative, pronouncement issued the Pope himself.
Apostolic Constitution
Usually appreciated "ap.con.," an Apostolic Constitution is generally regarded as the highest form of ecclesiastical legislative document issued by the Pope himself. Historically, the term Papal Bull has often been used to describe those documents which today might be termed Apostolic Constitutions, although the continuity is not absolute.
Apostolic Constitutions treat of the most fundamental questions in Church life and practice, but they do not necessarily have a universal scope. A classic example of an Apostolic Constitution would be Sacrae Discipline Leges (January 25, 1983) which promulgated the 1983 Code of Canon Law. The official texts of Apostolic Constitutions appear in the Acta Apostolicae Sedis and translations (which can be either Approved or unofficial) become available soon afterward.

Decree
A decree is a generic term for an official pronouncement announcing some decision of an authority, clarification of an issue or judgement of a court. Examples of the ecclesiastical use of the term would be a

decree of nullity, a decree of excommunication, a decree on the use of mustum (fresh grape juice) in place of wine at Mass, etc.

Decree: Generic term for an official pronouncement of a Church court or a decision, clarification, or administrative declaration of one in ecclesiastical authority.

Acta Sanctae Sedis

The Acta Sanctae Sedis or Acts of the Holy See was a monthly publication, issued in Rome, that contained many important pronouncements and decrees of the Holy Father or Roman Congregations. Although it was not an official publication at first, it was accorded official status in 1904 and then was superseded by the Acta Apostolicae Sedis in 1909.

Acta Sanctae Sedis: (Latin: Acts of the Holy See) The journal of record of the Holy See until 1909, when the name was changed to Acta Apostolicae Sedis.

Acta Apostolicae Sedis

The Acta Apostolicae Sedis (Acts of the Apostolic See) is the official journal of record for the Holy See. It was formally instituted by Pope St. Pius X in the Apostolic Constitution Promulgandi (September 29, 1908) and was first published on January 1, 1909. The AAS, as it is frequently abbreviated, superseded the Acta Sanctae Sedis and contains the authoritative texts of Apostolic Constitutions, encyclical letters and allocutions, records of papal and curial audiences, as well as major decrees and other documents issued by various departments of the Roman Curia. One of the most important uses of the AAS is for the formal promulgation of canon law, as specified by Canon 8. The AAS is published monthly, or as necessity warrants, by Liberia Editrice Vaticana and is available by subscription. It is also generally available in Catholic college and university libraries.

Acta Apostolicae Sedis : (Latin: Acts of the Apostolic See) The journal of record of the Holy See, containing official texts of papal pronouncements and decrees and the means of formal promulgation of Canon Law.

L'Osservatore Romano: The daily newspaper in Italian, begun in 1861, issued by the Holy See containing the official news and announcements from the Vatican, along with current events and editorials reflecting the opinions of the Holy See. There are weekly editions published in other languages, including English.

Privilege: 1. A special concession by authority, granting a favor (cc. 76-84; cf. Portiuncula, Privilege of the Faith). 2. A sacramental dispensation based on Holy Scripture (cf. Pauline Privilege, Petrine Privilege).

Privilege

The term privilege in canon law is derived from the Latin roots meaning "private law." A privilege, then, is a special grant by ecclesiastical authority by which a favor is bestowed (Canon 76). These favors may be granted to either physical or juridic persons by those possessing legislative power in the Church, or by their delegates. As a practical matter, such persons are diocesan bishops, religious superiors and various dicasteries of the Roman Curia.

Because privileges are exceptions to law, they are to be interpreted narrowly (cf. Canon Law, Interpretation of), but on the other hand, they should be interpreted in such a way that the beneficiary actually receives some favor (Canon 77). Privileges are presumed to be perpetual although personal privileges cease with the death of the beneficiary, and privileges attached to certain things or places (such as indulgences) generally cease with the destruction of the thing or place (Canon 78). Privileges do not cease when the one who issued them leaves office, unless the privilege was granted "only for so long as the grantor wills it," or words to that effect (Canon 81). Nor do they cease through non-use (Canon 82), and one is in no way bound to use a privilege if it was granted solely for that one's use (Canon 80).

Canon 79 of the 1983 Code of Canon Law specifies that privileges can be revoked by the issuing authority following certain formalities. It must be noted that privileges, because they are always favors, do not create a right in the beneficiary to have that favor continued against the will of the issuing authority. Canon 4 adds, however, that privileges granted by the Holy See, if they were still in use, remained in place after the promulgation of the new Code, unless they had been specifically revoked by the Code. Canon 83 is careful to emphasize, however, that any privilege ceases when the issuing authority determines that its continuation would become harmful. Canon 84 additionally directs that one who abuses a privilege is to be warned of the danger of such abuse and, that failing, the privilege may be revoked. If the privilege was granted by the Holy See, the same is to be notified of the abuse so that appropriate action can be taken.

Privileges should not be confused with dispensations, in part because the latter arise from executive, and not from legislative, authority in the Church. Dispensations generally tend to operate in a more restricted manner than do privileges. (Cf. Rescript.)

Rescript
Literally, a "writing back," a rescript is an administrative act issued in writing by a competent ecclesiastical superior, in response to a request for a privilege, dispensation or some other favor (cf. Canons 59-75).
Rescript : Written reply; an administrative act or "writing back," issued to a competent superior in response to a request for a privilege, dispensation, or some other favor. Papal dispensations are in the form of rescripts.

Indult
A special permission given by the Holy See for a person to deviate from a Church law. Permissions by indult can include dispensations, privileges, permissions or faculties.
Indult: A special permission given by the Holy See whereby the obligations of an ecclesiastical law can be waived for a person or group of persons.

Reverend Peter M.J. Stravinskas, Ph.D., S.T.L. Our Sunday Visitor's Catholic Encyclopedia. Copyright © 1994, Our Sunday Visitor. Brief, Apostolic (also Breve)

Reverend Peter M.J. Stravinskas, Ph.D., S.T.L. Our Sunday Visitor's Catholic Dictionary. Copyright © 1994, Our Sunday Visitor.

Whosoever Dies wearing this Scapular shall not suffer eternal fire
SCAPULAR PROMISE

whosoever dies wearing this scapular shall not suffer the fires of hell.

SCAPULAR PROMISE

CHAPTER 6

DOCUMENTED
MIRACLES OF THE
SCAPULAR

Chapter 6

Documented Miracles of the Scapular

A miracle is defined theologically as an event in the natural world but out of its established order and possible only by the intervention and exertion of Divine Power,

What proof do miracles offer us about the Vision of St. Simon Stock and the Scapular? The great Father of the Church, St. Augustine, may be cited:

1 *Miracles are the proper language of the Divinity, in the same way that words which men use, are their language.*

2 *It would be against all Divine Attributes for God to approve a lie with miracles.*

The words with which the Virgin promised St. Simon Stock that the Scapular would be a "Sign of Salvation" have been ratified by God many, many times in the language which He alone speaks, namely Miracles. Ancient books and modern publications are full of miracles which Our Lady of Mount Carmel performed on the sea, in fires, in war, in temptations, in sickness and on the death bed...Blessed Claude de la Colombiere wrote: *I venture to say that among all the pious devotions of the faithful to honor the Mother of God, there is no other so safe as Devotion to her Scapular, since no other has been confirmed by such wonderful and authentic miracles.* (1)

1) The very first Scapular Miracle was recorded by Peter Swanyngton, Secretary to St. Simon Stock:

On the Seventeenth of the Kalends of August, I accompanied Blessed Simon who traveled to Winchester to obtain from the Lord Bishop of the town, a Church Dignitary favorable to our religion, letters of recommendation to the Holy Father Pope Innocent IV. However, a horseman rode toward us from the village. It was Dom Peter of Lhynton, Dean of the Church of St. Helen of Winchester. He came to implore the Blessed Father to come to the aid of his brother who was dying in desperation. The dying man by the name of Walter was a man without shame who indulged in excessive behavior. Out of contempt he had distanced himself from the Sacraments during his scandalous life. He joined the practice of magic; with his habitual quarrelsome behavior, he became the scourge of his neighbors. Mortally wounded during a single combat with another noble, he understood well that the time had come for him to appear before the dreaded Tribunal of Justice. But the demons showed him the multitude of his crimes and he did not want to hear or speak of God or the Sacraments. On the contrary, he blasphemed ferociously and as loud as he could.

I am damned! Hell, avenge me of my assassin! When we arrived at his home we found a man in a state of rage, grinding his teeth and rolling his eyes wildly. One can say he was like a furious dog. When he seemed to be at the point of death and that he had lost his senses, the Blessed Father Simon made the sign of the cross and placed the holy "Habit" on the shoulders of the sick man, he turned his eyes towards Heaven and asked God to delay his impending death so that this poor soul, who was the price of the blood of Christ, would not become the prey of the devil. Suddenly, the dying man who was passing away quickly began to regain his strength and understanding: he spoke he cast out the demons, and marked himself with the Sign of salvation. He cried out wailing through his tears and said: *Miserable that I am! I am terrified of eternal damnation! My iniquities are numerous as the grains of sand on the shore of the sea! Have pity on me my Lord, you whose mercy exceeds justice. My Father, help me, I want to confess my sins!* (2)

2) The second Miracle narrated in the Office of St. Simon occurred many years after the first, for we find him now in the Convent of the Carmelites of Aylesford, so that it must have occurred some time after 1240:

The Saint had prepared himself for Holy Mass and had probably gone to the altar to begin the Holy Sacrifice. According to the rite of the Carmelites, the wine and water necessary for the celebration are given at the beginning of Mass. The devil, in order to put the Saint to confusion and if possible to prevent the celebration of the powerful mystery, caused the wine to disappear leaving in the cruet nothing but water. There was no more wine in the Convent at the time, hence the consternation of the brethren. St. Simon immediately understood the real cause of the extraordinary occurrence. He ordered the Brother who was serving the Mass to place before him on the altar the vessel that had previously contained the wine. Raising his eyes to Heaven, he besought Our Lord not to permit the devil to impede this holiest of all sacrifices. Confident that God had heard his prayer, he raised his hand and made the Sign of the Cross and lo! The wine once more filled the cruet, and Holy Mass proceeded.

These and many more miracles are related of St. Simon during his lifetime, and after death quite a number are mentioned in the documents sent to Rome about 1672, as having taken place through the invocation of the Saint and through the application of his relics to the sick and the afflicted. Those pertaining to the Scapular would occupy too much space for the present study; in fact they would require a complete treaties to discuss and explain them. (3)

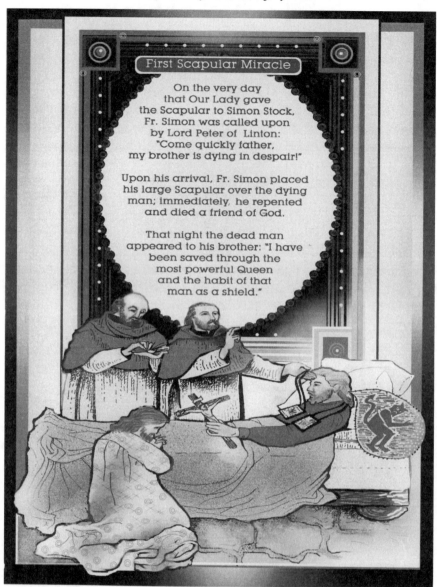

First Scapular Miracle

On the very day that Our Lady gave the Scapular to Simon Stock, Fr. Simon was called upon by Lord Peter of Linton: "Come quickly father, my brother is dying in despair!"

Upon his arrival, Fr. Simon placed his large Scapular over the dying man; immediately, he repented and died a friend of God.

That night the dead man appeared to his brother: "I have been saved through the most powerful Queen and the habit of that man as a shield."

St. Augustine wrote that the miracles of the apostles constituted a logical explanation of the belief in the Resurrection and Ascension of Christ *(De Civitate Dei. XXII, 5, "Si vero per Apostolos Christi...")* Likewise if one would deny the fact of the Scapular miracles, he must admit a moral miracle: that universal belief in the promise of the Scapular became firmly embedded in the Church without any miracles. (4)

3) Certain miracles of the Scapular are well considered singly: those instances especially of Scapulars found in tombs, incorrupt, where all other garments have perished or are in a state of decay:

There is the well-known case of St. John Bosco. Upon the opening of his tomb in 1929 the witnesses were struck silent, by the sight of the Brown Scapular alone intact among the rotted garments. (5)

4) Another such occurence in the 17th century was thus recorded by the pastor of the parish:

When Maria de Brune, wife of James Huterwulghe, having succumbed to the plague, died, she was buried in the Church of Lyswedegem. Eleven years afterward her husband died and the tomb was opened that he also might be buried there. Everything in it was found corrupted except the cranium and the larger bones. Nothing of the clothing remained, but the Scapular alone was intact, as if recent and new, not even a thread being harmed nor in any way changed in color. Brought to me from the cemetery in the presence of witnesses, it is here held in honor by all and every month, by decree of the most Reverend Bishop, processions with the statue of the most Blessed Virgin are held and a Plenary Indulgence granted. Thus I attest J. van Esch, Pastor in Lyswedegem. (6)

Father Joseph Hilgers, S.J., pointed out, the miracles of the Scapular place the protection of the Blessed Virgin, which is the object of the Promise, beyond factual doubt. Since the Blessed Virgin has most obviously indicated her pleasure through extraordinary manifestations of special protection during life for those who wear the Scapular, it reasonably follows that the benefit of her particular intercession will likewise be present at the supreme moment of all, the hour of death. (7)

5) A Soldier was hit by an iron bullet, thrown to the ground and he gets up healthy and safe:

In the year 1621, in Germany, during the tight siege of the fortress of Frankonthal [a mighty stronghold of the southern imperial domains] by the army of the Spanish King while those within the besieged fortress were gallantly defending her, one day an iron bullet from the protectors themselves, was shot and hit a soldier of the group of the Count of Verdugo in the chest, sending him to the ground. At the same time the same bullet landed next to his chest on the ground. Those who were present, watching him get up a few moments later, were astonished. When he was asked how such a thing could happen, he produced from under his shirt the Scapular of Our Lady of Carmel saying, *It is certain that I have been saved by means of this Holy Habit of the Most Glorious Virgin. They had recommended that I use it with lively faith from the first instance of the shooting of the muskets and cannon blasts of the enemy. May she be blest by all for all eternity.* (8)

6) A Great Miracle near Limoges in 1653 Source: The Documentation of P. Lejeune - edition Migne "Sacred Prayers," 1844, T. IV, sermon 18, col. 150:

In St. Julian, which is six leagues from Limoges, in the month of October during the year 1653, a Master Surgeon by the name of Leonard Tamin, a native of the village of Oradour received a blow to the heart with a sword which made a deep wound two fingers wide; and because he wore the Scapular and commended his life to the Holy Virgin, he did not die on the field but was given time to receive all the Sacraments and to give his testimony, having lived at least nine hours since the fatal injury.

I have seen the authentic declaration of the Vicar who administered the Sacraments attested to by many irreproachable witnesses. (8a)

7) A 17th century miracle:

Some years ago, in the *Carmelite Review,* one of the great miracles of the 17th century was recalled: In 1656, a noteworthy miracle occurred at St. Aulaye, in France, on the occasion of a mission there. It came to be recorded because the missionary fathers related it to the celebrated Father Lejeune. It was their testimony that at ten o'clock one evening during the mission, a house was discovered to be in flames. Each moment added new fuel to the fury of the flames. A missionary recalled that a similar fire that had raged at Periqueux about twenty years before was subdued when the Scapular was tossed into it and he resolved to invoke the aid of Our Lady of Mount Carmel. Quickly he called a boy whose faith and piety could not fail to be pleasing to the Queen of Heaven and said: *Take off your Scapular, cast it into the fire and we will see that the fire will be extinguished through Our Lady's power as evidenced by her Garment.* The young man felt so secure of the missioner's word that he immediately dashed off and rushing through the crowd, which parted to make way for him, he shouted: *Pray to the Blessed Virgin! I am going to put out the fire!* Running near the soaring conflagration he tossed his little Scapular into it. At that instant,the whole crowd saw the fire like a whirlwind in an immense brazier then slowly, slowly fall to finally die away. The next day the Scapular was found in the debris perfectly intact and uninjured though the pungent odor of smoke remained upon it. (8b)

8) A devotee of the Holy Scapular delights in the Promise of the Virgin Mary of Carmel to take out of Purgatory her devotees on the first Saturday after death:

A certain woman most devoted to our Lady of Carmel, died while devoutly wearing the Holy Habit, having done all that was required by the Confraternity of Sisters. The soul of the deceased was in purgatory. A few days after her death she appeared to one of her sisters and said: *Know, my sister, that according to the Divine Justice I should have been many years in Purgatory; but for the prayers and intercession of Mary Most Holy of Carmel, for being her devotee and having worn her Holy Scapular, I go today, Saturday, to enjoy the joys of Heaven. Try to be a devotee of Mary. She maintains for you the Promises she made to those devoted to her in her Confraternity.* (9)

9) The Miracle of the Scapular in our Hermitage of St. Anne close to Vienna, in 1676:

We have two sources of information for this miracle: The book of P. Raphael S. S. P. 699 and the Annales manuscripts of the Carmelite Province of Austria. We will follow the last source as it is more reliable and closer to the actual facts. On the 7th of October, 1676, a true miracle occurred close to our Hermitage of St. Anne, not far from Vienna in Austria. One day the home of a poor worker by the name of Andre Chrisantz caught fire. This house was a hut covered with thatch, close to the wall of our Hermitage. That year the weather was very dry. The fire threatened the Hermitage which was surrounded by trees. The Prior of the Hermitage was not at home that day. The Vicar Priest, seeing the imminent danger took a Scapular and threw it with great force into the fire, entrusting the Hermitage and the Friars to the protection of the Blessed Virgin. The fire was quickly subdued. Half an hour later, the worker returned home to find the burning embers, still red from the fire and the Scapular, surrounded by flames, was found completely intact. Not a thread was burned. He reported the miracle to his assistants, and he seized the Scapular and brought it to the Carmelite Convent. The fire was so completely extinguished that all could see that an adjoining house also covered with thatch was spared. After the Monastery chronicled the report of the Scapular Miracle, this Scapular with a certificate of authenticity of the miraculous phenomen, was transferred and entrusted to the Carmelites in Vienna. (10)

10) A confirmation from Heaven of the valor and grace of the Scapular in 1681 in Barcelona:

Source: The book by Angelus Serra - Spanish p. 252

Catherine Bosser died in Barcelona in 1681. Quite some time after her death, she appeared to her niece who was employed by the Rector of Cervallo in the Diocese of Barcelona. Her name was Madeleine Nicolas. Catherine asked her niece for her prayers, and begged her help to fulfill a promise that she had made. Madeleine asked Catherine where was Anne, the sister of the Rector who had also died. Catherine, who appeared to her, was also the sister of the Rector. She responded: *When my sister Anne died, I was present and also at [the Mass for] her internment and I attended other Masses also offered for her. She was taken up to Heaven the Saturday after her death, due to the Scapular that she wore of Our Lady of Mount Carmel.* She added: *As for myself, I was not in the Confraternity of the Scapular, but you who wear the Scapular, never abandon the Scapular, for it is a great truth that the very Holy Mother of Mount Carmel delivers the members of her Confraternity from Purgatory the Saturday after their death.* Madeline replied that the Rector would not believe her and that it would be better if Catherine could warn the Rector herself. Catherine replied that she could not do it, but assured her that it would be well believed. They hastened to fulfill the promise and prayed, and thus she [Catherine] was delivered from Purgatory.

The Vicar General of the Bishop of Barcelona examined the apparitions and approved them. His name was Doctor Molines. This was one of the most beautiful heavenly confirmations of the Privileges of the Scapular. One can suppose that the conditions imposed by the Blessed Virgin should be observed. (11)

11) In the year 1845, the *King of the Ocean*, left the London docks with a full complement of passengers for the far-off land of South Australia:

Amongst the passengers was a devout English Protestant clergyman, the Reverend James Fisher and his wife and their two children, James and Amelia, aged respectively about nine and seven. The sun had scarcely sunk beneath the western waters when a wild tornado swept the ocean from the northwest. The passengers were sent below. The Reverend Mr. Fisher with his family and others struggled to the deck and asked all to join in prayer for mercy and forgiveness as their doom seemed inevitable. Among the crew was a young Irish sailor, a native of County Louth, named John McAuliffe, who opened his vest and took from his neck a pair of Scapulars. He waved them in the form of a cross and then threw them into the ocean... The howling tempest calmed... but a wavelet washed over the side of the boat and cast near the sailor boy, the Scapulars he had thrown into the foam some minutes before! All was now calm. The Fishers approached the boy with deep reverence and begged him to let them know what those simple pieces of brown braid and cloth, marked B.V.M might signify. When told, they, then and there, promised to join the Faith which has for its protectress and powerful Advocate, the Virgin of Carmel. When they landed at Sydney (Australia) they were received into the Church by the then Father Paulding, afterwards Archbishop. (12)

SCAPULAR Miracle

In 1845, an Irish boy named John McAuliffe was on an English ship named the "King of the Ocean" in the middle of a deadly hurricane. All who were on board the ship feared for their lives.

Seeing the urgency of the situation, John McAuliffe removed his Brown Scapular and making the sign of the cross with it over the raging waves, threw it into the ocean. At that moment the wind calmed down; only one more wave washed over the deck, bringing with it the Brown Scapular which came to rest at the boy's feet!

WHOSOEVER DIES WEARING THIS SCAPULAR SHALL NOT SUFFER HELL FIRE.

12) When Our Lady gave the Scapular, she said that it would be not only a Sign of salvation but also a protection in danger. In the life of the Cure of Ars, St. John Vianney, there is an example which brings out this fact:

One day a young girl came to the Saint (John Vianney) to make her confession before entering the convent. He said to her: *You remember my child, a certain ball which you attended a short time ago? Yes, Father.*

You met a young man there, a stranger elegant of appearance and of distinguished bearing, who at once became the hero of the fete? And you wished he would invite you to dance? You were vexed and jealous when he preferred others to you?

You are certainly right, Father.

Do you recollect that when he left the assembly you thought you saw, as he walked two small bluish flames beneath his feet but you persuaded yourself that it was an optical illusion?

I remember it perfectly.

Well, my child, that youth was a demon. Those with whom he danced were in a state of serious sin! And do you know why he failed to ask you? It was owing to the Scapular which you did well not to lay aside and which your devotion to Mary impelled you to wear as your safeguard. (13)

13) In the life of Ven. Francis Yepes, Carmelite Tertiary and brother of St. John of the Cross, Hell's hatred for the Scapular is clearly brought out:

One night, Father Velasco, (his biographer tells us) while he was praying for the conversion of sinners, infernal spirits came to assail him with the most frightful temptations. Finally, seeing the uselessness of their efforts, they cried to him in rage: *What have we done to you that you torment us so cruelly? Why do you persuade so many persons to wear and to venerate the Scapular of Carmel? Wait until you fall into our power! You shall pay dearly for it!* Now, while he was flagellating himself, his Scapular was flicked off and he had no sooner hastened to pick it up and replace it than he heard a fury of demons, as though they felt cheated, crying: *Take it off! Take off the Habit which snatches so many souls from us!* They then cried that three things particularly torment them: the first is the name of Jesus; the second the name of Mary; the third, the Scapular of Carmel. (14)

14) Venerable Father de la Columbiere (now St. Claude de la Columbiere) tells us that a young person, who was at first pious and wore the Holy Scapular, had the misfortune to stray from the

path of virtue:

In consequence of bad literature and dangerous company, she fell into the greatest disorders and was about to lose her honor. Instead of turning to God and having recourse to the Blessed Virgin who is the refuge of sinners, she abandoned herself to despair. The demon soon suggested a remedy to her evils - the frightful remedy of suicide, which would put an end to her temporal miseries to plunge her into eternal torments. She ran to the river and still wearing the Scapular, threw herself into the water. But, oh wonder! She floated instead of sinking and could not find the death she sought. A fisherman who saw her hastened to give her assistance but the wretched creature prevented him, tearing off her Scapular, she cast it far from her and sank immediately. The fisherman was unable to save her but he found the Scapular and recognized that this sacred livery while she wore it had prevented the sinner from committing suicide. (15)

A 20th Century Miracle:

15) **In 1955 Father Aidan McGrath visited Aylesford, England. He had been, for many years, a missionary in China and had seen a flourishing Catholic community grow up around him.**

Then persecution came directed against the Legion of Mary (in China) of which he was head. Always, when in danger, he would go to the Carmel to ask for the Sisters' prayers. Fr. Aidan was arrested. In spite of the supernatural fortitude he had witnessed in the Christians, he confesses that he was craven with fear and fright and was miserable beyond words. They stripped him and beat him; they took his Breviary and Rosary and trampled on them. A raw impudently aggressive youth was his interrogator. They literally kicked their prisoners around. Fr. McGrath was wearing a Scapular and for three months they could not see it although it was not hidden by clothing and was plainly to be seen. He was thrown into a bare cell. From every side, came screams and the sound of beatings and of persons gone mad. Suddenly a great peace took possession of him. He lay down on the floor and fell asleep, and woke up refreshed in the morning. For over two years in the prison, that peace never left him. Father Aidan said: *I was brought up in the Faith and yet I felt I never knew Our Lady until that night in prison. Nor did I know what prayer really is until then.* (16)

Communism and Consecration

Today all the world is worried about Communism. Powerless, we have watched it grow, spreading unrest among the workers of the world, making a mockery of God, brutally crushing men and women in love with freedom, overthrowing the most sacred rights of man. Over thirty years ago Our Lady appeared to the children of Fatima and gave us her plan, her way of conquering Communism: the daily Rosary, daily sacrifice, Communions of reparation, the wearing of the Scapular. It is indeed interesting to note the well known fact, attested to by Generalissimo Franco himself, that the only defeat Communism has suffered was affected through the patronage and intercession of Our Lady of the Scapular. (17)

Communism and Our Lady of the Scapular

16) **Generalissimo Franco, leader of the Nationalist forces in the recent Civil War in Spain, publicly and officially ascribed the victory of his forces over the Communists to the special patronage of Our Lady of the Scapular:**

His first official command to his troops after their triumphal entry into Madrid was to march directly to the Church of Our Lady of the Scapular to thank her for their victory. At the very outset of the war, Francisco Franco dedicated his entire naval fleet to Our Lady of Mount Carmel. Throughout the war, the Scapular became almost the official insignia of the Nationalist troops.

The Carmelite convent at Burgos had to supply over half a million Scapulars for Franco's soldiers during the first year alone. Now it is not customary for a military general, however devout he may be in his personal life, to find the time and to take the trouble to emphasize so clearly the spiritual background of the cause for which his forces are fighting. Yet, these are the facts of history - undeniable inspiring facts. Who can dare to challenge Generalissimo Franco's declaration that the victory which he won was due solely to the patronage and intercession of Our Lady of the Scapular - especially when we remember that his was the first and only complete defeat ever inflicted upon the organized forces of atheistic Communism in its entire history? (18)

17) Our Lady has confirmed her promise with the most surprising facts:

One Sunday morning, on the way that leads to the village of Ars in France, a young lady dressed in black, walked along, her countenance signed with the deepest pain. She had tragically lost her husband a few days earlier. That poor man, after a life spent far from God, committed suicide by throwing himself off a railing of a bridge and drowned in the waters of the river. The widow could not find peace; she was afraid that her husband had been damned. She had done so much to convert him, but she was never able to do so. The day of their wedding she had given her husband as a gift, a small medal of Our Lady of Mt. Carmel which he had always worn around his neck even when he threw himself in the river. Every evening before going to sleep, he kissed that medal to make his wife happy, muttering a Hail Mary. Now that poor widow was on a pilgrimage to the parish priest of Ars, who enjoyed the reputation of sanctity in order to hear a word of consolation in the midst of her great pain. She arrived when the saint was descending from the pulpit after preaching at 11 o'clock. As he was leaving the Church, she tried to get close to him, to stop him but it was all in vain. He was surrounded by a sea of people that wanted to kiss his hand or touch his clothes. However, all of a sudden, the saintly priest stopped as if he was held back by an unexpected thought, looked for that woman through the crowd, caught her eye (remember, that they had never met each other) called her to himself all smiles and said: *He is saved! Your husband is saved!* She made a gesture of incredulity, *That is impossible. He was so evil and even ended badly!* However, the saint insisted, *No, no believe me. He is saved.* The lady could not believe it and for the third time, the parish priest of Ars said: *But I tell you, he is saved. The Madonna of Carmel reached him between the bridge and the water and inspired him to make an act of repentance.* (19)

18) In the City of Detroit, some years ago, lived a Catholic wife who was devoted to the Scapular and her non-Catholic spouse:

Many times he teased his wife about the Brown Badge she wore over her shoulders and finally she told him of Our Lady's Great Scapular Promises and of Our Lady's special protection to those who wear her Mount Carmel Scapular. The husband was greatly impressed and asked if he too might wear a Scapular. Although he realized that he would not gain the indulgences attached to the Scapular, he continued to wear it in honor of Our Lady. Some time later, he went fishing with a party of friends on Lake St. Clair. A storm came up rather suddenly and overturned their boat. The other men in the party were able to swim but the non-Catholic man could not. Each one tried his best to stay afloat but one by one they dropped below the surface and were lost. The non-Catholic, with Our Lady's Scapular over his shoulders held tightly to the front panel and the water seemed to come up no farther than the Scapular. When help arrived, the man was found with his head above water and his hands on his Scapular. He was taken to Receiving Hospital to recuperate. When he was released, he walked directly to the rectory of old St. Mary's Church which stands very close to the hospital and told the priest that he wished to enter the Catholic Church. (20) The following pages in this Chapter also contain two of the most recent modern day miracles: the Miracle of Eddie Cortez, in November of 2006, and the most recent published miracle of Fr. Higgins posted March 25, 2012.

There are countless miracles occurring even to this day, which would be impossible to record in the space of this research.

St. Luigi Orione

Era: 1872-1940

Saint Luigi Orione was born in Piedmont, Northern Italy, at Pontecurone, a village near Tortona on June 23, 1872. The young Luigi felt he wanted to be a priest and joined the Franciscans, but had to leave due to ill health. He was welcomed by St. John Bosco, but left the Salesians after a few years to become a seminarian in his own Diocese of Tortona.

While still a student, he started his life long work for those he loved most, namely the poor. He catechised a small group of boys and they followed him very much as children now follow priests, brothers and sisters as they go about their work. Don Orione drew people to himself throughout his life. They came to be with him; some to help him, others to be helped.

Don Orione loved everybody but the poor, the young, the elderly, the sick and people with disabilities were his special friends.

His apostolate embraces different types of work. In the British Isles at the time of his canonization in 2004 the Sons of Divine Providence ran several care homes for the elderly and people with learning disabilities, day centers and independent housing establishments. They have also founded and run missions in Kenya and Jordan for a number of years. In 2002 they founded a mission in India.

Throughout the world the apostolate includes schools, hostels for workers, hospitals, homes for the elderly, the disabled, the sick and the blind, learning centers, parishes and missions.

The ideal of Don Orione's life was to live and to die for the spiritual welfare of people, serving Our Lord Jesus Christ, the Mother Church and its head, the Pope. His motto was, *Do good always, to all, evil to none.*

He travelled far and wide, started new foundations at home and abroad and followed their progress. He died in Italy on 12th March 1940 after sending a loving message to the Pope. His last words were, *Jesus, Jesus, Jesus.* His body is incorrupt and can be venerated in Tortona.

At his canonization on May 16, 2004, Pope John Paul II said of him,

Passion for Christ was the soul of his bold life, the interior thrust of an altruism without reservations, the always fresh source of an indestructible hope. This humble son of a man who repaired roads proclaimed that only charity will save the world, and to everyone he would also say that perfect joy can only be found in perfect dedication of oneself to God and man, and to all mankind. http://www.papalartifacts.com/saint/66

In February of 2007, Mother Lodovica Pellegrini, Mother Foundress of the "Oblate Sisters of the Immaculate Heart of Mary," in Rome, Italy, gave this author a small pamphlet (untitled) containing daily prayers and the following Scapular Miracles attributed to Saint Luigi (Don) Orione:

Don Luigi Orione (now Saint Luigi Orione, founder of the "Little Work of the Divine Providence" 1872-1940), suffering from anxiety because of the looming eviction from the Mother House (Tortona), addressed Our Lady of Carmel (a statue):

At least You who have been a while in this House, pay the rent…!

A little later a stranger presented himself at the door and offered the necessary amount.

Don Orione was visiting the bedside of dying man and after comforting him, he praised the excellence of having the disposition to be a priest to all present. Next he looked for a small Habit of Our Lady of Carmel: he searched several times uselessly in his bags.

In turn, deeply recollected, he turned to prayer; then lifting his eyes up to Heaven and tracing a great Sign of the Cross on himself, he lowered his right hand to the bag at his chest and slowly began to extract a small Habit of Our Lady of Carmel, white as snow and ironed in a humanly impossible manner.

Don Orione blessed the Habit; He placed it around the seminarian's neck. The seminarian died that very day in almost the exact same way as Dominic Savio.

The Madonna wanted to perform this miracle so that a devout son of hers would be clothed in Her Habit!

The Devotion to Carmel is the most maternal Devotion experienced by the saints for soul and body.

It is the only Devotion that makes a formal Promise of quickly freeing us from Purgatory.

It has been confirmed by the greatest apparitions in history (Lourdes, Fatima…)

Millions upon millions of souls from every age and culture have made it a treasure and have obtained the mentioned graces and miracles. Thus it has poured out on the whole world a river of spiritual and temporal graces.

SCAPULAR TESTIMONIAL

I will share with you a brief testimonial, if you will. My mother, in a coma with weak vital signs, was expected to die at any time Wednesday afternoon. I left the hospital to drive to her apartment to get her Scapular to place around her neck. As I left the parking lot, a snow squall surrounded me, making it impossible to find street intersections that would lead me to her apartment. Deciding to drive home to another town, I followed the lights of a white Suburban out of town, unable to distinguish street, intersections or lanes. I would have turned back to try to find her apartment again, but the snow whirled to blind me.

Once out of town there was no more snow, wind, or storm Mother waited throughout the night for my return to her hospital bed. To place her Scapular around her neck. I arrived later than intended. Her vital signs did not warrant her being alive, but she was breathing heavily. I took the Scapular and placed it around her neck. I told her I was there, what I had done, and spoke through her coma, telling her she was now free to leave. She rolled her head to me, nodded her head, and stopped breathing. I am convinced she had waited for the Scapular.

Eternal rest grant unto her, O Lord, and let perpetual light shine upon her. May her souls and the souls of all the faithful departed, through the Mercy of God, rest in peace, Amen

By Richard D. Bowen, Mt. Pleasanat, Michigan
(taken from SOUL Magazine, July-August, 2001)

Scapular Miracle

Updated: Dec 2, 2011 9:49 PM

MCALLEN - Eddie Cortez is making progress, following an electrical accident back in 2006. He was shocked with 7200 volts at least twice.

His upper body was completely charred, except for the brown scapular of Mt. Carmel he was wearing the day of the accident.

Cortez says the scapular saved his life.

He's made at least 30 trips to San Antonio for treatment since NEWSCHANNEL 5 first interviewed him in 2007. He's had nearly a half dozen surgeries.

Doctors even implanted two expanders to create new skin to be used to reconstruct Cortez's face and neck. That surgery had some promising results.

Cortez says his faith is helping him through the difficult times. He's shared what he calls the Miracle of the Brown Scapular with several people. Some people criticize him, saying he was just looking for fame.

Cortez says he just wants people to know.

"I just want people to be aware of how my life was saved. Once I tell my story, they can draw their own conclusion," he says.

Man Believes Religious Medallion Saved His Life

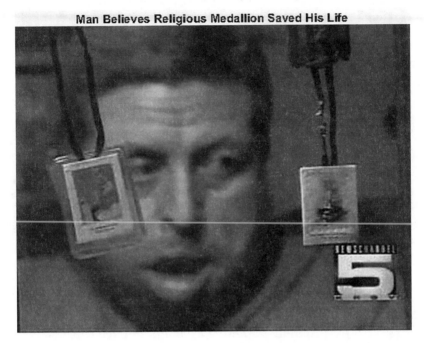

Updated: Dec 2, 2011 10:26 PM

MCALLEN - Eddie Cortez says there's no reason he should be here. Back in November 2006, he was shocked by a high-voltage line while working as an electrical contractor. He was burned over most of his body. All that's left is scars from the burns.

"As far as I got was just a thought, 'Do this.' And then everything went blank on me," he says. Cortez tells NEWSCHANNEL 5 a religious medallion he was wearing may have saved his life. "My scapular remained intact," he says. He is referring to his brown scapular of Mt. Carmel.

Following the accident, Cortez was taken to Brooke Army Medical Center in San Antonio. Doctors gave him less than a 20 percent chance to survive. But two months later, he was home. Cortez believes he was given a second chance for a reason. "I have something I haven't done yet, something I have to do," he says.

He faces another surgery in January.

Recently he met with Bishop Raymundo Pena and Father Robert Maher to see if his miracle can be recognized. Father Maher says we shouldn't be concerned about what something like this is called. "The question is: Do you believe God is watching over us," he asks.

Cortez says whatever the Church decides to call it, he already knows he's had his very own miracle.

Fr. Higgins: The Man I Saw Brought Back to Life

by H. HAMBROSE on Mar 25, 2012

Who doesn't enjoy a good BBQ with friends? When I was asked to a young couple's home for a Young Adult Ministry Home Mass and BBQ I packed my Mass kit and off I went. I arrived about 6:00 pm with a hearty appetite and was greeted by about 15 young people. Then the phone rang and everything changed. I had to drive about 10 miles to a hospital where there was an emergency call.

I drove quickly, thinking that the nurse in charge of the ER, Anne, would be waiting for me. I knew her and her husband and children from the parish. When I walked in I could see paramedics at the foot of the only occupied gurney there, so I hurried and walked in. "Sorry, Fr. John, you're too late. He's gone." Anne said, smiling. She had a lot of compassion, but also understood that I'd come as fast as I could. They were removing wires from an older man. I noticed that he was wearing a Brown Scapular, one of the old cloth ones. I reached and said "He's wearing an old fashioned Scapular". When I touched it there was a beep from a monitor, then another. The nurse, Anne, said "What did you do?" I said "Nothing!" She and another nurse jumped to work, reconnecting wires and calling for help. The Paramedics stood with their jaws dropped. The patient opened his eyes and said (in an Irish accent) "Oh, good, Father. I've been waiting for you. I want to go to Confession." I nearly fell over. I'd done nothing but seen and touched his Scapular. The next thing I knew they were working on him. He didn't get to go to Confession, but I gave him an emergency absolution as they worked. One of the Paramedics asked if I was OK and sat me in a chair.

A couple of weeks later the man came to me for Confession and told me that the doctor couldn't figure out what happened and had to tear up the Death Certificate he'd already started to fill out. The

Paramedics had come to see him in the hospital and shown him their notes. At the bottom of the page they'd written the time and place of his death and then in big bold letters had added "BROUGHT BACK TO LIFE BY GOD".

Miracles still happen. And no, I didn't do it. It just happened according to God's will. Why does He intervene in some cases and not in others? I really don't know. I haven't figured that out yet. But I do know that God has worked miracles in my life, the most important for me not being what He did for someone else, but what He has done over and over to bring me back from sin and death, through the Sacraments into His Covenant Relationship. That man still had to die a natural death to be raised from the dead into eternal life. The resurrection Jesus offers all of us is eternal too. And that's what we look forward to at Easter.

Father Higgins

http: / / www.stpeterlist.com/4546/fr-higgins-the-man-i-saw-brought-back-to-life/

The Brown Scapular
of Our Lady of Mt. Carmel

A Testimonial by:
Dr. Peter Torrice, DPM, Podiatrist
Clinton Township, Michigan, U.S.A.
November, 2012

Dr. Peter Torrice is a very distinguished, reputable and highly respected Doctor in his Community of Clinton Township, Michigan
and a very devout Catholic. Here is his testimony:

*I was enrolled in the Brown Scapular as a child and wore it devotedly.
As an adult, I was reintroduced to it once again about four years ago and
have been wearing it ever since. The following incident is true and took
place in 2012.*

*In November of 2012, while I was on vacation in Naples Florida, I was
standing innocently under a palm tree in front of a restaurant on the famous
5th Avenue. Suddenly I heard a loud explosion similar to a shotgun blast
or the sound of someone throwing a large firecracker at my right ear. I felt
something zip by my right shoulder and "explode" as it hit the ground near
my feet. Debris was flying in all directions and immediately many people
came running up to me to give me aid. People were asking me if I was ok and
I said I was but asked what just happened.*

*Three young Haitian men were particularly worried about my well be-
ing and immediately started shaking my hand in disbelief that I had survived
the event unscathed. The Doorman at the restaurant came up to me and put
his arm around me and asked if I realized what just happened. When I told
him I did not, he explained to me that it was the luckiest day of my life and
that I should go and buy a lottery ticket. I asked how so and he explained
to me that palm trees grow these very large and heavy Seed Pods that weigh
approximately 80 to 120 pounds. Occasionally, he explained, they fall from
the tree and do massive damage or severe injury to wherever they land. In
this instance, it brushed by my right shoulder about six inches from the
middle of my head. The bouncer explained that if that object had hit me in
the head it probably would have killed me or injured me to the point of severe
neurological injury.*

To this day, I <u>never</u> leave my home without wearing my Scapular.

Dr. Peter Torrice

INCORRUPT SCAPULAR MIRACLES

1) On January 10th, 1276, Blessed Pope Gregory X was laid to rest at Arezzo (Italy). In 1830 his remains were disinterred to be newly placed in a silver reliquary. There, in the old tomb, a small Scapular was lying over the pontiff's shoulders, incorrupt. It is now in perfect preservation, one of the great treasures of the celebrated Arezzo museum. (1)

****The Author personally traveled to the museum in Arezzo and obtained video footage of the incorrupt Scapular of Pope Gregory X in 2004

2) After the death of St. Alphonsus Liguori, there was a clamor for his canonization. When his body was solemnly exhumed, upon removal of the inner coffin where the body and Episcopal robes had decomposed, the Scapular lay incorrupt. (2)

****The Author personally traveled to Naples, Italy, to the house of St. Alphonsus, photographed, and obtained video footage of his incorrupt scapular in 2003. Photographs of the incorrupt Scapular of St. Alphonsus are on the following page.

3) Saint John don Bosco was buried in the Scapular in 1888 and in 1929 the Scapular was found under the rotted garments and remains of that great apostle and incomparable educator of youth, in perfect preservation. (3)

4) Incorrupt Scapulars of the parents of St. Therese of Lisieux, sealed until their canonization. Information: The Scapulars of Venerable Zelie and Louis Martin were found intact in their coffins, according to the Carmelite Sisters at the Carmel of Lisieux, France; see attached letter to Aileen O' Sullivan, friend of the Author, dated June 23, 2004. (4)

5) Pope Saint Pius X had commanded that his body should not be embalmed, contrary to the usual custom. When his tomb was opened his body was found to be incorrupt. Such a physical manifestation is often used by God to proclaim the victory of His Saints. In this case a further sign was added to confirm the great Pope's devotion to the Mother of God: the moment the tomb was opened and air admitted, all his sacred vestments disintegrated, but his Brown Scapular was found to be and still remains in a state of perfect preservation. (5)

Pasquale Vicidomini, custodian of the house of Saint Alphonsus
Liguori in Naples, Italy, is seen above holding the incorrupt scapular
of St. Alphonsus Liguori. The bottom pictures are the enlarged view
of the incorrupt scapular of St. Alphonsus Liguori.
(Photographed at Marianella, Naples in 2003 by the Author.)

The Incorrupt Scapular of St. John Bosco

St. John Bosco 1815-1888

St. John Bosco

St. John Bosco, in Italian, San Giovanni Melchior Bosco, by name, Don Bosco was born on August 16, 1815, Becchi, near Turin, Piedmont, kingdom of Sardinia, Italy. He was the pioneer in educating the poor and the Founder of the Salesian Order. He was ordained a Roman Catholic Priest in 1841 and through the influence of St. Joseph Cafasso, began to work to alleviate the plight of boys who came to seek employment in the city. He provided boys with education, religious instruction and recreation. He built a grammar school, a technical school and a Church. Don Bosco had a very special devotion to Our Lady of Mount Carmel and wore her Brown Scapular.

(St. John) Bosco died at dawn on the 31st of January, 1888, at the age of 73 and was buried in his priestly vestments and Scapular. Forty thousand (Martindale reports 100,000) people visited his body as it lay in the church at Turin, (Italy), and the entire city assembled to see him carried to his grave. It is said that more than 200,000 people at his funeral prayed to him. His work lives on in the Salesian Order he founded. His funeral was attended by thousands and very soon after there were popular demands to have him canonized. At the time of Don Bosco's death, there were 250 houses of the Salesian Society in all parts of the world, containing 130,000 children, and from which there annually went out 18,000 finished apprentices.

Many years later, his grave was opened, his body and sacred vestments in which he was buried were decayed, just dust, but the Brown Scapular that he was wearing was perfectly intact.

Photograph of incorrupt Scapular of St. John Bosco taken from *Lo Scapolare*, 5, A Cura Del Comitato Italiano VII Centenario Dello Scapolare, Roma, Via Della Conciliazione, 14-b, p. 214; http://www.marypages.com/DonBoscoEng.htm; Encyclopedia Britannica: St. John Bosco

Carmel de Lisieux + June 23rd, 2004
37, rue du Carmel
14100 Lisieux France
CCP PARIS 296-14V

Dear Aileen,

Thank you for your letter and details about your way of living.

Yes, that is correct that the Mt Carmel Scapulars were found intact in the coffins of Venerable Zelie & Louis Martin. All their remained items including these scapulars - are under seal - till their Beatification. We cannot open it beforehand.

With our prayers for Aylesford works and for your own intentions, we assure you of our best religious regards and thanks for your gift

Pray for us. Thank you

Your Carmelite Sisters

Louis and Zélie Martin,
parents of
Saint Thérèse of the Child Jesus
have been invoked under the title of
VENERABLE
since 26th March 1994.

On that day Pope John Paul II concluded the work of the process which was opened in 1956 in proclaiming the heroic vertues of the couple who were united in the sacrament of matrimony in 1858. The faithful are now invited to pray for a miracle to be obtained in order to open the way to their beatification.

The Good God gave me a father and a mother more worthly of Heaven than earth.

Saint Thérèse of the Child Jesus
Letter 261

CHAPTER 6 ENDNOTES

DOCUMENTED MIRACLES OF
THE BROWN SCAPULAR

1   *Take This Scapular,* Carmelite Fathers and Tertiaries, Carmelite Third Order Press, Chicago, 1949, pp. 41, 42, paraphrased.

2   *Le Scapulaire de Notre-Dame du Mont-Carmel est authentique.* P. Marie-Joseph du SacreCoeur, 1928, pp. 12 & 13

3   *The Scapular and Some Critics,* P. E. Magennis, O.C.C., 1914, Rome, p. 21

4   *The Credibility of the Scapular Promises,* by Christian Ceroke Rome, 1950, p. 152; footnote #100, De Civitate Dei,, XXII, 5 "Si vero per Apostolos Christi…"

5   *Ibid,* pp. 156-157; Chapter Four, footnote #108: "Il Beato Don Bosco e L'Abitino del Carmine," *Il Monte Carmelo,* (Giugno, 1929), p. 123. The information is taken from *Il Corriere d'Italia,* (19 Maggio, 1929)

6   *Ibid,* p, 157; Chapter Four, footnote #109, The text is a translation from the original testification, recently transcribed by a Belgian Carmelite, R.P.Archangelus a S. Regina, O.C.D. (The incident seems to have occurred in 1653.)

7   *Ibid,* p. 155

8   *Miracoli E Grazie Della Santissima Vergine Maria Del Carmine.* P. Simone Grassi, Carmelitano, Firenze, 1727, (p.25); Carm. Thaum. Ubi Supra, & Spec. Carm. T. 1. n. 2399

8a Miracles du S. Scapulaire au XVII siècle, R.P. Archange de la Reine du Carmel, O.C.D., Bruges, 1964, p. 86

8b Take This Scapular, Carmelite Fathers and Tertiaries, Chicago, 1949, pp. 43-44

9   *Miracoli E Grazie Della Santissima Vergine Maria Del Carmine* pp. 284-285; Capitolo XX: (Jo: Ang. Serra ubi Supra)

10 *Miracles du S. Scapulaire au XVIIme siecle.* R. P. Archange de la Reine du Carmel, O.C.D., Bruges, 1964, p. 110

11 *Ibid,* pp. 110-111

12 *Carm. Rev.* ,Vol. V, p. 338 cf. from Mary in Her Scapular Promise, John Mathias Haffert, 1942, pp. 120-121; Footnote # 8 - the author (of *Mary in Her Scapular Promise,* John Haffert) actually interviewed Mr. James Fisher, two hundred miles from Sydney.

13 *Take This Scapular,* Carmelite Fathers and Tertiaries, 1949, p. 23; *Annales du Carmel,* 1881, p. 199

14 *Ibid,* pp. 23, 24.

15 *Purgatory,* Fr. F. X. Shouppe, S. J., Tan Books and Publishers, 1973, pp. 373-374.

16 *Courage to Build Anew, The Story of the rebuilding of The Friars, Aylesford taken from the Newsletters of Fr. Malachy Lynch:* edited by Edwina Fielding, Westminster, 1968, p. 43.

17 *Take this Scapular,* Carmelite Fathers and Tertiaries, Carmelite Third Order Press, Chicago, 1949, p. 102; *Discourses on Our Lady,* O' Rafferty, p. 224.

18 *Leaves,* bi-monthly pub., Mariannhill Fathers, Detroit, MI taken from Take This Scapular, Carmelite Fathers and Tertiaries, Carmelite Third Order Press, Chicago, 1949, pp. 131-132.

19 *Vicarius Amoris,* Venerable Giuseppe Quadrio, *(a cura di Remo Bracchi)* Rome, 2011, pp. 99, 100; cf from *Memorie biografiche,* Don Bosco, June 15, 1864, translated.

20 *MARY,* Vol. 20, No. 2, March-April, England, 1959, p. 71: "Mary's Garment" – from the Scapular Confraternity Militant, Detroit, Michigan.

INCORRUPT SCAPULAR MIRACLES

1 *Mary in Her Scapular Promise,* John Mathias Haffert, 1942, p. 31; M.S. Harley 3, 383 (Bale's *Heliades*). In the list of confreres taken from Nic Cantilupe, we find: "...to these must be added the Popes Gregory X and Benedict XII, who Cantilupe assures us, wore the Scapular before their ascent to the Papal Throne". (Footnote #14, Chapter 3)

2 *Ibid,* p. 82

3 *Ibid,* p. 122 ;*Il Monte Carmelo,* XXI, Fasc. vii, p. 147

4 See attached Letter from the Carmel de Lisieux

5 *MARY,* Vol. 21, No. 4, July- August , 1960, p. 57

TOTA·PVLCRA

NON EST·IT·TE

ES·AMICA·MEA·ET·MACVLA

CHAPTER 7

PRIVATE
REVELATION
IN THE CHURCH

Chapter 7

Private Revelation in the Church

Extinguish not the Spirit. Despise not prophecies. But prove all things; hold fast that which is good. From all appearance of evil refrain yourselves. (1)

God continues to reveal Himself to individuals *not indeed for the declaration of any new doctrine of faith, but for the direction of human acts.* (St. Thomas Aquinas, *Summa Theologica* II-II q174 a6 reply 3)

Since it occurs after the close of Public Revelation, the Church distinguishes the content of such particular revelations to individuals from the deposit of Faith by calling it *private revelation.*

Private revelations are not considered binding on faith because everything God intended us to believe to hold the Catholic Faith has already been revealed to us in Public Revelation.

(Apparitions/Private Revelations: www.ewtn.com/expert/answers/apparitions.htm; *Authenticating Catholic Private Revelations.*) Pope Benedict XIV expresses as follows: *Although an assent of Catholic faith may not and cannot be given to revelations thus approved, still, an assent of human faith, made according to the rules of prudence is due them; for according to these rules such revelations are probable and worthy of pious credence.* (Pope Benedict XIV, 1675-1758, De. Serv. Dei Beatif.)

Approved private revelations are thus worthy of our acceptance and can be of great benefit to the faithful. The *Catechism of the Catholic Church* notes: *Guided by the Magesterium of the Church, the sensus fidelium knows how to discern and welcome in these revelations whatever constitutes an authentic call of Christ or his saints to the Church.* [CCC 67] (1a)

Before we proceed further, it is essential that we correct the dangerous error that since Fatima is a private revelation, it can be safely ignored. Shortly before his election to the papacy as Pope John

Paul I, Cardinal Luciani wrote in the Italian Blue Army magazine *Il Cuore Della Madre,* January 1978:

Someone may ask: so the Cardinal is interested in private revelations. Does he not know that everything is contained in the gospel, that even approved revelations are not articles of faith? I know all that perfectly well. But the following is also an article of faith contained in the gospel: "Signs will be associated with those who believe." (Mk, 16:17). If it is the fashion today to examine the signs of the times I think I may lawfully be allowed to refer to the sign of 13 October 1917, a sign to which even unbelievers and anti-clericals bore witness. And behind the sign itself, it is important to be attentive to the elements which this sign contains. (2)

Cardinal Ratzinger (before his Papacy) then Prefect of the Congregation for the Doctrine of the Faith said that indeed: *Private revelations add nothing to what a Christian must know from revelation (the Scriptures), but Marian apparitions approved by the Church in their known context reconfirm the urgency of penance, conversion, forgiveness and fasting. (3)*

Once again, we affirm that revelation proper ended with Christ and His Apostles. But does that mean that God has to remain silent, that He can no longer speak to His elect? Does it mean, as some believers think that He should remain apart and leave the world abandoned to itself? Did he not expressly say through his Prophet that He would pour forth of His Spirit on all flesh, that sons and daughters would prophesy, that old men would have visions in dreams...? (Acts 2:17; John 3:1-5) (3a)

THE CHURCH
AND THE SCAPULAR REVELATIONS

It is first to be noted that the mission of the Church is to propose the Universal Public Revelation committed to it by Christ. There are many devotions and feasts, the historical origin of which are believed to be Private Revelation. (For example), the public cult rendered to the Sacred Heart has been provoked by the revelations of Saint Margaret Mary. But it had in itself everything which was required for its approval; so that the revelations have only suggested the idea. (p. 33)

In 1832, the Miraculous Medal spread, as a result of the visions of Sister Laboure (St. Catherine Laboure) but while abstracting from the judgement it was necessary to bring to bear on the visions. It was sufficient to ascertain that the Devotion was good in itself. It was the same in the year 1846 for the Scapular of the Passion, due to the revelations of Sister Andriveau. (Pope) Pius IX approved it immediately, without demanding any official inquiry into its origin. (p. 34)

Those revelations which the Church permits to be published universally are to be understood according to the official teaching of the Church. (p. 36)

In Revelation which are promises of salvation, the only certain elements are those found in the Christian Revelation. They (for example, the promises of the Sacred Heart to St. Margaret Mary) can with certitude be considered addressed to the human race, to all the faithful only in the measure in which they concord with authentic teachings of Christian Revelation. And in this measure but in this measure only can one see in them an occasion of bringing to light certain truths traditionally possessed by the Church in at least an implicit manner since the apostolic age. (pp. 36-37)

Private Revelation is an aid to the Church to dispense her divine treasures: *These supernatural illuminations appear as an extraordinary means which Providence employs to instill powerful impulses in humanity, to speak only of the Church, it is assisted in this way to dispense wisely to the faithful the divine treasures of which it has the keeping and which at such time it left perhaps sleep.* As St. Thomas stated it: *At different times there have not been lacking those having the spirit of prophecy not indeed to propose new doctrines but for the direction of human acts.* (p.38)

One has but to recall Lourdes, La Salette, and Fatima which have given rise to shrines, prayers and practices of devotion throughout the world. (p. 39) It is clear, therefore, that devotions or feasts connected with private revelations are to be considered as based primarily on the teachings of the Catholic Faith according as they are suggested by revelation. Thus, the major consideration in the Scapular Devotion is that it begets a devotion to the Blessed Mother which is a confident reliance on her aid for eternal salvation and assistance after death in Purgatory on the plane of Catholic Faith. (pp. 41, 43) (4)

In a recent Apostolic Letter, His Holiness Pope Pius XII thus began his commendation of the Scapular Confraternity:

There is no one who is not aware how greatly a love for the Blessed Virgin Mother of God contributes to the enlivening of the Catholic Faith and to the raising of the moral standard. These effects are especially secured by means of those devotions which more than others are seen to enlighten the mind with celestial doctrine and to excite souls to the practice of the Christian life.

In the first rank of the most favored of these devotions, that of the Holy Scapular must be placed, a devotion which adapted to the minds of all by its very simplicity has become so universally widespread among the faithful and has produced so many and such salutary fruits. (5)

Therefore, in contrast to Public Revelation, Private Revelation has as its God-intended purpose not the revelation of new doctrine, but rather to encourage and lead the faithful to live the revealed truths of Public Revelation. Pope Saint John XXIII refers to this purpose of authentic Private Revelation in his 1959 address at the close of the Marian year:

The Roman Pontiffs...if they have been constituted the guardians and interpreters of the Divine Revelation contained in Scripture and Tradition also have the duty, when after mature examination, they deem it necessary for the common good of bringing to the attention of the faithful those supernatural lights which it pleases God to dispense freely to certain privileged souls, not for the purpose of presenting new doctrines, but rather to guide us in our conduct. (6)

Great indeed is Our trust in Mary. The resplendent glory of her "merits" far exceeding all the choirs of angels elevated her to the very steps of the throne of God." Her foot has crushed the head of the old serpent. Set up between Christ and His Church, Mary, ever lovable and full of grace, always has delivered the Christian people from their greatest calamities, ever rescued them from ruin. And likewise in our own day, Mary, with the ever merciful affection so characteristic of her maternal heart, wishes, through her efficacious intercession with God, to deliver her children from the sad and grief-laden troubles, from the tribulations, the anxiety, the difficulties and the punishments of God's anger which afflict the world because of the sins of men. (7)

The comparison between the Miracle of Elias on Mt. Carmel, in the Book of Kings I: 30-39 and the Miracle of the Sun of Our Lady at Fatima, taking place on October 13, 1917 in Fatima, Portugal is astounding. It is interesting to note, that according to the *Enciclopedia del Escapulario del Carmen,* (8) it is recorded by the ancient historian of the Order, Juan XLIV, Patriarch of Jerusalem, that the mystery of the Immaculate Conception, among other mysteries, were revealed to Elias in the little cloud that soared over the sea. (9) From that time on, he was called "Elias, the Prophet of the Immaculate."

The Miracle on Mount Carmel is strikingly similar to the Miracle of Fatima, at the climax of which Our Lady appeared as Our Lady of Mount Carmel. The Devotion to Our Lady of Mt. Carmel is rooted in the Old Testament: from the revelation of the Immaculate Conception in a cloud in the Old Testament, to her declaration in the flesh at Lourdes in the New Testament, each of Our Lady's apparitions are a continuation of the other.

In 1858, Our Lady appeared eighteen times at the grotto of Massabielle, near Lourdes, France, to a fourteen year old peasant girl, Bernadette Soubirous. **Our Lady would reveal her Immaculate Heart in 1917 at Fatima; at Lourdes she gave her name in this fashion:** *I am the Immaculate Conception.* So famous did the apparitions at Lourdes become that in 1907, Pope Pius X extended a feast in honor of Our Lady of Lourdes, February 11, to the Universal Church. (10)

On July 16th, 1251, Our Lady gave the Scapular to the world through St. Simon Stock. The first apparition of Our Blessed Lady to Bernadette Soubirous took place on February 11, 1858 at the Grotto at Massabielle, in Lourdes, France. She was visited by Heaven for a total of 18 days, ending with the final appearance of Our Lady on July 16, 1858, the Feast day of Our Lady of Mt. Carmel:

MOUNT CARMEL	LOURDES	FATIMA

927 BC: The mystery of the Immaculate Conception was revealed to the Prophet Elias in a cloud on Mt. Carmel, Palestine
July 16, 1251 AD: Our Lady appeared to St. Simon Stock, Carmelite Prior General, handing him the Scapular for the world.
July 16, 1858 AD: The Immaculate Conception appeared to St. Bernadette Soubirous at Lourdes for the last time,"
October 13, 1917 AD: Our Lady appeared at Fatima; during the Miracle of the Sun, and held down the Scapular to the world.

MOUNT CARMEL	LOURDES AND FATIMA
OUR LADY WAS REVEALED TO THE ELIAS IN A CLOUD, AS THE IMMACULATE CONCEPTION (Speculum Carmelitanum, 1680, n.22, p. 56)	OUR LADY OF LOURDES DECLARES: *"I AM THE IMMACULATE CONCEPTION."* THE CLOUD TAKES FORM IN LOURDES, FRANCE, 1858. (Pope Pius IX: *Ineffabilis Deus*, 1854)
ELIAS, MIRACLE OF FIRE ON MT. CARMEL IN PALESTINE, 927 B.C. (1Kings 18:38) ELIAS: "DESTROYER OF HERETICS" (III Kings)	OUR LADY, MIRACLE OF THE SUN, OCT, 13 1917 IN FATIMA The Great Sign in Heaven: Rev. 12:1:("*A Woman clothed with the sun,*") MARY: "DESTROYER OF HERESIES," Pope St. Pius V, *Consueverunt Romani*, 9/17/1569
MIRACLE OF FIRE PROVED GOD IS GOD (1Kings 18:39)	MIRACLE OF THE SUN PROVED GOD IS GOD. (October 13, 1930: Bishop of Fatima declares apparitions worthy of acceptance as of supernatural origin.)
MT. CARMEL: THE CLOUD BROUGHT THE SAVING RAIN OF WATER THAT FELL UPON THE EARTH, SYMBOL OF OUR LADY AND OF THE MOST CHOSEN GRACES. (1Kings 18:44,45)	AT THE GROTTO OF LOURDES, OUR LADY BROUGHT THE SAVING WATER OF MIRACLES AND GRACE. (January 18, 1862, Bishop of Tarbes recognizes apparitions at Lourdes as authentic in the name of the Church.)
ELIAS, THE GREAT PROPHET AND FOUNDER OF THE CARMELITE ORDER GAVE HIS MANTLE TO ELISEUS AFTER BEING TAKEN UP IN A FIERY CHARIOT. (2Kings 2:11-13)	MARY, QUEEN OF PROPHETS, GAVE US HER MANTLE, THE SCAPULAR THROUGH HER CARMELITE PRIOR GENERAL AND SUCCESOR OF ELIAS: ST. SIMON STOCK. (July 16, 1251)
ELISEUS RECEIVED THE MANTLE OF ELIAS AND HIS DOUBLE SPIRIT. (2Kings 2:15)	WE RECEIVE THE SCAPULAR, MARY'S SIGN OF SALVATION AND CONSECRATION TO HER IMMACULATE HEART. (Pope Pius XII, February 11, 1950)
ELIAS FOUNDED THE CARMELITE ORDER ON MT. CARMEL. (Bullarium Carmelitarum, Tom. III., p. 348) HIS FOLLOWERS BECAME DEVOTED TO THE IMMACULATE CONCEPTION.	OUR LADY APPEARDED AT FATIMA AS OUR LADY OF MT. CARMEL, DRESSED IN THE HABIT OF CARMEL, HOLDING THE SCAPULAR IN HER HAND AND OFFERING IT TO THE WORLD. (Interview of Fr. Howard Rafferty, O. Carm., with Sr. Lucia, the visionary of Fatima, August 15, 1950)
OUR LADY APPEARED TO THE SON OF ELIAS, ST. SIMON STOCK, GIFTING THE SCAPULAR TO THE WORLD ON JULY 16, 1251 WITH THE PROMISE: (*"Whosoever dies wearing this shall not suffer eternal fire."*)	OUR LADY'S FINAL APPEARANCE TO BERNADETTE OF LOURDES, WHO WORE THE SCAPULAR, WAS ON JULY 16, 1858. THE ANNIVERSAY OF THE BESTOWAL OF THE SCAPULAR.OF OUR LADY TO ST. SIMON STOCK
ELIAS WILL COME DOWN TO EARTH TO FIGHT THE FINAL BATTLE, (Mal. 4:1-5) *"Behold I will send you Elias the Prophet before the coming of the great and dreadful day of the Lord."*	OUR LADY GAVE US THE SCAPULAR TO PROTECT US IN THE FINAL BATTLE. IT IS THE "*SIGNUM MAGNUM*"(Pope Paul VI, May 13, 1967) (THE GREAT SIGN) AND SYMBOL OF HER SPIRITUAL MOTHERHOOD OVER ALL MANKIND!

"During the evening, the little Soubirous girl was again to be seen in the Church. In the morning, out of devotion to Our Lady of Mt. Carmel whose Scapular she had worn since her First Communion, she had approached the Holy Table for the third or fourth time," observes M. Estrade. For this fresh favor, she wished to renew her thanks. Now while praying, the voice of the *"all beautiful"* after more than three months silence, made

itself heard again in her heart. Quickly she had to go to the Grotto; she was expected there! *"She appeared to me in the usual place but did not say anything to me.* Bernadette declared. *Never have I seen her looking so beautiful!* (11)

Lourdes is the New Carmel where the cloud of a hidden Virgin takes form and the Immaculate declares herself. This new Mount Carmel of the West symbolizes a Virgin whom God no longer chooses to keep hidden. (12)

Father Petitot, O.P. says in his: *Apparitions de Notre-Dame a' Bernadette:*

Before the institution of pilgrimages to Lourdes there was no invocation more honored in all Christianity than that of Our Lady of Mount Carmel. At the time in which Bernadette lived, in all Christian families most children bore the Brown Scapular on their breasts. (13)

On the Silver Jubilee of *Our Lady of Lourdes,* twenty-five years to the day after Mary's last appearance to Saint Bernadette, representatives from every part of the Catholic World gathered at the grotto in the Pyrenees to honor the Virgin who had appeared there to declare that she was the Immaculate Conception. The Bishop of Nimes, a learned and saintly man, was the preacher. Addressing that great concourse inspired to the occasion he said:

Lourdes is the new Carmel where Mary has deigned to appear. Mary Immaculate appeared to the Prophet upon the lofty heights of Carmel, raising herself from the midst of the waves under the image of a light cloud. But at Lourdes the cloud assumes color it is transfigured, Mary is arrayed in light and splendor, she speaks and reveals her name, she designates herself, she declares: "I am the Immaculate Conception." (14)

PRIVATE REVELATION
CONCERNING
THE SCAPULAR DEVOTION

When in the continuation of time, as the hermits of Carmel were hunted by Islam as they passed into the West, the Blessed Virgin appeared to Saint Simon Stock to grant him the Holy Scapular as a guarantee of protection and a Sign of salvation. Barely 65 years later, she appeared to Pope John XXII to grant the Sabbatine Indulgence. She wanted again to appear in 1351 to her devoted servant, Saint Peter Thomas and assured him of the perpetuity of the Order of Carmel, a grace that the Prophet Elias had obtained from Jesus, transfigured on Mount Tabor. (15)

Blessed Grignion de Montfort, the apostle of the Scapular's silent lesson of *To Jesus through Mary,* made a prophecy. He said: *...But the power of Mary over all the devils will especially break out in the latter times, when Satan will lay his snares against her heel; that is to say, her humble slaves and her poor children, whom she will raise up to make war against him. They shall be little and poor in the world's esteem, and abased before all, like the heel, trodden underfoot and persecuted as the heel is by the other members of the body. But in return for this they shall be rich in the Grace of God, which Mary will distribute to them abundantly. They shall be great and exalted before God in sanctity, superior to all other creatures by their animated zeal, and leaning so strongly on the divine succor, that with the humility of their heel, IN UNION WITH MARY, they shall crush the head of the devil and cause Jesus Christ to triumph.*

Saint Teresa of Avila, Carmel's great reformer, was enabled to do more than make the prophecy which Blessed Grignion proclaimed. She had an actual vision of the latter days of the Church. St. Teresa says:

Once in prayer, with much recollection, sweetness and repose, I saw myself as it seemed to me, surrounded with angels and was close to God. I began to intercede with His Majesty on behalf of the Church and I was given to understand the great services which the Scapular family would render in the latter days.

On another occasion, when I was at Matins in choir, six or seven persons who seemed to me to be of this Family appeared and stood before me with swords in their hands. The meaning of that, as I think, is that they are to be defenders of the faith; for at another time, when I was in prayer, I fell into a trance and stood in spirit on a wide plain, where many persons were fighting with great zeal. Their faces were beautiful, and, as it were, on fire. Many they laid low on the ground and defeated others they killed. It seemed to be a battle with heretics. (16)

VISION OF THE VENERABLE ANNE CATHERINE EMMERICH:

I then saw another vision. I saw, after the hermits began to live in community, a monk on his knees in his cell. The Mother of God appeared to him with the Infant Jesus on her arm. She looked exactly like the statue that 1 had seen by the spring of the mountain. She gave him an article of dress in which was a square opening for the head to pass through. It fell in front over the breast. It was shining with light, the colors brown and white intermingling as in the vestment of the High Priest that Zacharias showed to Saint Joseph. On the straps that went over the shoulders were letters inscribed. Mary spoke to the monk. When she vanished and he returned to himself, he was filled with emotion on seeing himself clothed with the Scapular. I saw him assemble his brethren and show it to them. Then I had a vision of a Church festival on Mount Carmel. I saw in the choirs of the Church Triumphant as the first of the ancient hermits, and yet separated from them, Elias. Under his feet were the words, "Elias Prophet." I did not see these pictures one after another and I felt that a great number of years lay between them, especially between the vision of the reception of the Scapular and the feast, for the latter seemed to me to belong to our own day. Over the spring where once stood Mary's statue now arose a convent and its church. The spring was in the middle of the latter and above the altar was the Mother of God with the Infant Jesus just as she appeared to the hermit, living and moving in dazzling splendor. Innumerable little silken pictures hung at her sides attached in pairs by two cords and glancing like leaves of a tree in the sunshine in the splendor which radiated from Mary. The Holy Virgin was surrounded by the angelic choirs and at her feet, above the Tabernacle, wherein reposed the Blessed Sacrament, hung the large Scapular she had given the hermit in vision. On all sides were ranged choirs of holy Carmelites, men and women, the most ancient in white and brown striped habits, the others in such as are now worn. I saw too the Carmelite Order, monks and nuns of the present day celebrating the feast in their several convents, either in choir or elsewhere, but all upon earth. (17)

Venerable Anne Catherine Emmerich was an Augustinian nun, stigmatic and ecstatic, born September 8, 1774 at Flamsche, near Coesfeld, in the Diocese of Munster, Westphalia, Germany. She was a mystic whose visions were published in many books, some of which include: The Dolorous Passion of Our Lord Jesus Christ, and The Life of the Blessed Virgin Mary, according to the visions of Anne Catherine Emmerich. She died February 9, 1824. Six weeks after her burial, her body was found incorrupt. Beatification process started in 1982.(17a)

"Cries from a Suffering Soul"

On November 23, Sister Mary Seraphine, member of a Religious Community in Belgium saw her father (a suffering soul who had passed into Purgatory) but this time he seemed closer to her and her own suffering was thereby greatly increased. She felt as if she were all on fire.

Always obeying the directions of her Confessor and of her Superior, Sister Seraphine asked her father whether it was true that the torments of Purgatory surpassed in their intensity the sufferings of the martyrs. "It is but too true," was his reply. Then she inquired whether all members of the Confraternity of Our Lady of Mount Carmel that wore the Scapular are released from Purgatory on the First Saturday after their death. "Yes," he replied, if they have faithfully fulfilled all the conditions. She (Sister Mary Seraphine) died on Friday, June 23, the octave of the Feast of the Sacred Heart, at the early age of twenty-eight. (18)

Extracts of the Letter of S. E. Mgr. Theas, Bishop of Tarbes and of Lourdes, on the Occasion of the Centenary of the Apparition

(of Our Lady of Lourdes) on the 16th of July (1858):

On the 16th of July, 1858, towards the end of the day, the 18th apparition of the Immaculate Virgin to humble Bernadette took place. Thus on the 16th of July, the Church celebrates the Feast of Our Lady of Mount Carmel. The choice of this date for Our Lady's last visit to the Grotto reveals an intention of the Most Holy Virgin. Did she not want to draw our attention to the solemnity of July 16th and to remind us that the title of Our Lady of Mount Carmel was particularly dear to her heart? Did she not also want to express her predilection for the entire Order of Carmel, its spirituality, its Saints and Doctors and all who belong to Carmel under their diverse titles: the Carmelite Fathers, the Third Order Carmelites, and all those who have devotion to the Scapular of Our Lady of Mount Carmel?

Bernadette on the 16th of July, 1858, and before her First Holy Communion, always wore the Scapular; it is the guarantee of the particular protection of the Most Holy Virgin, according to the assurance that Our Lady had given to Saint Simon Stock when she granted to him the Holy Scapular. During the course of the 18th apparition, the prayers of Bernadette had all the characteristics of a Carmelite Oration. Silence, contemplation and love were the activities of this humble little Visionary." Let us remember and retain the words of Bernadette: *I have never seen her so beautiful!*

From his perspective, the Holy Father, Pope Pius XII, from whom Carmel has two *Letters* and two *Discourses* on the occasion of the Feast of the Seventh Centenary of the granting of the Scapular, deigned to address a strong evocative message to the pilgrims on the 16th of July in Lourdes, with links that unite Carmel to Lourdes and the grave intentions of the present hour at hand.

Know also how to be silent in your souls, dear children and you will be open to the contemplation of divine splendor fulfilled in Mary. Does not this paternal exhortation which we address to you on this Anniversary of the

Scapular, bring us back, moreover, to the spiritual lessons of the ancient and venerable tradition of Carmel?

What happened on July 16th 1858? On the Feast of Our Lady of Mount Carmel, the Virgin smiled upon us. At the heart of this last apparition the Immaculate Virgin appeared in silence to Bernadette and Bernadette contemplated her silently as well. The Holy Father took this occasion on the Feast of the Anniversary of the Scapular to teach us an important lesson: *You must also learn to contemplate in silence within your souls.* (19).

Why the Blessed Virgin Mary

The First World War was the principal turning point in the history of the twentieth century, now so nearly concluded. It was an unnecessary, pointless conflict among Western Christian nations with far more in common than the differences separating them. The totalitarian monsters of the future, Hitler and Stalin, were undreamed of – indeed, it was the First World War itself that did much to produce them. The First World War never should have started; once it was started, it should have been stopped within a few weeks or months. By any Christian moral standard as well as by any rational standard, the differences among the combatant nations were nowhere nearly sufficient to justify the blood being poured out. Nevertheless, the First World War went on for four appalling years, with millions of young men dying uselessly as they charged machine guns with their unprotected bodies to gain a few yards of blood-soaked ground. Nothing was accomplished by it all except almost to destroy civilization.

Worldwide Conflict

The principal nations involved in this war were France, Great Britain, Italy, Russia, Germany, and Austria. Despite its horrors, after two-and-a-half years only Catholic Austria sought to end it by peace negotiations early in 1917. Even then, the other governments all spurned the peace offers of Austria's holy Emperor Charles. The ghastly trench warfare continued. In February 1917, Germany began unrestricted submarine warfare in the Atlantic, with submarine torpedo assaults on ships carrying civilians including women and children. The United States entered the war in April, which had now become truly a worldwide conflict.

The least technologically advanced of the major combatants, Russia, seemed to be weakening most. The Tsar was overthrown in March and a new and very shaky provisional government came to power, but still it kept Russia in the war. The Germans decided to try to push Russia out of the war by helping to foment a revolution there. For that purpose they sent the Communist leader Lenin in a sealed railway train from Switzerland, where he was trapped, across Germany. Winston Churchill later compared this action to shipping a plague bacillus. Emperor Charles solemnly warned the German government against it, reminding them that "evil could only breed evil." They ignored him, and sent Lenin to Russia regardless.

Arriving in Russia in April 1917, Lenin announced immediately that he and his followers would make no compromises and give no support to any government they did not totally control. He called for the complete abolition of democracy, of any kind of elected gov-

World War I became a truly global conflict with the United States entry in April 1917, a month before Our Lady's first apparition at Fatima. Above, American soldiers in the Meuse-Argonne offensive on New Year's Day 1918, less than three months after the final Fatima apparition.

ernment. He called for the seizure of all private property and the transformation of the entire country under the rule of an all-powerful political party – his own Communist Party. He announced his unwavering purpose to make a revolution that would bring the whole world under the power of declared enemies of God. In only a little more than thirty years, Lenin and his successors had in fact gained power over one-third of the human race, enslaving and persecuting those they ruled with greater and longer-lasting evil than ever before known in history.

The Vicar of Christ during these years of horror was a frail wisp of a man, who never in his life would have been fit to charge a machine gun. But Pope Benedict XV's heart and mind and soul were not weak, only his body. Like the prophet Isaiah, he "cried out without ceasing."

In his first statement as pope, on September 8, 1914, he mourned the bloodshed and pleaded for a quick end to the war just begun – gently, lovingly, yet with a vein of iron, a reminder that all men, including rulers, will ultimately face a judge untouchable by propaganda or force. "The rulers of the peoples," Pope Benedict XV said, should "be satisfied with the ruin already wrought."

In his first encyclical, *Ad Beatissimi*, issued November 1, 1914, he asked sadly, surveying the ruthlessly and unnecessarily warring Christian peoples whom God had entrusted to his spiritual care: "Who could realize that they are brethren, children of the same Father in Heaven?" His encyclical closed with a call for prayer to Christ and to the Blessed Virgin Mary, "who bore the Prince of Peace."

On Christmas Eve 1914, in an unforgettable allocution to the cardinals, bish-

4

Came to Fatima

By Warren H. Carroll, Ph.D.

ops and other leaders of the Church in Rome, the pope cried: "May the fratricidal weapons fall to the ground! Already they are too bloodstained; let them at last fall! And may the hands of those who have had to wield them return to the labors of industry and commerce, to the works of civilization and peace."

The Pope Pleas for Peace

On May 5, 1917, Pope Benedict XV, in a letter to his secretary of state, recalled his repeated pleas for peace from the beginning of the war:

"Our earnestly pleading voice, invoking the end of the vast conflict, the suicide of civilized Europe, was then and has remained ever since unheard. Indeed, it seemed that the dark tide of hatred grew higher and wider among the belligerent nations, and drew other countries into its frightful sweep, multiplying ruin and massacre....Since all graces which the Author of all good deigns to grant to the poor children of Adam, by a loving design of his Divine Providence are dispensed through the hands of the most Holy Virgin, we wish that the petition of her most afflicted children, more than ever in this terrible hour, may turn with lively confidence to the august Mother of God."

The Ultimate Appeal

He directed that the invocation "Queen of peace, pray for us" be added permanently to the Litany of Loreto; and then, fixing his soul's gaze on her who had borne God in her womb and in her arms at Bethlehem, the loving mother of all Christians as she is the loving Mother of God, the "Pope of peace" made his ultimate appeal:

"To Mary, then, who is the Mother of Mercy and omnipotent by grace, let loving and devout appeal go up from every corner of the earth – from noble temples and tiniest chapels, from royal palaces and mansions of the rich as from the poorest hut – from every place where a faithful soul finds shelter – from blood-drenched plains and seas. Let it bear to her the anguished cry of mothers and wives, the wailing of innocent little ones, the sighs of every generous heart; that her most tender and benign solicitude may be moved and the peace we ask for be obtained for our agitated world."

The Blessed Virgin Mary heard, and answered – and not only by words, or by the granting of favors. She came herself, in person, eight days later, May 13, 1917, on a glorious spring day in the heart of Portugal, at Fatima, to the children Lucia, Jacinta and Francisco, to ask them to "say the Rosary every day, to obtain peace for the world, and the end of the war."

Russian Tragedy

Two months later, in her third appearance to the children at Fatima, she spoke specifically of the horror that was coming to Russia as a result of the tragedy of the First World War. By then the Communists, though never supported by more than a relatively small minority of the Russian people, were moving steadily toward power in the growing chaos of a nation torn apart by the horrors of the World War and by domestic violence. Our Lady said:

"I come to ask the consecration of Russia to my Immaculate Heart and the Communion of reparation on the first Saturdays. If they listen to my requests, Russia will be converted and there will be peace. If not, she will scatter her errors throughout the world, provoking wars and persecutions of the Church. The good will be martyred, the Holy Father will have much to suffer, various nations will be annihilated. In the end my Immaculate Heart will triumph. The Holy Father will consecrate Russia to me, and it will be converted, and a period of peace will be granted to the world."

Three months later, in the last of the Blessed Virgin Mary's Fatima apparitions, came the great Miracle of the Sun. The next month after that came the

Following continual rejection of his peace proposals by world leaders, on May 5, 1917, Pope Benedict XV called upon Mary, the Mother of Mercy, to end the war. Eight days later the Virgin Mary appeared at Fatima.

Communist Revolution in Russia which did indeed scatter errors, wars and persecutions throughout the world. Mary's warning and her promise resounded down the years. All over the world, millions of people prayed the Rosary as she had asked and pleaded for rescue from heaven. None prayed more devoutly and passionately than the victims of Communist rule in Eastern Europe and Russia, where although the Fatima prophecy was never allowed to be publicly mentioned, it was very widely known. It assured them that God appreciated their sufferings and accepted their sacrifices and in the end would deliver them from the enormous evil which held them in its grip.

Most of the Fatima prophecy has now been fulfilled. We can fully expect the conversion of Russia to come in the end, because the Mother of God promised it

FATIMA

It is absolutely certain that revelation as such was completed with Christ and His Apostles. What happens then if these private revelations confirm and emphasize certain truths that are found in this great revelation? This is exactly what happens with Fatima. Fatima confirms the existence of angels and of demons that the (Progressives) try to eliminate. Fatima confirms the mystery of the Eucharist which Modernists have stripped of all meaning. Fatima confirms the existence of Hell, which is simply denied today. Fatima requires prayer and penance, values to which people today consequently dispense themselves. (19a)

In the Old Testament, God repeatedly sent the Prophets to remind His people of their eternal destiny, to warn them and even punish them when they strayed from the path of salvation. Today, he sends the Queen of Prophets herself, entrusted with the same basic message: *Pray, do penance for your sins, amend your lives, or God will be compelled to let fall the arm of His Justice.*

In his Forward to the first edition of Sr. Lucia's Memoirs, Professor A. Martins, S.J., of Portugal writes:

Fatima reminds us that wars and cataclysms are God's punishment for our sins. Does not Holy Scripture say that Sodom was destroyed because there were not ten just men in it and Jerusalem, because it had not understood the message of peace? And what is meant by the Flood and the forty years of God's people in the desert and the captivity in Babylon? ...Fatima is an alarm signal to men to amend their lives. It is also a loving invitation for sincere contrition, an indispensable way to obtain pardon of God our Father. (19b)

On May 13, 1981, in St. Peter's Square, exactly 64 years after the first apparition of the Virgin Mary to the three shepherd children in Fatima, Portugal, Pope Saint John Paul II was shot by a Turkish gunman. One of the bullets that entered his body missed his central aorta by a few millimeters. Just before his surgery, he told the doctors: *Don't take off the Scapular* and the surgeons left it on. While he was in the hospital, he reviewed the Church's documentation of Fatima and the Third Secret of Fatima. He was convinced that Our Lady of Fatima had saved his life. In 1982, as a measure of his gratitude, he gave the bullet that was extracted from his abdomen to the Shrine; the bullet today forms part of the crown of the statue of the Virgin of Fatima. (19c)

On May 13, 2010, Pope Benedict XVI, now Emeritus Pope, in his homily, addressed an enormous crowd of Pilgrims, devoutly gathered at the feet of Our Lady of Fatima, on the Tenth Anniversary of the beatification of the shepherd children of Fatima, Jacinta and Francisco Marto with these words: *I too have come as a pilgrim to Fatima, to this "home" from which Mary chose to speak to us in modern times. I have come to Fatima to rejoice in Mary's presence and maternal protection… We would be mistaken to think that Fatima's prophetic mission is complete… In seven years you will return here to celebrate the centenary of the first visit made by the Lady "come from heaven", the Teacher who introduced the little seers to a deep knowledge of the Love of the Blessed Trinity and led them to savor God himself as the most beautiful reality of human existence… May the seven years which separate us from the Centenary of the Apparitions hasten the fulfillment of the prophecy of the Triumph of the Immaculate Heart of Mary, to the glory of the Most Holy Trinity.* (19d)

The maternal role of Our Lady has seldom been manifested so strongly as at Fatima. *The apparitions of Our Lady at Fatima,* said the Cardinal Patriarch of Lisbon, on 13 May, 1972, *are an eloquent expression for our times of the role the Virgin Mary fulfills in the mystery of the Word Incarnate and of the Mystical Body. She is the Messenger from Heaven who points the way to Jesus Christ, the only way, the truth and the life. She is the motherly heart who offers refuge to her children, to lead them to God by prayer and by penance. She is the cry of the supplication who begs of men not to offend God anymore, for He is already too greatly offended. The Virgin of Fatima is, after all, the Virgin of Nazareth, of Bethlehem, of Cana, of Galilee, of Calvary and of Pentecost, ever eager to give Christ to the world and the world to Christ.* (19e)

Today, Fatima stands as a shining symbol of hope in a world dominated by the spectre of mass apostacy from God…Venerable Archbishop Fulton J. Sheen wrote: *Devotion to Our Lady of Fatima is actually a petition to save man from nature made destructive through the rebellious intellect of man…How shall we overcome the spirit of Satan except by the power of that Woman to whom Almighty God has given the mandate to crush the head of the serpent?* (19f)

History has recorded as already having taken place many of the terrible disasters predicted by the Mother of God (at Fatima) in 1917. These things cannot be undone. But we still have the future ahead of us. It can be a happy future, filled with peace, if we live our lives according to the requests of Our Lady of Fatima and her "Peace Plan From Heaven":

1   Penance and Reparation, (to amend our lives, to fulfill our daily duties, according to our state in life and to obey the Commandments of God);

2   The Daily Rosary (Our Lady asked at Fatima for the recitation of the Rosary daily);

3   The Five First Saturday Devotions (going to Confession, receiving Holy Communion reciting five decades of the Holy Rosary and spending 15 minutes with Our Lady, meditating on the mysteries of the Rosary—all with the intention of making reparation to her);

4   Consecration to the Immaculate Heart of Mary through the wearing of the Brown Scapular as a sign of personal Consecration to her, and make acts of reparation to her Immaculate Heart.

Sister Lucia has said that all Catholics should wear the Brown Scapular as part of the Fatima Message. She said: *The Rosary and the Scapular are inseparable.* (19g)

Venerable Pope Pius XII, in his Apostolic Letter on the 7th Centenary of the Scapular Vision called the Scapular: *The Sign of our Consecration to the Immaculate Heart of Mary, which We in recent times have so strongly recommended.* (Pope Pius XII: *Letter: Neminem profecto latet,* February 11, 1950)

They should in a special manner consecrate themselves as children to the Mother of God, the Virgin of Carmel, honor her with the most fervent piety and fully entrust themselves to her most powerful patronage. If they act in this way, she will be their watchful comforter and most loving helper, not only during this life and on earth which is troubled by so many dangers and storms, but especially in the final hour of death; and if by chance they must be purified by the fire of Purgatory, she will be a source of Divine Grace and assistance.

(Venerable Pope Pius XII, *Letter: Ex obsequentissimis litteris,* "On the Occasion of the International Third Order Congress held at Fatima," August, 1957, April 3, 1957)

HEAVEN VISITS EARTH AGAIN! OUR LADY OF FATIMA

For six months in succession, from May 13 to October 13, 1917, Our Blessed Lady appeared to three shepherd children: Lucia, Jacinta and Francisco at the Cova d'Iria, in Fatima, Portugal.

The Miracle of the Sun: October 13, 1917, Fatima

The Apparitions (at Fatima) began on May 13, 1917 and continued each month until October 13, the day of the final Apparition ... Fr. De Marchi's account of the September Apparition ... (Our Lady said to Lucia): *Continue to say the Rosary every day to bring about the end of the war. Do not fail to be here on October 13 when St. Joseph will come with the Child to give peace to the world, Our Lord to bless the people, and then you will see my image as I am invoked as Our Lady of Sorrows, and as Our Lady of Carmel.* On October 13, the Blessed Virgin kept her promise to the children. (20)

During the official investigation made by the Diocesan Tribunal at the Asilo of the Sisters of St. Dorothy in Vilar, Lucy added the interesting detail that Our Lady held the Scapular in her hand: *It seemed to me that there followed another figure which appeared to be Our Lady of Carmel; for she held something hanging from her right hand.* (21)

October 13, 1917, during the Miracle of the Sun: The Mother of God manifested herself as *Brighter than the sun.* She opened her hands and made them reflect on the sun. As she ascended, the reflection of the light emanating from her own body continued to be projected on the sun itself. In other words, Our Lady shone more brightly than the sun. The little shepherds then beheld near the sun, the other promised visions. St. Joseph appeared with the Child Jesus blessing the world and with Our Lady robed in white with a blue mantle. St. Joseph and the Child Jesus made the Sign of the Cross with their hands. This vision vanished. Next they saw Our Lord and Our Lady (who appeared in aspect to be Our Lady of Sorrows).

Next came an apparition of Our Lady of Mount Carmel holding the Brown Scapular down to the world indicating (as Lucia later interpreted the gesture) that she still desired people to wear it as a sign of their Consecration to the Immaculate Heart of Mary. (22)

It was her last moving appeal to souls to wear her Scapular as a sign of Consecration to her Immaculate Heart. (22a)

The Brown Scapular of Our Lady of Mount Carmel

October 13, 1930: The cult of Fatima was officially recognized by the Bishop of the Diocese.

On May 13, 1931 the Portuguese hierarchy assembled at Cova da Iria, where, in the presence of 300,000 pilgrims from all parts of the nation, the new Patriarch, Dom Manual Goncalves Cardinal Cerejeira read an ACT OF CONSECRATION in which he publicly recognized the place of Our Lady of Mount Carmel in the Fatima message; there was no doubt in the Cardinal's mind about the Apparition of Our Lady of Mount Carmel. Here are some excerpts from his Act of Consecration:

... "Our Lady of the Rosary, whose heart is the true image of the heart of thy Son, thou has so perfectly lived the life of Jesus that the Savior shines in thy heart like the unveiled Sacrament" ..."

..."Our Lady of the Seven Sorrows, whose heart was pierced with a sword of sorrow, who in that heart didst endure all the sufferings of the Son, in order at the price of His blood and thy tears to win mercy for us and to save us from the fires of hell;"

... "Our Lady of Mount Carmel, whose maternal heart forgets none of thy children, eager to unite all with thee in paradise, even those whom we have already forgotten, thou relieves the sufferings of the souls in Purgatory, especially of the most abandoned ..."

Fatima therefore is a striking confirmation of the ancient pieties of the Rosary and the Scapular of Our Lady, both of which go back to the Ages of Faith when love for her permeated the whole of life and all found the beauty of life in her. (23)

His Excellency, Dom Joseph Alves Coreira da Silva, Bishop of Leira, on the occasion of the Seventh Centenary of the Scapular, addressed the following pastoral letter to his flock:

This year we celebrate the Seventh Centenary of the gift of the holy Scapular by the Blessed Virgin to her faithful servant Simon Stock (July 16, 1251)... it goes without saying that our motive in wearing the Scapular must not be pride or superstition, but a sincere and firm hope that the Blessed Virgin will grant us the grace of conversion and of final perseverance. (24)

August 15, 1950, the Feast of Our Lady's Assumption, Lucia gave an interview to Fr. Howard Rafferty, O. Carm.: (Fr. Rafferty): *Can we be sure she meant by her appearance dressed as Our Lady of Carmel and holding the Scapular that she wanted the Scapular as part of the Message?*

Lucy answered, *Yes.*

(Fr. Rafferty): *In giving the conditions of the Fatima Message, is it correct to say that the Scapular is one of the conditions?*

Lucy answered: *Yes, certainly.*

(Fr. Rafferty): *Is the wearing of the Scapular as important as the saying of the daily Rosary?*

Lucy answered: *Yes, the Rosary and the Scapular are inseparable.* (25)

And so it is that this triple manifestation was nothing more than a more distinct and a more tangible illustration of the title *Queen of the Most Holy Rosary.* (25a)

One can only hope that the faithful throughout the world will take to heart this message of the final Apparition and that the old pieties of the Rosary, of the Sorrows and of the Scapular will return to hold the place they once held in popular devotion. (26)

"IL CUORE CHE SI DONA A TUTTI" (A HEART GIVEN FOR ALL)

By: Emilio Marini, AMI Press, Washington, New Jersey, 1972

In 1917, Our Blessed Lady spoke these words at Fatima: "God wishes to establish in the world, devotion to my Immaculate Heart to obtain the conversion of Russia, in this way, she will be saved."

The Message of Fatima was preannounced by the Angel of Peace of Portugal, and by the Eucharist. It was then completed by Our Blessed Lady. From the first apparition of Our Lady, she manifested herself with a heart full of sadness, and in the sixth and last apparition, that of October 13, 1917, after the Miracle of the Sun, the three visionaries of Fatima (Lucia, Francisco, and Jacinta) saw Our Lady with the Holy Family, in the act of blessing the world, they also saw Our Lord blessing the people of the world and finally, after Our Lady revealed herself as Our Lady of the Rosary, she appeared in succession as Our Lady of Sorrows and Our Lady of Mount Carmel.

After the Rosary, the greatest weapon we have to fight against all the difficulties that hold back devotion to the Immaculate Heart of Mary is that of the Scapular. Our Lady held it in her hand during the last apparition at Fatima, therefore, Lucia said: "The Rosary and the Scapular are inseparable." This opinion of Lucia was validated during the Second Vatican Council (at the Marian and Marilogical Congress of 1964 in Republica Dominicana).

Wear the Scapular, recite the Rosary, and live the Morning Offering. Practicing the Five First Saturday Devotions in response to Our Lady's wishes will help us; and when a sufficient number of people follow Our Lady's requests, the world will experience the Triumph of the Immaculate Heart.

Protestant Christianity rejects Our Lady's role as Mediatrix...non Catholic Christians speak of the saving power of Christ, however, the Redemption itself depended on the consent of Our Lady in accepting to become the Mother of God.

This Sign of Consecration (the Scapular) becomes particularly efficacious when it is integrated with the habit of reciting the Rosary and the other pious practices requested by Our Lady at Fatima. This is, then, the principal reason why the Scapular and the Rosary are inseparable. (27)

PRIVATE REVELATION

In the early part of the 13th century, St. Dominic, St. Francis of Assisi and St. Angelus the Carmelite, accidentally met one day on a street comer in Rome (a Chapel still stands at this spot to commemorate this event). St. Dominic then uttered a famous prophecy: "To my Order, the Blessed Virgin will entrust a Devotion to be known as the Rosary and to your Order, Angelus, she will entrust a Devotion to be known as the Scapular. One day, through the Rosary and the Scapular, she will save the world." http://www.willingshepherds.org/Rosary.htm This story is found in a book on the scapular by Fr. Marianus Ventimiglia, published in 1773 in Naples. *Fatima, the Great Sign,* Francis Johnston, Rockford, Illinois, 1980, p. III

"THE ROSARY AND SCAPULAR ARE INSEPARABLE"

(Testimony of Lucia to whom Our Lady appeared at Fatima in 1917 with the Rosary and Scapular.)

Blessed Virgin Mary to Saint Dominic,
"One Day through the Rosary and Scapular I will save the World."

IMAGO CONFRATERNITATIS. B.V.
MARIÆ. DE MONTE CARMELI.

THE MAGNIFICENT BEAUTY OF CHRISTIAN ART

A work of art is a product of the creative capacity of the human being who in questioning visible reality, seeks to discover its deep meaning and to communicate it through the language of forms, color and sound. Art is able to manifest and make visible the human need to surpass the visible, it expresses the thirst and the quest for the infinite.

Towns and villages throughout the world contain treasures of art that express faith and beckon to us to return to our relationship with God. May the visits to places filled with art, then, not only be opportunities for cultural enrichment — that too — but may they become above all moments of grace, incentives to strengthen our bond and our dialogue with the Lord so that — in switching from simple external reality to the more profound reality it expresses — we may pause to contemplate the ray of beauty that strikes us to the quick, that almost "wounds" us, and that invites us to rise toward God.

BENEDICT XVI
GENERAL AUDIENCE

Castel Gandolfo Castel Gandolfo Wednesday, 31 August 2011

Sacred art, founded on Christian principles, faithfully expresses the simple and spontaneous piety of the faithful. Ever since the Council of Ephesus, it has pictured Mary as Queen and Empress, seated on a royal throne, adorned with royal emblems, crowned with a diadem, surrounded by angels and saints and dominating, not only the forces of nature but also the evil influence of Satan. Pictures and images of the Blessed Virgin Mary have always given expression to her royal dignity and have been noted for their artistic workmanship and beauty. (Pope Pius XII: Encycl. Ad caeli Reginam, October 11, 1954 Christian Art)

Under the reign of King (Saint) Constantine the Great in the 4th century, freedom to practice the faith was restored to the Christian world in Rome. His heroic efforts to restore freedom to the Christians to practice their faith openly, without fear of persecution, encompassed the renaissance of what we know today as "Iconography." Iconography or Christian Art was and still is used today, as a means of spreading the Gospel, Christianity and most beautifully, silent devotion to the Mother of God. In the early Christian Church, when faith in God could be practiced only in the Catacombs for fear of persecution and death, the ancient carvings and depictions scrawled into the rocks of the ground underneath the earth revealed the painful struggle of the early Christian Martyrs to cradle the Faith and were used as a means of historical recordings and of spreading the teachings of Christ.

St. Basil the Great spoke these precious words regarding religious art: *Among our senses, sight is the one that has the most efficient power to perceive sensible reality.* (1)

St. Gregory of Nyssa also revealed the importance of Christian Art: *For the silent painting speaks on the walls and does much good.* (2)

St. Nilus of Sinai, a disciple of St. John Chrysostom said: *Let the hand of the best painter cover both sides of the church with images from the Old and New Testaments, so that those who do not know the alphabet and cannot read the Holy Scriptures will remember, while looking at the painted representations, the courageous deeds of those who served God without malice, thus they will be encouraged to emulate the ever-memorable virtues of these servants of God who preferred the heavens to the earth.* (3)

Over 760 years of Scapular Devotion in the Church have brought us myriad images and paintings depicting the bestowal of the Scapular of Our Lady of Mt. Carmel to St. Simon Stock, images of Our Lady bestowing the Sabbatine Privilege to Pope John XXII, images of the holy souls having worn faithfully the holy habit, released into the arms of Our Blessed Mother and into everlasting paradise, images of our Beloved Mother and her Divine Son as Our Lady of Mt. Carmel, and hundreds of other numerous titles inspiring devotion and love and a change to the human heart.

In the pages following are two such famous images. The first is a photograph of a colossal painting found in the Church of San Martino in Corleone, Sicily. It was originally painted by Thomas de Vigilia, a Carmelite, in 1492, depicting the origins of the Devotion and is considered to be a "Document on the Sabbatine Bull," created in art, rather than written in text. Many of the faithful of that era were illiterate, unable to read, and the faith was then relayed through artistic depictions to inspire, educate and to disseminate the faith and true devotion to the Mother of God.

This painting is of great importance to the student of the Scapular. As a work of art, it is of much importance; but in its historic aspect, it is simply invaluable. Consider that the artist had seen copies of the old Bulls pertaining to the Sabbatine Privilege. The history of the Sabbatine Privilege had sunk so deeply in to the spiritual life of the people that it found representation in artistic work in the year 1492 and gives us a small idea of the popularity of the Devotion in the late 15th century and for many years before.

Fr. Daniel LoGrasso, who made a special study of the matters in question, has no doubt of the prevelance of the Devotion of the Sabatine Privilege in the whole of the century from the time of the confirmation by Alexander (V) until we find in artistic form, this Privilege and its history fully developed and expressed in a manner which to day could not be exceeded. There is a record of the presence of the copies of Bulls as well as the transumpta which seem to have been distributed through all the Convents of the Order in Sicily. (4)

Father Master Egidio Leoindelicato who lived in the second portion of the Sixteenth Century, dying between the years of 1592 and 1600 and who was an alumnus of the Convent of Sciarra writes: *From the authentic Bull were taken copies which were publicly displayed in the Carmelite Church of Sicily and the parts outside also.* Then he adds which is more to the subject in hand: *In particular there were copies in the Carmelite Churches in Palermo and Sciacca, and these I have seen with my own eyes and read.* (5)

The author of this work personally traveled to Corleone, Sicily, in 2004, to the Church of San Martino, to view and photograph this enormous painting and to have a video taped interview with the Pastor of the Church, Don Vincenzo Pizzitolo, who gave a very detailed history of the Devotion, the artist and the Bulls upon which this painting was designed.

Each picture surrounding the image of Our Lady, with her devoted Saints of Carmel standing below speaks the story of the Devotion, beginning with Our Blessed Lady presenting the souls devoted to the Holy Scapular to the Most Holy Trinity and ending with Pope John XXII, on his Pontifical Throne, surrounded by Bishops and Cardinals, handing the Document of the Sabbatine Bull to a Carmelite, who himself is surrounded by fellow Carmelite priests.

The second is a beautiful, breathtaking image of Our Lady of Mt. Carmel, discovered through a French book on the Devotion entitled: *Le Scapulaire de Notre-Dame du Mont-Carmel est authentique,* (P. Marie-Joseph du Sacre-Coeur, 1928, p. 68), found in a library in Rome which referred to the painting done by the disciples of Thomas de Vigilia in the Church of Our Lady of Mt.Carmel in Palermo, Sicily, in 1492. The author personally photographed this particular painting in the Church of Our Lady of Mt. Carmel, in Palermo as well, and may be found following the photograph of the above painting from the Church of San Martino in Corleone, Sicily. It depicts the story of Our Heavenly Mother's love for her children, her great desire to procure the salvation of their souls and the means by which to achieve this, the Brown Scapular. However, it silently and at the same time, magnanimously proclaims the tremendous dissemination of faith in the 15th century, the manifestation of the widespread indulgences and papal approbations granted, and the prodigious and towering expression of love and devotion of the people at that time for Our Lady of Mt. Carmel and for her Holy Scapular. Included in this Chapter as well, are photographs of other stained glass windows throughout the world of the Visions of St. Simon Stock and Pope John XXII and a photograph of the authentic copy of the Sabbatine Bull, from Messina, Sicily.

Photograph of the Document on the Sabbatine Bull 1492
Original Painting by Thomas de Vigilia
Venerated in the Church of San Martino Corleone, Sicily

The explanation of the side images of this painting are found on the following pages and are identical to the images found in the preceding pages explaining the painting in the Church of Our Lady in Mount Carmel, Palermo, Sicily (The author personally photographed this particular painting in Corleone in 2004.)

Photograph of a document on the Sabbatine Bull of 1492: Painting venerated in the Church of Carmine Maggiore in Palermo.

In this Chapter there is a photograph, taken by the author in April 2012, of an ancient painting found in the Church of Our Lady of Mt. Carmelo, in Palermo, Sicily.

The following article describing this painting and the eight images that surround it is found in and translated from the book: *Le Scapulaire de Notre-Dame du Mont-Carmel est authentique,* **by P. Marie-Joseph du Sacre-Coeur, Avignon, 1928, pp. 68-71.**

This ancient painting has the value of a perfectly authentic document.

It was recognized and decreed by the canon, Antonin Mongitore, the learned historian of all things pertaining to Sicily, in his work, "Palermo divoto di Maria" (Palermo, 1719, p. 167); and by the excellent art critic and archeologist, Msgr. Joachim Di Marzo, in his book, "La Pittura in Palermo Rinascimento" (Palermo, 1899). These two important authors affirm that Thomas de Viglia painted the portrait in 1492, following the signature and the date that this artist himself placed at the base of the frame: painted [by] Thomas de Viglia A.D. 1492.

Mongitore verified the signature and the date two hundred years ago, and Msgr. Di Marzo placed and consigned these into his book. "La Belle Arti in Sicilia," published in Palermo in 1862. But in 1868, after the expulsion of the religious, the venerated painting, having been despoiled by the rapacious hands of one who wished to decorate it, some pious faithful tried to restore it by a mediocre painter who, (alas!) replaced the ancient inscription with this one in crude Latin: "Painted by disciples of Thomas de Viglia in 1492; and, on the other side, inscribed his name: restored by Alosio Pizzillo in the year, 1868."

On the following page, first, we reproduce the entire painting, so one can judge the whole; the eight lateral subjects are then reproduced from the scale of the greatest, in view of their documentary importance.

Msgr. Di Marzo described, with deep knowledge, the central subject: "The Holy Virgin, in the middle, appears wonderful. She is standing in the heavens adorned with rays of gold, upon a crescent moon, with a nimbus of twelve stars above her head, turning toward those devoted to her with an air that is both majestic and full of tenderness. With a mantle enriched with flowers adorned with gold over white trim, enveloped with simple and gracious folds, the Virgin subtly reveals with one hand her maternal womb. Below her, kneeling on the ground strewn with flowers, are seen the prophets Elijah and Elisha in small dimensioned figures; they are old with long beards, each holding their characteristic signs, which for St. Elijah, is the sword of fire; two sons of the prophets dressed in Carmelite garb are at their side; the scene, placed between two mountain slopes, links the site of the convent of Saint Brocard to that of Mount Carmel. The two holy prophets are still depicted as small figures beholding the Virgin above the arc that supports the ledge of the frame.

"The eight little compositions that surround the Madonna, although they have suffered the injuries of time and an awkward restoration, call to mind, by their skillful composition, the art so full of life and truth of the fifteenth century." We are going to describe them by making use of the analysis provided by Msgr. Di Marzo and the learned P. Lo Grosso.

TO THE RIGHT LOOKING UPON THE HOLY IMAGE

I. – One sees some Carmelites deliberating, seated in a chapter hall, close to the church of the convent, while two of them, standing, withdraw to go solicit the confirmation of the Rule from Pope John XXII.

II. – John XXII, on his throne, in the middle of the seated cardinals, holds open the Collection of pontifical Bulls and Conciliar Decrees; he dismisses the two Carmelites, the order not having need of a new approval after that of Honorius III (1226), of Innocent IV (1247) and of the Council of Lyon (1274).

III. – John XXII is represented sleeping in a parade bed; then kneeling at the side of the bed wearing a cape and the tiara on his head: he gazes upon the Virgin who appears to him and dictates to him the conditions of the Sabbatine Bull. The painting assumes that the pope had this vision after his elevation to the sovereign Pontificate.

IV. – John XXII, at the pontifical throne, surrounded by cardinals and bishops, holds out the Sabbatine Bull to a kneeling Carmelite, who is surrounded by other Carmelite religious, on their knees, their hands crossed over their chests.

TO THE LEFT LOOKING UPON THE HOLY IMAGE

V. – In front of an altar, there rises a triptych representing: in the middle, God the Father above the Madonna who carries the divine Child; to the right and the left are St. Elijah and St. Elisha; a Carmelite, probably Blessed John Soreth, gives the habit and the veil to a virgin, who, with her companions, joins herself to Order, and he communicates to her the privilege of the Sabbatine Bull.

VI. – At the bottom of the scene, a great number of souls clothed with the holy Scapular and in flames; at the same time, there is above, a flock of other souls, taken from Purgatory by angels, being lifted up to Heaven. "This beautiful composition," says Mgr. Di Marzo, "is full of life and movement."

VII. – The Virgin appears in the heavens with open arms; she receives under her mantle the souls clothed with the holy Scapular and freed from Purgatory; a multitude of angels, which surround her, play diverse musical instruments, while at their feet two angels are blowing their long trumpets and seem to be calling other souls from Purgatory.

VIII. – The Virgin Mary presents to the Holy Trinity the souls devoted to the holy Scapular.

(Side Altar in the Church of Our Lady of Mount Carmel, Palermo Sicily, painted by the disciples of Thomas De Vigilia in 1492)

Stained Glass Window of Our Lady of Mount Carmel depicting the apparition to Saint Simon Stock and to Pope John the XXII granting the Sabbatine Privilege.

Found in the Basilica of Saint Therese of The Little Flower, San Antonio, Texas.

Basílica de Nossa do Carmo

BULLA SABATINA

São Paulo Basílica de Nossa Senhora do Carmo
 Our Lady of Mount Carmel Basilica Year: 1934 Brazil
 The Sabbatine Privilege is given to the Carmelite Order in 1322

(Pope John XXII-Born at Cahors in 1249; enthroned, 5 September, 1316; died at Avignon, 4 December, 1334)

Istam ergo sanctam Indulgentiam accepto, roboro et in terris confirmo, sicut, propter merita Virginis Matris, gratiose Jesus Christus concessit in coelis.

"This holy indulgence I therefore accept; I confirm and ratify it on earth, just as Jesus Christ has graciously granted it in heaven on account of the merits of the Virgin Mother."

O Papa João XXII promulga a Bula Sabatina que versa a respeito do santo escapulário de N.Sra.do Carmo.

Dedicated to Mary, Mother of God, Queen of Heaven:
"Our Lady of Mt. Carmel"
With love, honor, and eternal gratitude

"I brought you into the land of Carmel, to eat the fruit thereof, and the best things thereof." (Jer. ii. 7)

"Therefore, brethren, stand fast: and hold the traditions which you have learned, whether by word or by our epistle." (2 Thess. ii. 14)

(The above stained-glass window was donated by the Carmelites of Ireland and New York, U.S.A. and is in memory of the Reverend James Angelus Rabbitie, O.Carm., Director of the Carmelite Knock Pilgrimage 1935-1958 A.D. It can be found in the Parish of Our Lady of Knock, in Ireland.)

HISTORIA CHRONOLOGICA
Priorum Generalium
Latinorum totius
ORDINIS GLORIOSISSIMÆ
Dei Genitricis semperque Virginis
MARIÆ
de monte Carmelo

Translation:
**Chronological History of the Latin Prior Generals of the
Whole Order of the Most Glorious Ever-
Virgin Mother of God, Mary of Mount Carmel**
By
Fr. Mariano Ventimiglia
1723

Noster Princeps ELIAS, noster ELISÆVS, nostri Duces Filij Prophetarum
D. Hieronymus Ep. ad Paulinum

Translation:
Our Founder Elijah, Our Eliseus,
Leaders of our Sons of the Prophets

VI.

S. Simon Stochius Anglus

Electus Gñalis in Comitijs Ailesfordiæ habitis in Anglia 1245. Præfuit annis 20. Ad cælum migrauit Burdegalæ die 16 Maij 1265. Ætan: 100.

Translation:
Saint Simon Stock, Englishman
Elected General at the Chapter of Aylesford, England in 1245.
He governed for 20 years.
He entered into eternal life in Bordeaux on May 16, 1265
at the age of 100 years.

A Copy of the Sabbatine Bull

The Saturday Privilege of Sabbatine Promise of Our Blessed Lady, is contained in this copy of the Sabbatine Bull (found on the previous page), attributed to Pope John XXII in the year 1322.

Messina (Sicily) executed this copy at the end of the 15th century. He pictures a great multitude of the Christians who, together with the Carmelites, seek refuge under the protecting mantle of the Virgin. The help of Mary in the afterlife is represented as a mystery in three acts:

1   To the right in the lower portion a man is being saved from the mouth of Hell by our Lady,

2   Is sent to a Carmelite who clothes him in the Habit of Carmel, and

3   Ushers him into Heaven.

Although Historians reject the authenticity of the Sabbatine Bull, throughout the period of the growth of the Scapular Devotion among the people, the Popes repeatedly approved the Sabbatine Privilege and alluded to the (Sabbatine) Bull of 1322. (See Chapter 5 and Appendix 4 of this Book.) (6)

Many authentic copies of the Bull (of Alexander V, "Tenore cuiusdam," containing the Sabbatine Bull of John XXII) are conserved in Genoa, Messina, Trapani, (Sicily), in Majorca in Spain, and in the great Monastery of traspontina in Rome. (7)

CHAPTER 7 ENDNOTES
PRIVATE REVELATION IN THE CHURCH

1   Thess 5: 19-22

1a   www.ewtn.com/expert/answers/apparitions.htm

2   *Fatima, the Great Sign,* Francis Johnston, Rockford, Illinois, 1980, p. 2

3   *Her Glorious Title,* John Mathias Haffert, 1993, p, 32

3a   *Fatima, the Great Sign,* Francis Johnston, Illinois, 1980, p. 3

4   *The Credibility of the Scapular Promises,* a Dissertation, Rev. Christian P. Ceroke, O. Carm., Rome, 1950, pp. 33-47: The Church and the Scapular Revelations, paraphrased

5   *From the Apostolic Letter of His Holiness, Pope Pius XII on the Seventh Centenary of the Scapular vision,* issued February 11, 1950 in the Archives of the Order; *Neminem profecto latet; ibid,* pp.46, 47

6   Pope John XXIII, closing statement of 1959 Marian year, February 18, 1959, cf. *Introduction to Mary*, Mark Miravalle, S.T.D., California, 1993, p. 132, paraphrased

7   Pope Pius IX, Encylical: *Ubi primum*, February 2, 1849; *Papal Teachings; Our Lady*, the Benedictine Monks of Solesmes, 1961, pp. 56, 57

8   *Enciclopedia del Escapulario del Carmen*, by P. Simon Besalduch, 1931, p. 41, translated and paraphrased

9   Kings, III, 18:44

10   *Rediscovering Fatima*, Rev. Robert J. Fox, 1982, pp. 24, 25

11   *Saint Bernadette Soubirous*, 1844-1879, Abbé Francois Trochu, p. 179

12   *Mary in Her Scapular Promise.* John Mathias Haffert, 1942, p. 178

13   R. P. Petitot, O.P. *Apparitions de Notre-Dame á Bernadette*, cf. R. P. Eliseé de la Nativité O. C .D., *Etude Historique in Le Carmel* of July 1938, p. 328; *ibid*, p. 179

14   Mgr. Besson, *Lourdes and Carmel;* Carm. Rev., II, pp, 157, 193, 211; 14 *Chroniques du Carmel*, III, pp. 208, 394; *ibid*, p. 179

15   *Le Scapulaire de Notre Dame du Mont-Carmel est authentique*, P. Marie-Joseph du Sacre-Coeur, Avant-Propos, Avignon, 1928, Jean de Hildesheim (1re Partie, ch. VIII) *Defensorium* (1370), Cap. V

16   *Autobiography*, cf. *Analecta Ord. Carm.* V,411; *De Revelatione S. Theresiae quoad futura Ordinis nostri; Speculum Carmelitanum*, IX, pg. 790 N. B., (a) from *Mary in Her Scapular Promise*, John Mathias Haffert, 1942, pp. 200, 201, 202

17   *Les Chroniques du Carmel: II* pp. 210; *ibid*, p. 181-182; also, Carmelite Review Vol. 1, No. 7, July, 1893: "A Holy Sister's Vision"; p. 104

17a www.newadvent.org/cathen/05406b.htm

18   *Cries from a Suffering Soul*, taken from The *Housetops*, a Quarterly Magazine spreading the faith across the country, Volume XLVI, No. 3, Serial No. 87, St. Benedict Center ,Massachusetts, c. 2005, pp. 24, 28, 30

19   *Extracts of the Letter of S.E. Mgr. Theas, Bishop of Tarbes and of Lourdes, on the Occasion of the Centenary of the Apparition (of Our Lady of Lourdes), July 16, 1858* found in: *Le Scapulaire du Carmel*, Etude Historique, P. Elisee De La Nativite, O.C.D., 1958, pp. 87-90, 104

19a   *Fatima, the Great Sign*, Francis Johnston, Illinois, 1980, p. 3

19b *Ibid*, pp. 4, 5

19c www.michaeljournal.org/popefatima.htm; *The Pope of Our Lady of Fatima.*

19d Apostolic Journey of Pope Benedict XVI to Portugal on the occasion of the 10th anniversary of the Beatification of Jacinta and Francisco, young shepherds of Fatima Holy Mass, Homily of His Holiness Benedict XVI Esplanade of the Shrine of Our Lady of Fátima Thursday, 13 May 2010)

19e Fatima, the Great Sign, Francis Johnston, pp. 8, 9

19f *Ibid*, p. 12, cf: *Life is worth Living*, Second Series, "Fatima," p. 87n., and *The World's First Love*, Chap. 22

19g *Our Lady of Fatima's Peace Plan from Heaven*, 1950, Abbey Press, www.oocities.org/timothyc1/peace_plan.html

20 *Our Lady of Fatima and the Brown Scapular*. Rev. Killian Lynch, 1956, p. 10

21 Letter of Rev. Mother Lopes da Fonseca of September 2, 1950, Fatima Archives; *Our Lady of Fatima and the Brown Scapular*, Killian Lynch, O. Carm., Prior General, 1956, p. 12

22 *Rediscovering Fatima*, Rev. Robert J. Fox, 1982, p. 46

22a Catholic Voice, *On Devotion to Our Lady of Mount Carmel, July 16,* Dr. William A. Thomas, Ph.D., Issue 112, Ireland, July 7, 2013, pp. 26-27

23 *Our Lady of Fatima and the Brown Scapular,* Killian Lynch, O. Carm, Prior General, 1956, pp. 14-15, 17

24 *Our Lady of Fatima and the Brown Scapular,* Kilian Lynch, O. Carm. Aylesford, England, 1956, pp. 16, 17

25 *Ibid,* p. 13, 14

25a *Ibid,* p. 18

26 *Ibid,* p. 18

27 *Il Cuore Che Si Dona A Tutti, Emilio Marini,* AMI Press, Washington, New Jersey, 1972, pp. 7, 10, 119, 140, 143, 146

THE MAGNIFICENT BEAUTY OF CHRISTIAN ART

1 onbehalfofall.org/2013/02/06constantine-and-the-triumph-of-iconography, paraphrased

2 *Ibid*

3 *Ibid*

4 The Sabbatine Privilege of the Scapular, P. E. Magennis, pp. 115-116

5 *Ibid*, p. 117

6 This copy of the Sabbatine Bull is taken from *MARY*, Volume 23, No. 4, Camelite Fathers, Province of the Most Pure Heart of Mary, Rev. Howard Rafferty, O. Cam., Editor, Illinois, July-August 1962, pp. 22, 23

7 Taken from: *Bevi notizie sulla Bolla Detta Sabatina,* by Monsignor Francesco Gallo, Bishop of Avellino, Avellino, Italy, 1887, pp. 11,12

CHAPTER 8

OBSERVATIONS
OF THE AUTHOR

Chapter 8

Observations of the Author

Where Does the Truth Lie?

From the nature of His work, the Redeemer ought to have associated His Mother with His work. For this reason We invoke her under the title of "Coredemptrix." She gave us the Savior, she accompanied Him in the work of Redemption as far as the Cross itself, sharing with Him the sorrows of the agony and of the death in which Jesus consummated the Redemption of mankind.

Pope Pius XI Allocution to pilgrims from Vicenza, November 30, 1933 (The Coredemptrix; Greetings to pilgrims assembled in Rome for the Jubilee of the Redemption)

For in her is the beauty of life and
her bands are a healthful binding.
(Eccles. 6:31)

The authenticity of the Devotion to the Brown Scapular relies in great measure on the reality of the apparitions of Our Heavenly Mother to St. Simon Stock and to Pope John XXII. In the course of this investigation into the authenticity of the Visions, it was noted that the objections to the evidence thus far have stemmed from some Carmelite Communities themselves.

Publications throughout the world, predominantly penned by critical Historians have embraced the ideology of historical inaccuracy regarding the Visions, for example some of their objections are: lack of documentation, silence of noted historians in recording the Visions for a particular length of time, discrepancies in the dates, unauthentic copies and the list goes on.

The sources of information used by these Historians to deny the authenticity of the Visions and the ancient documentation reserved, not only in the Vatican, but in other Religious Communites throughout the world, (who still retain the traditional teaching on

271

the Scapular) include the writings of a 17th century Jansenist and Gallican, John Launoy, fomenter of the French Revolution, destroyer of Religious Communities, and a bitter adversary of the Holy See, whose work is cited to this day by certain 20th and 21st century Carmelite Historians.

But where does the truth lie and who is telling the truth? Does it lie within the Holy Roman Catholic Church, based on the centuries of Papal Approbation of the Visions, the authenticated miracles due to the wearing of the Scapular, Canonized Saints and the Blessed who have held in the highest esteem, the great Devotion to Our Blessed Mother and to her Promises? Does it lie with the authenticated Papal Bulls of the Solemn Pontiffs, dating back to the 14th century, indulgencing and confirming the ancient origins of the Devotion?

Or does it lie with the intellectual modern day historians, heavily influenced by the erroneous writings of critical scholars with questionable characters whose celebrated works have been condemned by the Church? Does it lie with the critics who have based their findings on their own intellectual doubt, rather than on historical facts, on their own personal opinion, rather than on the saintly unquestionable characters of trustworthy, reliable ancient historians? Does it lie with these scholars, who while claiming to have conducted their examination with tedious and scrupulous modern-day accuracy, have done nothing more than resurrect the ancient objections of the 17th century as a basis for their fallacious conclusions, and cloaked their findings in a sea of ambiguous terminology?

The course of this continual 15-year study has produced myriad personal observations of the assault on the validity of the Scapular Visions and the state of the Devotion, those who embraced and defended it and those who consistently deny it. Dear reader, discern with diligence the pages you have read and those that follow, for: *The weight of the evidence will very much depend upon the character of the witnesses.* (a)

1) THE SCAPULAR PROMISE HAS BEEN REMOVED FROM THE SCAPULAR ITSELF.

Please see photograph of the traditional Scapular with the Promise, indulgenced by many Holy Fathers and a recent scapular of the Carmelite Order with the changed words and note the following exerpt: *Some years ago in the United States, the Order produced a Scapular which on the reverse side from the usual picture of Our Lady, had the words: "PUT ON THE LORD JESUS CHRIST." One angry woman wrote demanding to know why we put what she termed "those Protestant words" on the Scapular. She did not know, of course, that "those Protestant words are in fact from Paul's letter to the Romans.*(1)

In my opinion: They may be the words of St. Paul to the Romans, but they are not the words testified to by numerous historians and affirmed by numerous Holy Fathers over the centuries of Our Lady's Promise: *Whosoever shall die wearing this habit, shall not suffer eternal fire.* (July 16, 1251) *Already in Baptism, Christians are "clothed with Christ" (Gal 3:27) but it is their duty thereafter to cooperate with Grace and thus increase their likeness to Our Lord by constantly imitating the virtues which shone in Him.* (1a) Romans 13:14 is also an extension of Galatians 3:27, referring to our Baptism, our rebirth with Christ.

2) THE SCAPULAR DEVOTION IS DISAPPEARING.

Please see the article from "Our Sunday Visitor:" *The Brown Scapular has had its recent detractors ...some say that the Scapular has seen its better days and that the faithful should no longer be governed by silly superstition.* (2)

In my opinion: Certain modern day Carmelite publications, periodicals, and websites, have cast a shadow of doubt (with words such as stories, legends, seemed, symbolic, etc.) on the authenticity of Our Lady's appearance to both St. Simon Stock, in which she bestowed the Scapular and its Promise and her appearance to Pope John XXII through which the Sabbatine Privilege was granted to the Universal Church (according to the Sabbatine Bull of the Pope John XXII, March 3, 1322). However, in the United States and Europe and elsewhere, these dubious publications have caused and are continuing to cause confusion and the systematic dissipation of the Devotion.

3) SOME OF THE OBJECTIONS OF LUDOVICO SAGGI, O. CARM., ARE PARALLEL TO THOSE OF JOHN LAUNOY WHO REJECTED THE SCAPULAR VISIONS IN 1642 AND WHOSE BOOKS WERE CONDEMNED AND PUT ON THE PROHIBITED LIST BY POPE ST. PIUS X. (3)

In my opinion: Please see the attached chart paralleling the objections of the Jansenist, John Launoy in 1642 and those of the modern-day objectors starting from 1887 to the 21st century. About thirty of the works of this 17th century Jansenist were banned by the ecclesiastical authorities and his work: *Dissertationes V. de Simonis Stochii Viso* etc. was <u>condemned</u> 18th April, 1689 AD.

The Index Librorum Prohibitorum published by authority of Pius X (1907) with Prefatio by Secretary of S. Ind. Congr., contains twenty-seven works of John Launoy. Many of them have been condemned more than once. (4)

4) THE SCAPULAR DEVOTION HAS TAKEN A "NEGATIVE DETOUR " EX POST FACTO, IN AMERICA, ALL OVER EUROPE AND IN OTHER PLACES.

In my opinion: The new interpretation of the Scapular Devotion and its origin as well as objections to the traditional teaching on the Scapular are expounded in several books and periodicals. Some examples are: "Carmel in the World," published by the Institutum Carmelitanum in Rome and various other Carmelite publications from France, England, Ireland, India and other countries throughout the world which the author has reviewed. Many objections seem to be coming from certain Progressives in the Carmelite Communities themselves.

5) THE MODERNISTS/OPPOSERS OF THE ORIGINS OF DEVOTION HAVE ESTABLISHED DOUBT IN THE SCAPULAR VISION AND THE SABBATINE PRIVILEGE.

Objection: Motives for a Scapular Vision Story: There are some reasons which would lead a Carmelite to concoct a story of a Vision of the Virgin Mary. St. Simon Stock is without doubt the most elusive personality in a group of eminent Englishmen at the time ... of whose life and. character we know almost nothing. The early references to Simon Stock in the catalogues of Prior-General by Grossi, imakes no mention of the Scapular Vision. No copy of the Bull has been found in the Vatican Archives and Ludovico Saggi demonstrated convincingly that the document was concocted around 1430 in Agrigento, Sicily, with the author taking as his model a similar Franciscan document relating to the Portiuncula Indulgence. (5)

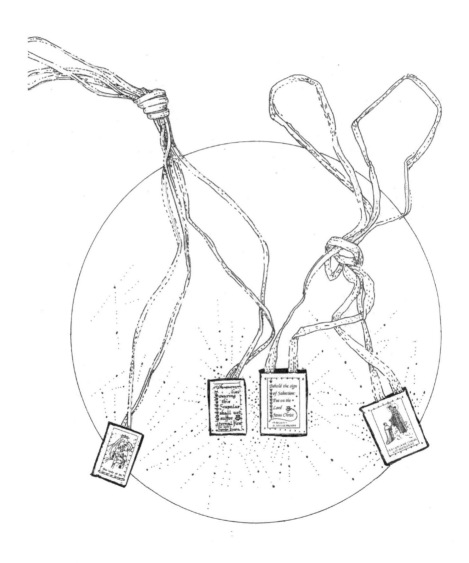

February 24, 1991 OurSunda

Unearthing a buried treas

It is time for the Brown Scapular to again be a part of

A landmark in the life of any Catholic boy or girl is the reception of First Holy Communion. Parents, pastors and catechists strive to ensure that the child is ready for this "greatest of - sacraments." Often decked out in new clothes amid family and friends, the child - after studying in Catholic school or CCD class - approaches the altar to receive Christ's Body and Blood for the first time.

One rite of passage that often accompanied the initial reception of the Holy Eucharist especially before the Second Vatican Council was the investiture and enrollment in the Brown Scapular of Our Lady of Mount Carmel. The parish priest, having instructed the children on the importance of Marian devotion and the meaning of the Brown Scapular, would bless the scapulars and place one on the shoulders of each student.

Unfortunately, this sacramental seems to have gone the way of other , pious practices such as Benediction of the Blessed Sacrament and the Nine First Fridays Devotion. Today, rarely is the scapular explained from the pulpit or teacher's desk. Even more unusual is the enrolling in the Brown Scapular of the faithful.

With the seeming advent of a renewed interest in the Mother of God

and the Rosary, it appears that the time has come for the Brown Scapular to be given its due.

Because of her privileges and utmost conformity to God's will, Mary pleases her Son more than any other creature could.

On July 16, 1251, Mary appeared to St. Simon Stock, an English Carmelite, and said: "Whosoever dies wearing this scapular shall not suffer eternal fire." She also made reference to what is now known as the "Sabbatine Privilege." This pious belief states that those who wear the Brown Scapular, observing chastity according to their state in life while daily reciting the Little Office of the Blessed Virgin Mary or performing some other similar work, will be assisted by Mary's intercession.and released quickly from purgatory. Anthony Buono, in the excellent "Dictionary of Mary," writes that Pope Pius XII in 1950 mentioned with approval the Sabbatine Privilege in the following words: "This most kind mother will not be tardy in using her intercession

ıy Visitor

sure of the Church

' the Catholic rite of passage

with God to open the gates of heaven as soon as possible for those of her children who are expiating theirfaults in purgatory, a trust which is based on the promise known as the Sabbatine Privilege."

Nearly seven centuries after the apparition to St. Simon, Mary was seen by three shepherd children in Fatima, Portugal. During her sixth appearance on Oct. 13, 1917, Mary held aloft the Brown Scapular; indicating her desire - as Lucia, one of the visionaries, would later say - that believers wear the scapular as a sign of their consecration to Mary's Immaculate Heart.

The Brown Scapular-has had its recent detractors - the Church's long-standing approbation notwithstanding; Some say that the scapular has seen its better days, and that the faithful should no longer be governed by silly superstition, albeit well-intentioned.

Authentic Brown Scapular devotion emphasizes that this sacramental demonstrates an entrusting of oneself to Mary. Because of her privileges and utmost conformity to God's will, Mary pleases her Son more than any other . creature could, To consecrate oneself to Mary implies a consecration to Jesus. As St. Louis de Montfort (1673-1716) once wrote, when we say "Mary," she says "Jesus." She un-

. Viewpoint

By Father Charles M. Mangan

.hesitatingly and unfailingly takes us to Christ and presents us as only a mother can .

The Rosary *and* the Brown Scapular are much-needed Marian • devotions in the modem world: Both promote purity. a virtue noticeably ııt a premium.

We who aspire to be disciples of Christ can give Him a marvelous gift: devoted sons and daughters of His mother. By our promoting this inexpensive piece of cloth and cord, souls may be won for heaven through our casual efforts, fueled by the maternal solicitude of the Mother of Jesus. (Information regarding the Brown . Scapular may be obtained from: Aylesford, The National Scapular Center, Darien,IL 60559-0065.) ～

Father Mangan is an associate pastor at St. Joseph Cathedral, Sioux Falls. S.D.

OBJECTIONS OF MODERN DAY CARMELITES 1967- 2005	OBJECTIONS OF JOHN LAUNOY 1642-1653 (and others)
1. The account of the vision is not found in the Catalogs of the Prior Generals.	1. Several texts vary from each other in attributing the Sabbatine Bull to Alexander III or the IV as found in the instrument notarized in Majorca.
2. In 14th century narrations referring to an intimate relationship between Mary and the Carmelites, the vision to St. Simon Stock is not spoken of.	2. The style of the Bull of John XXII (Sacrt. uti cul) is so different, not at all the one usually used by Roman Pontiffs in their official acts.
3. The written style of the Bull is not in the official style.	3. The variety of several circumstances in the vision and the variety of lessons in the Bull hinder the authenticity of the Sabbatine Bull itself among various authors.
4. There is no trace in the Papal Registers of the Bulls attributed to Alexander V and John XXII.	4. The Bull of Alexander V is not found in the Vatican Registers, therefore it is false
5. The official copy of the Bull of John XXII produced in Majorca has now been determined to be false.	5. The Bull of Alexander V carries the date from Rome. Therefore it is apocrophal because Alexander was never in Rome at least until after he became Pope.
6. The account of the vision is not written in the Acta Sanctorum.	6. There is manifested a contradiction in the words of the Virgin to John XXII when calling him: "Vicar of my Son," and then saying: "I will make you Pope."
7. The two visions associated with the habit of Carmel (The vision of Our Lady to St. Simon Stock granting him the Scapular and the Vision of Our Lady to Pope John XXII granting the Sabbatine Privilege) are determined to be false.	7. In assigning the years of the date of the Bull of John XXII there is a discrepancy between the authors and especially between P. Gregorio Nazianzeno and P. Marcantonio Casanate. (The two authors whom Launoy relied heavily upon)
8. In reference to the Sabbatine Bull, some expressions are not theologically correct- Saturday after death refers to space and time in eternity.	8. In the Bull of John XXII we find the use of the word Mercurri in place of Feria IV, which is not used ecclesiastically, therefore putting in doubt the authenticity of the Sabbatine Bull.
9. A Pope never refers in an official act to a Private vision for the granting of an indulgence or give concesions.	9. The promise made by the Blessed Virgin to John XXII of the liberation of souls devoted to her (Scapular) is absurd; the promise of descending to Purgatory to liberate them is ficticious.
10. The Decree of the Holy Office of 1613, reconfirmed on various occasions, prohibits talking about the Sabbatine Bull as a Papal Document which granted the Sabbatine Privilege.	10. If the Bull of John XXII (Sabbatine) really existed, then the biographers who wrote of the works of John XXII would never have neglected to speak of it. (4)
11. When was the Sabbatine Bull granted? Our Lady called John XXII: "Vicar of my Son, and then promised him: "I will make you Pope?	11. John Launoy declared the vision of St. Simon and of John XXII regarding the Scapular and the Sabbatine Bull unpreachable due to a lack docdumentary evidence.
12. Other difficulties come from the silence of the biographers... etc. (3)	The Sabbatine Bull is not contained in the collection of the great Bulls of the Roman Pontiffs. (4)

(6)

Observations of the Author

In my opinion: Pope Benedict XIV granted a plenary indulgence on May 11, 1751 in Solemn Commemoration of Our Lady of Mount Carmel; it was requested for "the giving of the Scapular to St Simon Stock." *(In memoriam tanti benefici)* The original copy of the Bull of Pope John XXII has been lost. However, official transcripts of it allow us to trace it back to an authenticated copy made in 1421.

Similar copies of the original Bull were approved by Popes Clement VII, St. Pius V, Gregory XIII and others as well. If we cannot rely on notarized copies guaranteed by several Popes, then we had better give up trying to prove almost any historical event for which we do not have notarized documents to support most of the data used in our histories. What also of *De festis,* the Treatise of Pope Benedict XIV, declaring the Visions to be true? (7) Consider the document of Pope Benedict XIV *(De festis...)* which states: **In the course of the 13th century we saw the death of St. Simon Stock, General of the Carmelite Order, a man of great holiness to whom many years before his death, the Holy Virgin had appeared to him and gave him the Scapular as a Sign of recognition of the Carmelite Order, with a particular guarantee of her special protection; therefore, after 50 years the Blessed Virgin appeared also to the Solemn Pontiff John XXII to nofity him of a special Indulgence, (Sabbatine) an Indulgence which the Pontiff himself promulgated then on the third day of March in the year 1322, and we believe the Vision to be true and as true, it should be retained so by all...This Vision is mentioned in the Roman Brevary.** (8)

And what of the words of Pope Saint John XXIII where he states: **John XXII: Jacques d'Euse de Cahor, was the Bishop of Avignon, who governed the Church for 18 years and died in 1334. He was a great Pontiff. His life was full of tribulations but rich in works and merits in all respects: a true servant of the Servants of God. He had, among others, the honor of canonizing St. Thomas Aquinas. Above all, he was very devoted to Mary. It is to him that history attributes the pious devotion of reciting an Our Father and Hail Mary at the chiming of the evening bells; to him also is attributed the Paternity of the "Sabbatine Privilege," so precious and dear to those who wear the Scapular of Our Lady of Mount Carmel.** (9)

Incidentally, regarding the statement by the Carmelites expressing confidence that Mary will seek grace for all who remain faithful to the Carmelite Vocation, the Holy Father, Pope Pius IX has stated in his *Brief* to Alfred Mombrun, author of *The Life of St. Simon Stock* dated October 23, 1869, the following:

This Scapular was not given solely for the use of the Carmelite

Order, but also for the good of the faithful who in conjunction with this religious Order would like to honor Mary in a special way.

What is to be said and done with the Apostolic Letters, Radio Discourses, etc. and ecclesial actions of these benevolent Holy Fathers regarding the Scapular over the centuries whose devotion to Our Lady and love of the Brown Scapular has given us these historical testimonials of their credence in the Visions? Did they not speak the truth? Are we to disregard their solemn pronouncements, invalidate and extinguish their sacred Indulgences and then truncate the supernatural roots of this beloved Devotion?

6) WITH THE DENIAL OF THE PROMISES, THE INTERCESSION OF THE MOTHER OF GOD AS MEDIATRIX IS REMOVED FROM THE SCAPULAR DEVOTION.

In my opinion: ... as Mediatrix of all Graces, Mary can grant the graces necessary for salvation to those who faithfully wear the Scapular as an external symbol of their internal devotion and dependence on the Mother of Jesus…The Scapular, then, is an external symbol of Marian devotion and dependency, of a continual Marian prayer that acknowledges Mary's intercessory role throughout this life and also in the purification of Purgatory that prepares the Christian for eternal life with God. (10) ... "to present the Scapular promise to the faithful one does not need the approbation of this or that critic; the approbation of the Church is perfectly adequate and is in fact preferable". (11)

"It is believed that she is the Mediatrix of all graces and the Spiritual Mother of men, who is intimately interested in their salvation and who may personally assist them to obtain it. It is believed that she herself may designate a particular Sign of her protection and a condition of obtaining it. It has been believed for more than four hundred years universally in the Church that SHE HAS DONE SO IN FAVOR OF THE BROWN SCAPULAR; AND UNIVERSAL EXPERIENCE HAS TESTIFIED TO THE FACT OF HER SPECIAL PROTECTION." (12)

See also the Letter of Pope Pius XII, *Superiore anno*, dated April 15, 1940 which states: "And since as St. Bernard declares: 'It is the Will of God that we obtain all favors through Mary,' let everyone hasten to have recourse to Mary." (13)

See also the document of Pope St. Pius X: *Ad diem illum laetissimum* dated February 2, 1904 which states: *It cannot of course be denied that the dispensing of these treasures is the particular and supreme right of Jesus Christ, for they are the exclusive fruit of His death, who by His Nature is the Mediator between God and man. Nevertheless, by this union in sorrow and suffering, as we have said, which existed between the Mother and the Son, it has been allowed to the August Virgin "to be the most powerful Mediatrix and Advocate of the whole world with her Divine Son."* (14)

7) ONE COULD EASILY CONCLUDE THAT WITHOUT THE PROMISE OF OUR LADY ATTACHED TO THE SCAPULAR: *(Whosoever shall die wearing this Scapular, shall not suffer eternal fire)* THE SCAPULAR THEN BECOMES JUST ANOTHER PIECE OF CLOTH.

In my opinion: with this teaching, the Scapular then carries no promise of eternal salvation. Why then would lay people wear it if it were not attached to a Promise? This consensus is found among many of the lay people. The most enduring reason that people wear it is because of the Promise that Our Lady gave to those who wear it. Removing the Promise has lead to the removal of the Scapular for many of the laity. According to the Venerable Francis Ypes, brother of St. John of the Cross, the devil once told him: *Take it off, take off the habit which snatches so many souls from us! Why Do We Wear the Scapular?* Garment of Grace, Et Verbum Catholic, Thursday, 5 May, 2011) www.etverbum.com/2011/05/why-do-we-wear-scapular.html "Our struggle is not against flesh and blood; it is not against an enemy whom we might leave helpless at our feet. Material weapons are of no use against the powers of darkness. No pact with men or nations will send Satan groveling in the dust. The weapons which will conquer him transcend the powers of man to make. They must be made in Heaven." *(Take This Scapular, Carmelite Fathers and Tertiaries,* Chicago, 1949, p. 18) *Oh Scapular, how many souls you snatch from us.* (Conc. X in Jubil. Carm. monachii habita, anno 1751; cf. *Sommes des Grandeurs,* Vol. V, pg. 421)

The devotion to the Brown Scapular turns in great measure on the reality of this apparition. If it cannot be depended upon to save its wearer from Hell, then it sails under false colours among Catholics... It is true that the wearing of the Brown Scapular still gives a share in certain privileges attached to the Order of Mount Carmel, but if the chief of all these Privileges turns out to be a fraud perpetrated by the Carmelites themselves, we can scarcely expect that much reliance will be placed upon the efficacy of the rest. It becomes a symbol of Devotion without anything tangible and trustworthy attaching to it except a vague and undefined impression that the wearer is in some sort of way under Our Lady's protection. (14a)

8) THE PROMISE OF ETERNAL SALVATION THROUGH THE INTERCESSION OF OUR LADY IS CALLED INTO QUESTION THROUGH THE OBJECTIONS OF THE MODERN SKEPTICS.

Objection: "Jesus is our link with spiritual reality; there is no mediator with the mediator."(15)

In my opinion: The Encyclical of Pope Leo XIII: *Fidentem Piumque,* dated September 20, 1896 states: *She is from whom Jesus is born: she is therefore truly His Mother and for this reason a worthy and acceptable "Mediatrix to the Mediator."* (15a) The question to be posed here may be: Could the above statement imply that the Progressives believe Our Lady has no intercessory role in God's plan for our eternal salvation? "The main purpose of the Scapular Devotion is to inculcate in the faithful the heavenly doctrine of the Church concerning Our Lady. This is its foundation." (16)

Pope Pius XI, in "Explorata res" February 2, 1923 said: *He will not taste death forever, who in his dying moments has recourse to the Blessed Virgin Mary. This opinion of the Doctors of the Church, which agrees with the mind of Christian people is confirmed by constant experience and is based above all on the fact that the sorrowful Virgin took part with Jesus Christ in the work of the Redemption.* (17)

The Scapular Promises prove the power of Our Blessed Mother to intercede for our eternal salvation. An attack on the Scapular is an attack on the Mother of God. In removing the supernatural nature of the Visions, the capability and the actuality of the Mother of God interceding for us for our eternal salvation as "Mediatrix of all Graces" is both denied and eradicated.

Pius XII said: "He whom the Blessed Virgin assists at his last hour will not suffer eternal death." In other words, he is promising that one devoted to her will not, as a matter of fact, reject that grace of perseverance. She, of course, whom Pope Benedict XV called "SUPPLIANT OMNIPOTENCE" will bring it about. It means that everything that God Himself can do by His inherent power, she can obtain by her intercession. (18)

On her part, the most holy Mother will not fail to intercede with

God that her children who in Purgatory are expiating their sins may, at the earliest possible moment, reach the Eternal Fatherland in accordance with the so-called Sabbatine Privilege. (19)

9) COUNTLESS DOCUMENTED MIRACLES OF THE SCAPULAR ARE BEING OVERLOOKED, IGNORED OR DENIED.

In my opinion: In a letter from the Carmelite Convent in Lisieux, France, the Carmelite Sisters have stated that the Scapulars of Venerable Zelie and Louis Martin, (parents of St. Therese of Lisieux) were found intact in their coffins, incorrupt. Their bodies and their clothing were decayed but the Scapulars only were found to be incorrupt. (20) The same may be said of the Scapular of St. Alphonsus de Liguori as well as the incorrupt scapular found in the coffin of Pope Gregory X in the Museum in Arezzo, Italy, personally photographed by the author and the Scapular of St. John Bosco which was discovered incorrupt in his coffin in 1929.

"Likewise, if one would deny the fact of the Scapular miracles, he must admit a moral miracle: that universal belief in the Promise of the Scapular became firmly embedded in the Church without any miracles. ...the miracles of the Scapular place the protection of the Blessed Virgin, which is the object of the Promise, beyond factual doubt. Certain miracles of the Scapular are well considered singly; those instances especially of Scapulars found in tombs, incorrupt, where all other garments have perished or are in a state of decay." (21)

Other books containing Miracles of the Brown Scapular are:

1 "Miracoli e Grazie della Santissima Vergine Maria del Carmine, P. Simone Grassi, Carmelitano," Firenze, MDCCXXVII

2 "Le Scapulaire de Notre-Dame du Mont-Carmel est authentique," P. Marie Joseph du Sacre Coeur, Avignon, France, 1928

3 "Histoire Des Miracles du Saint Scapulaire," Doctor J. Biroat, prieur de Cluny, Bruge, 1 Mai, 1963

4 "Miracles du S. Scapulaire au XVIIme siècle," R. P. Archange de laReine Du Carmel O.C.D. Carmel, Ezelstraat 28, 8000 Bruges, 1964

Fr. Howard Rafferty, a Carmelite, also produced a video tape in the United States in the 20th century on many of the amazing Miracles attributed to the protection of the Blessed Virgin Mary, through the Brown Scapular. The video is entitled: *Stories of the Brown Scapular.*

10) PRIVATE REVELATION WHICH IS THE BASIS OF THE SCAPULAR DEVOTION IS DISREGARDED AND DENIED IN DETERMINING THE AUTHENTICITY OF THE APPARITIONS.

Objection: When asked about the various visions, including the Fatima apparitions that might seem to confirm the Sabbatine Privilege, Morello said: *The Sabbatine Privilege or the historicity of the vision is not part of the deposit of faith. Private revelation cannot change that. People are free to believe it if they wish, but we cannot say that the Church teaches it and the Order clearly does not want to teach it as a part of the official catechesis.* (22)

In my opinion: *Extinguish not the spirit. Despise not prophecies, but prove all things, hold fast that which is good. From all appearance of evil refrain yourselves.* (1Thess.5, 19-22)

In passing judgment on pious traditions this must be borne in mind: that the Church acts so prudently in this matter that it does not allow such traditions to be narrated in books unless great caution has been employed and the narrative is premised by the declaration imposed by Urban VIII .... For the devotion based on any apparition, in as far as it regards the fact itself and is called relative, always implies as a condition the truth of the fact; but in so far as it is absolute, it is always based on the truth, for it is offered to the very persons of the Saints who are honored. (23)

In Sacred Scripture, the Letter of St. Paul to the Galatians, Chapter 1:11-12, is a direct reference for St. Paul receiving a (private) revelation from Jesus Christ Himself: *For I give you to understand, brethren, that the gospel which was preached by me is not according to man, for neither did I receive it of man, nor did I learn it, but by the revelation of Jesus Christ.* (24)

To repeat once again, from the Defense of the Scapular, found in Appendix 2,"Modern Day Objections and Responses," the above stated objection sounds strikingly similar to the statement of the 17th century Jansenist, John Launoy (who rejected the supernatural origins of the Scapular Devotion) when he said: *The Church is not ruled by private revelation and neither are the faithful to be ruled by it.* (25)

The Church approved the Devotion of the Sabbatine Privilege on the plane of Catholic doctrine: namely, it is a theologically sound opinion that the Blessed Virgin may assist souls in Purgatory on the day dedicated to her by the Church, thus she stabilized the Devotion, as she stabilizes all Devotions, by Catholic teaching. (26)

"To all the faithful who desired to obtain the assistance of Our Lady in Purgatory the Church recommended the devotion of the Sabbatine Privilege as it existed in the Confraternity of the Scapular of Our Lady of Mount Carmel." The Church exercised in the Decree on the Sabbatine Privilege her supreme spiritual authority to guide the devotional life of the faithful. She took the occasion of a belief in a private revelation existing in the Church to confirm the devotional practice to which it had given rise as one through which the devotional practice the faithful could hope for a suitable reward after death from the power of the Blessed Virgin with God. (27)

The place of the Scapular in the Fatima Apparitions: Our Lady told her (Lucia) that she would come as Our Lady of Mt. Carmel (on October 13, 1917) ... (Lucia's) interpretation was that the Scapular Devotion was pleasing to Our Lady and that she desired it to be propagated. Lucia said: *The Rosary and the Scapular are inseparable. The Scapular is a sign of Consecration to Our Lady.*

Pope Pius XII spoke of Fatima for the first time in an official Papal text, his Encyclical *Saeculo Exeunte Octavo,* **dated June, 13, 1940. In the text he stated:** *Let the faithful not forget, especially when they recite the Rosary, so recommended by the Blessed Virgin Mary of Fatima, to ask the Virgin Mother of God to obtain Missionary Vocations, with abundant fruits for the greatest possible number of souls.* **(www.miraclehunter.com/marian.../fatima/) On June 13, 1946, Venerable Pope Pius XII issued his Encyclical:** *Deiparae Virginis Mariae* **(an Encyclical by the Holy Father referring to a Private Revelation) in which he refers favorably to Our Lady's message at Fatima. (28)**

To deny the supernatural origins of the Scapular Devotion, based on the apparitions of Our Lady to Simon Stock, is in essence to deny the supernatural origins of Fatima, approved by the Church, where Our Lady appeared, during the Miracle of the Sun, on October 13, 1917 as Our Lady of Mount Carmel to the three children, holding down the Scapular to the world as an affirmation of her Scapular Visions to St. Simon Stock and to Pope John XXII.

The question here is: Are the Objectors to the authenticity of the origins of the Scapular Devotion saying that the numerous Holy Fathers' that have approved the authenticity of the Fatima apparitions are erroneous and that the authority of the Church to judge the authenticity of Private Revelation is incompetent?

Are we to ignore or reject Private Revelation approved by and founded on the doctrinal teachings of the Church that is attached to a Devotion deeply rooted in the Catholic Church for hundreds of years and confirmed by numerous Solemn Pontiffs? Are we to take the word of the Objectors who base their findings and have formulated their opinions based on the writings of a critical, erroneous and pronounced enemy of the Holy See, John Launoy?

11) THE ARGUMENTS AGAINST THE SCAPULAR DEVOTION ALONG WITH A LACK OF PROPER CATECHESIS HAVE WEAKENED THE DEVOTION TO A TREMENDOUS DEGREE.

In my opinion: Without the basics in the faith, the Devotion cannot be embraced; without a clear understanding of Our Lady's role in the economy of salvation, the Scapular Devotion will not be understood. My personal observation, to date, is that very few, if any, books are available in book stores recounting the traditional teachings of the Church on the Brown Scapular Devotion of Our Lady of Mount Carmel. It is hardly spoken of from the pulpit, generations of Catholic/Christians are unacquainted with and/or ignorant of the Scapular Devotion, of its Promise of eternal salvation and its Privilege and most especially in the basics of the Faith.

12) THE INTERCESSORY POWER OF THE MOTHER OF GOD HAS BEEN QUESTIONED THROUGH THE DENIAL OF THE SCAPULAR VISIONS.

In my opinion: The integrity of the Mother of God has been questioned and even defiled. The Scapular Devotion itself has not been denied only the Visions connected with it. However, when the Visions are denied and the origins of the Devotion are reconstructed, man is then placing himself above the power of God, who has worked undeniable, verifiable and unquestionable miracles through the vehicle of salvation delivered to the world through the loving hands of His Immaculate Mother and Queen, thereby challenging her "Suppliant Omnipotence" and her ability to obtain for us the salvation of our souls through her intercession.

13) NUMEROUS HISTORIANS WHO HAVE PROVIDED AUTHENTIC TESTIMONY AND SOLID SCHOLARLY RESEARCH ARE BEING IGNORED.

In my opinion: John Launoy was the first to attack the Scapular Visions in 1642, with his: *Dissertatio Duplex* and immediately John Cheron, O. Carm., responded to the defense of the Visions in the same year with his *Privilegiati Scapularis et visionis S. Simonis Stockii vindiciae.* Two other historians followed in the defense as well: Father Thomas Aquinas of St. Joseph, Carm. Disc: *Pro Sodalitio Sacri Scapularis,* 1648, and Fr. Hilibert Fesayus, O. Carm., *Duplex Privilegium Sacri Scapularis,* 1645. Many other historians have successfully supplied concrete historical documentation in favor of the authenticity of the Visions throughout the following years such as: William of Sanvico, 1290, John Grossi, 1398, Thomas Bradley-Scrope, 1450, Nicholas Calciuri, 1461, Baldwin Leersius, 1483, Arnold Bostius., 1499, John Palaeonydor, 1507, Giles Fabri, 1506, Menaldus of the Rosary, 1510, John Bale (who testified to having seen the Sabbatine Bull of John XXII, in the London Archives before it was burrned to the ground by Henry VIII), 1563, and most importantly, the Servant of God, Fr. Bartholomew Xiberta, 1950. (29)

14) THE ORIGIN OF THE SCAPULAR DEVOTION HAS BEEN TAKEN FROM OUR LADY.

In my opinion: One would wonder: Why the anxiousness for so long to try to disprove and deny the direct intercession of Our Lady for us through the Scapular Devotion, by challenging its supernatural orgins: the Visions, her promises, and her power to obtain for us the gift of Eternal Salvation? *Be sober and watch: because your adversary, the devil, as a roaring lion, goeth about seeking whom he may devour.* (1 Peter 5:8) *As the devil goes about seeking whom he may devour, so on the other hand, Mary goes about seeking whom She may save and to whom She may give life.* (29a)

15) WORDS SUCH AS "LEGEND, ELUSIVE, AMBIGUOUS, DOUBT AND SEEMED," ARE USED TO AID IN DIMINISHING THE AUTHENTICITY OF THE VISIONS.

Objection: *The legends of the Scapular Vision, then, and of the Sabbatine Privilege, arose at a time when similar stories were common currency when, in fact the fashion of the time almost demanded that each order should attribute, through some miraculous intervention, special efficacy to the habit* *its members wore.* (30) *St. Simon Stock is without a <u>doubt</u> the most <u>elusive</u> personality in a group of eminent Englishmen at the time…of whose life and character we know almost nothing.* (31)

In my opinion: In many publications put forth by certain Progressives in the Carmelite Community, extreme caution is placed in the mind of the reader regarding the authenticity of the Visions, creating doubt and cloaking the historicity in a veil of "legends," "fables" and "elusive" saints. The existence of St. Simon Stock is questioned in the greatest detail. (We quote again): A Brief from Pope Pius IX to Alfred Mombrun, author of "The Life of St. Simon Stock," dated October 23, 1869. His Holiness stated:

You are the author of "The Life of St. Simon Stock." We are most agreeable that the admirable virtues of this great saint, his zeal and the large and countless hardships he endured in Europe to spread the badge of the Order of Carmel, were not only capable of removing the indifference and the practical suppression where one plunged into the difficulties and hardships of the times, the cult of this great saint, but to sustain and increase the number of faithful for the Blessed Virgin Mary, either by the admirable examples of piety which was reflected in the life of St. Simon or either the marvelous testimonies of affection which he received from the Mother of God, affection which was above all manifested by the magnificent benefit of the Holy Scapular.

How could St. Simon have been "elusive" and "ambiguous," if the Holy Father spoke of him with much admiration, so much so as to acclaim the author of a book on the "Life of St. Simon Stock" by Alfred Monbrun? Finally, the authentic historical proofs of the historians and the supportive teachings of the Holy Fathers on the Scapular Devotion, especially those Documents which give the confirmation of the historicity of the Visions are monumental and must be carefully guarded:

That manner of speaking cannot be approved of in writings of Catholics, which, striving after a vicious novelty, seems to deride the piety of the faithful, and speaks of a new order of Christian life, new directions of the Church, new wants of the modern soul, etc. (32)

Would the numerous Holy Fathers who have richly indulgenced, affirmed, and confirmed the Scapular Devotion, and the Visions of Our Lady to St. Simon Stock and to Pope John XXII, issue Ecclesiastical legislation and Documentation from the Holy See on this Devotion for the past 763 years based on a legend? This very strongly implies the incompetency of the Papacy.

Consider the significant Documents issued by the Holy See in favor of the Scapular Devotion and the Visions by Several Popes, especially Venerable Pope Pius XII who left behind a "staggering amount" of writings on Carmel. His Documents on the Scapular Devotion are some of the most significant ever to come from the Holy See, for example: *Neminem profecto latet*, February 11, 1950. This letter has been aptly called, *the Charter of the Scapular Centenary celebration*. It is one of the most important Scapular documents ever to come from the Holy See. (32a) Again we repeat an exerpt from Pascendi Dominici Gregis, of Pope St. Pius X:

The Modernists pass judgement on the Holy Fathers of the Church even as they do upon Tradition. With consummate temerity they assure the public that the Fathers, while personally most worthy of all veneration, were entirely ignorant of history and criticism for which they are only excusable on account of the time in which they lived. (32b)

The following excerpt is taken from a Radio Broadcast to the International Mariological Congress, Venerable Pope Pius XII, regarding the "Errors to be Avoided:"

If these standards are strictly observed, Mariology will make genuine and permanent progress in inquiring ever more profoundly into the Blessed Virgin's gifts and dignity, and thus this study will go along the correct middle way, avoiding whatever falsely and intemperately goes beyond the bounds of truth, while keeping apart from those who are filled with a kind of unreasonable fear of conceding more than they ought to the Blessed Virgin, or as they frequently say, a fear that some honor and confidence is withheld from the Divine Redeemer Himself when His Mother is honored and invoked with all filial reverence. (33)

16) IN AN ON-LINE PUBLICATION ENTITLED: *THE CARMELITE SCAPULAR TODAY*, FROM CARMELITES. ORG, THE ARTICLE STATES THAT THE CONCLUSIONS DRAWN BY FR. XIBERTA ON PROVING THE HISTORICITY AND AUTHENTICITY OF THE SCAPULAR AND THE OVERALL RESULT OF HIS EFFORTS FROM A HISTORICAL POINT OF VIEW ON THE SCAPULAR VISION, ARE DESCRIBED BY THIS CONTEMPORARY

CARMELITE PUBLICATION AS "SOMEWHAT MEAGRE AND DISAPPOINTING." (34)

In my opinion: Again, are they referring to the same Fr. Bartolomeo Xiberta O. Carm., (1897-1967), who is now declared, "Servant of God," who was a Carmelite devoted entirely to the service of Jesus through Mary in the spirit of Elijah? Fr. Xiberta was one of the outstanding theologians of the last century, researcher, historian, teacher, and no doubt, the outstanding Carmelite theologian, who was present as a Consultant at the Second Vatican Council, and the only Carmelite who was on the Theological Commission. A book was written about his devotion to Mary: *Bartolome Maria Xiberta, Teologo de Nuestra Senora,* (Bartholomew Maria Xiberta, Our Lady's Theologian,) by Checa Arregui, O. Carm. Would he not have taken great precaution in assuring that his analysis of the ancient texts on the recorded Scapular Vision by several Carmelite historians and his conclusions were accurate? (35)

17) GENERALLY SPEAKING, AFTER REVIEWING ALL OF THE PAST AND CURRENT PUBLICATIONS IN OPPOSITION TO THE AUTHENTICITY OF THE VISIONS OF OUR LADY TO ST. SIMON STOCK AND POPE JOHN XXII, THE MAJORITY OF THE OBJECTIONS AGAINST THE TRADITIONAL TEACHINGS ON THE ORIGINS OF THE SCAPULAR DEVOTION AND THE VISIONS, ORIGINATE FROM THE PROGRESSIVE CARMELITES THEMSELVES.

In my opinion: It has been the author's observation over the past 14 years, that the majority of the publications, periodicals, books, pamphlets, and on line objections to the authenticity of the origin of the Scapular Devotion in regard to the Visions of Our Blessed Mother to St. Simon Stock and to Pope John XXII, are originating from certain Carmelite Community themselves. Appropriately speaking, the reader may discern for himself the source of the publications found in opposition to the authenticity of the Visions. Please see Appendix 2, "Ancient and Modern Day Objections to the Scapular Visions," and Appendix 3, "Publications in Opposition," in this book listing current Carmelite publications from different countries of the world, such as England, India, Italy, that expound and repeat many of the same objections of the past four centuries.

18) OBJECTION: THE STATEMENT IN AN ARTICLE IN THE CARMELITE DIGEST, 2001 SAYS: "IT IS NOW QUITE OBVIOUSLY HIGH TIME FOR THE CARMELITES FREELY AND FRANKLY TO RELINQUISH THESE PIOUS LEGENDS, UNABLE AS THEY EVIDENTLY ARE TO STAND UP UNDER SCRUTINY OF 'PRESENT-DAY HISTORICAL INQUIRY.'" (36)

In my opinion: It is interesting to note that "Present-Day Historical Inquiry," the application of modern day techniques in 20th and 21st century analysis used in determining the authenticity of the ancient documents of the Scapular Visions, have resulted in nothing more than the resuscitation of the identical objections of the 17th century Jansenist and Gallican, John Launoy, whose condemned works were written at a time when modern day techniques did not exist.

Though we are assured of the "scrupulous accuracy and scrutiny" of Fr. (Ludovico) Saggi's analysis in "La Bolla Sabbatina" in determining the inauthenticity of the Sabbatine Bull, his work, in my opinion, is quite dubious, weak, suspect and undoubtedly inaccurate if the critical approach of modern day scholarship produces nothing more than the regurgitation of the almost 400 year old, identical objections of a man whose fallacious works, distinguished by his "erroneous teachings" (27 of which were placed on *The Index Librorum Prohibitorum* [list of prohibited books] published by the authority of Pope St. Pius X, 1907) are the basis for the Contemporaries' rejection of the Scapular Visions.

(Please see: "The Weight of the Evidence will very much depend on the character of the witnesses," in Chapter 4 of this book regarding the *Index Librorum Prohibitorum*.) The critical approach of modern day scholarship to the history of the Scapular seems to have resulted in nothing more than a disreputable modification of the ancient errors of the past.

SABBATINE
PRIVILEGE FORBIDDEN

In my opinion: a *schism* has occurred within the Carmelite Community. The ancient 17th century objections of the Gallican and Jansenist thinker, John Launoy, has infiltrated into the 21st century Carmelite School of thought and the Contemporaries embracing it have challenged and obscured the traditional teachings on the origin of the Visions regarding the Scapular Devotion of Our Lady of Mount Carmel. Based on the collected resources of information for this book, the Opposition within the Order, through its publications and ecclesiastical actions, have hijacked the Devotion:

First, in an attempt to discredit the solid historical teachings and proclamations of the Church regarding the origins of this heavenly Devotion, by the manner described in the Encyclical of Pope St. Pius X, *Pascendi dominici gregis,* Sept. 8, 1907 ("On The Doctrine of the Modernists") and through what Pope Pius XII termed as: *an unreasonable fear of conceding more than they ought to the Blessed Virgin...* (Pius XII, R. M. to the International Mariological Congress, October 24, 1954: "Errors to be avoided")

Second, to sever any and all connections with the Mother of God regarding the origins of the Devotion, in so far as it may disprove the "Suppliant Omnipotence" (Pope Benedict XV, Epistle: *Decessorem Nostrum,* April 19, 1915), of the Queen of Heaven in obtaining all that she asks from her Son.

Third, to remove her association from the Scapular as the visible Sign, evidence, and concrete proof of Our Lady's Spiritual Maternity, and immeasurable power, as "Mediatrix of All Graces" and as "Coredemptrix" (Pope Saint John Paul II, Angelus, March 31, 1985) with Our Lord for the salvation of mankind.

Fourth, to eliminate through a disordered understanding of the Divine Mercy of God, the need for the post-mortem purification which the Church has dogmatically taught as Purgatory (P.R.F.) by the suppression of the Sabbatine Bull, and the Sabbatine Privilige.

Fifth, and most important of all, because the Scapular is the Visible Insignia of Christian Victory, the outward symbol of Mary's invisible, powerful mediation and her immeasurable role in the redemption of mankind; it is for our protection in battle (*And the dragon was angry against the woman and went to make war with the rest of her seed, who keep the commandments of God and have the testimony of Jesus Christ.*

292

Rev.12:17); and it is our identification as the *Seed of Mary*, the sign and symbol of Consecration to God through Her Immaculate Heart. *The Scapular will be for all, the sign of our Consecration to the Immaculate Heart of Mary.* (Pope Pius XII, A.A.S. 42, 1950)

In the final battle, it is by the Scapular, the Sign of eternal alliance with the *Woman* of Genesis (3:15) *who shall crush the head of Satan*, and the *Woman* of Revelation, (12:1) *clothed with the sun* that Lucifer will be rendered powerless against all humanity. The Victory is hers.

ROSARY FORGOTTEN

In my Opinion: If the Origins of the Brown Scapular Devotion, are allowed to decay in a sea of dust, so then will the Devotion itself, so then will all other approved Devotions in the Church, based on Private Revelation, such as the Rosary, which leads us closer to God:

…Devotion to Our Lady of the Rosary is most opportune for the needs of these times… we have desired to revive everywhere this devotion, and to spread it far and wide among the faithful of the world. (Pope Leo XIII, Encycl. *Vi è Ben Noto,* On the Rosary and Public Life, September 20, 1887).

We do not hesitate to affirm again publicly that We put great confidence in the Holy Rosary for the healing of evils which afflict our times. Not with force, not with arms, not with human power, but with Divine help obtained through the means of this prayer… (Pope Pius XII, Encycl. *Ingruentium Malorum,* Sept. 15, 1951, Feast of the Seven Sorrows of the Virgin Mary).

The Rosary has many times been proposed by my predecessors and myself as a prayer for <u>peace</u>. At the start of a millennium which began with the terrifying attacks of September 11, 2001, a millennium which witnesses every day in numerous parts of the world, fresh scenes of bloodshed and violence, to rediscover the Rosary means to immerse onself in contemplation of the mystery of Christ who *"is our peace."* (Pope Saint John Paul 1 II, Apostolic Letter: Rosarium Virginis Mariae, October 16, 2002)

The Rosary is a spiritual weapon in the struggle against evil, against all violence, for peace in hearts, in families, in society and in the world. (Pope Benedict XVI, Homily, *Pastoral Visit to the Pontifical Shrine of Pompeii,* Pompeii, Italy, October 19, 2008)

When Our Blessed Mother, appeared, as Our Lady of the Rosary, at Fatima, Portugal on May 13, 1917, she ended with these words: *Pray the Rosary everyday to obtain <u>peace</u> for the world <u>and</u> the end of the war.* The Scapular and the Rosary are one, for Sister Lucia of Fatima has said many times: *The Rosary and the Scapular are inseparable. (Our Lady of Fatima and the Brown Scapular,* Rev. Killian Lynch, O. Carm., Prior General, Aylesford, 1956, p. 14)

Sadly, evidence exists as well, that many Devotions based on private revelation, approved by the Church, have fallen victim to the quagmire of Modernism, and fallen prey to the promoters of the "Neo-Modernistic Age."

CHAPTER 8 ENDNOTES
OBSERVATIONS OF THE AUTHOR

a   Irish Ecclesiastical Record, Volume VIII, John E. Bartlley, O.C.C., Dublin, 1887, p. 795

1   *Carmel in the World,* Patrick Thomas McMahon, O. Carm., Vol. XLIII, N. 3, Rome, 2004, p. 187

1a Father Callan's Commentary on Romans 13:11-14 for the First Sunday of Advent

2   *Our Sunday Visitor,* February 24, 1991, by Fr. Charles Mangan

3   *La Bolla Sabbatina,* Ludovico Saggi, O. Carm., Roma, 1967, pp. 80-87; *Our Lady of the Place,* Emanuele Boaga, O. Carm., Roma, 2001, pp. 95-103

4   *The Scapular and Some Critics,* P. E. Magennis, O.C.C., Rome, p. 132

5   *The Carmelite Scapular Today,* Patrick Thomas McMahon, carmelites. org, pp. 2, 4

6   *Ristretto Della Vita di S. Simone Stock,* P.S. Mattei, Roma, 1873, pp. 123-139, OBIEZIONE DI GIOVANNI LAUNOY (and other modern day objectors)

7   *Vatican II Marian Council,* Fr. William G. Most, 1972, Ireland, pp.167, 168: (cf. Eugenius a S. Joseph, *Dissertatio Historica de Sacro Scapulari Carmelitico,* in *Analecta Ordinis Carmelitarum Discalceatorum* IV, 3

(January-March, 1930, p. 182), and *The Scapular and Some Critics*, P. E. Magennis, O.C.C., Rome, 1914, p. 150

8   *De Festis D.N. I C. et B. Mariae Vir.*. lib. II Cap. VI nn. 4.6.8. e 10 in: *Lo Scapolare, 2* A Cura Del Comitato Italiano, VII Centenario Dello Scapolare, Roma, p. 65

9   *L'Osservatore Romano,* Pope John XXIII at the Chiesa di S. Luigi dei Francesi, Roma, Venerdi 20 Febbraio 1959

10   *Introduction to Mary*, Mark Miravalle, STD., California, 1993, pp. 125,127

11   *The Credibility of the Scapular Promises, A Dissertation,* Christian P. Ceroke, O. Carme., Rome, 1950, p. 102

12   *Ibid,* pp. 102, 103

13   *Papal Teachings Our Lady,* The Benedictine Monks of Solesmes, 1961, p. 241

14   *Ibid,* p. 173, Pope St. Pius X: Encycl. *Ad diem illum laetissimum,* February 2, 1904

14a *De Visione Sancti Simonis Stock,* (Ven.) Bartholomaeus F. M. Xiberta, O. Carm., Rome, 1950, p. 15 cf. *The Month,* 58, (1886, III), 308

15   *The Carmelite Scapular Today,* Richard Copsey, O.Carm.; Journal of Ecclesiastical History, Vol. 50, No. 4, October 1999, carmelites.org., p. 2

15a Encycl. *Fidentem Piumque,* September 20, 1896 cf. *Papal Teachings, Our Lady* The Benedictine Monks of Solsemes, Boston, 1961, p. 148

16   *The Credibility of the Scapular Promises,* A Dissertation, Rev. Christian P. Ceroke, O. Carm, Rome, 1950, p. 47

17   *Papal Teachings on Our Lady,* The Benedictine Monks of Solesmes, Boston, 1961, p. 205: Pope Pius XI: Apost. Letter, *Explorata res est,* February 2, 1923 *The Brown Scapular,* Fr. William Most; www.ewtn.com/librarv/scriptur/scapular.tx Pope Benedict XV: *Epistle, Decessorem Nostrum,* April 19, 1915

18   Apostolic Letter of His Holiness, Pius XII on the Seventh Centenary of the Scapular Vision, February 11, 1950, in the Archives of the Order, *Neminem profecto* cf *Papal Teachings, Our Lady,* pp. 288-290

19   *Letter from the Carmel de Lisieux,* dated June 23, 2004 to a Third Order Carmelite, and personal friend of the author, Aileen O' Sullivan: See Chapter 8, "Testimonials of the Saints"

20   *The Credibility of the Scapular Promises, A Dissertation,* Christian P. Ceroke, O. Carm., 1950, pp. 152, 155, 156.

21   *The Carmelite Scapular Today,* carmelites.org, p.3; Summary of an article from Richard Copsey, "Journal of Ecclesiastical History," Vol. 50, No.4, October, 1999

22   *The Scapular and Some Critics*, P. E. Magennis, 1914, p. 10.

23   Galatians 1: 11-12, (Douay Rheims)

24   See endnote #36 in Appendix 2, "Responses to the Objections" under "Modern Day Objections and Responses"

25   *The Credibility of the Scapular Promises*, Rev. Christian P Ceroke, O. Carm., Rome, 1950, p. 51

26   *Ibid*, p. 52

27   *Our Lady of Fatima and the Brown Scapular,* Rev. Killian Lynch, O.Carm, Dublin, 1959, pp. 12, 13; *Rediscovering Fatima*, Rev. Robert J. Fox, Huntington, 1982, p. vii

28   *Take This Scapular,* Carmelite Fathers and Tertiaries, 1949, pp. 216-241; *Le Scapulaire de Notre-Dame du Mont-Carmel est authentique,* P. Marie Joseph du Sacre Coeur, Avignon, 1928, p. 63 (translated and paraphrased)

29   *St. Simon Stock - The Scapular Vision and the Brown Scapular Devotion,* Bede Edwards, Carmelite Digest, Vol. 16, No.3, Summer, 2001, p. 21

29a St. Bernardine, Marial. p. 3, s. 1. Cf Glorie, IX, 260 from: *Mary in Her Scapular Promise,* John Mathias Haffert, 1942, p. 110

30   *The Carmelite Scapular Today,* carmelites.org, p. 3

31   Pope Pius X: *Pascendi Dominici Gregis,* Encyclical on Modernism, *On the Doctrines of Modernists,* September 8, 1907, cf. *The Scapular and Some Critics,* P. E. Magennis, O.C.C., Rome, 1914, p. 9

32   Pope Pius XII, Radio Message to the International Mariological Congress, October 24, 1954 in: *Papal Teachings, Our Lady,* The Benedictine Monks of Solesmes, Boston, 1961, p. 408 *The Carmelite Scapular Today,* carmelites.org, p.3 www.carmelites.org/review/march2001/marchapril2001_9.pdf p. 2 CITOC, No. 4, October-December 2003, *Closure of the Diocesan Process of Canonization of Fr. Bartolomè Fanti M. Xiberta, O. Carm.;* CITOC, No. 3, July-September 2007, *Carmelite Presence at the Second Vatican Council;* The Carmelite Web Site – O.Carm; *Closure of the Diocesan Process for the Canonization of Fr. Bartholomew Fanti M. Xiberta, O. Carm:* http://www.ocarm.org/pre09/news/eng2803.htm Carmelite Digest: *St. Simon Stock – The Scapular Vision and the Brown Scapular Devotion,* by Bede Edwards, Vol. 16, No. 3, Summer, 2001, p. 23

32a *Pius XII and His Heritage to Carmel,* compiled by Brendan Hill, O. Carm., found in: *MARY,* Rev. Howard Rafferty, O. Carm., Editor, Volume 20, No. 4, July, August, 1959, p. 51

32b Pope Pius X: *Pascendi Dominici Gregis,* Encyclical on Modernism, *On the Doctrines of Modernists,* September 8, 1907

33   Pope Pius XII, Radio Message to the International Mariological Congress, October 24, 1954 in: *Papal Teachings, Our Lady,* The Benedictine Monks of Solesmes, Boston, 1961, p. 408

34   The Carmelite Scapular Today, carmelites.org, p. 3, www.carmelites. org/review/march2011/marchapril2001_9.pdf, p. 2

35   CITOC, No. 4, October-December 2003, *Closure of the Diocesan Process of Canonization of Fr. Bartolomè Fanti M. Xiberta,* O. Carm.; CITOC, No 3, July-September 2007, *Carmelite Presence at the Second Vatican Council;* The Carmelite Web Site—O. Carm.; *Closure of the Diocesan Process for the Canonization of Fr. Bartholomew Fanti M. Xiberta,* O. Carm.: http://www.ocarm.org/pre09/news/eng2803.htm

36   Carmelite Digest: *St. Simon Stock—The Scapular Vision and the Brown Scapular Devotion,* by Bede Edwards, Vol. 16, No. 3, Summer, 2001, p.23

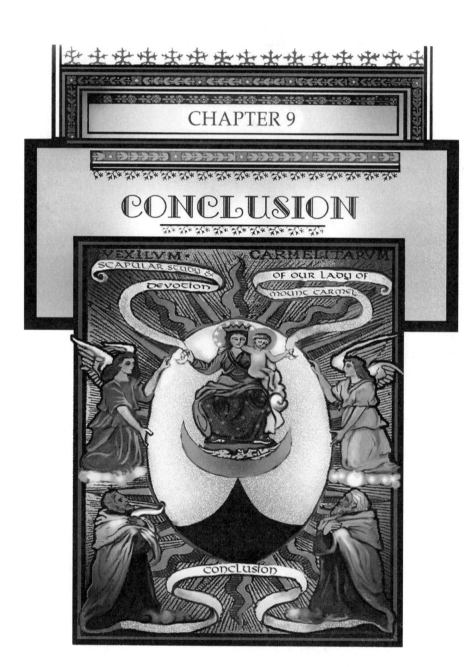

CHAPTER 9

CONCLUSION

Chapter 9

Conclusion

God has spoken through the countless miracles of the Scapular; Our Lady has come to us in the flesh to give us her Scapular with the Promise of eternal salvation and the pledge of her constant protection even beyond the grave; the Holy Fathers have acknowledged, approved and confirmed the authenticity of the Visions from the most ancient ecclesiastical pronouncements, to numerous contemporary Church documents in the 20th century; great Saints and Doctors of the Church have embraced the Scapular and acknowledged the authenticity of the Promises of the Blessed Virgin and countless, revered and reliable Professors, Doctors, Historians and witnesses have attested to the truth of the revelations of the Blessed Virgin. Who then would dare to contest these witnesses and judges and who can then say, that she did not make these Promises to St. Simon Stock and Pope John XXII?

In Conclusion: The Objectors and the Defenders have presented their cases and after reviewing the evidence, it may be justifiably determined (1):

1 The Queen of Heaven, "Suppliant Omnipotence" herself, did condescend to humanity, on July 16, 1251, to bequeath to us, her Garment of salvation, to identify us as her *seed*. It is the fruit of her love, the Promise of her protection, so that we, at the end of our sojourn in this Valley of Tears, may receive the Grace of Final Contrition at the moment of our death and be delivered from the pains of our purification on the first Saturday after our death, as she promised to Pope John XXII in granting the Sabbatine Privilege, to be accompanied by her to the glory of the Beatific Vision for all eternity.

2 The Vision of St. Simon was not an invention of Palaeonydor toward the close of the 15th century which is obvious from a series of witnesses which can be traced back to the middle of the 14th century....William of Sanvico, who about 1290 testified to the

299

Vision of the Blessed Virgin, proves that our tradition was not a simple fiction of the mid-14th century. Sanvico's proximity to the event, and the reliability of his chronicle, prohibit the rejection of his testimony...the historicity of the Scapular tradition is established by its remarkable conformity with the historical circumstances of St. Simon Stock's administration, even with facts that have come to light only recently...(2)

3   The approval of the Church and the Catholic world for centuries, the extraordinary miracles of the Scapular through the intercession of Our Lady and a sound, reliable and trustworthy historical investigation, prove that the Scapular Promises of Our Lady to St. Simon Stock and Pope John XXII, owe their origin, according to the tradition of the Church, to the unquestionable, verifiable, authentic and true revelations of the Blessed Virgin Mary. (3)

The information on the authenticity of the Scapular Visions of Our Blessed Mother to St. Simon Stock and to Pope John XXII is overwhelming. This book could not contain the vast amount of documented material and evidence that exists throughout the world. It is only a humble beginning to a continual lifetime of research on a subject so tender to the heart of Our Most Loving and Compassionate Mother Mary, Our Queen and Our Intercessor.

It is my hope, dear reader, that you will grow more in love with Our Heavenly Mother every day, and that you will treasure with all your heart, the gift from Heaven, given to us personally by the loving hands of Mary, Flower of Carmel, that you may choose to wear it lovingly as a sign of Consecration to Her Immaculate Heart and that you may avail yourself of the abundant spiritual benefits waiting for those who honor her and her Son through her Devotion and Sign of Consecration to Her Immaculate Heart, the *The Brown Scapular of Our Lady of Mount Carmel.*

THE GARMENT

And the Lord God made for Adam and his wife, garments of skins and clothed them. (Genesis 3:21-Douay Rheims)

The garment in Scripture is not only an article of clothing used in a physical maternal sense to cover the body and protect it from the elements of nature, it is, in a spiritual sense also a prefigurement, a symbolic representative of both the dignity, power, authority, inheritance and elevated status of the biblical figure, as well as the emotion, state or condition of the conscious soul.   In the Garden of Eden, Adam and Eve wore the garment of innocence and when they were cast out, they wore the garment of shame. (Genesis 3: Douay Rheims Bible parallel Haydock Commentary; www.veritasbible. com/drb/compare/haydock/Genesis_3), paraphrased

What spiritual benefit can possibly come from the putting on of a garment? What supernatural efficacy can a piece of cloth or material contain?   The answers to these questions can be found in the Holy Scriptures as well as in the historical facts in the life of the Church. (*The Scapular and Some Critics,* P. E. Magennis, Rome, 1914, p. 2)

Throughout the entire Old and New Testament and within the living spirit of the One, Holy, Catholic and Apostolic Church, examples abound of the sanctity, reverence and symbolism of the importance and power of the "garment" as a reflection of "Spiritual Maternity."

Now Israel loved Joseph above all his sons because he had him in his old age; and he made him a coat of diverse colors. (Genesis 37:3 D.R.)

And he gave him a multicolored garment as an excellent gift and proof of the love with which he accompanied him. Aaron, the first High Priest of the Sinai Covenant was also given a decorated coat/tunic as a sign of his priestly authority. (Ex. 28: 31-35) To the Fathers of the Church, Joseph's coat of many colors given him by his loving father as a sign of his authority over his brothers not only came to represent the gifts of power God gave His beloved Son but also the spiritual gifts God gave His Son's Bride, the Universal Church as a sign of her authority over the brotherhood of the human family. (http://www. agapebiblestudy.com/genesis/Lesson_16.htm);

THE PENTATEUCH PART 1: GENESIS
The Story of Joseph...paraphrased

Speak to the children of Israel and thou shalt tell them to make to themselves fringes in the corners of their "garments" putting in them ribbons of blue; that when they shall see them, they may remember all the commandments of the Lord, and not follow their own thoughts and eyes, going astray after diverse things. (Num. XV. 38, Douay Rheims; *The Sacramentals of the Holy Catholic Church, or Flowers from the Garden of the Liturgy,* Rev. William J. Barry, London, 1879, p. 204)

The word "garment" in this passage is "palliorum" in Latin. In this way, this "pallium" or "garment" became an article of ecclesiastical attire; it held the most important and dignified place among the articles of civil dress. Nor was it devoid of its sacred significance. It was a memorial of the Commandments of God and continence from worldly desires; (*ibid,* p. 205)

And it came to pass when he had made an end of speaking to Saul, the soul of Jonathon was knit with the soul of David and Jonathon loved him as his own soul...And David and Jonathon made a covenant for he loved him as his own soul and Jonathon stripped himself of the coat with which he was clothed and gave it to David and the rest of his garments. (First Book of Kings (1 Samuel 18:1, 3, 4)

Jonathon stripped himself of the robe that was upon him and gave it to David. To receive any part of the dress which had been worn by a sovereign or his eldest son and heir is deemed in the East the highest honor which can be conferred on a subject. (Jamieson-Fausset-Brown Bible Commentary; http://biblecommenter.com/1_samuel/18-4.htm)

Sacred Scripture and Church History clearly prove the fact that the outer "garment" (also referred to as a "pallium) of saintly personages was reverently preserved and sometimes worn by others. To assume the (garment) of another was to imbibe his spirit and profess to be his disciple. (*The Sacramentals of the Holy Catholic Church,* Rev. William James Barry, 1879, p. 205)

And the Lord said to him (Elias): Eliseus the son of Saphat of Abelmeula thou shalt anoint to be prophet in thy room...And Elias departing from thence found Eliseus and when Elias came up to him, he cast his "mantle" upon him. (III Kings xix, 16, 19)

The corresponding word for *mantle* (or garment) in the Latin Vulgate is *pallium*. When Elias was taken up in a chariot of fire, he dropped his (mantle) as a legacy to his faithful disciple and immediately Eliseus used it as the instrument of his miraculous powers. He struck the waters of the Jordan with the sacred garment and they were divided and the Prophet passed over dry shod. (*The Sacramentals of the Holy Catholic Church*, Rev. William James Barry, 1879, p. 206)

Thus, the mantle of Elias was at once the instrument whereby the double spirit which Eliseus had prayed for was imparted to him, the instrument whereby he was enabled to work the same miracles as Elias had wrought and the token whereby he was known and recognized as that Prophet's legitimate successor. (*The Rambler, A Catholic Journal and Review*, New Series, Vol. V., London, 1856, p. 64)

The Old Testament is rich with myriad examples on the significance and meaning of the "garment" as a sign of affiliation and of transmission of noble heredity passed on from one generation to the next.

In the New Testament, The Blessed Virgin Mary begins her role as a loving and protective Mother as she gently wrapped her "firstborn" in swaddling clothes and laid him in a manger:

And the angel said to them: "Fear not for behold I bring you good tidings of great joy that shall be to all the people: For this day is born to you a Savior, who is Christ the Lord in the city of David. And this shall be a sign unto you. You shall find the infant wrapped in swaddling clothes and laying in a manger." (Luke 2: 10-12)

It was a clothing of great significance, for she not only sought to physically nurture and shield her innocent child from the cold and the elements but she wrapped Him in a "garment" announced by the angel that would be a sign to the shepherds, a mark of His identification as the true Savior. (The Sacred Page: The Meaning of Jesus' Swaddling Clothes; http://www.thesacredpage.com/2008/12/christmas-star.html.) His clothing represented humility and yet a sign of His royalty and His identity as "Messiah," the Christ, the Son of David.

On the days when Jesus walked in Galilee, we read that the supernatural power passed from His garment to heal the sick and infirmed, thus apparently giving the sanction of the Son of Man to the great principle underlying the Devotion of the Scapular as well as of all other religious garments. (*The Scapular and Some Critics*, P. E. Magennis, O.C.C., Rome, 1914, p. 3)

And behold a woman who was troubled with an issue of blood twelve years came behind Him and touched the hem of His garment.

For she said within herself: If I shall touch only His garment, I shall be healed. But Jesus turning and seeing her said: "Be of good heart" daughter, thy faith hath made thee whole. And the woman was made whole from that hour. (Matthew 9:20-21 Douay Rheims)

Her faith is enriched by her expression of humility; she is conscious of being unworthy to touch Our Lord. "She touched the hem of His garment, she approached Him in a spirit of faith, she believed and she realized that she was cured… (It was the touch of His garment that healed her.) So we too, if we wish to be saved should reach out in faith to touch the "garment of Christ." (St. Ambrose, "Expositio Evangelii Sec. Lucam," VI, 56 and 58); Source: "The Navarre Bible: Text and Commentaries:, Catholic Caucus: Sunday Mass Readings, 07-01-12; Thirteenth Sunday.

After His passion, death and resurrection and before Our Lord ascended into Heaven, he empowered His apostles and their successors, the bishops and pastors of Christ's Church, with the command to continue His work on earth saying: *Going therefore, teach ye all nation; baptizing them in the name of the Father and of the Son, and of the Holy Ghost,* (Matthew 28: 19, D.R.) through His divinely instituted universal Sacrament of the One, Holy, Catholic and Apostolic Church.

For you are all the children of God by faith in Christ Jesus, for as many of you as have been baptized in Christ, have put on Christ. (St. Paul, Letter to the Galatians 3:26, 27) *But put ye on the Lord Jesus Christ and make not provision for the flesh in its concupiscence* (St. Paul, Letter to the Romans 13:14 Douay Rheims)

Christ Himself instituted all seven Sacraments of the Church, beginning with the Sacrament of Baptism when He, Himself was baptized in the Jordan River. Its use began when Christ and His disciples were baptizing. (John 3:4) The Sacrament became a precept when Our Lord expired on the Cross. The necessity of Baptism was proclaimed by the Savior after the Resurrection (Matthew 28:19, Mark 16:15) and its solemn promulgation took place on the day of Pentecost. (Acts 2:38, 39) (http://catholicharboroffaithandmorals.com/Baptism.html)

During the ceremonial administration of the Sacrament of Baptism, a white garment is used to represent *putting on Christ* in the words of St. Paul written above: (Galatians 3:26/27, Romans 13:14) Announcing that the believer has become a new creature having been clothed with Christ, the Priest places the white garment on the the new Christian (http://www.catholicdoors.com/courses/

304

baptism.htm)

The Catechism of the Catholic Church states in #1243: "The white garment symbolizes that the person baptized has "put on Christ," has risen with Christ." (Galatians 3:27) It is also a representation of the white burial cloth of our resurrected Lord that we have risen gloriously with Christ to a new life. The white garment of Baptism is the indelible mark of our identification with Christ, that we have been purified, sanctified, enlightened and clothed with a share in the divine life of Christ.

He that shall overcome shall thus be clad in white garments and I will not blot his name out of the book of life; I will confess his name before my Father and before His angels. (Rev. 3:5)

In the history of the early Church we see again and again how God charges with supernatural currents, places and things closely associated with the personalities of those who have loved Him and served Him with generosity. (*The Scapular and Some Critics,* P.E. Magennis, Rome, 1914, p. 4)

The great St. Athanasius gave his mantle to St. Antony; and when St. Paul, the hermit of Egypt prayed to St. Antony to bring it to his cell and to wrap his own body in it to bury him, St. Antony himself took the hermit's mantle from off his shoulders and ever afterwards wore it, we are told on all great occasions of solemnity. (Ibid, p. 64) Thus he professed that he held the same faith as Athanasius, the intrepid champion of the Divinity of the Eternal Word against the impious Arians. (*The Sacramentals of the Holy Catholic Church,* Rev. William James Barry, 1879, p. 206)

St. Luke recounts other events in the Acts of the Apostles which similarly recommend the institution of Sacramentals: (The Holy Scriptures tell us that) handkerchiefs and aprons touched by St. Paul, were carried to the sick and the diseases left them and the evil spirits departed:

And God wrought by the hand of Paul more than common miracles, so that even there were brought from his body to the sick, handkerchiefs and aprons and the diseases departed from them and the wicked spirits went out of them. (Acts of the Apostles, 19:11, 12, Douay Rheims); Opus Sanctorum Angelorum, Work of the Holy Angel (http://www.opusangelorum.org/English/Sacramentals.html)

These instances sufficiently prove that a certain religious meaning and value was attached in the estimation of the early Christians to the wearing of the garment of any great saint or doctor of the Church as though they were placed more immediately in communion with him to whom the garment had belonged. (*The Rambler, A Catholic Journal and Review, New Series*, Vol. V., London, 1856, p. 64)

Through the symbolism of the "Garment" we have received the inheritance of physical and spiritual maternity and the heredity of those who have gone before us. As the white garment of Baptism marks us with our identity in Christ as the adopted sons and daughters of God, so too, Our Heavenly Mother Mary, a brilliant reflection of the radiance of her Son, has spun a heavenly garment, an outward sign which carries the promise of her protection and of eternal salvation and marks us with the identification as her adopted children. A garment of recognition by Our Heavenly Mother, it is a gift to all of her children who want to be known, recognized and protected by her through the perils of this life, at the moment of our death, and into eternity.

The Brown Scapular of Our Lady of Mount Carmel is a Sacramental of the Holy Roman Catholic Church. As the Sacraments were all divinely instituted by Christ himself here on earth, the Sacramentals, sacred signs that signify effects obtained through the Church's intercession are usually instituted by the Church. They work through the power and prayers of the Church (*ex opera operantis Ecclesiae*) and through the pious disposition of the one using them. (http://www.fisheaters.com/sacramentalsintro.html)

Thus, for well-disposed members of the faithful, the liturgy of the sacraments and sacramentals sanctifies almost every event in their lives; they are given access to the stream of divine grace which flows from the paschal mystery of the passion, death, the resurrection of Christ, the font from which all sacraments and sacramentals draw their power. There is hardly any proper use of material things which cannot thus be directed toward the sanctification of men and the praise of God.

(Constitution on the Sacred Liturgy *Sacrosanctum Concilium* Solemnly Promulgated by His Holiness Venerable Pope Paul VI on December 4, 1963)

On July 16, 1251 the Queen of Heaven, accompanied by a multitude of angels in all majesty, appeared to her chosen priest, the Successor of Elias, his Carmelite Prior-General, St. Simon Stock, bequeathing to the world through him, her "Garment of Grace," the Habit of her Order the Scapular to be the material sign of her intercession and the vehicle of salvation for her adopted children: **This shall be the sign: whosoever shall die wearing this, shall not suffer eternal fire.**

Conclusion

The Church has recognized this gift from the Mother of God as useful for the salvation of her children. From the hands of her chosen priest, St. Simon Stock, it was delivered into the hands of Pope John XXII, the second Pope of Avignon educated by the Dominicans who in an apparition from the Queen of Heaven was directed to ratify on earth the Privilege that was granted by her Son in Heaven for all those who wear the Scapular called: *The Sabbatine Privilege.*

Through the inspiration of the Holy Spirit it was approved and confirmed by numerous Solemn Pontiffs throughout the Centuries until in the 20th century, Pope Saint John XXIII, a Secular Franciscan uniting himself across eight centuries of history to the last Pope that bore his name and proclaiming it for all the world, publicly authenticated and undeniably confirmed that his predecessor, Pope John XXII of Avignon was truly the "Father of the Sabbatine Privilege."(From a sermon of Pope John XXIII preached at St. Louis of France Church, Rome, February 18, 1959, for the closing of the Lourdes centenary year.)

Like the domestics of the wise woman whose praise is in the Book of Proverbs we are clothed with double garments to protect us against the cold winds and storms of spiritual and physical adversity: *She shall not fear for her house in the cold of snow: for all her domestics are clothed with double garments.* (Proverbs 31:21, 25; *The Sacramentals of the Holy Catholic Church...*, Rev. William James Barry, London, 1879, pp. 158, 159)

Because of her great love for us, Mary wraps us in the swaddling cloth of her Scapular, protects us from the tempestuous sea of earthly adversities, assists us at the agonizing door of death, safeguards us from the bonds of the roaring and everlasting fires of hell, delivers us into the purifying fires of salvation and accompanies us into Paradise so that we may be finally vested in the white garment of everlasting life, a garment that transcends all time and space, a garment predestined from all time from a *Woman* predestined from all eternity.

The Royal "Queen of Prophets," (Litany of Loreto) has woven a royal robe for her subjects. She is *The Woman of Genesis* (who will crush the head of Satan: Genesis 3:15: Douay Rheims) and *The Woman of the Apocalypse* (through whom the dragon is conquered Rev. 12:7-12 D.R.) who from beginning to end *accompanies the revelation of God's salvific plan for humanity.* (Redemptoris Mater, John Paul II, March 25, 1987)

Could it be that Almighty God has been preparing us from all time for the ultimate "garment," the garment that would bring about the conversion of our souls and shield us from the insidious attack of spiritual darkness in the final battle? It was to Elias that Our Lady was revealed in a cloud centuries before her birth, it was at Fatima centuries after her birth that Our Lady dressed in the habit of Carmel, held in her hands, the Scapular, the garment of her Order and the Order of Elias. Symbolic of the blood over the doors of the Jews during the Passover, Our Lady held out the Scapular to the crowd during the Miracle of the Sun, October 13, 1917, which foreshadowed a purification and a need for protection. This is offered to all who are consecrated to her and place themselves under her mantle of protection. When the Church passes through the period of purification leading to the Triumph of the Immaculate Heart, the Scapular will identify us in this future battle as Children of Mary, under her mantle of protection. (Speramus – We Hope, May 14, 2013, paraphrased)

For the Lord will pass through striking the Egyptians: and when he shall see the blood on the transom, and on both the posts, he will pass over the door of the house, and not suffer the destroyer to come into your houses and to hurt you. (Exodus 12:23 D.R.)

The mantle of Elias has been passed on to us, the garment of one chosen by God for the culminating confrontation with the powers of darkness. *Behold I will send you Elias the Prophet before the coming of the great and dreadful day of the Lord.* (Malachi 4:5 D.R.)

Like Eliseus who received the "double spirit" of his master, this garment from Heaven is the double spirit of Our Heavenly Mother, clothing us in the garments of her virtues, shielding us from spiritual and material danger and harm; it is for our protection, conversion, healing and salvation and to transform us into the fiery spirit of her Prophet in these tempestuous times of depravity and godlessness. The Queen of Heaven has spun this mighty shield to *defend us in the day of battle, And the dragon was angry against the woman and went to make war with the rest of her seed, who keep the commandments of God, and have the testimony of Jesus Christ.* (Revelation 12: 17, Douay Rheims)

In the words of the autobiography of St. Teresa of Avila, she said: *I was given to understand the great services which the Scapular family would render in the latter days.* (St. Teresa of Avila, See Chapter 7, footnote #16 in this book)

From the Garden of Eden to the Garments of the fallen nature of Shame, from the cloak of Elias that proclaimed the mighty power of God to the miraculous garments of many through which great blessings were bestowed, from the garment of new life that Baptism brings to the resurrected garments of eternal life, from the hem of His Garment to Her Garment of Grace stands a light brighter than the sun that shines as the resplendent light of the moon reflecting the glorious radiance of the King who has woven for us the garment of her heredity, to prepare us for this ultimate garment, her shield in battle with the powers of darkness, the sign of her love, protection, consecration and salvation: THE SCAPULAR!

In our battle against evil, may Mary Our Mother wrap us in her mantle. (Pope Benedict XVI, "Pontiff Praises wearing the Scapular," Castel Gandolfo, Italy, July 17, 2011)

CHAPTER 9 ENDNOTES

1   *The Credibility of the Scapular Promises*, Christian Ceroke, 1950, pp.191, 192, paraphrased

2   *Take This Scapular,* Carmelite Fathers and Tertiaries, Chicago, 1949, p. 242, taken from an article written by now, Venerable, Bartholomew F.M. Xiberta, O. Carm: *Annotations on the Status of the Scapular Question.*

3   *The Credibility of the Scapular Promises*, Christian Ceroke, 1950, pp. 191, 192, paraphrased

Appendix 1

RESCRIPTA AUTHENTICA

SACRAE CONGREGATIONIS

INDULGENTIIS SACRISQUE RELIQUIIS

PRAEPOSITAE

NECNON

SUMMARIA INDULGENTIARUM,

QUAE

COLLEGIT ET CUM ORIGINALIBUS IN ARCHIVIO SACRAE CONGREGATIONIS INDULGENTIARUM ACCURATISSIME CONTULIT

JOSEPHUS SCHNEIDER,

SOCIETATIS JESU SACERDOS, SACRAE CONGREGATIONIS INDULGENT. ET SS. RELIQ. CONSULTOR.

RATISBONAE, NEO EBORACI ET CINCINNATII.
SUMPTIBUS, CHARTIS & TYPIS FRIDERICI PUSTET,
S. SEDIS APOST. ET S. CONGREG. INDULG. ET RELIQ. TYPOGRAPHI.
MDCCCLXXXV.

Translation

Authentic Rescript of the

Sacred Congregation

presiding over

Indulgences and Sacred Relics

as well as

the Summary of Indulgences. …

1885

Sacra Congregatio Indulgentiis Sacrisque Reliquiis praeposita concessiones indulgentiarum contentas sive in Rescriptis proprie dictis sive in Summariis, prouti ista in hoc volumine jacent, post collationem cum originalibus in tabulario ejusdem Sacrae Congregationis adservatis peractam, uti authenticas recognovit et typis imprimi atque publicari posse permisit.

Datum Romae ex Secretaria ejusdem Sacrae Congregationis die 16 Decembris 1882.

Al. Card. **Oreglia a S. Stephano,**

(L. S.)   Praefectus.

Franciscus Della Volpe, Secretarius.

Translation

The Sacred Congregation presiding over Indulgences and Sacred Relics recognizes as authentic the concessions of indulgences and contained within this volume whether in Prescripts, properly speaking, or in Summaries—after being compared with the originals in the archives attained in the records of the same Sacred Congregation—and permits them to be printed and published.

Given in Rome by the Secretary of this same Congregation, December 16, 1882

Al. Cardinal Oreglia of St. Stephen,
Perfect
Francis Della Volpe, Secretary

RESCRIPTA AUTHENTICA

TRANSLATION FOR P. 475:

Other graces. The Privilege commonly called Sabbatine of the Supreme Pontiff John XXIII in the Bull, *Sic mihi*, March 3, 1322; approved and confirmed by Clement VII in *Ex clementi* of August 12, 1530; St. Pius V in *Superna dispositione* of Feb. 18, 1566, Gregory XIII in *Ut laudes* of Sept. 18, 1577, and also by others; as well as by the Supreme Roman and Universal Inquisition under Paul V on Jan. 20, 1613, decreed as follows: "The Carmelite Fathers are allowed to preach that the Christian people may piously believe that the souls of the brothers and associates of the Most Blessed Virgin Mary of Mount Carmel—namely, the souls of the brothers and associates of the Most Blessed Virgin Mary who have departed this life in charity, who have worn the garment [scapular] in life; observed chastity according to their state in life; and recited the Little Office [of the Blessed Virgin Mary]; or, if they don't know how to recite it, have observed the fast days of the Church, and abstained from meat on Wednesdays and Saturdays (unless it falls on the Feast of Our Lord's Nativity)—will be aided after their death by Mary's unceasing intercessions, devout offerings, merits and special protection, especially on Saturdays, the day dedicated by the Church to the Most Blessed Virgin."

Many other indulgences, which for the sake of brevity have been omitted, are contained in the Summary of indulgences of Ordinary Bulls, part. 2., p. 600).

Decree. This Summary, rightly recognized, and judiciously revised in conformity with authentic documents may be printed and promulgated everywhere. Given in Rome by the Secretary of the Sacred Congregation of Indulgences, December 1, 1866.

His Eminence M. Cardinal Panebianco, Prefect
Canon Philip Cossa, Substitute

Summarium indulgentiarum et gratiarum confratribus Beatae Virg. Mariae de Monte Carmelo a Summis Pontificibus concessarum.

Indulgentia plenaria sub conditione sacramentaliter confitendi, SS. Eucharistiam sumendi, et preces fundendi pro christianorum principum concordia, haeresum exstirpatione, sanctaeque Matris Ecclesiae exaltatione:

1. Die illa, qua quis recipiendo habitum, Confraternitatem ingreditur. (Paul. V. *Cum certas,* 30 Oct. 1606.)

2. In festo principali Commemorationis B. V. Mariae de Monte Carmelo die 16 Julii, vel Dominica immediate sequenti, aut alia ejusdem mensis juxta locorum consuetudinem. (Ibid.)

3. In mortis articulo, Poenitentiae et Eucharistiae Sacramentis susceptis, ad devotam SS. nominis Jesu invocationem ore, si fieri potest, sin autem corde. (Ibid.)

4. In una Dominica cujusvis mensis, interessendo processioni per Confraternitatem de Ordinarii loci licentia faciendae. (Idem *Piorum hominum,* 3 Aug. 1609, et *Alias volentes,* 19 Jul. 1614.)

5. Iis, qui praedictae processioni commode assistere non valent, si capellam respectivae Confraternitatis devote visitaverint. (Clem. X. *Commissae Nobis* 8 Maji 1673.)

6. Infirmis, captivis et peregrinis, qui hujusmodi capellam dicta Dominica visitare nequiverint, si Officium parvum B. M. V. aut quinquagies *Pater* et *Ave* recitaverint, et saltem contriti fuerint cum proposito confitendi, et sacram Communionem recipiendi quamprimum potuerint, quod adimplere omnino tenentur. (Clem. X. Bulla nuper citata.)

The Brown Scapular of Our Lady of Mount Carmel

Indulgentiae partiales. 1. *Indulgentia 5 annorum et totidem quadragenarum.* Semel in mense, si poenitentes et confessi SS. Eucharistiae Sacramentum sumpserint, et pro christianorum principum concordia, haeresum exstirpatione, et sanctae Matris Ecclesiae exaltatione oraverint. (Paul. V. *Cum certas* supra cit.)

2. *Item comitando SS. Sacramentum,* dum ad infirmos defertur, cum candela accensa, et pro iisdem pias ad Deum preces fundendo. (Ibid.)

3. *Indulgentia 3 annorum et 3 quadragenarum.* In qualibet ex festivitatibus B. M. V., quae celebrantur ab universa Ecclesia, confitendo, et SS. Eucharistiam sumendo in ecclesia vel capella Confraternitatis, et ut supra orando. (Ibid.)

4. *Indulgentia 100 dierum.* Corpora defunctorum tam confratrum et consororum, quam aliorum ad sepulturam associando, ac pro eorum animabus Deum exorando. Officium parvum B. M. V. devote recitando. Assistendo Missis aliisque divinis Officiis in ecclesia vel capella Confraternitatis. Pauperes hospitio recipiendo, aut eis in eorum necessitatibus vel periculo peccandi existentibus auxilium ferendo. Pacem cum inimicis propriis, vel alienis componendo. Devium aliquem ad viam salutis reducendo. Ignorantes Dei praecepta et ea, quae sunt ad salutem, edocendo, aut aliud quodcumque pietatis vel caritatis opus exercendo. (Ibid.)

Omnes et singulae indulgentiae praedictae per Paulum V. concessae animabus purgatorii per modum suffragii possunt applicari. (Clem. X. *Cum sicut accepimus,* 2 Jan. 1672.)

Gratiae nuper concessae. [1]) 1. Omnes confratres et consorores, si in locis versantur, ubi nulla Carmelitani Ordinis reperiatur ecclesia, omnes indulgentias ab Apostolica Sede ejusdem Ordinis ecclesiis concessas lucrari possunt, si vere poenitentes et confessi, ac sacra Communione refecti, respectivam parochialem ecclesiam statis diebus devote visi-

---

[1]) Gratiae olim concessae, praeter promissiones B. Simoni Stock a SS. Virgine factas, sunt: 1. Indulgentiae personales praedictae; 2. Participatio omnium bonorum spiritualium N. Ordinis ex Bulla Clem. VII., *Ex Clementi,* 12 Augusti 1530; 3. Facultas in articulo mortis recipiendi absolutionem generalem cum plenaria indulgentia, etc. ut supra.

taverint, ac reliqua injuncta pietatis opera rite in Domino praestiterint. (Pii IX. Brev. 15 Jan. 1855.)

2. Omnes et singulae Missae, quae in suffragium celebrantur confratrum et consororum, eodem gaudent privilegio, ac si in altari privilegiato celebratae fuissent. (S. C. Indulg. 22 Jun. 1865.)

Aliae gratiae. Privilegium vulgo dictum *Sabbatinum*, a Summis Pontificibus Joan. XXII. Bulla *Sic mihi*, 3 Mart. 1322; Clemente VII., *Ex Clementi*, 12 Aug. 1530; S. Pio V. *Superna dispositione*, 18 Febr. 1566, Greg. XIII., *Ut laudes*, 18 Septembr. 1577, aliisque approbatum et confirmatum, necnon a S. Romana et Universali Inquisitione sub Paulo V., die 20 Jan. 1613, decreto tenoris sequentis:

„Patribus Carmelitanis permittitur praedicare, quod populus christianus possit pie credere de adjutorio animarum fratrum et confratrum Sodalitatis Beatissimae Virginis de Monte Carmelo, videlicet Beatissimam Virginem animas fratrum et confratrum in caritate decedentium, *qui in vita habitum gestaverint et castitatem pro suo statu coluerint, Officiumque parvum recitaverint, vel si recitare nesciant, Ecclesiae jejunia observaverint, et feria quarta, et Sabbato a carnibus abstinuerint (nisi in iis diebus Nativitatis Domini festum inciderit),* suis intercessionibus continuis, piisque suffragiis et meritis ac speciali protectione, post eorum transitum, praecipue in die Sabbati, qui dies ab Ecclesia eidem Beatissimae Virgini dicatus est, adjuturam.“

Aliae multae indulgentiae, quae brevitatis causa omittuntur, in Summario indulgentiarum Bullarii Ordinis part. 2. pag. 600. continentur. [1])

---

[1]) *Obligationes confratrum ad supradicta consequenda:* 1. Ut quis s. scapulare a sacerdote deputato cum solitis caeremoniis recipiat.

2. Ut illud semper super humeros portet; et si fuerit attritum, aliud sive benedictum, sive non benedictum absque alia nova caeremonia assumendum est.

Obligationes particulares pro consequendo privilegio Bullae Sabbatinae: 1. Ut servetur castitas secundum proprium statum.

2. Ut scientes legere, quotidie recitent Officium parvum B. M. V. in Breviario Romano appositum; nescientes vero legere, Ecclesiae jejunia observent, ac diebus Mercurii et Sabbati abstineant ab esu carnium, excepto die Natalis Domini. Ob justam tamen causam confessarius, habens specialem facultatem, in aliud pium opus commutare potest.

476 IV. Summaria indulgentiarum

Decretum. Hoc Summarium rite recognitum, et authenticis documentis, revisorum judicio, conforme repertum, imprimi posse, et ubique promulgari permittitur. Datum Romae ex Secretaria Sacrae Congregationis Indulgentiarum die 1 Decembris 1866.

Ant. M. Card. Panebianco, Praef.
Philippus Can. Cossa, Substit.

- -

ACTA
SANCTAE SEDIS

EPHEMERIDES ROMANAE

A SSMO D. N. PIO PP. X

AUTHENTICAE ET OFFICIALES

APOSTOLICAE SEDIS ACTIS PUBLICE EVULGANDIS

DECLARATAE.

Volumen XLI

ANNO 1908

ROMAE

DIRECTIO	ADMINISTRATIO
VIA GICLIA, 141.	VIA S. NICCOLÒ DA TOLENTINO, 74.

Eeprinted with the permission of Libreria Editrice Vaticana

JOHNSON REPRINT CORPORATION
111 Fifth Avenue, New York, N.Y. 10003

JOHNSON REPRINT COMPANY LTD.
Berkeley Square House, London, W1X6BA

TRANSLATION:

ACTS OF THE HOLY SEE, VOL. 51 (1908)

SUMMARY

of the indulgences, privileges and indults granted by the Roman Pontiffs to the Confraternities of the Holy Scapular of the Blessed Virgin Mary.

(pp. 609-610)   III. Privilege

1. The Privilege of the Supreme Pontiff, John XXII, commonly called Sabbatine, has been approved and confirmed by Clement VII in *Ex clementi* of August 12, 1530; St. Pius V in *Superna dispositione* of Feb. 18, 1566, Gregory XIII in *Ut laudes* of Sept. 18, 1577, and also by others; as well as by the Supreme Roman and Universal Inquisition under Paul V on Jan. 20, 1613, which decreed as follows: "The Carmelite Fathers are allowed to preach that the Christian people may piously believe that the souls of the brothers and associates of the Most Blessed Virgin Mary of Mount Carmel—namely, the souls of the brothers and associates of the Most Blessed Virgin Mary who have departed this life in charity, who have worn the garment [scapular] in life; observed chastity according to their state in life; and recited the Little Office [of the Blessed Virgin Mary]; or, if they don't know how to recite it, have observed the fast days of the Church, and abstained from meat on Wednesdays and Saturdays (unless it falls on the Feast of Our Lord's Nativity)—will be aided after their death by Mary's unceasing intercessions, devout offerings, merits and special protection, especially on Saturdays, the day dedicated by the Church to the Most Blessed Virgin."
2. Each and every Mass, which is celebrated in support of the confraternity, enjoys the same privilege as if it had been celebrated on a privileged altar.
3. The faculty for general absolution with a plenary indulgence at the moment of death can be bestowed upon sodalities, or, if they lack this, on any approved confessor.

The Sacred Congregation presiding over Indulgences and Sacred Relics approved the present Summary taken from authentic documents and graciously allowed it to be printed and published.

Granted in Rome by the Secretary of the same Congregation on July 4, the first of the pontificate.

D, Panici, Archbishop of Laeodicea, Secretary

Appendix 1

SUMMARIUM

**Indulgentiarum, privilegiorum et indultorum confratribus
S. Scapularis B. M. V. de Monte Carmelo a Romanis Pontificibus concessorum.**

Confratres, qui legitime acceperunt S. Scapulare a sacerdote deputato per PP. Generales Ordinis Fratrum B. M. V.
de Monte Carmelo aut de eorum assensu a PP. Provincialibus, et illud semper super humeros gestant, consequuntur
sequentes indulgentias, et infrascriptis privilegiis et indultis
gaudent.

I. INDULGENTIA PLENARIA

*Si confessi ac S. Synaxi refecti sodales ad mentem Summi
Pontificis oraverint:*

1. die illa, qua, accipiendo S. Scapulare, confraternitatem ingrediuntur;

2. in festo commemorationis B. M. V. de Monte Carmelo, die 16 Iulii, vel una eiusdem mensis Dominica, iuxta
locorum consuetudinem;

3. eodem die *quoties* ecclesiam vel publicum sacellum
visitaverint, ubi S. Scapularis sodalitium canonice erectum reperitur;

4. in una ex Dominicis cuiusvis mensis, si processioni a
confraternitate, de Ordinarii licentia, peragendae interfuerint;

5. in festo Pentecostes;

6. die commemorationis Defunctorum Ordinis Carmelitis (15 Novembris, vel, si Dominica fuerit, die 16);

7. in mortis articulo, si uti supra dispositi, vel saltem
contriti, SS. Iesu nomen ore si potuerint, sin minus corde
devote invocaverint.

The Brown Scapular of Our Lady of Mount Carmel

II. INDULGENTIAE PARTIALES

1. *Quinque annorum totidemque quadragenarum:*

   d) semel in mense, die cuiusque arbitrio eligenda, qua sodales confessi ac S. Synaxi refecti iuxta intentionem Summi Pontificis oraverint;

   ô) si SS. Sacramentum, dum ad infirmos defertur, cum candela accensa et pro iisdem pias ad Deum preces fundendo, comitati fuerint.

2. *Trium annorum totidemque quadragenarum* in qualibet ex festivitatibus B. Mariae V., quae in universa Ecclesia celebrantur, si sodales confessi et S. Synaxi in ecclesia vel capella confraternitatis refecti fuerint et ad mentem Summi Pontificis oraverint.

3. *Trecentorum dierum* pro abstinentia singulis feriis IV «et Sabbatis per annum.

4. *Centum dierum* quotiescumque aliquod pietatis vel caritatis opus còrde saltem contrito ac devote sodales exercuerit.

5. Si confratres, corde saltem contrito ac devote, ecclesiam vel capellani sodalitii visitaverint :

   d) *septem annorum totidemque quadragenarum* quibuslibet infra annum feria IV et Sabbato;

   b) *trecentorum dierum* quocumque alio anni die.

Omnes et singulae praefatae indulgentiae, excepta pie-maria in mortis articulo lucranda, etiam animabus fidelium •defunctorum applicari possunt.

III. PRIVILEGIA

i. Privilegium, vulgo dictum *Sabbatinum,* Summi Pontificis Ioan. XXII, a Clemente VII *Ex clementi* 12 Aug. 1530, S. Pio V *Superna dispositione* 18 Feb. 1566, Gregorio XIII *Ut laudes* 18 Sept. 1577, aliisque approbatum et confirmatum ; nec non a S. Romana et Universali Inquisitione sub

Appendix 1

Paulo V, die 20 Ian. 1613, decreto tenoris sequentis: «Patribus Carmelitanis permittitur praedicare quod populus christianus possit pie credere de adiutorio animarum fratrum et confratrum sodalitatis Beatissimae Virginis Mariae de Monte Carmelo, videlicet Beatissimam Virginem animas fratrum et confratrum in charitate decedentium, qui in vita habitum gestaverint et castitatem pro suo statu coluerint, Officiumque parvum recitaverint, vel, si recitare nesciant, Ecclesiae ieiunia observaverint, et feria quarta et Sabbato a carnibus abstinuerim (nisi in iis diebus Nativitatis Domini festum inciderit), suis intercessionibus continuis piisque suffragiis et meritis ac speciali protectione, post eorum transitum, praecipue in die Sabbati, qui dies ab Ecclesia eidem Beatissimae Virgini dicatus est, adiuturam ».

2. Omnes et singulae Missae, quae in suffragium celebrantur confratrum, eodem gaudent privilegio ac si in altari privilegiato celebratae fuissent.

3. Absolutio generalis cum indulgentia plenaria in articulo mortis sodalibus impertiri potest a facultatem habente, vel, eo deficiente, a quovis confessario approbato.

IV. INDULTA

1. Omnes confratres, si in locis versantur ubi nulla Carmelitani Ordinis reperiatur ecclesia, omnes indulgentias ab Apostolica Sede eiusdem Ordinis ecclesiis concessas vel concedendas lucrari possunt, si, ceteris conditionibus adimpletis,, parochialem ecclesiam statis diebus devote visitaverint. Ubi. autem existit aliqua confraternitatis ecclesia, hanc tenentur sodales ad easdem indulgentias lucrandas visitare, nisi plusquam unius milliarii spatio distet.

2. Sodales qui menstruae processioni commode assistere nequeunt, *plenariam indulgentiam* sub n. 4 relatam lucrari valent, si, ceteris positis conditionibus, capellani respective confraternitatis eadem die visitaverint.

323

Ex S. C. Indulgentiarum et SS. Reliquiarum

3. Ubi processio praedicta locum non habet, vel confraternitas erecta non reperitur, confratres *plenariam memoratam indulgentiam* Dominica III cuiusque mensis lucrantur, si, ceteris adimpletis, quamcumque ecclesiam vel publicum oratorium visitaverint.

Sacra Congregatio Indulgentiis Sacrisque Reliquiis praeposita praesens Summarium ex authenticis documentis excerptum approbavit typisque imprimi ac publicare benigne permisit.

Datum Romae, e Secretaria eiusdem S. Congregationis, die 4 Iulii i po S.

f D. Panici, Archiep. Laodicen., *Secretarius.*

Indulgentia pro invocatione ad SS. Cor Iesu.

Très Saint Père.

Le prêtre G. Braillard, aumônier des Religieuses de la Visitation, dans le diocèse de Bordeaux, humblement prosterné aux pieds de Votre Sainteté, La supplie de daigner accorder une indulgence à tous les fidèles qui réciteront l'invocation suivante: *Cœur Sacré de Jésus, je crois à votre amour pour moi*

Et que Dieu etc.

Ex audientia SSmi, die 2p Iulii ipoy.

Sanctissimus Dominus Noster Pius PP. X universis christifidelibus, quoties praefatam invocationem corde saltem contrito ac devote recitaverint, indulgentiam trecentorum dierum, defunctis quoque applicabilem et in perpetuum valituram, be^ nigne concessit. Contrariis quibuscumque non obstantibus.

Datum Romae, e Secretaria S. Congregationis Indulgentiis Sacrisque Reliquiis praepositae, die 18 Iulii 1908.

S. Card. CRETONI, *Praefectus.*

f D. Panici, Archiep. Laodicen., *Secretarius.*

————••ol^go^O————:—

Dogmatic Constitution on the Church Lumen Gentium

Pope Paul VI, November 21, 1964

Chapter 8, #67:

This most Holy Synod deliberately teaches this Catholic doctrine and at the same time admonishes all the sons of the Church that the cult, especially the liturgical cult, of the Blessed Virgin, be generously fostered and the practices and exercises of piety, recommended by the Magisterium of the Church toward her in the course of centuries be made of great moment and those decrees, which have been given in the early days regarding the cult of images of Christ, the Blessed Virgin and the saints, be religiously observed... (1) *It is our conviction that the Rosary of Mary and the Scapular of Carmel are among the recommended practices.* (2) *Following the study of Sacred Scripture, the Holy Fathers, the doctors and liturgy of the Church and under the guidance of the Church's Magisterium, let them rightly illustrate the duties and privileges of the Blessed Virgin which always looks to Christ, the source of all truth, sanctity, and piety.*

Apostolic Constitution of Pope Paul VI Indulgentiarum Doctrina

*WHEREBY THE REVISION
OF SACRED INDULGENCES IS PROMULGATED*

January 1, 1967

n. 17—The faithful who use with devotion an object of piety (crucifix, rosary, scapular or medal) properly blessed by any priest, can acquire a partial indulgence.

But if this object of piety is blessed by the Supreme Pontiff or any Bishop, the faithful who use it devoutly can also acquire a plenary indulgence on the feast of the holy Apostles Peter and Paul, provided they also make a profession of faith using any legitimate formula. (3)

NATIONAL CONFERENCE OF CATHOLIC BISHOPS

Behold Your Mother
A Pastoral Letter on the Blessed Virgin Mary, November 23, 1973

We view with great sympathy the distress our people feel over the loss of devotion to our Lady and we share their concern that the young be taught a deep and true love for the Mother of God. We Bishops of the United States wish to affirm with all our strength the lucid statements of the Second Vatican Council on the permanent importance of authentic devotion to the Blessed Virgin, not only in the Liturgy, where the Church accords her a most special place under Jesus her Son, but also in the beloved devotions that have been repeatedly approved and encouraged by the Church and that are still filled with meaning for Catholics. As Pope Paul has reminded us, the Rosary and the Scapular are among these tested forms of devotion that bring us closer to Christ through the example and protection of His Holy Mother. (4)

Homily of Pope St. John Paul II, Fatima, Portugal, May 13, 1982

*The appeal of the Lady of the Message of Fatima is so deeply rooted in the Gospel and the whole of Tradition that the **Church feels that the Message imposes a commitment on her.** In its Dogmatic Constitution on the Church (**Lumen Gentium**) and its Pastoral Constitution on the Church in the Modern World (**Gaudium et Spes**) the Second Vatican Council amply illustrated the reasons for the link between **the Church and the world of today.** Furthermore, its teaching of Mary's special place in the mystery of Christ and the Church bore mature fruit in Paul VI's action in calling Mary **Mother of the Church** and thus indicating more profoundly the nature of Her union with the Church and of Her care for the world, for mankind, for each human being, and for all the nations: what characterizes them is her motherhood. Today John Paul II, successor of Peter, continuer of the work of Pius, John, and Paul, and particular heir of the Second Vatican Council, presents himself before the Mother of the Son of God in her Shrine at Fatima. **We are truly blessed that Our Lady has come in our time at Fatima. May all men be grateful to you, O Sweet Mother Mary.*** (5)

DIRECTORY ON POPULAR PIETY AND THE LITURGY PRINCIPLES AND GUIDELINES

Vatican City, December, 2001

Prepared by the Congregation for Divine Worship and the Discipline of Sacraments, December, 2001

Inculturation and Popular Piety

91. <u>Popular piety is naturally marked by historical and cultural factors</u>. The sheer variety of its expressions is an indicator of that fact. It reflects forms of popular piety that have arisen and been accepted in many particular Churches throughout the ages, and are a sure sign of the extent to which the faith has taken root in the hearts of particular peoples, and of its influence on the daily lives of the faithful. Indeed, "popular piety" is the first and most fundamental form of the faith's "inculturation" and should be continually guided and oriented by the Liturgy, which, in its turn, nourishes the faith though the heart. (103) The encounter between the innovative dynamism of the Gospel message and the various elements of a given culture, is affirmed in popular piety. (104).

92. The adaptation or inculturation of a particular pious exercise should not present special difficulties at the level of language, musical and artistic forms, or even of adopting certain gestures. While at one level pious exercises do not concentrate on the essential elements of the sacramental life, at another, it has to be remembered, they are in many cases popular in origin and come directly from the people, and have been formulated in the language of the people, within the framework of the Catholic faith.

The fact that pious exercises and devotions express popular sentiment, does not, however, authorize personalistic or subjective approaches to this material. With due respect for the competence proper to local Ordinaries or the Major Superiors of religious orders in cases involving devotions connected with their Orders, the Conference of Bishops should decide in matters relating to pious exercises widely diffused in a particular country or in a vast region.

Great vigilance and a deep sense of discernment are required to ensure that ideas contrary to the Christian faith, or forms of worship vitiated by syncretism, are not insinuated into pious exercises though various forms of language.

It is especially necessary to ensure that those pious exercises undergoing adaptation or inculturation retain their identity and their essential characteristics. In this regard, particular attention must always be given to their historical origin and to the doctrinal and cultic elements by which they are constituted.

Directory on Popular Piety and the Liturgy
Congregation for Divine Worship and the
Discipline of Sacraments, December, 2001

Pious Exercises
Recommended by the Magisterium

The Brown Scapular and other Scapulars

205. The history of Marian piety also includes "devotion" to various scapulars, the most common of which is devotion to the Scapular of Our Lady of Mount Carmel. Its use is truly universal and undoubtedly, it is is one of those pious practices which the Council described as "recommended by the Magisterium throughout the centuries." (255)

The Scapular of Mount Carmel is a reduced form of the religious habit of the Order of the Friars of the Blessed Virgin of Mount Carmel. Its use is very diffuse and often independent of the life and spirituality of the Carmelite family.

The Scapular is an external sign of the filial relationship established between the Blessed Virgin Mary, Mother and Queen of Mount Carmel, and the faithful who entrust themselves totally to her protection, who have recourse to her maternal intercession, who are mindful of the primacy of the spiritual life and the need for prayer.

The Scapular is imposed by a special rite of the Church which describes it as "a reminder that in Baptism we have been clothed in Christ, with the assistance of the Blessed Virgin Mary, solicitous for our conformation to the Word Incarnate, to the praise of the Trinity, we may come to our heavenly home wearing our nuptial garb."(256).

The imposition of the Scapular should be celebrated with "the seriousness of its origins". It should not be improvised. The Scapular should be imposed following a period of preparation during which the faithful are made aware of the nature and ends of the association they are about to join and of the obligations they assume."(257). (6)

ENDNOTES

1   Dogmatic Constitution on the Church, *LUMEN GENTIUM*, Solemnly Promulgated By His Holiness, Pope Paul VI, November 21, 1964 Chapter 67

2   Letter from Pope Paul VI: *In Dominica Republicana,* February 2, 1965, appointing Cardinal Silva of Santiago, Chile, Papal Legate to the Mariological and Marian Congresses held in Santo Domingo, March 1965.

3   *Apostolic Constitution of Pope Paul VI,* Indulgentiarum Doctrina, January 1, 1967

4   *Behold Your Mother,* A Pastoral Letter on the Blessed Virgin Mary, United States Catholic Conference, Washington, D.C., November 21, 1973, Paragraph 93, p. 35, cf. *The Wonders She Performs,* Louis Kaczmarek, Virginia, 1986, pp. 100, 103

5   Homily of Pope John Paul II, Anniversary of the Apparitions at Fatima, Portugal, May 13, 1982, cf. *L'Osservatore Romano,* July 17, 1982

6   http://www.vatican.va/roman_curia/congregations/ccdds/ documents/re_con_ccds_doc_2002, 183-207; Chapter Five: "Veneration of the Holy Mother of God," Directory on Popular Piety and the Liturgy, Principles and Guidelines, prepared by the Congregation for Divine Worship and the Discipline of Sacraments, December 2001

CONGREGATION FOR DIVINE WORSHIP
AND THE DISCIPLINE OF THE SACRAMENTS

DIRECTORY
ON POPULAR PIETY AND THE LITURGY

PRINCIPLES AND GUIDELINES

Vatican City
December 2001

Chapter Five

VENERATION OF THE HOLY MOTHER OF GOD

Some Principles

183. Popular devotion to the Blessed Virgin Mary is an important and universal ecclesial phenomenon. Its expressions are multifarious and its motivation very profound, deriving as it does from the People of God's faith in, and love for, Christ, the Redeemer of mankind, and from an awareness of the salvific mission that God entrusted to Mary of Nazareth, because of which she is mother not only of Our Lord and Saviour Jesus Christ, but also of mankind in the order of grace.

Indeed, "the faithful easily understand the vital link uniting Son and Mother. They realise that the Son is God and that she, the Mother, is also their mother. They intuit the immaculate holiness of the Blessed Virgin Mary, and in venerating her as the glorious queen of Heaven, they are absolutely certain that she who is full of mercy intercedes for them. Hence, they confidently have recourse to her patronage. The poorest of the poor feel especially close to her. They know that she, like them, was poor, and greatly suffered in meekness and patience. They can identify with her suffering at the crucifixion and death of her Son, as well as rejoice with her in his resurrection. The faithful joyfully celebrate her feasts, make pilgrimage to her sanctuary, sing hymns in her honour, and make votive offerings to her. They instinctively distrust whoever does not honour her and will not tolerate those who dishonour her"(208).

The Church exhorts all the faithful - sacred minister, religious and laity - to develop a personal and community devotion to the Blessed Virgin Mary through the use of approved and recommended pious exercises(209). Liturgical worship, notwithstanding its objective and irreplaceable importance, its exemplary efficacy and normative character, does not in fact exhaust all the expressive possibilities of the People of God for devotion to the Holy Mother of God(210).

184. The relationship between the Liturgy and popular Marian piety should be regulated by the principles and norms already mentioned in this document(211). In relation to Marian devotion, the Liturgy must be the "exemplary form"(212), source of inspiration, constant reference point and ultimate goal of Marian devotion.

185. Here. it will be useful to recall some pronouncements of the Church's Magisterium on Marian devotions. These should always be adhered to when elaboration new pious exercises or in revising those already in use, or simply in activating them in worship(213). The care and attention of the Pastors of the Church for Marian devotions are due to their importance, since they are both a fruit and an expression of Marian piety among the people and the ecclesial community, and a significant means of promoting the "Marian formation" of the faithful, as well as in determining the manner in which the piety of the faithful for the Blessed Virgin Mary is moulded.

186. The fundamental principle of the Magisterium with regard to such pious exercises is that they should be derivative from the "one worship which is rightly called Christian, because it efficaciously originates in Christ, finds full expression in Christ, and through Him, in the Holy Spirit leads to the Father"(214). Hence, Marian devotions, in varying degrees and modes, should:

- give expression to the Trinitarian note which characterises worship of the God revealed in the New Testament, the Father, Son and Holy Spirit; the pneumatological aspect, since every true form of piety comes from the Spirit and is exercised in the Spirit; the ecclesial character, in virtue of which the faithful are constituted as the holy people of God, gathered in prayer in the Lord's name (cf. Mt 18, 20) in the vital Communion of Saints(215);
- have constant recourse to Sacred Scripture, as understood in Sacred Tradition; not overlook the demands of the ecumenical movement in the Church's profession of faith; consider the anthropological aspects of cultic expressions so as to reflect a true concept of man and a valid response to his needs; highlight the eschatological tension which is essential to the Gospel message; make clear missionary responsibility and the duty of bearing witness, which are incumbent on the Lord's disciples(216).

Times of Pious Marian Exercises

Celebration of feast

187. Practically all Marian devotions and pious exercises are in some way related to the liturgical feasts of the General Calendar of the Roman Rite or of the particular calendars of dioceses and religious families. Sometimes, a particular devotion antedates the institution of the feast (as is the case with the feast of the Holy Rosary), in other instances, the feast is much more ancient than the devotion (as with the *Angelus Domini*). This clearly illustrates the relationship between the Liturgy and pious exercises, and the manner in which pious exercises find their culmination in the celebration of the feast. In so far as liturgical, the feast refers to the history of salvation and celebrates a particular aspect of the relationship of the Virgin Mary to the mystery of Christ. The feast, however, must be celebrated in accordance with liturgical norm, and bear in mind the hierarchal difference between "liturgical acts" and associated "pious exercises"(217).

Appendix 1

It should not be forgotten that a feast of the Blessed Virgin, in so far as it is popular manifestation, also has important anthropological implications that cannot be overlooked

Saturdays

188. Saturdays stand out among those days dedicated to the Virgin Mary. These are designated as *memorials of the Blessed Virgin Mary(218)*. This memorial derives from carolingian time (ninth century), but the reasons for having chosen Saturday for its observance are unknown(219). While many explanation have been advanced to explain this choice, none is completely satisfactory from the point of view of the history of popular piety(220).

Prescinding from its historical origins, to-day the memorial rightly emphasizes certain values "to which contemporary spirituality is more sensitive: it is a remembrance of the maternal example and discipleship of the Blessed Virgin Mary who, strengthened by faith and hope, on that great Saturday on which Our Lord lay in the tomb, was the only one of the disciples to hold vigil in expectation of the Lord's resurrection; it is a prelude and introduction to the celebration of Sunday, the weekly memorial of the Resurrection of Christ; it is a sign that the "Virgin Mary is continuously present and operative in the life of the Church"(221).

Popular piety is also sensitive to the Saturday memorial of the Blessed Virgin Mary. The statutes of many religious communities and associations of the faithful prescribe that special devotion be paid to the Holy Mother of God on Saturdays, sometimes through specified pious exercises composed precisely for Saturdays(222).

Tridua, Sepinaria, Marian Novenas

189. Since it is a significant moment, a feast day is frequently preceded by a preparatory triduum, septinaria or novena. The "times and modes of popular piety", however, should always correspond to the "times and modes of the Liturgy".

Tridua, septinaria, and novenas can be useful not only for honouring the Blessed Virgin Mary through pious exercises, but also to afford the faithful an adequate vision of the positions she occupies in the mystery of Christ and of the Church, as well as the the role she plays in it.

Pious exercises cannot remain indifferent to the results of biblical and theological research on the Mother of Our Saviour. These should become a catechetical means diffusing such information, without however altering their essential nature.

Tridua, septinaria and novenas are truly preparations for the celebration of the various feast days of Our Lady, especially when they encourage the faithful to approach the Sacraments of Penance and Holy Eucharist, and to renew their Christian commitment following the example of Mary, the first and most perfect disciple of Christ.

In some countries, the faithful gather for prayer on the 13th of each month, in honour of the apparitions of Our Lady at Fatima

Marian Months

190. With regard to the observance of "Marian months", which is widespread in the Latin and Oriental Churches(223), a number of essential points can be mentioned(224).

In the West, the practise of observing months dedicated to the Blessed Virgin emerged from a context in which the Liturgy was not always regarded as the normative form of Christian worship. This caused, and continues to cause, some difficulties at a liturgico-pastoral level that should be carefully examined.

191. In relation to the western custom of observing a "Marian month" during the month of May (or in November in some parts of the Southern hemisphere), it would seem opportune to take into account the demands of the Liturgy, the expectations of the faithful, their maturity in the faith, in an eventual study of the problems deriving from the "Marian months" in the overall pastoral activity of the local Church, as might happen, for example, with any suggestion of abolishing the Marian observances during the month of May.

In many cases, the solution for such problems would seem to lay in harmonizing the content of the "Marian months" with the concomitant season of the Liturgical Year. For example, since the month of May largely corresponds with the fifty days of Easter, the pious exercises practised at this time could emphasize Our Lady's participation in the Paschal mystery (cf. John 19, 25-27), and the Pentecost event (cf, Acts 1, 14) with which the Church begins: Our Lady journeys with the Church having shared in the novum of the Resurrection, under the guidance of the Holy Spirit. The fifty days are also a time for the celebration of the sacraments of Christian initiation and of the mystagogy. The pious exercises connected with the month of May could easily highlight the earthly role played by the glorified Queen of Heaven, here and now, in the celebration of the Sacraments of Baptism, Confirmation and Holy Eucharist(225).

The directives of *Sacrosanctum Concilium* on the need to orient the "minds of the faithful...firstly to the feasts of the Lord, in which, the mysteries of salvation are celebrated during the year"(226), and with which the Blessed Virgin Mary is certainly associated, should be closely followed.

Opportune catechesis should remind the faithful that the weekly Sunday memorial of the Paschal Mystery is "the primordial feast day". Bearing in mind that the four weeks of Advent are an example of a Marian time that has been incorporated harmoniously into the Liturgical Year, the faithful should be assisted in coming to a full appreciation of the numerous references to the Mother of our Saviour during this particular period.

Appendix 1

Pious Exercises Recommended by the Magisterium

192. This is not the place to reproduce the list of Marian exercises approved by the Magisterium. Some, however, should be mentioned, especially the more important ones, so as to make a few suggestions about their practise and emendation

Prayerfully Hearing the Word of God

193. The Council's call for the "sacred celebration of the word of God" at significant moments throughout the Liturgical Year(227), can easily find useful application in devotional exercises made in honour of the Mother of the Word Incarnate. This corresponds perfectly with the orientation of Christian piety(228) and reflects the conviction that it is already a worthy way to honour the Blessed Virgin Mary, since it involves acting as she did in relation to the Word of God. She lovingly accepted the Word and treasured it in her heart, meditated on it in her mind and spread it with her lips. She faithfully put it into practise and modelled her life on it(229).

194. "Celebrations of the Word, because of their thematic and structural content, offer many elements of worship which are at the same time genuine expressions of devotion and opportunities for a systematic catechesis on the Blessed Virgin Mary. Experience, however, proves that celebrations of the Word should not assume a predominantly intellectual or didactic character. Through hymns, prayers, and participation of the faithful they should allow for simple and familiar expressions of popular piety which speak directly to the hearts of the faithful"(230).

Angelus Domini

195. The *Angelus Domini* is the traditional form used by the faithful to commemorate the holy annunciation of the angel Gabriel to Mary. It is used three times daily: at dawn, mid-day and at dusk. It is a recollection of the salvific event in which the Word became flesh in the womb of the Virgin Mary, through the power of the Holy Spirit in accordance with the salvific plan of the Father.

The recitation of the *Angelus* is deeply rooted in the piety of the Christian faithful, and strengthened by the example of the Roman Pontiffs. In some places changed social conditions hinder its recitation, but in many other parts every effort should be made to maintain and promote this pious custom and at least the recitation of three *Aves*. The *Angelus* "over the centuries has conserved its value and freshness with its simple structure, biblical character [...] quasi liturgical rhythm by which the various time of the day are sanctified, and by its openness to the Paschal Mystery"(231).

It is therefore "desirable that on some occasions, especially in religious communities, in shrines dedicated to the Blessed Virgin, and at meetings or conventions, the *Angelus* be solemnly recited by singing the *Ave Maria*, proclaiming the Gospel of the Annunciation"(232) and by the ringing of bells.

Regina Coeli

196. By disposition of Benedict XIV (2 April 1742), the *Angelus* is replaced with the antiphon *Regina Coeli* during paschaltide. This antiphon, probably dating from the tenth or eleventh century(233), happily conjoins the mystery of the Incarnation of the Word (*quem meruisti portare*) with the Paschal event (*resurrexit sicut dixit*). The ecclesial community addresses this antiphon to Mary for the Resurrection of her Son. It adverts to, and depends on, the invitation to joy addressed by Gabriel to the Lord's humble servant who was called to become the Mother of the saving Messiah (Ave, gratia plena).

As with the *Angelus*, the recitation of the *Regina Coeli* could sometimes take a solemn form by singing the antiphon and proclaiming the Gospel of the resurrection.

The Rosary

197. The Rosary, or Psalter of the Blessed Virgin Mary, is one of the most excellent prayers to the Mother of God(234). Thus, "the Roman Pontiffs have repeatedly exhorted the faithful to the frequent recitation of this biblically inspired prayer which is centred on contemplation of the salvific events of Christ's life, and their close association with the his Virgin Mother. The value and efficacy of this prayer have often been attested by saintly Bishops and those advanced in holiness of life"(235).

The Rosary is essentially a contemplative prayer, which requires "tranquillity of rhythm or even a mental lingering which encourages the faithful to meditate on the mysteries of the Lord's life"(236). *Its use is expressly recommended in the formation and spiritual life of clerics and religious*(237).

198. *The Blessing for Rosary Beads*(238) indicates the Church's esteem for the Rosary. This rite emphasises the community nature of the Rosary. In the rite, the blessing of rosary beads is followed by the blessing of those who meditate on the mysteries of the life, death and resurrection of Our Lord so as to "establish a perfect harmony between prayer and life"(239).

As indicated in the *Benedictionale*, Rosary beads can be blessed publicly, on occasions such as a pilgrimage to a Marian shrine, a feast of Our Lady, especially that of the Holy Rosary, and at the end of the month of October(240).

199. With due regard for the nature of the rosary, some suggestions can now be made which could make it more proficuous.

On certain occasions, the recitation of the Rosary could be made more solemn in tone "by introducing those Scriptural passages corresponding with the various mysteries, some parts could be sung, roles could be distributed, and by solemnly opening and closing of prayer"(241).

200. Those who recite a third of the Rosary sometimes assign the various mysteries to particular days: joyful (Monday and Thursday), sorrowful (Tuesday and Friday), glorious (Wednesday, Saturday and Sunday).

Where this system is rigidly adhere to, conflict can arise between the content of the mysteries and that of the Liturgy of the day: the recitation of the sorrowful mysteries on Christmas day, should it fall on a Friday. In cases such as this it can be reckoned that "the liturgical character of a given day takes precedence over the usual assignment of a mystery of the Rosary to a given day, the Rosary is such that, on particular days, it can appropriately substitute meditation on a mystery so as to harmonize this pious practice with the liturgical season"(242). Hence, the faithful act correctly when, for example, they contemplate the arrival of the three Kings on the Solemnity of the Epiphany, rather than the finding of Jesus in the Temple. Clearly, such substitutions can only take place after much careful thought, adherence to Sacred Scripture and liturgical propriety.

201. The custom of making an insertion in the recitation of the Hail Mary, which is an ancient one that has not completely disappeared, has often been recommended by the Pastors of the Church since it encourages meditation and the concurrence of mind and lips(243).

Insertions of this nature would appear particularly suitable for the repetitive and meditative character of the Rosary. It takes the form of a relative clause following the name of Jesus and refers to the mystery being contemplated. The meditation of the Rosary can be helped by the choice of a short clause of a Scriptural and Liturgical nature, fixed for every decade.

202. "In recommending the value and beauty of the Rosary to the faithful, care should be taken to avoid discrediting other forms of prayer, or of overlooking the existence of a diversity of other Marian chaplets which have also been approved by the Church"(244). It is also important to avoid inculcating a sense of guilt in those who do not habitually recite the Rosary: "The Rosary is an excellent prayer, in regard to which, however, the faithful should feel free to recite it, in virtue of its inherent beauty"(245).

Litanies of the Blessed Virgin Mary

203. Litanies are to be found among the prayers to the Blessed Virgin recommended by the Magisterium. These consist in a long series of invocations of Our Lady, which follow in a uniform rhythm, thereby creating a stream of prayer characterized by insistent praise and supplication. The invocations, generally very short, have two parts: the first of praise (*Virgo clemens*), the other of supplication (*Ora pro nobis*).

The liturgical books contain two Marian litanies(246): *The Litany of Loreto*, repeatedly recommended by the Roman Pontiffs; and the *Litany for the Coronation of Images of the Blessed Virgin Mary*(247), which can be an appropriate substitute for the other litany on certain occasions(248).

From a pastoral perspective, a proliferation of litanies would not seem desirable(249), just as an excessive restriction on them would not take sufficient account of the spiritual riches of some local Churches and religious communities. Hence, the Congregation for Divine Worship and the Discipline of the Sacraments recommends "taking account of some older and newer formulas used in the local Churches or in religious communities

which are notable for their structural rigour and the beauty of their invocations"(250)
This exhortation, naturally, applies to the specific authorities in the local Churches or religious communities

Following the prescription of Leo XIII that the recitation of the Rosary should be concluded by the Litany of Loreto during the month of October, the false impression has arisen among some of the faithful that the Litany is in some way an appendix to the Rosary. The Litanies are independent acts of worship. They are important acts of homage to the Blessed Virgin Mary, or as processional elements, or form part of a celebration of the Word of God or of other acts of worship.

Consecration and Entrustment to Mary

204. The history of Marian devotion contains many examples of personal or collective acts of "consecration or entrustment to the Blessed Virgin Mary" *oblatio, servitus, commendatio, dedicatio*). They are reflected in the prayer manuals and statutes of many associations where the formulas and prayers of consecration, or its remembrance, are used.

The Roman Pontiffs have frequently expressed appriciation for the pious practice of "consecration to the Blessed Virgin Mary" and the formulas publicly used by them are well known(251).

Louis Grignon the Montfort is one of the great masters of the spirituality underlying the act of "consecration to Mary". He " proposed to the faithful consecration to Jesus through Mary, as an effective way of living out their baptismal commitment"(252).

Seen in the light of Christ's words (cf. John 19, 25-27), the act of consecration is a conscious recognition of the singular role of Mary in the Mystery of Christ and of the Church, of the universal and exemplary importance of her witness to the Gospel, of trust in her intercession, and of the efficacy of her patronage, of the many maternal functions she has, since she is a true mother in the order of grace to each and every one of her children(253).

It should be recalled, however, that the term "consecration" is used here in a broad and non-technical sense: "the expression is use of "consecrating children to Our Lady", by which is intended placing children under her protection and asking her maternal blessing(254) for them". Some suggest the use of the alternative terms "entrustment" or "gift". Liturgical theology and the consequent rigorous use of terminology would suggest reserving the term *consecration* for those self-offerings which have God as their object, and which are characterized by totality and perpetuity, which are guaranteed by the Church's intervention and have as their basis the Sacraments of Baptism and Confirmation.

The faithful should be carefully instructed about the practice of consecration to the Blessed Virgin Mary. While such can give the impression of being a solemn and perpetual act, it is, in reality, only analogously a "consecration to God". It springs from a

Appendix 1

free. personal. mature. decision taken in relation to the operation of grace and not from a fleeting emotion It should be expressed in a correct liturgical manner to the Father. through Christ in the Holy Spirit. imploring the intercession of the Blessed Virgin Mary. to whom we entrust ourselves completely. so as to keep our baptismal commitments and live as her children The act of consecration should take place outside of the celebration of the Eucharistic Sacrifice. since it is a devotional act which cannot be assimilated to the Liturgy It should also be borne in mind that the act of consecration to Mary differs substantially from other forms of liturgical consecration

The Brown Scapular and other Scapulars

205. The history of Marian piety also includes "devotion" to various scapulars, the most common of which is devotion to the Scapular of Our Lady of Mount Carmel. Its use is truly universal and, undoubtedly, its is one of those pious practices which the Council described as "recommended by the Magisterium throughout the centuries"(255).

The Scapular of Mount Carmel is a reduced form of the religious habit of the Order of the Friars of the Blessed Virgin of Mount Carmel. Its use is very diffuse and often independent of the life and spirituality of the Carmelite family.

The Scapular is an external sign of the filial relationship established between the Blessed Virgin Mary, Mother and Queen of Mount Carmel, and the faithful who entrust themselves totally to her protection, who have recourse to her maternal intercession, who are mindful of the primacy of the spiritual life and the need for prayer.

The Scapular is imposed by a special rite of the Church which describes it as " a reminder that in Baptism we have been clothed in Christ, with the assistance of the Blessed Virgin Mary, solicitous for our conformation to the Word Incarnate, to the praise of the Trinity, we may come to our heavenly home wearing our nuptial garb"(256).

The imposition of the Scapular should be celebrated with "the seriousness of its origins. It should not be improvised. The Scapular should be imposed following a period of preparation during which the faithful are made aware of the nature and ends of the association they are about to join and of the obligations they assume"(257).

Medals

206. The faithful like to wear medals bearing effigies of the Blessed Virgin Mary. These are a witness of faith and a sign of veneration of the Holy Mother of God, as well as of trust in her maternal protection.

The Church blesses such objects of Marian devotion in the belief that "they help to remind the faithful of the love of God, and to increase trust in the Blessed Virgin Mary"(258). The Church also points out that devotion to the Mother of Christ also requires "a coherent witness of life"(259).

Among the various medals of the Blessed Virgin Mary, the most diffuse must be the "Miraculous Medal". Its origins go back to the apparitions in 1830 of Our Lady to St. Catherine Labouré, a humble novice of the Daughters of Charity in Paris. The medal was struck in accordance with the instructions given by Our Lady and has been described as a "Marian microcosm" because of its extraordinary symbolism. It recalls the msytery of Redemption, the love of the Sacred Heart of Jesus and of the Sorrowful Heart of Mary. It signifies the mediatory role of the Blessed Virgin Mary, the mystery of the Church, the relationship between Heaven and earth, this life and eternal life.

St. Maximillian Kolbe (+ 1941) and the various movements associated with him, have been especially active in further popularizing the miraculous medal. In 1917 he adopted the miraculous medal as the badge of the "Pious Union of the Militia of the Immaculate Conception" which he founded in Rome while still a young religious of the Conventual Friars Minor.

Like all medals and objects of cult, the Miraculous Medal is never to be regarded as a talisman or lead to any form of blind credulity(260). The promise of Our Lady that "those who were the medal will receive great graces", requires a humble and tenacious commitment to the Christian message, faithful and persevering prayer, and a good Christian life.

The "Akathistos" Hymn

207. In the Byzantine tradition, one of the oldest and most revered expressions of Marian devotion is the hymn "Akathistos" - meaning the hymn sung while standing. It is a literary and theological masterpiece, encapsulating in the form of a prayer, the universally held Marian belief of the primitive Church. The hymn is inspired by the Scriptures, the doctrine defined by the Councils of Nicea (325), Ephesus (431), and Chalcedon (451), and reflects the Greek fathers of the fourth and fifth centuries. It is solemnly celebrated in the Eastern Liturgy on the Fifth Saturday of Lent. The hymn is also sung on many other liturgical occasions and is recommended for the use of the clergy and faithful.

In recent times the Akathistos has been introduced to some communities in the Latin Rite(261). Some solemn liturgical celebrations of particular ecclesial significance, in the presence of the Pope, have also helped to popularize the use of the hymn in Rome(262). This very ancient hymn(263), the mature fruit of the undivided Church's earliest devotion to the Blessed Virgin Mary, constitutes an appeal and invocation for the unity of Christians under the guidance of the Mother of God: "Such richness of praise, accumulated from the various forms of the great tradition of the Church, could help to ensure that she may once again breath with "both lungs": the East and the West"(264).

http://www.vatican.va/roman_curia/congregations/ccdds/documents/rc_con_ccdds_doc_2
0020513_vers-direttorio_en.html#Chapter%20Six

Appendix 2

ANCIENT AND MODERN DAY OBJECTIONS TO THE SCAPULAR VISIONS

DISSERTATIO DUPLEX:
UNA DE ORIGINE ET CONFIRMATIONE PRIVILEGIATI SCAPULARIS CARMELITARUM ALTERA DE VISIONE SIMONIS STOCHII PRIORIS AC MAGISTRI GENERALIS CARMELITARUM

(Dissertation Duplex [On the Vision of Simon Stock, Prior and Teacher: Double Dissertation] John Launoy, (Joanne De Launoy) Paris, 1642, pp. 8-24 and Addenda Paginae 39. Post Illa Verba

SOME OBJECTIONS OF JOHN LAUNOY: 1642

Two documents of the two Popes were produced: the one of John XXII, the other of Alexander V of which the revelation of the Mother of God (of the Carmelite Scapular) is asserted first and then its confirmation.

But many dispute the faith and authenticity of both. What follows pertains to the document or Bull of John XXII.

I.   The first is that the beginning of the Bull carries two different meanings: John, Bishop, Servant of the Servants of God, to each and every one of the Christian faithful, etc., and "As in the most sacred height of Paradise such sweet melody of the Angels is found etc".

II. The second is the discrepancy of the years which this Pontifical Bull is certified Gregory Nazianzus of St. Basil presents the text as dated March 3, first year of the Pontificate (which would seem to be the year 1317...) But Marcus Antonius de Cazanate records the writing as dated during the sixth year of the Pontificate (1322), which can be read...on the margin of p. 7.

III. The third is that the Most Blessed Virgin appeared to John XXII while he had already been made Pontiff (which is shown from the Bull to which Gregory Nazianzus of St. Basil and Marcus Antonius de Cazanate refer) but the account of Paleonydorus which is the more ancient of the two, wrote that the apparition of the Virgin took place before the Pontificate of John.

IV. The fourth is that the author of the Bull departs from the common style of John XXII: for indeed all the extravagances, privileges and Bulls of this Pope (which are found at the end of 6 of his decrees) such as *Calendis* [first day of the month] *Nonis* [the ninth day], *Idibus* [the fifteenth day] are continually confirmed yet the Sabbatine Bull is certified the 3rd day of March.

V. The fifth is the great variety of the context of the revelations which this altered collection will make evident to readers. For...something beyond what is honest they will never give. And indeed since no true copy and original text of a Bull of John ever had [these] under his name, the original storytellers invented what they wanted and in the style they wanted.

VI. The sixth is this: If the Bull of John XXII rests on a sound origin, nothing explains why it winds up in Genoa, (as claimed) Messina, Barcelona, Valencia and other Spanish cities but not in Avignon.

VII. The seventh is that it is impious to say or even to think that this Bull of John XXII believed to come from the Most Blessed Virgin would present deception. Nevertheless, this we clearly show to be the case. The Mother of God promised John XXII to deliver him from adversity (if he wished this). John did (as the Bull makes clear), but the Mother of God did not fulfill what was promised, as the history of the time shows; John indeed was not immune from adversity.

VIII. The eighth is that they lead to speaking of the Virgin ineptly, which is a manifest sign of insolence; this should not be done in any way on account of the honor of the Virgin. But this is the way Marcus Antonius de Cazanate speaks who remembers the

Bull of John dated the sixth year of his Pontificate.

IX. The ninth is: if this Bull of the Mother of God truly concerns revelation, there is no doubt except that John XXII and those who wrote for him come forth in the same way against Ludwig of Bavaria, against the pseudo-pope, etc. [The point here is the Bull is inconsistent in its rejections of certain people, some of whom deserve to be condemned and some who don't].

X. The tenth is: if the words granted to the Virgin are those (at least those liberated from Purgatory) *are led back to the Holy Mountain of glorious eternal life,* where likewise sing *those in heaven enjoying the eternal fruits of blessedness, established in the sight of God and standing firm in the most pure love of Him*...why does John XXII hesitate for so long to say whether the souls of the deceased (who after death have nothing to be purged)—having gone immediately into heaven—have contemplated the God of the universe (as He is)? Why do they not hold to a certain faith in the Mother of God, which according to the authority of his revelation and the privileges granted will remove doubt for anyone whatsoever?

XI. The eleventh is: if up to the year 1409 the genuine copy of the Bull of John existed, how in the year (as they wish) that Alexander V confirmed and issued his Bull did men, not lacking in diligence, come to lose such a noble copy? Why did the Sabbatine Privilege, of 1316 or 1322, by 1409 not have one author affirming it; whereas some 60 years before it had infinite numbers praising it?

XII. The twelfth is: If because of this revelation, the Pope confirmed [the Bull] in the presence of the brothers of the Carmelite Order, if he did so freely and unhindered, if he endowed it with many privileges: why is it not contained in the great *Bullarium* of the Roman Pontiffs? Why has not even one of the Carmelite writers of this time given clear witness?

XIII. The thirteenth is: The ancient record and prerogatives of this Order were brought back, and in these no Bull of Alexander V and John XXII is mentioned; is this not a most manifest sign that neither Bull was produced from these authors from that time up to the present?

XIV. The fourteenth is: The (Sabbatine) Bull and instrument or copy made in Majorca has been confirmed by many to be a forgery.

RISTRETTO DELLA VITA DI S. SIMONE STOCK ED APOLOGIA DELLA BOLLATINA SABATINA

(Abridgement of the Life of St. Simon Stock and the Defense
of the Sabbatine Bull, by: P.S. Mattei of the same Order;
Rome - Tipografia Cuggiani, Santini E.C, Piazza della Pace
Num. 35, 1873, pp. 126-139

OBJECTIONS: 1873

I.   Some disagree among themselves in attributing the Bull
     to Alexander III or Alexander IV as found in the notarized
     document in Majorca. (p.126)

II. In assigning the years to the date of the Bull of John XXII, there is
     discrepancy among authors and especially between Fr. Gregory
     Nazianzus of St. Basil and Fr. Marcantonio Casanate. (p.127)

III. The style of the Bull of John XXII, *Sacratissimo uti culmine* is
     different in that it is one never customarily used by this Pontiff
     in his acts. (p.128)

IV. In opposition to the authenticity of the Bull is the variety of
     some circumstances of the Vision and the variety of the reading
     of that same Bull by various authors. (p.129)

V.   There is a manifest contradiction in the words of the Virgin to
     John XXII when she calls him, *Vicar* of her Son and then says to
     him: *I am making you Pope.* (p.130)

VI. In the Bull of John XXII, there is found the term, *die Mercurii*
     [Wednesday] in place of *Feria IV* {Day 4} which is not employed
     in Ecclesiastical usage, placing in doubt the authenticity of the
     Bull. (p.133)

VII. If the Bull was in existence there would not be missing mention
     of those authors who dealt with the deeds of John XXII, just as
     there would not be missing mention of the ancient Carmelite
     writers such as Thomas Walden, Battista Mantovano and not
     even to mention of Trithemius of the defense of the Carmelites
     and likewise the ancient *Speculum Ordinis* from which one
     should conclude that they believed it to be apocryphal. (p.133)

VIII. The promise made by the Blessed Virgin of the liberation of souls of her devotees from Purgatory is absurd. The promise of the descent into Purgatory itself is fictitious. (p.135)

IX. The Bull of Alexander V carries the date of Rome. Therefore it is apocryphal since Alexander never was in Rome at least after being made Pope. (p. 136)

X. The Bull of Alexander V is not found in the Vatican Records, therefore it is something imaginary. (p.138)

THE ORIGIN OF THE SCAPULAR

Fr. Benedict Zimmerman, Irish Ecclesiastical Record, Vol. XV, January to June, Fourth Series, Dublin, 1904

THE ORIGIN OF THE SCAPULAR —A CRITICISM

Fr. Herbert Thurston, S.J Irish Ecclesiastical Record, Vol. XVI, July to December, Fourth Series, Dublin, 1904

OBJECTIONS: 1901-1911

I. The most serious objection to the authenticity of Alexander's Bull is its being dated from St. Mary Major at Rome. Alexander V never was in Rome. (p. 342, Fr. Zimmerman)

II. All these considerations are too damaging for the Bull of Alexander V to be accepted as genuine…(p. 342, Fr. Zimmerman)

III. Arnold Bostius, in his work "The Patronage of Our Lady," says not a word about the Sabbatine Indulgence: a sure proof that he had not yet heard of it…and his silence in that work on the Sabbatine Privilege implies that not only he but also his friends were ignorant of the subject. (p.333, Fr. Zimmerman)

IV As to the Sabbatine Promise, we have already expressed our conviction that the words of Our Lady really were: "I shall descend into Purgatory "subito" at once, (not Sabbato), after their death. (p. 349, Fr. Zimmerman)

V.   Can we with these facts before us regard the story of St. Simon Stock's Vision as anything more than a pious legend? (p. 59, Fr. Thurston)

VI. The first suggestion of any special privilege being attached to the wearing of the Carmelite Habit, in whole or in part, cannot be traced further back than the 14th century. (p. 69, Fr. Thurston)

VII. We have a very valuable account preserved to us of an early Confraternity erected by the Carmelites in Florence at the close of the 13th century. I cannot in their statutes find the slightest trace of any wearing of habit or Scapular. (p. 74, Fr. Thurston)

VIII. Fr. Thurston seriously questioned the authenticity of the Fragment of Peter Swanyngton and pointed out that the document was historically worthless, as the original manuscript was never revealed by Fr. Cheron. ("The Modern Controversy," cf. *The Credibility of the Scapular Promises*, Rev. Christian P. Ceroke, O. Carm., Rome, 1950, p. 25)

IX. In 1904, (Fr. Benedict Zimmerman) treated the question of the Sabbatine Bull, agreeing with other authorities as to its falsity. (*Ibid*, p. 24)

X.   He (Fr. Herbert Thurston) concluded with the suggestion that the attribution of the Scapular Promise to Our Lady in sermons required reservations in the face of the documentary difficulties. (*Ibid*, p. 26)

XI. In the view of Launoy, contemporaneous documentary evidence for the fact of the Vision of St. Simon and the authenticity of the Sabbatine Bull were necessary, and the only true criteria for the acceptability of the fact of the Visions. Fr. Thurston required documentary evidence "critically established" as the primary criterion for the acceptability of the fact. (Ibid, pp. 28, 29) (paraphrased)

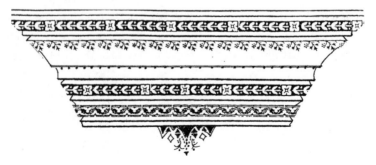

LA BOLLA SABBATINA

(The Sabbatine Bull)
Setting-Text-Time
by
Ludovico Saggi, O. Carm. Roma, Institutum Carmelitanum, 1967,
pp. 75-87

OBJECTIONS: 1967

I.   When was the Bull granted? Here the more serious difficulties begin to be made. (p. 81)

II.   In the text of the Bull, the Madonna calls John by the name of Pope, saying *Vicar of my Son* and she promises to him *I am making you Pope.* How could he be made Pope if he has already been Pope for six years? (p. 81)

III. Another difficulty comes from the silence of biographers and of defenders of the Pope on such an important particular of Marian protection. (p. 82)

IV.   Moreover, everyone who has familiarity with Papal Documents of such kind realizes the uniqueness of the case of a Pope speaking expressly of making concessions following a private vision. This is also realized from the strangeness of the text. (pp. 81, 82)

V.   We have seen how the narration contained in the "Bull" is presented in a way a Papal act is not. Perhaps the papal "varnish" was added only in order to have the account emerge as true in itself even if the apparition was given to a person different than John XXII with a similar narration. It's possible but who can affirm it? (p. 87)

VI.   Neither do we know the author. We fall into complete anonymity and pure possibility; actually in one possibility, there is still need of a correct interpretation given that in 1613 it was said by the Congregation of the Index that it was not dealing with an indulgence and it prohibited speaking about a personal descent of the Madonna into Purgatory. (p. 87)

VII. To whom was the Bull given? (p. 81)

VIII   Is this a notarized document? The one who saw it judged it as it was presented. Can we place it into doubt today? (p. 74)

IX.   How did the strangeness of the text come about? Nor is it worth much to say that the text came to us corrupted. (p. 82)

X.   The "document from Majorca" was not made in Majorca. (p. 84)

XI.   A final difficulty: a similar grant of indulgences seems to have been given a few years before by the Decree of Clement V, the immediate predecessor of John XXII, contained precisely in the *Clementine*. The "Sabbatine Bull" cannot be accepted as authentic. The arguments to the contrary are too serious in regard to John XXII and Alexander, whether IV or V is of little consequence (pp. 82, 83, 84)

LA BOLLA SABBATINA
Ambiente – Testo – Tempo

Ludovico Saggi, O. Carm. (Carmelite Historian) Roma, 1967

OBJECTIONS: 1967

Cited by Ludovico Saggi, specifically referencing John Launoy in"La Bolla Sabatina:"

I.   John De Launoy – the most noted of the deniers (of the Visions of Our Lady to St. Simon Stock and Pope John XXII) justifiably inquired: *A genuine copy of a Bull or certain document may be produced; wherefore error, if error is in the edition, is corrected, otherwise, a Bull, howsoever counterfeited, is no Bull. Likewise, a document is not defended as true or legitimate if altered in any way or rejected for errors in printing or by scribes.* (1)

II.   John de Launoy said there would be need to prove what really happened with regard to what took place at Majorca in 1421. This is because various elements do not correspond. (2)

III   Who and where was Alexander V? He was the pope who left from the Council of Pisa on June 26, 1409 (the third pope living at the same time during the Western Schism). Since the Bull was dated December 7 of the first year, it would have been December 7, 1409. Well now, Alexander V was never in Rome as Pope. In order to save his "Bull" he had recourse to authors poorly informed who wrote that he was in Rome, since Rome is wherever the Papal See is. In a particular way it was so for Alexander who ardently desired to go there. (3)

IV.   When was the Bull granted? Here the more serious difficulties begin to be made. The official date is March 3, year VI of the pontificate of John XXII that is 1322. In the text of the Bull the Madonna calls John with the name of the Pope, saying to him: *Vicar of my Son* and she promises to him: *I am making you Pope.* How does she make him the Pope if he has already been Pope for six years? (4)

V.   Another difficulty comes from the silence of the biographers and the defenders of the Pope on an article so important for Marian protection. And it should be noted that among the defenders of John against Ludovicus the Barbarian were also the Carmelites. Actually, while members of the Order are full of gratitude for the privileges obtained from him [John XXII], especially for the extension of the "Super cathedram," they are silent on this Carmelite intervention of Mary. (5)

VI.   "The Sabbatine Bull" cannot be accepted as authentic. There are too many grave arguments to the contrary such that John XXII and Alexander, whether IV or V is of little importance; the document of Majorca was not made in Majorca. There is doubt with respect to the time in which transcriptions A and B were made. (6)

VII. The document lacks the authentification of the signature and sign of a notary made by superior authority; the sign of the notary is manual. The dating which follows the Bull of John XXII is very strange. (7)

VIII. It is worthwhile to note the reintroduction of the mention of the Sabbath, the addition of the words, *et meritus* to the text of *Ex clementi* and the attribution to John XXII of the words that in reality are those of Clement VII. (8)

Appendix 2

ENDNOTES

OBJECTIONS OF LUDOVICO SAGGI
DIRECTLY AND INDIRECTLY CITING
IDENTICAL OBJECTIONS OF JOHN LAUNOY

1   JOANNES DE LAUNOY, *De Simonis Stochii viso, de sabbatinae bullae privilegio et de scapularis Carmelitarum sodalitate dissertiones V*; 3a ed., Parisiis, 1663, 134; "La Bolla Sabatina," Ludovico Saggi, p. 29

2   LAUNOY, *De Simonis Stochii viso,* 185, *Ibid*, p. 248

3   LAUNOY, *De Simonis Stochii viso,* 138-154; *Ibid*, p. 79

4   "La Bolla Sabatina," p, 298, indirect reference to *De Visione Simonis Stochii,* John Launoy, 1642, pp.8-24, objections II and III; identical objection of John Launoy's "Negative Argument"

5   *Ibid*, p. 299, indirect reference and similarities to *De Visione Simonis Stochii, objections of John Launoy,* pp. 8-24

6   "La Bolla Sabatina," Ludovico Saggi, pp. 300-301; indirect reference and identical objections as those in *De Visione Simonis Stochii, John Launoy,* pp. 8-24

7   *Ibid*, p. 62, footnote #92; LAUNOY, *De Simonis Stochii viso,* pp. 70-72

8   *Ibid*, p. 255; indirect reference and similarities to *DeVisione Simonis Stochii,* pp. 8-24

OUR LADY OF THE PLACE

by
Emanuel Boaga, O. Carm,
Edizioni Carmelitane, Roma, 2001

OBJECTIONS: 2001

I.   There is no trace in the papal registers of the Bulls attributed to Alexander V or John XXII. (p. 102)

II.   Therefore, Fr. Ludovico Saggi concluded rightly that the Majorca document is false and the Sabbatine Bull contained in it cannot be accepted as authentic. (p. 102)

III.   In the references to the "Sabbatine Privilege" we find some expressions that are not exact from the theological point of view (the indication of the Saturday after death and Purgatory are applications of criteria of space and time to eternity). (p. 103)

IV   As we have already demonstrated this Bull was not authentic. The content of the document contains contradictions that are both theological and juridical. The decree of the Holy Office of 1613 reconfirmed on various occasions afterwards, prohibits talking about this Bull as a Papal document which grants this Privilege. (p. 166)

V.   The content of this Privilege was approved and confirmed by the Popes from Clement VII onwards (1530). The Popes allowed that people should speak about immediate liberation from Purgatory especially on Saturdays, not because of an indulgence, but through the love of Mary for those who are devoted to her. Therefore the "Sabbatine Privilege" has to be based on the doctrine of the Spiritual Motherhood of Mary for humankind and her Universal Mediation without any reference to the Bull or to Pope John XXII. (p. 166)

VI.   The narration of the Vision is contained in the Catalogue of the Saints (from the beginning of the 15th century), but there is no reference to it in the Catalogue of Prior Generals (up to the 14th century). (p. 99)

VII.　No one knows where the Vision took place nor the day nor the year. In 1642 the Carmelite John Cheron published two Fragments (published in defense of the prior attack on the Scapular Visions by John Launoy in 1642) which he said came from Peter Swanyngton, Simon Stock's secretary. In both of these writings, Cambridge was indicated as the location of the Vision and the date was the 16th of July, 1251. Historical criticism today is able to show that the Fragments mentioned above are false and cannot be taken seriously. (p. 101)

VIII　It is curious to observe that John XXII before he became Pope and during his time as Pope denied, as a theologian, the existence of Purgatory and only as his death was approaching did he accept this doctrine. (p. 103)

IX.　It is unusual for a Papal document. A Pope never referred in official acts to private visions in order to grant indulgences or any other type of favour. (p. 103)

X.　The frequent visits of Mary to the religious living on Mount Carmel, because of its closeness to Nazareth, is considered a Marian Legend as is the virginity of Elijah (Elias), Elisha, and the sons of Prophets. (p. 104)

XI.　Various apparitions of the Blessed Virgin to religious and Saints of the Order (St. Simon Stock, St. Peter Thomas, etc.) and to the Popes (Honorious III, John XXII, etc) are now considered a Marian Legend. (p. 104)

ANTOLOGIA DELLO SCAPOLARE

a cura di
Giampiero Molinari, O. Carm., Roma, 2001

OBJECTIONS: 2001

I. The story of the Vision is not found in the Catalogue of the Prior Generals (end of the 14th century). In the 14th century, even the narrative reference of the "intimate" relations between Mary and the Carmelites does not speak of the "Vision." On the contrary, the story is present in all the editions of the Catalogue of Saints in the beginning of the 15th century. (pp. 172-173)

II. Nothing is known about the place of the apparition, of the year and the day of the Vision. The Carmelite Jean Cheron in 1642 published two false Fragments attributed to Peter Swanyngton, Secretary to St. Simon that give Cambridge (England) as the place and July 16, 1251 as the date. Since this has been clearly proven to be false by historical criticism, it cannot be taken seriously. (p. 173)

III. Furthermore it could not have taken place in the year 1251 because if the Simon of the Vision was also the [Superior] General, it would have taken place either before 1249 or in 1254-1255 or later between 1257 and 1266. (p. 173)

IV. The date of July 16 was chosen by Cheron in order to coincide with the liturgical feast of the Solemn Commemoration. But he did not know that this feast was first celebrated on July 17 and that this occurred from the beginning for a motive completely independent of the "Vision." The link between the Solemn Commemoration and Scapular is rather late. (sec. XVI-XVII) (p. 173)

V. The location of Cambridge cannot be confirmed because it is based only on the false document of Cheron. Aylesford has come to be indicated in our era (1949 to be precise), but without proof and thus as mere hypothesis. (p. 173)

VI. On the historicity of the Vision of Simon Stock, the opinion of the scholars is divided between the affirmative (traditional position of B. Xiberta), and the negative (position of B. Zimmerman.) (pp. 173-174)

VII. In truth, the analysis of the elements of the recorded sources demonstrates that the question of the historicity of the Vision is very problematic and that, with scientific honesty, one should say with P. (Ludovico) Saggi: "It is not proven that it is false. But the alleged proofs for its historicity are not satisfactory." (p. 174)

VIII. It is presently held that in the Middle Ages, visions and assertions similar to that of Simon Stock circulated also about Scapulars or Habits of other religious orders and the faithful wearing these habits became affiliated to promises of eternal salvation. (p. 174)

IX. This salvation linked to the habit, before the "Vision of Simon Stock" for the Carmelites is found in the visions of the respective founders or otherwise of the Madonna bound to the habit for the Benedictines, Dominicans, and Franciscans. (p. 174)

X. The Vision of Simon Stock therefore is classified in medieval mentality with regard to the religious life, considered as a way to secure eternal salvation. To comprehend its Marian relevance in its entirety it must be placed in the context of Marian patronage. (p. 174)

GARMENT OF GRACE

A Historical Appreciation of the
Carmelite Scapular
by
Patrick Thomas McMahon, O. Carm.,
Carmel in the World 2004, Vol. XLIII, N. 3,
Roma, 2004, pp. 175-188

OBJECTIONS: 2004

I.   No where in the Constitution is there any reference to a supernatural origin for the Scapular. (p.1 80)

II. The lack of any mention of the Scapular Vision from its alleged 1251 occurrence, until the end of the 14th century, some 150 years later and the unfamiliarity of any Carmelite of this period with the story raises serious questions about the historical basis of the legends. (p. 181)

III. In the years after World War II, the Carmelite scholar Ludovico Saggi clearly demonstrated that the alleged Bull of John XXII had not been issued from the Avignon chancery in 1322 but was rather a forgery from the Agrigento region of Sicily in the early 15th Century. (p. 182)

IV. The Portuguese Inquisition had condemned the Sabbatine Privilege as heretical in 1609; when the Order appealed to the Holy See, silence was imposed on all parties and the Carmelites were forbidden to preach the Privilege (an obedience which they generally ignored). (p. 182)

V.   During the celebration of the Anniversary of the Scapular, Pope John Paul II, for his part, wrote of the importance of the Scapular to him personally but mentioned neither the Sabbatine Privilege nor the Vision of Simon Stock although he recognized that the celebration "is taking place according to a venerable tradition of the Order itself, on the 750th Anniversary of the Bestowal of the Scapular." (p. 184)

VI. There are still many Catholics who think that the Brown Scapular has in itself some power to save those who wear it from Hell or to deliver them from Purgatory. (p. 176)

VII. The historicity of the Sabbatine Bull and its accompanying Privilege has been discredited with more certainty than the apparition to Simon Stock. (p. 182)

VIII. It was long troubling to historians how John XXII could have been told by Our Lady that she would free souls from Purgatory on the First Saturday after their deaths when John XXII himself did not believe in the doctrine of Purgatory. (p. 182)

IX. Stories of visions with the Blessed Virgin or various saints conferring habits on religious orders and introducing various sacramentals abound in medieval literature. Most are clearly inventions and can be traced to the rather extravagant preaching of medieval clergy anxious to win esteem and alms for their Orders. (p. 181)

The Brown Scapular of Our Lady of Mount Carmel

Carmelite Friars

63 East End Road
East Finchley
London
N2 0SE

Tel: 020-8346-1458
Fax: 020-8343-0942
http://www.carmelite.org

17th March 2004

Dear Aileen,

Many thanks for the letter and I will do my best to answer your queries. Luckily, I wrote an article for the *Journal of Ecclesiastical History* a few years ago and it has just been reprinted in our own journal *Carmelus*, so I am enclosing an offprint for you to read.

The article does not deal directly with the supposed papal bull of John XXII but there is some discussion of it on pages 79-81. The best account by far is found in two articles by Fr. Ludovico Saggi, O.Carm. published in 1966-67. His conclusion was that the bull is a forgery and probably produced in Agrigento, Sicily, around 1430. There never has been any record of the bull by John XXII in the papal archives and the emergence of the supposed "bull" in 1430 seems to have been inspired by a desire of some Sicilian Carmelite for the Order to have a similar privilege to the Portiuncula privilege of the Franciscans.

The story of the Scapular Vision is more complicated and I have tried to trace out the development of the legend in my article. My basic conclusion is that we have fairly good evidence for the existence of a saintly prior general, Simon Stock, who was English, died in 1265 and was buried in Bordeaux. After his death, a cult built up at his tomb in Bordeaux which attracted pilgrims. Sometime around 1400, a separate story emerged, probably in Belgium, about an unknown English Carmelite called Simon who had a vision in which Our Lady made the scapular promise. This new Simon is not a prior general nor is there any reference to his being buried in Bordeaux but quite quickly the association is made between the two Simons and it is claimed that they are the same person. After that, the legend grows, miracle stories are added and also the *Flos Carmeli*. The legend is communicated to Bordeaux in 1426 by the prior of Ghent who goes to ask for relics of Simon and Bordeaux quickly becomes another centre for spreading the legend. Etc. etc.

My apologies for being somewhat critical of the historical veracity of the two legends but the same is true for many other medieval stories. This does not invalidate the wearing of the scapular as a sign of devotion to Our Lady -- we place ourselves under her protection not because of a vision but because the Carmelites have always trusted in her patronage of the Order. The scapular is a sign of devotion and also a sign of affiliation to the Carmelite Family. As for the rest, we trust in Our Lady to be a Mother for us.

With all my best wishes and I hope you are enjoying a well-deserved retirement in Ireland. With all my prayers and best wishes,

Yours sincerely in Carmel,

Richard

Fr. Richard Copsey, O.Carm.

THE CARMELITANA COLLECTION

carmelitanacollection.com/about.php
A Catechesis on the Brown Scapular 2008 site by Orionlex

OBJECTIONS: 2008

I. One can say that on February 11, 1858, Bernadette Soubirous had an experience in which she *perceived* the Blessed Virgin standing in a grotto at Lourdes. The question then from the historical perspective, is not whether Mary appeared to Simon Stock and gave him the Scapular, but rather did Simon Stock *perceive* the Mother of God bestowing this sign of her protection on him and his brothers in Carmel?

II. It is the Carmelite Order – not the Blessed Virgin – who gives the Scapular to the faithful and invites the faithful to share our charism in expectation of the graces won by Christ and bestowed on Carmel and its members through the intercession of the Mother of God.

III. In the Nineteen Forties and Fifties they even encouraged wild stories and unfounded legends to popularize a Devotion that had been gutted of its original meaning.

IV. The story of the Vision of the Blessed Virgin Mary to Pope John XXII at Avignon conferring the Sabbatine Privilege of her Promise to deliver from Purgatory on the Saturday following death the souls of any who died in the Scapular has been shown by scholars to be based on an inauthentic Papal Bull forged in Sicily in the first half of the 15th century. Thus the Sabbatine Vision and Privilege, too, are without any historical foundation. These Visions then cannot be seen as historical events.

V. No one seems to know about the Vision until the very end of the 14th century–almost a century and a half after it supposedly happened.

VI. It is not possible to say that the stories of Simon Stock receiving the Scapular from the Blessed Virgin Mary are any older than the end of the 14th century a century and a half after the Vision supposedly took place.

VII. The Order should seek to revoke permission for any but Carmelite Religious to enroll the faithful in the Confraternity and enroll only those who are committed to actual and active membership in a Confraternity.

THE BRITISH PROVINCE OF CARMELITE FRIARS

Heritage and Archive, Origins of the Carmelite Order, 2013 Saints of Carmel: St. Simon Stock – Friar www.carmelite.org

&

CITOC NEWS

Order of the Brothers of the Most Blessed Virgin Mary of Mount Carmel: St. Simon Stock, Religious (M), Thursday, May 16, 2013 (THE ORDER OF CARMELITES - www.ocarm.org Curia Generalizia dei Carmelitani, Via Giovanni Lanza 138, 00184 Rome, Italy 2013)

OBJECTIONS - 2013

I.   The Carmelites have a very unique background. Unlike most Religious Orders, we have no Founder.

II   So, we have no Francis or Dominic or Benedict (or even a Teresa as have the Discalced Carmelites) to whom we can look as a Founder. This means that God's founding gift to the Order (the Charism) is not found in a person or a particular book but in a community of people.

III.   Around 1400, a separate <u>legend </u>emerged in the Low Countries of a "Holy Simon" who had a Vision of Our Lady, in which she appeared to him bearing the Scapular and promised: "This is a Privilege for you and your brethren: whoever dies wearing it, will be saved."

IV   The combined account quickly became elaborated with imaginary biographical details of Simon's life, such as his birth in Kent, his living for some years as a hermit in the trunk of a tree and his authorship of the Flos Carmeli, a beautiful Carmelite hymn to Our Lady (which is, in fact, found in the 14th century and hence predates the *legend*).

V. The <u>legends</u> surrounding Saint Simon—*particularly the so-called Scapular Vision*—have been extensively researched by the leading historian of the British Province, Fr. Richard Copsey, O. Carm., whose research has been published in the third volume of the *Carmel in Britain* series, published by Saint Albert's Press.

VI. In the 16th century, the cult of Saint Simon Stock was made a part of the Liturgical Calendar for the whole Order, his feast being usually celebrated on 16th May. The feast was omitted in the recent reform of the Liturgical Calendar after Vatican II but has been now reintroduced.

VII. Although the historicity of the Scapular Vision is rejected the Scapular itself has remained for all Carmelites a sign of Mary's motherly protection and as a personal commitment to follow Jesus in the footsteps of his Mother, the perfect model of all his disciples.

RESPONSES TO THE OBJECTIONS

This section begins with the immediate response of the First Defenders of the Scapular against the assault of John Launoy in 1642.

DEFENDERS OF THE SCAPULAR VISIONS AND THE DEVOTION

PRIVILEGIATI SCAPULARIS ET VISIONIS S. SIMONIS STOCKII VINDICIAE

John Cheron, O. Carm. Bordeaux, 1642: (First book written in defense of the Scapular and against the attack of John Launoy)

John Cheron thus replied to Launoy's charge that the truth was endangered: *If truth, as he (Launoy) wrongly thinks be endangered by such an assent, the Roman Pontiffs are in this great danger since they have granted the faculty to the General of the Carmelites to erect and institute the Confraternity of the Scapular everywhere, extending Plenary Indulgences, that through the outpouring of the treasury of the Church, they may entice, induce and join in the wearing and fellowship of the Scapular. God, who by this Scapular has extinguished the devouring flames, calmed the wild waves of the sea, prevented shipwrecks, cured the incurable, broken bonds and chains, restored the dead to life, heretics to faith, sinners to all appearances in despair to a sincere aversion from creatures and conversion to the Creator and has worked innumerable other miracles and works them daily, supports a lie.* (1)

DUPLEX PRIVILEGIUM SACRI SCAPULARIS ORDINIS ET CONFRATERNITATIS GLORIOSAE VIRGINIS MARIAE DE MONTE CARMELO SEU RESPONSIO AD JOANNIS LAUNOY DISSERTATIONES

Philibertus Fesysus, O. Carm. (Aix, 1645) 1645, op. cit, p. 63,

He summed up his argument against Launoy's denial of the fact of the Vision of St. Simon: *That it is contrary to common opinion, to the opinion of the theologians, to a very ancient tradition, to the Declaration of the Cardinals of the Sacred Congregation of Rites, to reason and propriety.* (2) All three (of the above writers) appealed to the fact of the numerous miracles in the Scapular Devotion. (3)

PRO SODALITIO SACRI SCAPULARIS ADVERSUS DUPLICEM DISSERTATIONEM I. LAUNOY

Thomas Aquinas of St. Joseph, O.C.D. (Tutelae, 1648)

In the mind of Thomas Aquinas of St. Joseph, O.C.D. who wrote the second work to appear against the *Dissertatio Duplex* (of John Launoy), a denial of the fact of the apparitions resulted in an attack against the Confraternity itself. *But since we have heard that some "lovers of novelty" triumphing in that book, give it prominence so that it might possibly extinguish the love for the Holy Scapular burning in the hearts of the faithful.* Fr. Thomas Aquinas based his reply, which was concerned with the documentary objections of Launoy on the inseparability of the Confraternity and the Scapular Vision of St. Simon: *For on that apparition and that gift of the Scapular as on its primary foundation, the Confraternity is founded.* To Launoy's claim that the Vision was "fidei inexploratae" (of unexamined or uninvestigated faith), Thomas Aquinas responded that the fact of universal belief which included popes, cardinals, bishops and theologians was sufficient examination.

It may and must be considered to be examined in the list of those things confirmed by the consent of the Church. (4)

SCAPULARE PARTHENICO-MARIANUM ILLUSTRATUM ET DEFENSUM

Theophilus Raynaud, S.J. (Paris, 1654) He rebuttled Launoy's second book "De Viso." He took the same position as the previous Carmelite writers, taking his arguments both from the concrete fact of the Devotion and using historical evidence according as it was available. His book seems to have carried great weight. (5)

Pope Benedict XIV considered the Vision of St. Simon to be certain and to be held as certain by all. His judgment included the authenticity of the Fragment of Swanyngton. (p. 23) In a Pontifical Document, recognizing the work of Theophilus Raynaud, in defense of the Scapular and the Sabbatine Bull, the Pontiff stated: *Verum tum Bullae Sabbatinae. tum rerum dictarum "VERITAS" apud Theophilum Ravnaudum vindicantur* which means: *Both the truth of the Sabbatine Bull and the truth of what it says [were judged] (to be) "True" by Theophilus Raynaud.* (6)

Thus in concrete, the Promise (given by Our Blessed Mother to St. Simon Stock) constitutes the motive for the practice of the Devotion and determines the significance of the Scapular. (7)

In 1884, *The Catholic Dictionary* (Addis and Arnold) a product of lay converts, rejected both the Vision of St. Simon and the Sabbatine Privilege on the grounds of documentation. The authority was John Launoy whose dissertations, in the opinion of the writers, were a work of "wonderful learning." The articles in the Dictionary were criticized and rejected by **Joseph Clarke, SJ.** He thus summed up his point of view: *The historical evidence we have adduced is sufficient to establish the authenticity of the story of Our Lady's appearance and Promise to St. Simon Stock. Its general reception all over the Catholic world, its promulgation by the* Ecclesia docens *and its acceptance by the* Ecclesia discens *is also proof enough of the supernatural origin of the Scapular. The repeated approbations of Popes and Roman Congregations and finally the official insertion of the story in the Breviary would leave no doubt about the matter even if other proof were not forthcoming.* (8)

Appendix 2
ENDNOTES

DEFENDERS OF THE SCAPULAR VISIONS
AND THE DEVOTION

1   *The Credibility of the Scapular Promises,* Rev. Christian P. Ceroke, Rome, 1950, p. 17

2   *Ibid,* p. 18

3   *Ibid,* p. 19

4   *Ibid,* pp. 17-18

5   *Ibid,* p. 22

6   Benedict XIV, *De Servorum Dei Beatificatione,* Prato, 1841, t. IV , p.II c. IX, n. 10, p. 185; and "Le Scapulaire de Notre Dame du Mont-Carmel est authentique," P. Marie Joseph du Sacre Coeur, Avignon, 1928, p. 87

7   *The Credibility of the Scapular Promises,* Rev. Christian P. Ceroke, Rome, 1950, p. 96

8   *Ibid,* p. 23

OBJECTIONS AND RESPONSES
TAKEN FROM:

A *Ristretto Della Vita Di S. Simone Stock* Per il P. S. Mattei, 1873

B *La Divozione Illustrata dello Scapolare Della B. V. Maria* P. Enrico Maria, 1876

C *Vita di San Simone de Stock.* Alfred Mombrum, 1884

D *Coleccion De Instrucciones.* R. P. Brocardo de Sta. Teresa, 1895

I. OBJECTION: The promise that the Blessed Virgin makes to John XXII of the liberation of the souls of her devotees from Purgatory is absurd and the promise of the descent into Purgatory is fictitious.

RESPONSE: To these two objections of Natale Alessandro, which are united into one, I respond briefly that the Promise of liberation presupposes the conditions otherwise necessary for satisfying the Divine Justice and after all, the Promise consists in the greater help that the Virgin administers by her merits and intercession. The descent then to Purgatory should not be understood materially but morally, not as an absolute patron but as an intercessor. (1)

II. OBJECTION: The Bull of Alexander V is not found in the Vatican records therefore, it is imaginary (false).

RESPONSE: Documents should not be rejected as imaginary whose originals do not exist if from them authentic copies are conserved. And therefore the fact that the Bull of Pope Alexander V is not found in the *Regestra Pontificum* does not prove it is apocryphal and invented as our adversaries wish. Chacon, cited by me more than once, asserts that the above-mentioned Pontiff Alexander V, in his very brief Pontificate, emanated various Bulls, although not all are known, nor are the originals conserved. (2)

III. OBJECTION: The Bull of John XXII, through other investigations, has never been found, and for this reason, it is not acknowledged in the Collections of the Bulls, Encyclicals and Decrees of the Pontiffs, through which they deduce that it is and should be considered apocryphal!

RESPONSE: It cannot be denied that the signature of Pope John XXII cannot be found, but one cannot therefore, conclude that it never existed and that the Bull of this Pontiff is apocryphal and imaginary; on the contrary, we have numerous arguments to demonstrate the authenticity. And indeed in the first place, there exists a Bull of Pope Alexander V issued hardly 87 years after that of John in which this Pope transcribes the Sabbatine Bull word for word by autograph and which he claims to have seen and examined with diligence: *Per nos visi et diligenter inspecti* [seen and diligently inspected by us]. Finally, this Bull of John XXII was acknowledged as authentic by almost all the writers who speak of it before the 16th century, in which there was doubt of any truth. Indeed, of this grace speak the celebrated Giovanni Bacone, Giovanni Ornebio, Guglielmo Reufu or Rebuffo, Tommaso Lombe, William of Sanvilliac, Gualtero Hunte, ALL WRITERS WHO LIVED BEFORE THE SAID 16th century. (3)

This is how the learned Antonio Sandero expresses himself on the Sabbatine Bull: "With regard to the Privilege of the Sabbatine Bull, it is divine, not human; celestial, not earthly; so that even the words of Arnauld of Chartres in his SEVEN WORDS of the LORD can be most aptly applied to it: "Mary, our Mother asks, the Son approves the Father decrees." This Privilege was given in Heaven…it was brought to earth by the Holy Virgin; it was confirmed and promulgated by Pope John XXII, as we have in these words of the Bull: *I, therefore, accept, approve, and confirm on earth this holy indulgence as graciously granted to them by Jesus Christ from Heaven through the merits of his Blessed Mother, and this is why the Sacred Congregation of Rites quite properly calls the Scapular "a celestial habit."* (4)

IV. OBJECTION: Some variations are found in different editions and so in them the same date is assigned in diverse ways.

RESPONSE: The variations of some terms in ancient writings is not a valid argument for placing their authenticity in doubt. In fact, in editions of authors and in those of the Church Fathers one often finds some variations which were there originally or from the differences of the copies, translations and especially from the ignorance or inadvertence of the copyists or the printers; this even happens also in the books of Sacred Scripture, such that some variations occur in many texts but from these no Catholic would argue for their falsity on the basis of some variations of time and place that are attributed to the same events. (5)

V. OBJECTION: The argument that derives from the diversity of style existing between this Bull (Sabbatine) and the other proper ones of this Pope, because one observes in this one a dictation more humble and of greater obscurity and baseness of style when compared to those that have a greater choice of words, greater clarity of expression and greater sublimity of concepts!

RESPONSE: To this point one responds that the diversity of style in a work of the same author provides no reason for not attributing any of them to him if there are not other arguments sufficiently strong for this. In fact with respect to the letters of St. Paul, scholars observe that in some of them there exists a notable difference of style from others of the same Apostle. (6) The strange irregularities of style and expression that pervade the Bull, instead of being any proof of its being a forgery, are a strong argument that it is genuine. What forger would be foolish enough to depart from the general style of the Roman Bullarium? (6a)

VI. OBJECTION: In the Bull of John XXII, the term *die Mercurii* [Wednesday], is used in place of *Feria IV* [Day Four], which not being of Ecclesiastical use places the authenticity of the Bull in doubt.

RESPONSE: Before the 13th century it was rare to refer to the days of the week with the terms Monday, Tuesday, Wednesday, etc. but after the above-mentioned century it became frequent as the often-cited Vaines (*Dictionn. Raisonn. De Diplomatiq*) testifies. Consequently it should not present any obstacle, nor harm the authenticity of the deed to have something in this form of the 14th century, such as the Bull in question. (7)

VII. OBJECTION: Some differ among themselves in attributing the Bull either to Pope Alexander III or to Pope Alexander IV as found in the notarized documents in Majorca.

RESPONSE: The response is that this presents no difficulty, since everyone sees in the blink of an eye that this is a material error of memory, either on the part of the writers or the notary who compiled the document of Majorca. It would in fact be ridiculous to have a case of confirming a Bull of 1322 if one wished to have it issued by a Pope created in 1159, Pope Alexander III, or otherwise by a Pope of 1254 such as Alexander IV. (8)

Appendix 2

VIII. OBJECTION: In assigning the years of the date of the Bull of Pope John XXII there is discrepancy among the authors, and especially between Fr. Gregorio Nazianzeno da S. Basilio and Fr. Marcantonio Casante.

RESPONSE: First of all, I need to warn once and for all that one cannot give much weight to the authority of P. Casante, nor do I intend to give it much value because, by common consent of writers, even of the Order, he was more anxious to accumulate facts than to make good choices and to distinguish true facts from those that are suspect or false; in conclusion, he does not have a reputation as an exact historian and this is why he was even censured by the Holy Congregation. With regard to the diversity of the time assigned to the emanation of the Bull, some indicate the first year of the Pontificate of John XXII and others the sixth year and various reasons can be assigned. That there is a falsity in the date of a copy—even though authentic—does not prove the falsity of the original. One can then complete the proof by other means, cited by me above: "The citation does not reject an authentic copy as false in the absence of the original with which it could be compared." (9)

IX. OBJECTION: The Bull of Pope Alexander V carries the date of Rome therefore it is "apocryphal" since Alexander was never in Rome, at least after being made Pope.

RESPONSE: Apart from the very probable mistake made by a copyist, we must confess there is very little in the difficulty proposed for it would not be outside the range of possibility that the Bull did bear the place of publication as Rome for there was not absent from the mind of Alexander the fixed idea of proceeding to Rome and at once. The Romans were already prepared for him and were ready to restore to him all his authority. The fact that the place of promulgation is noted as Sancta Maria Maggiore is quite in accordance with the usage of the times for all the Papal documents or rather most of the documents of the time were so promulgated. (9a)

In such sad circumstances, in order to appease the anger of Heaven against Christendom, Pope Alexander implored, as Pope John XXII did before, the powerful protection of Mary confirming the Sabbatine Bull in a special Bull *dated December 7, in Rome, at St. Mary Major, in the first year of our pontificate* (1409). Before contesting this difficulty, one must take into account the following facts: This Pontiff was elected on June 26, 1409 in Pisa and consecrated on the 7th of the following July and he died in Bologna on the 3rd of May, 1410. (10)

X. OBJECTION: There is a manifest contradiction in the words of the Virgin to John XXII: while she calls him, "Vicar of her Son," she then says to him, "I am making you Pope."

RESPONSE: Before responding to this alleged difficulty it is appropriate to caution that it is a question among writers whether the Vision took place when John was not yet Pope or after [he was Pope]. In either hypothesis, it doesn't matter whether one gives greater weight to one or the other; the explanation of the contested words becomes so genuine that it allows no room for the supposed contradiction. And here is the demonstration. Let us suppose with some that the words of the Virgin were spoken to Pope John before he was Pope, except in the mind of God; in such a case these expressions, "Vicar (or *vicari*) of my beloved son" were spoken in the sense of anticipation of the prediction of what will be accomplished insofar as God has already determined. There will certainly not be absent in the Sacred Scriptures—well-understood in the Vulgate version—examples in which the present may be taken to intend the past, as there are not absent cases that use the present to denote the future. (11)

XI. OBJECTION: If the Bull had been in existence there would not be lacking mention of it by those authors who dealt with the actions of John XXII, just as there would not be lacking mention of it by ancient Carmelite writers, such as Thomas Walden, Battista Mantovano, and neither would the Treatise of the Defense of the Carmelites not mention it and likewise the ancient, *Speculum Ordinis*. From this should it not be concluded that they believed it apocryphal?

RESPONSE: Walden did not speak of the Bulls of John and Alexander because of his growing attention to the points of controversy against Wyclif, which did not demand that he have anything to do with [the Bulls]. Mantovano not only did not take up the Bulls in question but still many other things as well; for matters close at hand are undertaken with greater ease! Therefore, are they all false? Mantovano was content to rapidly name various Pontiffs, and the many which he does not name confirms that he had already done them. (12)

Appendix 2

ENDNOTES

RESPONSES TO THE OBJECTIONS

All Objections and most Responses are taken from *Ristretto Della Vita di S. Simone Stock*, **P. S. Mattei, Roma, 1873, and** *La Divozione Illustrata Dello Scapolare Della B. V. Maria Del Carmine*, **P. Enrico Maria del SS. Sacramento, Oneglia, 1876**

1   Ristretto Della Vita D. S. Simone Stock, Apologia delle lettere Apostoliche del Papa Giovanni XXII., P. S. Mattei, Roma, 1873, Roma, p. 135

2   *Ibid*, p. 138

3   Apud *Lezana Maria Patrona* Cap. 5, P. Federico *Divoto del Carmine,* p. 1, cap. 10, in *La Divozione Illustrata dello Scapolare Della B. V. Maria Del Carmine,* P. Enrico Maria, Del SS. Sacramento, Oneglia, 1876, pp. 34, 35, 36

4   *Vita di San Simone Stock,* Alfredo Mombrum, Siena, 1884, p. 156

5   *La Divozione Illustrata Dello Scapolare Della B.V. Maria Del Carmine,* P. Enrico Maria Del SS. Sacramento, Oneglia, 1876, pp. 36-37

6   *Ibid*, p. 38, 39

6a *The Month,* A Catholic Magazine and Review, Vol. LVIII, September-December, 1886, p. 489, paraphrased

7   *Ristretto Della Vita di S. Simone Stock,* P. S. Mattei, Roma, 1873, p. 133

8   *V Sandini Vitae Pontificum. etc.;* in *Ristretto della Vita di S. Simone Stock,* P. S. Mattei, Roma, 1873, p. 126

9   *Vaines Diction. raison. de Dipolomatique Tom. I.* p. 211, *ibid*, pp. 127-128

9a *The Sabbatine Privilege of the Scapular,* P. E. Magennis, Ord. Carm., New York, 1923, p. 49

10 *Escapulario de N.S. Del Carmen; Coleccion de Instrucciones:* R. P. Brocardo de Sta. Teresa, Vitoria, 1895, pp. 228-229

11 *Ristretto della Vita di Santo Simone Stock.* P. S. Mattei, Roma, 1873, pp. 130-132

12 *Ibid*, pp. 133-134

A DEFENSE OF THE BROWN SCAPULAR: A REFUTATION OF THE "CATHOLIC DICTIONARY" PUBLICATION BY ADDIS AND ARNOLD, NEW YORK, 1893, P. 820

taken from

THE MONTH

A Catholic Magazine and Review,
Vol. LVII, May-August, 1886, p. 306

THE IRISH ECCLESIASTICAL RECORD

Volume VIII, No. 1, January, 1887, Dublin, Third Series, p. 799

The title page of the Catholic Dictionary, by Addis and Arnold, 1893 states specifically: "A Catholic Dictionary - obtaining some account of the "Doctrine, Discipline, Rites, Ceremonies, Councils and Religious Orders of the Catholic Church. It also claims in its "Preface to the First Edition" that its goal in the work submitted to the Dictionary is intended to meet a practical want, namely of a **single, trustworthy source of information** on points of Catholic doctrine, ritual and discipline and is written by Catholics. The work was granted a *Nihil obstat* which certifies that the limits of Catholic orthodoxy have been observed.

The definition and explanation of the "Scapular" can be found on page 820 of the above named Catholic Dictionary which contains an abundance of inaccurate information regarding the Scapular, as well as critical opinions expressed regarding the authenticity of what the Catholic Church had taught on the Scapular for 642 years up to the time this Dictionary was formulated.

I. OBJECTION: The explanation of the Scapular on page 821 of the above Catholic Dictionary Publication, specifically asks the questions:

Two statements, then, have to be examined. Is there any proof that the Blessed Virgin appeared to St. Simon Stock and made the promise related above? (Whoseover dies clothed in this Scapular shall not suffer the fires of hell...) and is the Sabbatine Bull genuine and the story it tells true?

The Catholic Dictionary then goes on to state: *Launoy, (John) in a dissertation of "wonderful learning" to be found in the second volume of his collected works (the edition we have used is dated 1731, "Coloniae Allobrogum") proves by a superabundance of reasons that the Bull of John XXII is a clumsy forgery and that of Alexander V another forgery made to cover the former. The autograph has never been found nor has it any place in the Roman "Bullarium." Its authenticity is unhesitatingly denied by the great Bollandist Papebroch in his reply to the attacks made upon him by the Carmelites and by Benedict XIV. He alludes, we suppose, to the style of the Bull, which as Launoy points out betrays in many ways the hand of the imposter. (1)*

RESPONSE: The authenticity of this Bull has also been denied by Launoy, but the reasons he alleges for this denial have been shown by the authors we have quoted to be groundless. A very complete answer to these objections may be read in the *Bibliotheca Carmelitana* (T. 1, p. 51, et seq.). An authentic copy of this Bull signed by public notaries, judges, etc., who testify that they have compared it with the original and found it to correspond, was deposited in the archives of the Carmelite Fathers at Genoa, as may be learned from the *Speculum Carmelitanum* (T. 1, L. V., p. 543, cap. xii., et seq.) where a copy of it is given and where its authenticity is clearly demonstrated. Other authentic copies were deposited at the Carmelite Convents of Messina, Mechlin, Cologne, Antwerp, Rome and other places, as is proved in the *Speculum Carm.* (Tom. 1, cap. xii., p. 543) (2) (A copy of the Sabbatine Bull executed in Messina may be found in Chapter 7 under, "The Magnificent Beauty of Christian Art," in this Book)

Regarding the apparition of Our Lady to St. Simon Stock granting the Scapular to the world, it is mockingly questioned, inaccurately referenced, and insultingly criticized in the Catholic Dictionary article under the subtitle: Scapular.

But certain elements of the attack on the Devotion are pointed out within this Catholic Dictionary publication, by Fr. R.F. Clarke, author of an article on the defense of the Scapular entitled: *The Catholic Dictionary and the Brown Scapular* found in *The Month"* in Appendix 3 of this book and are worth noting. He says:

The Article on the Brown Scapular is one which we read with pain and with dismay… we should cast aside the volume of the work of a "weak-kneed Catholic," weak-kneed not only as regards his practical devotion and loyalty to what the Church approves, but feeble in the extreme in his power of historical criticism…it is more than this: it is inaccurate and unfair; it makes statements at variance with truth; it displays an ignorance of the facts of the case; it is careless and inexact throughout; IT IS BASED ON THE CONDEMNED WRITINGS OF A DISLOYAL AND BITTER ENEMY OF THE HOLY SEE. (John Launoy) (3)

John Launoy was one of those bitter adversaries of the Holy See and of the Religious Orders who unhappily sprung up in considerable numbers under the baneful influence of Gallicanism. He was a …most disloyal Catholic, the opponent of authority, the sympathizer with false doctrine, who made it his object to vilify and defame the Religious Orders, to assail their privileges, to pour out his venom on them on every possible occasion. (4)

If M. Launoy was a man of "wonderful learning," (as he is referred to in the above Addis and Arnold Catholic Dictionary article), he was also a man of wonderful malice and full of a wonderful hatred of the Holy See. (5)

Is this the man who is to be taken as our guide in a matter like this? Is this half-hearted Catholic, this enemy of Rome, this quarrelsome mischief-maker, this friend of heretics, to be quoted with unqualified approval in a matter which concerns the privileges of one of the most venerable of those Religious Orders that he hated? Is this unhappy Gallican to be spoken of with admiration on a subject in which he at least indirectly impugnes the dignity and privilege of the Holy Mother of God? (6)

But, this is not all…The very work which is thus praised and quoted (of John Launoy) is actually one condemned by the Church, one which has been, in company with M. Launoy's other productions on the Index of Prohibited Books for the last (over) two hundred years! (7)

A work which lies under the Church's ban, which unless special permission has been obtained, no Catholic can read without sin where the Index is promulgated, is brought forward as a standard authority and recommended to Catholics as justifying the rejection of Our Lady's gift to her faithful children of Mount Carmel! (8) Any attack on the Scapular is indirectly an attack on the power and privileges of the Holy Mother of God. (9)

As in many of the objections found in this Appendix, the pattern is clear. At the basis of the modern day objections are the identical disputes of the 17th century Jansenist, John Launoy. He is still quoted today, both directly and indirectly. (See Chapter 4 in this book.) This scornful attitude of John Launoy and his critical judgements toward the Visions has spread like a cancerous disease in the hearts and the souls of the Progressives from whom these 20th and 21st century objections are issued.

It is a sad state when a publication, such as the Catholic Dictionary in the 19th century, as well as many other current modern day Catholic publications can no longer be trusted to speak the truth but instead expound the errors of an enemy of Rome (John Launoy) and cultivate the very objections he spewed forth to substantiate, quote and support their derision of the Scapular Devotion in their indirect attack on the Mother of God still happening to this very day.

It will greatly benefit the reader to review the defending articles in "The Irish Ecclesiastical Record," and "The Month," found in "Publications in Defense" Appendix 3 in this book. It will help to enlighten the reader to the truth, repair the damage done to the Devotion and restore faith in the authenticity of the Scapular Visions and in the never ending love and care that the most noble and merciful Queen of Heaven has for her suffering children on earth and in Purgatory.

ENDNOTES

RESPONSES TO THE OBJECTIONS:
IN DEFENSE OF THE BROWN SCAPULAR
A REFUTATION OF THE CATHOLIC DICTIONARY
A PUBLICATION ON THE BROWN SCAPULAR
BY ADDIS AND ARNOLD, LONDON, 1893

1   *The Catholic Dictionary,* William E. Addis, Thomas Arnold, M.A., London, 1887, p. 744, and in 1893, p. 821

2   *The Irish Ecclesiastical Record,* Volume VIII, No. 1, January, 1887, Dublin, Third Series, p. 799

3   *The Month,* A Catholic Magazine and Review, Vol. LVII, May-August, 1886, p. 306

4   *Ibid,* p. 314

5   *Ibid,* p. 314

6   *Ibid,* p. 314

7   *Ibid,* p. 315

8   *Ibid,* p. 315

9   *Ibid,* p. 307

THE SABBATINE PRIVILEGE OF THE SCAPULAR

1322 A.D. – 1922 A.D.,
P. E. Magennis, Ord. Carm., New York, 1923,
pp. 131-135, paraphrased.

In Defense of the Sabbatine Bull against some objections of John Launoy
[from his *Dissertatio Duplex, 1642*]:

I. OBJECTION: The beginning of the Bull carries two different meanings: John, Bishop, Servant of the Servants of God, to each and every one of the Christian faithful, etc., and "As in the most sacred height of Paradise such sweet melody of the Angels is found etc."

RESPONSE: His first objection is founded on a comparison of the two authors who have treated extensively of the Sabbatine Bull: namely Gregorius Nazianzenus a Sancto Basilio and Marcus-Antonius de Casanate, who John Launoy believed were the first to address the Bull—an erroneous belief. Each has produced a copy of the Bull and undoubtedly there are very many discrepancies in the two versions. With all the knowledge that has been acquired in regard to ancient documents, it is just as hopeless as ever to get two copies made by different scribes to agree in everything. There is no doubt that the substantial part of the Sabbatine Privilege is contained in both of the versions compared by Launoy. There is no doubt that both attribute the Bull to John XXII. There is no doubt that the contents of the one are much the same as the contents of the other even though phrases as to context and form are widely different.

II. OBJECTION: The discrepancy of the years which this Pontifical Bull is certified: Gregory Nazianzus of St. Basil presents the text as dated March 3, first year of the Pontificate (which would seem to be the year 1317...) But Marcus Antonius de Casanate records the writing as dated during the sixth year of the Pontificate (1322).

RESPONSE: The error as to the date is of no importance. In the English translation of the Regestra (1305-1342), copies of the Bulls are to be seen where the year is missing and others where even the month is not reproduced. No one would dream of rejecting those copies for the reason of a variation in registration.

III. OBJECTION: The author of the Bull departs from the common style of John XXII.

RESPONSE: To this point one responds that the diversity of style in a work of the same author provides no reason for not attributing any of them to him if there are not other arguments sufficiently strong for this. In fact with respect to the letters of St. Paul, scholars observe that in some of them there exists a notable difference of style from others of the same Apostle. The strange irregularities of style and expression that pervade the Bull, instead of being any proof of its being a forgery, are a strong argument that it is genuine. What forger would be foolish enough to depart from the general style of the Roman Bullarium? (Please see *Responses to the Objections,* answer V. page 368, in this section.) Launoy objects to the word *Mercurio* as indicating the more recent reproduction or fabrication of the Bull and insists that the use of the word was not known in the ecclesiastical documents of John's time. The opponents of Launoy point out that the word is used in the Council of Florence, in the Lateran Council and the Tridentine Council.

IV. OBJECTION: The Mother of God promised John XXII to deliver him from adversity (if he wished this). John did (as the Bull makes clear), but the Mother of God did not fulfill what was promised, as the history of the time shows; John indeed was not immune from adversity.

RESPONSE: Launoy tried to prove that John XXII was overcome by his enemies and that the Mother of God did not fulfill her promise to protect him from his adversaries. However, only the opposite was true; John died at a ripe old age and did not seem eager to leave the chair of Peter. He had the satisfaction of seeing (his enemy) the anti-Pope, on his knees with a cord around his neck at the feet of John XXII, weeping, confessing his sins, and detained as a prisoner in Avignon, where he died three years later. No one can doubt that the victory of John XXII over this and many of his other adversaries was complete.

V. OBJECTIONS: The ancient record and prerogatives of this Order were brought back, and in these, no Bull of Alexander V and John XXII is mentioned.

If up to the year 1409 the genuine copy of the Bull of John existed, how in the year (as they wish) that Alexander V confirmed and issued his Bull did men, not lacking in diligence, come to lose such a noble copy?

RESPONSE: Fr. Zimmerman, a 20th century Carmelite authority published a work using the same objections (as those of John Launoy) against the authenticity and genuinity of the Sabbatine Bull. Many other contemporary 20th and 21st century Carmelite authorities have published similar works using the same objections as John Launoy to discredit the authenticity of the Bull. It is easy to conclude how long these objections have been used against those who wish to believe in the traditional account of the Sabbatine Privilege. These contemporary Carmelite authorities are repeating the identical errors of John Launoy, who has completely erred in his treatment of the Scapular including the Sabbatine Privilege and in many other of his condemned works, including those listed in the Index Librorum Prohibitorum of Pope Pius X, where the Dissertation of Launoy (on the Scapular Devotion) still appeared. Nevertheless, Catholic (and Carmelite) authorities have cited his work without even the slightest indication (or concern) that it has been proscribed by the ecclesiastical authorities.

(The Objections of John Launoy are taken from *Dissertatio Duplex De Origine et confirmation privilegiati Scapularis Carmelitaru, altera De Visione Simonis Stochii Prioris ac Magistri,* Joanne de Launoy, Paris, 1642. The Responses are taken from *The Sabbatine Privilege of the Scapular,* 1322 A.D. – 1922 A.D., P. E. Magennis, Ord. Carm., New York, 1923, pp. 131-135, paraphrased.)

ENCICLOPEDIA DEL ESCAPULARIO DEL CARMEN

P. Simon M. Besalduch, Barcelona, 1931, pp. 261-283
(Objections and Responses)

I. OBJECTION: Does it deal with an authentic or apocryphal Bull?

RESPONSE: The profound Carmelite theologian, Juan de Santo Tomas, Portuguese, was one of the two commissioned by the Order to defend the Sabbatine Privilege in the Roman Curia, which was much discussed in Portugal during the pontificate of Paul V. He made his first argument in the brilliant dissertation, which he made before the most eminent Cardinals who needed to settle the growing controversy with his unimpeachable judgment, as they thus ruled in favor of the Carmelites:

John XXII, Supreme Pontiff issued his Sabbatine Bull to us in 1322; Alexander V later confirmed this, and Clement VII as well; this was once again called to mind and confirmed by Gregory XIII. Therefore, these later confirmations prove the first, which is equally found in them. And this truth is firm; and over the course of the centuries it has established outstanding piety for our entire religious Order, and faith and Marian devotion for the people of the whole world. (1)

II. OBJECTION: If the original of the Sabbatine Bull does not exist, how can its authenticity be proved?

RESPONSE: Rather, how does one advise an author [who asks]: "Where are the originals of the books of David and Solomon? Where are the originals of the Gospels?" They have disappeared ... and, nevertheless, all admit these aforementioned books as true. By way of logic, you will be able to repeat here the following conclusion: therefore, even if the original does not exist, the Sabbatine Bull is authentic, and it is real in all its parts by the fact that we refer to it, because it is thus evident in the Bulls of other Pontiffs and in copies legitimately authorized and exempt from all suspicion. (2)

III. OBJECTION: But the style and circumstances of the Sabbatine Bull of John XXII are out of harmony with other Bulls of the same

Pope, and [with] the discrepancy of facts among Carmelite writers how can one not consider one or the other as indicating falsehood?

RESPONSE: With regard to the discrepancy of dates observed in some copies, it is sufficient to note that, inasmuch as all of these are in perfect harmony with regard to their substance, the variations in dates can and should be attributed to the error of secretaries, copyists, and printers, as St. Jerome advised in reference to his writings: "If you discover any errors in writing, or some description missing, which hinders you from reading the meaning, you should not impute these to me, but to those unskilled scribes and copyists who write, not what they find, but what they understand, and while strange errors strive to be corrected, their own are displayed." (3)

IV. OBJECTION: Do not the variations noted in some of the copies constitute a difficulty against the authenticity of the Sabbatine Bull?

RESPONSE: Gathering together, on our subject, the final words of the authorized testimony, we will say that, taking note of the different copies of the Sabbatine Bull, and in spite of the word changes and errors that are accidental or of mere form, in what affects the substance of the event, the universal belief of the Christian people is "an argument that proves its authenticity." (4)

V. OBJECTION: How can one harmonize the locutions of the Virgin in her apparition to John XXII, calling him, "Vicar of her Son," and promising "to make him Pope?

RESPONSE: "Vicar of my beloved Son," signifies the divine election concerning the Papacy that the Virgin revealed to her devoted follower, Cardinal Ossa (John XXII). "I am making you Pope" means that the Virgin promises that he will be Pope. There are those who interpret these words "I am making you Pope" in the sense that the Virgin, by her prayers, was leading him to the peaceful possession of the Papacy, disturbed by the antipope, Peter of Corvaro (Nicholas V) and the Emperor Louis of Bavaria; and this interpretation seems to be confirmed by the clause found between the two spoken locutions: "Thus I will free you from your adversary."(5)

VI. **OBJECTION: Why does the Sabbatine Bull use the word "Wednesday" (*mercurio*) to designate the fourth day of the week, when the use of the Church is to use numbers for the days, which in our case, would be to say the "fourth day?"**

RESPONSE: On the point of the "use of the Church" here are some brief words that summarize how many authorities and witnesses we could have cited for our proposition: The councils themselves, given breath by the Holy Spirit, indicated a future session to take place on a certain day, by the accepted words of Monday, Tuesday, Wednesday, Thursday, Friday, etc. without any sign of scruples, as can be seen in the Council of Constance, Florence, the last Lateran [Lateran V] and Trent. (6)

VII. **OBJECTION: There is a silence among several ancient writers of the Order who should have had an occupation with the Sabbatine Privilege. Does not that cause suspicion of falsehood regarding the (Sabbatine) Bull which contains the Privilege?**

RESPONSE: We have the negative argument or silence of which we deal elsewhere, showing that it has no probative value and force especially in matters of history. The fact that the Epistle of St. Paul to the Romans does not speak of the Episcopacy of Saint Peter in Rome does not signify that the Prince of the Apostles was not in Rome. The fact that Saint Thomas Aquinas left us nothing written on the Rosary of his Saintly Founder does not mean that the origin attributed the devotion of the Rosary is false. The fact that Saint Bonaventure does not say one word in his writings of the Portiuncula proves nothing against the truth and authenticity of this Privilege.

What does it matter that several writers have not written on the Sabbatine Privilege when there are others from the same time period who have occupied themselves with it and have defended it.

There were several others who lived in proximity to the Pontificate of John XXII: for example, John Baconthorpe who died 24 years after the publication of the Sabbatine Bull (1346), William of Sanvico (1348) and Tomas Lombe who wrote in 1387. See more names of Carmelite Writers who have spoken of the Sabbatine Privilege in Chapter VI, Num. 73 found in *Enciclopedia del Escapulario Del Carmen,* P. Simon Besalduch, 1931 and in the Appendix of *Bibliografia del Escapulario del Carmen.* (7)

The devotion of Pope John XXII to Our Blessed Mother was

extraordinary. He was so devoted to the Carmelite Order, that among his predecessors, no other Holy Father enriched it with so many Privileges as he did.

Everyone who has studied the proceedings of the Roman Curia knows how great is the caution exercised in granting or confirming privileges having their origin in disputed facts or visions of doubtful authenticity. If a Pope confirms the Indulgences granted by one of his predecessors to some special devotion, he thereby implicitly approves the devotion and acknowledges the authenticity of the previous grant. (8)

But Pope after Pope has approved the Sabbatine Indulgence and thereby has implicitly accepted the substance of the Bull in which the Indulgence was contained. It would indeed be strange if an impudent "forgery" of this kind was allowed by one Pope after another to pass current without rebuke, and not only without rebuke, but as the ground for a continual repetition and confirmation of the favors which were originally granted to the Catholic world on the strength of such an "infamous fraud". Clement VII, Paul III, St. Pius V, Gregory XIII, Clement X, Innocent XI all appear as the Protectors and Defenders of these Carmelite favors. (8a)

The belief in the Sabbatine Indulgence and in the Sabbatine Bull is firmly and deeply rooted in the hearts of the Catholics all over the world. Firmly and deeply rooted, by God's mercy, it will ever remain, as long as time shall last. (8b)

(For further information and proof of the authenticity of the Scapular Visions please refer to *Enciclopedia del Escapulario del Carmen,* by P. Simon M. Besalduch, Barcelona, 1931)

The Sabbatine Bull differs, in form and in style, from ordinary Bulls; but this difference can derive from the fact that John XXII—in as much as he alone had had the Vision—put himself into the writing under impressions still vivid of joy and wonder, while other Bulls are made later, by secretaries and writers and those deputed, which always, insofar as possible, follow the ordinary forms. Whatever may be the case, the Pope [John XXII], with a most beautiful warrant, descends from the Vision of the Divine Majesty to the contemplation of the most sacred humanity of Jesus Christ; he then passes from the songs and hymns of the Angels, with these spirits altogether praising God, to the Queen of the Heaven, glorified amid all the heavenly courts, invoked and honored by the Church Militant, and especially by all those of the Carmelite Order; finally he comes to himself and begins the narration of the Vision of the Promise and the Authorization he had received from her. (9)

Pope Saint John XXIII: *It was likewise pleasing to us (in choosing the name John) to feel united across six centuries of history, to the last of the numerous Pontiffs of this name, John XXII ... the Bishop of Avignon, who governed the Church for 18 years and died more than ninety years of age in 1334. This was a great Pontiff. His life was full of tribulations, but rich in works and merits in every way; a true servant of the Servants of God. He was very devoted to Mary; to him history attributes the fatherhood of the Sabbatine Privilege, so precious and so dear to those who wear the Scapular of Our Lady of Mount Carmel.* (10)

ENDNOTES

RESPONSES TO THE OBJECTIONS

1   Apud Villiers. *Bibl Carm.*, t. II, col. 124; in *Enciclopedia Del Escapulario Del Carmen.* P. Simon M. Besalduch, Barcelona, 1931, p. 278

2   *Ibid*, pp. 279, 280

3   *Ep. 71 ad Lucinium.; ibid*, pp. 280-281

4   *Ibid*, pp. 281-282

5   *Ibid*, pp. 282- 283

6   Villiers, *Bibl Carm.*, 1.c., 6. *ibid*, p. 283

7   *Ibid*, pp. 283, 284

8   *The Month*, A Catholic Magazine and Review, *The Catholic Dictionary and the Sabbatine Indulgence,* by R.F. Clarke, Vol. LVIII, September-December, 1886, p. 492

8a *Ibid*, p. 492

8b *Ibid*, p. 494

9   *Vita di San Simone de Stock,* Alfredo Mombrun, 1884, pp. 142-143, translated

10 Pope John XXIII a the closing of the Jubilee of Lourdes, February 18, 1959; *Osservatore Romano*, Friday , Feb. 20, 1959. (The above photograph of Our Lady's appearance to Pope John XXII granting the Sabbatine Privilege is taken from *Histoire Des Miracles du Saint Scapulaire,* Doctor J. Biroat, prieur de Cluny, Bruges, 1963)

Both the Objections and the Responses are taken from *Enciclopedia Del Escapulario Del Carmen*, P. Simon M. Besalduch, Barcelona 1931, found on the above listed pages.

MODERN DAY OBJECTIONS AND RESPONSES 2004

I. OBJECTION: In the text of the Bull the Madonna called John by the name of the Pope, saying to him: "Vicar of my Son" and she promised him, "I am making you Pope:" how could he be made Pope if he already is [the Pope] for six years? (1)

RESPONSE: Some exemplars of the Bull have, instead of the phrase, "I made thee," the phrase, "I am making thee Pope," in the present tense, but the meaning carries more naturally the sense of past time, "I made you Pope." As we observed already it seems that it should more likely read: "I have made you, Pope, than "I am making you," as the Venerable Father Giovanni di Gesù e Maria, and others observe, who maintain that it should be believed that the Vision happened after the election of John XXII to the papacy; but even if one prefers the other opinion, nevertheless, one can say that Mary Most Holy might have already called him "Vicar of her Son," in the sense that he was bound to be elected Pope by her maternal mediation. (2)

Also … God permitted an English Carmelite, an apostate under Henry VIII, to give testimony to the truth: this unfortunate soul was named John Bale: "John XXII, he says, before his elevation to the papacy, had an admirable vision, as he testified himself in a Bull, in which it was revealed that during the dispute of the Cardinals the Virgin would make him Pope and free him from his adversaries"; he likewise says in another part: "I read, both in England and Belgium, the said apparition, with indulgences and nothing of hatred, and [of] the liberation of souls from Purgatory, in a certain Bull which was renewed under Clement VII in Rome in 1530." (3)

II. OBJECTION: Other difficulties come from the silence of biographers and defenders of the Pope on a particular matter of such importance for Marian protection. (4)

RESPONSE: Launoy thus formulates this negative argument: "If an event, which is not lacking in importance, has been passed over in silence by all the writers, and there was not any memorial that has passed on the memory during a period of around two hundred years from the time in which the event is said to have taken place, it ought to be considered false." Launoy then reduces to 150 years the delay that he already fixed as 200. Luke, the author of the Acts of the Apostles, speaks for a long time about the establishment of Christianity in Antioch, that metropolis of the East, which was a gathering of the whole world (*totius orbis compendium*), as has been said; he names his evangelists (Acts 11: 19-30), but he says not a word about the preaching of St. Peter, nor of the foundation of the See of Antioch by the Prince of the Apostles four years after the Ascension of our Lord, facts affirmed by a very ancient tradition, reported by Eusebius, St. Jerome, Origen, and later authors, but about which the witness is never weakened by the silence of St. Luke, even though he is a contemporary. Moreover no contemporary witness can be produced to establish that St. Peter was the First Bishop of Rome. (5)

III. OBJECTION: The Sacred Congregation of the Inquisition in Rome, after a lengthy study, issued a decree on January 20, 1613, outlining what the Carmelites were permitted to preach. The decree was accompanied by a recommendation that the Carmelites "shall not mention the Sabbatine Bull in order that the term may be forgotten." (6)

RESPONSE: Launoy considered this decree to condemn both the Sabbatine Bull of John XXII and the apparition. This opinion has been shown to be false by the simple fact that the Church, when conceding the Sabbatine Privilege to the Scapular Confraternity by the Decree of Paul V, has premised it by citing first the (Sabbatine) Bull of John XXII "Sic mihi. 3 Mart. 1322". (See: RESCRIPTA AUTHENTICA, Summaria Indulgentiarum, December 1, 1866, pp. 475, 476, under Section II, Chapter 1B in this book; see also a copy of the Sabbatine Bull executed from Messina, found in Chapter 7, under "The Magnificent Beauty of Christian Art" in this book.)

Benedict XIV stated that it was unnecessary for him to weigh the arguments for and against the authenticity of the Bull as the question was wisely settled by the decree of Paul V. He explained as follows: *"The Second Lessons in the Roman Breviary agree with this Decree all of those things which could create difficulty both in the Vision of St. Simon Stock and in the Sabbatine Bull have been removed both by the wise observations of learned men and the Decree of the Roman Pontiff."* (The Decree of January 20, 1613). (7)

IV. OBJECTION: There are some reasons which would lead a

Carmelite to concoct a story of a vision of the Virgin Mary. If they were to appeal to the ordinary faithful, the Carmelites needed to have some special privilege for their own habit and Scapular and the Story of the Vision to "Holy Simon" inserted in the catalogue of saints satisfies this need. Clearly, the Carmelite story is modeled on Dominican and Franciscan claims and it is difficult not to see it as an attempt to claim equal spiritual value for the Carmelite Scapular. (8)

RESPONSE; It would certainly not be necessary to defend the truth of this Vision because they are so few in number who, with intemperate criticism, still place it in doubt – for not even their doubts and false arguments can in anyway lessen or dampen the piety of the true devotees. After Swanyngton, and eight other writers, the first being Paleonidoro, had ascertained, by their volume the truth of the above-mentioned revelation, the Vision of St. Simon Stock was 600 plus years in counting; moreover, it was admitted and believed as authentic by all the people just as it was, in the 1st century [of its occurrence], by those who were there then, and this devout faith is so deeply rooted throughout the whole Catholic world. (9)

V. OBJECTION: The first recognizable account of the Simon Stock Legend is found in a brief catalogue of Carmelite Saints included in the Viridarium composed sometime between 1413 and 1426, by the Prior General, John Grossi. (10)

RESPONSE: The Scapular Vision is also alluded to from the mouth of St. Simon himself, and by Pope John XXII, who was elected in the year 1316, fifty-one years after the death of St. Simon. In his Bull, *Sacratissimo uti culmine*, 1322, better known as the Sabbatine Bull, he informs us that the Blessed Virgin appeared to him and told him that they who enter the Holy Order and wear the sign of the Holy Habit (the Scapular) shall enjoy certain privileges. William of Sanvico (from the province of the Holy Land written about 1290) wrote: *And so the Virgin Mary revealed to their Prior that they should fearlessly approach the Supreme Pontiff, Innocent because they would obtain from him a salutary remedy for their troubles.* (11)

Fr. Bartholomew Xiberta, (now declared Servant of God) (in his monumental work: *De Visione Sancti Simonis Stock,* Rome, 1950) has traced the earliest biography of St. Simon, not to John Grossi, but to an official catalogue or legendary of Carmelite saints which is found in various versions, the lengthier and later of which exists in manuscripts dating from the second half of the 14th century...which is therefore even older, and must have been written at a time much closer to the event than was formerly realized. It is brief, factual and sober. There are no grounds in historical criticism for doubting any of the facts it relates about the life of St. Simon Stock. (11a)

The revelation of the Virgin to the Prior General of the Order about which Sanvico speaks, is the famous and most glorious apparition of July 16, 1251, as is the date of the Bull which has mentioned it. (12)

VI. OBJECTION: The last serious attempt to vindicate the Historicity of the Scapular Vision was made...a quarter of a century ago by Fr. Bartholomew Xiberta, O.Carm. (1897-1967)...a distinguished scholar and a great Carmelite...(who) failed in its purpose. (13)

RESPONSE: Servant of God, Fr. Bartholomew F. Xiberta, O. Carm., (was) the greatest living authority on Scapular history. After years of critical research, he concludes: *Having studied the documentary evidence, one sees how the arguments against the historicity of the Vision of St. Simon Stock collapse one after the other...I dare to affirm that the Vision of St. Simon which preceded the Scapular Devotion has the support of more historical documents than one would expect to find.* (13a) Fr. Bartolomew Xiberta O. Carm., (1897-1967), is now declared, "Servant of God," and was a Carmelite devoted entirely to the service of Jesus through Mary in the spirit of Elijah. Fr. Xiberta was one of the outstanding theologians of the last century, researcher, historian, teacher, and no doubt, the outstanding Carmelite theologian, who was present as a Consultant at the Second Vatican Council, and the only Carmelite who was on the Theological Commission. A book was written about his devotion to Mary: *Bartolome Maria Xiberta, Teologo de Nuestra Senora, (Bartholomew Maria Xiberta, Our Lady's Theologian,)* by Checa Arregui, O. Carm.<cerni. Fr. Xiberta wrote a "monumental" work on the authenticity of the Scapular Vision entitled: *De Visione Sancti Simonis Stock,* 1950, establishing the historical foundation for the Authenticity of the Scapular Vision and St. Simon Stock. (14)

VII. OBJECTION: The Brown Scapular Devotion, as we know it today, dates no further back than the latter half of the 16th century and owes its popularity largely to Giovanni Battista Rossi who was Prior General from 1564 to 1578. Needless to say, at that time,

and since, great emphasis was laid on the promise that was put in Our Lady's mouth by the legend: "Whosoever dies wearing this will be saved," and also the Sabbatine Privilege still held on to the popular imagination of the assurance of release from Purgatory on the Saturday after death. (15)

RESPONSE: It was the Servant of God, Fr. Bartholomew F. M. Xiberta, who established a solid and accurate historical foundation for the earliest recording of the Scapular Vision, in his monumental work: *De Visione Sancti Simonis Stock,* Rome, 1950, and in his article: *Annotations on the Status of the Scapular Question.* Fr. Xiberta concluded that the Vision of St. Simon Stock was authentic, and based on a sound historical foundation. Again, as read in #VI above, Fr. Xiberta was an outstanding Carmelite Theologian who was present at the Second Vatican Council and the only Carmelite who was on the Theological Commission at the Vatican Council. Please read #XVI further below in this Appendix for a more detailed description of Fr. Xiberta's findings. (16)

VIII. OBJECTION: The document of Majorca is certainly false and therefore the "Sabbatine Bull" contained in it cannot be considered authentic. (17)

RESPONSE: The first, and most ancient transcript, which appeared a little more than 11 years after the publication of the Bull of Alexander V, is that one made on the Island of Majorca in 1421 by P. Alfonso de Theramo by means of the Notary Public, Paolo de Rubengerio di Piacenza (*Paulus de Rubengeso de Placentia*) in the presence of various witnesses, who all signed the solemn act, which can be found included in another also notarized and solemn (act), which is often spoken of as the second transcript. (18) (also): The original of the Bull of Alexander V was also transferred to England as we learn from the authentic copy of it made January 2, 1421 at the instance of Alphonsus de Theram, an Englishman, then Prior of the convent of Captun in the Island of Majorca, afterwards Prior of the convent of Coventry, England, who then took the original to be kept in the archives of the General in London. This copy was solemnly reduced to public form before notaries, and judges, and kept at Genoa. Of this we are informed by Palaeonydorus, Bostius, Leersius and in *Vide Speculum,* Carm.,T.1, p. 562, n. 2204. (19)

IX. **OBJECTION: The Order does not have one founder, but it refers to the Prophet Elijah and the Virgin Mary as inspirational models.** (20).

RESPONSE: Many supreme Pontiffs, in their letters and in their Bulls, have spoken of the Carmelities as imitators, followers, and sons of the Prophet, Elijah, and the Church in her Liturgy does not fail to acknowledge this opinion; and, as confirmed by Benedict XII, she has permitted, in the great Basilica of St. Peter in Rome where the statues of all the Holy Founders of Religious Orders are found, that of St. Elijah also to be erected with the following inscription, which proves the tradition of the Carmelites: *To St. Elijah, the Prophet, the Founder of the Universal Order of the Carmelities this is erected by the Decree of June 26, 1725.* (21) Also, Pope Sixtus IV, in his Bull: *Dum Attenta,* dated Nov. 28th, 1476, B. I. 428, stated these words: *The Most Glorious Virgin Mary, who by virtue of the Holy Spirit brought forth Jesus Christ, is the same Virgin who "produced the family" of the Blessed Virgin Mary of Mount Carmel.* Pope Gregory XIII, in his Bull: *Ut Laudes,* dated Sept. 18th 1577 also stated: *She brought forth the Order of Carmel and nourished it at her breasts.* (21a)

X. **OBJECTION: This seems unusual in a pontifical document. A pope never refers to a private vision in official acts granting indulgences or making other concessions.** (22)

RESPONSE: See "Chronology of Events," 1421, the Bull of Alexander V contains the Bull of John XXII relating the Vision of Our Lady granting the Sabbatine Privilege, also Clement VII and several other Popes who have granted indulgences and concessions found in the "Chronology of Events" in Chapter 3 in this book, based on the Visions and also the Decree of the Holy Office of Pope Pius X, dated December 16, 1910. A.A.S., III, p. 23 in which the Holy Father specifically mentioned the Sabbatine Privilege. "With the outbreak of the terrible Muslim persecutions in Palestine, the Madonna appeared on Mt. Carmel to make known her desire that the Carmelites move *en masse* to the West where some Convents were already open. These, well known for their sanctity, were soon diffused throughout Europe, but a new storm stirred up against the Order and it came to be suppressed; but the Most Holy Virgin soon came to their assistance, and on January 30, 1226 she appeared to Pope Honorius III and not only dissuaded him from his decision to suppress the Order but enjoined him to approve the Rule of St. Albert of Jerusalem presented by St. Brocardo." (23) (There are numerous examples such as these that exist). Also: already before the Vision of St. Simon Stock, she appeared to Pope Honorius III to order him to take the Institute of Carmel under his protection (*The Roman Breviary*, 16 of July and all the historians of Carmel). (24)

> A Pope did refer to a private vision in an official papal text, in an encyclical: *Saeculo Exeunte Octavo,* (encyclical of Venerable Pope Pius XII on the Eighth Centenary of the Independence of Portugal, June 13, 1940). In the text he stated: *Let the faithful not forget, expecially when they recite the Rosary, so recommended by the Blessed Virgin Mary of Fatima to ask the Virgin Mother of God to obtain missionary vocations with abundant fruits for the greatest possible number of souls.* www. miraclehunter.com/marian.../fatima/

XI. **OBJECTION: "The Church...over the last 50 years, has examined its Rites and Rituals, simplified them, suppressed some, revised others and made changes necessary to keep us focused on the Cross and Resurrection of Christ as the single origin of our salvation. In this light, the Fathers of Vatican Council II clearly stated that our approach to the Sacramentals of the Church has changed."** (25)

RESPONSE: FROM THE "DIRECTORY ON POPULAR PIETY AND THE LITURGY": *The fact that pious exercises and devotions express popular sentiment, does not, however, authorize personalistic or subjective approaches to this material. With due respect for the competence proper to local Ordinaries or the Major Superiors of religious orders in cases involving devotions connected with their Orders, the Conference of Bishops should decide in matters relating to pious exercises widely diffused in a particular country or in a vast region.*

It is especially necessary to ensure that those pious exercises undergoing adaptation or inculturation retain their identity and their essential characteristics. In this regard, particular attention must always be given to their historical origin and to the doctrinal and cultic elements by which they are constituted. **(Issued by the Congregation for Divine Worship and the Discipline of Sacraments, Vatican City, December, 2001, #92)**

Misreading of Vatican II led to "collapse" in Marian Devotion, Studies! Devotion to Mary "collapsed" in some parts of the United States after the Second Vatican Council even though the council fathers had upheld her critical place within the Catholic Faith said a leading American expert in Marian Studies. Even though bishops felt

Mariology, like the church as a whole, needed to be renewed in light of tradition, liturgy and the Bible, later an "over rationalist" historical approach reduced the role of the Holy Spirit and marginalized most forms of devotion, Father Phalen said. While popular piety may have suffered in some parts of the West, Cardinal Amato said Popes Paul VI, John Paul II, and Benedict (XVI) did much to enrich and invigorate Marian reflection and tradition. (25a)

Vatican II's call for renewal did not break with tradition, Pope says! *The Second Vatican Council's call for "Renewal" did not mark a break with tradition or a watering down of the faith, but reflected Christianity's lasting vitality and God's eternal presence,* Pope Benedict XVI said. *This renewal does not mean a break with tradition, rather it expresses a lasting vitality,* he said. *Renewal doesn't mean watering down the faith, lowering it to fit modern fads or trends, or fashioning it to fit public opinion or one's own desires, "rather it's the contrary,"* he said. (25b)

NATIONAL CONFERENCE OF CATHOLIC BISHOPS:

A Pastoral Letter on the Blessed Virgin Mary: Behold Your Mother, **Nov. 21,1973** *We Bishops of the United States wish to affirm with all our strength the lucid statements of the Second Vatican Council on the permanent importance of authentic devotion to the Blessed Virgin, not only in the Liturgy, where the Church accords her a most special place under Jesus her Son, but also in the beloved devotions that have been repeatedly approved and encouraged by the Church and that are still filled with meaning for Catholics. As Pope Paul (VI) has reminded us, the Rosary and the Scapular are among these tested forms of devotion that bring us closer to Christ through the example and protection of His Holy Mother.* (26)

Many people in our day, decades after Vatican Council II, (wrongly) think the Catholic Church is changing its teachings. However, this is not true! Vatican II "Proposes Again" the Decrees of Trent: #24: "Taken up to heaven she [Mary] **did not lay aside this saving office but by her manifold intercession continues to bring us gifts of eternal salvation**." #9 states: "The Faithful who use with devotion an object of piety (crucifix, cross, rosary, scapular, or medal) after it has been duly blessed by any priest, can gain a parital indulgence. #46: *This Sacred Council accepts loyally the venerable faith of our ancestors in the living communion which exists between us and our brothers who are in the glory of Heaven or who are yet being purified after their death; and it proposes again the decrees of the Second Council of Nicea, of the Council of Florence, and of the Council of*

Trent. Statement #46 mentions that Vatican Council II concurs with and reaffirms again "the Decrees" of Trent (1545 to 1563) (26a)

XII. OBJECTION: "The Historicity of the Sabbatine Bull and its accompanying Privilege has been discredited with more certainty than the apparition to Simon Stock." (27)

RESPONSE: "The existence and authenticity of the Bull of John XXII is confirmed by the authority of the Pontiffs who have made mention of confirming it; the existence of the Sabbatine Bull is corroborated by the approval of the Breviary, the *Bullarium*, and other Books. Under the day of July 16th in the Carmelite Breviary we have, the SOLEMN COMMEMORATION OF THE BLESSED VIRGIN MARY, the most important feast of the Carmelite Order and of ancient custom. In 1673 the Sacred Congregation of Indulgences and Relics solemnly approves the Collection of Indulgences granted by various popes, naming there, among the Indulgences granted to the Carmelite Order and its affiliated Confraternities, those that are based on the Sabbatine Bull. At this time, the compilation of the same Collection falls into place through the work of Cardinal Bona, with special mention of the Sabbatine Privilege and all that was confirmed by Clement X. (28)

Charles Drelincourt, born in the year 1595, a minister of the so-called reformed church in Charenton, in a book he composed on the honor that should be allotted to the Most Blessed Virgin, says that, "the Bull of John XXII was authentically confirmed by Alexander V." (29)

Although the Privilege and the Indulgence of the Sabbatine Bull was granted and confirmed by Jesus Christ in Heaven it was necessary that the Supreme Pontiffs, his Vicars, approve, corroborate, and confirm them on earth; because our Lord does not exercise ecclesiastical jurisdiction exteriorly over mortals. The Indulgence of the Portiuncula that Jesus Christ granted to his Great Servant, Francis, needed to be accepted and confirmed equally by the Sovereign Pontiffs. (30)

XIII. OBJECTION: In the years after World War II, the Carmelite Scholar Ludovico Saggi clearly demonstrated that the alleged Bull of John XXII had not been issued from the Avignon chancery in 1322, but was rather a forgery from the Agrigento region of Sicily in the early 15th century. (31)

RESPONSE: The Second Constitution of Alexander (V) as found in the *Carmelite Bullarium* is the one in reference to the Sabbatine Bull. A note mentions that the Constitution is taken from an authentic copy which is in the archives of the Order in Rome. The introduction to this copy is addressed to the Prior General and all the brothers and sisters as well as the members of the Confraternity, and it testifies that an authentic copy of the said Bull of John XXII, of happy memory, has been seen and examined, the copy of which is then reproduced. The Bull of John XXII still preserves the clausula *Datum Avinione 3 die Martii, Pontificatus nostri anno sexto,* and the Constitution of Alexander V carries the place and date thus, *Datum Romae, septima Decembris apud S. Mariam Majorem Pontificatus nostri anno primo.* The two years of interregnum (1314-1316) are of interest to those who have studied the Sabbatine Devotion, for it was during those years that John had the Famous Vision, although the actual Bull bears the date of several years afterwards. This is easily intelligible and seems to bear witness to the affinity between the Sabbatine Bull and the Sabbatine Privilege.

Benedict XIV clearly teaches and defends the authenticity of the Sabbatine Bull....citing: *All the difficulties that could be brought against both the Vision of St. Simon Stock and the Sabbatine Bull have been removed, both by the wise disquisition of learned men and by the Decree of the Sovereign Pontiff.*

There are other Bulls to the same effect from other Sovereign Pontiffs in different ages of the Church. It is worthy of remark that many of these Bulls mention the two fundamental Bulls of John XXII and Alexander V., approve of them, and ratify their contents. These Popes would not surely quote these two Bulls, give them their approbation, and make them the foundation of their own if there was any doubt of their authenticity.

To these authorities we may add that of the Sacred Congregation of Rites which has approved the Lessons of the Second Nocturn of the Breviary for the Feast of the Solemn Commemoration of the Blessed Virgin of Mount Carmel; and the Decree of the Congregation of the Inquisition under Paul V., February 15, 1613, both confirmative of the privileges of the Sabbatine Bull. We may (also) add the authority of the theological faculties of different universities. (32)

XIV. **OBJECTION: There are still many Catholics who think that the Brown Scapular has in itself some power to save those who wear it from hell or to deliver them from purgatory.** (33)

RESPONSE: Of the days when Jesus walked in Galilee, we read that the supernatural power passed from His garment to heal the sick and infirm thus apparently giving the sanction of the Son of Man to the great principle underlying the Devotion of the Scapular, as well as of all other religious garments. (34)

XV. **OBJECTION: "We know that Private Revelation can neither add to nor detract from the Deposit of Faith. The Sabbatine Privilege or the Historicity of the Vision is not part of the Deposit of Faith. Private revelation cannot change that."(35)**

RESPONSE: The above statement sounds strikingly similar to the statement of the 17th century Jansenist, John Launoy, who initiated a ruthless assault on the authenticity of the Scapular Visions in 1642. He wrote: *The Church is not ruled by private revelation and neither are the faithful to be ruled by it.* (36) In Sacred Scripture, the Letter of St. Paul to the Galatians, Chapter 1:11-12, is a direct reference for St. Paul receiving a direct (private) revelation from Jesus Christ himself: *For I give you to understand, brethren, that the gospel which was preached by me is not according to man for neither did I receive it of man, nor did I learn it; but by the revelation of Jesus Christ.* (37) [On the role of Private Revelations in the Church see CCC #67]

XVI. **OBJECTION: Current research on the Scapular Vision itself does not support its Historicity. Fifty years ago Bartolomeo Xiberta suggested that we needed to move away from a strictly historical approach and try to discover the kernel of faith contained in the story.** (38)

RESPONSE: Fifty years ago, (the now declared Servant of God) Bartolomeo Xiberta, "one of the outstanding theologians of the last century, and no doubt the outstanding Carmelite Theologian," wrote a monumental work entitled: *De Visione Sancti Simonis Stock,* Rome, 1950, for the upcoming occasion of the Seventh Centenary of the famous Vision of St. Simon Stock which gave a new aspect to the "problem" of the Historicity of the Vision. Fr. Xiberta has traced the earliest biography of St. Simon, not to John Grossi (died c. 1434), but to an official catalogue or legendary of Carmelite Saints which is found in various versions, the lengthier and later of which exist in manuscripts dating from the second half of the 14th century...and must have been written at a time much closer to the event than was formerly realized. It is brief, factual and sober. There are no grounds in historical criticism for doubting any of the facts it relates about the life of St. Simon Stock." (The above words were written by Fr. Joachim Smet, O. Carm. and were published in the Catholic Herald issue dated September 29, 1950.) (39)

To quote the words of now "Servant of God," Fr. Xiberta in his article: *Annotations on the Status of the Scapular Question,* he said: **Objections made three centuries ago and lately renewed by clever writers have infected the modern mind with the idea that the devotion rests on a pious fiction, or at least on insufficient arguments.** In this article, Fr. Xiberta prepared a factual, concise, and accurate presentation of historical evidence based on his analysis, comparison and conclusion of the collection of ancient texts on the Authenticity of the Vision of St. Simon. (See Chapter 5: *Responses to the Objections*). He concludes with four powerful facts based on the discovered historical evidence which he says "can overthrow every thesis against the historicity of the Scapular Vision." Fr. Xiberta closes the article with these words: *In consideration of these conclusions, I am compelled to affirm that the Vision of St. Simon Stock, which occupies so dominant a place in the Scapular Devotion, is as solidly founded on historical evidence as could be expected. Let anyone who is so minded belittle faith in the Vision; lest, however, he make himself ridiculous, let him do so before the bar of history.* (40)

XVII. **OBJECTION: During the celebration of the anniversary of the Scapular, Pope John Paul II, for his part, wrote of the importance of the Scapular to him personally, but mentioned neither the Sabbatine Privilege nor the Vision of Simon Stock, although he recognized that the celebration "is taking place, according to a venerable tradition of the Order itself, on the 750th Anniversary of the Bestowal of the Scapular. (41)**

RESPONSE: On the 24th of September, 1983, at the end of a Mass celebrated with members of the 1983 General Chapter of the Carmelite Order, the newly elected Father General, Fr. John Malley, asked the Holy Father, Pope St. John Paul II to say a few words to those present. Pope John Paul II said: *You are the oldest Order in the world because you descend from no one less than the Prophet Elias...You are a great and very old family. You are linked to St. Simon Stock, the saint of the Scapular...* (41a)

Also, in the Osservatore Romano Newspaper, Pope John Paul II, in 1988 did mention the vision of St. Simon Stock when he referred to a venerable tradition identified with "St. Simon Stock" rooted in the Christian people, with much spiritual fruit which is the Scapular of Our Lady of Mount Carmel. The commemoration of the 750th Anniversary of the Bestowal of the Scapular in 2001 is in itself, a silent recognition and confirmation by Pope St. John Paul II of the Authenticity of the Vision of St. Simon Stock, or the Anniversary itself would not be taking place. (42)

XVIII. OBJECTION: The Portuguese Inquisition had condemned the Sabbatine Privilege as heretical in 1609; when the Order appealed to the Holy See, silence was imposed on all parties, and the Carmelites were forbidden to preach the (Sabbatine) Privilege (an obedience which they generally ignored). (43)

RESPONSE: First of all, a Book of Indulgences written by a Carmelite Father, which included the Sabbatine Privilege, was prohibited by the Master of the Sacred Palace in the year 1603. The prohibition was not serious. It only suspended the circulation of the book until it amended in some particulars. The Portuguese Inquisitor believed the Sabbatine Privilege was intended. (43a)

It is interesting to note also that among the objections to the Sabbatine Privilege in other countries in Europe at the time of the controversy in 1609, was one from the King of Spain, through the keeper of the royal exchequer that the abstinence commanded by the Sabbatine Privilege (one of the conditions to gain the Privilege is to abstain from flesh meat on Wednesday, Friday, and Saturday) deprived the Portuguese treasury of 30,000 scudi per annum (per year). (44)

All objections to the Sabbatine Privilege were brought forward and referred to different Universities for examination. The Sabbatine Privilege was referred to the University of Salamanca in 1566, (the unanimous decision was that the Sabbatine Bull and those of the other Sovereign Pontiffs relating to it were authentic,) to the Holy Office and to the University of Bologna in 1609 (who gave a similar attestation) confirming the Bull of John XXII. This is signed by six doctors and others. (45)

The whole question was committed to a Commission and on the 30th of June, (1610-1611) the answers of the Commission were given: ...The Indulgences according to the tenor of the Bulls of Clement and

Paul and Gregory could be preached; they were at liberty to preach that the Devotion had been very much favored by the Popes, and that it was richly endowed with Indulgences for the living as well as for the dead...the judgment of the Commission was laid before the Cardinals of the Holy Office in 1612. Eleven Cardinals took part in this consultation. Cardinal Bellarmine took part in the deliberations and openly espoused the side of the Carmelites, urging that they were quite right in their preaching according to the tenor of the Bulls...finally, it was intimated to the Commissary-General of the Carmelites that the doctrine in regard to the assistance given on the First Saturday after death to the souls of the deceased members of the Confraternity could be piously believed. (45a)

Even the King of Portugal had petitioned Pope Paul V not to reject the Privilege of the Sabbatine Bull. The authenticity of the Sabbatine Bull was full discussed before the Holy Office in 1613. St. Robert Bellarmine, who was the most influential of the Cardinals deciding the question of the Sabbatine Privilege by the Decree of 1613, laid down the principle of the authority of the Church. He said: *It cannot be denied to the Carmelite Fathers to preach...according to the tenor of the Bulls.* (46) So then, the Decree of the Congregation of the Inquisition, issued under Pope Paul V, (decided on January 20, 1613) and (confirmed and dated by the Supreme Pontiff, Paul V on February 15th, 1613), (46a) confirmed the privileges of the Sabbatine Bull (47) satisfying all the objections brought forward against the Sabbatine Privilege.

On the 18th of March, in the year 1922, His Holiness Pope Pius XI issued a *Letter* on the Occasion of the Sixth Centenary of the Sabbatine Privilege, in which he called the Sabbatine the greatest Indulgence of them all. The *Letter* of the Holy Father was accompanied by one from the Cardinal Secretary of State conveying his congratulations on the "Sixth Centenary of the bestowing of the "Sabbatine Privilege." (48)

ENDNOTES
MODERN DAY OBJECTIONS AND RESPONSES 2004

1   *La Bolla Sabbatina,* Ludovico Saggi, O. Carm., Roma, 1967, p. 81

2   *La Divozione Illustrata Dello Scapolare Della B. V. Maria Del Carmine,* P. Enrico Maria Del SS. Sacramento, 1876, Oneglia, pp. 29, 42

3   *Escapulario de N.S.Del Carmen, Coleccion de Instrucciones.* R. P. Brocardo de Sta. Teresa, 1895, pp. 232-233

4   *La Bolla Sabbatina,* Ludovico Saggi, O. Carm., Roma, 1967, p. 82

5   *Le Scapulaire de Notre-Dame du Mont-Carmel est authentique.* P. Marie-Joseph du Sacre-Coeur, 1928, pp. 98, 99

6   *The Carmelite Scapular Today,* from the summary of an article by Richard Copsey, O. Carm, Journal of Ecclesiastical History, Vol. 50, No. 4, October 1999; carmelites.org

7   *The Credibility of the Scapular Promises* Rev. Christian P Ceroke, O. Carm., 1950, p. 50; see also SUMMARIUM Indulgentiarurn et Gratiarum, December 1, 1866 in Chapter I, "Synthesis of the Devotion"

8   *The Carmelite Scapular Today,* from the summary of an article by Richard Copsey (see # 6 above) p. 4

9   *La Divozione Illustrata Dello Scapolare Della B.V. Maria Del Carmine.* P. Enrico Maria, 1876, pp. 9, 10, 12

10   *The Carmelite Scapular Today,* p. 2 (see #6, 8 above); www.carmelites. org/review/march2001/marchapril2001_9.pdf

11   *Take This Scapular,* Carmelite Fathers and Tertiaries, 1949, p. 222; Also read: *The Meaning and Use of the Scapular of Our Lady of Mt. Carmel,* The Bishop of Salford, 1893, p. 9

11a *The Catholic Herald.co.uk:* ST. SIMON STOCK SIR- a newspaper article written by Fr. Joachim Smet, O. Carm, published in the Catholic Herald on September 29, 1950

12   *Enciclopedia del Escapulario Del Carmen* P. Simon M. Besalduch, 1931, p. 146

13   *St. Simon Stock—The Scapular Vision and the Brown Scapular Devotion,* by Bede Edwards, *Carmelite Digest,* Vol. 16, No. 3, Summer, 2001, p. 20

13a *Your Brown Scapular,* Rev. E. K. Lynch, O. Carm., Westminster, MD, 1950, p. 12

14   CITOC, No. 4, October-December 2003, Closure of the Diocesan Process of Canonization of Fr. Bartolome `Fanti M. Xiberta, O. Carm.; CITOC, No. 3, July-September 2007, Carmelite Presence at the Second Vatican Council; *The Carmelite Web Site – O.Carm*; Closure of the Diocesan Process for the Canonization of Fr. Bartholomew Fanti M. Xiberta, O. Carm: http://www.ocarm.org/pre09/news/eng2803. htm

15   *St. Simon Stock – The Scapular Vision and the Brown Scapular Devotion,* by Bede Edwards, *Carmelite Digest,* Vol. 16, No. 3, Summer, 2001, p. 23, paraphrased

16   *Catholic Herald.co.uk, the archive: ST. SIMON STOCK SIR – The letter by Mr. Derek W. Whifield,* originally printed in the 29th September 1950 issue of the Catholic Herald, article written by Fr. Joachim Smet, O. Carm. Collegio di Sant'Alberto, Via Sforza Pallavincini, 10, Rome; *Take This Scapular,* Carmelite Fathers and Tertiaries, Chicago, 1949, *Annotations on the Status of the Scapular Question,* by Bartholomew F. M. Xiberta, O. Carm., pp. 213-243

17   *Antologia dello Scapolare,* Giampiero Molinari, O. Carm., Roma 2001, p.175

18   *Ristretto Della Vita di S.Simone Stock,* P. S. Mattei, Roma, 1873, pp. 83-84;

19   *The Irish Ecclesiastical Record: The Brown Scapular and the Catholic Dictionary,* Vol. VIII, 1887, p. 800

20   *Antologia dello Scapolare* Giampiero Molinari, O. Carm, 2001, p. 185

21   *La Divozione Illustrata dello Scapolare Della B. V. Maria Del Carmine* P. Enrico Maria Del SS. Sacramento, 1876-Notizie Preliminary p. 1, see also: *Sacre Instruttioni Per beneficio de Divoti del S. Scapolare Della Gloriosissima Sempre Vergine Maria,* R. P. F. Gabrielle Ferri da Bologna Carmel, 1656, pp. 7, 8, 11

21a   cf. *Mary in Her Scapular Promise,* John Mathias Haffert, 1942, p. 146, footnotes 1, 2, found on p. 244 of the References

22   *Antologia dello Scapolare,* Giampiero Molinari , O. Carm, Roma 2001, p. 176

23   *Alla Madre di Dio,* Raffaela Impronta, Napoli, 1956, pp. 6, 7

24   *Escapulario de N.S. Del Carmen;* R.P. Brocardo Sta. Teresa, 1895, p. 201

25   *Garment of Grace,* in *Carmel in the World,* Patrick Thomas McMahon, O. Carm., Rome, 2004, p. 177

25a   *Catholic News Service: Misreading of Vatican II led to "collapse in Marian devotion, studies,* Fr. James Phalan, President of the Mariological Society of America, September 7, 2012; http://www.catholicnews. com/data/stories/cns/1203755.htm.

25b   *Catholic News Service: Vatican II's call for renewal did not break with tradition, pope says,* Pope Benedict XVI, October 12, 2012; http:// www.catholicnews.com/data/stories/cns/1204312.htm

26   *National Conference of Catholic Bishops, A Pastoral Letter on the Blessed Virgin Mary: Behold Your Mother,* Nov. 21, 1973, p. 35, #93

26a   *Vatican Council II,* (Official Teachings of Roman Catholicism). Statements #9, #24, and #46 can be verified by consulting Volumes 1 and 2 of the book, *Vatican Council II* printed by Costello

Publishing Co., Northport, New York. Austin Flannery, O.P., is the general editor and each volume contains the Nihil Obstat and the Imprimatur. The editions are: 1984 (Vol. 1) and 1982 (Vol. 2); http://www.evangelicaloutreach.org/official.htm

27   *Garment of Grace*, inside: *Carmel in the World*, Patrick Thomas McMahon, O. Carm, Rome, 2004, p, 182

28   *Ristretto Della Vita di S. Simone Stock,* P.S. Mattei, Roma, 1873, pp. 89, 96, 109

29   *Escapulario de N.S.De Carmen; Coleccion de Instrucciones.* R.P. Brocado de Sta. Teresa, Vitoria, 1895, p. 233

30   *Ibid*, pp. 193-194

31   *Garment of Grace*, inside: *Carmel in the World,* Patrick Thomas McMahon, O. Carm, Rome, 2004, p. 182

32   *Sabbatine Privilege of the Scapular* P. E. Magennis 1923, pp. 27, 42, 43; Irish Ecclesiastical Record., Vol. VIII, 1887, p. 803, 807: *The Brown Scapular and the Catholic Dictionary*

33   *Garment of Grace*, inside: *Carmel in the World,* Patrick Thomas McMahon, O. Carm, Rome, 2004, p. 176.

34   *The Scapular and Some Critics,* P. E. Magennis, O.C.C, Rome, 1914, p. 3

35   *The Carmelite Scapular Today,* carmelites.org, (on-line periodical), p. 2

36   *De Viso*, John Launoy, pp. 65-66, 1642, taken from *The Credibility of the Scapular Promises*, Rev. Christian P. Ceroke, Rome, 1950, p. 116, footnote #39

37   Galatians 1: 11-12, Douay Rheims

38   *The Carmelite Scapular Today,* on-line Carmelite publication: carmelites.org: Summary of an article by Richard Copsey, O. Carm., which was printed in the "Journal of Ecclesiastical History," Vol. 50, No. 4, October 1999, www.carmelites.org/review/march2001/marchapril2001_9.pdf

39   *Catholic Herald.co.uk, the archive*: *ST. SIMON STOCK SIR – The letter by Mr. Derek W. Whifield,* originally printed in the 29th September 1950 issue of the Catholic Herald, article written by Fr. Joachim Smet, O. Carm., Collegio di Sant'Alberto, Via Sforza Pallavincini, 10, Rome.

40   *Take This Scapular,* Carmelite Fathers and Tertiaries, Chicago, 1949, *Annotations on the Status of the Scapular Question,* by Bartholomew F. M. Xiberta, O. Carm., pp. 213-243

41   *Carmel in the World,* Vol. XLIII, N. 3, 2004: *Garment of Grace; a Historical Appreciation of the Carmelite Scapular,* Patrick Thomas McMahon, O. Carm., p. 184

41a   Pope John Paul II *Address to Carmel,* 24.IX.84, *Carmel in the World,* 1984, Rome, Institutum Carmelitanum Vol. XXIII, pp. 5-6, *Ballinasmale Carmelite Abbey, 1288-1870,* by Stephen Josten, O. Carm., 16 July, 1984, pp. 9, 10

42   *Osservatore Romano Newspaper,* Monday-Tuesday, 25th-26th July, 1988: *La Vergine Madre di Dio "Flos Carmeli" possiede la bellezza di tutte le virtu,* translated

43   *Carmel in the World,* Vol. XLIII, N. 3, 2004, p. 182, *Garment of Grace,* Patrick Thomas McMahon, O. Carm., p. 182

43a   *The Sabbatine Privilege of the Scapular,* P. E. Magennis, Ord. Carm., New York, 1923, p. 85

44   *The Ecclesiastical Review,* A Monthly Publication for the Clergy, Vol. LVI, Philadelphia, 1917, p. 165, footnote #12

45   *The Irish Ecclesiastical Record,* A Monthly Journal, John E. Bartley, O. C. C., Third Series, Vol. VIII, Dublin, 1887, pp. 803, 804

45a   *The Sabbatine Privilege of the Scapular,* P. E. Magennis, New York, 1923, pp. 86-88

46   *The Credibility of the Scapular Promises,* Rev. Christian P. Ceroke, Rome, 1950, pp. 163, 164, 167, 171; (46a): *MARY* Vol. 23, No. 3, Illinois, 1962: *Sabbatine Privilege,* by Fr. Gabriel N. Pausback, O. Carm., p. 62

47   *The Irish Ecclesiastical Record,* John E. Bartley, O. C. C., 1887, p. 803, paraphrased

48   *The Sabbatine Privilege of the Scapular,* 1322 A.D. to 1922 A.D., P. E. Magennis, Ord. Carm., New York, 1923, Forward: *Letter* of His Holiness Pope Pius XI on the Occasion of the Sixth Centenary of the Sabbatine Privilege, paraphrased.

ADDED OBJECTIONS AND RESPONSES TO THE AUTHENTICY OF THE SCAPULAR VISIONS OF OUR LADY TO ST. SIMON STOCK AND POPE JOHN XXII 2004

I. **OBJECTION:** The "Negative Argument:" the silence of some **Carmelite historians in recording the Scapular Visions.** (1)

RESPONSE: Granting that some Carmelite historians are silent about the Scapular, that is no argument against its authenticity as long as there are other Carmelites equally trustworthy who mention it in their works. If that kind of argument were valid, many most important events both in sacred and profane history might be denied or called into question. Thus the mission of the Archangel Gabriel to the Blessed Virgin, to announce to her that she was chosen by God to be the Mother of the Messiah, is recorded by St. Luke in his gospel, while the other Evangelists make no mention of that august event. Would it, therefore, be lawful to call it into question? (2)

II. **OBJECTION: The Bull of John XXII has no place in the Roman Bullarium.** (3) **There is no trace in the papal registers of the Bulls attributed to Alexander V or John XXII** (4)

RESPONSE: Does it follow hence, that it must be a forgery? By no means! There are many other Bulls issued by Sovereign Pontiffs that have no place in the Roman Bullarium and yet their authenticity and the privileges conceded by them have not been questioned. John XXII reigned as Pope for nineteen years and during that long period, transacted many important negotiations and issued many Bulls and yet only a few of them are now in existence. The rest have been lost. When we consider the stormy times in which he lived, that the Popes were obliged to live in exile at Avignon exposed to the attacks of their enemies, we can easily account for the loss of these documents. Alphonsus Chiaconius in his "History of the Popes" relates that the heretics and enemies of the Church invaded the palace of John XXII and with violent hands opened the public archives, and destroyed the documents of the Apostolic Chancery, chiefly those issued under John.

The Roman Bullarium does not profess to embrace all the Bulls ever issued. The first who compiled the Roman Bullarium was Laertius Cherubinus. He collected the Bulls from the reign of St. Leo the Great to that of Sixtus V. There are many Bulls of preceding Popes, however, not contained in this Bullarium and few indeed of John XXII and of Alexander V. Spondanus and Bzorius in their annals, (Ad an. 1409), Renatus Choppin and others cite many Bulls of Alexander V, not one of which is mentioned in the Bullarium of Cherubinus. (5)

III. **OBJECTION: It is curious to observe that John XXII before he became Pope and during his time as Pope, denied, as a theologian, the existence of Purgatory and only as his death was approaching did he accept this doctrine. Therefore the reference to Purgatory is strange from a theologian who denies its existence.** (6)

RESPONSE: Purgatory, (Latin: purgare, to make clean, to purify), in accordance with Catholic Teaching is a place or condition of temporal punishment for those who, departing this life in God's Grace, are not entirely free from venial faults, or have not fully paid the satisfaction due to their transgressions. (6a)

Consider the *Letter* of Pope John XXII: *Nequaquam sine dolore* to the Armenians, November 21, 1321 (On the Destiny of the Dead):

[The Roman Catholic Church teaches]…*Truly the souls of those who, after receiving the Sacrament of Baptism, have not fallen into any stain of sin at all, as well as those who, after having contracted the stain of sin, are PURIFIED - either while they remain in their bodies or after they have departed them - are immediately received into Heaven. The souls, however, of those who die in mortal sin or with original sin only descend immediately into Hell; to be punished, though, with different pains and in different places.* (worth noting, "and in diverse places", suggests "Limbo.") (6b)

Contrary to the already then common theological understanding, John XXII upheld the opinion that the souls of the dead, remaining "under the altar of God," enjoyed only the vision of the human nature of Christ and came to enjoy the fullness of beatitude only after the General Judgement. In 1333, John XXII also wrote a short treatise in support of his position. King Philip VI of France initiated an examination. It began on December 19, 1333. Subsequently, the Pope also convoked a commission of cardinals and theologians, which induced him to declare to the Consistory on January 3, 1334 that he would retract his thesis since it was found to be in opposition to the common doctrine of the Church. On December 3, 1334, one day before his death, in the presence of the College of Cardinals, he solemnly retracted his thesis with the words handed down in this *Bull: Ne super his,* which was published by his successor, Benedict XII:

We therefore confess and believe that the purified souls separated from the body are gathered together in heaven, in paradise and the kingdom of Heaven with Christ in the company of the angels, and that they, according to the common precept, clearly see God and the divine essence face to face, insofar as the state and the condition of the separated soul allows. (6c)

Pope John XXII NEVER denied the existence of Purgatory. He held the belief that Heaven will be entered only after the Last Judgement; that Heaven is attained only when the body and soul are united on the last day. He held this opinion as a Theologian before his elevation to the Papacy, and maintained this belief throughout his Pontificacy. The public statements he made to this same effect were made in three sermons preached at Avignon. These statements were made only in a sermon, as a private individual and with no intention of binding the consciences of the Christian world, and it was not, at that time, opposed to a formal dogma, as it had not yet been defined.

"The Church formulated her Doctrine of Faith on Purgatory especially at the Councils of Florence (1431) and Trent (1545)." (Catechism of the Catholic Church, Part one, The Profession of Faith, Article 12, "I Believe in Life Everlasting," #1031)

IT IS IMPORTANT TO EMPHASIZE, HOWEVER, THAT IT WAS ONLY AFTER THE DEATH, OF JOHN XXII THAT HIS SUCCESSOR, POPE BENEDICT, XII ISSUED HIS PAPAL BULL: *BENEDICTUS DEUS,* "On the Beatific Vision," January 29, 1336 defining the doctrine of the Beatific Vision: that the souls of the faithful departed go to their eternal reward immediately after death or purgatory. (7)

Pope John XXII was a strong man in health and action. In his later years, he was a Professor of Civil and Canon Law in his native city of Toulouse. He was tutor to the son of the King, who himself afterwards became King under the name of Charles II. He was also the tutor of Louis, whom he later canonized as St. Louis of Toulouse, and he canonized St. Thomas Aquinas as well. He was the "Author of the Sabbatine Bull," and the "Father of the Sabbatine Privilege." There was much evidence of his practical devotion to the the Mother of God, both in the privileges (he) granted and the manner of their granting. The volumes of Regesta, preserved in the Secret Papal Archives, containing sixty thousand (according to other computations nearer eighty thousand), documents, bear witness to the world-wide labors of John XXII. Among his many achievements, he indulgenced the pious custom of saluting the Blessed Virgin with "three Hail Marys" in honor of the Angelical Salutation which according to tradition took place about the hour of sunset. He also indulgenced the "Salve Regina." To this may be added the Pope's devotion and generosity in giving an indulgence to those who would pronounce the name of Mary with the proper dispositions. No one could question his great devotion to the Blessed Virgin, for he has given ample proof of it. He gave us evidence not only of his devotion to the Blessed Mother, but it is also a strong proof that when John spoke of the Mother of God, he did not confine himself to cold prose, and was not afraid to speak in language that was as elevated as it was sublime; no matter how exaggerated it may appear…it is a wonderful expression of devotion. He reigned from 1316 to 1334, and it has been noted by more than one of his biographers that on the removal of his body to another part of the Cathedral in the year 1759, that his body was found intact. (7a)

IV. OBJECTION: Therefore, Fr. (Ludovico) Saggi concluded rightly that the Majorca document is false and the Sabbatine Bull contained in it cannot be accepted as authentic. (8)

RESPONSE: The original of the Bull of Alexander V was transferred to England as we learn from the authentic copy of it made January 2nd 1421, at the instance of Alphonsus de Theram, an Englishman, then Prior of the Convent of Captun, in the island of Majorca, afterwards Prior of the Convent of Coventry, England, who then took the original to be kept in the archives of the General in London. This copy was solemnly reduced to public form, before notaries and judges, and kept at Genoa. Of this we are informed by Palaeonydorus, Bostius, Leersius, etc. An old authentic MS. Copy, written in 1484, and kept at the Carmelite Convent, Mechlin, gives us similar information. (This was attested to in: V. Spec. Carm. T. I. Pars. III, p. 511, n. 2158 and it is confirmed by Fr. Paul of All Saints, in his Clavis Aurea, p. 2, c. 27). (9)

V. OBJECTION: Simon Stock is an elusive 13th century Carmelite Saint; the details of his life and even the fact of his existence have aroused considerable controversy over the centuries. (10)

RESPONSE: "After the (Second Vatican) Council, the Scapular Devotion suffered the same "crisis of rejection" that so many other practices and teachings of the Catholic Church underwent.

First, it was said that St. Simon Stock never existed. As a consequence, his feast day, which had been celebrated on May 16th, the date of his death was expunged from the liturgical calendar.

Second, if he never existed, then we must do away with the feast of Our Lady of Mt. Carmel and the Scapular Devotion. The effort was then made by a liturgical committee to expunge Our Lady of Mount Carmel from the liturgical calendar, but the Latin American Bishops protested so vehemently that the feast was kept, however, on the condition that nothing be mentioned about the Scapular.

"One of the internationally renowned Mariologists of (the) (Carmelite) Order, Father Nilo Geagea from Lebanon, then set about doing a very thorough research into the whole history of devotion to Mary in our Order."

"The result of his years of study is a huge wonderfully researched and documented volume published by the Teresian Historical Institute in 1988, so it is a fairly recent study. The title of the book is: *Maria Madre e Decoro del Carmelo*, (written by Fr. Nilo Geagea, O.C.D., Rome, 1988)"

"Through painstaking demonstration, Father Nilo shows how even the most intransigent critic could not put into reasonable doubt the historical existence of St. Simon Stock. St. Simon Stock's feast day was, in fact, restored by the Congregation for Divine Worship and the Sacraments in 1979. (10a)"

Simon Stock, the Saint of the Scapular of Our Lady of Mt. Carmel, was born in the County of Kent, England, in the year (1165 AD.) From his tenderest years his thoughts turned to God, and his piety was such as to indicate his remarkable future. At the age of twelve years, urged on by the Spirit of God, he left home and retired to the solitude of the woods. He lived solely on wild herbs, drank only water, and passed his days and nights in prayer before a crucifix and an image of the Blessed Virgin. Lost in Divine contemplation, he frequently forgot to sustain himself with food, so Heaven intervened to supply him with the food necessary to keep him alive, as his body wasted with the severest mortification.

He was a man of extraordinary energy and of dauntless courage. In the year 1245, he was elected Prior General of the Carmelite Order. Our Blessed Lady gave the Holy Scapular to St. Simon Stock at the Monastery of Cambridge on the 16th of July, 1251. Our Divine Lord showed his approbation of the holy life of Simon by bestowing on him the gift of miracles. Many more miracles are related of St. Simon during his lifetime, and after death; quite a number is mentioned in the documents sent to Rome about 1672, as having taken place through the invocation of the Saint, and through the application of his relics to the sick and the afflicted. His wondrous work for the Order of Carmel was not less than a miracle and his frequent visions of the Blessed Virgin and his conversations with her, of which we have contemporary and corroborative evidence, give us some idea of the supernatural in his life. He died on the 16th of May, 1265 at the age of 100. He was buried at the Cathedral of Bordeaux, and was almost immediately cultivated as a saint. Pope Nicholas III granted that an Office might be celebrated in his honor on the anniversary of his death each year in that city. This office was extended to the entire order by Paul V. (11)

The Holy Virgin promises here to liberate from Purgatory the members of the Confraternity of the Holy Scapular the First Saturday after their death, and this either by descending in person into Purgatory, or, what is more likely, through the ministry of Angels. This liberation can take place either by a free intervention or by means of the satisfaction that Mary, by her prayers will graciously offer on behalf of their souls; also it can take place by means of the application of a part of her satisfactory merits hidden in the treasury of the Church; or, finally it can be obtained by her Divine Son who Himself, by an exceptional disposition on behalf of her, applies to them her satisfactory merits, which shape the aforementioned Treasury. Although the terms used to express Mary's favor of liberating the Confraternity members from Purgatory seem to suggest that she should descend personally to liberate them, they are not intended in this material sense; although the term *descend* is used in the Sabbatine Bull, it is also used many times in Sacred Scripture in the sense of helping, assisting, liberating, as when the Lord says: *I have seen the affliction of my people in Egypt and I have heard their cries caused by the harshness of their taskmasters ... and I have descended to liberate them from the hands of the Egyptians*. In the same way, the descent of Mary is a moral descent, which expresses nothing more than the effect of her power to provide comfort to men. (12)

Nevertheless, when we say as a general thesis that Mary liberates from Purgatory the Confraternity members of the Holy Scapular, *the First Saturday* after their death, there is nothing in this that is repugnant to reason or faith; indeed, parents in their families, in light of their state, reserve certain days to confer their graces, their favors; the Holy Church likewise in her Bull of a Plenary Indulgence, determines the day in which the certain Indulgence will profit for the remission of the temporal punishment due to sins. So why should Mary, the Mother in Glory, not be able to obtain from her Divine Son that He loose in Heaven what the Pontiffs, as His Vicars, loose on earth, since, according to the order established in the Holy Church, she makes these same Pontiffs trustees, depositors, and executors or promulgators of His promises and His favors? (13)

ENDNOTES
ADDED OBJECTIONS AND RESPONSES

1   Chief argument of John Launoy, 1642 *Dissertatio Duplex*, identical Argument of Ludovico Saggi, O. Carm: *La Bolla Sabbatina* Ludovico Saggi, Roma, 1967, p. 82 translated and paraphrased

2   Defense against the Negative Argument: *The Brown Scapular and the Catholic Dictionary, II Irish Ecclesiastical Record,* Volume VIII, Third Series, 1887, No. l, Dublin, pp. 1008, 1009

3   Objection: absence of Bull from Bullarium,from: *The Catholic Dictionary,* Addis & Arnold, 1887, p. 744

4   Objection: absence of Bull from Bullarium, from: *Our Lady of the Place,* Emanuele Boaga, O. Carm., Roma, 2001, p. l02

5   Defense against the absence of the Bull of John XXII in the Roman Bullarium, *Irish Ecclesiastical Record,* Vol. VIII, 3rd Series, 1887, Dublin, pp. 804, 805

6   Objection against the credibility of Pope John XXII, from *Our Lady of the Place,* p. 103

6a   *Catholic Encyclopedia:* Purgatory-New Advent.org

6b   *Heinrich Denzinger-Enchiridion symbolorum difinitionum et declarationum de rebus fidei et morum,* Latin-English, edited by: Peter Hunermann, Co-edited by Robert Fastiggi (translator for this book) and Anne Englund Nash, Ignatius Press, San Francisco, 2012, p. 294, #925

6c *Ibid,* p. 301: Pope John XXII, Bull: *Ne super his,* December 3, 1334, on the *Retraction of John XXII on the Beatitude of the Saints,* #991

7 Defense of Pope John XXII: "Fr. Hardon Archives-Christ to Catholicism-Chapter IX, Papal Infallibility, CATHOLIC ENCYCLOPEDIA: Purgatory; New Advent.org: Pope Benedict XII; New Advent.org: Pope John XXII, paraphrased http://www.therealpresence.org/archives/Church_Dogma/Church_Dogma_031.htm

7a *The Sabbatine Privilege of the Scapular 1322 A.D. – 1922 A.D.,* P. E. Magennis, Ord. Carm., New York, 1923, pp. 25, 26, 28, 36, 37, paraphrased

8 Objection against the Majorca document containing the Sabbatine Bull of Pope John XXII from *Our Lady of the Place,* p. 102

9 Defense of Majorca Document containing Sabbatine: *Irish Ecclesiastical Record,* Vol. VIII 1887, p. 800

10 Objection to the existence of St. Simon Stock from: *The Carmelite Scapular Today,* Carmelites.org, p. 3

10a Zenit: Brown Scapular: a "Silent Devotion," by Father Kieran Kavanaugh, O.C.D., printed July 16, 2008

11 Defense of the existence of St. Simon Stock from: *The Scapular and Some Critics,* P. E. Magennis, O.C.C., Rome, 1914, pp. 13, 19, 20, 21 and *The White Friars,* Rev. P. R. McCaffrey, Ord. Carm., Dublin, 1926, pp. 29, 48, 49, 54, 55, 57 paraphrased

12 *Vita di San Simone Stock,* Alfredo Mombrum, 1887, pp. 148-149

13 *Ibid,* p. 153, 154

ADDED RESPONSES TO THE OBJECTIONS AGAINST THE AUTHENTICITY OF THE VISION OF OUR LADY TO ST. SIMON STOCK 2004

Several of the Publications in Opposition to the Brown Scapular have consistently repeated the same objections of John Launoy against the authenticity of the Visions of Our Lady to St. Simon Stock and to Pope John XXII. Although we have given sufficient evidence in response to these objections, so much more evidence exists to the authenticity of the Visions, that it bears bringing to light.

I. **OBJECTION: In 1642 the Carmelite John Cheron published two Fragments which he said came from Peter Swanyngton, Simon Stock's Secretary. In both of these writings, Cambridge was indicated as the location of the Vision and the date was the 16th of July, 1251. Historical criticism today is able to show that the Fragments mentioned above are false and cannot be taken seriously. (1)**

RESPONSE: Regarding the "Fragments," or document of Swanyngton, (Secretary to St. Simon Stock), reproduced by Fr. John Cheron, in defense of the attack of John Launoy against the Scapular, Fr. R. F. Clarke answers:

The document in which Swanyngton wrote at the dictation of St. Simon Stock, (recording the Scapular Vision of Our Lady) was, as we have seen, preserved in the archives of the Carmelites at Bordeaux and printed for the first time by Fr. John Cheron when the controversy arose which the enemies of the Carmelites stirred up against the Scapular. Fr. John Cheron was Prior of the Convent, and though we have no particulars of his life, yet the fact of his election by his religious brethren to this important office is sufficient proof of the high esteem in which he was held. Our adversaries would have us believe that this document never existed at all. They would have us accept the utterly improbable, the ludicrous hypothesis that a distinguished man, high in office in his Order, or one of his fellows, forged this manuscript narrative and that it has been accepted from that day to this by the Christian world, has been quoted over and over again, approved by Popes, sanctioned by Roman Congregations, spread abroad among the faithful by written documents, and by continual sermons and exhortations, although all the while it was a fraud and imposture.

But the testimony of Fr. Cheron does not stand by itself. The MS. in the Vatican is a well authenticated document of which a copy was made officially in 1635. It dates from the end of the 13th century (or at least the beginning of the 14th century.) Even Launoy does not venture to deny its existence, he simply tries to destroy its authority...nor is this the only testimony to the Scapular before the end of the 14th century. There are no fewer than three other accounts or allusions to the apparition of an earlier date than the "Viridarium" of John Grossi of Toulouse. In the "Speculum Carmelitanum," by Fr. Daniel, quotations are given distinctly confirming the apparition from four different sources. (2)

To read the entire context of these four sources mentioned above, please refer to "The Month" pp. 318-324, found in Addendix 3 of this book, under: "Publications in Defense."

II. **OBJECTION: The lack of any mention of the Scapular Vision from its alleged 1251 occurrence until the end of the 14th century, some 150 years later, and the unfamiliarity of any Carmelite of this period with the story raises serious questions about the historical basis of the legends.** (3)

RESPONSE: In opposition to the positive testimony of existing documents, (John) Launoy relies upon the feeble and negative argument derived from the silence of certain writers who in his opinion ought to have mentioned the Scapular. This method of argumentation is a favorite one with the sceptic bent on destruction. (4) (The objection stated above may be found in Appendix 3, "Ancient and Modern Day Objections to the Scapular Visions," which we have already addressed at length. This same objection has been found in publications dating from the time of the Dissertation of John Launoy in 1642 in which he attacked the Scapular Visions, to the above cited Carmelite publication of 2004).

We are all familiar with it in the mouth of the Protestant controversialist. If St. Peter was Bishop of Rome how is it that he is not mentioned in St. Paul's Epistle to the Romans? If Our Lady was conceived without sin, how is it that so important an exception to the general law is omitted by the Apostle when declaring the universality of original sin? This style of argument is the more mischievous because in many cases it can only be refuted by a hypothesis, and such a refutation sounds like a confession of weakness. Happily, however, we are able to refute M. Launoy far more satisfactorily than by such considerations as these. (5)

But, again, (we repeat) granting that some Carmelite historians are silent about the Scapular that is no argument against its authenticity, as long as there are other Carmelites equally trustworthy who mention it in their works. Thus, the mission of the Archangel Gabriel to the Blessed Virgin to announce to her that she was chosen by God to be the Mother of the Messiah, is recorded by St. Luke in his gospel, whilst the other Evangelists make no mention of that august event. Would it therefore, be lawful to call it into question? (6)

Please See: *The Month,* in Appendix 3 for a complete defense against the arguments of John Launoy, which are a reflection of the arguments of certain modern day Carmelite Historians in the 21st century.

ENDNOTES

ADDED RESPONSES TO THE OBJECTIONS AGAINST THE AUTHENTICITY OF THE VISION OF OUR LADY TO ST. SIMON STOCK

1 *Our Lady of the Place,* Emanuele Boaga, O. Carm., Roma, 2001, p. 101

2 *The Month,* A Catholic Magazine and Review, VOL. LVII, May-August, London, 1886, pp. 318-324

3 *Carmel in the World, Garment of Grace,* Vol. XLIII, N. 3, Rome, 2004, p. 181

4 *The Month,* A Catholic Magazine and Review, Vol LVII, May-August, 1886, p. 315

5 *Ibid,* pp. 315, 316

6 *The Irish Ecclesiastical Record,* Vol. VIII, No. 1, January, Dublin, 1887, pp. 1008, 1009

A DEFENSE OF THE BROWN SCAPULAR AGAINST:
"The Carmelitana Collection" A Specialized Library in Carmelite Studies found on the Carmelite Website 2008:

http://carmelitanacollection.com/catechesis.php

Below are objections against the Authenticity of the Visions taken from the above Carmelite website. Its defense follows:

I. **OBJECTION:** *Did Our Blessed Lady appear to Saint Simon Stock and give him the Brown Scapular? The long-standing tradition of the Church has approved this Vision as an acceptable cult, but that does not authenticate it as a historical experience. For example, one can say that on February 11, 1858, Bernadette Soubirous had an experience in which she perceived the Blessed Virgin standing in a grotto at Lourdes. The question then from a historical perspective, is not whether Mary appeared to Simon Stock and gave him the Scapular, but rather did Simon Stock perceive the Mother of God bestowing this Sign of her protection on him and his brothers in Carmel.* (1)

RESPONSE: Let us look for a moment at the definition of the word "perceive." To perceive is to use the senses to acquire information about the surrounding environment or situation; it is an attitude or understanding based on what is observed or thought and lastly, it is the neurological process of acquiring and mentally interpreting information from the senses. (2) It is not synonomous with the truth and implies that truth is relative and is determined upon the individual's interpretation of the material acquired through the senses. Perception is often times, an individual's self-deception, not his truth. (3)

These approved Visions in the Church are presented as perceptionary illusions. The French Novelist, Gustave Flaubert once said: *There is no truth, there is only Perception.* (4) This philosophy bears a strikingly similar resemblance to the ancient heresy known as *Docetism*...which comes from the Greek word *dokesis* meaning "to seem." It dates back to the time of St. Ignatius of Antioch (circa 107/110) and was the greatest heresy that faced Ignatius at the time. It held that the Son of God only "seemed" or "appeared" to take on human flesh but actually did not...it suggests that the human appearance of Christ is more illusion and has no objective reality. Christ's human nature was not real but only apparent. (This is the position of the Docetists.) (4a)

The above objection then also implies a denial of the *Dogma of the Assumption* (4b) (and also of the *Resurrection*) indicating that the human and historical appearance of Our Lady, who was assumed into Heaven both body and soul, and who would then appear both in body and soul, was not flesh and blood but was merely an illusion perceived in the minds of St. Bernadette Soubirous and St. Simon Stock, two holy and meritorious Saints who have been acclaimed and venerated in the Catholic Church for centuries.

In the eyes of the Docetists, if the humanity of Christ was just an illusion, so too would be His Passion, Suffering, Death and Resurrection, all things in the Church would then be an illusion including the presence of His most Holy Mother Mary, body and soul, in her approved apparitions to the world. This means our salvation, too, would have been an illusion. At the time that supernatural interventions occur, it is to be expected that Divine Providence will supply adequate signs for their discernment. God is not bound by the principles of historical criticism. Since private revelation is under the dominion of God, it is He who chooses the concrete circumstances and the concrete motives of credibility. (5) The authority of the Holy Roman Catholic Church only is responsible for determining the authenticity of a vision and establishing its place, as a vehicle of sanctification in the devotional life of the Church. To imply a perception is to undermine the authority of the Church.

To suggest that the Vision of Our Blessed Mother to Bernadette of Lourdes was a perception in the mind of an imaginative child and to attempt to detach the apparition of Our Lady to Bernadette and to St. Simon Stock, as an historical experience appears to be a classic example of the infiltration of the philosophical position of relativism, in the "postmodern mindset"of the contemporary Progressives.

The Solemn declaration by Bishop Laurence, the Bishop of Tarbes, (responsible for determining the authenticity at the time of the Apparitions at Lourdes) states: *We judge that Mary Immaculate, the Mother of God, really did appear to Bernadette Soubirous on eighteen occasions from 11th of February 1858 at the Grotto of Massabielle, near the town of Lourdes, that these apparitions bear the characteristics of truth; that the faithful can believe them as true. We humbly submit our judgment to the judgment of the Sovereign Pontiff, who is responsible for governing the Universal Church.* (6)

Regarding the numerous healings and cures through the miraculous waters of the spring, the Bishop concluded: *There is thus, a direct link between the cures and the Apparitions, the Apparitions are of divine origin, since the cures carry a divine stamp. But what comes from God is truth! As a result, the Apparition calling herself the Immaculate Conception, that Bernadette saw and heard, is the Most Holy Virgin Mary! Thus we write: "The finger of God is here."* (7)

Therefore, Bernadette did not have an experience in which she perceived the Mother of God in the Grotto at Massabielle, in truth, Bernadette SAW the Mother of God in the Grotto at Massabielle.

St. Simon Stock himself was a person of verifiable historicity, Prior General of the Carmelite Community in the 13th century he was a man of great sanctity, filled with love and devotion for the Mother of God. His Holiness, Blessed Pope Pius IX, wrote these words in a Preface written for the book: *La Vie de St. Simon Stock,* (The Life of St. Simon Stock) by Alfred Monbrun:

This most extraordinary gift of the Scapular from the Mother of God to St. Simon Stock, brings its great usefulness not only to the Carmelite Family of Mary, but also to all the rest of the faithful who wish, affiliated to that Family, to follow Mary with a very special devotion. (8)

St. Simon Stock was born in the County of Kent, England, 1165. He was born into a very distinctive family where his father was Governor. His mother consecrated him to the Holy Virgin when he was still in her womb. In 1177, when he was 12 years old he reportedly went to live in a hollow oak trunk, drinking only water and eating only herbs and wild apples. In that solitary dwelling in the woods he practiced many mortifications of the body and became noted for his sanctity of life. The Blessed Virgin seems to have been the object of his intense devotion and she communicated frequently with him. According to a venerable tradition, the Queen of Heaven appeared to him promising him that soon hermits from Palestine would land in England. She added that he should join these men whom she considered her servants. He followed the summons of the Mother of God and entered the Carmelite Order in 1212 and he became Vicar General of the Carmelite Order of the West in 1215. In 1237, he went to the Holy Land where he lived for six years

(1237-1243) on Mount Carmel.

In 1245 St. Simon Stock was elected Prior-General of the whole Carmelite Order. Simon Stock pleaded with the Virgin Mary through constant prayer and many tears to defend this Order that was consecrated to her. On July 16, 1251 Our Blessed Mother appeared to St. Simon Stock and bestowed upon him the Scapular with the Promise that *whosoever shall die wearing this (Scapular) shall not suffer eternal fire.* The Virgin Mary revealed to the Prior General that they were to approach Pope Innocent to receive a remedy for the difficulties in the Order. It is a historical fact that (soon after the Vision) Innocent IV issued a papal letter (of protection) for the Carmelites, January 13, 1252 at Perugia. Thus, we see that in less than six months after the Vision of St Simon Stock, the Carmelites were protected in an efficacious manner by the Pope. From there he established the First Scapular Confraternity. The devotion to the Brown Scapular then spread throughout the world.

As said before, Our Divine Lord showed his approval of the holy life of Simon by bestowing on him the gift of working miracles. Two miracles can be found in the Lessons of His Office for the 16th of May. Many more miracles are related of St. Simon during his lifetime and after death quite a number are mentioned in the documents sent to Rome about 1672 as having taken place through the invocation of the Saint and through the application of his relics to the sick and the afflicted. He died on May 16th at the age of 100 years while he was visiting his monasteries in Bordeaux, France. He was buried in the cathedral of that city and honored among the saints soon after his death. Pope Nicholas III granted an office to be celebrated in his honor at Bordeaux on the 16th of May. His feast was introduced in 1411 and in 1435 his feast was put in the choral books of the monastery at Bordeaux. It was introduced before 1458 into Ireland and probably at the same time, into England. In 1564, his feast was approved by the Holy See and extended throughout the Carmelite Order. His remains were transferred to Ayelsford, England in 1951. He was never formally canonized. However, not only was he confirmed as a man of sanctity by Pope Pius IX, but he is also defended in the both Treatise of Pope Benedict XIV in: *De Festis Domini Nostri Jesu Christi et Beatae Mariae Virginis,* and in *De Servorum Dei Beatificatione et Beatorum Canonizatione.* (8a)

The testimonies of his contemporaries, the recordings of ancient Carmelite historians throughout the Centuries, the Papal Approbations including that of Pope Benedict XIV who embraced the Brown Scapular devotion affirming the authenticity of the Visions, with many other Solemn Pontiffs, the numerous indulgences granted by the Church, the outstanding recorded miracles performed through the intercession of Our Lady and her Brown Scapular, the instantaneous spread of this Universal Devotion to the Mother of God throughout the world and the establishment of the Brown Scapular as a Sacramental of the Church, could never have possibly been achieved based on a perception; they in fact, serve to verify, in truth, the Apparition of Our Holy Mother to Saint Simon Stock as a historical event authenticated by the inexhaustible recordings of documented miracles, still continuing to this day, through the Brown Scapular of Our Lady of Mount Carmel. Therefore, Simon Stock did not perceive the Mother of God bestowing this Sign of her Protection on him and on his brothers in Carmel, he SAW the Mother of God bestowing her protection on him and on his brothers in Carmel.

The Carmelitana Collection continues
in its objections to the authenticity of
the apparitions of Our Blessed Mother to
St. Simon Stock and to Pope John XXII:

II. **OBJECTION:** *Well, what about the various statements of the Popes over the centuries about the Scapular. Don't they prove the historicity of the vision? Frankly no. Over the years, many Popes have encouraged the wearing of the Brown Scapular. Some have repeated the stories and legends concerning St. Simon Stock or the Sabbatine Privilege. No one has ever claimed that these statements enjoy the privilege of infallibility. They do not meet the criterion which the First Vatican Council set down for Papal statements to be infallible. The statements should be considered doctrinally sound, but that does not mean that they are historically accurate. Papal infallibility pertains to faith (doctrine) and morals it does not extend to history or to the sciences. ...We cannot say that Our Lady made any promises to Saint Simon Stock or to Pope John XXII regarding this sacramental.* (9)

RESPONSE: To say that statements made by the Holy Fathers over the centuries concerning St. Simon Stock or the Sabbatine Privilege *do not enjoy the privilege of infallibility and do not meet the criterion which the First Vatican Council set down for Papal statements to be infallible* implies that it is permissible to dissent from the *Apostolic Letters, Briefs, Bulls,*

Decrees, Indulgences granted by the Church, etc. issued by the Solemn Pontiffs, on behalf of the Scapular and the Sabbatine Privilege, or any other Church Documents not related to Infallibility and are not to be accepted as Magisterial teaching. This falls under the following error:

Error No. 22 of the *Syllabus of Pius IX: A Collection of Errors Proscribed in Diverse Documents of Pius IX, Published December 8, 1864:* (Denzinger – H - #2922)

ERROR: *The obligation by which Catholic teachers and writers are absolutely bound is restricted to those matters only that are proposed by the infallible judgement of the Church to be believed by all as dogmas of the faith.* (9a)

The Scapular Promises may not enjoy the privilege of Papal Infallibility, but they enjoy the privilege of Papal Authority. The Popes have never made any formal "ex cathedra" pronouncements concerning the Scapular. But they have made pronouncements similar to Encyclicals indicating the mind of the Church on the Scapular. The Holy Father may speak as an individual in a matter that concerns the whole Church. To contradict him in such an expression would be imprudent and against the mind of the Church. His approval, even as an individual, of any devotion in the Church is a kind of visible trademark of God attesting to the genuineness of that devotion. We cannot separate from the Holy Father his unique character as Vicar of Christ. As the Vicar of Christ on earth, he speaks with the authority of God. Pontiffs for many centuries have given their own private testimonies to the Scapular, confirming its power and value as a sacramental par excellence. (9b) No private individual has the authority to determine definitely and officially which private revelations are true and which are not, and which Magisterial teachings are to be adhered to, and which are not. To suggest error and incompetency on the part of the Holy Fathers in "repeating stories and legends concerning St. Simon Stock or the Sabbatine Privilege" without sufficient investigation is to infer the failure of the local Bishop and the Church to properly investigate and determine the authenticity of the Visions and all other Visions of Our Lady including Fatima and to challenge the authority of the Church as a whole, in its judgement of all Private Revelation.

Consider the Document of Pope Pius X: *Pascendi Dominici Gregis:*

The Modernists pass judgment on the Holy Fathers of the Church even as they do upon Tradition. With consummate temerity they assure the public that the fathers, while personally most worthy of all veneration, were entirely ignorant of history and criticism for which they are only excusable on account of the time in which they lived.

Finally, the Modernists try in every way to diminish and weaken the authority of the ecclesiastical Magisterium itself by sacrilegiously falsifying its origin, character, and rights, and by freely repeating the calumnies of its adversaries. They seize upon professorships in the seminaries and universities and gradually make of them chairs of pestilence.

Under their own names and under pseudonyms they publish numbers of books, newspapers reviews, and sometimes one and the same writer adopts a variety of pseudonyms to trap the incautious reader into believing in a multitude of Modernist writers.

They are to be found among the laity and in the ranks of the clergy, and they are not wanting even in the last place where one might expect to meet them, in Religious Communities.

Under the sway of certain a priori conceptions, they destroy as far as they can the pious traditions of the people and bring into disrespect certain relics highly venerable from their antiquity. (10)

The concepts of Modernism and Relativism were condemned by our beloved Holy Father, Pope Pius X, in the above exerpts, taken from his Encyclical on Modernism "On the Doctrines of Modernists:" *Pascendi Dominici Gregis,* September 8, 1907.

As the finger of God was at Lourdes, so it was at the Monastery at Cambridge on July 16, 1251, the day the world received the precious gift of the Scapular through the hands of Our Lady's beloved servant, the Successor of Elias, and Prior General of the Carmelite Order, St. Simon Stock, bringing forth miraculous cures, healings, conversions, but above all the promise of eternal salvation if Our Lady's requests were heeded. Could these rich fruits of the miraculous intervention of the Queen of Heaven have been the result of an illusionary "perception"?

The apparitions of the Mother of God at Lourdes and the Apparition to St. Simon Stock and Pope John XXII are events in the public domain and cannot be the fabrication of an individual. To discount an event, we would have to discount the witness of all the people involved. (11)

When it comes to God it is not negotiable; such truth is not relative to culture or time, it is outside the influence of man. (12) God alone is the source of absolute Truth for He alone is the "Way, the Truth, and the Life." (John 14:7)

ENDNOTES

1   http://carmelitanacollection.com/catechesis.php
2   http://www.bing.com/Dictionarysearch?
    q=define+perception&qpvt=m

3   http://ecoggins.hubpages.com/hub/Perception-is-an-Individuals-Self-Deception

4   http://thinkexist.com/quotes/gustave_flaubert

4a   Early Understanding of Jesus; the truth decoded: *Ignatius of Antioch* (d.circa 107/110),by Rev. Thomas G. Weinandy, O.F.M., paraphrased http://www.thetruthdecoded.org/au/Ignatius-of-Antioch.php; *The Navarre Bible,* Catholic Letters, James, Peter, John Jude, Dublin, New York, 2003, p. 152

4b   Apostolic Constitution of Pope Pius XII, *Munificentissimus Deus,* Defining the Dogma of the Assumption, November 1, 1950

5   *The Credibility of the Scapular Promises,* Rev. Christian P. Ceroke, O. Carm., Rome, 1950, pp. 83, 84

6   http://www.indefenseofthecross.com/Lourdes.htm

7   http://www.indefenseofthecross.com/Lourdes.htm

8   Preface written by Pope Pius IX from: *La Vie de St. Simon Stock,* Alfred Monbrun, cf. *Mary in Her Scapular Promise,* John Mathias Haffert, New Jersey, 1942, p. 11

8a   Biographical references include: *The Scapular and Some Critics,* The Vision (1251 AD – 1500 AD), P. E. Magennis, O.C.C. Rome, 1914, Chapter 4-Chapter 7: pp.13-33; http://www.ewtn.com/library/MARY/SIMONSTO.HTM; http://www.newadvent.org/cathen/13800a.htm (about Simon Stock); NZ Grand Priory of the Order of St. Lazarus– Our Lady of Mount Carmel; http://www.miraclehunter.com/marian_apparitions/approved_apparitions/aylesford/index.html from The Miracle Hunder: Marian Apparitions: Our Lady of Mt. Carmel

9   http://carmelitanacollection.com/catechesis.php;

9a   *Syllabus of Pius IX: A Collection of Errors Proscribed in Diverse Documents of Pius IX, Published December 8, 1864,* "Propositions of the Syllabus," 2922, #22, cf. *Heinrich Denzinger,* Compendium of Creeds, Definitions, and Declarations on Matters of Faith and Morals, Peter Hunermann, co-edited by Robert Fastiggi and Anne Enlund Nash, Ignatius Press, 2012, p. 593

9b   *Take This Scapular,* Carmelite Fathers and Tertiaries, Chicago, 1949, pp. 78-79

10   *Pascendi Dominici Gregis,* Pope Pius X, September 8, 1907, #42, #43

11   http://www.seekingtruth.co.uk/truth.htm

12   http://www.seekingtruth.co.uk/truth.htm

A DEFENSE OF
THE BROWN SCAPULAR DEVOTION
A RESPONSE TO SOME OF THE
OBJECTIONS OF 2013

The British Province of Carmelite Friars –
Heritage and Archive,
Origins of the Carmelite Order
Saints of Carmel: St. Simon Stock - Friar
www.carmelite.org; and CITOC News –
Order of the Brothers of the Most Blessed Virgin
Mary of Mount Carmel: St. Simon Stock, Religious
(M), Thursday, May 16, 2013

I. OBJECTION: The Carmelites have a very unique background. Unlike most Religious Orders, we have no Founder.

RESPONSE: The Carmelites consider the Prophet Elias as the Founder of their Order, and produce satisfactory proofs to sustain their opinion. This tradition is so ancient, says Father Alexis-Louis of St. Joseph, that its origin has never been assigned. It has been respected by the Church, for the statue of Elias has a place in the Basilica of St. Peter's at Rome, amongst the founders of religious orders. The following inscription, given by Benedict XIII himself, is upon it: *Universus Ordo Carmelitarum fundatori suo sancto Eliae prophetae erexit.* (The entire Order of Carmelites has erected this to the holy Prophet Elias, its Founder). (Chapter 1, the Order of Mount Carmel: http://www.ccacarmels.org/blog/chapter-1-the-order-of-mount-carmel)

II. OBJECTION: Around 1400, a separate legend emerged in the Low Countries of a "Holy Simon" who had a Vision of Our Lady, in which she appeared to him bearing the Scapular and promised: "This is a Privilege for you and your brethren: whoever dies wearing it, will be saved."

RESPONSE: Servant of God, Fr. Bartholomew F. Xiberta, O. Carm., (was) the greatest living authority on Scapular history. After years of critical research, he concludes: *Having studied the documentary evidence, one sees how the arguments against the historicity of the Vision of St. Simon Stock collapse one after the other...I dare to affirm that the Vision of St. Simon which preceded the Scapular Devotion has the support of more historical documents than one would expect to find.* (See #VI, page 388, MODERN DAY OBJECTIONS AND RESPONSES 2004- in this Section.)

III. **OBJECTION: The legends surrounding Saint Simon - particularly the so-called Scapular Vision - have been extensively researched by the leading historian of the British Province, Fr. Richard Copsey, O. Carm., whose research has been published in the third volume of the *Carmel in Britain* series, published by Saint Albert's Press.**

RESPONSE: To quote the words of now "Servant of God," Fr. Xiberta in his article: *Annotations on the Status of the Scapular Question,* he said: *Objections made three centuries ago and lately renewed by clever writers have infected the modern mind with the idea that the devotion rests on a pious fiction, or at least on insufficient arguments.* In this article Fr. Xiberta prepared a factual, concise and accurate presentation of historical evidence based on his analysis, comparison and conclusion of the collection of ancient texts on the Authenticity of the Vision of St. Simon. (See Appendix 3: *Responses to the Objections.*) He concludes with four powerful facts based on the discovered historical evidence which he says "can overthrow every thesis against the historicity of the Scapular Vision." Fr. Xiberta closes the article with these words: *In consideration of these conclusions, I am compelled to affirm that the Vision of St. Simon Stock, which occupies so dominant a place in the Scapular Devotion, is as solidly founded on historical evidence as could be expected. Let anyone who is so minded belittle faith in the Vision; lest, however, he make himself ridiculous, let him do so before the bar of history.* (See #XVI, page 395, MODERN DAY OBJECTIONS AND RESPONSES 2004 in this Section.)

IV. **OBJECTION: Although the historicity of the Scapular Vision is rejected, the Scapular itself has remained for all Carmelites a sign of Mary's motherly protection and as a personal commitment to follow Jesus in the footsteps of his Mother, the perfect model of all his disciples.**

RESPONSE: According to the Doctrinal Statement on the Brown Scapular of Our Lady of Mount Carmel, dated November 29, 1996, issued by the Congregation for Divine Worship and the Discipline of Sacraments it is stated: *During one of its difficult times, the order asked to get full recognition and stability within the Church. Mary, Patroness of Carmel, seemed to have answered this plea with a vision to the English Carmelite St. Simon Stock. She held in her hand the scapular and assured the holy prior general, saying: "This is a privilege for you and the order: whoever dies wearing this Scapular will be saved."* [The 1996 Doctrinal Statement did not reject The Scapular Vision] (Venerable Bartholomew Xiberta, O. Carm., *De Visione S. Simonis Stock oma.* 1950. 3 11.)

A TRUE parent begets children, nourishes them, clothes them, educates them, and gives them their identity in society by giving them a family name. Mary has done all these things to show how she truly is a mother to those whom she has adopted by Her Scapular contract. "The Most Glorious Virgin Mary, who by virtue of the Holy Spirit brought forth Jesus Christ, is the same Virgin who *produced the family* of the Blessed Virgin Mary of Mount Carmel" (Pope Sixtus IV). (1) She then nourished this family; "She brought forth the Order of Carmel and nourished it at her breasts," says Gregory XIII. (2) (Saint Joseph, Father and Model Taken from MARY IN HER SCAPULAR PROMISE by John Haffert with *Imprimatur* and *Nihil Obstat*, 1942) (1) Dum Attenta, Nov. 28th, 1476, B. I. 428. (2) Ut Laudes, Sept. 18th, 1577.

Fr. Bartholomew F. M. Xiberta O. Carm.
"Servant of God"
1897-1967

The closure of the diocesan process for the canonization of Fr. Bartholomew F. M. Xiberta, O. Carm., took place in Barcelona, Spain. A copy of the Acts of the Process will be sent to Rome to the Congregation for the Causes of Saints where the next steps will take place. (1) Fr. Xiberta was a Carmelite priest, known as "one of the outstanding theologians of the last century, and no doubt, the outstanding Carmelite Theologian." He was present at the Second Vatican Council, and was the only Carmelite there who was on the Theological Commission. As a member of the Commission, he had a role in presenting the original document. (2) Fr. Xiberta wrote his doctoral dissertation called *Clavis Ecclesiae,* on the Sacrament of Penance. The chief purpose of his dissertation is to demonstrate its essential significance for the penitent as an act of reconciliation with the Church. (3)

Fr. Xiberta's work was strongly influenced by Cardinal Franz Ehrle, (who was Prefect of the Vatican Library, from 1895 – 1914) (4) and the Jesuit, Maurice de la Taille, who wrote "The Mystery of Faith," regarding the Most August Sacrament and Sacrifice of the Body and Blood of Christ. Maurice de la Taille's work was quoted by Archbishop Fulton J. Sheen in his own book: "Calvary and the Mass."

Servant of God, Fr. Bartholomew Xiberta also wrote, a monumental work on the authenticity of the vision of St. Simon Stock entitled: *De Visione Sancti Simonis Stock,* Rome, 1950. This book was written on the occasion of the Seventh Centenary of the famous vision of St. Simon Stock (Our Lady bestowing the Scapular with the promise that "…

whosoever shall die wearing this, shall not suffer eternal fire). Fr. Xiberta traced the earliest biography of St. Simon to a version written much closer to the event of the bestowal of the Scapular, July 16, 1251, than was formerly realized. It is brief, factual and sober. In Fr. Xiberta's work, there are no grounds in historical criticism for doubting any of the facts it relates about the life of St. Simon Stock. (5)

On the following page is an article written by Fr. Xiberta and reproduced in its entirety. It is entitled "Annotations on the Status of the Scapular Question," and is followed by a collection of texts, in the order that they were brought to light, by Carmelite Historians, containing documentary proof by Fr. Xiberta, of the authenticity of the vision of St. Simon Stock (6)

ENDNOTES

1   http://www.ocarm.org/pre09/news/eng2803.htm

2   CITOC: July – September 2007: History

3   *The Ecclesiastical Review,* A Monthly Publication for Clergy, Vol. LXVII, July – December, 1922, p. 212

4   BAV – Vatican Library: Historical Notes

5   CatholicHerald.co.uk: *St. Simon Stock Sir-The Letter by Mr. Derek W. Whitfield,* originally printed September 29, 1950, paraphrased

6   *Take This Scapular,* 1949, p. 213: *Annotations on the Status of the Scapular Question,* by Fr. Bartholomew F. M. Xiberta, O. Carm.

Annotations on the Status of the Scapular Question

By

(Servant of God) Bartholomew F. M. Xiberta, O. Carm.

For some years now, the question of the Scapular has been the subject of a spirited discussion which has tended to diminish the ardor of the devotion. Although no solid argument militates against the tradition, debates and doubts have resulted in this deterioration. What is to be done about it?

This warning, which Father Gabriel Wessels made repeatedly in the *Analecta*, can be applied to the present state of things. Objections made three centuries ago and lately renewed by clever writers have infected the modern mind with the idea that the devotion rests on a pious fiction, or at least on insufficient argument. It frequently happens that we Carmelites, ourselves overwhelmed by the denials of others, hesitate to push the devotion to the fore; or that, desiring to defend it, we learn how one or another document previously used as proof is now rejected by critics, and we do not know where to turn. It happens, also, (which is worse) that, to avoid unpleasant controversies, the Scapular devotion is cloaked in silence. This is especially unfortunate since its intrinsic worth, when stripped of the historical facts upon which it is based, seems less than the value of the other universal Marian devotion, the Rosary.

To improve these conditions, it is incumbent upon all of us to promote the cause of the devotion with increased fervor. At the same time, however, we must satisfy the critical requirements of our age; for otherwise, those in charge of souls will scarcely continue to recommend the Scapular; and, if their efforts are wanting, it will necessarily follow that the devotion will grow weak among the faithful and lose its universal character. It seems to me that the best way of satisfying critical requirements is to discard the apologetic method for the time being, and to place the facts simply before all in such a manner that the status of the question will become clear and each one may judge the case for himself.

It is, indeed, an unpleasant task to commit ourselves to a discussion of this nature, one in which we allow to hang in the balance a thing we love with our whole hearts. But the necessity lies before us, and it must be faced.

One of the major duties in a critical examination of the Scapular question is to present the problems objectively and to indicate the specific point involved in each. It is a fact that recent controversies have so complicated its history that those who can devote only a limited amount of study to it are prone to lose heart. An outstanding reason for this is that many of those participating in the arguments missed the point at issue in particular questions. It often happened that, when they discussed secondary matters, they thought the main issue was endangered; and, when they had finished the argument, no one knew what conclusions had been reached as to the main issue.

The main issue confronting those studying the Scapular question is this: what reasonable grounds for belief does this devotion of the Scapular, which promises final salvation to the faithful, enjoy on the basis of St. Simon's vision in 1251 or thereabouts? This question has two aspects, the historical and the doctrinal. The former requires that we determine with what degree of certitude, if any, we can claim that the events alleged in defense of the devotion actually happened. The doctrinal part has, again, a twofold aspect: first, concerning its harmony with faith and sound theological reasoning; second, concerning its intrinsic value as an aid to Catholic piety.

In the present article, we treat the historical problem only. It will be of assistance to present, at the outset, a general survey of the controversies obtaining here, for a knowledge of these is the first step toward accurately determining the status of the entire question.

GENERAL SURVEY OF THE CONTROVERSIES

When this Carmelite devotion passed beyond the bounds of the Order itself, to become part of the public practice of the Church, its foundations were already deeply rooted in the past; consequently, it was exposed to the criticism of those who were unwilling to accept it unless its extraordinary origin was investigated. Such a position is entirely reasonable and justifiable; for the Order can neither demand nor expect that what it offers to the faithful as an established fact be accepted without examination. There were two distinct series of controversies waged over the Scapular: one occurred with the endeavor to obtain the public approval and safeguards of ecclesiastical authority; the other was debated by experts in Church history. It is the latter contest we now attempt to explain, setting aside for the moment the favorable points that might be drawn from the former.

Two controversies of this kind have been carried on by historians: John Launoy instigated the first in the middle of the 17th century; the other is still going on in our time.

THE CONTROVERSY OF LAUNOY

By the middle of the 17th century, the Scapular devotion had undergone the examination of Church authorities, had passed this test successfully, and had been widely propagated. Carmelites had written untiringly in an effort to spread and explain it; so much so, in fact, that Launoy could write: "For a hundred years the vision of Simon Stock has been enshrined in an almost infinite number of books. However, due to the fact that no one questioned it, Carmelite writers had not concerned themselves with bringing the historical arguments before the public." In 1642, John Launoy, a doctor of the Paris schools put an end to this unchallenged spread of the devotion.

The occasion for his attack was Father Mark Anthony Alegre de Casanate's work, *Carmelitici decoris Paradisus,* which had already been placed on the Index by the Holy See and was condemned also by the University of Paris. Launoy's first book was entitled: *Dissertatio Duplex,* one concerning the origin and confirmation of the Scapular privileges of Carmelites; the other concerning the vision of Simon Stock, Prior and Master General of the Carmelites. In it, he set out to prove that St. Simon's vision was "fidei inexploratae"—specifically, that it had no earlier vindicator than John Palaeonydor (toward the close of the 15th century); that it lacked the marks of a true revelation; and that the bulls of John XXII and Alexander V on the Sabbatine Privilege were fraudulent.

In the same year, 1642, Father John Cheron, a Carmelite of Bordeaux attempted to refute Launoy's arguments. His book was followed by two others: Father Thomas Aquinas of St. Joseph, Carm. Disc., and Father Philibert Fesayus, O. Carm.

These rebuttals compelled Launoy to examine more carefully the history of the Order, which he had entirely ignored when writing his first dissertation; and, when he had read *Speculum Carmelitarum,* by Father Baptist Venetus de Cathaneis, he returned to the attack writing five new dissertations which were published in 1653 and again in 1663.

While the quarrel raged on unabated, Carmelite writers produced more books. Father Leo of St. John published several editions of his work, *The Alliance of the Virgin regarding the privileges of the Holy Scapular of the Carmelites*. Father Irenaeus of St. James achieved the more valuable *Theological Tract concerning the Singular protection of the Virgin*. Father Matthias of John followed, still later, Father Paul of All Saints, and Daniel of the Virgin Mary.

Father Theophilus Raynaud, S. J., joined forces with the Carmelites, supporting the Scapular tradition. The fact that this was written by one not of the Order gave it greater prestige and value.

Public opposition to the Scapular continued, however, in spite of these efforts. Three disputations were held in the Paris schools: in 1674, at the Sorbonne, by Claude Blouin; in 1677 at the College de Nacarre, by Noel Varet; and at the Ecole des Jacobins, by Noel de Bertigeres. But these debates do not appear to have had any great influence.

May I state here confidently: although, from the time of Launoy, the Scapular could no longer be an undisputed inheritance, that struggle terminated to its advantage. For the result was that learned men accepted it with greater knowledge of the case and, therefore, more freely. Besides the contribution of Theophilus Reynaud to this happy ending, the following renowned authors outside the Order became patrons of the devotion: Blessed Claude de la Columbiere, S.J., Benedict XIV; and even Daniel Papebroch, who although greatly stirred up over the antiquity of the Order, nevertheless openly signified his approval of the Scapular devotion.

RECENT CONTROVERSIES

For two centuries the devotion remained practically in the same state in which it was left by the 17th century controversies. Even during the 19th century, as far as I can judge, just as its adversaries appealed to the arguments of Launoy, so those who defended it, such as Father Thomas de Chaix, O. Carm., Father Brocards of St. Teresa, O.C.D., and Father Richard Clark, S. J., offered the same arguments as their predecessors. But, as critical requirements became more exacting and knowledge of the Middle Ages increased, the day came when the problems and difficulties of the question were again brought up for judgement. Then, too, many historical documents of our Order, hitherto unknown, had been brought to light, and this also contributed to the reopening of the discussion.

Appendix 2

Father Benedict of the Cross Zimmerman, Ord. Carm. Disc., an exceptionally distinguished authority on Carmelite history, propounded a new statement of the question. But (alas!), too anxious to satisfy the "critics" and rather inclined to exaggerate unfavorable features, he often boldly discounted the traditions of the Order and favored the opponents. He untiringly vindicated St. Simon's vision as being historically true; as a matter of fact, he produced testimonials previously unknown to verify it. Yet he ventured to reconstruct the circumstances and alter the meaning of the vision in a manner contrary to commonly accepted views. He began to write on the Scapular in 1901.

Meanwhile, Father Herbert Thurson, S. J., in the course of conducting a searching inquiry into the historical foundations of devotions, assailed the history of the Scapular, using Father Zimmerman's monographs as a basis. His first article, "The Origin of the Scapular, A Criticism," appeared in the "Irish Ecclesiastical Record, XVVI, July 1904, pp. 59-70. Father Zimmerman replied briefly (Sept., p. 259). Father Thurston submitted "The Scapular Tradition and its Defenders" (June, 1911). Both articles appeared in the same periodical.

Working along the same lines, the Abbe Louis Saltet, Professor at the Catholic Institute of Toulouse, attempted to prove that the Swanyngton fragments were a fraud concocted by Fr. Cheron.

These continual attacks provoked the defenders of the tradition to a counteraction; the more so because encyclopedias and other popular reference works commonly accepted the verdicts of unfavorable critics as final.

Father Marie Joseph of the Sacred Heart, O.C.D., published a pamphlet, in several languages, refuting the opinions of Father Zimmerman. In 1911, he launched the periodical *Etudes Carmelitaines,* for which he constantly supplied material sustaining the traditional claims of the Order. In the first year of its publication he himself, submitted two articles against the diatribes of Abbe Saltet. Other refutations appeared in it also: Father Hyacinth Derken, O. Pr.; Father Marie-Amand of St. Joseph, O.C.D. Father Patrick of St. Joseph, O.C.D., whose work we speak of next, also wrote many articles for it. In 1914, it reprinted the defense of the Sabbatine Bull, which Father Placidus M. Del Pilar, O.C.D., had previously published in Spanish.

Father Patrick of St. Joseph Rushe strove to defend and amplify the historical foundations of the Scapular in a number of articles, published in the Irish Ecclesiastical Record, which were translated into French for *Etudes Carmelitaines.*

Father Gabriel Wessels, O. Carm., purposely avoiding the discussion, compiled documents for our *Analecta* that practically nullified the argument from silence.

Father Elias Magennis, O. Carm., took upon himself the task of discussing all the arguments the opponents had brought to bear on the Scapular.

Father Titus Brandsma, O. Carm., gave a very clear survey of the difficulties and arguments in the Netherland publication *Der Katholiek.*

Since these writings, scattered about as they were in various periodicals and books, had given rise to some confusion, Father Zimmerman and Father Thurston each discussed the question once again to explain their own definitive positions. Many other articles and books were written to instruct the faithful.

THE TESTIMONY OF HISTORY FOR
THE VISION OF ST. SIMON STOCK

From the controversies, we turn to the historical basis of the Scapular devotion. Our task is to provide the reader with the evidence for its historicity so that he may determine with what degree of certitude it can be held as an historical fact.

Inasmuch as documentary evidence is the source for the devotion's origin, it is of the first importance in our investigation. While granting it first place, we must remember that this historical certainty which is our objective should not be entrusted to a set of documents alone; for we are dealing with an occurrence that blossomed into a living tradition. We evaluate a tradition of this kind as we do every living thing: not solely from what we learn of its origin, but also from our knowledge of its full development. It often happens that we have no evidence for the origin of a tradition; yet its vitality, as revealed in the fact that it had become part and parcel of Catholic life is sufficient testimony of its trustworthiness. Certainly there is nothing unreasonable in the acceptance of a devotion which, far from remaining stagnant at its origin, has become an institution within the Catholic Church. For we may admit with reason that, since the greater part of the past is hidden from us, our own ignorance concerning its origin does not of itself militate against it.

On the other hand, this reasonable attitude must not be allowed to lessen the importance of recourse to historical documentation, since this alone gives us *positive* historical certitude; and positive certitude, if it is possible, is always to be preferred. For it is one thing to accept an event on faith; another to know positively that it is true. Therefore, we undertake here to supply the documentary proof of the vision of St. Simon Stock. We do not touch upon the Sabbatine Bull, as that requires a separate treatise.

THE DOCUMENTS

The collection extends to the end of the 15th century. Several later texts are added for the sake of clarity. In order to avoid any appearance that we are prejudicing the case, the documents are placed in the order in which they were brought to light. Consequently, those from very old sources are put first; those attributed to earlier authors (especially the Swaynyngton fragments), but which reach us through later sources, follow after.

WILLIAM OF SANVICO
(from the Province of the Holy Land; work written about 1290)

Chronica de multiplicatione religionis Carmelitarum...Ch. 7 cf. Analecta III, 302-315; VII 186; the text is taken from Daniel's Speculum, I, 103:
The devil, therefore, seeing that the more he tried to prevent the spread of this Order the more it flourished in different parts of the world, stirred up in his great anger the rectors and curates of the parish churches against the brethren....When they besought the lord bishops to restrain the curates from imposing these obligations, many bishops, taking the part of the rectors, recounted certain sophistical reasons to the effect that the curates had just cause against the brethren.

"The brethren, therefore, seeing that they could find no favor with the prelates, humbly besought their Patron, the Virgin Mary that she who had brought them to these places would free them from these diabolical temptations."

"And so the Virgin Mary revealed to their Prior that they should fearlessly approach the Supreme Pontiff, Innocent, because they would obtain from him a salutary remedy for their troubles

The Brown Scapular of Our Lady of Mount Carmel

JOHN GROSSI
(from the province of Toulouse;
became General in 1399; ob. ca. 1434)

Viridarium, part II (sect I) De sanctis patribus. The text of this work differs greatly in the manuscript codices and in its two editions: the old "Speculum Carmelitanum" published at Venice in 1507 and the new "Speculum" published at Antwerp in 1680. It would seem that the differences must be attributed in great part to the continual additions of the author himself. There seem to be two recensions: a short one, which is given in the Venice edition; and a longer one, which many codices and the Antwerp edition contain, though with many variant readings. In addition, the Vatican codex lat. 3813, ff. 12v-13r has a hagiography of St. Simon which is certainly taken from the "Viridarium" and seems to be a harmonized text. We give all three designated thus: Grossi-1, the short redaction of the Venice edition; Grossi-2, the life from the Vatican codex lat. 3813; Grossi-3 the longer redaction from the Antwerp edition.

Grossi-1 "The ninth was St. Simon of England, the sixth General of the Order; who continually besought the most glorious Mother of God to defend with some privilege the Order of Carmelites, which enjoys the special title of the Virgin, saying most devoutly: 'Flower of Carmel, Blossoming Vine, Splendor of heaven, Child-bearing Virgin none like to thee, Mother mild Whom no man didst know, upon thy Carmelites privileges bestow, Star of the Sea.'

"The Blessed Virgin appeared to him with a multitude of angels, holding in her blessed hands the scapular of the Order and saying: 'This will be for you and for all Carmelites privilege, that he who dies in this will not suffer eternal fire, that is, he who dies in this will be saved.'

"While the said General Simon was visiting the province of Gascony, he died in the convent of Bordeaux, where his body rests: and therefore he is named by some St. Simon of Gascony, by others St. Simon of Bordeaux; but he is more correctly called St. Simon of England, where he was born."

Grossi-2 "The sixteenth was St. Simon Stock, an Englishman, the sixth General of the Order...(there follows an account of his solitary life in the trunk of a tree, his entry into the Order, election as General, graces obtained from the Holy See; passing over the miracles, however, it goes to the vision:)

"St. Simon continually besought the glorious Virgin Mother of God to defend with some singular privilege the Order of the Carmelites, which is distinguished by the special title of the Virgin, saying most devoutly every day in his prayers: Flower of Carmel...etc.

"The Blessed Virgin Mary holding the Scapular of the Order, appeared to the blessed man with a multitude of angels and said: This will be for you and for all Carmelites a privilege: he who dies in this will not suffer fire for eternity, that is, he who dies in this will be saved.

"By reason of this great privilege many princes of the English realm, like blessed Edward, King of England, the second after the conquest, who established these brethren at Oxford, giving his own palace for their convent...(the sentence breaks off).

"The body of St. Simon Stock, illustrious for many miracles, rests at the convent of Bordeaux.

"Mark that in olden times for love of this privilege noblemen put on the scapular of the Carmelite Order at the hour of death and died in it. Amen."

Grossi-3 "St. Simon Stock, an Englishman, sixth General of the Order...(there follows the same account of his life as before, but with two miracles added: the water changed into wine, and the restoring to life of a fried fish; then it goes into the vision.)

He frequently besought the glorious Virgin Mother of God, the Patron of the Order, to defend with a privilege those who are distinguished by her title, saying most devoutly every day in his prayers: Flower of Carmel....etc.

"On a certain occasion, therefore, while he was devoutly praying this prayer, the glorious Virgin Mary Mother of God appeared to him with a multitude of angels, holding in her hand the Scapular of the Order and saying: This will be for you and for all Carmelites a privilege: he who dies in this habit will be saved. And she gave him the Scapular. Whence the verses:

If anyone dies in the sign of the Order, by a benign right,
He is freed from torment and enjoys heavenly places.
Simon asked this of the dear Virgin:
Afterwards he died, rising to wondrous joys.

"By reason therefore of this great privilege many princes of the English realm, as Edward, King of England, the second after the conquest (who established these brethren at Oxford, giving them his own palace for their convent), likewise the Lord Henry, Duke of Lancaster (who is reported to have been renowned for many miracles), and also many other nobles of this realm secretly wore the Scapular of the Order: in which they afterwards died.

"While St. Simon was visiting in the province of Gascony, he died in the hundredth year of his age on May 16 in the convent of Bordeaux: where his body, illustrious for many miracles, rests. And therefore he is termed by some Simon of Gascony: by others he is styled St. Simon Stock of Bordeaux: but he would be more correctly termed and named St. Simon Stock of England (where he was born)."

THOMAS BRADLEY-SCROPE
(made Bishop of Dromor, Ireland, in 1450)

There are two texts, one at Cambridge University Library, ms. FF. 6. 11, ff. 42-43; the other in *Tractatus de fundatione...Ordinis fratrum glor. Dei Genitricis semperque Virg. Mariae de Monte Carmelo,* ch. 2, Concerning the Habit of the Order. The first we designate Bradley-1, the second Bradley-2.

Bradley-1: "The fourteenth was St. Symon of England, who was the sixth General of the Order of Carmelites; who continually besought the most glorious Mother of God to defend with some privilege the Order of Carmelites: who continually besought the most glorious Mother of God to defend with some privilege the Order of Carmelites: who continually besought the most glorious Mother most devoutly: "Flower of Carmel....

"The Blessed Virgin Mary appeared to him with a multitude of angels, holding in her blessed hands the scapular of the ancient Order of Carmelites and saying: 'This will be for you and for all Carmelites a privilege, that he who dies in this will not suffer eternal fire, that is, he who does in this will be saved.'

"While the General St. Symon was visiting the province of Gascony, he died in the convent of Bordeaux, where his body rests: and therefore he is named by some St. Symon of Bordeaux, but he is more correctly called St. Symon of England, where he was born."

Bradley-2: "At that time there was a holy man in this Order, Simon Stock by name, an Englishman, who continually besought the glorious Mother of God to defend with some privilege the Order of Carmelites, which enjoys the special title of the Virgin, saying most devoutly: 'Flower of Carmel, Blossoming Vine, Splendor of heaven, Child-bearing Virgin, none like to thee, Mother mild Whom no man didst know, upon thy Carmelites Privileges bestow, Star of the Sea.'

"The most Blessed Virgin appeared to him with a multitude of angels, holding in her blessed hands the scapular or cloak (cucullam) of the ancient Order of Carmelites with a small capuce (caputio) reaching to the belt, and saying: 'This will be for you and for all Carmelites a privilege, that he who dies in this will be saved; she gave it to him.'

"Simon, devoutly taking it, laid aside the large capuce with its scapular or his cloak *(caputium grossum de scapulari seu cuculla sua)* and added to the scapular another capuce of his own according to the form of the capuce which he had received from the B. Virgin; both he and all Carmelites to the present day use this scapular day and night for the habit of their profession."

NICHOLAS CALCIURI
(from the province of Sicily; work written in 1461)

Vita de Sancti e Romiti del Monte Carmelo. The author was from the convent of Messina in the province of Sicily. Previously unknown, he wrote also *Fioretti del sancto monte Carmelo.* Both works are in manuscript at Florence in the Discalced Carmelite convent.

"The most holy brother Simon, general from the province of England, devoutly besought every day the Virgin Mary to defend and favor with some singular privilege the Carmelite Order, which is distinguished by her special title. Raising his voice sweetly every day, he said this holy prayer: 'Flower of Carmel and blossoming vine, splendor of heaven and child-bearing Virgin, none like to thee, mother mild, whom no man didst know, upon thy Carmelites some privilege bestow, star of the sea.'

"And the most glorious Virgin Mary appeared to the blessed Simon with a great multitude of angels and held in her hand the scapular of the Order and said these words: 'This will be for you and for all Carmelites a privilege. And he who dies with the scapular will not suffer the pain of fire for eternity and he who dies with this will be saved.'

"And the blessed brother Simon with great reverence took the Scapular from the hands of the glorious Virgin Mary, and thereupon she disappeared.

"Many miracles were done with this holy Scapular, the cure of many blind and of many deaf and of many crippled and of many other infirmities."

The Brown Scapular of Our Lady of Mount Carmel

BALDWIN LEERSIUS
(Arras, ob. 1483)

Collectaneum exemplorum, written after 1477 as it mentions two convents of nuns founded by B. Francis Ambosia. The text is taken from Daniel's *Speculum,* part II, nn. 1496 ff.

Chapter IV. How the B. Virgin Mary appeared to St. Simon Stock and gave the Scapular.

"St. Simon, surnamed Stock, so called from the place in England where he was born, and sixth general of the Order, a man of great self-restraint and devotion, especially to the B. V. Mary, illustrious in his lifetime for many miracles, frequently besought with humility and recollection the glorious Virgin Mother of God, singular patron of the Order of Carmelites, to defend still more with a privilege those who are distinguished by her title, saying with a most devout heart every day in his prayer: 'Flower of Carmel, Blossoming Vine, Splendor of heaven, Child-bearing Virgin, None like to thee, Mother mild whom no man didst know, Upon thy Carmelites, privileges bestow, Star of the Sea.'

"On a certain occasion therefore while he was devoutly praying this prayer, the glorious Virgin Mother of God appeared to him with a multitude of Angels, holding in her hand the scapular and saying: 'This will be for you and for all Carmelites a privilege: he who dies in this habit will be saved, etc. she gave him the Scapular: whence are the verses:

If anyone dies in the sign of the Order, by a benign right,
He is freed from torment and brought to heavenly places,
Simon asked this of the dear Virgin,
Afterwards he died, rising to wondrous joys."
(There follows the approbation of the Rule, from Grossi).

Chapter V. How the B. Virgin drew many to affection for the Order and freed them from dangers.

"By reason of this privilege given to St. Simon, many princes of England, especially Edward, King of England (who gave his own palace at Oxford to the brethren, establishing it as a convent out of the fervent zeal he had for the Blessed Virgin Mary) took the scapular of the Order and died in it. For the Blessed Virgin drew him more to devotion in a certain danger which he escaped by her prayers: as is told fully in the confirmatory bull of the Oxford monastery of the brothers of the Blessed Mary of Mount Carmel (Cf. Bullarium, III, 21).

"Likewise we read how King Louis of France was freed from a danger of the sea by the merits of the glorious Virgin Mary and how from the affection that he had for the Blessed Virgin he secretly wore the habit of the Order and died in it, and how he brought the brethren from Mount Carmel to France and settled them at Paris, building a beautiful cloister.

"Likewise the Lord Henry, Duke of Lancaster, by the same miracle granted to St. Simon, took the Scapular and died in it illustrious for many miracles.

"Also, Angela, daughter of the King of Bohemia, who from childhood desired to serve God and the glorious Virgin in chastity and devotion, wore the holy habit of the Order out of reverence for the glorious Virgin, in which, resplendent by many miracles, she holily and piously died: her body is honorably buried in the Church at Prague.

"Likewise Frances, Duchess of Britanny, prompted by the intense zeal which she had for the Blessed Virgin, preparing to leave the world, carefully examined the rules of many Orders, but was inclined toward none save the Order of the Blessed Mother of God, Mary of Mount Carmel: devoutly entering it and living in it holily and piously, she greatly enriched the Order, building in Britanny two convents of nuns and endowing them with goods: with whom in all sanctity and devotion she still perseveres. And there is no doubt but that she was drawn to this by the merits of the Blessed Mary Mother of God."

ARNOLD BOSTIUS
(Ghent, ob. 1499)

He described the vision several times, both in *De patronatu B.V. Mariae* written in 1479 and in *Speculum historiale* written about 1490. Four excerpts follow from Lezana and Daniel of the Virgin Mary.

De Patronatu B.V.Mariae, ch. 10s "Since Blessed Simon Stock, an Englishman, Prior of the whole Carmelite company...loved Mary... very intimately, he besought her for a long time to enrich the holy Order Carmel, which is singularly distinguished by the glorious title of her name, with some special mark of favor, and to defend it with a particular privilege, saying to her with a most devout heart every day among his other prayers: 'Flower of Carmel, etc.'

"The most bountiful Virgin, second after her Son in command of heavenly things, (appeared) to her ardent lover...accompanied by an angelic host, her garment wrapped in light...(He extols what a great privilege it was for Simon to look upon the beauty of Mary and continues):

"Would you not believe that this vision was his whole reward?...it was not sufficient for Mary...She held the Scapular of your Order in her hands...My dearly beloved son, receive the sign of my fraternity; this will be for you and for all Carmelites a privilege: he who dies in this will not suffer eternal fire.

"O singular privilege and wondrous sign that will remain continually without end...

"The news of the deed gradually became known, the rumor of the miracle spread, the unusual event aroused those who heard of it, it became famous among the people of God, all were filled with wonder and happiness, and by reason of this great and singular privilege many men and women of great condition, seizing the arms and shield of the Queen of Heaven hastened to the Order of Carmel and were marked with the holy habit as with a special sign of fraternal union and a pledge of future inheritance...Many devout persons of both sexes and of different condition and states...desired to guard themselves...secretly wearing the scapular of our Order during life...in which they afterwards holily died; and to the present day it is honored by many with great devotion in different parts of the world."

Speculum historiale, I. IV, ch. 18: from the Speculum, I, p. 284s "(In place of the upper garments *superhumeralium*) the B. Virgin gave the Scapular to St. Simon Stock: who while he was worthily governing the Order as its sixth Prior General, continually besought the glorious Mother of God to defend with some singular privilege the Order of Carmelites, which enjoys the special title of the Virgin, frequently saying most devoutly in his prayers: 'Flower of Carmel, Blossoming Vine, Splendor of Heaven, Child-bearing Virgin, none like to thee, Mother mild whom no man didst know, Upon thy Carmelites Privileges bestow, Star of the Sea.'

"The most holy Mother of God appeared to him with a multitude of angels, holding in her blessed hands the Scapular; she gave it to him saying: 'This will be for you and for all Carmelites a privilege...'"

Speculum historiale, 1. VII. ch. 18: from the Speculum, I, p. 288: "For the most blessed Mother of God appeared to him with a multitude of angels holding in her blessed hands the Scapular in a less bulky form than was worn before, with a small capuce reaching to the belt only in the back; and she gave it to him saying: 'This will be for you and for all Carmelites a privilege, he who dies in this will not suffer eternal fire, that is, he who dies in this with due obedience to the Order will be saved.'

"Simon, gently taking it from Our Lady with thanks, laid aside his own large capuce with its Scapular or cloak (caputium suum grossum cum scapulari seu cuculla), and then put on the capuce with the Scapular exactly according to the form he had received from the Virgin. For both he and all Carmelites to the present day use this Scapular night and day for the habit of their profession. And therefore it is prescribed concerning it in the rubric of the ancient statutes of our Order on the Divine Office: We strictly prohibit that any brother dare to celebrate Divine services without his capuced Scapular...

"Having ruled our holy Order dutifully for almost fifty years, after many miracles which the Lord worked through him, he died full of days while he was visiting the province of Gascony in the hundredth year of his age on May 16, 1265, in the convent of Bordeaux, where his body, illustrious for many miracles, rests."

Speculum historiale, 1. *VII,* ch. 20: from Lezana, *Annales, IV,* 332: "He unceasingly besought the glorious Virgin Mary, singular Patron of the Order of Carmelite brothers, to defend with some singular privilege the Order of Carmelite brothers, which is distinguished by her title, and when he had frequently prayed for this, afterwards he fervently added: 'Flower of Carmel, etc.'

"On a certain occasion therefore, while he was saying this prayer with a most devout heart, the most Blessed Mother of God suddenly appeared to the blessed man, and holding in her hands a becomingly worked scapular of a brown color, said: 'This will be for you and for all Carmelites who are now in the world or will be at a future time a singular privilege: for he who dies in this will be saved, and will never see eternal torment, that is, he who dies in what this garment signifies will be saved.' We have spoken of its meaning above.

"Blessed Simon therefore, taking the Scapular from Our Lady with thanks, devoutly put it on: for both he and all Carmelites to the present day use this Scapular night and day for the habit of their profession."

JOHN PALAEONYDOR
(Convent of Mechlin, Ob. 1507)

Fasciculus Trimerestus, 1. III, ch. 8, published at Moguntia, 1497 Venice, 1570, and in Daniel's *Speculum,* I, pp. 229-273. The text is taken from this last edition, p. 258:

"B. Simon...unceasingly besought Mary to defend with some singular privilege the Order, which is distinguished by her title, and to adorn it in praise of herself and for the edification of the faithful, frequently praying: 'Flower of Carmel...etc.

"The bountiful Virgin Mother of God did not fail her ardent lover, but accompanied by an angelic host and wrapped in light, she appeared to him saying: 'My most beloved, receive this Scapular of your Order, the sign of my Confraternity, for you and for all Carmelites, a privilege, he who dies in this will not suffer eternal fire. Behold the sign of salvation, a help in danger a pledge of peace and eternal covenant.'

"The news of the deed gradually became known, the rumor spread from England to foreign countries, the event became famous among the people of God. And so by reason of this great and singular sign of salvation and privilege of eternal peace many men and women of great state, seizing the arms and shield of the Queen of Heaven, dedicated themselves to the Order of Carmel: as Louis, King of France, Edward, King of England, the Lord Henry, Duke of Lancaster, illustrious for many miracles, Henry, Earl of Northumberland, Angela, daughter of the King of Bohemia, Joan and Anne of Toulouse and many others of different provinces wore the holy habit of the Order, the Scapular, night and day. Many others who took the habit in these times were healed of various illnesses."

GILES FABRI
(Prior of Brussels, ob. 1506)

Chronicon Ordinis. The work is lost. The text is taken from Zimmerman's article in the *Analecta (Disc.)* from the collectanea of Bale, Oxford, ms. Bodley, 73, f. 111r.

"The heavenly Virgin, accompanied by a host of celestial beings, appeared to him in prayer, holding in her hands a becomingly worked Scapular of a brown color, and giving it to him she said: 'This will be for you and for my brethren who are now and will be for all time, a singular privilege, that he who dies in this will be saved.'

"Symon put on the Scapular he received not without thanks and gave it to his brethren to wear. And he died...

"When the Virgin's promise to Symon became known, many princes used the Scapular out of devotion to the Virgin, especially Edward, whom Mary (drew) to devotion through a certain danger which he escaped by the protection of the Virgin; see the bull of John. Many are buried in this habit after the great example of these men. Important persons wear this Scapular with great faith at the hour of death or when about to go into battle. In the Kingdom of France on the feasts of Mary, noblemen dressed in white wear the Scapular on their shoulders as in a fraternity united to the Order. The Roman Pontiffs have granted a remission of a third part of their sins to those entering the Order. The wearing of this Scapular sometimes heals the illness of the body."

MENALDUS OF THE ROSARY
(Bordeaux, Provincial of Gascony, ob. ca. 1510)

Vita S. Simonis Stock. Our text is Zimmerman's transcription from Bale's *collectana*, British Museum, ms. Harley, 1819, f. 131r-v.

"Meanwhile, (namely, while Simon was getting his baccalaureate at Oxford), the devil cunningly stirred up the bishops and curates against him and his brethren, so that they laid heavy burdens upon them as Pharoah once repressed the Israelites. On four of them especially they laid burdens...

"Inasmuch as the holy father had a presentiment that this was done through the work of the devil, he called a general chapter and consoled his brethren and comrades, saying that they must have recourse to the divine aid; and he imposed a three day fast on bread and water, and decreed that the priests were to celebrate their masses with all devotion and the rest of the brethren were to recite the psalter.

"But the most holy father himself, standing in the midst of his people like another Moses, prayed for those committed to his care, and turned the anguish of his mind toward the most Blessed Virgin (who was his Patron), saying: 'O Flower of Carmel...'

"When he had frequently repeated this, at the approach of the third day of the prescribed fast the most holy Virgin came toward him at dawn with a great retinue of angels and virgins, bringing the habit with her. For before that time the Carmelite brothers used only the tunic and the white cloak.

"'Take, she said, for he who dies in this will be saved. This will be for you and yours a privilege.' And immediately she added: 'Send the brethren to the Roman Pontiff, for I shall render him so favorable to you that he will confirm your privilege and repress the rashness of the bishops and curates.' Having said this, the Virgin disappeared.

"When morning come therefore the chapter was assembled and he told the brethren all that had happened; and they, rejoicing exceedingly with great joy and being in admiration, gave thanks to God and His Mother.

"Meanwhile, two of the brethren, the clerics Reginald and Peter, were chosen to go to the council at Lyons.

"Meanwhile, the news of the privilege granted to the habit of the Carmelites went out through all England, and because of it many noblemen were clothed in it so that dying in it, they might be saved. Among these King Edward the second secretly wore the habit all the days of his life, and he gave the Order his own castle he owned at Oxford, to be made into a convent. Henry, the first Duke of Lancaster, and many others were clothed in it.

"And so when the holy father had reached the hundreth year of his age, etc."

JOHN BALE
(Englishman, ob. 1563)

Anglorum Heliades, ch. 18, British Museum, ms. Harley 3838; the work was written at the instance of Leland before the suppression of the monasteries but after the author had gone over to Henry VIII.

"Simon received from Innocent through the Virgin Mother of God, a remedy against the encroachments of those in high places." From Siber de Beka

"At that time the Carmelites were compelled to ask for new letters of recommendation. But first to calm the disquieted spirits of the bishops and curates, Simon called a meeting of the fathers and imposed three days of fasting and prayer upon all. And like another Moses standing in the midst of his people he admonished them to direct their anguish to God and the Virgin Mary...Bursting forth into these words: 'Flower of Carmel...'

"When he had frequently repeated this, after the fast when light was seen to arise, the Queen of the heavens...was seen to bring from Heaven the habit of the Order. Bestowing it upon Simon, she said: 'You need not be fearful. Behold this Scapular of your Order, the pledge of fraternal love, for you and for all yours, a privilege: whoever will die in this, provided he is worthy, will not feel eternal fire. This is a sign of solace, a shield in adversity, a solemn covenant of peace.'

"She said this partly that the pusillanimous might not be troubled by her deed and partly that detractors might not have an occasion for calumny. For they frequently declared that those who had taken another kind of garment than the one that had been worn by the brethren in general should be condemned."

And the pious Mother added: "Send some of your brethren to the Roman Pontiff...After speaking a few more words, she immediately disappeared.

"Simon put the pledge he had received upon his shoulders, then distributed it for the brethren to use. Fearlessly, they approached the Pontiff, Innocent, in the year of our salvation, 1252, and they suffered no repulse."

THE FRAGMENTS OF PETER SWANYNGTON
From the *Vindiciae* of John Cheron, Bordeaux, 1642; Magennis, *Scapulare B.M.V.* pp. 26-30.

Fragment 1: "Blessed Simon, weighed down with old age, enfeebled by rigorous penance, and bearing in his heart the troubles of all the brethren, used to pray without ceasing throughout the night even to the dawn; while he was thus praying, consolation came to him from Heaven, which he related to us at our assembly as follows:

'Dearest brethren: Blessed be God who does not abandon those who trust in Him and does not spurn the prayers of his servants; Blessed be also the most Holy Mother of Our Lord Jesus Christ, who, mindful of ancient days and the tribulations which have befallen many of you beyond measure, as you did not attend that all who wish to live piously in Christ Jesus will suffer persecutions: sends you a message which you will receive with joy in the Holy Spirit. May He guide me that I may make it known as it behooves me to speak:

'While I was pouring out my soul in the sight of the Lord, though I am but dust and ashes, and while I was beseeching with all confidence my Lady, the Virgin Mary, that as she willed to call us her brothers, so she would show herself a Mother, snatch us from temptation, and by some sign of grace, recommend us to those who are persecuting us, while saying to her with sighs:

'Flower of Carmel, blossoming vine, splendor of Heaven, Child-bearing Virgin none like to thee, Mother mild whom no man didst know, Upon thy Carmelites privileges bestow, Star of the Sea.'

"She appeared to me with a great company, and holding the Habit of the Order, said, 'this will be for you and for all Carmelites a privilege, he who dies in this will not suffer eternal fire' and because her glorious presence delighted me beyond measure and I, miserable one, could not withstand her majesty, she disappeared, saying that I should send to the Lord Innocent, the Vicar of her Blessed Son, who would grant us a remedy for our troubles.

'Brethren, store up this message in your hearts, strive to make your election sure by good works and never be found wanting; watch in thanksgiving for so great a mercy, pray without surcease that the word made known to me may redound to the praise of the Most Holy Trinity, the Father, Jesus Christ, the Holy Spirit, and the ever Blessed Virgin Mary.'

"To the Brethren in other places who were very dejected he sent the same message by means of a letter of consolation, which I, unworthy man, wrote down an as the man of God dictated, that they might also give thanks in prayer and perseverance. Cambridge on the day after the division of the Apostles, 1251.

Fragment II: "On the 17th day before the Kalends of August (July 16), while the aforesaid Simon was on his way to Winchester with myself as a companion to obtain a letter of introduction to the Pontiff, the Lord Innocent the fourth, from the Lord Bishop of Winchester who was favorable to our Order, the Lord Peter of Linton, Dean of the Church of St. Helen at Linton, met us in great haste *(celeri vectura)*, beseeching the Blessed Father to come with all speed to the aid of his brother who was dying in despair; his name was Walter…The B. Father Simon, making the sign of the Cross, laid his habit upon the sick man and lifting up his eyes to Heaven, asked God for mercy, that one redeemed by Christ might not become the prey of the devil, and suddenly, the dying man, regaining his strength…said…Father, help me, I wish to make my confession.

"…And about the eighth hour of the night he peacefully breathed forth his soul. He appeared to his Brother who was doubtful of his salvation, saying that all was well with him and that he had escaped the wiles of the devil through the post powerful Queen of the Angels with the Habit of the Blessed Man as a shield.

"The news of this event spread through the whole city. The said Lord Peter of Linton immediately put everything down in writing for the Venerable Bishop of Winchester, and awaited his opinion in so unusual a matter. The Lord Bishop being amazed at this and having consulted his advisers, determined to question Blessed Simon concerning the power of his Habit. He appeared before the Lord Bishop and obeying his commands, concealed nothing. The Lord Bishop commanded that everything be written down under his authentic seal; and the aforesaid Lord Peter, because of the miracle wrought by the glorious Virgin Mary on behalf of his brother, established the Brethren at Winchester, granting them land and building a very suitable and spacious monastery for our Order.

"When these facts became known throughout England and abroad, many cities offered us places for foundations and many Princes sought to be affiliated to this Holy Order for the sake of participating in its graces, desiring to die in the holy Habit of the Order, so that by the merits of the glorious Virgin Mary they might have a happy death. And so gradually the Order of the Blessed Virgin Mary of Mount Carmel began...to spread..."

SHORTER ALLUSIONS TO THE VISION OF ST. SIMON
M. Gerard of Edam (Harlem), *De antiquitate, habitu titulo et regula ord. Carm.* (In Daniel's *Speculum* I, 318, from the ms. of Mechlin. Work written about 1470):

"...Simon Stock, a holy man, General of the Order,
While in earnest prayer to the inviolate Virgin Mary
Received the Scapular in England's pleasant clime.
And we remember that as he took the habit she said
That he who dies in this would without doubt be saved."

Peter Bruno, *Tabulare ordinis Fratrum Deiferae V. Mariae de M. C.* (In Daniel's *Speculum,* I, 207-210, from the edition of 1474, Theodore Martins, Aelst):

"Point VI, The giving of the habit...And so we see that the Carmelites are dressed in scapulars; as the holy Simon Stock tells us, they joyfully received the Scapular they wear from the virginal hands (at which time for his great devotion to the Virgin Mary he also

looked upon her as a Prelude to his great reward." From the ms. of Mechlin (1484), f. lv in Daniel's "Speculum:"

"...Simon the Englishman asked of the Mother of Christ,
The aid of the Mother and his Scapular."

"Laurence Burell, (Durom, ob. 1505), *Carmina de illustribus Carmelitis.* (cf. Monumenta, p. 412; *De scriptoribus* O. Carm., p. 5):

"Simon of England, the shepherd of Carmel's glory
Received from the Mother of Christ a holy reward.
His heroic integrity made him beloved of all,
And his modest life kept him dear to God.
He who dwelt in an oak-tree now lives on the beautiful Olympus,
For he was a leader and a teacher of the people."

John of Hildesheim, *Defensorium* (In Daniel's *Speculum,* I, p. 159):

"The privilege of eternal life he gives to the professed,
He is the saving leader; he is the way and the guide,
He is the sign of succor for his companions."

B. Nonius Alvares Pereira, in his letter to Father Alphonse of Alfama, 1392: (29)

"In the first place I kiss your holy Scapular, inestimable gift of the Mother of God, who brought it from Heaven for the defense of her friars because of the great affection which ever since her lifetime she had for them."

CONCLUSIONS FLOWING FROM
ANALYSIS AND COMPARISON OF THE TEXTS

We may now summarize the conclusions flowing from our analysis and comparison of the texts:

1   The accounts of the vision fall into two families, one of which is composed of Menaldus of the Rosary, Bale, and Swanyngton Fragment I. We may term this the Bordeaux family.

2   The accounts outside of the Bordeaux family reduce themselves

to the prototype found in Grossi-1 and Bradley-1. The real author of this prototype is certainly earlier than John Grossi.

3   John Cheron's statement that William Coventry is the author of the primitive text is in complete accord with the findings of historical scholarship.

4   The question as to whether or not the Bordeaux family contains elements of an earlier origin than the primitive text cannot be decided by textual analysis alone, but must be determined by other indications.

FOUR FACTS

I think that our historical evidence establishes four facts which can overthrow every thesis against the historicity of the Scapular vision:

• That the vision was not an invention of Palaeonydor toward the close of the 15th century is obvious from a series of witnesses which can be traced back to the middle of the 14th century.

• William of Sanvico, who about 1290 testified to the vision of the Blessed Virgin, proves that our tradition was not a simple fiction of the mid-fourteenth century. Sanvico's proximity to the event, and the reliability of is chronicle, prohibit the rejection of his testimony.

• The independence of Sanvico and Coventry indicate that the account of the mid-fourteenth century was not a mere elaboration of Sanvico's statement of the vision.

• Finally, the historicity of the Scapular tradition is established by its remarkable conformity with the historical circumstances of St. Simon Stock's administration, even with facts that have come to light only recently.

In consideration of these conclusions I am compelled to affirm that the vision of St. Simon Stock, which occupies so dominant a place in the Scapular devotion, is as solidly founded on historical evidence as could be expected. Let anyone who is so minded belittle faith in the vision; lest, however, he make himself ridiculous, let him do so before the bar of history.

(Servant of God, Fr. Bartholomew F. M. Xiberta, O. Carm.

COPY OF THE SABBATINE BULL

Taken from: *The Credibility of the Scapular Promises,*
Rev. Christian P. Ceroke, Rome, 1950
APPENDIX II pp. 85-93

Authentic Transcript of the Sabbatine Bull (The original Latin text may be found in "Biblioteca Vaticana": Diversa Cameralia S. Pii V 1568-1571, Armadio 29, tomo 238 fol. 16-19 – There follows an English translation of the principal features of the document. The translation is taken from P.E. Magennis, O. Carm., *The Sabbatine Privilege of the Scapular* (New York, 1923) pp. 13-19. This *Transumptum* was made in 1567.)

Vitellotius, by the Divine Mercy, Cardinal Deacon of St. Mary's in Via Lata and Vitellius, Chamberlain of the Holy Roman Church, to each and everyone who shall see, read or hear this present document of the authentic Transcript, unending greeting in the Lord.

Know ye that lately in the Apostolic Chamber, on behalf of the Right Reverend Master John Baptist of Ravenna, Prior General of the whole Carmelite Order, there hath been brought forward and duly shown a certain document of a Transcript which was composed in the Latin language on parchment and bore the signature of the Rev. Jerome Manegat, Vicar of the Bishop of Barcelona, writ by his own hand (as hath appeared therein), which was published, moreover, and signed by Master Francis Aquilo, Notary Public of Barcelona under the date of the fourth day of September in the year of Our Lord, One Thousand Five Hundred and Sixty-seven.

Now the tenor of the said document is as follows:

To each and everyone who shall see these presents of this public document, who shall read or hear the same, be it manifest and known that WE Jerome S.U.D., a Canon of the Church of Barcelona, and in spiritual affairs Vicar General of the Bishop of Barcelona, in accordance with the request, desire and command made to us on behalf of the Right Rev. Master John Baptist Rossi of Ravenna, Prior General for the time being of the Whole Order of Carmelites, by a special messenger of the court of our Vicariate did summon and caused to be summoned before us a certain suitable and unalterable day, hour and place (all of which are indicated below) all those whom either singly or collectively, whether in common or separately we thought it expedient to be present, as well as their representatives, that they might see and hear the transcription, reproduction and arrangement in legal form of a certain public instrument of a transcription, written on parchment and authenticated by the public notaries – which is also inserted hereinunder – or that they might state or allege a reasonable cause, if such they had, why such steps should not be taken.

Now on the day and at the time aforesaid there appeared before us the Reverend Br. Magnalbrocon, Prior of the monastery of the Blessed Mary of Mount Carmel in the city of Majorca and claiming to be the representative of the Most Rev. Father General, he handed a certain letter of summons which had been duly affixed to the doors or gates of the episcopal palace of Barcelona by the above-mentioned messenger. But whereas the person so summoned did not appear, the aforesaid Rev. Father charged them with contumacy and asked that they should be adjudged as such. He further requested and required that the aforesaid document of the transcript which he showed and presented to us in its original form and style should be reduced to public and legal form by us.

Now we, on our part, not rashly but in accordance with the promptings of justice did judge as contumacious those who had been summoned but did not appear and in face of their contumacy we did call unto ourselves the aforesaid document of the transcript. Wherefore, having held in our own hands, having seen it, read it, examined it and authenticated it, having found it free from legal defect or dubious in any part, but on the contrary, whole and in every wise entire, we did therefore cause it to be transcribed and copied and reduced to legal form through the instrumentality of Francis Aquilo, notary and clerk of the court of our Vicariate.

Now the substance of this Transcript is as follows: - This is a transcript faithfully made at Barcelona of a certain other transcript public and authentic of certain apostolic letters, executed on parchment, authorized and certified, as doth appear hereinunder, free from defect or erasure, or doubtful in any of its parts, wholly without blemish or suspicion of same, of which said document here follows the content.

In the name of God. Be it known to all and several who will examine the collection of these presents that we, John Barcelo, Doctor of Canon Law, Canon of the See of Tarraco and on behalf of the most Rev. Father in Christ, and Lord Lewis de Borgia, by the Divine Mercy Cardinal Priest of San Marcello and Archbishop of Valentina, in spiritual and temporal affairs vicar general and general official in the city and diocese of Valentina, sitting as judge unto the rendering of justice in the consistory of the court of our Vicariate, did see and hold in our hands, did read and carefully examine a certain public instrument which was duly written on paper and bore the seal of the university of the noble city of Messina, the same being without fault or erasure or suspicion thereof, but perfect in every way as doth also appear evidently from said document itself of which document herein follow the contents:

On the sixteenth day of April of the third Indication, on behalf of the Carmelite Convent be it known that the hereinunder contained transcript of the contents of the Apostolic Bulls (also given herein) which have been granted and conceded to the convent of the Carmelites, hath been written and copied at the instance of the Venerable Master de Bratzullo, Doctor in Sacred Science and Prior of the Carmelite Convent of Messina. Now the content of the said transcript is as follows:

To wit. I.H.S. In the name of Our Lord Jesus Christ, Amen. In the year of Our Lord's Incarnation one thousand four hundred and twenty–one, in the month of January and on the second day of the said month, which is also of the fifteenth Indication in the days of our most serene and noble Lord and King, Alfonso, by the grace of God renowned ruler of Aragon, Sicily, Valentia, the Islands of Majorca, Sardinia and Corsica, Count of Barcelona, Duke of Athens and Neopatria, Count of Rossilion and Cocitania, in the sixth year of his auspicious reign, Amen. We, Peter of Terranova, judge, and Paul de Rubingerio of Piacenza, by the Imperial authority everywhere, and of the whole of the royal island of Majorca, ordinary judge and notary public and we the witnesses whose names appear below, having been called on and specially invited thereunto by a public document make known and bear witness that the venerable and godly Brother Ilde Alfonso de Theramo of the kingdom of England, Prior of the convent of Captuna of the Order of the Blessed Mary of Mount Carmel, did present unto us and cause to be publicly read a certain Papal Bull of Pope Alexander V of blessed memory, said Bull having been obtained by the said Order. Now this Bull we did see and read and examine with care and its style and contents are as follows:

The aforesaid venerable Prior did desire and request from the above-mentioned persons acting in the capacity of judge and notary public in these parts that we might cause to be reduced to legal form and copied the aforesaid bull, inasmuch as the present and future interest of the said Order make such claim.

Now we, in accordance with request of said petitioner, in that his requirement was reasonable and just – and hence not to be gainsaid –

did have reduced to its present public form and copied, the aforesaid bull with leaden seal affixed as it stood. We further took care that the sense thereof might not be altered by any addition, subtraction or other change whereby the sense might suffer, but that the original might be faithfully reproduced, so that the same trust might be put in this present public transcript as in the original aforesaid bull itself.

Now the entire substance of the Bull is as follows:

Alexander, Bishop and servant of the servants of God, to each and all of these who are faithful of Christ and who either in this our day or in the time to come shall see the presents, greetings and apostolic blessing.

By these our present letters we do make citation of the substance of a certain privilege emanating from our Predecessor of blessed memory, John XXII, the document of which privilege we have seen and carefully examined, whereby for future time greater sureness may be had in regard to same. Now the said privilege was given to our dear children in Christ to wit, the Prior General and brethren, the daughters, sisters and associates of the brotherhood styled of Mount Carmel, and the substance of the said privilege is as follows:

John, Bishop and servant of the servants of God, to the faithful of Christ, collectively and individually, <u>as hath been aforesaid.</u> As though in the most sacred heights of paradise, the so sweet and charming harmony of the angels is heard. While the sense of sight is also delighted and Jesus is seen adorned with the glory of His Father. For He saith: I and the Father are one....He who seeth me, seeth also the Father...and the choir of the angels ceaseth not to say, Holy, Holy, Holy. Even so, the Assembly ceaseth not to pour forth praise to the Virgin on high: Virgin, Virgin, Virgin be thou our mirror alike and example. For she is adorned with the gift of grace, as holy church singeth,....Mary, full of Grace and Mother of Mercy...So that hill which is reputed of the Order of Carmel, praising with song and extolling and telling of this mother of grace...Hail, Queen of Mercy and our hope,..So as I prayed on bended knee, the Virgin of Carmel seemed to me to speak these words: Oh, John, John, Vicar of my well-beloved Son, I shall snatch thee as it were from thy foe. Thee, who art Pope, I make my vicar for the solemn gift which I have obtained by favor with help of my prayers, sought from my Son. So it behoveth thee to grant favor and confirmation ample to my holy and devout Order of Carmel, which took its rise with Elias and Eliseus on the mountain of that name. That whoso maketh the profession, whoso observeth the rule drawn up by my servant Albert the Patriarch, whoso unfailingly sheweth obedience thereunto...and that which has been approved by my dear son Innocent, so that thou mayest accept through the Vicar of my Son on earth, what my Son hath prepared and ordained in Heaven. That he who shall have persevered in holy obedience, poverty, and chastity, or shall enter the Holy

Order, shall be saved. And if others, for the sake of devotion shall enter the holy religion, bearing the sign of the sacred habit, and calling themselves associates of either sex of my aforesaid Order, they shall be freed and absolved from a third part of their sins on what day they enter the aforesaid Order, promising chastity, if a widow be in question; and pledging troth to virginity, if a virgin; if married, observing marital faith unbroken, as holy mother church doth ordain. So let the professed members of the said Order be freed from punishment and from guilt on what day they go from this world; so that with hastened step they may pass over Purgatory.

I, the Mother of Grace, shall descend on the Saturday after their death and whoso I shall find in Purgatory, I shall free, so that I may lead them unto the holy mountain of life everlasting. Tis true that you brothers and sisters are bound to recite the Canonical Hours, as it behoveth, according to the rule given by Albert. Those who are ignorant must lead a life of fasting on those days on which holy church doth so ordain. Moreover, unless through some necessity they be involved in some difficulty, they must abstain from flesh meat on Wednesday and Saturday, except on the Birthday of my Son." Now when these words had been the uttered, the sacred vision departed.

Therefore, I accept that holy indulgence I guarantee it and confirm it, even as though the merits of the Virgin Mother of Grace, Jesus Christ granted it in Heaven. Be it therefore forbidden to all to make void this document of our indulgence or statute or decree, or to go against it by any rash endeavor. But if any one presume to make such an attempt, be it known that he shall incur the anger of the Almighty God, and of the Holy Apostles Peter and Paul.

Given at Avignon on the third day of March.

Given at Avignon on the third day of March in the sixth year of our pontificate.

Let no one therefore, <u>as hath been said</u>, etc.

Given at Rome on the seventh day of December in Santa Maria Maggiore, in the first year of our Pontificate.

Wherefore for future reference and unto the security of the said Order the present copy has been duly made and signed with my usual seal, as is even used by me as Notary public. It has also been signed in the handwriting of the Judge and of the witnesses whose names appear below. Done at Majorca, on the day during the month and Indiction indicated hereinunder.

I, Peter Terranova, by the authority of the Emperor everywhere, and of the entire kingdom of the Island of Majorca, ordinary judge and notary public, having been asked with regard to the aforesaid, did write my name and signed with my wonted seal.

Appendix 3

PUBLICATIONS
IN DEFENSE

FOLLOWING ARE SOME PUBLICATIONS USED IN DEFENSE OF THE SCAPULAR VISIONS OF OUR LADY TO ST. SIMON STOCK AND TO POPE JOHN XXII:

1   *The Month*, A Catholic Magazine and Review, "The Catholic Dictionary and the Brown Scapular," Vol. LVII, May-August, 1886

2   *The Month*, A Catholic Magazine and Review, "The Catholic Dictionary and the Sabbatine Indulgence," Vol. LVIII, September-December, 1886

3   *The Irish Ecclesiastical Record*, A Monthly Journal, "The Brown Scapular and the Catholic Dictionary, I and II" Third Series, Vol. VIII, 1887

4   *The Irish Ecclesiastical Record*, A Monthly Journal, under Episcopal Sanction, "The Scapular Promise from the Historical Standpoint," Vol. XXIX, Fourth Series, January to June, 1911

The Brown Scapular of Our Lady of Mount Carmel

A Catholic Magazine and Review.

Per menses singulos reddens fructum suum,
et folia ligni ad sanitatem gentium.
(*Apoc.* xxii. 2.)

VOL. LVII.

MAY—AUGUST.

1886.

LONDON:

OFFICE OF THE MONTH, 48, SOUTH ST., GROSVENOR SQ.

LONDON: BURNS & OATES.   DUBLIN: M. H. GILL & SON.

AGENTS FOR AMERICA: MESSRS. JOHN MURPHY AND CO., BALTIMORE.

Appendix 3

Contents.

The Catholic Dictionary and the Brown Scapular.

IT has always been our desire to avoid domestic controversy in THE MONTH. Against those without we are ever ready to take up our weapons, and, albeit in friendly form as far as may be, to drive back the enemies of the Church. But we have no desire to enter on any of the disputes respecting moot points of canon law and ecclesiastical history, moral or dogmatic theology, which stir up interminable strife. The time and efforts of the combatants, the energies which might have been employed and employed with advantage against heretics and unbelievers, have often ere now been wasted on fruitless wrangling, to which at last the Holy See itself has had again and again to put an end by imposing silence on the disputants. Even where the disputed point is one of real importance, involving weighty issues, it is outside the province of a Catholic magazine intended for general circulation to be a partisan in a contest which may be necessary, but is always to be regretted.

But there are exceptions to every rule. There are occasions when we are compelled, however reluctantly, to attack those to whom we desire to show all honour and respect. There are subjects on which we cannot keep silence, even though we are forced to assail writers to whom in other respects the Catholic body owes on many grounds a debt of gratitude, and who have done good service to the Catholic cause. Slowly and unwillingly we enter on the task, slowly and unwillingly in so far as it is always painful to say a word against those whom we recognize as friends, those whose loyalty cannot be questioned, and whose learning and ability give a weight to their words. But yet not slowly or unwillingly when we forget the personal qualities of those whom we assail, and look to the question on which they have laid themselves open to attack. Not slowly or unwillingly when the privileges of one of the greatest of the Religious Orders of the Church are impugned, and the veracity of their members called in question. Not slowly or unwillingly when a slur is cast upon a devotion dear to Catholic hearts, a devotion which an ever widening experience proves to have been, under God's mercy, the means of saving innumerable souls.   Not slowly or unwillingly when the point involved affects either directly or indirectly the honour due to the Holy Mother of God.   *Amici auctores, magis amica Maria.*

The title of our article will explain the reasons we give for our mingled reluctance and anxiety to write it.   The *Catholic Dictionary* supplies a want long felt among all English-speaking Catholics.   Its articles are in general full of solid information and prudent discretion.   They display a wide knowledge of history and canon law, and for the most part a sound theological temper.   They put before the world information on Catholic matters which was scarcely attainable before by ordinary English readers.   The articles are written generally speaking in an impartial judicious spirit which no one can fail to admire.   The authors of the work are men highly esteemed, and justly esteemed, for their literary ability and historical knowledge.

But there is one article in the book which sadly disfigures the volume in which it is found.   The article on the Brown Scapular is one which we read with pain and with dismay.   We should not like to say that it deserves any theological note of censure, but certainly if we read it alone and apart from the rest, we should cast aside the volume as the work of a "weak-kneed Catholic,"—weak-kneed, not only as regards his practical devotion and loyalty to what the Church approves, but feeble in the extreme in his power of historical criticism.   Nay, it is more than this : it is inaccurate and unfair ; it makes statements at variance with truth ; it displays an ignorance of the facts of the case ; it is careless and inexact throughout ; it is based on the condemned writings of a disloyal and bitter enemy of the Holy See.   There seems to be (we do not say there is) in the mind of the writer a secret dislike to and suspicion of the Scapular as an encouragement to popular superstition, and this even while he coldly praises it and admits that no Catholic can doubt its piety and utility.   He seeks to rob it of that quasi-sacramental character which invests it with such a practical value in the eyes of the faithful.   He treats it as only a visible mark of devotion to Mary, a sign that the wearer intends "to live a Christian life, and so by living in Jesus Christ to prove himself worthy to have Mary for his Mother."   But it is no longer a gift from Mary's own hands, giving him who carries it a *claim* to her protection: it is no longer supernatural in its origin. The promise that one who wears it faithfully, and dies with it upon him, will not be allowed to fall into the flames of Hell, is pooh-poohed as a bit of superstition, or at least unreliable under the light of modern criticism. The further promise of escape from Purgatory on the Saturday after death, under certain conditions which are not difficult to fulfil, is dismissed as a clumsy forgery. There is no sufficient evidence that our Lady appeared to St. Simon Stock at all; there is no reason for thinking that she made any promise to him respecting it. There is no proof that the Scapular dates from him. The only contemporary Life of the Saint cannot be found. If it exists, the story of the apparition seems to have been interpolated. The Sabbatine Bull of John the Twenty-second is a forgery: that of Alexander the Fifth is another forgery to cover the former. The Carmelites are at the bottom of it all. They have simply thrown dust in the eyes of the faithful. They refused to show this precious Life to the Jesuit who asked to see it. They forged, invented, interpolated, recklessly and without scruple, for the glorification of their Order, and succeeded at last in imposing on the Catholic world and obtaining the general acceptance of the story of the Brown Scapular and of the extraordinary privileges that it carries with it.

All this is not stated plainly and explicitly as we have put it, but it is the legitimate and necessary inference from the assertions contained in the article. If no other reason led us to refute the statements made, our love and veneration for the great Carmelite Order would be more than a sufficient motive. We cannot sit quietly by and see them insulted in such fashion as this. But we have a further motive for writing, one which we know every Carmelite in the world would wish to see preferred even to the honour of his own illustrious and venerable Order. Any attack on the Scapular is indirectly an attack on the power and privileges of the Holy Mother of God. Under plea of applying to a popular superstition the laws of enlightened criticism, one of the most fruitful sources of devotion to Mary is impugned. It thus becomes the bounden duty of every Catholic to protest against the appearance in a Catholic Dictionary of an article anti-Catholic in spirit, and to reassert in unmistakeable terms the honour due to the most holy Scapular, which the whole Christian world regards as the personal gift of Mary to her children, carrying with it privileges almost miraculous to those who wear it as a pledge of their devotion to her. If we are rather late in the field, it is because it is only recently that our attention has been called to the article on the Scapular and that we have discovered the tainted sources from which its argument is derived.

We shall not attempt to quote in full the article which we are impugning. We shall merely give the more objectionable passages contained in it. The *Catholic Dictionary* is on the shelves of most educated Catholics, who can verify for themselves the accuracy of our quotations and the absence of any sort of garbling or misconstruction of its words. It first repeats "the story told" of the origin of the Scapular, of the appearance of our Lady to St. Simon Stock, and of her promise made to him that "no one dying in this Scapular shall suffer eternal misery." The Sabbatine Bull of John the Twenty-second, the vision that was its occasion, is next mentioned, and the two apparitions are then discussed separately. We shall confine ourselves at present to the former of these questions, postponing to a future article the celebrated Sabbatine Bull. What we have to decide is whether there is sufficient evidence to justify or to compel our acceptance of the story of the apparition of our Blessed Lady to the English Carmelite in the thirteenth century, and to give us full confidence in the assurance made to him that the Scapular that she placed in his hands should ensure the salvation of all who are wearing it at the moment of their death.

Now the devotion to the Brown Scapular turns in great measure on the reality of this apparition. If it cannot be depended upon to save its wearer from Hell, then it sails under false colours among Catholics. If it cannot be shown that such a promise was really made, if there is ground for supposing that the whole thing is an invention and a pious fraud, the Brown Scapular ceases to merit the implicit confidence it receives from the faithful. It is true that it still gives a share in certain privileges attached to the Order of Mount Carmel, but if the chief of all these privileges turns out to be a fraud perpetrated by the Carmelites themselves, we can scarcely expect that much reliance will be placed on the efficacy of the rest. It becomes a symbol of devotion without anything tangible and trustworthy attaching to it, except a vague and undefined impression that the wearer is in some sort of way under our Lady's protection. To place an absolute reliance on it, to cherish it with loving and undoubting confidence in its efficacy, to regard it as the pledge of our perseverance, the mark whereby our Lady will recognize us as having a certain claim to her all-powerful intercession at the hour of death, becomes a silly superstition. It may even generate a false presumption, and encourage the sinner in false hopes and most dangerous expectations of a help from Mary that she has never promised to give. The sinner may persuade himself that he is safe of his salvation if only he wears to the last this magical Scapular, and may thus put off repentance until too late, on the ground that his Scapular will prevent his falling into the fires of Hell.

The general tendency of the article we are discussing is to crush, or at least to discountenance, this " idol " of confidence in the Brown Scapular. It would have us throw to the winds the idea that we may rest assured of the salvation of those who die with the scapular around their necks. It allows the piety and utility of the institution, and that it is a visible token that the wearer owns himself one of our Lady's children, but the words of Bossuet to this effect are quoted, in which he takes care to add that Mary will be our Mother " if we live in our Lord Jesus Christ "—a pious sentiment the truth of which is undeniable, but in which we read between the lines that Scapular or no Scapular, Mary will not answer for the safety of the sinner. Benedict the Fourteenth is also quoted as admitting that too many abuse these symbols, or badges, by a misplaced confidence in them.

Now, it is perfectly true that such an abuse of the Brown Scapular is one theoretically possible, and in the controversy with heretics various Catholic writers are careful to point out that unless in the heart of the dying sinner there is present the love of God and contrition for sin, nothing in the world can save his soul. *If* a Catholic continues in a state of sin up to the moment when his soul leaves his body, to Hell he must go, Scapular or no Scapular. *If* he has not made that act of submission to God and aversion from sin, which is the condition of eternal salvation, the Scapular will not act as a charm. Nay, the very graces it carries with it would only increase his damnation, by reason of his greater guilt in rejecting them. We must be very explicit on this point, else we should justly lay ourselves open to the charge of what would really be a most degrading and demoralizing superstition. To suppose that aught can avail to deliver from Hell save love to God and faith in Jesus Christ, would be a most abominable and damnable doctrine. We must not allow any mistake as to this.

But this is not the point at issue. The question is not whether a Catholic wearing the Scapular and dying in sin would lose his soul. Every one must admit that he would. The real question is whether any Catholic who wears the Scapular up to the moment of death does die in a state of sin. This is the real meaning of our Lady's promise—that every one who dies with this Scapular upon him shall previously obtain from God the grace of contrition ; that his devotion to the Holy Mother of God, evidenced in his wearing of her badge and livery, shall earn for him such good dispositions at the hour of his death, that in virtue of them, through the merits of our Lord and Saviour Jesus Christ, he shall be received into the Kingdom of Heaven.

It may be objected that this too is a demoralizing doctrine, that it encourages men to remain in sin because forsooth by wearing the Scapular, they can ensure their conversion before their death. They can indulge in every possible vice, and yet need not fear, since saving grace can be obtained, and Heaven can be purchased by the very simple device of putting on a little bit of brown stuff in honour of the Mother of God before they die.

We answer to this, that it is equally demoralizing to teach the sinner that every one who makes a genuine act of contrition at the last moment of his life will certainly enjoy the eternal bliss of Heaven, whatever may have been the abominations of his past life. Yet every Catholic knows full well that this is true. How is it that this is not an encouragement to sin ? For the simple reason that Catholics know that a just God watches over us, and that he who abuses the mercy of God to continue in sin will in the end fail of obtaining that necessary contrition. If a man trusts to a death-bed repentance, and avails himself of it to go on sinning, the death-bed repentance will probably never take place. The sinner will be struck down of a sudden. He will have no time for repentance—or delirium or insensibility will creep over him before the arrival of the priest—or it may be that he will, in punishment of his presumption, have lost the power of making an act of contrition at all—or even if he make one, some subsequent temptation will overcome him, and the devil will regain his victim before the last moment comes.

Now it is just the same with any one who should abuse the privilege of the Scapular. If God has granted this privilege to Mary, He will not allow His Holy Mother to be insulted by her Scapular being made an excuse for sin. To trust presumptuously to it is no less dangerous than to trust presumptuously to a death-bed repentance. The Scapular in which the sinner trusts will somehow disappear. The strings will break, and he will lose it, and will not take the trouble to provide himself with another. Very often he will himself tear it off under the influence of an evil conscience and a heart hardened against God. Somehow or other, when the hour of death arrives, it will be gone. The vanished Scapular will be, through his own fault, the just punishment of continuance in sin.

As a matter of fact, we do not believe that there is any practical danger of Catholics placing any undue confidence in the efficacy of the Scapular. We certainly have never encountered an instance. The tendency is quite the other way. One of the strongest practical arguments in favour of the privilege attaching to it is that a continuance in sin almost always carries with it the voluntary or involuntary abandonment of the Scapular. We could quote instances without number which have come under our own experience. Often a Catholic who intends to commit mortal sin will deliberately take off his Scapular. Bad he may be, but not so bad as to insult the Holy Mother of God by wearing her uniform while he is outraging her Divine Son. More often the indifference to holy things which is one of the effects of sin will make him careless, and one day he will forget or neglect to resume it after it has been taken off. Somehow or other, and many of my readers will confirm the truth of what I am saying from their own knowledge, the abandonment of the Scapular is one of the most certain signs which accompanies wilful persistency in wrong-doing and a determined resistance to the grace of God.

All this does not prove that we *must* believe in the efficacy of the Scapular; it only proves that we *may* believe in it with the most implicit confidence, without laying ourselves open to the charge of superstition or of encouraging a dangerous abuse. But it proves more than this, it proves that there is a certain connection between the presence of grace in the soul and the wearing of the Scapular, and between the loss of grace and the loss of the Scapular. This at least points to the further conclusion that he who wears it to the end will either retain or recover the grace of God before he die, and this again confirms the fact of the apparition and of the promise made, which we shall now proceed to establish on sufficient and more than sufficient evidence.

But first of all we must do the disagreeable work of demolition. We cannot reconstruct till we have cleared the ground of the rubbish accumulated by the *Catholic Dictionary*, which dismisses the positive evidence in favour of the apparition as follows:

> As to the fact of the apparition to Simon Stock, it is accepted by Benedict the Fourteenth, Papebroch, and Alban Butler, on the faith of a "Life" of the Saint by Swaynton, who was his secretary and wrote the story of the apparition at his dictation. A fragment of this "Life" was produced from the archives at Bordeaux and printed by one of the Carmelites—viz. Cheronensis. We may observe that the Carmelites refused a sight of this "Life" to Papebroch. (See Bollandist Acta SS. Maii, tom. iii.)

This paragraph is quite inaccurate (to say the least), both in its facts and in its insinuations.

1. The apparition is not accepted by Benedict the Fourteenth on the faith of a "Life" of the Saint by Swaynton.

If the reader will refer to the passage where Benedict the Fourteenth discusses the question, he will find that there is no mention of a "Life" by Swaynton at all. His words are as follows :

> We believe the vision to be true, and think that it ought to be held as true by all men. For it is accurately reported by Suvaningron (*sic*), who was the friend and secretary of B. Simon, and says that he received it from his own lips. "This vision I, unworthy as I am, wrote at the dictation of the man of God." The MS. account of it was formerly hidden away in the archives at Bordeaux. From this obscurity it was extracted when these controversies were at their height, and was printed by Father John Cheron, Prior of the House at Bordeaux, in his *Vindiciæ Scapularis*, pp. 157 seq.[1]

There is not a single word about a "Life" of the Saint. Benedict the Fourteenth simply speaks of a MS. account of the apparition taken down by his secretary, and kept in the Carmelite archives. The "Life" which is brought forward as the basis of the story, in order that it may be discredited, and through it the devotion to the Scapular, is a pure fiction. It was either invented by the enemies of the Carmelites, or arose out of a misapprehension respecting the nature of Swaynton's document, which was simply a written testimony to the truth of the vision, discovered in the archives of Bordeaux, and printed

[1] Cf. Benedict the Fourteenth, *de Festis B.M.V.* ii. c. vi. p. 269.

by Father John Cheron (not Cheronensis, as the *Dictionary* calls him) in his *Vindiciæ Scapularis.*[2]

2. There is no sort of foundation for the statement that "the Carmelites refused a sight of this 'Life' to Papebroch." It seems that Father Papebroch was asked to insert in the *Acta Sanctorum* a Life of St. Simon Stock by Father Roland, who was Prior of the Carmelite Monastery at Valenciennes, but refused to accept it because the Carmelites objected to the notes and animadversions which would have been inserted by one whom they, rightly or wrongly, already regarded as inclined to look unfavourably on the antiquity and privileges of their Order. He seems, moreover, to have been possessed with the same idea about the existence somewhere or other of a Life (or at least of certain *Acta*) written by Swaynton, and this impression confirmed his unwillingness to accept without dispute the Life by Roland, which was written a century and more after the Saint's death. But in the *Acta Sanctorum* to which the writer in the *Catholic Dictionary* refers, there is not a word about the alleged " refusal," or anything that admits of any such interpretation.[3]

The writer now proceeds to a further disparagement of the alleged apparition.

Next, to understand the force of Launoy's arguments for regarding this passage in the "Life," if it be authentic, as an interpolation, we must remember that the miracle is represented as gaining immediate notoriety. These are Swaynton's or pseudo-Swaynton's words : " The story running through England and beyond it, many cities offered us places in which to live, and many nobles begged to be affiliated to this holy order, that they might share in its graces, desiring to die in this holy habit." If so, the silence of Carmelite authors for more than a century after is remarkable. Simon Stock died in 1250. Ribotus, Provincial in Catalonia (about 1340), in his ten books "On the Institution and Remarkable Deeds of the Carmelites," ignores it. So does Chimelensis in two books specially designed to glorify the Order ("Speculum Historiale" and "Speculum Ordinis Carmeli "), and so do three other authors of similar books quoted by Launoy. Strangest of all, Waldensis, a Carmelite, an Englishman, and writing in England ("De Sacramentalibus "), tries hard to prove

---

[2] Father Daniel, in his *Speculum Carmelitanum*, where he gives an elaborate account of the various lives of the saint that have been written, makes no mention whatever of any "Life" of St. Simon Stock by Swaynton, but simply of the story of the scapular being given to the saint from Heaven (*Historia de Scapulari cælitus ei dato*). At the same time a careless reader might easily mistake the drift of the passage, and this is the probable origin of the misapprehension.

[3] Cf. *Acta Sanctorum*, Maii, Pars iii. p. 750.

the religious habit a sacramental, and speaks particularly of the Carmelite habit and the form which it is given. Nothing could have been more to the point than Swaynton's story, but he never alludes to it. The vision is mentioned, apparently for the first time, so far as is known for certain, by Grossus, a Carmelite of Toulouse, in his "Viridarium" (1389), then by Paleonidorus ("Antiq. Ord. Carm.," vi. 8, apud Launoy), published in 1495. It is right to add, however, that the Carmelites claimed the support of an anonymous MS. in the Vatican said to have been written early in the fourteenth century.

Before we discuss in detail the plausible insinuations of this paragraph, we should like to say a word about M. Launoy, the author whom the writer has taken for his authority and source of information. In an earlier part of the article which we shall deal with hereafter, he speaks of M. Launoy's dissertation as one of "wonderful learning." Having enlisted the readers' sympathies and invested him with all the weight that we duly attach to a man so remarkable, he quite forgets to tell us that M. Launoy was one of those bitter adversaries of the Holy See and of the Religious Orders who unhappily sprung up in considerable numbers under the baneful influence of Gallicanism. We have no right to brand him as an actual heretic, but he was at least a most disloyal Catholic, the opponent of authority, the sympathizer with false doctrine, who made it his object to vilify and defame the Religious Orders, to assail their privileges, to pour out his venom upon them on every possible occasion.[4] If M. Launoy was a man of "wonderful learning," he was also a man of wonderful malice and full of a wonderful hatred of the Holy See. Is this the man who is to be taken as our guide in a matter like this ? Is this half-hearted Catholic, this enemy of Rome, this quarrelsome mischief-maker, this friend of heretics, to be quoted with unqualified approval in a matter which concerns the privileges of one of the most venerable of those Religious Orders that he hated ? Is this unhappy Gallican to be spoken of with admiration on a subject in which he at least indirectly impugns the dignity and privilege of the holy Mother of God ?

[4] The following is a choice specimen of the language used by M. Launoy of the members of the Religious Orders. Speaking of the work of Father Raynaud, S.J., he says : " I and others have read his book and re-read it, but we find in it nothing at all except abuse borrowed from taverns and houses of ill-repute (*quæsita ex tabernis et prostibulis maledicta*), and wondrous lies (*portenta mendaciorum*) which not even the Devil, the parent of all calumniators, would belch forth, since he would be afraid to show himself so openly and stupidly in his true character." (*De vera causa secessus St. Brunonis in eremum Præf.*, p. 15).

But this is not all. There is a further consideration which makes us scarcely able to believe that a Catholic dictionary should take as the basis of one of its articles the "wonderful learning" of M. Launoy. The very work which is thus praised and quoted is actually one condemned by the Church, one which has been, in company with M. Launoy's other productions, on the Index of Prohibited Books for the last two hundred years! It seems to us a scandalous thing that one whose writings the Church has solemnly declared unfit for perusal should be accepted as an authority respecting a devotion dear to every Catholic heart, and one which is a source of unceasing honour to God's Holy Mother all over the Catholic world. A work which lies under the Church's ban, which, unless special permission has been obtained, no Catholic can read without sin wherever the Index is promulgated, is brought forward as a standard authority and recommended to Catholics as justifying the rejection of our Lady's gift to her faithful children of Mount Carmel!

M. Launoy's character, and the condemnation of his work, are quite sufficient to render his arguments not only suspicious, but valueless, and we should be quite justified in passing them over in silence. But we are dealing with the *Catholic Dictionary*, not with the Jansenist writer, and we will therefore examine these arguments in themselves.

We should be quite justified in passing them over on another ground. In opposition to the positive testimony of existing documents, M. Launoy relies upon the feeble and negative argument derived from the silence of certain writers who in his opinion *ought* to have mentioned the Scapular. This method of argumentation is a favourite one with the sceptic bent on destruction. We are all familiar with it in the mouth of the Protestant controversialist. If St. Peter was Bishop of Rome, how is it that he is not mentioned in St. Paul's Epistle to the Romans? If our Lady was conceived without sin, how is it that so important an exception to the general law is omitted by the Apostle when declaring the universality of original sin? This style of argument is the more mischievous because in many cases it can only be refuted by an hypothesis, and such a refutation sounds like a confession of weakness. If an author whose works are not in our hands is cited as omitting certain facts which he ought to have mentioned if he had known them, we are driven to suggest *possible* reasons why he may have omitted them. We may be absolutely certain of the truth of the facts, but we are at a disadvantage when we urge a *supposed* reason for his silence, which may or may not have been the true reason. The sceptic knows this, and this sort of appeal *ad ignorantiam* often serves him as an effective method of destructive criticism. Happily, however, we are able to refute M. Launoy far more satisfactorily than by such considerations as these. Of the three authors adduced by the writer in the *Catholic Dictionary*, we are able to give a good account of two, while the third is the distorted offspring of M. Launoy's ignorance or carelessness, cited more carelessly still by the *Catholic Dictionary*.

We will take first of all the one whose silence carries the greatest weight with the assailants of the story respecting the supernatural origin of the Scapular, Thomas Waldensis. The Carmelites of other countries (such is the argument of Launoy) might perhaps have been ignorant of the wonder that had taken place in England ; but even if their silence can be thus explained, the omission of any mention of the Vision in the works of Thomas Waldensis, the Englishman who is defending the sacramental or quasi-sacramental character of the religious habit against the blasphemies of the Wickliffites, is quite conclusive. It is impossible that he should not have known of this wondrous vision, or that, knowing it, he should have neglected so triumphant an argument in his favour. Here the writer in the *Catholic Dictionary* follows blindly in the steps of the "wonderful learning" of its Gallican authority and his condemned works.

The answer to this is a very simple one. So far from this story being suitable to the work of Thomas of Walden, nothing would have been more inopportune than its introduction into a controversial work such as he was engaged upon. He was battling with heretics, the bitter enemies of the Religious Orders and religion in general. To drag in the account of this supernatural vision would have been most imprudent. It would have been a veritable casting of pearls before swine. It would only have provoked his opponents to fresh blasphemies against all things sacred, and especially against the Holy Mother of God. What should we say of a Catholic writer who should adduce some of the most wonderful miracles adduced by St. Alphonsus in the *Glories of Mary* by way of refuting the objections of Protestants to Catholic devotion to our Lady ? When we are engaged in combating those who deny the essentials of our holy religion, we meet them on their own ground, by facts which they cannot deny, by arguments within their comprehension ; we do not bring forward untimely those extraordinary favours which God in His mercy sometimes vouchsafes to His saints. Thomas Netter, of Walden, like a wise man kept his own counsel, and shrank from exposing to the obloquy of the blasphemer the token of love that the Order of Carmel had received from the Holy Mother of God.

We next come to Father Philip Ribot (or Riboti), Provincial of Catalonia. For a long time we sought in vain for the treatise referred to, but at length, through the courtesy of the Carmelite Fathers, we have had an opportunity of consulting it. We will give a brief account of its contents, and leave our readers to judge whether the silence of its author respecting the apparition to St. Simon Stock is any sort of argument against the reality of the vision. Father Ribot's book is simply a digest of the writings of four celebrated writers who preceded him: John, Bishop of Jerusalem in the fifth century, St. Cyril of Constantinople (A.D. 1170), Gulielmus de Sanvico (or Samuco) who lived towards the end of the thirteenth century, and Sibertus de Beka who lived at the beginning of the fourteenth. Of these, De Sanvico wrote on the multiplication of the Order in the East, and the subsequent destruction of the monasteries there, and De Beka (or Beke) treated of the Carmelite Rule. Ribot's work has nothing original in it. It is a mere compilation. It treats of the institution of the Order, of its gradual advance, of its history in Palestine, of its transference to Europe, of its Rule, of the proper shape and meaning of the habit, of the official privileges derived from various Popes. But there is not a word in it of what we may call the devotional side of the Carmelite Rule or of Carmelite confraternities, any more than in the writers from which it is derived. St. Simon Stock is, as far as we have seen, nowhere mentioned in its pages. It is simply a dry record of historical facts or discussion of the various laws and customs pertaining to the Order. To have dragged in the apparition would have been as much out of place in Ribot's work[5] as in Thomas of Walden's.

Our third author, whose silence is conclusive against the Scapular, is Joannes Chimelensis, who we suppose is to be identified with the Joannes Chimetensis of M. Launoy. But who

---

[5] Ribot's work is inserted in the *Speculum Carmelitanum* of Father Daniel, pars i. p. 229.

was Joannes Chimetensis? We are sorry to disparage the "wonderful learning" of M. Launoy, but after many inquiries we are driven to the conclusion that the writer whom he calls Joannes Chimetensis is none other than Joannes de Ciminetho, who lived in 1336, and belonged to the Convent at Metz, and therefore bore the name of *Metensis*. M. Launoy apparently muddles up the two names. The *Catholic Dictionary*, as usual, follows him blindly, except that it introduces the additional inaccuracy of changing his name to Chimelensis. Now when we turn to the account of the work of this Joannes de Ciminetho in the *Speculum Carmelitanum*, we find that it is a brief history of the Order, and seems to be a mere repetition in another form of the facts given by Ribot and other early Carmelite writers. The Editor of the *Speculum* gives as his reason for not inserting it that all that is contained in it has already been given by other authors. Hence there is no more reason why John of Metz should tell the story than Philip of Catalonia or any other of those who wrote the history of the Carmelite Order or the account of its official privileges.[6]

It seems that Launoy never can have seen the work, much less the writer in the *Catholic Dictionary*. Yet the latter does not hesitate to discredit an author whose work is clearly unknown to him. Chimelensis—the imaginary Chimelensis—was the author of "two books specially designed to glorify the Order." We must protest against the groundless insinuation against the good Carmelite, which we read between the lines. If the motive attributed to a writer is "to glorify the Order" to which he belongs, the ground of our confidence in him is cut away from under our feet. It implies that to such an one the interests of truth are secondary to the glorification of the body of which he is a member. It implies that if the story about which he is silent had not been utterly unknown in his day, he would certainly have thrust it, *per fas et nefas*, into his book.

We now come to the positive evidence in favour of the apparition, evidence which establishes its authenticity by proofs so irrefragable that nothing but ignorance or a determined theological bias could fail to be convinced by them.

1. The document in which Swaynton wrote at the dictation of St. Simon Stock was, as we have seen, preserved in the archives of the Carmelites at Bordeaux, and printed for the first time by Father John Cheron when the controversy arose which the

---

[6] *Spec. Carm.*, pars 2, p. 206, n. 885. The work of Joannes de Ciminetho was printed at Venice in the *Speculum magnum Ordinis Carmelitani*, fol. 50 seq.

enemies of the Carmelites stirred up against the Scapular. Father Cheron was Prior of the convent, and though we have no particulars of his life, yet the fact of his election by his religious brethren to this important office is sufficient proof of the high esteem in which he was held. Our adversaries would have us believe that this document never existed at all. They would have us accept the utterly improbable, the ludicrous, hypothesis that a distinguished man, high in office in his Order, or one of his fellows, forged this manuscript narrative, and that it has been accepted from that day to this by the Christian world, has been quoted over and over again, approved by Popes, sanctioned by Roman Congregations, spread abroad among the faithful by written documents, and by continual sermons and exhortations, although all the while it was a fraud and imposture. It is sometimes said, and said with considerable truth, that none are so credulous as those who profess to believe nothing. Certainly it requires a good deal of credulity to suppose that the origin of the world-wide confidence in the Brown Scapular was a paper forged by an unscrupulous monk. It requires more credulity still to believe that the monk who committed such a crime was a man of literary ability and distinction, Superior of a convent in a large city of Catholic France, to whom was entrusted the task of vindicating this great Carmelite devotion. It requires most credulity of all to imagine that Almighty God could allow hundreds of learned and holy men and with them thousands and tens of thousands of pious Catholics to be deceived by such an imposture, and on the strength of it to attribute to the Brown Scapular an efficacy which it does not possess.

But the testimony of Father Cheron does not stand by itself. The MS. in the Vatican, of which the author of the article we are discussing speaks as if the claim put forward in its behalf by the Carmelites were at least exceedingly doubtful, is a well-authenticated document, of which a copy was made officially in 1635. It dates from the end of the thirteenth (or at least the beginning of the fourteenth) century. Even Launoy does not venture to deny its existence, he simply tries to destroy its authority by reminding his readers of the vast amount of rubbish which the Vatican Library, like the net which draws every kind of fish, had gathered into its archives. Nor is this the only testimony to the Scapular before the end of the fourteenth century. There are no less than three other accounts of or allusions to the apparition of an earlier date than the *Viridarium* of Grossi of Toulouse. To say that it is mentioned for the first time by him is not only a gratuitous statement, but one in direct contradiction with the facts of the case. In the *Speculum Carmelitanum*, by Father Daniel, quotations are given distinctly confirming the apparition from four different sources.

The first of these is the MS. in the Vatican,[7] which contains a brief life of St. Simon Stock, in which the following passage occurs. St. Simon used constantly to pray the glorious Mother of God to fortify with some singular privilege the Order of the Carmelites, which was specially distinguished by the title of the Virgin herself, repeating daily in his prayers, with most devout voice, "O Flower of Carmel, Flowering Vine, Glory of Heaven, Virgin who alone didst bear a Son, gentle Mother, who knewest not man, give favour to thy Carmelites, O Star of the Sea." To this blessed man, the Blessed Virgin Mary appeared with a multitude of angels, holding in her hands the Scapular of the Order, and said : "This shall be a special favour to thee and to all the Carmelites. He who dies in this shall not suffer the fires of Hell."[8] This MS. was attested by eye-witnesses who read it and copied it out in the presence of Horatius Justinianus, Qualificator of the Sacred Office, 1635.

The second is a MS. in the Library of Barthelot, Bishop of Damascus, quoted by Gononus in the *Lives of the Fathers of the West*, book iv. It tells the story in almost the same words.

The third is a MS. in the Convent of the Carmelites at Malines, containing records of the chief events in the Order in elegiac verse, in which the following lines occur :

> Anglicus iste Simon petit a Christi genetrice,
> Præsidium Matris ac Scapulare suum.[9]

The fourth is the testimony of William of Coventry (1348), who, in his *Scutum Carmelitanum*, gives an account substantially the same as that of the Vatican MS.

All these are prior to Grossi, who, in fact, borrows *verbatim* the account of William of Coventry, simply adding to the

---

[7] N. 3813.

[8] "Sanctus vero Simon gloriosam Dei Genitricem jugiter deprecabatur, ut Carmelitarum ordinem speciali insignitum ipsius Virginis titulo, aliquo singulari privilegio communiret, dicens quotidie voce devotissima in suis orationibus, Flos Carmeli, vitis florigera, splendor cœli, Virgo puerpera singularis : Mater mitis, sed viri nescia, Carmelitis da privilegia, stella maris. Beata Maria Virgo cum multitudine Angelorum ipsi B. viro apparuit, Scapulare Ordinis ipsius manibus tenens, et dixit: Hoc erit tibi et cunctis Carmelitis privilegium, in hoc moriens æternum non patietur incendium." (*Speculum Carmelitanum*, pars iii. p. 521.)

[9] Quoted in the *Vinea Carmeli*, p. 560, n. 1,000.

promise, he who dies in this shall not suffer the fire of Hell, the explanatory words, that is, he who dies in this shall be saved (*in hoc moriens salvabitur*).

2. But the vision has a far more reliable warranty than the general belief of the account given of its origin. From the first time that it was brought under the notice of the Holy See, the action of the Popes has been distinctly in favour of the fact of the apparition, and as time went on they have adopted it as their own and professed both implicitly and explicitly their belief and confidence in its reality. The Indulgences and privileges granted to all who belonged to the Sodality of Our Lady of Mount Carmel, were an implicit approval of the foundation on which that Sodality rested, even though no express mention is made of it. To say nothing of John the Twenty-second and Alexander the Fifth (since their Bulls are attacked as forgeries by the *Catholic Dictionary*), Clement the Seventh in the Bull *Ex Clementi* (Aug. 12, 1530, *Bull. Rom.* Clemens VII. n. 38), comfirms the privileges granted by his predecessors. So too does Pius the Fifth in 1566, Gregory the Thirteenth in 1577, and Paul the Fifth in 1606. Now if there grows up in the Catholic world a devotion to some shrine or place of pilgrimage, where countless miracles are reported to occur and favours to be granted to the faithful, and if the Holy Father grants to all who frequent that shrine or visit that place of pilgrimage, rich and large Indulgences, we are justified in attributing to him an approval of it and a recognition of the reality of the facts whence it has had its origin. In the same way, when we find Pope after Pope confirming the privileges granted by their predecessors to all who wear this sacred Scapular, it is impossible to believe that they one and all are taken in by a pious fraud, or support a Confraternity founded on a pure fiction, an imaginary vision blasphemously invented and presumptuously attributed to one whose fame of sanctity gave force to his words and ensured the acceptance of anything narrated by him and written down at his dictation.

But one of the Popes goes beyond a mere implicit approbation. During the Pontificate of Paul the Fifth, the Carmelites asked for the insertion in the Roman Breviary of a clearer and more explicit account of the origin of the Sodality of the Brown Scapular. The matter came before the Congregation of Rites, and Cardinal Bellarmine was instructed by the Pope to draw up a fresh set of Lessons for the second nocturn. The second of these

Lessons speaks with no faltering voice. "The Blessed Virgin not only gave to the Order of Carmel their name and afforded them her protection, but also the badge (*insigne*) of the sacred Scapular, which she bestowed on Blessed Simon the Englishman, that by this heavenly dress this sacred Order might be distinguished and protected from all evils that were gathering round it." The third Lesson goes on to say how the privileges of the Order are extended to all who are received into the Sodality (*Societas*) of the Scapular, and how our Lady comforts in Purgatory and delivers thence those who have fulfilled the conditions imposed upon them during life. This Office was sanctioned by the Pope, and by his authority inserted in the Carmelite Breviary.

3. But there is yet another argument establishing the vision of St. Simon Stock, and one which cannot be rejected by any loyal Catholic. All over the world the Brown Scapular is not only a popular, but an universal devotion. Not only is it dear to the faithful, but their confidence in it is unlimited. They accept it as the gift of Mary. Bishops recommend it to their dioceses,[20] missioners preach it, priests explain it, catechists instruct the children under their care respecting it : one and all they give the same account of it ; one and all they profess and inculcate

---

[20] We cannot refrain from quoting a few words from *The Meaning and Use of the Scapular of our Lady of Mount Carmel*, by the Bishop of Salford (Burns and Oates, price 1d.). "While praying one night to the Blessed Virgin with the greatest devotion and humility, and saluting her as 'the Flower of Carmel, the flowering Vine, the Splendour of Heaven, the Star of the Sea,' and many other titles, St. Simon Stock received a visit from the Blessed Virgin herself, holding in her hand the Carmelite habit, which she offered to him, saying, 'This is the pledge of the privilege granted to thee and to all Carmelites : he who shall piously die wearing this habit shall be preserved from eternal flames.' This happened on the 16th July, 1251 " (pp. 8, 9). "No confraternity has ever received a greater number of approbations from the Sovereign Pontiffs than this of the Scapular. Nineteen Popes have confirmed and approved it by publishing some forty Bulls and Rescripts in its favour. A number of the Popes have been members of the Confraternity. The Benedictines, Franciscans, Dominicans, and Jesuits have been, with the Carmelites, its defenders and propagators. When the devotion was attacked in 1609, Father Aquaviva, the General of the Jesuits, not only defended it, but wished the members of the Society to use and recommend the devotion of the Scapular as one most pleasing to the Blessed Virgin and most useful to the faithful. In this country, where there were over forty houses of White Friars, or Carmelites, before the suppression of the monasteries, there was undoubtedly great devotion to Our Lady of Mount Carmel. Kings and Queens of England and of Scotland (before the apostacy of the sixteenth century), and innumerable multitudes of persons of every condition of life throughout Christendom, have worn and still wear the Scapular. In Ireland it has been the comfort and the joy of the people for centuries, especially during the long night of persecution " (pp. 10, 11). We strongly recommend this little manual to all our readers.

their absolute confidence in its celestial origin ; one and all they confirm by their own experience the truth of the promise made, that none wearing it fails to die well ; one and all bear testimony that the hardened sinner, sooner or later, loses or throws off his scapular. *Securus judicat orbis terrarum.* In spite of the attacks made upon it by Gallicans and other enemies of the Holy See, in spite of the insinuations of the *Catholic Dictionary*, this absolute reliance remains, and will ever remain, ineradicably fixed in the hearts of the faithful children of Holy Church. What the *Ecclesia docens* teaches in every country and every age, what the *Ecclesia discens* accepts and approves, what Catholic instinct, the unfailing touchstone of truth in things spiritual, pronounces to be in accordance with the ways of God's Providence, and what an ever increasing experience confirms and ratifies, cannot be rejected without the greatest peril, except where invincible ignorance excuses.

4. We have only one fact more to clench our argument. We do not cast it in the teeth of the authors of the *Catholic Dictionary*, since we believe they wrote before it was known to them. Among the Offices lately granted to England by our Holy Father Pope Leo the Thirteenth, is the Office of St. Simon Stock. On the 16th of May, Mass is said in his honour in every church in England and his Office recited by every priest throughout the country. The Collect of the Mass and the Lessons for the Office have the sanction and approval of the reigning Pope. Now, if ever there was a Ruler of the Church whose wise and prudent moderation was slow to admit into official records anything to which objection could be taken, it is he who now sits in Peter's Chair. If ever there was an earnest advocate of a thorough and searching historical criticism, it is our present Pontiff. Even non-Catholics admit his astonishing prudence, his well-balanced judgment, his scholar-like discrimi-nation, his instinct for historical truth. Already he has given orders for changes in certain Lessons of the Breviary, because the statements made therein were not certain matters of fact. The whole tendency under his Pontificate is to an ever increasing accuracy of historical criticism. We do not say that the Pope makes himself responsible for every statement of fact in a new lesson, but we do say that overwhelming evidence is required to justify the rejection of what is recommended to the faithful with this authority. Now the new Collect for the feast of St. Simon is distinct enough ; the Third Lesson of the Second

324   *The Catholic Dictionary.*

Nocturn of his Office is more distinct still. The Collect is as follows :

> May Thy people, O Lord, dedicated to Thee and Thy Virgin Mother, rejoice in the solemnity of the blessed Simon : and as through him they have obtained a mark of so great protection, so may they attain the gifts of eternal predestination. Through Jesus Christ our Lord, &c.

The words of the Lesson are these :

> As he [Simon] was praying, the Blessed Virgin, to distinguish his Order, which rejoiced in bearing her sacred name, from the rest by some special privilege, she herself appeared to him, accompanied by a multitude of angels, holding in her hand the Scapular of the Order, and saying, " This shall be for thee a sign, and for all the Carmelites a special privilege, that he who devoutly dies in this shall not suffer eternal burning."

To sum up. The historical evidence we have adduced is sufficient, and more than sufficient, to establish the authenticity of the story of our Lady's appearance and promise to St. Simon Stock. Its general reception all over the Catholic world, its promulgation by the *Ecclesia docens*, its acceptance by the *Ecclesia discens*, is also proof enough of the supernatural origin of the Scapular. The repeated approbation of Popes and Roman Congregations, and finally the official insertion of the story in the Breviary, would leave no doubt about the matter even if other proof were not forthcoming. On the other hand, the account given of the Scapular by the *Catholic Dictionary* is based on a malicious, scandalous work, condemned by Rome, the author of which was a dangerous, scurrilous, and disloyal character. It abounds with inaccuracies (to give these statements a gentle name), and displays an animus derogatory to the dignity of the Holy Mother of God and insulting to the venerable Order of the Carmelites. It is a blot upon the pages of the *Catholic Dictionary*. The excellence of the work in other respects makes us hope that its authors will speedily disown this unfortunate production, and remove from their pages an article which is likely to be very mischievous to the ignorant and ill-informed, and to disgust all well-informed and loyal Catholics, all faithful servants of Mary and honest lovers of Truth.

R. F. CLARKE.

THE MONTH

A Catholic Magazine and Review.

Per menses singulos reddens fructum suum,
et folia ligni ad sanitatem gentium.
(*Apoc.* xxii. 2.)

VOL. LVIII.

SEPTEMBER—DECEMBER.

1886.

LONDON:

OFFICE OF THE MONTH, 48, SOUTH ST., GROSVENOR SQ.

LONDON: BURNS & OATES.   DUBLIN: M. H. GILL & SON.

AGENTS FOR AMERICA: MESSRS. JOHN MURPHY AND CO., BALTIMORE.

THE MONTH.

The Catholic Dictionary and the Sabbatine Indulgence.

THE Scapular of our Lady of Mount Carmel is regarded by Catholics in general as carrying with it two extraordinary privileges. They believe that all who devoutly wear it at the moment of their death will not be allowed to fall into the flames of Hell, and they also ascribe to it the character of a pledge of the deliverance from the flames of Purgatory, by our Lady's mediation, on the Saturday next after their death, of all who not only wear it devoutly, but also practise continually and without fail certain other prescribed devotions. Of the first of these privileges we spoke in our last article. We pointed out that the gift of eternal salvation made to all who wear the Scapular at their death, is based on an authentic apparition of our Blessed Lady to St. Simon Stock, and we gave the proofs establishing its authenticity and justifying our perfect confidence in the promise made to the Saint. The second of these privileges will occupy us in our present article. It is known generally by the name of the Sabbatine Indulgence. It is a plenary and perfect Indulgence and remission of all punishment due to sin, available on the first Saturday after the death of him who gains it, releasing him then and there from Purgatory and admitting him straightway to the joys of Heaven. This privilege, like the former, appeals to our Lady's own promise, made however, not to St. Simon Stock or any of his Order, but to Pope John the Twenty-second. This Pope, in a Bull issued in 1322, and addressed to the Carmelite Order, relates the vision he had seen and proclaims the Indulgence which our Lady committed to his hands for the benefit of her children.

On the authenticity of this Bull depend the hopes of all those who have laboured to gain the Sabbatine Indulgence. The *Catholic Dictionary* declares it to be a clumsy forgery. If this is so, the sooner the imposture is dragged to the light the better. It would be a cruel thing to encourage the pious children of the Church to place their confidence in a document which is the forged invention of some designing knave, and to assure the dying client of our Lady of Mount Carmel that his Patroness would, ere one or two short days had passed, come to his relief amid his sufferings and set him free from his place of banishment, when all the time no such assurance was given, no such deliverance is to be hoped for.   Surely it were inexcusable for those who could have prevented it to allow the deceit to continue.; surely it were more inexcusable still for those who must have been conscious of the fraud to repeat and repeat again the fallacious promise, trusting to the silence of the voiceless dead not to betray the cruel deception practised upon them ; surely it were most inexcusable of all to encourage the Christian world to ascribe to the Vicar of Jesus Christ so important a pledge and promise, when all the time it was fabricated by some unscrupulous forger.

This, however, is what the writer in the *Catholic Dictionary* would have us believe has been the history of the Sabbatine Indulgence.   Yet he cannot deny its general acceptance as true all over the world. Insolent and clumsy forgery as it is shown to be, on abundant and superabundant grounds, by the wonderful learning of M. Launoy, condemned even by a Jesuit critic as at least worthy of grave suspicion, it is nevertheless, strange to say, more firmly rooted now than ever in the hearts of the faithful. It is reproduced in every manual of our Lady of Mount Carmel, and none says a word against it ; it is preached from a thousand Christian pulpits, and none challenges its truth ; it is set forth as authentic in the writings of saints and theologians, and no warning voice declares the heartless fraud.   It is a source of hope and consolation to every son and daughter of Carmel, but no authoritative utterance reveals that the hope it imparts is vain and the consolation grounded upon it is a thing of nought.   The Roman authorities, so far from an indignant condemnation of the Bull, have actually put upon the Index the work in which it is depicted in its true character.   The Carmelites, instead of protesting against the unscrupulous fraud, have with continually increasing joy and exultation seen it accepted more and more widely, as time went on, for a genuine pronouncement of the Vicar of Jesus Christ.   In spite of advancing criticism, in spite of the historical spirit, in spite of the onslaught alike of Gallican doctor and Jesuit historian, and even of Benedict the Fourteenth himself, the Sabbatine Bull is still received as genuine, and the Sabbatine Indulgence still regarded as worthy of all confidence.

We shall pursue the same plan in our present article as in the last. First of all we shall say a few words on the theology of the subject, then we shall examine the character of the statements made respecting the Bull in the *Catholic Dictionary*, and we shall then look at the question on its own merits and see what opinion we ought to hold respecting it, apart from any statement or mis-statement by which the writer may have prejudiced our judgment.

First of all it is important clearly to understand what was the promise made, and what the nature of the Indulgence called Sabbatine. We cannot do better here than quote the account in the *Catholic Dictionary* of the supposed origin of the Indulgence and the conditions necessary for gaining it. It is substantially correct, introduced though the vision is as a "marvel," and a marvel which, as we shall presently see, turns out in the opinion of the author of the article in the *Catholic Dictionary* to be an arrant imposture.

Another marvel is related by John the Twenty-second in the famous Sabbatine Bull. The Blessed Virgin, he says, appeared to him, and, speaking of the Carmelites and those associated to them by wearing the scapular, promised that, if any of them went to Purgatory, she herself would descend and free them on the Saturday following their death. "This holy Indulgence," says the Pope, "I accept, corroborate, and confirm, as Jesus Christ for the merits of the glorious Virgin Mary granted it in heaven." To gain this privilege it is necessary to observe fidelity in marriage or chastity in the single state. Those who read must recite the Office of the Blessed Virgin, unless already bound to the Divine Office; those who cannot, must abstain from flesh meat on Wednesdays and Saturdays, unless Christmas falls on one of these days. So the Sabbatine Bull, as given in the Carmelite "Bullarium."

The only objection that might be made on theological grounds to the promise made in this Bull, is on the ground of its almost extravagant generosity. The conditions seem so easy and the privileges so magnificent. We read of those who are condemned for long years, and decades, and even centuries, to the purgatorial fire, nay, of some who will deem themselves very happy to escape therefrom on the very day of the final Judgment. The Church, by sanctioning the foundation of anniversary Masses to perpetuity, leads us to believe that long indeed will be the sufferings of some who nevertheless in the end will see the face of God for ever in perfect bliss. How then is it possible that by so simple a condition as the daily recital of our Lady's

Office, this protracted term of agonizing punishment should be reduced to a matter of some six or seven days at most ? Does it not seem to lessen our sense of the heinous nature of sin and our dread of its awful consequences, if they can be evaded on such easy terms as these ?

This question is the more interesting because it is one which introduces to us the varied difficulties raised against Indulgences and indulgenced prayers. Without attempting to enter on this wider field, which has indeed been so often traversed by theologians, we may nevertheless do well to point out how futile is the objection in this particular case. The first rejoinder which suggests itself is the counter-question : Are the conditions laid down so easy of fulfilment ? Is the observance of chastity so easy a matter, whether it be in the single or the married state ? We must remember that it includes not merely words and actions, but thoughts as well. A single unchaste thought deliberately indulged, even though it be but one in the course of long years, forfeits the claim to this prompt deliverance. Is the external condition one which can be fulfilled without any hardship or self-denial ? The recital of our Lady's Office is easy enough now and again, just once or twice, at such times and on such days as may be selected without inconvenience, and when superabundant leisure leaves many an hour unoccupied. But to persevere in the constant recital day by day for long years, never to omit the self-imposed task whether at home or abroad, in days of recreation or times of continual labour, to perform it faithfully in spite of weariness and the tedium which in the course of time arises to deter ordinary men from the oft-repeated words—all this requires a courage and a patience amounting almost to heroism.

But however easy the conditions (and here it is that we touch once more on the difficulty attaching to all Indulgences), there is one most valuable and practical lesson that such a promise as this teaches—a double lesson bringing out two facts of the Divine government that all men are prone to overlook. The first of these is the desire on the part of Almighty God to substitute mercy for justice, if only men will give Him the least opportunity or excuse for doing so. In all the most terrible of His judgments He seems to act reluctantly. He gives fresh chances to the unrepentant sinner, waits to see whether he will not turn from his evil way, entreats him not to compel Him to pour out the vials of His wrath and to execute the terrors of

His judgment—forgives him fully and freely, and receives him back to His favour, if there be present in his soul the faintest spark of supernatural love and true contrition. Much more is this the case with those who are inexpressibly dear to the Sacred Heart of our Lord, and whom He has predestined to be with Him for ever in Heaven, who are united to Him by the bonds of charity, and are glorious and beautiful in His sight. How reluctantly (to speak in human fashion) does He leave them to suffer in the purgatorial flames of Divine justice! How many a chance He has given them in life to pay off the heavy debt on the easiest possible terms, if only they would have accepted it! How He sorrows (if God could sorrow) that they must, in accordance with the irrefragable law of justice, work off that penalty that their sins have merited! How He rejoices to find some excuse for admitting them without delay to Paradise! It is this wonderful preference for mercy over justice that shines forth in the Sabbatine Indulgence. Through the hands of our Lady, the Mother of Mercy, He extends to all who have worn until their death her sacred Scapular, and fulfilled the conditions imposed, a perfect remission of all the punishment which would have been their lot had not their loyalty and perseverance earned for them this speedy entrance into the joy of their Lord.

The other practical piece of theology involved in the Sabbatine Indulgence is the comparative facility with which sin may be atoned for in this life, as compared with the penalty to be paid when life is over, even by those who have no serious sin upon their conscience. Even if the conditions required are not so simple as may at first sight appear, yet how light and easy as compared with the conditions of long and patient endurance of the purgatorial fire and of the loss of God. If St. Paul tells us that the sufferings of this life are not worthy to be compared to the glory that is to be revealed in us, we may supplement his words by saying that they are not worthy to be compared with the agony of the sufferings of Purgatory. But to gain the Sabbatine Indulgence there is no question of suffering at all, except so far as theologians tell us that prayer is a "penal" work; all that is required is that the law of God be observed, and in honour of our Lady her Office read. To recite this Office day by day ought to be regarded as a pleasure and privilege by the devout client of Mary. So small a gift to God, and so incomparably generous a reward! So trifling, so minute a sacrifice of inclination and ease, and as recompense, or rather as one of the many recompenses granted in return by the liberality of God, the forgiveness of a debt for which justice would have required long years of tribulation and separation from God in the house of darkness and the cleansing fire !

We must however proceed to our task of rejoinder to the writer in the *Catholic Dictionary*. It is not on intrinsic grounds that he attacks the Sabbatine Indulgence. He does not lay to its charge any false theology or danger to faith or morals. It may be perfectly orthodox or excellent in its encouragement to Catholic piety. But all this counts for nothing if it has no foundation in fact. If the alleged Bull of John the Twenty-second was never issued by him at all, if our Lady never appeared to him and made no such promise as is asserted, if the whole story is an invention, then it is useless to talk of the generosity of God which this Indulgence manifests to men, or of the practical benefit it confers on those who seek to avail themselves of it. The point at issue really is the evidence for our Lady's promise having been really made. Everything turns on this, and it is here that the contention lies between the writer in the *Catholic Dictionary* and ourselves. We will first quote his words, and then discuss them in detail.

He tells us that there are two statements to be examined.

1. Is there any proof that the Blessed Virgin appeared to St. Simon Stock and made the promise related above ?

2. Is the Sabbatine Bull genuine, and the story it tells true ?

He then continues—

We take the latter question first because it may be despatched very quickly. Launoy, in a dissertation of wonderful learning, to be found in the second volume of his collected works (the edition we have used is dated 1731, " Coloniæ Allobrogum "), proves by a superabundance of reasons that the Bull of John the Twenty-Second is a clumsy forgery, and that of Alexander the Fifth another forgery made to cover the former. The autograph has never been found, nor has it any place in the Roman " Bullarium." Its authenticity is unhesitatingly denied by the great Bollandist Papebroch in his reply to the attacks made upon him by the Carmelites and by Benedict the Fourteenth (" De Fest." lxxiv. lxxvii.). The latter says it is as hard, perhaps harder, to believe in this Bull than in the story of the chapel built on Mount Carmel in honour of the Blessed Virgin during her life. He says he could give more reasons against it than he cares to produce, and arguments drawn " from things [in the Bull] which want all appearance of truth." He alludes, we suppose, to the style of the Bull, which, as Launoy points out, betrays in many ways the hand of the impostor. (*Catholic Dictionary*, art. Scapular.)

All this sounds very formidable, and is put in so clear and convincing a way, that the unsophisticated reader can scarcely fail to be at least shaken in his confidence in the Sabbatine Bull and the Indulgence therein promised. There is a superabundance of reasons for distrusting it. These reasons prove it to be a forgery, and may be found in a dissertation proceeding from the pen, not of some shallow assailant of the Church, but of a Doctor of Paris and a man of wonderful learning. This so called Papal Bull is not to be found in the official collection which alone contains the genuine utterances of the Roman Pontiffs. The great Jesuit historian and editor of the *Acta Sanctorum*, assailed by the Carmelites, unhesitatingly pronounces it to be an imposture. Benedict the Fourteenth, the great Canonist, who himself sat on St. Peter's Chair, rejects it as a pure fiction, and, by way of expressing his incredulity, says it is as hard or harder to believe than the wonderful story of a chapel built on Mount Carmel to our Blessed Lady during her lifetime. Like the great Launoy, he has a superabundance of proofs of the Bull being unauthentic, so many that he does not care to produce them all —proofs extrinsic and proofs intrinsic, among the latter the absence not merely of all truth but of all appearance of truth in the contents of the Bull, by which he means that the style of the Bull clearly indicates the hand of the unscrupulous forger.

Now who would believe that from first to last there is scarcely a statement in the paragraph that we have just quoted and then paraphrased which is in accordance with fact, save the loss of the original copy of the Bull and its consequent absence from the *Bullarium Romanum*, a fact which, as we shall see presently, is not difficult to be explained ? The writer ascribes to Benedict the Fourteenth what he never said—nay, he gives clear signs of never having read what he wrote on the subject. Benedict the Fourteenth does *not* deny the authenticity of the Bull at all. He does *not* say that he could bring more reasons against it than he cares to produce, or imply that its style betrays the impostor. He does *not* compare the apparition to John the Twenty-second with the tradition of the chapel on Mount Carmel in order to show that the former is unworthy of belief.

But we must prove our points one by one. We spoke in our last article of M. Launoy's character, and a further investigation of his works does not improve his reputation. He is one of those industrious men who have acquired a large store of historical erudition, but unfortunately employs that erudition on the wrong side. He seems to delight in building up a series of plausible objections to all the pious beliefs which, though they do not come within the sacred circle of dogmatic facts, are nevertheless so closely united with these, or are so generally accepted by the faithful, or have such solid evidence in their favour, that to attack them is at least a just cause of offence to pious ears. The fact that his works are, to the amount of twenty-one several dissertations, on the *Index*, shows the man's character, and the necessity of receiving his statements with caution, and with greater caution still every conclusion he draws from his real or alleged facts. In the treatise in which he discusses the Brown Scapular, and which is one of those selected for condemnation, he accumulates seventeen different reasons why the Sabbatine Indulgence is to be rejected. To go through these and answer them one by one would be a most wearisome and unprofitable task. They are most of them utterly trivial, and even where they have some plausibility, they invariably rest not on a certain but on a probable argument. The writer in the *Catholic Dictionary* would have us accept them wholesale, and assures us that M. Launoy proves by a superabundance of reasons that the Bull is a clumsy forgery. The only answer we need make to this sweeping and unfounded statement is the counter statement that M. Launoy proves nothing of the kind, and we appeal to any of our readers who may be sceptical on the subject to examine for himself the arguments of the Gallican Doctor. We invite him to weigh in the balance of impartial logic the abundance and superabundance of elaborate arguments which M. Launoy piles up, in the hope that the mere accumulation of reasons adduced may by sheer force of quantity turn the scale against the Bull he is attacking. Not that they have any sort of claim upon us, inasmuch as we are answering the *Catholic Dictionary*, and the writer in the *Catholic Dictionary* does not produce any of them. *Quod gratis asseritur gratis negatur.* If I am told that a learned man proves a point against me by a superabundance of proof, I am justified in refusing to be moved by the bold assertion if none of these superabundant proofs are adduced. If I find that the learned man is a very suspicious character, it is scarcely worth while wasting my time on his arguments.

But the writer in the *Catholic Dictionary* confronts us with an adversary of a very different calibre from M. Launoy. No less an authority than Benedict the Fourteenth is brought forward as the adversary of the Sabbatine Bull. If this were really the case, we allow that it would indeed be a severe, if not a fatal, blow to our cause. To so distinguished a Canonist we listen with profound respect. His every word carries the greatest weight. Even though he had not the same evidence in favour of the Sabbatine Indulgence that we have now, yet his judgment, his learning, his experience, his instinctive power of discerning the true from the false, would make us hesitate before we should presume to differ from one over whose words his subsequent elevation to St. Peter's Chair throws a shadow of Pontifical authority.

Now three different assertions are attributed to Benedict the Fourteenth, respecting the Sabbatine Bull of John the Twenty-second. Happily for the honour of the Sabbatine Bull, un-happily for the credit of the *Catholic Dictionary*, all these are directly at variance with what Benedict the Fourteenth says. We will quote them one by one and compare them with the original.

(1) The authenticity of the Bull is unhesitatingly denied by Benedict the Fourteenth.

We are sorry to have directly to contradict the writer in the *Catholic Dictionary*, but what is here stated is distinctly the reverse of the fact. Benedict the Fourteenth gives the opinions in favour of and against the Bull with most judicial impartiality ; he himself pronounces no distinct opinion whatever. Nowhere does he unhesitatingly reject it, or reject it at all. We cannot prove our assertion by quotation, because detached phrases and sentences prove little or nothing, but from first to last there is not a single word in the dissertation of Benedict the Fourteenth condemnatory of the Bull. We invite our readers to read carefully through the discussion,[1] and they will be able to judge for themselves.

(2) The latter [Benedict the Fourteenth] says it is as hard, perhaps harder, to believe in this Bull than in the story of the chapel built on Mount Carmel in honour of the Blessed Virgin during her life.

This quotation is perfectly correct as far as the words quoted are concerned. At the same time it is utterly misleading in the impression it necessarily leaves on the mind of the reader. Half the sentence is omitted which completely reverses the

[1] *De Festis B.M.V.* II. vi. pp. 267, seq. Prati, 1843.

drift of the whole.   The natural inference from the above words is the exact opposite of that which follows from the argument of Benedict the Fourteenth.   If the words in the *Catholic Dictionary* mean anything at all, they mean that the story of the chapel is incredible, and the authenticity of the Sabbatine Bull more incredible still.   Now Benedict the Fourteenth says the very opposite.   He argues from the credibility of the Sabbatine Bull to the credibility of the story of the chapel. He classes together (and here the omission in the *Catholic Dictionary* is most unfair), in the same sentence, and as being on a similar footing of credibility, the vision of St. Simon Stock and the Bull of John the Twenty-second, and from the greater difficulties which attach to them, credible though they are, he leaves the reader to infer that the lesser difficulties attaching to the story of the chapel are not necessarily fatal to its truth. He has already given the arguments *pro* and *con* in the matter of the chapel on Mount Carmel, and has declined to throw in his lot either with its assailants or its defenders.   He tells us that its existence may be described as an object of pious belief, and adduces the lessons in the Roman Breviary, in which it is mentioned with the qualifying clause, "as is said" (*ut fertur*). He regards its existence as credible, not as certainly established, and he then passes on to the vision to St. Simon Stock and the Sabbatine Bull, with the remark that they involve, if not a greater, at least an equal difficulty with the story of the chapel built on Mount Carmel.   Now, as he subsequently pronounces the vision of our Lady to St. Simon Stock to be true, and expresses it as his opinion that all the faithful ought to regard it as true, and in the same breath mentions the Sabbatine Bull as sharing with the vision to Simon difficulties greater than those which surround the chapel on Carmel, what would be more utterly misleading than to adduce his words as unfavourable to the authenticity of the Bull?

(3) He [Benedict the Fourteenth] says that he could give more reasons against the Bull than he cares to produce, and arguments drawn "from things (in the Bull) which want all appearance of truth." He alludes, we suppose, to the style of the Bull, which, as Launoy points out, betrays in many ways the hand of the impostor.

We will translate as literally as possible the passage on which the above sentence is based.   It is not easy to see the precise meaning of one expression contained in it; at all events we have read it and re-read it without being able to come to any definite conclusion. This, however, we can assert, that whatever be its exact meaning, it does *not* mean what the writer in the *Catholic Dictionary* asserts. Benedict the Fourteenth's words are as follows :

But now after examining the Vision (to St. Simon Stock), we ought to have weighed the Bull of John the Twenty-second, which is called the Sabbatine Bull, because the Blessed Virgin promised that she would free from the fire of Purgatory, on the first Saturday after their death, all who have faithfully practised the Carmelite devotion to Mary. We touched on this subject above. But much more would have had to be brought forward if we thought it of advantage to collect, for the purpose of tearing its authority to pieces, all those arguments which can be drawn from certain circumstances which are destitute of all probability (*omni verisimilitudine carentibus*), as for instance, that the original copy of it has never been found, and that this Bull has never been approved by the Roman Pontiffs *in forma specifica*, and only, as the common expression is, *in forma communi*. It is enough to remark that the quarrels respecting this Bull were cut short by the wise decree of Paul the Fifth, which even Launoy approved and praised.[2]

There is nothing in all this, about " more reasons against the Bull than he cares to produce," nothing to imply that Benedict the Fourteenth has at his disposal "arguments drawn from things (in the Bull) which want all appearance of truth." What he really says is that he would have to bring forward a number of other points, if he thought it conduced to truth to quote all the arguments based on improbabilities. His attitude to these arguments is not that they are a reserve which he could employ against the Bull if it were not sufficiently shown to be unauthentic, but that they are arguments from probability which are not worth adducing in a cause where the Holy See has imposed silence on the disputants, and where

[2] " Nunc vero post Visionis examen expendenda esset Bulla Joannis XXII. quæ ideo Sabbathina appellatur, quod B. Virgo pollicita sit, se quotquot Carmelitano Mariæ cultui addicti fuerint, primo post eorum obitum Sabbatho a Purgatorii igne erepturam. Nonnihil de ea superius attigimus. Multo tamen plura essent afferenda, si nobis videretur conducibile, ad ejus auctoritatem convellendam, omnia ea, quæ ex quibusdam rebus omni verisimilitudine carentibus prodeunt, huc conferre argumenta ; cujusmodi sunt illa, quod nunquam ejus repertum sit autographum ; et nunquam *in forma specifica*, nec nisi, ut vulgo dicitur, *in forma communi* a Romanis Pontificibus ea Bulla approbata sit. Satis fuerit illud admonere, coortas in Lusitania de ea Bulla contentiones, et inde ad totum, Christianum Orbem diffusas, quarum historiam tradidit Paulus ab Omnibus Sanctis *in Clavi Aurea* part. 2. cap. 15. sapientissimo Decreto tandem diremisse Paulum V. Pontificem, quod vel ipse probavit collauda-vitque Launojus " (Bened. XIV. *De Festis*, p. 270).

he himself has no intention of expressing an opinion. The ingenious twist given to his words in the *Catholic Dictionary* makes them at variance with the position which Benedict the Fourteenth takes up throughout the discussion.

In the same way, the words, "in the Bull," which are slipped in in a parenthesis, completely change the meaning of what Benedict the Fourteenth says. They imply that the Bull contains things manifestly untrue. The things alluded to by the Pontiff are things external to the Bull. So far from alluding to the *style* of the Bull, as the writer in the *Catholic Dictionary* would have us suppose, he gives two instances—the form in which the Bull has been subsequently approved (to this we shall allude presently), and the loss of the original copy of it. Both of these are extrinsic arguments, and have nothing to do with anything in the Bull.

So far for Benedict the Fourteenth. We now come to the final authority quoted against the Bull.

Its authenticity is unhesitatingly denied by the great Bollandist Papebroch in his reply to the attacks made upon him by the Carmelites.

Although it is true that the opinion of Father Papebroch is adverse to the Bull, yet it is too much to say that he "unhesitatingiy denies" its authenticity. Our writer does not seem, to judge from the article in the *Dictionary*, to have read Father Papebroch's Dissertation. In the list of the authorities given at the end of the article as the sources whence it has been compiled, there is no mention of it. Father Papebroch brings forward arguments in abundance which seem to him to make against the authenticity of the Bull. In some passages he speaks very strongly respecting it; yet in the end all that he says respecting it is that he regards it *with suspicion*,[3] and that he considers that there is a *moral* certainty against it,[4] and that he agrees with Launoy that it *seems* to be fictitious.

In weighing the authority of Father Papebroch, and deciding how far it is conclusive against the Bull, we have to remember the position of the editors of the *Acta Sanctorum*. The *Acta Sanctorum* owe their universal acceptance and undisputed authority to the elaborate care with which their authors have excluded everything which could not at the

---

[3] "Suspecta est mihi" (*Bull. Sabbatina Papebroch Resp.* p. 291).

[4] "Non vacat mihi nunc deducere minutim argumenta quibus suppositionem moraliter certam ostendere non sit difficile " (*Ibid.* p. 289).

time they wrote stand the severest test of historical criticism. They entered on their task in a spirit of official scepticism which, painful as it sometimes is to the affectionate devotion which clings to some pious and cherished tradition, furnishes nevertheless the strength of their position, and ensures to him who relies upon their authority a security that would have been wanting if a single fable or doubtful story had been admitted without note or comment into their volumes. They determined to come before the world, ready to challenge it on its own grounds, and to invite the most searching inquiry into their every statement. The end at which they aimed, and which every year that passes pronounces them to have been successful in attaining, was to present lives of the saints absolutely trustworthy, and requiring on the part of the reader no further research into original authorities to know whether the statements made could be absolutely relied upon or not.

Under these circumstances and with this end in view, they very rightly rejected any document for which proof positive was not forthcoming, or in which they discerned any suspicious signs of weakness. Such signs Father Papebroch detected in the Sabbatine Bull, and therefore he very rightly refused to admit it as authentic.

All through the Dissertation he is apologetic and on the defensive. He is justifying himself for his incredulity, and he does not appear to regard the evidence as perfectly and finally conclusive. In this, as in all else, there is a very marked contrast between the Bollandist and the Gallican Doctor. Launoy is so obscure as in some passages to be quite unintelligible. His wonderful learning seems to make him muddleheaded. He brings forward reasons that are no reasons at all, and in place of open argument substitutes personal attacks on his opponents. There is an unmistakeable animus in all that he writes. Father Papebroch is beautifully clear in style, and writes in a dispassionate spirit of impartial historical criticism. He knows perfectly well what he means, and says it in a way that makes it quite plain to his readers. There is nothing personal in his method of attack, and he abounds in apologies for the attitude he is bound to assume. Every argument carries weight, and if we do not agree with his conclusion, it is only because we have the advantage of subsequent experience. If Father Papebroch had lived in the present day, we feel sure he would have been among the first to admit the authenticity of the Bull in spite of the many apparent reasons existing against it. If M. Launoy had lived in the present day, we cannot feel the same confidence that he would have thrown in his lot with the consentient voice of the Catholic world.

We will allow that certainly there did exist in the seventeenth century evidence which might seem to outweigh the *a priori* improbabilities of its being forged, and that Papebroch had reason for regarding it with suspicion. But to grant as true in the seventeenth century all this is very different from granting the possibility of its being true in the present day. The two centuries that have passed have changed the whole aspect of the question. What a critic a hundred and fifty or two hundred years ago was justified in admitting, as at least the more probable hypothesis, has now been placed in a very different position. Time has tried the Sabbatine Bull. The instinct of the Catholic world has declared itself in its favour. The calm judgment that was impossible when the storm was raging is possible now, and the calm judgment of the faithful at large has been such that the arguments once urged against the Bull have lost their value now. They are swept away by the stream of continuous approval of Popes and Bishops, saints and theologians, from that day to this.

But our task would not be complete unless we gave our reasons for regarding the arguments of Father Papebroch as inconclusive in the present day. We do not say that the authenticity of the Sabbatine Bull is even now regarded by learned men as absolutely beyond all doubt. We have heard it questioned by those whose authority on such subjects was great, and there are some who altogether refuse to accept it. If we ourselves thoroughly believe it to be what it professes to be, we are but stating our own conviction, and we leave it to our readers to judge for themselves whether the arguments we adduce in its favour are sufficient, and our explanation of the difficulties connected with it satisfactory. We should be sorry to thrust down the throats of our readers a matter of opinion as if it were a certain fact. What we complain of in the *Catholic Dictionary* is not that it pronounces a judgment unfavourable to the Bull, but that it misquotes and misrepresents the great authority whom it adduces in support of its own view. We have done with our charges against it, and are now dealing with the general question. We are anxious to remove any suspicion that might still linger in the minds of our readers that there still remain unanswerable difficulties in the absence of the autograph of the Bull, in its absence from the *Romanum Bullarium*, and in the strange awkwardness of its style. These are facts which are undeniable, and facts which need explanation. Perhaps the best course we can pursue is to give what appears to us the most natural hypothesis respecting the origin and history of the Bull, the one which without any violence falls in with the established facts, and at the same time removes all the difficulties which Father Papebroch puts forward.

The vision of our Blessed Lady to John the Twenty-second took place at Avignon in the year 1322. She appeared to him while he was kneeling in prayer, and promised that all who enter the holy Order of Carmel, or are affiliated to it, shall on the day of their reception be freed from a third part of all their sins, and if they persevere in it till death, observing faithfully the obligations of their state in life, and reciting daily the Canonical Hours prescribed by rule, that she will descend on the Saturday after their death and free all those whom she shall find in Purgatory, and bring them to the Sacred Mount of eternal life.

The new privilege thus conferred upon the Carmelite Order was one which the Pontiff would, as a matter of course, communicate in the first instance to those to whom it immediately concerned. To the Carmelite Fathers at Avignon we naturally suppose that John the Twenty-second detailed the wondrous vision. To them he would entrust the task of committing it to writing. To them by word of mouth he would tell the story and the commands of our Lady that he was instructed to impart. It would be their privilege to draw up the required document and present it to the Holy Father for his approval. It would be to them that would belong the grateful work of framing the Bull in which he told the story, and in his capacity of Supreme Pontiff granted the Indulgence which he alone could officially bestow, and confirmed the privileges which came from our Lady through him. This would account for the style of the Bull—for its simplicity and ruggedness, nay, for its awkward Latinity and ungrammatical construction. We are quite ready to allow that the Pope did not himself write a word of it save his signature and possibly the concluding sentence. If it were necessarily the work of the Pope himself, or had been drawn up in the accustomed manner by the officials of the Congregation of Indulgences, it would be indeed impossible to explain its extra-

488   *The Catholic Dictionary*

ordinary clumsiness and its solecisms, and we should be inclined to throw in our lot with Father Papebroch, and agree with his opinion that it could not possibly be genuine.

This document, having received the signature of Pope John the Twenty-second would then pass into the hands of the Carmelite Fathers. The local authorities would, as a matter of course, communicate it to the Father General of the Order, who at this time was resident in England.[5] To England, therefore, the Bull would be forwarded, to be deposited in the archives. What became of the original copy of it we do not know. The probability is that it perished, along with countless other documents treasured up by the Religious Orders, at the hands of the sacrilegious barbarians who pillaged the various convents and monasteries in the reign of Henry the Eighth.

It was many years before the Bull became generally known. It was not promulgated till it was written many years after, and this it is which seems to the adversaries of the Bull so inexplicable. But it appears to us a wise economy not to proclaim at once to all the world the extraordinary privilege conferred. The Order had many enemies, who would take occasion to malign them. It is not the habit of Religious Orders to publish their privileges on the housetops. When Leo the Thirteenth lately confirmed and renewed the privileges of the Society of Jesus, they kept to themselves all knowledge of this signal mark of His Holiness' love. It was only through others that it became known at all. Six hundred years ago men were more careful than they are now, and exercised greater reserve and caution. Perhaps the Pope had entrusted to the Fathers his desire that they should be very prudent in their use of the Bull. Perhaps it was decided in the councils of the leading authorities of the Order that for a time it would be better to exercise the economy which has been so frequent a shield against those who are jealous of the privileges of the favoured servants of God, and who delight to trample under foot the precious jewels that God vouchsafes to bestow upon His saints out of the treasure-house of Heaven. Whatever the cause, it is perfectly true that we hear nothing of this Bull of John the Twenty-second till many years

---

[5] From the time of St. Simon Stock the archives of the Carmelite Order were in London. Several Carmelite writers, speaking of various Papal Bulls affecting their Order, use the expression, *Hunc bullam vidi in Conventu Carmelitarum Londini* (*Spec. Carm.* iii. 512).

after. The Carmelite authors pass it over in silence, and it is not until nearly a century later that it makes its appearance in various convents of Italy and Sicily. In fact, it seems likely that it remained buried in the Carmelite archives until the original copy of it had been presented to Alexander the Fifth in the year 1409, and confirmed by him in that second Bull, which the opponents of the Sabbatine Indulgence are compelled to declare, to be in common with that of John the Twenty-second, a clumsy forgery. The necessity of supposing a double forgery is a very weak point in the cause of those who impugn the Bull. To suppose one forgery in or about the year 1322, and another eighty-seven years after with the view of rehabilitating the former is at least a rather improbable supposition. If both were forged together in the time of Alexander the Fifth, it was rather a roundabout and elaborate proceeding to forge one document which was supposed to be eighty-four years old, and then to forge another declaring the former genuine, and testifying to its having been subject to the personal inspection of the Pope who issued the second. Besides, we can scarcely avoid attributing the forgery to some member of the Order in whose favour the document was issued, and what could be more utterly improbable, more insulting to a great Religious Order than to suppose that there was an organized conspiracy among them to execute a shameless forgery and impose it on the Christian world as the work of the Vicar of Jesus Christ?

Such are a few of the difficulties which surround the hypothesis of forgery. They are far greater than those which have to be met by those who accept the Bull as genuine. They seem to us in themselves to turn the balance in its favour. But we have in addition strong positive evidence in favour of its being genuine. We have no doubt that to what we are about to adduce a great deal more might be added, but we think there is at least enough to convince our readers that they may accept the Bull with greatest confidence.

1. Our first argument is one which we take out of the very mouths of our opponents. The strange irregularities of style and expression that pervade the Bull, instead of being any proof of its being a forgery, are a strong argument that it is genuine. What forger would be such an idiot as to go out of his way to depart from the general style of the Roman *Bullarium?* It is true he might be weak in his Latin, and in

spite of his anxiety to be accurate, might be guilty of uncon-
scious solecisms, though even here it is morally impossible that,
on the hypothesis of the opponents of the Bull that the
document was forged, the forgers should be so foolish as to put
forward so indifferent a Latinist to compile the Bull.   But it is
absolutely impossible that an unscrupulous forger, sitting down
to imitate the Papal Bulls, should after the usual heading
commence with the words:

As on the sacred heights of Paradise so sweet a melody is found,
tuned to the beatific vision, while Jesus is seen united to the Eternal
Father, and says, " I and the Father are one; he who sees Me sees the
Father," and the choir of angels ceases not to cry, Holy, Holy, Holy—
so the assembly ceases not to pour forth its praises to the Blessed Virgin
in her exaltation, saying, "Virgin, Virgin, Virgin, be our pattern and
our example."   For she is surrounded by the bestowal of graces as the
Holy Church sings: Full of grace and Mother of mercy.   Thus of high
esteem is held that Mount of the Order of Carmel, extolling and praising
this Mother of graces, and saying, Hail Queen, Mother of mercy and
our hope.

Thus I was praying on my bended knees when the Virgin of Carmel
appeared to me, and uttered the following words, &c.[6]

With a hundred Bulls before him, none of them affording any
sort of parallel to this extraordinary commencement, no
impostor would have been so mad as to wander away from
the beaten track into this unparalleled narration of the
appearance.   But on the supposition of the story having been
written down by one of the Carmelites to whom the Pope
narrated it, the extraordinary wording of the Bull is natural
enough.

2. Whenever any forged document has been successfully
circulated and widely received as genuine, we never find that
its success is lasting.   It may for a time be regarded even by
men of ability and learning as trustworthy; it may gain credit

---

[6] " Sacratissimo uti culmine Paradisi angelorum tam suavis et dulcis reperitur
melodia, modulamine visionis, dum paterno Jesus Numini circumspicitur adunatus,
dicente Domino: Ego et Pater unum sumus; et qui videt me, videt et Patrem meum;
et angelorum chorus non desinit dicere Sanctus, Sanctus, Sanctus; ita Synodus non
cessat laudes effundere celsæ Virgini, dicendo: Virgo, Virgo, Virgo, sis speculum
nostrum pariter et exemplum.   Quoniam munere munitur gratiarum, sicut sancta
cantat Ecclesia; Gratia plena et Mater misericordiæ.   Sic ille mons reputatur de
Carmelo Ordine cantibus extollendo, et hanc gratiarum Genitricem commendando et
dicendo ; Salve Regina, Mater misericordiæ et spes nostra.   Sic mihi flexis genibus
supplicanti Virgo visa fuit Carmelita, sequentem effata sermonem " etc.

even among those in authority; it may escape suspicion for a few years more or less. But as time goes on it somehow or other loses its influence. The Forged Decretals had in their favour the large admixture of genuine documents with which they were mixed up; they were drawn up with remarkable ability; they had every appearance of being genuine. Yet how completely did they pass, as time went on, into the oblivion they deserved! Now there is no trace left of them, no interest taken in their history, save that they are a valuable stalking-horse to the Protestant controversialist. In the same way some of our readers may have seen the supposed grant of complete exemption from Purgatory attaching to the daily repetition, for a space of fourteen years, of certain prayers in honour of the Passion. It was circulated as one of the promises of our Lord to St. Bridget. But it would not bear the test of criticism, and though it is not condemned as false, yet the absence of sufficient proof has caused it to be set aside by the faithful generally, even though it is possibly true and genuine. Any privilege that lacks sufficient foundation is always gradually discredited as years go on by the infallible instinct of the Church. If, on the other hand, we find that any supposed grant of spiritual favours and privileges gains in its hold over Catholic consciences, and in its acceptance by those who teach with authority, there can be little doubt that it is worthy of all confidence: if it passes unchallenged from mouth to mouth, if it is found in popular books of devotion, and none declare it to be unreliable, if the good works it inculcates are practised all over the world, in the full belief that they will gain the favour promised, and no priest or bishop warns his flock that the promise is of doubtful authority, and therefore the favour one which cannot be reckoned on with certainty, then the silence on the part of the *Ecclesia docens* is in itself a very strong evidence in favour of the promise made being genuine and authentic, and the *Ecclesia discens* has a right to say "*Lex orandi, lex credendi.* The devotion I am practising with the implicit sanction of authority is one which I have right to believe is sanctioned by Almighty God Himself." Now this is essentially the case with the Sabbatine Indulgence. Take any book of popular devotion, and you will find it spoken of as an undoubted fact. Turn to a summary of recognized Indulgences, and it is sure to be there. What would be thought of a bishop who should discountenance it, or of a theologian who should warn the faithful against it? Every country in the world contains hundreds and thousands of pious souls who are striving to gain it. Are they all the victims of a heartless fraud and a clumsy forgery?

3. Our third argument is based on the attitude of the Popes to the privileges of the Scapular. Every one who has studied the proceedings of the Roman Curia knows how great is the caution exercised in granting or confirming privileges having their origin in disputed facts or visions of doubtful authenticity. If a Pope confirms the Indulgences granted by one of his predecessors to some special devotion, he thereby implicitly approves the devotion and acknowledges the authenticity of the previous grant. If he approves the Bull granting the Indulgences or privileges *in forma specifica*, this means that he makes himself responsible for all that was contained in the previous Bull; if he does so *in forma communi*, this means that he confirms the grant of his predecessors without necessarily adopting as his own the details of the Bull, or giving them his own personal authority. To approve the Bull of John the Twenty-second *in forma specifica* would have pledged the Pope who approved it to every detail of the narrative respecting our Lady's appearance of which the great part of it consists, and without a Divine revelation who would venture to answer for the exactness of each little circumstance of the apparition?

But Pope after Pope has approved the Sabbatine Indulgence, and thereby has implicitly accepted the substance of the Bull in which the Indulgence was contained. It would indeed be strange if an impudent forgery of this kind was allowed by one Pope after another to pass current without rebuke, and not only without rebuke, but as the ground for a continual repetition and confirmation of the favours which were originally granted to the Catholic world on the strength of such an infamous fraud.

Clement the Seventh, Paul the Third, St. Pius the Fifth, Gregory the Thirteenth, Clement the Tenth, Innocent the Eleventh, all appear as the Protectors and Defenders of these Carmelite favours. Above all, a Decree of the Inquisition issued by the command of Paul the Fifth, February 25, 1613, declares in express terms that the substance of the Sabbatine Bull of John the Twenty-second can be devoutly believed by the faithful, and may be preached by the Carmelite Fathers as worthy of all confidence.[7]

[7] " Patribus Carmelitanis permittatur prædicare, quod populus christianus possit pie credere de adjutorio animarum Fratrum et Confratrum Sodalitatis Beatissimæ Virginis Mariæ de Monte Carmelo, videlicet, Beatissimam Virginem animas Fratrum

and the Sabbatine Indulgence. 493

4. The various conditions named in the Bull have been at various times submitted to the Sacred Congregation of Indulgences for information and direction respecting their fulfilment. Thus a Decree of June 22, 1842, declares that in the concession of the power to invest in the Scapular there is not necessarily contained the power to change the recital of the Office of our Lady into some other good work in case of necessity. An answer of the same Congregation of August 18, 1868, declares that a Priest or Religious saying his or her ordinary Office with that intention, and fulfilling the other conditions, gains the Sabbatine Indulgences. The original concession is always taken for granted. No doubt respecting it ever seems to cross the minds of the Sacred Congregation. What plainer proof could we have than this of the universal belief of the whole Catholic world that the Sabbatine Indulgence is no fiction but a reality, and that the document on which it is based is accepted as a matter of course by those in authority at Rome ?

Our space forbids other testimonies that we would fain have added. We can only refer our readers to *Maurel des Indulgences*, Art. v. n. 74 ; Schneider (*Die Ablasse ihr Wesen und Gebrauch*, pp. 412—425) ; St. Alphonsus (*Glories of Mary*, c. viii. § 2) ; Ven. Father de Colombière (*Sermon on the Scapular*), all of whom declare plainly and unhesitatingly their confidence in the genuine character of the Bull and in the promises made therein. It is impossible that the universal conviction prevailing respecting the Bull should lack foundation, or that Popes and Saints and Canonists should all have been deceived respecting it.

We do not say that the evidence will necessarily appear to every one as convincing as it does to ourselves. We do not presume to say a word against those who may still be incredulous, but this we say without hesitation, that we are persuaded that their incredulity is the result of a partial view of the question, founded on the abnormal and extraordinary character of the Bull, and on other circumstances which at first

et Confratrum in caritate decedentium, qui in vita habitum gestaverint, et castitatem pro suo statu coluerint, Officiumque Parvum recitaverint, vel si recitare nesciverint, Ecclesiæ jejunia observaverint, et feria quarta et sabbato a carnibus abstinuerint, nisi ubi in iis diebus Nativitatis Domini festum inciderit, suis intercessionibus continuis, suisque suffragiis et meritis, et speciali protectione post eorum transitum, præcipue in die sabbati (qui dies ab Ecclesia eidem B.V. dicatus est) adjuturam. Quod Decretum fuit publicatum die 15 Februarii 1615 in palatio S. Officii a D. Marcello Filonardo, assessore ejusdem S. Officii" (On trouve la traduction de ce Décret, au IVᵐᵉ Chapitre, pag. 247). The Decree was approved December 1, 1886, by the Congregation of Indulgences.

sight seems to cast very grave suspicions upon it. But if there are any who have been deceived by the article in the *Catholic Dictionary* and its strange misquotations from Benedict the Fourteenth, we have at least said enough to show them that the great canonist and theologian is in no sense the adversary of the Bull. On the general question every one is free to form his own opinion. At the same time the faithful children of our Lady of Mount Carmel may rely with the most perfect confidence on the promises made to her faithful servant John the Twenty-second. If here and there a critically-minded person raises objections, the consensus of the faithful pronounces very distinctly against him, as in the case of the vision of St. Simon Stock. Here we can apply the maxim, *Securus judicat orbis terrarum.* The belief in the Sabbatine Indulgence and in the Sabbatine Bull is firmly and deeply rooted in the hearts of the Catholics all over the world. Firmly and deeply rooted, by God's mercy, it will ever remain, as long as time shall last.

R. F. CLARKE.

THE IRISH

ECCLESIASTICAL RECORD

A Monthly Journal,

UNDER EPISCOPAL SANCTION

THIRD SERIES.

VOLUME VIII.—1887.

" Ut Christiani ita et Romani sitis."

" As you are children of Christ, so be you **children of Rome**."

Ex Dictis S. Patricii, **Book of Armagh,** fol. 9

DUBLIN :

BROWNE & NOLAN, NASSAU-STREET.

1887.

Nihil Obstat.

GIRALDUS MOLLOY, S.T.D.,

CENSOR DEP.

𝕴mprimatur.

✠ GULIELMUS,

Archiep. Dublin., Hiberniae Primas.

BROWNE & NOLAN, STEAM PRINTERS, DUBLIN.

503

Contents.

on Inchiquin's lineage, and possibly some material point has not been recorded.

The island of St. Connell lies at present outside the parish of Inniskeel. Half a century ago itself and the adjoining districts were ceded to Ardara in exchange for certain town-lands lying near Glenties. So the people of both parishes look to it with equal pride, and visit it with equal reverence. We feel sure that the lesson its great saint teaches as well as the benediction they obtain, will stand the children of Boylagh in good stead as the ages roll on. This said, we have com-pleted a little vacation tribute of homage and gratitude, long since intended, to St. Connell and St. Dallan.

PATRICK O'DONNELL.

THE BROWN SCAPULAR AND THE *CATHOLIC DICTIONARY.*

THE distinguished honor paid to the Scapular of our Lady of Mount Carmel by the Holy See, in the recent Decree relative to its investiture, which appeared in the July number of the RECORD for the present year, furnishes us with an occasion for comment on an article in the *Catholic Dictionary*, compiled by the Rev. W. A. Addis, and Mr. Thomas Arnold, M.A., under the word "Scapular."

It is true that two able papers, written by the Rev. Father Clarke, S.J., Editor of the *Month*, in refutation of the article in the *Catholic Dictionary*, have already appeared in that periodical, for which the clients of our Lady of Mount Carmel owe a deep debt of gratitude to that pious and learned Editor. But as the RECORD circulates in many places in Ireland, to which the *Month* does not reach, and as we purpose to meet the objections in our own way, it will not be deemed out of place if we supply the readers of the former, with an answer to the difficulties raised against the devotion of the Carmelite Scapular by the *Catholic Dictionary*. We do this all the more eagerly, because this devotion is so widely spread amongst Irish Catholics, and is so dear to them.

It is indeed unaccountable how an article so un-Catholic and so repugnant to the feelings and belief of Catholics, could have found its way into the pages of a Catholic dictionary.

We might expect such teaching in a work avowedly hostile to Catholic devotional practices; but certainly not in a Catholic book. Although freely admitting that nothing could be farther from the intention of the compilers of the *Catholic Dictionary*, than to throw any discredit on devotional practices sanctioned by the Church, yet we are bound to assert that the article in question has that tendency.

Having given a brief description of the devotion of the Scapular, the writer of the article says, " Two statements, then, have to be examined. Is there any proof that the Blessed Virgin appeared to St. Simon Stock and made the promises related above ? Is the Sabbatine Bull genuine, and the story it tells true ? " He then adds, " We take the latter question first, because it may be despatched very quickly." He does indeed despatch it very quickly, but we must add very unsatisfactorily.

Now let us examine the authorities the writer adduces, to prove that the Bulls of John XXII. and Alexander V. are not genuine; for the weight of the evidence will very much depend on the character of the witnesses.

The first he brings forward is Launoy, a doctor of the College of Sorbonne, who died at Paris in 1678. Now it is well known that his works are distinguished by their sceptical and erroneous teaching. Nearly all of them have been proscribed by the Sacred Congregation of the Index. He is called by Benedict XIV., in his work on the Canonization of Saints, a most pronounced enemy of the Roman Pontiffs and the Apostolic See. Alluding to a theological opinion of Launoy's, he designates it—

" Temerarium profecto et contumeliosum in Christi vicarium dictum ! quod a solo Launojo proferri poterat, utpote Romanorum Pontificum et Sedis Apostolicæ hoste apertissimo, ex quo ipsius opuscula a Sacra Indicis Congregatione fuerant merito proscripta."[1]

[1] *Act de Canon. Ser. Dei.* Lib. I., c. 44., n. 18.

No doubt Launoy was a man of great learning, but he turned it to bad account. He held weekly conferences at his residence in Paris, at which opinions were taught so subversive of society, and the authority of the Church, that the King was obliged to interdict them in 1636. He next made war on religious orders, canonized saints, and some of the most cherished devotions of the Church ; employing his acrimonious pen in endeavouring to discredit them by false objections and unfounded imputations.

He wrote also against the Formulary of Alexander VII. condemnatory of Jansenism ; and he is accused of altering, with incredible audacity, texts which he quoted in proof of his theory. Most of his reasonings too are not more just than his quotations (V. *Dictionnaire Universel des sciences Ecclésiastiques* Tom. 2, P. 1230). Being generally of a negative character, to give them the appearance of solidity he published a work on the force of negative arguments (*De auctoritate negantis argumenti*). He has been greatly praised by Protestants, and his works have been reproduced by them, no doubt, because of his anti-catholic and anti-papal tendencies.

In his work entitled *De Simonis Stokii viso, de Sabbatinae Bullae Privilegio et de Scapularis Carmelitarum Sodalitate Dissertationes quinque*, this cynical and unscrupulous critic attacked, to use the words of Benedict XIV., with inexpressible fury the vision to St. Simon Stock and the Bull of John XXII. "Adversus utramque quasi quodam, qui satis verbis explicari non potest, furore invehitur Launojus in Dissertationibus suis."[1]

To show the lengths to which the man's morbid desire for attacking admitted facts carried him, and the kind of arguments he used, we may mention that he stoutly maintained that St. Thomas Aquinas was not the author of the *Summa Theologica*. The matter is thus related by Benedict XIV. and we give it here because it is much to our present purpose.

"Denique magnis olim animorum motibus agitabatur controversia utrum Summa Theologica S. Thomae Aquinatis ab eo fuerit

[1] Benedict XIV. *de Festis*, T. 2, P. 330 Lovanii 1761. This book by Launoy is on the Index.

composita, an potius a Vincentio Bellovacensi. Joannes nempe Launojus, *more suo*, sententiae adhaerebat quae favet Bellovacensi, innixus sermone Clementis VI. qui S. Thomam laudans, anno 1323, ad solemnia ejusdem recens canonizati et ejus operum indicem retexens Theologicae Summae non meminit, sed cum eruditus ex Dominicana Familia Theologus, Jacobus Echard, in libro de S. Thomæ Summa suo auctori vindicata (P. 439 et seq.) clarissime demonstraverit in eodem Clementis VI. sermone Summam S. Thomæ esse commemoratam."

And the learned Pontiff adds :

" Ex his omnibus plene evincitur serio perpendendum esse ante omnia an negotium sit redactum ad punctum argumenti negativi ; cum aliquando fidenter asseri contingat, nullum aequaevum auctorem rem retulisse, quamvis non desint qui retulerint."[1]

Now this Launoy is the authority that furnishes the writer of the article in question with a " superabundance of reasons " to show that the Bull of John XXII. and that of Alexander V. are forgeries. Of course Launoy could supply " *more suo* " as Benedict XIV. designates his methods, a "superabundance" of what he calls "reasons," for denying facts admitted by all reasonable people. How many historical facts could stand the test, if the methods employed by Launoy were to prevail ? Why even the most sacred and fundamental truths of religion have been attacked in the same way, by unbelieving and heretical writers who have furnished, in their own opinion and in the opinion of those who believe with them, a superabundance of "reasons" against doctrines which they do not wish to admit, but which are held by all Catholics.

The "reasons" supplied by Launoy against the authenticity of these Bulls, have been over and over again completely refuted by various learned writers. To quote them here would not only exceed the space allowed us in these pages, but would fill volumes. We can, however, refer the reader who wishes to follow this subject more fully, to works in which the objections and difficulties internal and external, historical and theological, raised against these Bulls are fully and completely answered and refuted, viz. : *Speculum Carmelitanum*, by the Rev. Fr. Daniel of the Virgin Mary (T. 1,

---

[1] Act de Canon, Ser. Dei, l. iii., c. x., n. 5.

798 *The Brown Scapular and the Catholic Dictionary.*

L. V., p. 3, Antverpiae, 1653); *Vinea Carmeli seu Historia Ordinis Eliani*, by the same author (Pars V., cap. iv. et seq.); *Bibliotheca Carmelitana*, by the Very Rev. Cosma of St. Stephen (T. 1, p. 52, et seq.); *Historico-Sacra et Theologico-Dogmatica Dissertatio de Vera Origine et Progressu Monastices* (Nolae, 1697), by the Very Rev. John Feyxoo de Villalobos; *Scapulare Marianum illustratum et defensum*, by the distinguished Jesuit writer Fr. Theophilus Raynaud; Benedict XIV. *de Festis*, P. 2, c. 76, et seq., also *De Beatificatione et Canoniz. Sanctorum* (L. 4, p. 2, cap. ix., n. 10). Also the works of Ven. P. John the Baptist de Lazana, G. Colvener, John Palaeonydorus, Arnold Botius, John Cheron, Iraeneus of St. James, Paul of All Saints, and others.

The writer of the article in question says that the autograph of the Sabbatine Bull has never been found. Not since it was lost, but is that a proof that it never existed? If that test were applied to other rights and privileges, how few of their claims could be proved? Why, if it were lawful to make the comparison, the autographs of the most authentic documents in the world, the Holy Scriptures, are not now in existence. Would it therefore be lawful to conclude that they are apocryphal?

If the original of the Sabbatine Bull has been lost, we have unquestionable testimony that it existed, that its loss can be satisfactorily accounted for, and that authentic copies of it have been taken, some of which are at present in existence.

The first witness who testifies to its existence is Alexander V., who tells us that he saw it himself, examined it carefully, was convinced of its authenticity, and in order to put its existence beyond future cavil, he embodied it in a Bull of his own, in which he renews and confirms the privileges contained in it :—

"Tenore cujusdam privilegii fel. record. Joannis XXII. Praedecessoris nostri, dilectis filiis, Priori Generali et Fratribus et dilectis in Christo Filiabus sororibus confratribus, et Confratriae Fratrum dicti ordinis Carmelitarum concessi, *per nos visi et diligenter inspecti, de dicto originali sumpto*, ut de ipso in posterum certitudo plenior habeatur, praesentes fecimus annotari, qui talis est."

Then follows the text, *in extenso*, of the Sabbatine Bull—"*Sacratissimo uti culmine*, &c. ¹Datum Romae 7 Dec. 1409." Apud Mariam Majorem.[1]

The authenticity of this Bull has also been denied by Launoy, but the reasons he alleges for this denial have been shown by the authors we have quoted to be groundless. A very complete answer to these objections may be read in the *Bibliotheca Carmelitana* (T. 1, p. 51, et seq.) An authentic copy of this Bull signed by public notaries, judges, &c., who testify that they have compared it with the original and found it to correspond, was deposited in the archives of the Carmelite Fathers at Genoa, as may be learned from the *Speculum Carmelitanum* (T. 1, L. V., p. 543, cap. xii., et seq.) where a copy of it is given, and where its authenticity is clearly demonstrated. Other authentic copies were deposited at the Carmelite Convents of Messina, Mechlin, Cologne, Antwerp, Rome, and other places, as is proved in the *Speculum Carm.* (Tom. 1, cap. xii., p. 543).

John Palaeonydorus in his work *Fasciculus Tripartitus*, cap. xi., Arnold Botius in his *Speculum Hist.*, cap. vii., Baldinus Leersius in his *Collectaneum Exemplorum*, cap. vi., and others inform us, that the original of the Bull of John XXII., was conveyed to England, and an authentic copy of it kept at Genoa. This fact is also attested by a witness who will not be suspected of any bias in favour of the Bull, viz., Balaeus, a renegade Carmelite Friar, who was named by Edward VI., Bishop of Ossory in Ireland. In his Catalogue of British writers, at the name N. Trineth, in the appendix, alluding not in friendly terms to the vision of John XXII., he thus writes:

"Istam apparitionem, &c., in quadam Bulla legi in Anglia; quae etiam Romae an. 1530 sub Clementi VII. renovata fuit."

Theophilus Raynaud, the illustrious Jesuit writer, also gives clear testimony to the same fact. He thus writes in his work on the Scapular (Part 2, p. 2):—

"Joannes autographum Carmelitis ipsis tradidit, tamquam ad eos maxime attinens. Carmelitae autem variis apographis confeetis

---

[1] Vide *Speculum Carmelitanum*, T. 1, p. 3, L. V., n. 2,161.

800   *The Brown Scapular and the Catholic Dictionary.*

et huc illucque transmissis, autographum ipsum ad Generalem Praepositum, cujus in Anglia sedes ordinaria erat, deferri curarunt, apud eum, in generali ordinis Tabulario cum aliis, magni momenti, Diplomatibus aut Instrumentis asservandum."

The original of the Bull of Alexander V. was also transferred to England as we learn from the authentic copy of it, made Jan. 2nd, 1421, at the instance of Alphonsus de Theram, an Englishman, then Prior of the Convent of Captun, in the island of Majorca, afterwards Prior of the Convent of Coventry, England, who then took the original to be kept in the archives of the General in London. This copy was solemnly reduced to public form, before notaries, judges, &c., and kept at Genoa. Of this we are informed by Palaeonydorus, Botius, Leersius, &c.[1] An old authentic MS. copy, written in 1484, and kept at the Carmelite Convent, Mechlin, gives us similar information. These words are added to it—

" Haec est Bulla Joannis XXII. quam Alexander V. confirmat, cujus originale dicitur fore in Anglia et in Conventu Januens (Genoa) ejus Instrumentum authenticum." (V. *Spec. Carm.* T. L. Pars. III., p. 544, n. 2158.)

It is confirmed by Fr. Paul of All Saints, in his *Clavis Aurea* (p. 2., c. 27) where he writes thus :—

"Singulari vero Divinæ Providentiæ beneficium adscribendæ videtur, quod Alexander in suum Diploma, Bullam Joannis verbatim integreque retulerit, quod paucis post annis, videlicet 1421, Diplomatis Alexandri publicum, authenticumque Majoricæ instrumentum conficeretur, ad instantiam R. P. Alphonsi de Theramo Angli, qui autographum, seu Bullam originalem, Alexandri, quam Judicibus et Notariis legendam, inspiciendamque, ut iidem testantur, exhibuit, atque, in Angliam ubi Prioris munere fungebatur, erat asportaturus, una cum Bulla Joannis adservandam."

It may be asked why were these original and valuable documents brought to England and deposited there ? The answer is, that, at that time, England was the most important and flourishing province of the Carmelite order, and the seat of the Prior General. There too were held many general chapters, in the first of which, after their

---

[1] Vide *Speculum Carm.*, T. 1, p. 562, n. 2204.

transmigration from Syria, St. Simon Stock was elected
General. There too the latter was favoured with the
heavenly vision in which he received the Scapular. The
province too was remarkable for the number of its houses
and the learning and piety of its members. Before the
suppression of the monasteries by Henry VIII. it contained
fifty-six convents and fifteen hundred religious. In attestation of these facts we may quote Pitsæus (*Lib. de viris illus.
Angliæ agens de Carm.*). He says :—

" In Anglia plusquam in quacumque alia Europæ parte hunc
ordinem floruisse constat; magisque abundasse et numero monas-
teriorum et doctorum virorum copia."

Also Nicholas Herpfeldus, an English historian (*Hist.
Ang., sec.* 14, c. 17.) Having enumerated many men of
other orders illustrious for their piety and learning, he thus
concludes :—

" Sed hos omnes et ceteros hoc seculo non modo singulos, sed
universos non tantum exaequant, sed longe, ni fallor, in hac scriptionum
palaestra, et laude librorum laborumque, magnitudine superant
Carmelitæ."[1]

In the Convent of London were kept from the time of St.
Simon Stock, the archives of the order in which were preserved important documents, treasures, apostolic diplomas
and Bulls granted to the order. In proof of this, we can refer
to the writings of John Grosius, John Bacho, Thomas Bradley,
Bishop of Dromore, Leersius.[2]

From these writers we learn that some of the most important Bulls granted to the order were kept in the archives of
the London Convent, the library of which was the largest and
most valuable in London, as we read in the *Bibliotheca
Carmelitana*, (T. II., p. 473). " Bibliotheca Carmelitarum
Londinensium deperiit, multitudine et antiquitate superans
omnes quotquot erant Londini 1420."

But alas! these glorious days of the Church in England
were sadly changed by the wicked Henry VIII. Having
rebelled against the Holy See, because it would not comply
with his unlawful demands, he cast his avaricious eyes on the

[1] V. *Spec. Carm,* T. 1., p. 562. [2] *Spec. Carm.* T. 1., p. 562, n. 2204.

rich monasteries, and resolved to replenish his coffers and those of his needy and greedy nobles, with their property. We need not go into the sad story of the suppression of those monasteries and the confiscation of their property. In this general destruction, the great Carmelite library of London shared the common fate of the other religious houses. It was taken possession of by the enemy ; its archives, documents, papal diplomas and Bulls relating to the order deposited there, were all seized, scattered or destroyed. It is not surprising, then, that, in this general overthrow and destruction, the original of the Sabbatine Bull, and that of Alexander V. which were deposited there, should be lost or destroyed.

That such was the fate of these Bulls, we have the testimony of George Colvenerius, Doctor of S. Theology and Chancellor of the University of Douay. In his work *Kalendarium Marianum* (Douay, 1638), he writes as follows, under the 7th December :—

" Hac die datum est Romae diploma apud S. Mariam Majorem Alexandri V. Pontificis, quae confirmat Bullam Joannis XXII."

And afterwards he adds these words concerning the originals :—

" Diploma originale Joannis XXII. et Alexandri V. in Anglia periisse, ubi maxime florere hic solet ordo et Praepositus ordinis residere, ubi et commune totius congregationis erat Archivium, quod heretici violenta manu effregerunt."

P. F. Daniel of the Virgin Mary, gives us similar testimony in his great work *Speculum Carmelitanum* (T. I., p. 562, c. 15).

But if these important Bulls have been lost or destroyed, many authentic copies of them remain as we have already seen. They have, too, been confirmed and ratified by many Popes. The first to do so was Clement VII. In his Bull " Ex clementi Sedis Apostolicae," he, by name, cites those of John XXII. and Alexander V., solemnly approves them, and ratifies their contents. This Bull is dated at St. Peter's, Rome, August 12th 1530 (Vide *Bullarium Romanum Cherub*. T. 1, p. 683, item *Bullarium Carm*. Pars 2, p. 47, et seq.) Also that of Paul III. " Provisionis Nostrae," 1534 (*Bullar. Carm*. T. 2, p. 68) of Paul IV. in his Bull dated 30th May, 1556, in which

The Brown Scapular of Our Lady of Mount Carmel

he expressly cites those of John XXII., Alexander V., Clement VII., Paul III., and Julius III., and confirms them (*Bullar. Carm.* T. 2. p. 107); of Pius V. in his Bull " Superna dispositione, 1566 ; and of Gregory XIII. " Ut laudes," Rome, 18th September, 1577, in which he confirms the concessions of his predecessors, amongst whom he expressly mentions the names of John XXII. and Alexander V.[1]

There are other Bulls to the same effect from other Sovereign Pontiffs in different ages of the Church which it is unnecessary to cite here. Now, it is worthy of remark that many of these Bulls mention the two fundamental Bulls of John XXII. and Alexander V., approve of them, and ratify their contents. These Popes would not surely quote these two Bulls, give them their approbation, and make them the foundation of their own if there was any doubt of their authenticity.

To these authorities we may add that of the Sacred Congregation of Rites, which has approved the lessons of the second nocturn of the Breviary for the feast of the solemn commemoration of the Blessed Virgin of Mount Carmel; and the decree of the Congregation of the Inquisition, under Paul V., February 15th, 1613, both confirmative of the privileges of the Sabbatine Bull.[2]

To the proofs we have already given of the authenticity of the Bulls in question, we may add the authority of the theological faculties of different universities. An agitation having been raised in Spain about the year 1566, against the devotion of the scapular, the matter was referred to the University of Salamanca for consideration. Four of its most learned doctors were deputed to examine it, and their unanimous decision was that the Sabbatine Bull and those of the other Sovereign Pontiffs relating to it, were authentic, and that the Carmelites could enjoy the privileges contained in them. (*Spec. Carm.* T. 1, p. 567).

The College of Sorbonne gave similar attestation. Eight of its learned doctors having examined the Bulls and considered the question, solemnly declared :—

" Indulgentiam Sabbatinam juxta tenorem Pauli V. publicandam asserandamque. August 19th, 1648."—(*Spec. Carm.* T. 1, p. 561.)

Bullar. Carm., T. 2, p. 194.   [2] V. *Spec. Carm.*, T. 1, p. 491.

work the author ably defends the Sabbatine Bull against
Launoy and Papebroch, and puts its authenticity beyond
question.   At page 641 of the same book he accuses and con-
victs Papebroch of following, imitating, and quoting Launoy,
the enemy of the Holy See, the contemner of Papal Bulls, the
calumniator of saints and religious orders, the sneerer at and
reviler of religious practices, whose works have nearly all
been condemned by the Sacred Congregation of the Index.
In support of the accusations he quotes the celebrated Jesuit
writer Theophilus Raynaud, who thus describes the character
of Launoy—

"Probat deinde Raynaudus Launoyum esse turbidum, inquietum
garrulum, truculentum, alienae famae lanium, necnon infrunitum
calumniatorem ac mendacem, omni proinde fide humana indignum."

Then our author adds—

"Quae Papebrochium non videntur potuisse latere.   Unde satis
mirari non possum, quod hominem adeo infamem, cujus omnia fere
opuscula ab Ecclesia sunt damnata, pro se citari audeat, dum Joannis
XXII. Bullam a successoribus *proprio motu et ex certa scientia,* toties
confirmatam, cum isto solo calumniatore et sedis Bullarum Pontificae
contemptore, in opusculo ejus damnato proclamat esse *nullius fidei.*"

When we consider that the Sabbatine Bull has been
approved and confirmed by many Popes, that it has been
examined and sanctioned by the theological faculties of universities, that the objections raised against it have been again
and again refuted by many able and learned writers, the fact
that Papebroch agrees with Launoy in affirming that it is of
doubtful authenticity has very little weight indeed, especially
as the work containing Launoy's "superabundance of reasons" is condemned by the Holy See.

The writer of the article next produces two passages from
Benedict XIV. (or rather the pious and learned Cardinal
Lambertinus, for he had not been elevated to the Pontifical
throne when he wrote the words quoted) which seem to bear
the interpretation, that the learned Cardinal held that the
Sabbatine Bull was of doubtful authenticity.   Nothing could
be more injurious to the memory of that great Pontiff than
such an insinuation, for it is well known, that he took up his
pen to defend it against the attacks of Launoy and Papebroch.
We cannot admire the candour of the writer in quoting these
passages, whilst at the same time he leaves unquoted other

passages of the same learned Pope in which he clearly affirms that it is genuine.

First let us see if these quotations bear the meaning the writer of the article would have us infer. " It is " thus runs the quotation " as hard, perhaps harder to believe in this Bull than in the story of the chapel built on Mount Carmel in honour of the Blessed Virgin during her life." But there is no difficulty in believing the latter, for it is an historical fact, supported by the authority of the Sacred Congregation of Rites, the received tradition of the whole order, and the testimony of different trustworthy writers, as may be seen in *Speculum Carm.* (T. 1. pars 2, page 355, n. 1455 et alibi). The next quotation is "He says he could give more reasons against it than he cares to produce and arguments drawn from things (in the Bull) which want all appearance of truth." The words "in the Bull" is a gloss of the writer. The writer then adds "He alludes we suppose to the style of the Bull which as Launoy points out, betrays in many ways the hand of the impostor."

Benedict XIV. says more reasons could be produced against the Bull if it should appear to him profitable or expedient (si nobis videretur conducibile). But evidently he did not deem it profitable to produce them. But what were these reasons? According to the writer of the article, they were, he supposes, some of Launoy's, which we may add, have been condemned by the Holy See, and refuted by many able and learned writers.

Now, Benedict XIV. clearly teaches and defends the authenticity of the Sabbatine Bull, both in his work *De Festis*, and his other great work *De Servorum Dei Beatificatione*, &c· In the former work (Tom. 2, p. 326, cap. lxx. et seq., Lovanii· 1761), having stated reasons in favour of the Bull, in chapter 78, he says: " all the difficulties that could be brought against both the vision of St. Simon Stock and the Sabbatine Bull, have been removed, both by the wise disquisitions of learned men and by the decree of the Sovereign Pontiff."[1]

[1] " Ea omnia, quae tum in B. Stokii visione tum in Sabbatina Bulla difficultatem creare poterant, et sapientibus doctorum virorum animadversionibus, et Romani Pontificis decreto sublata sint."

516

In the latter work he writes also in favour of the scapular. Having alluded to the difficulties raised against it by Launoy and Papebroch, he adds: "But the genuineness of the Sabbatine Bull, and many things in vindication of the aforesaid matters (viz., the privileges of the scapular) can be read in the work of Theophilus Raynaud, entitled *Scapulare Marianum illustratum.*" (Tom. 7.)[1]

It is clearly evident, therefore, that Benedict XIV. was a strenuous defender of the Sabbatine Bull and its privileges.

We have said, we think, enough to prove that the strictures against the Sabbatine Bull contained in the first question discussed in the article of the *Catholic Dictionary* are groundless, and contrary to the belief and instincts of Catholics. With the editor's permission, we purpose in another article, to examine the difficulties raised on the second question discussed in the *Catholic Dictionary*, viz.: " The Vision of the Blessed Virgin to St. Simon Stock, and and the promises made to him."

JOHN E. BARTLEY, O.C.C.

THE MOZARABIC RITE.

OVERRUN as continental Europe now is with tourists of every kind and of every nation, Spain is comparatively speaking unknown. Yet there is much in this country to interest anyone, and to a Catholic few lands could be more fascinating. Among the most interesting spots in Spain is the conical hill, almost surrounded by the Tagus, on whose summit is Toledo, the See of the Primate of Spain. Its cathedral is unique, in that the Divine Office is always recited in it by two choirs according to two Rites. The Office of the Roman Rite is said in the magnificent *Coro;* and in a small chapel, the *Capilla Muzaraba,* situated at the

[1] " Sed Bullæ Sabbatinæ veritas et multa pro dictarum rerum vindicatione legi possunt apud Theophilum Raynaudum in opusculo cui titulus *Scapulare Marianum.*" (V. *Act de Beat.*, &c., L. iv., Pars. 2, cap. ix., no. 10).

THE IRISH
ECCLESIASTICAL RECORD

A Monthly Journal,

UNDER EPISCOPAL SANCTION

THIRD SERIES.

VOLUME VIII.—1887.

" Ut Christiani ita et Romani sitis."
" As you are children of Christ, so be you children of Rome."
Ex Dictis S. Patricii, **Book of Armagh,** fol. 9

DUBLIN :

BROWNE & NOLAN, NASSAU-STREET.

1887.

Nihil Obstat.

GIRALDUS MOLLOY, S.T.D.,

CENSOR DEP.

𝕴𝖒𝖕𝖗𝖎𝖒𝖆𝖙𝖚𝖗.

✠ GULIELMUS,

Archiep. Dublin., Hiberniae Primas.

BROWNE & NOLAN, STEAM PRINTERS, DUBLIN.

Contents.

" wishing joy " to God in the fruition of His infinite glory; the offering of felicitations on His privilege of eternally feasting His eyes on His own ineffable beauty; and lowly, worshipful congratulation on the endlessness and unalterability of His supreme sway. It lovingly protests that our hearts are made happy in the knowledge that this absolute plenitude of happiness can, through all unending ages, suffer no diminution, no overclouding, no limiting of the faculty to confer and necessitate beatitude worthy of an infinitely perfect God. It goes further, and, applying itself to the consideration of how it may prove the genuine and unaffected sincerity of those protestations of love, it becomes *affective efficax* and, as far as may be, *effective efficax* as well. It labours to remove from the soul all that could be offensive to the presence of God, and devises against future offence such anxiously and affectionately contrived provisions as give assured promise of stability in His service.

" TUNC AMABO DEUM PERFECTE si Deo velim ista bona, ideo, quia Deo bona sunt . . . Si orem et quantum est in me, impediam, ne offendatur, quia propter infinitam bonitatem suam, id est, propter illas infinitas perfectiones quas habet, dignissimus est non offendi, sed super omnia amari, coli, honorari." (La Croix.)

C. J. M.

THE BROWN SCAPULAR AND THE *CATHOLIC DICTIONARY—*II.

IN a former paper on this subject we gave the character of Launoy and his writings. We showed that he was animated by a spirit of bitter hostility to the Holy See, canonized saints, religious orders, and Catholic devotional practices; that his facts were often groundless, his arguments unsound, his conclusions false, and we may add too that his works have, nearly all, been condemned by the Holy See.

As the difficulties raised in the second part of the article on the Scapular in the *Catholic Dictionary*, are drawn from this poisoned source, we might dismiss the subject summarily by stating that they have no solid foundation, and are unworthy of serious consideration.

For the satisfaction, however, of our readers, we purpose to take up each point separately, examine its merits, and ascertain its value.

The writer in the *Catholic Dictionary* says :

"As to the fact of the apparition to St. Simon Stock, it is accepted by Benedict XIV., Papebroch, and Alban Butler on the faith of a 'Life' of the Saint by Swaynton, who was his secretary, and wrote the story of the apparition at his dictation."

It is a high compliment, no doubt, to Swaynton that the apparition is believed on his authority by such grave writers as Benedict XIV., Alban Butler, and a critic so severe as Papebroch.

The writer seems here to imply, however, that these grave authors accepted the truth of the apparition on the sole authority of Swaynton. Such cannot be the case, as in their writings they refer to other motives and authorities in support of their belief. Thus Benedict XIV., in his work *De Festis* (T. 2, cap. 70, et seq.), as well as in his work *De Canoniz. Sanct.* (L. 4, p. 2, cap. 9, n.:10) refers to the authors of the *Vinea Carmeli, Spec. Carm., Clavis aurea* and the *Scap. Marianum.* Alban Butler, in his life of St. Simon, says that Benedict XIV. and Fr. Cosmas de Villiers refute Launoy on the testimonies of several ancient writers of the order.

That Papebroch had other motives for believing in the apparition and the devotion of the Scapular, besides the authority of Swaynton, is evident from passages in his reply to Fr. Sebastian of St. Paul's strictures on him. In this work he thus writes :—

"Quod ad Deiparæ verba attinet, de qualicumque ordinis habitu, *in quo moriens aeternum non patietur incendium;* ego in illis nullam video difficultatem. Ea enim Patres Carmelitæ tam commode exponunt, ut facile evadant omnem justam reprehensionem . . . . Improbus porro sit qui neget, multis Romanorum Pontificum gratiis ac privilegiis ornatam, multis etiam divinis beneficiis comprobatam fuisse, istam Scapularis Mariani devote gestandi religionem." (V Art xx., n. 28.)

1006   *The Brown Scapular and the Catholic Dictionary.*

Alban Butler in his life of St. Simon says in reference to the devotion of the Scapular:

"Several Carmelite writers assure us that he (St. Simon) was admonished by the Mother of God in a vision, with which he was favoured on the 16th of July, to establish this devotion."

We may conclude, therefore, that these authors had other motives, besides the authority of Swaynton's life of the saint, for their belief in the apparition to St. Simon.

The writer says that the Carmelites refused Papebroch a sight of this life. This does not seem to affect very much the matter under consideration, but we may add that if they thought he would treat it as he did other portions of their history to which he had access, they were perfectly justified in doing so.

The writer continues thus:

"Next, to understand the force of Launoy's arguments for regarding this passage in the 'Life' if it be authentic, as an interpolation, we must remember that the miracle is represented as gaining immediate notoriety."

Here the writer casts a doubt on the authenticity of this life without giving any reason for so doing. He then gives Swaynton's, or, as he calls him, pseudo-Swaynton's words. Why pseudo? Is he not as real as any personage that figures in history? He is quoted and alluded to by several historians who have written on the Scapular, and his life is recorded in the *Bibliotheca Carmelitana*, amongst the distinguished men of the Carmelite Order. These are Swaynton's words:

"The story running through England and beyond it, many cities offered us places in which to live, and many nobles begged to be affiliated to this holy order. that they might share in its graces, desiring to die in this holy habit."

The writer then adds:

"If so, the silence of the Carmelite authors for more than a century after is remarkable."

Whilst not admitting that the silence of Carmelite authors for more than a century after, is a valid argument against a fact that was received generally, not only throughout

England, but also in other countries, we deny that they were silent on the subject for more than a century after.

St. Simon Stock died on the 16th of May, 1265, at the Carmelite Convent of Bordeaux, whilst on his visitation there, and not in 1250, as is represented in the *Catholic Dictionary*. Not only Swaynton, his cotemporary, but other Carmelite authors, relate the story of the vision within the century after the saint's death, as we shall show further on.

The writer in the *Catholic Dictionary*, using Launoy's argument, says that Ribotus, Provincial in Catalonia (about 1340), in his ten books on the institution and remarkable deeds of the Carmelites, ignores it.

True, he is silent about it, because it did not come within the scope of his work. He wrote an apology for the Carmelites on questions at that time disputed, namely, the antiquity of the order, its hereditary succession from the Prophet Elias, its confirmation, title, &c., which facts were to be proved by the testimony of the ancient writers from whom he quoted, and not by the recent heavenly-given benefit of the Scapular, concerning which there was at that time no controversy. The same may be said of the silence of the other Carmelite authors quoted by the writer from Launoy, viz., Chimilensis, or rather, Chimetensis and others. They wrote on the origin of the order, its founder, its succession from the Prophet Elias, its title, confirmation, &c., which were questions in their time disputed. But it did not come within the aim of their works, nor would it promote the end they had in view to treat of the recent and undisputed fact of the vision to St. Simon. Papebroch gives a similar reason for his silence concerning the vision when reproached by Fr. Sebastian of St. Paul, for not mentioning it in his notice of the saint's life. These are his words:

"Importunus est qui mihi vitio vertendum putat, quod de B. Simone breviter agens in Majo, maluerim tacere de Scapulari . . . Importunissimus porro est, quisquis putat, debuisse me late excurrere in commendationem praedictae devotionis, cum id alienum sit ab operis nostri instituto." (*Resp. ad Exhib.*, &c., Pars. 2, p. 381.)

The writer seems to attach great importance to the

1008   *The Brown Scapular and the Catholic Dictionary.*

silence of the great English Carmelite theologian Waldensis, for he says :

> " Strangest of all, Waldensis, a Carmelite, an Englishman, and writing in England (*De Sacramentalibus*) tries hard to prove the religious habit a sacramental, and speaks particularly of the Carmelite habit and the form which it is given."

To this we answer that it would have been altogether outside the question were Waldensis, in his controversy with the heretics on the sacraments and sacramentals, to allude to the vision to St. Simon, which they would not admit. He wrote, no doubt, about the Carmelites and the holy habits or garments of religious in general, but it was more to defend them against the attacks of the heretics, than to explain their privileges. Hence in his work on Sacramentals, chap. 25, he mentions some of the rules of the Carmelite order, and proves that monastic rules are not repugnant to the Gospels as Wickliffe contended. In the 89th chapter he defends the antiquity of the Carmelite order, and the title of Brothers of the Blessed Virgin, both of which questions were impugned by Wickliffe. In the 92nd chapter he writes of and defends the holy habits or garments of religious in general, against which the same heretic declaimed. It would seem that this was a fitting occasion for alluding to the vision in which St. Simon received the scapular from the Blessed Virgin. But as his adversary rejected all such visions, Waldensis prudently omitted any reference to it, and instead had recourse for his proofs and illustrations to the Holy Scriptures, such as the hem of our Lord's garment, the cloak of Elias, and the like, the miraculous power of which Wickliffe would not dare deny. Hence it is easy to understand why Waldensis makes no allusion to the vision of St. Simon in his controversies with the Wickliffites.

But granting that some Carmelite historians are silent about the Scapular, that is no argument against its authenticity, as long as there are other Carmelites equally trustworthy who mention it in their works. If that kind of argument were valid, many most important events, both in sacred and profane history, might be denied or called into question. Thus the mission of the Archangel Gabriel to the Blessed

Virgin, to announce to her that she was chosen by God to be the Mother of the Messiah, is recorded by St. Luke in his gospel, whilst the other Evangelists make no mention of that august event. Would it, therefore, be lawful to call it into question? The institution of the Rosary by St. Dominick is narrated by many writers, and yet the great Dominican authors St. Thomas, Durandus and Cajetanus make no allusion to it in their works. Is it, therefore, of doubtful origin? We could illustrate this subject by many other examples from both sacred and profane history, if space would permit. But it is unnecessary, as the weakness of such reasoning is evident to all.

The next statement in the article in question is as follows :

" The vision is mentioned, apparently for the first time, so far as is known for certain, by Grossus, a Carmelite of Toulouse, in his *Viridarium* (1389)," then by Paleonidorus. (*Antiq. Ord. Carm.* vi. 8, apud Launoy).

We now proceed to show that there are many Carmelite authors antecedent to the time of both Grossus and Palaeonydorus, who relate the vision to St. Simon.

First of all it is related by the saint himself in a letter addressed to all his brethren. This holy man, by the angelic purity of his life and his great devotion to the Mother of God, merited this heavenly favour. We are told that at the early age of twelve years, he retired into the solitude of the desert and there for twenty years led a most austere life. Having been divinely inspired to embrace the rule of the Carmelite order, some members of which at that time had arrived from the Holy Land, he sought and readily obtained admission amongst them. He was sent to the University of Oxford to make his ecclesiastical studies, which he did with great success, and in due time was admitted to Holy Orders. At a general Chapter held at Aylesfort, Kent, in 1245, he was unanimously elected General of his order, which he ruled with great prudence for twenty years. On the authority of this holy man, a canonized saint of the Church, who was chosen on account of his great wisdom to be Prior General of his order, we have the story of the apparition of

Appendix 3

the Blessed Virgin. He was not one likely to be deceived or to deceive others.

His order being greatly persecuted, he constantly prayed to his holy Patroness to protect it and give it some mark of her special favour. In answer to these prayers she deigned to give him the Scapular as a badge of her special protection.

The next who relates this vision is Swaynton, the saint's secretary, confessor and companion in his visitations. We are told by Pitsœus in his work *De Scriptoribus Angliæ*, (p. 346), that he was an English Carmelite, a Doctor of Theology and Professor in Oxford, afterwards taught sacred literature in Bordeaux, and was distinguished in every branch of knowledge. His life is written in the *Bibliotheca Carm.* (T. 2, p. 603). We there read that he was author of many works on sacred subjects, and amongst others he wrote a life of St. Simon in which he records the vision. The passage in which it is related is too long for insertion here, but may be seen in the *Spec. Carm.* (T. 1, para. 3, N. 2077). It will be sufficient to quote a few points.

Swaynton tells us that the saint narrated to his assembled brethren, the apparition, saying amongst other things:

> "Fratres charissimi, benedictus Deus qui non dereliquit sperantes in se, et non sprevit preces servorum suorum . . . Cum effunderem animam meam in conspectu Domini, quamvis sim pulvis et cinis; et in omni fiducia Dominam meam Virginem Mariam deprecarer, quod sicut volebat nos appellari Fratres suos, monstraret se Matrem, eripiendo nos de casu tentationum et aliquo signo gratiæ nos recommendo erga ipsos, qui nos persequebantur . . . Apparuit mihi cum grandi comitatu, et tenendo habitum ordinis, dixit: *Hoc erit tibi et cunctis Carmelitis privilegium. In hoc moriens, aeternum non patietur incendium* . . . Fratres, conservando verbum istud in cordibus vestris, satagite electionem vestram certam facere per bona opera et numquam deficere; vigilate in gratiarum actione pro tanta misericordia, orantes sine intermissione, ut sermo mihi factus clarificetur ad laudem sanctissimæ Trinitatis, Patris, Jesu Christi, Spiritus Sancti et Virginis Mariæ semper benedictæ."

Swaynton here relates a miracle effected through the instrumentality of the Scapular, the day after the vision. The saint, accompanied by Swaynton, was journeying to Winton, where there was a man named Walter, who had led a very wicked life and was now dying in despair. The dean of the

The Brown Scapular and the Catholic Dictionary. 1011

church of St. Helen, at Winton, brother of the dying man, besought the saint to come to him and endeavour to procure his conversion. The saint accordingly came, and having prayed, laid on him the holy Scapular. The dying man was immediately changed. He sought pardon for his sins, begged to receive the sacraments, and died a happy death. In gratitude for this conversion the aforesaid dean founded a Carmelite monastery at Winton.

This miracle was the happy occasion of the further confirmation of the vision. The report of it having reached the ears of the Bishop of Winton, he sent for the saint, and questioned him as to the power of the Scapular, &c. Having satisfied himself as to the truth of the apparition, he ordered the narrative to be committed to writing, and authentically signed and sealed. (*V. Spec. Carm.,* T. 1, pars. III., p. 519.)

In the year 1348, less than a century after the death of St. Simon, we have another Carmelite author, William of Coventry, relating it in his work *Scutum Carmelitarum.* His words are :

" S. Simon de Anglia Generalis Ordinis sextus, qui Dei gloriosissimam Genitricem jugiter deprecabatur, ut Carmelitarum Ordinem, qui speciali gaudet ipsius Virginis titulo, aliquo communiret privilegio . . . . Cui Beatissima Virgo cum multitudine Angelorum, apparuit, scapulare ordinis in benedictis suis manibus tenens et dicens: *Hoc erit tibi et cunctis Carmelitis privilegium ; quod in hoc moriens, æternum non patietur incendium.*" (*V. Bibliotheca Carm.* T. 2, p. 759.)

In the same century (1360) John Wilson, in his *Martyrologium Anglicanum,* thus writes :

"Decima sexta Maii Burdigalis in Guasconia, depositio S. Simonis Confessoris et Generalis Carmelit. in Anglia ; quo orante B. Virginem Mariam, illa apparuit ipsi cum comitatu Angelorum ferens scapulare sui ordinis in manibus et dixit: quod quicumque mortuus fuerit in isto ordine salvus erit." ;(*V. Biblioth. Carm.* T. 2, p. 759, et *Spec. Carm.* T. 1, pars. III., pp. 521 et 529.)

The Scapular is also alluded to by Pope John XXII, who was elected in the year 1316, fifty-one years after the death of St. Simon. In his Bull " Sacratissimo uti Culmine," or as it is called the Sabbatine Bull, he informs us that the Blessed Virgin appeared to him and told him that they who enter

1012   *The Brown Scapular and the Catholic Dictionary.*

the holy order and wear the sign of the holy habit (the Scapular) shall enjoy certain privileges. John was favoured with this vision as a reward for his great devotion to the Mother of God, and in answer to his prayers to her, that God would avert the evils with which the Church was menaced and deliver him from his enemies. This vision and promise corroborate and confirm the promise made to St. Simon in favour of those who wear the Scapular.

The next Carmelite writer who refers to the Scapular is John of Hildesheim in his *Defensorium Ordinis Dei Virginis Mariæ de Monte Carmeli*, written in 1370. Although this work treats chiefly of the ancient history of the order, in some verses of the last chapter, he thus alludes to St. Simon, the Scapular, and its prerogatives.

> " Dat superna professis commoda vitae
> Est salvificus Prior ; est et vita superstes
> Stat pro signo de subveniendo sodali."
>
>   (*V. Spec. Carm.* T. 1., pars. 2, p. 159.)

The Carmelite author who next gives us an account of the vision is John Grossus, who flourished in 1389. According to the writer in the *Catholic Dictionary*, he was the first apparently to mention it, as far as is known for certain. We have seen, however, such is not the case, as others before him, at least equally authentic, have alluded to it. This author, in his work *Viridarium*, gives a brief outline of the life of St. Simon, in which he thus relates the vision:

> " Whilst devoutly praying to the glorious Virgin Mary, Mother of God, she appeared to him surrounded by a multitude of Angels, holding in her hand the Scapular of the Order, and saying, ' *This shall be to you and to all Carmelites a privilege; he who dies in this habit shall be saved.*' "

He then adds these verses :—

> "Si ordinis in signo moritur quis jure benigno
> Solvitur a pœnis, fruiturque locis peramœnis
> Hoc impetravit Simon a Virgine chara
> Postea migravit scandens ad gaudia clara."

After him we have in 1430, Thomas Bradley, an English Carmelite, who was appointed Bishop of Dromore in Ireland by Pope Eugene IV. He was also Apostolic Legate. In the second chapter of his tract *De fundatione, &c. Ordinis Fratrum Glorios. Dei Genitricis Virginis Mariae de Monte Carmeli*, he thus refers to the vision :

> " Erat tunc vir sanctus in religione praedicta, Simon Stock nomine natione Anglicus, qui Dei gloriosam Genitricem jugiter deprecabatur, ut Carmelitarum ordinem, qui speciali gaudet ipsius Virginis titulo, aliquo communiret privilegio . . . Cui Beatissima Virgo cum multitudine Angelorum apparuit, scapulare . . . in benedictis manibus suis tenens et dicens: Hoc erit tibi et cunctis Carmelitis privilegium, quod in hoc moriens aeternum non patietur incendium."

Balduinus Leersius, a Carmelite writer who flourished in 1460, also refers to the vision in the fourth chapter of his *Collectaneum Exemplorum.* His words are :

> " S. Simon sextus Generalis Ordinis, Vir Magnae abstinentiae et devotionis, specialiter ad Beatam Virginem Mariam : multis in vita clarens miraculis : saepius Virginem Gloriosam Dei Genitricem, ordinis Carmelitarum Patronam singularem, deprecabatur humiliter et attentius, ut titulo suo insignitos pariter communiret privilegio . . Quodam ergo tempore dum devote oraret, Virgo gloriosa Mater Dei cum multitudine Angelorum ei apparuit, Scapulare in manu tenens et dicens: *Hoc erit tibi signum et cunctis Carmelitis privilegium : in hoc habitu moriens salvabitur, &c.*, ei Scapulare tradidit. (*V. Spec, Carm.*, T. 1, pars. 3, p. 367.)

Again we have the Carmelite, Peter Bruyne, Prior of the Convent of Ghent. In the sixth chapter of his *Tabulare Ordinis Fratrum*, &c., which was printed in 1474, he thus refers to the Scapular :—

> "Itaque indui Scapularibus aspicimus Carmelitas ; qui, sancto tradente Simone Stock, Virgineis tentum manibus Scapulare (quando suae devotionis in Virginem Mariam, veluti cujusdam praemii praeludio, Mariam etiam aspexerat) mirum in modum alacres induendum susceperunt." (*V. Spec. Carm.*, T. 1, p. 2, p. 209.)

The next important witness we shall quote is Arnold Botius, a Carmelite of Ghent, a renowned theologian, philosopher, orator and poet, who flourished in 1480. He is thus described by the Abbot Trithemius in his book on ecclesiastical writers :

> " Arnoldus Botius, natione Teutonicus, Ordinis Fratrum Beatae Mariae semper Virginis de Monte Carmeli, Conventus Gandensis ; vir in divinis scripturis studiosus et eruditus et in saecularibus litteris egregie doctus, Theologus, Philosophus, Orator et Poeta praeclarus ingenio acutus, eloquio disertus, vita et conversatione devotus."

1014   *The Brown Scapular and the Catholic Dictionary.*

In the sixth chapter of his *Speculum Historiale*, written in 1494, this author alludes briefly to the vision of the Blessed Virgin to St. Simon and his receiving from her hands the Scapular. But in his larger work *De Patronatu Bmac. Virginis Mariae*, he devotes a whole chapter, the tenth, to St. Simon, the Vision, his reception from her hands of the Scapular and its privileges.

The last author we shall quote is John Palaeonydorus, a Carmelite of Mechlin, who published in 1497 a history of the Carmelite order entitled *Fasciculus Tripartitus*. In the third book, seventh chapter, of that work, he gives an account of the Vision of St. Simon, in which he received the Scapular from the Blessed Virgin as a sign of privilege to all Carmelites. He also records the fame which this apparition gained, not only in England, but also in foreign countries, and the numbers of distinguished persons who sought to be invested with the holy habit.

There are many other writers, Carmelites and others, who in different ages of the Church have given us histories of this vision, but we abstain from mentioning them, as we have already, we hope, attained our object, which was to meet the objection in the *Catholic Dictionary*, viz., " The vision is mentioned apparently for the first time, so far as is known for certain, by Grossus, a Carmelite of Toulouse, in his *Viridarium* (1389), then by Paleonidorus (*Antiq. Ord. Carm.* vi. 8, apud Launoy), published in 1495." We have shown that there are many other trustworthy writers who have related the vision to St. Simon before Grossus and Palaeonydorus.

The writer thinks it right to add, however, that the Carmelites claimed the support of an anonymous MS. in the Vatican, said to have been written early in the fourteenth century.

This document, although spoken of thus lightly is of the highest authenticity. It was rigorously examined and approved of by learned Cardinals. It was examined and read in 1635 by the most illustrious Horatius Justinianus and exhibited to the judges of the Holy Office. After a diligent examination they found that its authenticity could not be shaken, and consequently approved of it by their decree, as is related by Irenæus of St. James in his theological tract, cap. 1, § 5 (*V. Exhibitio errorum, &c.*, by Fr. Sebastian of St. Paul, art. 20, p. 550).

There are other old MSS., ancient verses, seals, &c., which prove the constant belief of the faithful in the devotion of the Scapular. In an old MS. which belonged to the Carmelite convent of Mechlin, written in 1484, and containing memorials of the order, there is an epigram on some of its saints, in which St. Simon and the Scapular are thus alluded to :

" Anglicus iste Simon petit a Christi Genitrice
Praesidium matris ac Scapulare suum."
V. Vinea Carmeli, p. 560.

In a convent of the Blessed Virgin near Alost in Flanders, founded about 1351, there was an old seal of the order, possessed from the time of the foundation, on which was represented a figure of the Blessed Virgin in the act of giving the Scapular to St. Simon (*V. Spec. Carm.*, pars. iii., p. 521.)

Another important piece of evidence in favour of the vision is an old canonical Office of St. Simon, written in 1435, in the books of the choir of the Carmelite Convent at Bordeaux, where the body of the saint was buried. It was used there in manuscript for many years, and afterwards printed at Bordeaux in 1580. In this Office there is frequent mention made of the privileges of the Scapular, particularly in the hymns and prayer. In the sixth lesson of Matins there is a full description of the apparition (*V. Vinea Carmeli*, p. 430, where a copy of it may be seen.)

The writer says, " No Catholic, Launoy as little as anyone, doubts the utility and piety of the institution." It is very magnanimous, no doubt, on the part of Launoy and his admirers to admit so much, after having done their utmost, though in vain, to prove that it is of doubtful authenticity.

As to the danger, alluded to, of abuse by a misplaced confidence in the Scapular, we have no fear. Such, too, was the impression of so weighty an authority as Papebroch, who thus expresses himself on the point :

"Neque nata sint (sicut calumniantur nonnulli) stolidam fiduciam ingerere peccantibus adipiscendae salutis, quomodocumque ducatur vita." (*V. Resp. ad Exhib. errorum, &c.*, art. 20, n. 28).

Instead of tending to cause any neglect of the more important duties of religion, it promotes their observance; for the rules of the Sodality enjoin in a special manner such essential virtues and good works as prayer, purity, fasting, mortification, the reception of the sacraments, &c. It is known, too, that it exercises a most salutary influence on those who wear it, as they hold themselves bound, in a special manner to imitate the virtues of their holy Patroness, and to avoid everything unworthy of one wearing her holy Scapular.

Much more might be said in favour of this devotion did the space at our disposal permit. We hope, however, we have attained our present purpose which is merely to meet the difficulties raised against this devotion by the article in the *Catholic Dictionary.*

JOHN E. BARTLEY, O.C.C.

BOSSUET AND CLAUDE.

THE conference of Bossuet with Claude dates from a distance as a fact of history, but it must be ever interesting, more especially to ecclesiastics, to witness, even in history, a polemical encounter between two champions, who in their respective spheres ranked so high amongst the celebrated men who adorned the age in which they lived, and of whom the " great nation " is so justly proud.

The portrait of the illustrious Bishop of Meaux is drawn by Massillon in describing him as " a man of vast and specially favoured genius, of a candour that ever characterises great souls, and minds of the highest order, the ornament of the Episcopate, in whom the clergy of France will for ever feel honoured, a Bishop in the midst of a court, a man

THE IRISH

ECCLESIASTICAL RECORD

𝔄 𝔐𝔬𝔫𝔱𝔥𝔩𝔶 𝔍𝔬𝔲𝔯𝔫𝔞𝔩, 𝔲𝔫𝔡𝔢𝔯 𝔈𝔭𝔦𝔰𝔠𝔬𝔭𝔞𝔩 𝔖𝔞𝔫𝔠𝔱𝔦𝔬𝔫

VOLUME XXIX

JANUARY to JUNE, 1911

𝔉𝔬𝔲𝔯𝔱𝔥 𝔖𝔢𝔯𝔦𝔢𝔰

DUBLIN

BROWNE & NOLAN, LIMITED, NASSAU STREET

1911

Appendix 3

Nihil Obstat:

TERENTIUS O'DONNELL, S.T.D.,

Censor Dep

Imprimi potest:

✠ GULIELMUS,

Archiep. Dublinen.,

Hiberniae Primas.

THE 'SCAPULAR PROMISE' FROM THE HISTORICAL STANDPOINT

IN a recent number of the I. E. RECORD, special attention was drawn to the Indult empowering the Congregation of Rites to grant faculties to Bishops, superiors-general, and priests ' to bless and endow medals with the privileges and indulgences hitherto associated with scapulars.'[1] The question as to how the new legislation may affect the Scapular of Our Lady of Mount Carmel, because of the well-known promise attaching to the wearing of the same, was left in abeyance ' until the matter is placed beyond doubt by some authentic pronouncement.' Meanwhile, the editor kindly allows me to avail myself of the present opportunity to fulfil a promise given to his readers on a former occasion when referring casually to the recognized official sources of reliable information concerning the vision vouchsafed to St. Simon Stock.[2]

At first sight the task does not appear to present any great difficulty, but I then expressly stated that these sources, as quite distinct from the authority usually quoted by other writers, had not yet been so much as mentioned in certain articles published in the I. E. RECORD a few years ago.[3] Readers will remember that in those contributions much was said about a particular document upon the authenticity of which arguments in favour of the historical truth of the promise almost exclusively depended; to be refuted, however, with apparent ease, in a critical article written in reply.[4] Personally, I cannot say that the method adopted by either of the writers appealed to me as being of a kind to test adequately the

---

[1] I. E. RECORD, December, 1910. Reference is made to the Sabbatine Privilege further on.

[2] Ibid., January, 1911, p. 31.

[3] Ibid., May, 1901, p. 385 ; February, March, and April, 1904, pp. 142, 206, 331.

[4] Ibid., July, 1904, p. 59.

evidential value of so important a document, purporting to be a verified copy of an ancient MS. discovered at Bordeaux in the course of the seventeenth century, and which again disappeared in such circumstances as to arouse the suspicions of those 'somewhat sceptically disposed.' I did not find it very reassuring to notice that manifest mistakes made in connexion with this document, by one of the two writers concerned, were described by the other as a 'hopeless muddle,' and attributed to the Carmelites of the fourteenth century—'of the time in fact when the legend originated!'[1]

However, the original MS. being no longer available for scientific examination, I have undertaken to demonstrate from the positive evidence of other medieval documents still extant the historical truth of the 'Scapular Vision'; and I will ask the reader to bear in mind the essential points of the narrative found in the tomb of St. Simon Stock at Bordeaux by Father John Chéron, who testified to its having been written by Peter Swanyngton, the contemporary and intimate friend of the saint :—

Cum effunderem animam meam in conspectu Domini . . . et in omni fiducia Dominam meam Virginem Mariam deprecarer, quod sicut volebat nos appellari Fratres suos, monstraret se matrem, eripiendo nos de casu tentationum, et aliquo signo gratiae nos recommendando erga ipsos qui nos persequebantur, dicendo illi cum suspiriis : Flos Carmeli, Vitis florigera, Splendor coeli, Virgo puerpera singularis ; Mater mitis, sed viri nescia, Carmelitis da privilegia, Stella maris : apparuit mihi cum grandi comitatu, et tenendo habitum Ordinis dixit : ' Hoc erit tibi et cunctis Carmelitis privilegium. In hoc moriens aeternum non patietur incendium.' Et . . . disparendo dixit, quod mitterem ad dominum Innocentium, benedicti Filii sui Vicarium, qui de gravaminibus remedium praestaret. . . . Idem verbum [continues Swanyngton] mittebat ad fratres qui erant in aliis locis valde tristes, per consolatoriam, quam ego immeritus, homine Dei dicente, scribebam, ut similiter gratias agerent, orando et perseverando. Cantabrigiae in crastinum Divisionis Apostolorum, 1251.[2]

---

[1] I. E. RECORD, July, 1904, p. 65.
[2] *Speculum Carmelitanum*, i., 518 ; *Vinea Carmeli*, p. 439.

Here, at least, we have the principal details of the Scapular Vision as accepted by the Carmelites of the seventeenth century; and these they submitted with the utmost confidence when exhorting the faithful to filial reliance on the truth of our Lady's wondrous promise :—

(*a*) Down to the year 1251 the White Friars, in England especially, suffered grievous hardships.

(*b*) So oppressive had their trials become at that date, the Prior-General of the Order, St. Simon Stock, could only implore the Blessed Virgin, as chief patroness of the Carmelites, to intervene miraculously, granting some special sign of her powerful protection.

(*c*) Our Lady appeared to him and gave the habit of the Order as the desired pledge : attaching thenceforth to the wearing of it a most consoling promise ; and instructing St. Simon to appeal forthwith to Pope Innocent IV. for succour against their oppressors.

(*d*) The saint took immediate steps to have so great a favour made known to the religious generally ; and a striking miracle, wrought at Winchester, is associated with the ensuing popularity of the White Friars throughout England. This is recorded by Swanyngton as a subsequent event ; but I thought it well to include everything of distinct importance, in order that the critical reader may judge for himself as to whether Father John Chéron could be fairly accused in this wise : ' Having come across some sort of account a century or more older than his time, he chose to assume that it was a contemporary narrative, attributed it to Swanyngton, and manipulated it ' accordingly.[1]

Seeing that it is now my purpose to establish these points quite independently of the narrative of Peter Swanyngton, and even of the authorities quoted in his *Collections*[2] by John Bale ; of course those who would still maintain a sceptical attitude towards the Scapular Vision must be prepared to explain upon what rational grounds they could

---

[1] I. E. RECORD. July, 1904, p. 64.
[2] MS. Harley, 3838.

reject such *historical* facts as I am about to submit for genuinely critical investigation; for these facts are so recorded by the respective writers, whom I shall consult in contemporary MS. copies of their works, as to convey the impression of absolute certainty; and it would be simply impossible to think of fraud or credulity in conjunction with their names. As for the source of *their* information, there can be but one opinion; but it might seem too like ' begging the question ' were I to insist upon it at this stage.[1]

As ' an eye-witness ' of the events which he himself describes, a prominent place is due to the evidence of William de Sanvico, who furnishes a vivid narrative of the expulsion of his brethren from the Holy Land, A.D. 1238-1241, and of the troubles that awaited them in Europe. A seventeenth-century version of this most important narrative was mentioned by a former contributor to the I. E. RECORD when treating of the ' Scapular Promise '; but nothing was said of the ancient MS. copies of the treatise known to be in existence.[2] However, it is not my wish to complain of this omission; but I must draw attention to the painfully laboured effort then made to convict de Sanvico of historical inaccuracy, because the particular date which he assigns did not happen to bear out rather a bewildering surmise on the part of the contributor to whom I refer: that the Scapular Vision really occurred just ten years later than the time specified by Peter Swanyngton. (Whence the ' hopeless muddle ' in chronology ascribed to the medieval Carmelites!)[3] In a subsequent article it was admitted that de Sanvico had given the correct date after all; that it had been verified at some official source of information.[4] Freely confessing my own inability to

---

[1] But I shall have occasion to allude to the matter again. In the meantime I may refer the reader to the *Speculum Carmelitanum*, t. ii. n. 1478, p. 413. Indeed, a detailed vindication of Father John Chéron's memory suggests the theme for a special and particularly interesting article.

[2] I. E. RECORD, May, 1901, p. 385, n. 2.

[3] Ibid., p. 404.

[4] Ibid., February, 1904, p. 152.

follow the argument designed to show that this only confirmed the plausibleness of the surmise in question, I will
here quote the passage as occurring in the version of de
Sanvico's narrative issued A.D. 1370; and it is now taken
from a contemporary transcript [1] :—

Videntes ergo fratres quod super praemissis [hardships] non
poterant cum praelatis favorem invenire, Virginem Mariam
eorum patronam humiliter deprecabantur, ut quae ipsos ad
regiones illas pervenire fecerat a praemissis diabolicis tenta-
tionibus eos eriperet. Virgo itaque Maria priori eorum revelavit
ut ad summum pontificem Innocentium intrepide fratres sui
accederent ; quia ab eo salubre remedium contra praemissa
gravamina reportarent. Ad ipsum ergo tunc Perusii com-
morantem accedentes, fratres ipsi exposuerunt gravamina quae
curati eis inferebant, et favorem modicum quem super praemissis
praelati eis impendebant. Pontifex autem praedictis fratribus
compatiens scripsit praelatis Idibus Januarii, A.D. 1252, mandans
eis ut super praemissis pium favorem fratribus impenderent et
molestatores eorum per censuram ecclesiasticam appellatione
postposita compescerent. . . . Sicque paulatim hanc religionem
in diversis fidelium regionibus per Europam multiplicabant.[2]

. Now, it must be borne in mind that William de Sanvico
was himself a member of the Order at the very date
mentioned in his narration. His object in writing was to
leave a formal record of the circumstances in which his
brethren in religion had been expelled from the Holy Land
(A.D. 1238-1241), and as to how their presence was actively
resented in Europe—in England principally—until the
intervention of Pope Innocent IV. on their behalf. To my
mind this passing allusion to our Lady's apparition to
St. Simon Stock—the then Prior-General of the Order—
is proof positive of the fact of that supernatural favour
being already thoroughly well known, not only to the
Carmelites themselves, but to the faithful generally, when
de Sanvico wrote his relation ; and, remembering the
purpose which he had in view, I should unhesitatingly

---

[1] MS. A. 9. 241.—I. E. RECORD, January, 1911, p. 44.
[2] In a former chapter (iii.) de Sanvico makes express mention of the
Carmelites in England.

pronounce any more detailed account of such an event as being entirely out of place in a narrative of this kind.[1] Nevertheless, even from this casual reference we learn :—

(a) At a specified date the Carmelites were enduring certain grave trials.

(b) It was then their Prior-General had a vision, during which he received particular instructions from the Blessed Virgin for the encouragement and consolation of the religious.

(c) Because of these instructions the Carmelites laid their case before Pope Innocent IV.—to receive immediate succour at the hands of that Pontiff (A.D. 1252).

(d) The prosperity of the Order in Europe (and especially in England) followed gradually, apparently as a matter of course . . . It would be superfluous to invite comparison of these facts with those recounted in connexion with the selfsame event by Peter Swanyngton.

No one could dream of questioning the importance of de Sanvico's testimony as to the fact of St. Simon Stock having been favoured by a vision from the Blessed Virgin at a trying juncture in the history of the Carmelite Order ; for his evidence is confirmed by the Bull of Pope Innocent IV. issued on that occasion, and for the very purpose assigned.[2] But we have just seen that were it not for this corroboration, de Sanvico's veracity as a witness would stand seriously impugned in the opinion of some recent writers; because of his having so emphatically stated that the opposition to his brethren in Europe had begun to wane from the year 1252. I am not aware of any effort having hitherto been made to show that even independently of the Bull of Pope Innocent IV. the authenticity of the narrative, in this respect, might be easily vindicated from other contemporary sources. Take, for example, the

---

[1] This narrative was written in the latter half of the thirteenth century; but the exact year is not known, the annalists submitting various dates as probable, still merely conjectural.

[2] In the I. E. RECORD, February, 1904, p. 152, this Bull is cited as 'No. 5,563, in Elie Berger's edition' of the Register of Pope Innocent IV. I prefer to quote from the transcript given in the version of de Sanvico's narrative, issued A.D. 1370, MS. A. 9, 241.

English *State Papers* of that period. It is surely significant that prior to the same year (1252) we meet with no mention from which we could infer that the Order had made the least material progress in the country; although it is quite certain that isolated communities of the Hermits of Carmel had settled in England since A.D. 1212, when their austere mode of life was embraced by St. Simon Stock; while we have de Sanvico's own assurance of their number being considerably augmented there after the year 1238.[1] I do not forget that these facts clash with the conjectures of critics who rely solely on the authority of John Bale for their information concerning the history of the Carmelites; and indeed I have wondered how they would manage to reconcile their very dogmatic assertions on the subject with what Bale himself states so positively: that he had seen and examined an ancient MS. clearly demonstrating the fact of the growing fame of the Carmelites throughout Europe as early as the year 1220.[2] I may add, incidentally, that John de Horneby—who successfully upheld the claims of his Order at Cambridge—produced conclusive evidence to show that these religious had already been established in Cyprus long before the end of the twelfth century.[3]

However, the prospects of the English White Friars became much brighter, undoubtedly, from the date mentioned by de Sanvico; for preserved among the Patent Rolls of King Henry III. we still have the official record of their having secured the royal protection (for the first time, so far as I can ascertain), A.D. 1252, the 'Letters' granting the same being 'sine termino cum hac clausula: Et rogamus quod cum ad vos venerint elemosinas petituri, eis de bonis vestris misericorditer erogetis.'[4] In the circumstances I do not think that even the most exacting critic would venture to brush aside the issue of this patent as a mere 'striking coincidence': that it admits of an inter-

---

[1] Cambridge MS. (University Library). Ff. 6, 11, f. 42.
[2] *Scriptores Britanniae*, vol. i. p. 260; ibid., p. 269.
[3] MS. Bodley, e Mus. 86, f. 212b.
[4] Patent Roll 37, Henry III., m. 21, Public Record Office, London.

pretation different from the one which I claim it bears, marking a most desirable change in the condition of the Carmelites in England immediately after our Lady's vision to St. Simon Stock. William de Sanvico piously traces the intervention of Pope Innocent IV. on that occasion to a supernatural favour ; to what are we to attribute the very opportune mediation of King Henry III. ?

But the inaugurator of hostile criticism of the Scapular Devotion in the seventeenth century—the 'famous and somewhat sceptical French scholar, J. Launoy,' to quote from an article in the I. E. RECORD[1]—denied that this vision was to be associated with any such promise as that insisted upon by Father John Chéron and other contemporary Carmelites.[2] Moreover, if there had been a promise of this kind de Sanvico had here an excellent opportunity of mentioning so extraordinary a privilege : 'Loquendi tamen locum fuisse vel opportunissimum, quis negaret ? ' Certain writers of the present day consider the same question equally pertinent, citing the omission as a forcible argument based on the 'negative evidence of history '! Besides, being in the Holy Land at the time, de Sanvico could only have acquired his information at ' second-hand,' so to speak, from those religious of the English province whom he may have met, later on, at some general chapter of the Order—sufficiently reliable witnesses, I should have thought ; if I may not refer to the consoling tidings conveyed to the Carmelites generally by Peter Swanyngton, acting on the express injunction received from St. Simon Stock.

It was Launoy's taunt that he could find no authoritative pronouncement on the question—the testimony of some one who in virtue of his official capacity had so spoken about the origin of the Scapular Promise as to remove every vestige of doubt concerning its authenticity from the strictly historical point of view. As for Father John Chéron's discovery, it has been stated that ' the

---

[1] July, 1904, p. 62.
[2] Joannis Launoii, *Dissertationes V., De Simonis Stochii Viso*, etc., ed. iii. Paris, 1663, p. 12. I do not think that his other treatise on the Scapular, *Examen du Privilège d'Alexandre V.*, etc., has yet been removed from the Index.

VOL. XXIX.—18

appearance of this *deus ex machina* was hailed by him and others with ill-concealed derision ' ; but our informant apparently forgot to add how Launoy treats the evidence furnished by a very renowned Prior-General of the Carmelite Order, already distinguished among his contemporaries A.D. 1370—the date of that version of de Sanvico's narrative from which I have quoted; and little more than one hundred years after the death of St. Simon Stock.[1] The famous French scholar openly jeers at this evidence : first declaring and *trying* to prove that the witness was not trustworthy ; but subsequently modifying this opinion, as he felt satisfied that the record in question had been forged by the Carmelites after the witness's death.[2] It so happens that I myself am in a position to show how very much mistaken Launoy was in this respect, at least.

The Prior-General referred to was Father John Grossi, destined to render services of incalculable worth to Christendom by his successful efforts to end the Great Western Schism—one of the most trying crises in the whole history of the Church. He was Superior-General of one of the two sections of the Order in the year 1389 ; and although now of advanced age, he found himself unanimously elected Prior-General of all the Carmelites in a Chapter specially convened, A.D. 1411, after the long, sad estrangement between the religious acknowledging the authority of Pope Urban VI. and his successors, and those who had proclaimed themselves 'Clementines.' It was m .inly through Grossi's instrumentality that the blessings of peace and union had been restored to the Order—a happy augury of what should happen at the Council of Constance later on. Furthermore, in order to insure the permanency of this revival of monastic fervour in his own Order, Grossi wrote the well-known *Viridarium* for the instruction and edification of the religious.[3] It was his object to illustrate

---

[1] I. E. RECORD. July, 1904, p. 62.

[2] Launoy, *De Simonis Stochii Viso*, p. 16 ; ibid. p. 39, et passim.

[3] I have come across several medieval MS. copies of this most important work, but circumstances did not admit of my examining them very closely, had I then occasion to do so. Fortunately, in view of recent events, there is an admirable copy preserved in the Bodleian Library (MS. Laud. Misc. 722, f. 113), which I am utilizing for my present purpose.

the ideal of the true Carmelite's life by the examples of certain saints of the Order who had attained to preeminent holiness simply by the observance of a Rule that contained an epitome of the traditions handed down to them from the days of the Prophet Elias.[1] Amongst others was St. Simon Stock, who obtained for them so great a privilege at the hands of the Blessed Virgin, in virtue of those selfsame traditions, appealing to her on behalf of his brethren then sorely tried throughout Europe. But Grossi takes it for granted, manifestly, that all members of the Order would be well aware of the event to which he thus briefly refers, dwelling, however, on certain details of the vision that supplement the incidental allusion made to the same extraordinary favour by William de Sanvico.

He knew that he could further the purpose which he had in mind when writing the *Viridarium* by speaking of his own recent experience in England, where he had witnessed some of the marvellous results of our Lady's promise ; and in doing so he has left a reliable account of the actual sense in which the Scapular Devotion was understood by the faithful generally within Grossi's own memory, which, as we shall now see, brings us very close to the time of St. Simon Stock.[2]

Remembering the responsible position held in the Order by John Grossi A.D. 1389, surely it is not too much to assume that he had then attained the fiftieth year of his age ? Otherwise, how could he himself have so pathetically pleaded the ' burden of years ' in order to be relieved of the office of Prior-General long before the death of one of his most enthusiastic admirers amongst the English White Friars, the celebrated Thomas Walden, who died in 1430 ?[3] At all events, we have positive evidence to

---

[1] I. E. RECORD, January, 1911, p. 41.

[2] It is not pleasant to have to say that the evidential value of Grossi's testimony has been so represented recently as to obscure completely the importance of its bearing on the authenticity of the Scapular Promise, recalling, in fact, Launoy's uncritical comments.

[3] MS. Harley, 3838, f. 82b ; MS. Bodley, 73, f. 98.

show that certain Carmelites who had been professed in the Order before the death of St. Simon Stock were still living A.D. 1338, which merely implies, after all, that these religious had now reached their ninetieth year—by no means a wonderful age.[1] Consequently, had there ever been the slightest misgiving about the exact interpretation of the Scapular Promise, many of John Grossi's own contemporaries could testify to what they themselves had heard from the lips of those venerable men concerning so remarkable an event in the history of the Order.

However, there is nothing in the *Viridarium* to lead us to infer that this was how Grossi verified the facts which he records with such absolute conviction of their authenticity. Hence, I submit that he had access to some source of reliable information, intimately known to himself and his coevals, including the renowned Walden : some such letter, for instance, as that to which reference is made in the MS. discovered by Father John Chéron at Bordeaux. Of course those who rely on the authority of the somewhat sceptical Launoy will not be prepared to admit the reasonableness of this conjecture, since the famous French scholar bluntly accuses the Carmelites of a subsequent age of having ' manipulated ' the *Viridarium* after the death of both Walden and Grossi : ' nec tunc immerito dicetur, eam [the fame of the Scapular Vision] assutam esse ab iis, qui post Waldensis obitum Swaingtoni historiam, et Grossi *Viridarium* transcripserunt.'[2] So sure was Launoy that the silence of Thomas Walden (erroneously assumed) argued this atrocious fraud, he bases upon it his chief argument against the veracity of the Scapular Promise : ' Hoc, iterum dico, prae ceteris argumentum me convincit.'[3] But we have seen that Walden did not die until the year 1430, whereas the aged Grossi survived until A.D. 1434. Now, the copy of the *Viridarium* preserved in the Bodleian Library dates from

---

[1] MS. Selden, supra, 41, 4, cap. x. ; also *Speculum Ordinis*, ed. 1507. De Hildesheim's treatise.
[2] *De Simonis Stochii Viso*, p. 16,
[3] Ibid.

the year 1426, and from it the following passage has been transcribed [1] :—

Saepius vero Virginem gloriosam Dei Genitricem patronam Ordinis deprecabatur (St. Simon) ut suo titulo insignitos comuniret privilegio. . . . Sic demum Beata Virgo cum multitudine angelorum beato viro apparuit Scapulare Ordinis in manibus suis tenens et dicens : ' Hoc erit tibi et cunctis Carmelitis privilegium in hoc moriens salvabitur.' Ratione hujus magni privilegii diversi proceres regni Angliae, utpote dictus Edwardus Rex Angliae Secundus post Conquestum, qui fratres praedictos fundavit Oxoniis dans illis proprium palatium pro conventu, Dominus Henricus dux Lancastriae primus, qui miraculis multis dicitur claruisse, et multi alii nobiles hujus regni praedicti Scapulare Ordinis in vita clandestine portaverunt in quo postea obierunt. [2]

This testimony—and nothing could be more explicit—simply amounts to a statement of well-known facts, even including reference to the popularity of the Scapular Devotion in England ; for the religious generally would have been aware that Grossi had visited that country in his official capacity, a fact formally attested to by the Royal Letters of Protection granted to him on that occasion, and which we find recorded on the Patent Rolls of the period, A.D. 1412.[3] So we are assured, on reliable authority, once more :—

(*a*) That St. Simon Stock had occasion to implore our Lady's miraculous intervention during some crisis in the history of the Carmelite Order.

(*b*) That the Blessed Virgin appeared to him, and gave the Scapular of his Order as a sign of her special protection, attaching a promise to the wearing of the same.

(*c*) That all the faithful might participate in this promise,

---

[1] MS. Laud. Misc. 722, fol. 113. In calce, ' Explicit origo cum vita de sanctis fratribus Ordinis Beatae Mariae Dei Genitricis de Monte Carmeli. Anno Domini, Mo.CCCCo.XXVIo.' Conf. ' Viridarii, Pars Secunda,' in the *Speculum Carmelitanum* (Antwerp, A.D. 1680), t. i. pars ii. p. 139.

[2] MS. Laud. Misc. 722, fol. 114b.

[3] Patent Roll, 14 Henry IV., m. 10. This is a most important and interesting document, and is preserved in the Public Record Office, London.

and many began to wear the Scapular of the Carmelites *secretly*.

(*d*) That it was in virtue of this promise benefactors became so devoted to the Order, particularly in England.

Here the critical student of the question may well ask himself : In face of this evidence how could Father John Chéron have been accused of ' manipulating ' the MS. found in the tomb of St. Simon Stock at Bordeaux ? He, at least, knew that Grossi's *Viridarium* had been written and transcribed before the death of Thomas Walden, during whose life, according to the sceptic Launoy, the White Friars would not have dared to exploit such a fraud !

Seeing, therefore, that the influence of the famous French scholar extends to our own times, and that Launoy challenged his readers to search the works of Walden for confirmation of the Scapular Promise, it may prove instructive if I dwell a little longer on this aspect of the case, since I am by no means inclined to admit Walden's silence on the subject ; in fact, he was the very first to furnish a most valuable clue to the solution of the only difficulty which I myself had experienced in connexion with the Scapular Devotion—the express reference made to the Carmelite habit in the book *On the Institution of the First Monks* and in the *Ancient Constitutions* of the Order. I do not forget the opinion of that modern German writer, quoted on a former occasion in the I. E. RECORD,[1] who believed that the Carmelites ' had no scapulars in the beginning of the Order ' ; but the following testimony is far more reliable, and has come down to us from the year 412 :—

Superhumeralibus etiam prisci Religionis professores tempore legis veteris utebantur. . . . Erat autem superhumerale vestis sine manicis, usque ad renes descendens, in utroque latere aperta, brachiis etiam ea nudatis, cujus posterior pars in humeris copulabatur parti anteriori. Novae autem legis tempore huic vesti in apertura colli junctum fuit caputium, tegens caput, et scapulas. Quam nostrae Religionis professores . . . usque

---

[1] July, 1904, p. 73. note 2.

nunc (A.D. 412) summa cum diligentia diebus ac noctibus indesinenter gestabant.[1]

Furthermore, the reason why this particular garment (the scapular) should be worn constantly with such scrupulous care is immediately assigned by John of Jerusalem : because it denotes obedience—the basis of the monastic virtues. In the very next chapter (xlvii.) he explains the mystical meaning of the white mantle worn by the Carmelites from the beginning, and concerning which, likewise, some extraordinary statements have been made in the I. E. RECORD by writers unaware, or unmindful, of certain historical facts recorded by St. Cyril of Constantinople.[2] So, too, is it to the book *On the Institution of the First Monks* that we must trace that distinction between the scapular as *habitus professionis* and the white mantle as *signum religionis* to be found in the writings of the medieval Carmelite doctors, which has been entirely ignored by certain modern critics who prefer to rely on the authority of the seventeenth-century opponents of the Order.[3]

Turning to the most ancient copy of the Carmelite Constitutions to hand—those approved of at the General Chapter of the year 1324—this is what we read in the sixth Rubric ('De dormitione Fratrum') : 'Statuimus quod fratres in tunica et Scapulari dormiant supracincti, sub poena gravis culpae. Exceptis infirmis quorum relinquimus arbitrio ut Scapulare induant vel deponant.'[4] But this, undoubtedly, is taken from the *Ancient Constitutions* of the Order quoted by the renowned Baconthorpe and several of his contemporaries, and which date from the days of

---

[1] I. E. RECORD, January, 1911, p. 39, note 1; MS. A. 9, 241; ibid. p. 44.
[2] Ibid., July, 1904, p. 72 ; cont. ibid. January, 1911, p. 47; *Liber S. Cyrilli Constan.* cap. ii.
[3] *Signum religionis* rather refers to the object for which the particular Order was founded, *ad venerationem Virginis Deiparae*, in the case of the Carmelites, as John Baconthorpe shows so clearly in his beautiful treatise on the subject. MS. Laud. Misc. 722, fol. 122. See I. E. RECORD, July, 1904, p. 72. But John de Horneby proves conclusively that it is not the mantle, *sed Scapulare (quod) est habitus professionis meae.*—MS. Bodley, e. Mus. 86, fol. 101b.
[4] MS. Add. 16372, British Museum.

St. Brocard, who is said to have compiled them by drawing largely upon the book of the Patriarch John.[1]

Hence my own difficulty to understand how this statute became affected by the promise attaching to the scapular from the time of St. Simon Stock until I came across the explanation in the *Doctrinale Fidei*, the best known of all Walden's works; for he instances this very Rubric against the Wyclifites, and in doing so elucidates the meaning : ' Nostri Carmelitae in tunica candida et Scapulari *nocturno* ' [dormiunt].[2] This express mention of a special scapular for use during sleep reveals that even in Walden's time a custom prevailed in the Order to interpret the Rubric in a more rigorous sense ; because what had formerly been worn, day and night, as the emblem of monastic obedience was now revered as the most appropriate sign chosen by the Blessed Virgin to be the vehicle of her reassuring promise. And no longer would the religious avail themselves of that clause (*exceptis infirmis*) which modified the ordinance in case of necessity. New legislation on the subject was introduced later on ; but even at the present day the Constitutions of the Discalced Carmelites afford a good illustration of how the custom to which I allude became obligatory in the Order in the course of time : ' Fratres dum cubant, Scapulari *parvo* utantur . . . nullus sanus, vel aeger, suum habitum, hoc est Scapulare, exuat, sed aegrotantibus *tenuius* permittetur.'[3]

Having ventured to mention the difficulty suggested to my own mind in this connexion, I must take care not to leave the reader under the impression that there is anything conjectural about the solution thus derived from the *Doctrinale Fidei*. Nor could I demonstrate this more satisfactorily than by adducing the unimpeachable testimony of another of the famed Walden's contemporaries—the Venerable Thomas Bradley, chosen by Pope Eugene IV. to proceed to Rhodes as Apostolic Legate, and afterwards to bear the burden of the episcopate as Bishop of Dromore

---

[1] I. E. RECORD. January, 1911. p. 40.
[2] T. iii.. col. 4, A. f. 130b.
[3] Pars i. cap. x., *De Fratrum Indumentis*, nn. 17, 19.

in Ireland.[1] He had already acquired great renown throughout England while Walden himself was still Superior of the White Friars of that province ; and his works include several most valuable treatises concerning the history of the Carmelite Order, in one of which the Scapular Promise is dealt with as follows :—

Cui (St. Simon Stock) Beatissima Virgo cum multitudine Angelorum apparuit, Scapulare, seu Cucullam antiqui Ordinis Carmelitarum cum parvo caputio usque ad cingulum descendens in benedictis manibus suis tenens, et dicens : Hoc erit tibi, et cunctis Carmelitis privilegium, quod in hoc moriens aeternum non patietur incendium, id est, in hoc moriens salvabitur, tradidit. Quod ipse Simon devote suscipiens caputium grossum de Scapulari seu cuculla sua deposuit, et caputium suum aliud juxta formam caputii, quod a B. Virgine receperat Scapulari addidit ; quo etiam Scapulari tam ipse, quam omnes alii Carmelitae usque in hodiernum diem die nocteque pro habitu suae professionis utuntur.[2]

I may remark that, in this instance, Bradley was treating of the Carmelite habit in detail, and merely refers to the Scapular Vision in order to explain certain alterations which had been introduced by St. Simon Stock. He, too, speaks of the promise as of unquestionable authenticity, while in another place he mentions the ' Winchester miracle' when speaking of the monasteries founded for the White Friars in England: 'Wyntonyae fundator Dominus Petrus de Wyntonia Praepositus Ecclesiae Sanctae Helenae, Wyntoniensis : qui propter miraculum sibi per gloriosam Virginem Mariam ostensum, Fratres ibidem fundavit.'[3]

---

[1] In Ware's *Bishops* (Harris, Dublin, 1739), vol. i. p. 261 sqq., it is stated that Bishop Bradley succeeded to the See of Dromore, A.D. 1434, and resigned in 1440. But this is not borne out by the note in MS. Harley 211, fol. 191, which appears to have been written by Bradley himself : ' Orate pro anima Thomae Bradley quondam anachoreta in conventu Fratrum Carmelitarum Norwic. Et postea, A.D. 1448, factus est Episcopus Dromor. in Hibernia et Sanctae Romanae Ecclesiae Legatus.' Of course he may have been consecrated before the death of Pope Eugene IV. (A.D. 1447). Conf. *Dict. Nat. Biogr.*, vol. li. p. 147.
[2] Conf. *Speculum Carmelitanum*, vol. i. pt. ii. p. 192. Cambridge MS. Ff. 6, 11, f. 42.
[3] See the *Speculum Carmelitanum*, vol. i. pt. ii. p. 184, which also contains an excellent summary of the Cambridge MS., University Library, Ff. 6, 11 ; ibid. pp. 190-194, et passim.

Appendix 3

a dispute. Being required to deal with the subject according to rigorously critical methods, of course all such irrelevant issues had to be eliminated during my investigations, with the result that I found no difficulty whatever in often condensing a whole treatise into a few pages ; and even in these latter rarely perceived anything bearing directly on the question of the monastic traditions of the Carmelites, or on the vision of our Lady to St. Simon Stock.[1]

It was by this process I at length laid bare the absolutely gratuitous assertions upon the refutation of which many writers of the Order simply wasted their industry, instead of insisting upon a far more satisfactory cause being assigned for the rejection of the testimony of those witnesses whose authority should appeal to the most exacting critics of even our own times.[2] For the rest, there was always the ' negative evidence of history ' to urge against the pretensions of the Carmelites, concerning which argument I may quote what struck me as a very prudent reservation—based on Mabillon's familiar admonition[3]— made in the I. E. RECORD a few years ago : ' No one knows better than the present writer how delicately the *argumentum a silentio* should be handled on account of the extremely unsatisfactory state of our old records' ;[4] although, in the circumstances, it might have been more appropriate to suggest Bellarmine's forcibly expressed conviction : ' Respondeo nihil concludi ex argumentis ab auctoritate negativa, et plus creditur tribus testibus affirmantibus, quam mille nihil dicentibus.'[5]

Well, I have now submitted the evidence of my own three witnesses, who were manifestly unaware of the historical importance of those casual references to what they themselves regarded as a matter of indisputable fact

---

[1] I happen to have by me a very valuable collection of works occasioned by that controversy, some of them exceedingly rare.

[2] Especially the testimony of those quoted in my article on 'The Monastic Traditions of the Carmelites.' I. E. RECORD, January, 1911.

[3] See *Traite des études monastiques*, p. ii. c. xiii.

[4] I. E. RECORD, March, 1904, which the reader may compare with the opinion expressed in the *Monumenta Historica Carmelitana*, p. 343 : ' Magis tamen me movet silentium auctorum.'

[5] *De Rom. Pontif.*, l. ii. cap. 8.

upon whose authority I should implicitly rely, had I never heard of Swanyngton's narration. It is hardly necessary to add that I am quite convinced of the authenticity of the MS. found at Bordeaux, utterly rejecting the assumption of its having been ' manipulated ' in any way by the discoverer.[1] Were it permissible, I could submit some interesting illustrations from personal experience to show that equally opportune discoveries have been made in our own days by those engaged in [historical research, one instance being, if anything, somewhat more remarkable than the case of Father John Chéron. For I myself have been instrumental in bringing to light an original document, numbered among ' hopelessly lost ' MSS. for several hundred years, and deemed of vital importance to a particular cause in which I happened to be very intimately concerned at the time of the discovery. I do not know whether the cause to which I refer would meet with hostile criticism at the hands of those writers who have professed themselves no less sceptical than Launoy concerning the Scapular Promise, nor whether they would insist upon either my superiors or myself producing the original document in question, once we should have volunteered our express assurance of its genuineness and identity.[2]

As for the Sabbatine Indulgence, considered from the historical standpoint, I have not space at my disposal to deal with the subject in a manner that would be likely to prove acceptable to my readers. The distinguished Jesuit theologian who replied to Launoy's attack on the Scapular Devotion quotes Baconthorpe and de Horneby, the contemporaries of Pope John XXII., to establish the authenticity of the privilege as described in verified copies of the famous Papal Bull proclaiming the extraordinary new favour granted to the clients of Our Lady of Carmel.[3] He does so, because these renowned English White Friars

---

[1] See I. E. RECORD, July, 1904, p. 64.

[2] Of course this article has received the formal approval of the Superior-General of the Discalced Carmelites. (Romae, 25 Januarii, 1911.)

[3] ' Scapulare Partheno-Carmeliticum.' See note at the end of this article, p. 287.

enjoyed special opportunities of consulting official documents relating to the history of their Order, which were then kept in the archives of the London monastery. Launoy would complain of the negligence of the Carmelites of the sixteenth century in their having failed to preserve the actual Bull announcing the Sabbatine Indulgence.[1] Those acquainted with the history of the suppression of the English monasteries may be inclined, like myself, to regard this as very unreasonable ; even if they did not know of the existence of a number of authentic copies, including several made in the course of the fifteenth century.[2] As a matter of fact, the evidence shows that verified copies of important documents of this kind were at once distributed among the principal monasteries of the Order to insure their contents being conveyed to the religious with the least possible delay.[3] I could cite the testimony of John Grossi himself to this effect ;[4] or that of the apostate Bale, whose authority seems of such moment to recent critics of the Scapular Devotion, adding that even after his sad defection he still upheld the authenticity of the Bull of Pope John XXII., utilizing it in one of his most scurrilous diatribes against the Papacy.[5]

Bale, unhappily, was but one of those wretched men who were then endeavouring to deaden the voice of con-science by calumniating all priests and religious steadfast

---

[1] *De Sabbatinae Bullae Privilegio*, op. c. p. 111.

[2] I may mention the three copies at the Vatican which I have not yet examined ; so I cannot say, for certain, whether they are merely transcripts of a much later date.

[3] John Bale speaks of copies of the ' Sabbatine Bull ' which he himself had seen, *tam in Anglia quam in Hannonia*, and we may assume it was from the former he transcribed the copy given in MS. Harley, 1819, f. 61b. This does not appear to have occurred to the writer in the I. E. RECORD, April, 1904, pp. 331 sqq. In note 17 to the same article a useful quotation is given to show why many original Papal Bulls are not to be found in the *Regesta* (*Papal Registers*, vol. i. pref.).

[4] Rouen MS. No. 772 : ' Regula Fratrum Ordinis B.M. de Monte Carmeli per Innocentium Papam Quartum correcta, qui sedit anno MCCXLVII., cujus Bullam ego Frater Joannes Grossi, Prior-Generalis. vidi in conventu Londoniarum et Coloniae.' Further positive evidence of Grossi's visit to England !

[5] ' Istam apparitionem cum inauditis indulgentiis, et animarum a purgatorio liberationibus, in quolibet ejus festo et in sabbatorum Missis, in quadam Bulla legi. . . . Quae etiam Romae anno Domini 1530, sub Clemente VII. renovata fuit '—(*Scriptores Britanniae*, vol. i. p. 401).

in their sacred calling. So that if he, or any of those other apostates, suspected the possibility of forgery in such a connexion, is it credible that he would have omitted to chronicle the fact of what he would stigmatize as a fraud (or 'fable') being encouraged by the Holy See for the infamous reason which he actually assigns?[1] It forms no part of my task to enter on a defence of the Sabbatine Indulgence, especially just now, when the new legislation regarding scapulars encourages the faithful to avail themselves all the more fervently of this great privilege, dating back to the pontificate of John XXII., as every truly critical student of the question is well aware.[2] However, should anyone desire to weigh the evidence as presented by an 'independent witness,' I have already indicated a work which meets Launoy's frivolous objections in detail.[3] And if I have singled out the French sceptic

---

[1] 'Procuratione pecuniaria.' ibid. See I. E. RECORD, January, 1911, p. 98.

[2] 'Sabbatino, quod dicunt, Scapularis B.M.V. de Monte Carmelo Privilegio non excepto'—(*Acta Apostolicae Sedis*, vol. iii. p. 23, die 15 Decembris, 1910).

[3] *Scapulare Partheno-Carmelitanum Illustratum, et Defensum*, A. R. P. Theophilo Raynaudo, Societatis Jesu Theologo. Romae M.DCC.XXX. This work was first published A.D. 1653. The learned author treats of the Confraternity of the Brown Scapular also (ibid. p. 186), and proves very conclusively, I think, that St. Louis of France *did* wear the habit (or Scapular) of the Carmelites. It is interesting to note that I have lately come across an original 'Charter' granted to the chaplain of the Confraternity Altar in St. John's Church by Robert Brussone, Prior of the White Friars of Perth, 28th of March 1508.' (Archives of King James the Sixth's Hospital, Perth; cont. *The Ecclesiastical Annals of Perth* (Fittis), under A.D. 1508.)
Father Raynaud follows Bellarmine in warning his readers of the dangers, and 'de inanitate argumenti ducti ab auctoritate negativa,' p. 188. I add this because it has been suggested that one might reasonably expect to find some allusion to the origin of the Scapular Devotion in ancient Manuals (the Ordinances, etc.) of the Confraternity (I. E. RECORD, July, 1904, p. 74). I failed to grasp the reason for any such expectation; and after having consulted a number of Manuals of this kind—'Antiquissimae Archi-Confraternitatis S. Mariani Scapularis'—I discovered nothing bearing on the subject, except in a single instance, where a copy of the Sabbatine Indulgence was inserted at the end. ('Bulla Sabbathina,' Augustae, A.D. 1740.) If asked, what about those various guilds connected with Carmelite churches in the Middle Ages:—such as the 'Confraternity of Goldsmiths' in the church of the Carmelites at Avignon, A.D. 1413 (Carpentras MS. No. 886, and the Avignon MS., No. 1959, f. 1)—I should say that, in my opinion, they were quite similar to the 'Commercial' and other sodalities attached to churches of the Order at the present day.

for particular notice in this paper, it is because compared
with his attack on the Scapular Devotion I should pronounce
the difficulties raised by later critics—notably those occuring to certain recent writers—as trifling in the extreme.
Still, even doubts of this nature may occasion disquiet
in the minds of readers not in a position to consult
authoritative sources of information, or unsuspicious of
latent fallacies upon which the most specious arguments
are often based.

JAMES P. RUSHE, O.D.C.

PUBLICATIONS IN OPPOSITION

TO THE AUTHENTICITY OF THE SCAPULAR VISIONS OF OUR LADY TO ST. SIMON STOCK AND TO POPE JOHN XXII:

1). *DISSERTATIO DUPLEX: UNA DE ORIGINE ET CONFIRMATIONE PRIVILEGIATI SCAPULARIS CARMELITARUM ALTERA DE VISIONE SIMONIS STOCHII,*

Prioris ac Magistri, Generalis Carmelitarum, Joanne De Launoy, *Theologo Parisiensi,* (Paris), 1642, p. 9:

"The third is: The Most Blessed Virgin appeared to John XXII (while he had already been made Pope) while based on Paleonydorus (as Gregory Nazianzus, A.S. Basilius & Marcus confide from what the (Sabbatine) Bull writes) the apparition took place before the Pontificate of John."

2). *DE VISIONE SIMONIS STOCCHI, DE SABBATINAE BULLAE PRIVILEGIO ET DE SCAPULARIS CARMELITARUM SODALITATE DISSERTATIONES V*

Joanne De Launoy, *Lutetiae Parisiorum,* 1653.

Various elements of the dates of the copies of the (Sabbatine) Bull in Majorca and Agrigento do not correspond to when they took place and must be proven.

3). A CATHOLIC DICTIONARY

William E. Addis and Thomas Arnold, M.A., New York, 1887, pp. 744 -745. (Scapular)

"Is there any proof that the Blessed Virgin appeared to St. Simon Stock and made the promise related above? *(This will be a privilege for you and for all Carmelites; no one dying in this Scapular will suffer eternal burning.)* Launoy, in a dissertation of wonderful learning to be found in the second volume of his collected works (the edition we have used is dated 1731, "Coloniae Allobrogum"), proves by a

556

superabundance of reasons that the Bull of John XXII is a clumsy forgery and that of Alexander V another forgery made to cover the former. The autograph has never been found, nor has it any place in the Roman "Bullarium." Its authenticity is unhesitatingly denied by the great Bollandist Papebroch in his reply to the attacks made upon him by the Carmelites and by Benedict XIV ("De Festis"). "As to the fact of the apparition to Simon Stock...the silence of Carmelite authors for more than a century after is remarkable. The Vision is mentioned apparently for the first time, so far as known for certain by Grossus, a Carmelite of Toulouse in his "Viridarium" (1389)....

4). *LA BOLLA SABBATINA*
Ludovico Saggi, O. Carm., Roma, 1967, p. 82.

"Another difficulty comes from the silence of the biographers and defenders of the pope on a particular matter so important for Marian protection. And it is noted that among the defenders of John against Louis of Bavaria there were also Carmelities. In the text of the Bull, the Madonna refers to John with name of pope, saying to him: 'Vicar of my son' and she promises him 'I am making you pope;' but how can she make him pope if he's already been pope for six years?"

5). THE CARMELITE SCAPULAR TODAY
(carmelites.org) Articles taken from the "Journal of Ecclesiastical History," Richard Copsey, O. Carm. Vol 50, No. 4, Rome, October, 1999

"Scholarship has disproved the historicity of the Sabbatine Bull of John XXII granting the so-called Sabbatine Privilege. Ironically, this is not a post-Vatican II thing," McMahon (Patrick) said, *The definitive research on the subject was done by a Carmelite historian, Ludovico Saggi in the fifties and sixties.* (p. 3)

When asked about various visions including the Fatima apparitions that might seem to confirm the Sabbatine Privilege, Morello (Fr. Sam Anthony) said: *We know that private revelation can neither add to nor detract from the deposit of faith. The Sabbatine Privilege or the historicity of the vision is not part of the deposit of the faith. Private revelation cannot change that.* (p. 3)

No copy of the Bull (Sabbatine) has been found in the Vatican Archives, and Ludovico Saggi demonstrated convincingly that the Document was concocted around 1430 in Agrigento, Sicily, with the author taking as his model, a similar Franciscan document relating to the Portiuncula Indulgence. The Sacred Congregation of the

Inquisition in Rome, after a lengthy study, issued a Decree on January 20, 1613 outlining what the Carmelites were permitted to preach. The Decree was accompanied by the recommendation that the Carmelites shall not mention the Sabbatine Bull in order that the term may be forgotten. (p. 4)

6). THE CARMELITE SCAPULAR: HISTORY AND DEVOTION

by Fr. Paul D'Souza, O.C.D., Institute of Philosophy Vijayanagar, Bangalore, India.

All things considered, there is no mention of the Scapular Vision in the present Carmelite Proper even on the Solemn Commemoration of Our Lady of Mt. Carmel. In the post-Vatican revision of the liturgical calendar, the memory of Simon Stock which was earlier celebrated with explicit mention of the Vision was totally suppressed. However, in 1979 once again the Carmelites were permitted an optional memory on condition that no mention be made of the "problematic Scapular Vision."

Eventually, the Scapular of Carmel came to be one of the most highly indulgenced objects in the Catholic Church before the Second Vatican Council. Today, however after the post-Vatican revision of indulgences, objects and things are no longer as important as human acts.

7). ST. SIMON STOCK; THE SCAPULAR VISION AND THE BROWN SCAPULAR DEVOTION

by Bede Edwards; an article from the Carmelite Digest, Vol. 16 No.3, Summer 2001

Fr. (Ludovico) Saggi's doubt as to the identification of Prior General Simon Stock or Simon of England with the English Carmelite said to have received the Scapular from Our Lady, is not shared by other Carmelite historians. (p. 17)

The legends of the Scapular Vision, then and of the Sabbatine Privilege arose at a time when similar stories were common currency, when, in fact, the fashion of the time almost demanded that each Order should attribute, through some miraculous intervention, special efficacy to the habit its members wore. (p. 21)

The Brown Scapular Devotion, as we know it today, dates no further back than the latter half of the 16th century and owes its popularity largely to Giovanni Battista Rossi who was Prior General from 1564 to 1578. Needless to say, at that time and since, great emphasis was laid on the Promise put into Our Lady's mouth by the legend that "whoever dies wearing this will be saved," and also on the Sabbatine Privilege, that despite much official caution and verbal quibbling, continued to hold on to the popular imagination of the assurance of release from Purgatory on the Saturday after death. (p. 23)

It is now quite obviously high time for the Carmelites freely and frankly to relinquish these pious legends, unable as they evidently are to stand up under the scrutiny of present-day historical inquiry. (p. 23)

8). ANTOLOGIA DELLO SCAPOLARE
a cura di Giampiero Molinari, O. Carm., Roma, 2001

The Document of Majorca is certainly a forgery and therefore "the Sabbatine Bull" contained in it cannot be accepted as authentic. (p. 175) This appears unusual in a Pontifical Document. In official acts a pope never refers to a private vision to grant indulgences or make other concessions. (p. 176). It's interesting to note that John XXII before being pope and during his pontificate denied, as a theologian the existence of Purgatory, proposing a prior opinion on the Beatific Vision. (p. 176) In reference to the "Sabbatine Privilege" there are also found expressions that do not exist on a theological level (the indication of the Saturday after death and the descent of the Madonna into Purgatory are applications of spatio-temporal criteria to eternity). (p. 177) The Order does not have One Founder, but refers to the Prophet Elijah and the Virgin Mary as inspirational models. (p. 185)

9). OUR LADY OF THE PLACE
Emanuele Boaga, O. Carm., Roma, 2001

When it comes to the historicity of Simon Stock's Vision the opinions of the experts are divided. Indeed, an analysis of the information from the sources shows that the question of historicity is a complex one and from the point of view of intellectual honesty we may agree with Ludovico Saggi: *It has to be said that it is not possible to prove that the Vision is false, but at the same time the proofs offered for its historical validity are not sufficient.* (p. 101) There is no trace in the papal registers of the Bulls attributed to Alexander V or John XXII. Therefore Fr. Saggi concluded rightly that the Majorca Document is false and the Sabbatine Bull contained in it cannot be accepted as authentic. (p. 102) In the references to the "Sabbatine Privilege" we find some expressions that are not exact from the theological point of view (the indication of the Saturday after death and the descent of Our Lady into Purgatory are applications of criteria of space and time to eternity. (p. 103)

10). MARY AND THE BROWN SCAPULAR,

Fr. Hugh Clarke, O. Carm., Faversham, Kent, 2002

The origins of the Scapular Devotion are to be found in the desires of lay people during the Middle Ages to be closely associated with the Carmelite Order and its spirituality. (p. 20)

If the promises of the protection and final perseverance promised to St. Simon Stock and the speedy liberation from Purgatory in the Bull—**now known to be inauthentic**—of Pope John XXII are to be understood rightly, they cannot be seen in isolation from the living of a life of allegiance to Jesus Christ, a life lived within the teaching of the Church. (p. 23)

11). SIMON STOCK AND THE SCAPULAR VISION

Essay by Richard Copsey, O. Carm., Carmelus, Vol. 49, 2002

No one has ever found a copy of the Bull (Sabbatine) in the Vatican Archives and Ludovico Saggi demonstrated convincingly that the Document was concocted around 1430 in Agrigento, Sicily. The fact that the Bulla Sabbatina contains no reference to the Scapular Vision and that its author felt the need to fabricate a further Marian appearance would indicate that the Simon Stock story had not reached Sicily by 1430. (p. 79)

Perhaps the time has come to accept the Vision as a later invention which was subsequently attached to the Prior General, Simon Stock. (p. 83)

12). CARMEL IN THE WORLD, VOL. XLIII, N. 3

Patrick T. McMahon O. Carm., Roma, 2004: "Garment of Grace: A Historical Appreciation of the Carmelite Scapular"

There are still many Catholics who think that the Brown Scapular has in itself, some power to save those who wear it from Hell or to deliver them from Purgatory. (p. 176) No where in the constitution is there any reference to a supernatural origin for the Scapular. (p. 180)

The historicity of the Sabbatine Bull and its accompanying Privilege has been discredited with more certainty than the apparition to Simon Stock. It was long troubling to historians how John XXII could have been told by Our Lady that she would free souls from Purgatory on the First Saturday after their deaths when John XXII himself did not believe in the Doctrine of Purgatory. (p. 182)

PUBLICATIONS IN DEFENSE

OF THE AUTHENTICITY
OF THE SCAPULAR VISIONS
OF OUR LADY TO
ST. SIMON STOCK AND
POPE JOHN XXII
THE SABBATINE BULL

1). *PRIVILEGIATI SCAPULARIS ET VISIONIS S. SIMONIS STOCKII VINDICIAE*

John Cheron, O. Carm., Bordeaux, 1642: (First book written in defense of the Scapular and against the attack of John Launoy)

John Cheron thus replied to Launoy's charge that the truth was endangered: *If truth, as he (Launoy) wrongly thinks be endangered by such an assent, the Roman Pontiffs are in this great danger since they have granted the faculty to the General of the Carmelites to erect and institute the Confraternity of the Scapular everywhere, extending Plenary Indulgences, that through the outpouring of the treasury of the Church, they may entice, induce and join in the wearing and fellowship of the Scapular. God, who by this Scapular has extinguished the devouring flames, calmed the wild waves of the sea, prevented shipwrecks, cured the incurable, broken bonds and chains, restored the dead to life, heretics to faith, sinners to all appearances in despair to a sincere aversion from creatures and conversion to the Creator and has worked innumerable other miracles and works them daily, supports a lie.*

2). *DUPLEX PRIVILEGIUM SACRI SCAPULARIS ORDINIS ET CONFRATERNITATIS GLORIOSAE VIRGINIS MARIA DE MONTE CARMELO, SEU RESPONSIO AD JOANNIS LAUNOY DISSERTATIONES*

Philibertus Fesysus, O. Carm., (Aix, 1645) 1645, op. cit, p. 63, (Third book written against Launoy, in defense of the Scapular).

He summed up his argument against Launoy's denial of the fact of the Vision of St. Simon: *That it is contrary to common opinion, to the opinion of the theologians, to a very ancient tradition, to the Declaration of the Cardinals of the Sacred Congregation of Rites, to reason and propriety.*

3). *PRO SODALITIO SACRI SCAPULARIS ADVERSUS DUPLICEM DISSERTATIONEM I. LAUNOY*
Thomas Aquinas of St. Joseph, O.C.D (Tutelae, 1648)

In the mind of Thomas Aquinas of St. Joseph, O.C.D. who wrote the second work to appear against the *Dissertatio Duplex* (of John Launoy) a denial of the fact of the apparitions resulted in an attack against the Confraternity itself. *But since we have heard that some "lovers of novelty" triumphing in that book, give it prominence so that it might possibly extinguish the love for the Holy Scapular burning in the hearts of the faithful.*

4). *SCAPULARE PARTHENICO-MARIANUM ILLUSTRATUM ET DEFENSUM*
Theophilus Raynaud, S.J. (Paris, 1654)

He rebuttled Launoy's second book "De Viso." He took the same position as the previous Carmelite writers, taking his arguments both from the concrete fact of the Devotion and using historical evidence according as it was available. His book seems to have carried great weight.

5). *SACRE ISTRUTTIONI PER BENIFICIO DE DIVOTI DEL S. SCAPOLARE DELLA GLORIOSISSIMA SEMPRE VERGINE MARIA NOSTRA SIGNORA DEL CARMINE*
R.P. F. Gabrielle Ferri da Bologna Carmel, Bologna, 1656

Then there remains from the Virgin the privileged Carmelite Habit [Scapular] by which the one who wears it devoutly will be kept free of dangers in the present life; [and receive] most powerful assistance to die well and be liberated from the flames of Purgatory particularly on the Saturday after death. The privileges and graces are all united by an ingenious pen in this little verse: *Now I protect you; in death I pray for you; after death, I rescue you.* (pp. 103-104)

6). *NOTIZIA ISTORICA DELL'ORIGINE*
Ven.Archiconfratenita Del Sacro Scapolare di Maria SSma Del Carmine, Privilegi Della Medesima Grazie E Singolari Favori Accordati Dalla Vergine Santissima a tutti gli ascritti presso Giuseppe Brancadoro Via Della Gatta N. 9, Roma, 1843

Chapter Four: Of the Great and Singular Sabbatine Privilege

For since the privileges described here of our Most Holy Mother Mary are so great and singular for those who serve under her Garment of the Holy Scapular, the Sabbatine Privilege should be esteemed in a most special way. Since her maternal and ardent love will not bear seeing her dear and beloved children suffer the flames of Purgatory, she promised to liberate them promptly from this trial and especially on the First Saturday after their death as the day the Church particularly consecrated to her, as she herself revealed to Pope John XXII to whom she appeared in Avignon commanding him to publish this Privilege, assigning to him also these obligations which are all held as indispensable for enjoying this most singular favor. The same Pontiff, with his Bull of March 3, 1322, published this Privilege which has been confirmed by many Supreme Pontiffs and also by the Congregation of the Holy Office on Feb. 16, 1613, and by the Sacred Congregation of Rites with more Decrees (p.17)

7). *RISTRETTO DELLA VITA DI SIMONE STOCK*
L'Apologia Della Bolla Sabatina, per il P. S. Mattei dell'Ordine medesimo, Roma, 1873

The difficulties that we encounter to dissuade others are proposed by John Launoy and Natale Allesandro; others are more modern, but sooner or later they all have the same origin. Shortly before the middle of the 17th century, Launoy or Launojo flung himself "with an unrelenting furor"— to use the words of Benedict XIV (*Delle feste della B. Vergine* chap. 6, p. 286 Venice, 1749)—against the Vision of St. Simon Stock and against the Sabbatine Bull in his work, *De Simonis Stockii Visio, de Sabatinae Bullae Privilegio, et de Scapularis Carmelitarum Sodalitate, Dissertationes Quinque* [On the Vision of Simon Stock, the Privilege of the Sabbatine Bull and the Scapular of the Sodality of the Carmelites, Five Discussions]. But before putting his reasons on display it would be helpful to know a little about the character of this noteworthy theologian, or rather we will say a most harsh critic, called by his nationals, *The opponent of Saints who had taken more of them from Heaven than ten Popes canonized.* Launoy was a terrible critic [so says Argonne, *Melanges d'Histoire et de Literature*, Vol.1, p. 274 (Paris, 1701) Vol. 3.120, pp. 123-124].

8). *VITA DI SAN SIMONE DE STOCK*
Alfredo Mombrum, Siena, 1884

Here is how the learned Antonio Sandero expresses himself about the Sabbatine Bull: *With regard to the Privilege of the Sabbatine Bull, it is divine not human; celestial, not earthly; so that even the words of Arnauld of Chartres in his seven words of the Lord can be most aptly applied to it: Mary, our Mother asks, the Son approves, the Father decrees. This Privilege was given in Heaven ... it was brought to earth by the Holy Virgin; it was confirmed and promulgated by John XXII as we have in these words of the Bull: "I, therefore, accept, approve and confirm on earth this Holy Indulgence as graciously granted to them by Jesus Christ from Heaven through the merits of his Blessed Mother and this is why the Sacred Congregation of Rites quite properly calls the Scapular "a Celestial Habit." (Vita di San Simone Stock,* Alfredo Mombrum, 1884) (p. 156)

9). *BREVI NOTIZIE SULLA BOLLA DETTA SABATINA*
Monsignor Francesco Gallo, Vescovo di Avellino, (Bishop of Avellino) 1887

Alexander V closed the mouth of those bold ones who dared to subvert the genuine character of this Great Privilege, after the most minute and diligent examination, he solemnly published, with his Bull, the confirmation of that of John XXII with the following words: *Hold to this Privilege by whatever means...* and many authentic copies of this Bull were conserved in Genoa, Messina, Trapani, Majorca in Spain, and in the great monastery of Traspontina in Rome. (pp.11, 12)

10). *THE CARMELITES AND THE BROWN SCAPULAR*
A.E. Farrington, D.D., OCC., Dublin, 1891

Another voice in favor of this (Scapular) Promise is that of God, Himself. God never authorizes error or deceit by miracles; it would not be in keeping with His Sanctity to do so. Now of all the practices of piety in honour of Mary, none has been more visibly authorized by splendid miracles. It would go beyond the object of this work to record them. It would take volumes to tell them all and so we must be content with a mere outline of them.

11). *THE MEANING AND USE OF*
THE SCAPULAR OF OUR LADY OF MOUNT CARMEL
By the Bishop of Salford, (made Cardinal Archbishop of Westminster), Salford, 1893:

...St. Simon Stock received a visit from the Blessed Virgin herself, holding in her hand the Carmelite Habit, which she offered to him saying: *This is the Pledge of the Privilege granted to thee and to all Carmelites: He who shall piously die wearing this habit shall be preserved from eternal flames.* This happened on the 16th July, 1251. In a circular addressed to all the members of his Order, he made known this extraordinary Vision, and at the same time said: *Brethren, make your election sure by good works and never faint. Watch and offer thanksgiving to God for so much mercy; pray without ceasing, so that the words spoken by the Blessed Virgin to me may be glorified to the praise of the most holy Trinity, Father, Son, and Holy Ghost, and of the ever Blessed Virgin Mary.*

12). *THE IRISH ECCLESIASTICAL RECORD*
Volume XXIX, Fourth Series, January to June, Fr. James P. Rushe, O.C.D., Dublin, 1911:

As for the Sabbatine Indulgence, considered from the historical standpoint, I have not space at my disposal to deal with the subject in a manner that would be likely to prove acceptable to readers. The distinguished Jesuit theologian who replied to Launoy's attack on the Scapular Devotion quotes Baconthorpe and de Horneby, the contemporaries of Pope John XXII, to establish the Authenticity of the Privilege as described in verified copies of the famous Papal Bull proclaiming the extraordinary new favour granted to the clients of Our Lady of Mt. Carmel. He does so, because these renowned English White Friars enjoyed special opportunities of consulting official documents relating to the history of their Order, which were then kept in the archives of the London Monastery. Launoy would complain of the negligence of the Carmelites of the Sixteenth Century in their having failed to preserve the actual Bull announcing the Sabbatine Indulgence. Those aquainted with the history of the suppression of the English monasteries may be inclined like myself to regard this as very unreasonable, even if they did not know of the existence of a number of authentic copies, including several made in the course of the 15th century. As a matter of fact, the evidence shows that verified copies of important documents of this kind were at once distributed among the principal monasteries of the Order to insure their contents being conveyed to the religious with the least possible delay. I could cite the testimony of John Grossi himself to this effect or that of the apostate Bale, whose authority seems of such moment to recent critics of the Scapular Devotion, adding that even after his sad defection he still upheld the authenticity of the Bull of Pope John XXII, utilizing it in one of his most scurrilous diatribes against the Papacy. (pp. 285-286)

Bale, unhappily was but one of those wretched men who were then endeavouring to deaden the voice of conscience by calumniating all priests and religious steadfast in their sacred calling. So that if he or any of those other apostates, suspected the possibility of forgery in such a connection, is it credible that he would have omitted to chronicle the fact of what he would stigmatize as a fraud (or fable) being encouraged by the Holy See for the infamous reason which he actually assigns? It forms no part of my task to enter on a defense of the Sabbatine Indulgence, especially just now when the new legislation regarding Scapulars encourages the faithful to avail themselves all the more fervently of this Great Privilege, dating back to the pontificate of John XXII as every truly critical student of the question is well aware. (pp. 286, 287)

13). *THE SCAPULAR AND SOME CRITICS: THE VISION*

P.Magennis, O.C.C., Rome, 1914:

Benedict XIV, before ascending the Papal throne, was known as Prospero Lambertini, Cardinal Archbishop of Bologna. In the year 1740 A.D., he published in Bologna, a kind of commentary on the Feasts of Our Lord and the Blessed Virgin for the use of his own Ecclesiastics: *Annotazioni sopra le Feste di Nostro Signore e della Beatissima Vergine second l'ordine del Calendario Romano.* Under the heading *Della Festa della Beata Vergine del Carmine,* we have, amongst other matters, bearing on the Feast, an interesting reference to the Scapular Vision of St. Simon Stock. His opinion of the Scapular Vision of St. Simon Stock is just as clearly declared *(par. 76 P.S.). As to the Vision, we quite willingly admit it, and we believe, too, that everyone should admit it.* (pp. 146, 147)

14). *MOUNT CARMEL—ABRIDGEMENT OF CARMEL—ITS HISTORY AND SPIRIT*

Carmelites; Burns Oates and Washbourne, London, 1923

There is no doubt that the marvelous Privilege of the Scapular granted to St. Simon Stock at the Monastery of Cambridge, contributed largely to the popularity which the Order familiarly called "White Friars" then enjoyed and the veneration felt for this great Saint, favored with the gifts of miracles and prophecy, greatly aided the extension of the Order in England. The kings were most favorable to it and Edward II, above all loaded it with privileges.

15). *SPIGHE DEL CARMELO; RICORDO DEL VI CENTENARIO DEL "PRIVILEGIO SABATINO"*

Palermo, Carmine Maggiore, 1923 "LA BOLLA SABATINA":

[Pope John XXII regarding the Sabbatine Bull]: *I therefore, accept this indulgence; I reinforce it; and I confirm it on earth, yes—just as through the merits of the Virgin Mother it is fitting that Jesus Christ grant it from*

Heaven. Hence, it is not licit for any man to annul this Bull of our Indulgence or our Statute and our Order or to boldly contradict it. Whoever presumes to attack it, should know that he incurs the indignation of the Almighty God and the Blessed Apostles Peter and Paul. Given at Avignon the third of March, the sixth year of our Pontificate (namely 1322) (p. 72). We have the text (of the Sabbatine Bull) in an authentic transmission given in the Bull of Alexander V (p. 72).

16). *THE SABBATINE PRIVILEGE OF THE SCAPULAR*
1322-1922, P. E. Magennis, O. Carm., New York, 1923

Our opinion in reference to the Bull is clearly stated and though we have weighed well the objections that are called classic against it, we still remain faithful to the opinion that the Sabbatine Bull was issued by John XXII and had for its origin a Vision of the Blessed Virgin who desired to give a token of greater love to her clients. (p. 11)

17). *THE SCAPULAR DEVOTION*
Origin, Legislation and Indulgences attached to the Scapulars, Most Rev. P. E. Magennis, O. Carm., Dublin, 1923

Decree of Pope Pius X: *For the future all the faithful already inscribed or who shall be inscribed in one or other of the real Scapulars approved by the Holy See by what is known as regular enrollment, may instead of the cloth Scapulars, one or several wear on their persons, either round the neck or otherwise, provided it be in a becoming manner, a single medal of metal through which by the observance of the laws laid down for each Scapular they shall be enabled to share in and gain all the spiritual favors not excepting what is known as the SABBATINE PRIVILEGE OF THE SCAPULAR OF OUR LADY OF MT. CARMEL and all the privileges attached to it.* (pp. 46-47)

18).*THE WHITE FRIARS:*
AN OUTLINE; CARMELITE HISTORY
by Rev. P. R. McCaffrey, Ord. Carm., Dublin, 1926

This Vision (of Our Lady to St. Simon Stock) was vouchsafed the saintly General at the Carmelite Convent of Cambridge. What is certain is that, on recovering from his ecstasy, he felt himself constrained to make known so momentous a favor in the interests of the salvation of souls and that he wrote to all the convents of his Order a detailed account of the Vision. Popular devotion to the

Holy Scapular, as it is officially named was undoubtedly propagated shortly after the date of the Vision. (p. 55)

19). *LE SCAPULAIRE DE NOTRE DAME DU MONT CARMEL EST AUTHENTIOUE*
P. Marie-Joseph du Sacre Coeur, Avignon, 1928

Alexander V completely inserts the Sabbatine Bull of John XXII, *Sacratissimo uti culmine*, into the Bull *"Tenorum cujusdam privilegii"* of December 7, 1409 in order to give to the first, an even more ample, more undeniable certitude for the future and Alexander V gives assurance of having seen and diligently examined the original of the Sabbatine Bull. (p. 61)

The testimony of William of Sanvico on the recourse to the pope directly confirms the historical fact of the apparition of the Virgin to Simon Stock at the same time it solidly supports the granting of the Privilege of the Scapular to the Holy Prior in the same apparition, for it places outside of doubt the authenticity of the letter of Swanyngton. (p. 20)

The principal difficulty opposed to the Scapular is what is called in historical criticism "The Negative Argument of the Silence of Contemporaries" among whose adherents the most determined is Launoy. Thus, Launoy formulates this negative argument. The author of the Acts of the Apostles, St. Luke speaks at length about the establishment of Christianity at Antioch, that metropolis of the Orient, *totius orbiscum compendium* [a compendium of the whole world], as was then said; he names his evangelists (Acts 11: 19-30), but he does not say a word about the preaching of St. Peter, nor of the foundation of the See of Antioch by the Prince of the Apostles four years after the Ascension of Our Lord, facts affirmed by a tradition going back to ancient times reported by Eusebius, St. Jerome, Origen and later authors but whose first witness is not weakened by the silence of St. Luke, even though he is contemporary. (pp. 97-99)

20). *ENCICLOPEDIA DEL ESCAPULARIO DEL CARMEN*
por El P. Simon M. Besalduch, Carmelitano Calzado, Corcega, 415 Barcelona, 1931

Chapter XIV: The Authenticity of the Bull.

Summary: The Original and the copies. The pontifical document that is of equal worth as the original, the entire text of the Bull of Alexander V which literally contains the Sabbatine Bull of John XXII,

Notes and commentaries, Bulls and other pontifical documents that confirm the Authenticity of the Sabbatine Bull, The Liturgy, Ancient Documents of the Order, Testimonies of strangers, the tradition and the unanimous sense of the faithful, Summary and Conclusion. (p.257)

Can one extract some proof of the Holy Liturgy in favor of the Authenticity of the Privilege of the Sabbatine Bull?

In the readings of the Divine Office of the great Feast of Carmel (July 16) we read how the Virgin of Consolation, with truly maternal affection toward the souls of those in her Confraternity will, while they are in Purgatory, lift them up as soon as possible to Heaven (Reading VI): *Not only in this world has the Most Blessed Virgin adorned the Order itself with receiving so many favors, but truly in the other...she is moved with maternal affection toward [her] children enrolled in the society of the Scapular [and] while they are being purified by the fires of Purgatory it is piously believed that they are raised to the light and enter their heavenly home as soon as possible.* These words were composed by the illustrious Cardinal St. Robert Bellarmine of the Company of Jesus and approved with the other parts of the Office after a mature examination by the Sacred Congregation of Rites. (pp. 266-267)

21). *MARY IN HER SCAPULAR PROMISE*
John Mathias Haffert, New Jersey, 1942

That the Mother of God appeared to Saint Simon Stock promising that anyone who died in her Scapular would not suffer eternal fire, is as certain as the fact that George Washington defeated Cornwallis in 1781 in Yorktown. There are documentary proofs; the Catholic Church has propagated the Devotion for seven centuries, and more miracles have been worked through the Brown Scapular than through almost any other Sign this world has ever had. While one miracle, one operation above the power of nature is God's word, innumerable miracles are decidedly a bit of divine emphasis. Hence we might say that one has more ground for believing in the Scapular Promises than for believing in the defeat of Cornwallis or the signing of the Declaration of Independence. Besides documents, we have the word of the two greatest authorities in existence: God and His Church. (p. 25)

22). *TAKE THIS SCAPULAR*
Carmelite Third Order Press, Chicago, 1949 "Annotations on the Status of the Scapular Question," by (Servant of God) Fr. Bartholomew F. M. Xiberta, O. Carm.

Objections made three centuries ago (against the Scapular Devotion) and lately renewed by clever writers have infected the modern mind with the idea that the Devotion rests on a pious fiction or at least on insufficient argument. It happens also (which is worse) that to avoid unpleasant controversies, the Scapular Devotion is cloaked in silence. (p. 213)

23). *DE VISIONE SANCTI SIMONIS STOCK*
(Servant of God) Bartholomaeus F M. Xiberta O. Carm., Romae 1950

Conclusion: from what has been said the following seems to be drawn out:

1 The vision of St. Simon came to us confirmed by the testimony of two sources, one of which existed by a document of the 13th century itself, the other in fact from the first decade of the 14th century.

2 Wherefore that which they were saying before: that this vision recently was introduced without witnesses, today not even any type of question can be proposed (p. 216)

24). *THE CREDIBILITY OF THE SCAPULAR PROMISES*
Christian P. Ceroke, O. Carm., A Dissertation.... Rome, 1950

St. Robert Bellarmine, who was the most influential of the Cardinals deciding the question of the Sabbatine Privilege by the decree of 1613, laid down the principle of the authority of the Church. He said: *It cannot be denied to the Carmelite Fathers to preach according to the tenor of the Bulls.* (pp.163-164) In other words, the Privilege itself rested on Papal Authority, which the Holy Office had no intention of revoking. (p. 166) Consequently the Privilege, in a reduplicative sense, as a particular Privilege of the Scapular Confraternity cannot be denied. As such, it may be revoked only by the authority of the Church. It is not, therefore sufficient to say that the Sabbatine Privilege rests merely on the general theological principle assuring its spiritual value but on the authority of the Church as a particular benefit of the Scapular Confraternity, which no other Confraternity or Sodality or Society as such enjoys. (p. 167)

The Revelations, themselves, and what has followed from centuries of their acceptance in the Church is nothing more than a concrete expression of the Spiritual Maternity and Mediation of the Blessed Virgin. (p. 173)

Concerning the Sabbatine Privilege, therefore, the Decree of the

Holy Office of 1613 must be admitted to regulate the entire question, including the historical aspect. No one may gainsay the Decree unless he wishes to place himself above the authority of the Church, (p. 173, 174)

25). *YOUR BROWN SCAPULAR*

Rev. E. K. Lynch, O. Carm., Westminster, Md., 1950

Seven centuries of Christian Devotion have helped to reveal the hidden treasures of the Scapular. The Scapular is a Sign of our special adoption by the Mother of God. (p. 32)

The conclusion (was) reached by (Servant of God) Fr. Bartholomew F. M. Xiberta, O. Carm., who is the greatest living authority on Scapular History. After years of critical research he concludes: *Having studied the documentary evidence one sees how the arguments against the historicity of the Vision of St. Simon Stock collapse one after the other...I dare to affirm that the Vision of St. Simon which preceded the Scapular Devotion has the support of more historical documents than one would expect to find.* (p. 12)

26). *LA S. MESSA DELLA MADONNA DEL CARMINE - LA S. MESSA DEL 16 LUGLIO E LA MESSA SABATINA*

Collana VII Centenario dello Scapolare 1951

"The Liturgy of the Mass of the Solemn Commemoration of the Most Holy Mary of Carmel"

"The Sabbatine Privilege:" Among the spiritual favors granted to the sons and daughters of Carmel (The Religious of the First and Second Orders and those of the Third Order) inscribed in to one or more type of Habit [Scapular] and *The Sabbatine Privilege*: Dating from the beginning of the 14th century, at that time when the Holy See after the death of Clement V was absent [from Rome] and in residence in Avignon, the Queen of Heaven appeared to the pious Jacques d'Euse who would be soon raised to the throne of St. Peter with the name of John XXII and ordained him to promulgate, as soon as he was elected pope, a document by which was granted to all Carmelites a special Privilege, that of prompt liberation from Purgatory if they had observed the following conditions:

A). Chastity according to their state [of life].

B). Recitation of the Office of the Blessed Virgin or the Divine Office.

For those who cannot read or had an appropriate commutation

of the above-mentioned recitation from a Confessor: A) chastity according to one's state of life; B) abstinence from meat of Wednesdays and Saturdays, except when one of these days falls on the Nativity of Our Lord Jesus Christ." (pp. 5-6)

The proper of the Holy Mass which we report and the Votive Mass of the Blessed Virgin of Mount Carmel is recited or sung every Saturday in all Carmelite Convents. In some convents, it is also recited on Wednesdays. All the parts of the Holy Mass record the singular Sabbatine Privilege and the Preface above all others. The said Votive Mass is privileged and left only for first class feasts of the Lord and some other times. (p.19)

27). *LO SCAPOLARE 2*
edited by the Italian committee for the VII Centenary of the Scapular, Roma –Via Della Conciliazione, 14B 1951

Pope Benedict XIV: Therefore, after 50 years the Blessed Virgin appeared also to the Supreme Pontiff John XXII and made known to him many indulgences that she had petitioned from her Son, Jesus Christ for the brothers and sisters of the Carmelite Order, indulgences that the same Pontiff then promulgated on March 3, 1322, and this is what is called: "The Sabbatine Privilege." (p. 65) (Defestis D.N.I.C. et B.Mariae Virg., lib. II, cap . VI, nn. 4,6,8, e 10)

28). *ROSARIO E SCAPOLARE -*
LA MADONNA LI VUOLE UNITI
P. Teofano Di S. Teresa Del Bambino Gesu, O.C.D., Roma, 1955

Given the explicit approval by the Church to the Promise of Final Perseverance, to the Sabbatine Privilege, to the total Consecration of love to Mary that the Scapular brings and to the intense Marian life that, as a consequence, it requires and promotes, the faithful are certain not to fall into error by their devotion to the Scapular of Carmel; I am practically certain of the goodness of the doctrine and of the most particular real spiritual value of the Scapular of Carmel. (p. 18)

29). *VITA FRACTUM DEL SANCTO MONTE CARMELO*
Nicola Calciuri O.C., Tusciae, (1466) P. Graziano Di Santa Teresa O.C.D., 1955

"On the vision of the most Holy Brother Simon of the Order of the Virgin Mary of Holy Mount Carmel: The most Holy Brother Simon, General of the English Province, prayed devoutly everyday to the

Virgin Mary whom the Carmelite Order assigned the special title of…

> Carmelite Flower
> and flowering summit
> Splendor of Heaven
> and Virgin who gave birth,
> in a singular way; merciful Mother;
> never knowing man; to your Carmelites
> give such privilege, Star of the sea.

And the most glorious Virgin Mary with a great multitude of angels appeared to Blessed Simon, and she held the Scapular of the Order in her hands and spoke these words: *This will be for you and for all Carmelites a Privilege. And whoever dies with this Scapular will not experience the pain of fire; and whoever dies with it will be saved* (p. 404) [168].

30). *ALLA MADRE DI DIO REGINA DELL 'UNIVERSO GLORIA LETIZIA ONORE DEL POPOLO NOSTRO MADRE DELLE MADRE IN CIELO ASSUNTA*

Raffaele Improta dal Carmine di S. Giovanni a Teduccio, Napoli, luglio 1956

But the Most Holy Virgin does not reward only according to the Promises made to St. Simon Stock; she wishes to add another Particular Privilege for those who have put on their Holy Scapular: "The Sabbatine Privilege," that is, the prompt liberation from the pains of Purgatory on Saturday, revealed to Pope John XXII, Jacques D'Euse, a Frenchman, most devoted to the Madonna, who on March 3, 1322 promulgated the Bull connected to it, which was confirmed by Clement VII, St. Pius V, and Gregory XIII. (p. 8)

31). *OUR LADY OF FATIMA AND THE BROWN SCAPULAR*

Kilian Lynch, O.Carm., Prior General, Ayelsford, England, 1956

On the Feast of our Lady's Assumption, August 15, 1950, Lucia (the visionary of Fatima) gave an interview to the Rev. Fr. Howard Rafferty, O. Carm. (Here is an exerpt): Fr. Howard asked: *In giving the conditions of the Fatima Message, is it correct to say that the Scapular is one of the conditions?* Lucia answered: *Yes, certainly. The Rosary and the Scapular are inseparable.* (pp.13, 14)

But Our Lady did not say anything when she appeared as our Lady of Mt. Carmel. Can we be sure she meant by her appearance dressed as

Our Lady of Carmel and holding the Scapular that she wanted the Scapular as part of the Message? Lucia answered *Yes. The Scapular is a Sign of consecration to Our Lady.* (p. 13)

32). *PAPAL TEACHINGS - OUR LADY*
by The Benedictine Monks of Solesmes, the Daughters of St. Paul, Boston, Massachusetts, 1961

Neminem profecto, (Pope Pius XII), to the Superior General of the Carmelites, February 11, 1950:

For this reason we have been glad to hear that as the Seventh Centenery of the institution of this Scapular of the Divine Mother of Mount Carmel approaches, the Carmelite brethren (calced and discalced) have decided to hold solemn celebrations in honor of the Blessed Virgin Mary. We who have always nourished an ardent love toward the Holy Mother of God and since our early childhood have been admitted into the Confraternity of the said Scapular, do heartily recommend this devout project and we confidently hope that, with God's favor, it will produce abundant spiritual fruits. Indeed, this is not a small matter; it is a question of the attainment of eternal life in virtue of the most Blessed Virgin's Promise; therefore, it is an extremely important project on which it behooves all concerned to proceed with prudence. (pp. 288, 289)

33). *HISTOIRE DES MIRACLES DU SAINT SCAPULAIRE*
Dr. J. Biroat, prieur de Cluny, *Cum permissu superiorum,* Bruge, 1 mai, 1963, P. Archange de la Reine du Carmel, O.C.D. Translated

The report of Nicholas Calciuri: This Carmelite friar of Sicily is a precious witness. His province accepted hermits who experienced the Marian interventions in the East and lived with St. Simon Stock. Here is the testimony on the subject of the miracles of the Scapular: *With this holy Scapular many miracles took place, the healing of many of the blind and deaf and many afflicted and otherwise infirm.* The sense is clear. By the Scapular, God performed many miracles: the blind see, the deaf hear and from many other maladies people recover their health. In the same way the Virgin wishes to manifest to the Christian even before 1461 the supernatural value of her gift to Carmel: the Scapular. She obtained so many miracles. They did not remain hidden. (p. 47)

34). *VATICAN II MARIAN COUNCIL*
Fr. William G. Most, Professor at Loras College, St. Paul Publications, Ireland, 1972

The historical evidence for this Vision (of Our Lady to St. Simon

Stock) is quite good. So tremendous a Privilege as this should be more than enough to make all eager to take up the Scapular Devotion. But here is another Privilege associated with the Scapular: The Sabbatine Privilege. The Privilege was announced in a Bull of Pope John XXII, dated March 3, 1322. (1)

The original copy of the Bull of Pope John XXII has been lost. Many documents of that Pope have been lost. However, official transcripts of it allow us to trace it back to an authenticated copy made in 1421. If we cannot rely on notarized copies guaranteed by several Popes then we had better give up trying to prove almost any historical event. For we do not have notarized documents to support most of the data used in our histories. (pp. 164, 167, 168)

- Cf. Eugenius a S. Joseph, *Dissertatio Historica de Sacro Scapulari Carmelitico*, in: *Analecta Ordinis Carmelitarum Discalcatorum* IV, 3, (January-March, 1930) p. 182

35). *THE GLORIES OF MARY*
by St Alphonsus Liguori, Illinois, 1977

The promise made by our Blessed Lady to Pope John XXII is well known. She appeared to him and ordered him to make known to all that on the Saturday after their death she would deliver from Purgatory all who wore the Carmelite Scapular. (p. 208)

36). *INTRODUCTION TO MARY - THE HEART OF MARIAN DOCTRINE AND DEVOTION*
Dr. Mark Miravalle, S.T.D., California, 1993

Pope Pius XII spoke of the powerful spiritual effects of wearing the Scapular in the following discourse:

How many souls even in circumstances which, humanly speaking, were beyond hope have owed their final conversion and their eternal salvation to the Scapular which they were wearing! How many more, thanks to it have experienced the motherly protection of Mary in dangers of body and soul? (Pope Pius XII, Discourses and Radio Broadcasts, Vol. 12, 1950-51, p. 165) p. 126

The Spiritual benefit of the Scapular Devotion is well summarized by Pope Pius XII in a 1950 Apostolic Letter: *We are not concerned here with a light or passing matter but with the obtaining of eternal life itself which is the substance of the Promise of the Most Blessed Virgin which has been handed down to us....But not for this reason may they who wear the Scapular think they can gain eternal salvation while remaining slothful and negligent of spirit, for the Apostle warns us: "In fear and trembling shall you work out your salvation."* (Phil. 2:12) (pp. 127, 128)

37). *NELLA FAMIGLIA DI MARIA.*
I PAPI E LO SCAPOLARE DEL CARMINE
A Cura Della Provincia Italiana Dei Carmelitani, Roma, 1996

John XXIII, some months after his elevation to the supreme pontificate, on February 18, 1959 in a visit to the Church of San Luigi dei Francesi in Rome, while speaking of his predecessor John XXII and calling to mind his devotion to the Madonna, added: *To him was the fatherhood of the Sabbatine Privilege, so precious and dear to those who wear the Scapular of Our Lady of Mount Carmel.* (p. 31)

Pius IX said: (In a *Brief* written to Alfred Mombrun, author of The *Life of St. Simon Stock): The life of St. Simon Stock was accepted so much more because of what was written by you… because the admirable virtues of this man and his zeal … can not only intensify devotion to this great man but also stimulate and promote devotion and honor toward the most blessed Virgin … by means of the stupendous testimony given to him by the Mother of God, and especially by the eminent benefit of the Holy Scapular, granted to him for use not only for the Carmelite Family but also for those other members of the faithful who might wish to honor her by the particular veneration of this Religious Order.* (p. 17)

38). *THE SCAPULAR OF*
MT. CARMEL TRADITIONS MONASTIOUE
By a Monk of Saint Joseph Abbey, France, c. 1998

The Magisterium of the Church has in fact confirmed many times and with the utmost formality, the contents of this Bull, i.e. the "SABBATINE PRIVILEGE." (p. 19)

Appendix 4

PAPAL DOCUMENTS CONFIRMING THE SCAPULAR VISIONS

John XXII

Birth name	Jacques Duèze or d'Euse
Papacy began	1316
Papacy ended	December 4, 1334
Predecessor	Clement V
Successor	Benedict XII
Born	1249 Cahors, France
Died	December 4, 1334 Avignon, France

Other

Pope John XXII: Jacques Dueze or d'Euse:

Papacy: 1316 - 1334

Summary of Contents:

1). The Bull, Pope John XXII, *Sacratissimo uti culmine*, dated March 3, 1322, is found in the *Bullarium Carmelitanum, Pars Prima.*

It is known as "The Sabbatine Bull," which mentions a privilege, obtained from Christ, by the Blessed Virgin, in favor of those who wear her Scapular . The Mother of God appeared to the Pope, asking him to promulgate the indulgence that was granted by her Son to the Church, through her intercession, in favor of all those who wear the Scapular, with certain conditions to be followed. Following is an excerpt from the translation of the "Transumptum authenticum" of the Sabbatine Bull as taken by Father Gabriel Wessells from the "Bibliotheca Vaticana:

"So let the professed members of the said Order be freed from punishment and from guilt on what day they go from this world; so that with hastened step, they may pass over Purgatory. I, the Mother of Grace, shall descend on the Saturday after their death and whoso I shall find in Purgatory, I shall free, so that I may lead them unto the holy mountain of life everlasting..."

The original text follows and is in Latin.

(Excerpt of Bull, found in the "Transpumptum authenticum," (Bibliotheca Vaticana: Diversa Cameralia S. Pii V. 1568-1571), is taken from The Sabbatine Privilege of the Scapular, 1322-1922, P. E. Magennis, Ord. Carm., New York, 1923, p. 18)

BULLARIUM

CARMELITANUM

PLURES COMPLECTENS SUMMORUM PONTIFICUM CONSTITUTIONES

Ad Ordinem Fratrum Beatiſſimæ, ſemperq; Virginis Dei Genitricis MARIÆ de Monte Carmelo ſpectantes,

Nunc primò in lucem editum, duaſque in partes diſtinctum

A FRATRE ELISEO MONSIGNANO

Ejuſdem Ordinis Procuratore Generali.

PARS PRIMA

Duplici Indice exornata.

ROMÆ, MDCCXV.

Ex Typographia Georgii Plachi, Cælaturam Profitentis, & Characterum Fuſoriam, apud S. Marcum.
SVPERIORVM FACVLTATE.

FR. PETRUS THOMAS
S A N C H E Z

Sacræ Theologiæ Magister, Romani Cleri Exami-
minator, Collegii Ecclesiastici de Urbe perpetuus
Lector, nec non humilis Prior Generalis, Visi-
tator, & Commissarius Apostolicus totius Ordi-
nis Fratrum Beatissimæ, semperque Virginis Dei
Genitricis Mariæ de Monte Carmelo Antiquæ
Observantiæ Regularis.

BUllarium Carmelitanum, studio ac labore
A.R.P. Magistri Elisei Monsignani, ejusdem
Nostri Ordinis Procuratoris Generalis confectum
summoperè commendantes, tenore præsentium
facultatem impartimur, ut typis mandetur, si
iis, ad quos spectat, ità videbitur.
Datum Romæ in Conventu S. Mariæ Transpontinæ 25. Martii 1715.

> *Fr. Petrus Thomas Sanchez Generalis*
> *Carmelitarum.*

Imprimatur,

Si videbitur Reverendiss. Patri Sacri Palatii Apostolici Magistro.

> *N. Archiepiscopus Capuæ Vicesgerens.*

Imprimatur.

Fr. Gregorius Selleri Ord. Prædicat. Sacri Palatii
Apostolici Magister.

I N.

2 Cupientes igitùr, ut Ecclefia Religiosorum Virorum Fratrum Ordinis Beatæ Mariæ de Monte Carmeli de Bononia congruis honoribus frequentetur, & à Chriftifidelibus jugitèr veneretur: omnibus verè pœnitentibus, & confeſſis, qui ad dictam Ecclefiam in quolibet feſto ipſius Ecclefiæ, necnon in feſtivitatibus Domini noſtri Jeſu Chriſti, videlicèt Nativitatis, Circumciſionis, Epiphaniæ, Paraſceves, Reſurrectionis, Afcenſionis, Pentecoſtes, Trinitatis, & Sacramenti ejuſdem; & in omnibus, & ſingulis Feſtivitatibus Beatæ, & Glorioſæ, femperque Virginis Mariæ; & in omnibus, & ſingulis diebus Dominicis totius anni; æ in feſtivitatibus Sanctorum Michaelis Archangeli, Joannis Baptiſtæ, Inventionis, & Exaltationis Sanctæ Crucis, Beatorum Apoſtolorum Petri, & Pauli, & omnium aliorū Apoſtolorum, & Evangeliſtarum; Laurentii, Vincentii, Georgii, Donini, Clementis, Blaſii, Nicaſii, & Dionyſii Martyrum; Nicolai, Martini, Ægidii, Eligii, Leonardi, Sixti, Donati, Benedicti, Bernardi, Dominici, & Franciſci Confeſſorum; Auguſtini, Hieronymi, Gregorii, Ambroſiique Doctorum; & Sanctarum Mariæ Magdalenæ, Marthæ, Catharinæ, Margaretæ, Cæciliæ, Luciæ, Agathæ, Agnetis, Barbaræ, Scholaſticæ, ac undecim millium Virginum; Annæ, & Eliſabeth Viduarum; & in Commemoratione Omnium Sanctorum, & Animarum; & in Dedicatione ipſius Ecclefiæ, & Altarium, ac per Octavas prædictarum feſtivitatum; & in ſingulis diebus à Septuageſima uſquè ad Paſcha; ac in

Miſſa B. M. V. in Sabbato. omnibus, & ſingulis diebus Sabbathi ad Miſſam, quæ ſolemnitèr celebratur ibidèm in honore Beatæ Mariæ Virginis, cauſa devotionis, peregrinationis, vel orationis acceſſerint; aùt qui Corpus Chriſti, aùt Oleum Sacrum fecuti fuerint, cùm portatur infirmis; feù qui Miſſis, Prædicationibus, & aliis Divinis Officiis, Exequiis, & fepulturis Mortuorum in dicta Ecclefia, vel ejus Cœmeteriis interfuerint; aut qui in ſerotina pulfatione Campanæ flexis genibus tèr Ave Maria devotè dixerint; vèl fratribus ejuſdem Ecclefiæ infirmitate gravatis, aùt laborantibus in extremis;

necnon qui ad ædificationem, fabricam, luminaria, ornamenta, & alia dictæ Ecclefiæ neceſſaria, five durantibus ibidèm Capitulis generalibus, & Provincialibus per ſingulos dies, de bonis ſibi à Deo collatis manus porrexerint adjutrices; necnon qui extremis laborantes, dictæ Ecclefiæ, vel Fratribus dictæ Domus quicquam fuarum legaverint facultatum, quotiefcumque præmiſſa, vèl præmiſſorum aliquid fecerint; de omnipotentis Dei mifericordia, & Beatorum Petri, & Pauli Apoſtolorum ejus authoritate confiſi, ſinguli noſtrum ſingulas dierum quadragenas de injunctis eis pœnitentiis mifericorditèr in Domino relaxamus; dummodò Diœceſani voluntas ad id acceſſerit, & conſenſus. In cujus rei teſtimonium has litteras ſigillorum noſtrorum fecimus appenſione muniri.

Datum Avinione Anno Domini milleſimo trecenteſimo vigeſimo, die decima menſis Iulii, Pontificatus Sanctiſſimi Patris, ac D.N.D. Ioannis Divina Provid. Papæ XXII. Anno quarto.

CONSTITUTIO V.

Ex tranſumpto authentico, quod extat in Archivio Ordinis; & ex Hippolyto Marraccio in Pontificibus Marianis Romæ impreſſis apud Franciſcum Caballum Anno 1642.

SVMMARIVM.

Continet Privilegium, quod paſſim appellatur Sabbatinum, à Clemente VII., Pio V., Gregorio XIII., & aliis poſteà confirmatum.

IOANNES EPISCOPUS
Seruus Seruorum Dei.

Vniverſis, & ſingulis Chriſtifidelibus &c.

1 SIc mihi flexis genibus ſupplicanti Virgo viſa fuit Carmelita, ſequentem effata ſermonem: O Ioannes, ò Ioannes, Vicarie mei dilecti Filii, veluti te à tuo eripiam adverſario, te Papam *An.1322. 3.Mart.*

62   *Ioannes Vigesimus secundus.*

pam facio, folemni dono Vicarium meis juvantibus fupplicationibus à dulciffimo Filio meo petens, quod gratiosè obtinui, iftam gratiam, & amplam meo fancto, ac devoto Carmelitarum Ordini confirmationem habeas præconcedere, per Eliam, & Elifeum in Monte Carmelo inchoato.

2 Quod unufquifque profeffionem faciens, Regulam à meo Servo Alberto Patriarcha ordinatam obfervabit, & per meum dilectum Innocentium approbatam, ut verus mei Filii Vicarius debeat in terris affentire, quod in Cœlis meus ftatuit, & ordinavit Filius, quòd qui in fancta perfeverabit obedientia, paupertate, & caftitate, vel qui fanctum intrabit Ordinem, falvabitur. Et fi alii devotionis caufa in fanctam ingrediantur Religionem, fancti habitus fignum ferentes, appellantes fe Confratres, & Confrorores mei Ordinis prænominati, liberentur, & abfolvantur à tertia fuorum peccatorum portione, à die, quo præfatum Ordinem intrabunt; Caftitatem, fi vidua eft, promittendo; Virginitatis, fi Virgo eft, fidem præftando; fi conjugata, inviolatam matrimonii confervationem adhibendo, ut Sancta Mater Ecclefia imperat; Fratres profeffi dicti Ordinis fupplicio folvantur, & culpa, die, quo ab hoc feculo ifti recedunt, properato gradu accelerant Purgatorium.

3 Ego Mater gloriofa defcendam Sabbato poft eorum obitum, & quos invenero in Purgatorio, liberabo, & eos in Montem fanctum vitæ æternæ reducam. Verùm, quod ifti Confratres, & Confrorores, teneantur dicere Horas Canonicales, ut opus fuerit, fecundùm Regulam datam ab Alberto; illi, qui ignari funt, debeant vitam jejunam ducere in diebus, quos facra jubet Ecclefia (nifi neceffitatis jàm traditæ impedimento) Mercurio, ac Sabbato debeant fe à carnibus abftinere, præterquàm in mei Filii Nativitate, & hoc dicto, evanuit ifta fancta vifio.

4 Iftam ergò fanctam Indulgentiam accepto, roboro, & in terris confirmo; ficùt propter merita Virginis Matris gloriofæ Iefus Chriftus conceffit in Cœlis. Nulli ergò hominum liceat hanc paginam noftræ Indulgentiæ, feù Statu-

ti ordinationem irritare, vèl ei aufu temerario contraire. Si quis autèm hoc attentare præfumpferit, indignationem Omnipotentis Dei, & Beatorum Apoftolotum Petri, & Pauli fe noverit incurfurum.

Datum Avenione tertia die Martii, Pontificatus noftri Anno fexto.

Authenticum tranfumptum decreti Sanctæ Rómanæ, & Univerfalis Inquifitionis Anno 1613. fub Paulo V. editi circà Privilegium Bullæ Sabbatinæ. Extat Romæ in Archivio Ordinis.

1 NOs Supremi Tribunalis Sanctæ Inquifitionis in hoc Lufitaniæ Regno Confiliarii, per præfentes litteras notum facimus, juffu Sanctiffimi D. Papæ Pauli V. Anno 1613. editum fuiffe decretum in Congregatione Illuftriffimorum Cardinalium Inquifitorum, cujus nos certiores facti fumus per epiftolam Illuftriffimi Cardinalis Millini miffam ad Dominum Generalem Inquifitorem hujus Regni eodèm Anno 1613. die 20. Ianuarii. Quià verò Reverendus Admodum Pater Magifter Fr. Martinus Monifius Provincialis Ordinis B. Virginis Mariæ de Monte Carmeli in hoc Regno à Nobis poftulavit authenticum ejufdem decreti tranfumptum; quo Religiofis ejufdem fui Ordinis innotefcerent in eo contenta, aliifque juftis de caufis juffimus hoc ipfum authenticum tranfumptum ei tradi per Nos fubfcriptum, figilloque Sanctæ Inquifitionis munitum. Eft autèm hujufmodi.

2 Patribus Carmelitanis permittatur prædicare, quòd Populus Chriftianus poffit piè credere de adjutorio animarum Fratrum, & Confratrum Sodalitatis Beatiffimæ Virginis de Monte Carmelo, videlicèt, Beatiffimam Virginem animas Fratrum, & Confratrum in charitate decedentium, quæ in vita habitum geftaverint, & caftitatem pro fuo ftatu coluerint, Officiumque parvum recitaverint, vèl fi recitare nefciunt, Ecclefiæ jejunia obfervaverint, & feria quarta, & Sabbato à carnibus abftinuerint (nifi ubi in iis diebus Nativitatis Domini feftum inciderit) fuis interceffionibus continuis, piifque fuffragiis, & meritis, ac fpeciali protectione poft earum tranfitum, præcipuè in die Sabbati.

An. 1613.
20. Ian.

585

Ioannes Vigesimussecundus. 63

bati, qui dies ab Ecclesia eidem Beatissimæ Virgini dicatus est, adjuturam.

Quod decretum Ego Simon Lopez Se-
cretarius Consilii Generalis S. Officii In-
quisitionis egi, traduci ex originali, quod
in secreto ejusdem Consilii Generalis ex-
tat, illudque lucubratum, unà cum for-
mulario hìc mecum consignato, & cum pro-
prio originali concordat.

Datum Ulyssippone, subscriptumque à
Dominis supradicti Consilii 14.die Iunii,
Anno Domini 1628.

> Simon Lopez.
> Gaspar Pereira. D.Ioan da Silva.
> Francisco Barretto.
> Collationatum cum me Notario Ga-
> spare Clementi.

CONSTITUTIO VI.

Ex Originali cum Sigillo plum-
beo in Archivio S.Chrysogoni.
n.I I.Tit.Religion.

SVMMARIVM.

Facultatem concedit Priori Generali, &
Fratribus Carmelitis recipiendi locum
in Provincia Romandiolæ.

IOANNES EPISCOPUS
Servus Servorum Dei.

Dilectis Filiis Priori Generali, &
Fratribus Ordinis Beatæ Mariæ
de Monte Carmeli, salutem,
& Apostolicam Benedi-
ctionem.

An.1322. INtèr ceteros Ordines in agro plà-
kal. Aug. tatos Ecclesiæ, sacrum vestrum
Ordinem gerentes in visceribus charitatis, ad ea vigilantèr intendimus, ac
opem, operamque solicitam benigniùs
impertimur, per quæ dictus Ordo pro-
speris successibus affluat, & votivis pro-
ficiat incrementis. Ex tenore siquidèm
vestræ Nobis exhibitæ petitionis accepimus, quod in diversis Provinciis pauca loca numero acquisita per Vos hactenùs obtinetis, quodque in nonnullis Ci-
vitatibus, Villis, & locis insignibus dictarum Provinciarum Fratres vestri Ordinis per ipsarum Civitatum, & Villa-
rum fideles Populos, ut in eis de novo

loca recipiant, cùm instantia requirun-
tur. Quarè Nobis humilitèr supplica-
stis, ut Vobis super hoc benignam licentiam concedere de speciali gratia
misericorditèr dignaremur.

2 Nos igitùr attendentes, quòd vestra Sacra Religio, sub qua virtutum
Domino devotum, & sedulum impen-
ditis famulatum, ex suæ institutionis
exordio ad robur, & fulcimentum erecta fidei orthodoxæ, per insignium gratiam meritorum, & sacræ Prædicationis
doctrinam, uberes hactenùs in universali Ecclesia honestatis fructus protulit,
& salutis: Et proptèr hoc Religionem
ipsam, & Professores ipsius in locis, in
quibus ex ipsis fructus expectatur ube-
rior, propagari, affectuosiùs cupientes,
volentesque præmissorum consideratio-
ne gratiam Vobis facere specialem: Vestris supplicationibus inclinati, recipiendi unum locum infrà Provinciam Romandiolæ, & in eo Ecclesiam, seù Oratorium, Domos, & Officinas necessa-
rias, juxtà morem ipsius Ordinis construendi, & morandi in illis, ac in eis
solemnitèr celebrandi, ut ibidem Auctore Domino possitis Vobis, & aliis
proficere ad salutem: necnòn habendi
Cœmiterium in eodem loco, & Ecclesiasticam Sepulturam liberam habendi; fe-
lic. record. Bonifacii Papæ VIII. Prædecessoris nostri, qua cavetur, nè Religiosi Mendicantes in aliqua Civitate,
Castro, vel Villa, seù loco, locande novo recipiant absque Sedis Apostolicæ
licentia speciali, faciente plenam, & expressam de inhibitione hujusmodi mentionem, & alia quacumque contraria,
Constitutionibus nequaquàm obstantibus, plenam, & liberam concedimus
Vobis auctoritate præsentium facultatem sine juris præjudicio alieni.

3 Nulli ergò omninò hominum liceat hanc paginam nostræ Concessionis
infringere, vel ei ausu temerario contraire. Si quis autem hoc attentare præsumpserit, indignationem Omnipotentis Dei, & Beatorum Petri, & Pauli
Apostolorum ejus, se noverit incursurum.

Datum Avinione Kal. Augusti, Pontificatus nostri Anno sexto.

586

CON-

Appendix 4

Pope Alexander V

Birth name	Peter of Candia or Petros Philargis (Greek)
Papacy began	June 26, 1409
Papacy ended	May 4, 1410
Predecessor	Pope Gregory XII?
Successor	Pope Martin V?
Born	1339
Died	May 3, 1410, Bologna, Italy

Pope Alexander V: Petros Philargis

Papacy: 1409 – 1410

Summary of Contents:

---

1). The Bull, *Tenorem cujusam privilegii*, dated December 7, 1409, found in the *Bullarium Carmelitanum Pars Prima*.

The Bull of Pope Alexander V both contained and confirmed the Sabbatine Bull of Pope John XXII. Alexander V was the first witness to testify to the existence of the Sabbatine Bull of John XXII, he tells us that he saw it himself, examined it carefully, was convinced of its authenticity, and in order to put its existence beyond future objections, he embodied it in a Bull of his own, in which he renews and confirms the privileges contained in it.

It was during the reign (of Alexander V) that the Carmelites became united under one General. Pope Alexander V nominated John Grossi, Professor and Master of Theology, to be Superior-General of the whole Order. It was John Grossi who wrote the Viridarium, the Catalogue of the Saints, and who recorded the vision of Our Blessed Mother to St. Simon Stock, as has been previously presented in Chapter 3(B) of this book, under "John Launoy versus John Grossi.

The original text follows and is in Latin.

(Cited from The Irish Ecclesiastical Record, Vol. VIII, Dublin, 1887, p. 798; The Sabbatine Privilege of the Scapular, 1322- 1922, P. E. Magennis, New York, 1923, p. 43))

BULLARIUM
CARMELITANUM
PLURES COMPLECTENS SUMMORUM
PONTIFICUM CONSTITUTIONES

Ad Ordinem Fratrum Beatissimæ, semperq;
Virginis Dei Genitricis MARIÆ
de Monte Carmelo spectantes,

Nunc primò in lucem editum , duaſque
in partes diſtinctum

A FRATRE ELISEO MONSIGNANO

Ejuſdem Ordinis Procuratore Generali .

PARS PRIMA
Duplici Indice exornata .

ROMÆ, MDCCXV.

Ex Typographia Georgii Plachi, Cælaturam Profitentis,
& Characterum Fuſoriam , apud S. MARCUM.
SVPERIORVM FACVLTATE.

589

FR. PETRUS THOMAS
S A N C H E Z

*Sacræ Theologiæ Magifter, Romani Cleri Exami-
minator, Collegii Ecclefiaftici de Urbe perpetuus
Lector, nec non humilis Prior Generalis, Vifitator, & Commiffarius Apoftolicus totius Ordinis Fratrum Beatiſsimæ, femperque Virginis Dei
Genitricis Mariæ de Monte Carmelo Antiquæ
Obfervantiæ Regularis.*

BUllarium Carmelitanum, ftudio ac labore
A.R.P. Magiftri Elifei Monfignani, ejufdem
Noftri Ordinis Procuratoris Generalis confectum
fummoperè commendantes, tenore præfentium
facultatem impartimur, ut typis mandetur, fi
iis, ad quos fpectat, ità videbitur.

Datum Romæ in Conventu S.Mariæ Tranfpontinæ 25. Martii 1715.

*Fr. Petrus Thomas Sanchez Generalis
Carmelitarum.*

Imprimatur,

Si videbitur Reverendifs. Patri Sacri Palatii Apoftolici Magiftro.

N. Archiepifcopus Capuæ Vicefgerens.

Imprimatur.

Fr. Gregorius Selleri Ord. Prædicat. Sacri Palatii
Apoftolici Magifter.

I N-

-compefcendo, invocato ad hoc, fi opus fuerit, auxilio brachii feeularis. Non obftante prædicta, quæ incipit *Omnis utriufque fexus*, & aliis Conftitutionibus Apoftolicis contrariis quibufcumque.

Datum Pifis 4. Idus Octobris, Pontificatus noftri anno primo.

CONSTITUTIO II.

Ex tranfumpto authentico, quod extat Romæ in Archivio Ordinis. F. n. 1, tit. Communia Ordinis.

SVMMARIVM.

Inferit Bullam Privilegii Sabbatini.

ALEXANDER EPISCOPUS
Servus Servorum Dei.

Univerfis, & fingulis Chriftifidelibus tam præfentibus, quàm futuris præfentes litteras infpecturis, Salutem, & Apoftolicam Benedictionem.

An. 1409.
9. Decem.

1 TEnorem cujufdam privilegii fel. recor. Joannis XXII. Prædecefforis noftri dilectis Filiis Priori generali, & Fratribus, & dilectis in Chrifto Filiabus, Sororibus, & Confratribus Confratriæ Fratrum dicti Ordinis Carmelitarum conceffi, per Nos vifi, & diligenter infpecti, de dicto originali fumptum, ut de ipfo impofterum certitudo plenior habeatur, præfentibus fecimus annotari, qui talis eft.

JOANNES EPISCOPUS
Servus Servorum Dei.

Univerfis, & fingulis Chriftifidelibus &c. *ut prædictum eft.*

2 Sacratiffimo uti culmine paradifi Angelorum tam fuavis, & dulcis reperitur melodia, modulamine vifionis dum paterno Jefus numini circunfpicitur adunatus dicendo, Domine: Ego, & Pater unum fumus, & qui videt me, videt, & Patrem meum, & Angelorum Chorus non definit dicere: Sanctus, Sanctus, Sanctus; Ita Synodus non ceffat laudes effundere celfæ Virgini dicendo: Virgo, Virgo, Virgo;

Sis fpeculum noftrum, pariter, & exemplum. Quoniam munere munitur gratiarum, ficut Sancta cantat Ecclefia, Gratia plena, & Mater Mifericordiæ. Sic ille mons reputatur de Carmelo Ordinem cantibus extollendo, & hanc gratiarum Genitricem commendando, & dicendo: Salve Regina Mifericordiæ, & fpes noftra.

Sic mihi flexis genibus fupplicanti Virgo vifa fuit Carmelita fequentem affata fermonem: O Joannes. O Joannes. Vicarie mei dilecti Filii, veluti à tuo te eripiam adverfario, te Papam facio folemni dono Vicarium meis coadjuvantibus fupplicationibus dulciffimo meo Filio petens; quod gratiosè obtinui, Iftam gratiam, & amplam meo fancto, ac devoto Carmelitarum Ordini, confirmationem debeas præconcedere, per Eliam, & Elifeum in Monte Carmeli inchoato.

Quod unufquifque qui profeffionem faciens, Regulam à meo fervo Alberto Patriarcha ordinatam confervabit, & inviolatam obtinebit, & per meum dilectum Filium Innocentium approbatam, & veri mei Filii Vicarium debeat in terris affentire, quod in Cælis meus ftatuit, & ordinavit Filius; quòd qui in fancta perfeverabit obedientia, paupertate, & caftitate, vel qui fanctam intravit Ordinem, falvabitur; Et fi alii devotionis caufa in fanctam ingrediantur Religionem, fancti habitus fignum ferentes, appellantes fe Confratres, & Confrorores mei Ordinis prænominati, liberentur, & abfolvantur à tertia eorum peccatorum portione, à die quo præfatum Ordinem intrabunt; Caftitatem, fi viduæ eft, promittendo; virginitatis, fi eft virgo, Fidem præftando; fi eft conjugata, inviolati confervationem matrimonii adhibendo, ut Sancta Mater imperat Ecclefia: Fratres profeffi dicti Ordinis fupplicio folvantur, & culpa, & die quo ab ifto feculo recedunt, profperato gradu accelerant purgatorium.

Ego Mater gratiosè defcendam Sabbato poft eorum obitum, & quot inveniam in purgatorio, liberabo, & eos in Montem Sanctum vitæ æternæ reducam. Verum quòd ipfi Confratres, & Confrorores teneantur Horas dicere

Joannes Vigesimustertius. 167

dicere Canonicales, ut opus fuerit, secundùm Regulam datam ab Alberto. Illi, qui ignari funt, debeant vitam jejunam ducere diebus, quos facra jubet Ecclesia,nisi necessitatis causa aliqui essent traditi impedimento: Mercurio, & Sabbato debeant se à carnibus abstinere, præterquam in mei Filii Nativitate: & hoc dicto evanuit ista Sancta Visio.

Istam ergo Sanctam Indulgentiam accepto, roboro, & in terris confirmo, sicut propter merita Virginis Matris gratiosè Jesus Christus concessit in Cœlis.

Nulli ergo omnino hominum liceat hanc paginam nostræ indulgentiæ, seu statuti, & ordinationis irritare, vel ei ausu temerario contraire; si quis autem hoc attentare præsumpserit: indignationem Omnipotentis Dei, & BB. Apostolorum Petri, & Pauli se noverit incursurum.

Datum Avinione 3. die Martii, Pontificatus nostri anno sexto.

Nulli ergo &c. *ut prædictum est.*

Datum Romæ, septima Decembris apud S. Mariam Majorem, Pontificatus nostri anno primo.

JOANNES XXIII

Italus, patria Neapolitanus, Balthaffar Cossa antea vocatus S. R. E. Diaconus Cardinalis tit. S. Eustachii, Bononiæ 17. Maii 1410. Summus Pontifex pronunciatur. Sedit annos 6,, & dies 15., postea deposuit Papatum in Concilio Constantiensi.

Fundatio Conventus Incisæ in Provincia Lombardiæ.

An.1413. 16. Mar.

Concessit hic Pontifex Fratri Emmanueli de Incisa Priori Provinciali Provinciæ Lombardiæ licentiam fundandi Cœnobium in Terra Incisæ Aquensis Diœcesis, sub Vocabulo Beatæ Mariæ de Monte Carmelo. Sub. Dat. Romæ apud S. Petrum XVII. Kal. Aprilis. Anno tertio. *Ex lib. de litte-*

ris DD. *Cardinalium*, & *de provisionibus Prælatorum. Anno tertio. fol.*15.

CONSTITUTIO UNICA.

Ex Reg. Vat. lib. 2. de diverfis formis ann.5. fol.255.

SUMMARIUM.

Constituuntur Conservatores, & *Judices Fratrum Mendicantium.*

JOANNES EPISCOPUS
Servus Servorum Dei.

Venerabili Fratri Episcopo Streginen., & dilectis Filiis Streginen., ac Arosien. Ecclesiarum Præpositis &c.

1   Frequentes hactenùs, imò innumerosæ quodammodo de diversis mundi partibus Venerabilium Fratrum nostrorum Episcoporum, aliorumque Superiorum Prælatorum, nec non dilectorum Filiorum Rectorum, Curatorum, & parochialium Sacerdotum querelæ contra dilectos Filios Prædicatorum, & Minorum Ordinum Fratres Apostolicæ Sedis jamdudum excitarunt, nostrumque clamorosis insinuationibus excitare, & fatigare non cessant auditum: quodque iidem Fratres Decretalem dudum editam a fel.rec.Bonifacio Papa VIII. Prædecessore nostro, quæ incipit: *Super Cathedram* &c.; ac deindè per piæ mem. Clementem Papam V.Prædecessorem nostrum in Viennensi Concilio innovatam temerè observare non curant, sed ipsam transgredi non verentur, in ejusdem Sedis contemptum, animarum suarum periculum, & eorumdem conquerentium, & Ecclesiarum Parochialium prejudicium, & gravamen.

2   Intelleximus quoque: quòd plerumque præfatis dictorum Prædicatorum, & Minorum nec non Eremitarum S. Augustini, & Carmelitarum, ac Servorum Beatæ Mariæ dicti S. Augustini Ordinum Fratribus, in cujus Ordinis dictorum Eremitarum personis idem Prædecessor Bonifacius Decretalem præfatam, in qua tantum ipsis Prædicatorum, & Minorum cavetur Ordinibus,

per

An.1414. 28. Aug.

Clement VII

Birth name	Giulio di Giuliano de' Medici
Papacy began	November 19, 1523
Papacy ended	September 25, 1534
Predecessor	Adrian VI
Successor	Paul III
Born	May 26, 1478 Florence
Died	September 25, 1534 (age 56) Rome, Italy

Pope Clement VII: Giulio di Giuliano de'Medici

Papacy: 1523 – 1534

Summary of Contents:

1). The Bull: Pope Clement VII, *Ex Clementi Sedis Apostolicae*, dated August 12, 1530, found in the *Bullarium Carmelitanum, Pars Secunda.*

In his Bull, Pope Clement VII, by name, cites the previous Bull of John XXII almost word for word, and in the Bull of Alexander V., regarding the Sabbatine Privilege, solemnly approves and confirms them, and ratifies their contents and approves all the graces and privileges of the Order. The only change in these Bulls is, that Clement does not speak of the descent of the Virgin in Purgatory, which has been already mentioned, but says, the holy Virgin will aid, etc. The original text follows and is in Latin.

(Cited from The Irish Ecclesiastical Record, Vol. VIII, Dublin, 1887, p. 802); (The Carmelites and the Brown Scapular, A.E. Farrington, Dublin, 1891, p. 130)

B.ULLARIUM
CARMELITANUM

PLURES CONTINENS SUMMORUM PONTIFICUM
LITTERAS ET CONSTITUTIONES

Ad Ordinem Fratrum Beatiſſimæ, ſemperque
Virginis Dei Genitricis MARIÆ
de Monte Carmelo ſpeɛtantes

Nunc primùm in lucem editum, duasque
in partes diviſum

A FRATRE ELISEO MONSIGNANO

Ejuſdem Ordinis Procuratore Generali.

PARS SECUNDA
Duplici Indice inſtruɛta.

Præmittitur brevis Additio ad Primam Partem.

ROMÆ, MDCCXVIII.

Typis Georgii Plachi, Cælaturam Profitentis, & Charaɛterum
Fuſoriam, apud S. MARCUM.
SVPERIORVM PERMISSV.

NOS FR. CAROLUS CORNACCIOLI

Sacræ Theologiæ Magifter & Doctor, humilis Prior Generalis, nec non Vifitator & Commißarius Apo-ftolicus totius Ordinis Fratrum Beatiffimæ, femper-que Virginis Dei Genitricis Mariæ de Monte Car-melo antiquæ Obfervantiæ Regularis.

AUctoritate noftra, præfentium tenore licentiam concedimus Admodum Reverendo Patri Ma-giftro Elifeo Monfignano ejufdem noftri Ordinis Procuratori Generali typis mandandi Partem Se-cundam *Bullarii Carmelitani*, fi iis, ad quos fpectat, ita vifum fuerit. In quorum fidem &c. Datum Romæ in Conventu S. Mariæ Tranfpontinæ die 7. Septem-bris 1718.

Fr. Carolus Cornaccioli Generalis Carmelitarum.

Fr. Joannes Francifcus Orlandi Provincialis Romæ & Secretarias Ordinis.

IMPRIMATUR,

Si videbitur Reverendiffimo Patri Magiftro Sacri Palatii Apoftolici.

T. Epifc. Eracleæ Vicefgerens.

IMPRIMATUR.

Fr. Gregorius Selleri Sac. Palatii Apoftolici Magifter Ordinis Prædicatorum.

INDEX

Clemens Septimus.

CLEMENS PAPA VII.

Universis, & singulis Christifidelibus presentes litteras inspecturis Salutem, & Apostolicam Benedictionem.

An.1530.
8. Febr.

1 Licèt aliàs felicis recordationis Julius Papa II. Prædecessor noster eò quòd in Vigilia Sancti Martini Civitatem nostram Bononiensem tunc suam, per alios occupatam recuperaverat, plenariam Indulgentiam Ecclesiam Domus Sancti Martini Bononien. Ordinis Carmelitarum annis singulis, quandoque vivæ vocis oraculo, quandoque verò per litteras in forma Brevis concesserit, ac piæ *Conf.33* memoriæ * Leo Papa X.etiam Prædecessor noster eamdem Indulgentiam plenariam cum facultate deputandi Confessores omnibus utriusque sexus Christi fidelibus Ecclesiam ipsam annis singulis visitantibus, perpetuis futuris temporibus duraturam concesserit: tamen cum instaret Annus Jubilæi Anni MDXXV. omnes plenarias Indulgentias cum facultate deputandi Confessores durante dicto anno Jubilæi proximè præteriti, & deinde ad beneplacitum nostrum suspendimus; Et propterea dicta Indulgentia adhuc suspensa existit. Quare pro parte Prioris, & fratrum dictæ Domus Nobis fuit humiliter supplicatum, ut beneplacitum prædictum revocare, ac aliàs in præmissis opportunè providere de benignitate apostolica dignaremur.

2 Nos itaque in memoriam recuperationis dictæ Civitatis, hujusmodi supplicationibus inclinati, Beneplacitum nostrum, & suspensionem hujusmodi per præsentes revocamus, & annullamus; incontrarium facientibus non obstantibus quibuscumque.

Datum Bononiæ sub anulo Piscatoris die 8. Februarii 1530. Pontificatus nostri anno septimo.

XXXVI.

Ex originali sub plumbo. Romæ in Archivio Ordinis.

SUMMARIUM.

Confirmantur privilegia, gratiæ, & exemptiones Ordini, ejusque Confratribus, & Consororibus concessa.

Vid. infra in Paulo V.& Constitutionem Clementis X. Commisse Nobis anno 1673. 8. Maii.

CLEMENS EPISCOPUS
Servus Servorum Dei.

Ad perpetuam rei memoriam.

An.1530.
12. Aug.

EX Clementi Sedis Apostolicæ provisione, nec non personarum Deo devotarum sub Religionis jugo, & regulari castimonia Domino militantium pia devotione provenire dinoscitur, ut Romanus Pontifex quandoque per Prædecessores suos Romanos Pontifices pro personarum earumdem, ac illarum Locorum felici successu, & quiete, ac Christi fidelium piis operibus vacantium, animarum salute, concessa approbet, & innovet, ac innovata communiat, & alia de novo concedat, prout in Domino conspicit salubriter expedire.

1 Sanè pro parte dilectorum filiorum Nicolai Audet Generalis, ac Provincialium, & Priorum Domorum Ordinis B. Mariæ Virginis de Monte Carmelo, nec non Confratrum utriusque sexus Confraternitatum in Ecclesiis Domorum ejusdem Ordinis institutarum Nobis nuper exhibita petitio continebat, quòd aliàs fel.rec. * Joannes XXII. & * Alexander V. *Conf.5.* Romani Pontifices prædecessores nostri *Conf.2.* universis, & singulis Christi fidelibus, qui Confraternitatem de Monte Carmelo ingredi seu Confratrum Confraternitatum hujusmodi numero ascribi, ipsiusque Ordinis statuta observare, ac habitum dicti Ordinis deferre, seq; Fratres, & Sorores dicti Ordinis appellare; Ita quòd si mulier, Virgo castitatem, vidua verò continentiam, conjugata autem matrimonii jura, prout S. Ecclesia præcipit, tempore earum ingressus inviolabiliter servare velle promitterent, & observarent, tertiam partem suorum peccatorum in Domino

48 *Clemens Septimus:*

mino relaxarunt, ac ipfa gloriofiffima Dei Genitrix femper Virgo Maria ipforum Confratrum, feu Religioforum, ac Sororum animas poft eorum tranfitum fuis interceffionibus continuis, piis fuffragiis, & fpeciali protectione adjuvabit; quòdque Confratres ipfi gratiarum earumdem Prædecefforum participes fieri volentes, horas canonicas juxtà formam ab Alberto Patriarcha dicto Ordini conceffam, & ordinatam recitare; ignari verò litterarum, diebus, quibus S. Ecclefia jejunare præcipit, jejunare, nec non quarta feria, & Sabbato toto tempore vitæ eorum, preterquam die, qua aliquam ex feriis prædictis Nativitatem Domini Noftri Jefu Chrifti occurrere contigerit, à carnibus abftinere deberent; Ac etiam nonnulli alii Romani Pontifices etiam Prædeceffores noftri quamplura, & diverfa privilegia, immunitates, exemptiones, præfertim quartam funeralium Presbyteris fecularibus non folvendi, ac indulta, indulgentias, & peccatorum remiffiones, ac gratias d. Ordini, illiufque Fratribus, Monialibus, Sororibus, & utriufque fexus perfonis, ac Monafteriis Monialium, & Domibus Sororum, eorumque Ecclefiis, & Locis quibufcumque etiam per modum extenfionis, feu communicationis, ac aliàs cefferunt, prout in diverfis eorumdem Prædecefforum litteris defuper confectis dicitur pleniùs contineri. Quare pro parte Generalis, Provincialium, Priorum, & utriufque fexus Confratrum prædictorum afferentium, refrigefcente in dies fidelium devotione, Domos Fratrum, & Sororum, ac Monafteria hujufmodi non modica reparatione indigere, & propterea fideles ipfos ad temporalia bona pro hujufmodi reparatione concedenda fpiritualibus bonis, & gratiis invitare oportere, ac ad id inducere neceffe fore, Nobis fuit humiliter fupplicatum, ut privilegia, indulta, immunitates, exemptiones, & gratias, ac alia prædicta approbare, & innovare, & inviolabiliter obfervari mandare, illaque pro potiori cautela de novo concedere de benignitate apoftolica dignaremur.

2 Nos igitur dicti Ordinis, quem præ cæteris in vifceribus gerimus charitatis, profperum, & tranquillum ftatum, ac animarum falutem paterno zelantes affectu, hujufmodi fupplicationibus inclinati, Joannis, & Alexandri, ac aliorum Præ-

decefforum noftrorum litteras, ac per eofdem prædeceffores omnia, & fingula privilegia, immunitates, exemptiones etiam non folvendi *Quartam funeralium* Presbyteris fecularibus, quoad fratres Domorum in poffeffione Quartam ipfam non folvendi exiftentes dumtaxat, ac indulta, indulgentias citra plenarias, peccatorum remiffiones, & gratias Ordini, & illius fratribus, monialibus, fororibus, & utriufque fexus Confratribus, & perfonis, Domibus, Monafteriis, Ecclefiis, & locis quibufcumque etiam per modum extenfionis, feu communicationis, & aliàs quomodolibet etiam per Nos, & Sedem apoftolicam conceffa, quorum omnium tenores præfentibus pro fufficienter expreffis, & infertis haberi volumus, auctoritate apoftolica, tenore præfentium approbamus, & innovamus, ac perpetuæ firmitatis robur obtinere, & inviolabiliter obfervari debere.

3 Ipfofque fratres, moniales, forores, perfonas, Monafteria, Domos, Ecclefias, & alia loca hujufmodi, omnibus, & fingulis privilegiis, immunitatibus, exemptionibus, indultis, indulgentiis, citra tamen plenarias, peccatorum remiffionibus, & gratiis quibufvis Congregationibus dicti & aliorum Ordinum etiam Mendicantium Fratribus, & perfonis, ac Confraternitatibus fuæ profeffioni non contrariis, aliifque Ordinibus quibufcumque etiam non Mendicantium quomodolibet conceffis, & concedendis in genere, uti, frui, & gaudere poffe, atque debere in omnibus, & per omnia, perindè ac fi eis conceffa fuiffent, decernimus. Nec non potiori pro cautela ea omnia etiam de novo concedimus.

4 Ipfiufque Ordinis Fratres ab Inquifitoribus hæreticæ pravitatis penitus eximimus, & fub noftra, ac d. Sedis Protectione fufcipimus, ac eifdem Inquifitoribus fub excommunicationis latæ fententiæ, & officiorum fuorum privationis pœnis diftrictè inhibemus, ne de dd. Fratribus etiam ratione criminis hærefis quoquomodo fe intromittere præfumant. Decernentes irritum, & inane quidquid per eos fcienter, vel ignoranter contigerit attentari.

5 Omnibufque & fingulis utriufque fexus Confratribus, ut quilibet eorum aliquem Presbyterum idoneum fecularem, vel cujufvis Ordinis etiam Mendican-

Concedit privileg. aliorum Ordinum

Hoc privilegium revocatur in Conf. st. Pii IV. apud Cherubinum.

Facultas eligendi Confeffarium, qui eos abfolvat &c.

cantium, & de Obſervantia Regularem in ſuum poſſint eligere Confeſſorem, qui vita eis comite, eos, & eorum quemlibet à quibuſvis, etiam majoris excommunicationis, ſuſpenſionis, & interdicti, aliiſque Eccleſiaſticis ſententiis, cenſuris, & pœnis à jure, vel ab homine quavis occaſione, vel cauſa pro tempore latis, & quibus etiam pro tempore irretiti fuerint, etiamſi illorum abſolutio Sedi prædictæ ſpecialiter, vel generaliter (præterquàm per litteras in Cœna Domini legi ſolitas) reſervata foret, ac quorumcumque votorum, & Juramentorum, nec non Eccleſiæ præceptorum tranſgreſſionibus, perjuriorum, ſimoniæ, & homicidii mentalis, vel caſualis reatibus, manuum violentarum in quaſuis perſonas Eccleſiaſticas (non tamen Epiſcopos, vel eorum ſuperiores) de præterito injectionibus, jejuniorum, horarum Canonicarum, Divinorum officiorum, ac pœnitentiarum injunctarum in toto, vel in parte omiſſionibus, omnibuſque aliis eorum peccatis, criminibus, exceſſibus, & delictis quantumcumque gravibus, & enormibus, etiam talibus, propter quæ Sedes prædicta meritò conſulenda foret, in caſibus d. Sedi qualitercumque reſervatis, exceptis contentis in dd. litteris Cœnæ Domini, ſemel in vita, & in mortis articulo; de aliis verò d.Sedi non reſervatis caſibus, totiens quotiens opportunum fuerit, eorum confeſſionibus diligenter auditis abſolvere, illiſque pro commiſſis pœnitentiam ſalutarem injungere. Vota verò quæcumque, (ultramarino, viſitationis Liminum Beatorum Petri, & Pauli Apoſtolorum de Urbe, ac S. Jacobi in Compoſtella, nec non Religionis, & Caſtitatis votis dumtaxat exceptis) in alia pietatis opera commutare, & juramenta quæcumque ſine tertii præjudicio relaxare, ac omnium eorum peccatorum ſemel in vita, & in mortis articulo, ut præfertur, etiamſi tunc non ſubſequatur, plenariam remiſſionem, & abſolutionem, auctoritate apoſtolica impendere poſſit.

6 Liceatque omnibus, & ſingulis utriuſque ſexus Confratribus prædictis & cuilibet eorum habere Altare portatile cum debitis reverentia, & honore, ſuper quo in locis ad hoc congruentibus, & honeſtis etiam non ſacris, & quavis, etiam apoſtolica auctoritate interdictis, ſeu tempore ceſſationis à Divinis, dummodo cau-

ſam non dederint hujuſmodi interdicto, ſeu ceſſationi, & per eos non ſtet, quominùs pareatur apoſtolico interdicto, etiam antequam illuceſcat dies, circa tamen diurnam lucem, ſeu circa meridiem, cum qualitas negotiorum pro tempore ingruentium id exegerit, in eorum præſentia, clauſis januis, excommunicatis, & interdictis excluſis, non pulſatis Campanis, & ſubmiſſa voce Miſſas, & alia Divina officia per Sacerdotes ſeculares, vel Regulares hujuſmodi celebrare: ac quocumque tempore Euchariſtiam, & alia Sacramenta Eccleſiaſtica a quocumque maluerint Presbytero idoneo, & ubicumque ſine Rectoris Parochialis Eccleſiæ præjudicio recipere, & adminiſtrare liberè, & licitè valeat. Etſi contingat, eos, vel eorum aliquem tempore interdicti hujuſmodi ab humanis decedere, corpora eorum Eccleſiaſticæ, cum aliquali honeſta tamen funerali pompa, tradi poſſint ſepulturæ.

7 Quòdque ſingulis quadrageſimalibus, & aliis cujuslibet anni temporibus, & diebus Stationum Baſilicarum, & Eccleſiarum almæ Urbis Romæ, & extra illius muros, unam, vel duas Eccleſias, aut unum, duo, vel plura Altaria in partibus illis, ubi eos, ſeu eorum aliquem reſidere, ſeu quò declinare contigerit, quas, vel quæ ipſi vel quilibet eorum duxerint eligendas, vel eligenda, devotè viſitando, tot, & ſingulas, ac ſimiles indulgentias, & peccatorum remiſſiones conſequantur, quas conſequerentur, ſi ſingulis diebus eaſdem ſingulas d. Urbis, & extra eam, Eccleſias pro Stationibus hujuſmodi deputatas perſonaliter viſitarent.

8 Inſuper etiam omnibus utriuſque ſexus Chriſtifidelibus, qui pro monaſteriorum, & domorum reparatione, ac Fratrum hujuſmodi ſuſtentatione manus porrexerint adjutrices, ſupradictas indulgentias conſequi poſſint, & conſequantur. Omnibus verò, & ſingulis aliis Chriſtifidelibus utriuſque ſexus, qui dictum Ordinem, illiuſque Domos, & Monaſteria, Fratres, Sorores, & Moniales hujuſmodi, ſuis eleemoſynis, & ſubſidiis pro tempore juverint, & manutenuerint, ut ipſi, & quilibet eorum, omnium precum, ſuffragiorum, eleemoſynarum, jejuniorum, orationum, Miſſarum, horarum Canonicarum, diſciplinarum, peregrinationum, & cæterorum ſpiritualium bo-

50 *Clemens Septimus,*

bonorum, quæ pro tempore in universali Sacrosancta Ecclesia militante fiunt, in perpetuum participes fiant, & omnibus ejus meritis gaudeant; ac omnibus aliis, qui gratiis eorumdem Confratrum gaudere voluerint, aliquam eleemosynam, sive charitatem, prout eis, ac Præsidentibus Confraternitatum hujusmodi visum fuerit, dando, & largiendo, gratiarum hujusmodi participes fiant indulgemus. Non obstantibus constitutionibus, & ordinationibus apostolicis, ac dicti Ordinis statutis, & consuetudinibus etiam juramento, confirmatione apostolica, vel quavis firmitate alia roboratis, nec non privilegiis, indultis, & litteris apostolicis per quoscumque Romanos Pontifices prædecessores nostros, ac Nos, & Sedem prædictam etiam motu proprio, & ex certa scientia, ac de apostolicæ potestatis plenitudine, & cum quibusvis irritativis, annullativis, cassativis, revocativis, modificativis, præservativis, exceptivis, restitutivis, declarativis mentis, attestativis, ac derogatoriarum derogatoriis, aliisque efficacioribus, efficacissimis, & insolitis clausulis quomodolibet etiam pluries concessis, confirmatis, & innovatis, quibus omnibus, etiamsi pro illorum sufficienti derogatione, de illis, eorumque totis tenoribus specialis, & individua, ac de verbo ad verbum, non autem per clausulas generales idem importantes mentio, seu quævis alia expressio habenda, aut exquisita forma servanda forent, & in eis caveatur expressè, quòd illis nullatenus derogari possit, illorumque omnium, nec non quarumcumque, etiam in forma Brevis, litterarum occasione præmissorum quomodolibet confectarum, & quorumcumque in eis contentorum tenores præsentibus pro sufficienter expressis, ac de verbo ad verbum insertis, nec non modos, & formas ad id servandos pro in individuo servatis habentes hac vice dumtaxat, illis aliàs in suo robore permansuris, harum serie specialiter, & expressè derogamus, nec non omnibus illis, quæ præfati Prædecessores in eorum litteris voluerunt non obstare, cæterisque contrariis quibuscumque. Volumus autem, quòd præsentium transumptis manu alicujus publici Notarii subscriptis, & sigillo alicujus personæ in Dignitate Ecclesiastica constitutæ munitis, eadem prorsus fides in Judicio, & extrà adhibeatur, quæ præsentibus originalibus adhiberetur, si fœrent exhibitæ, vel ostensæ.

Nulli ergo omnino hominum liceat hanc paginam nostrorum approbationis, innovationis, concessionis, exemptionis, susceptionis, Inhibitionis, Decretorum, Induli, derogationis, & voluntatis infringere, vel ei ausu temerario contraire. Si quis &c.

Datum Romæ apud S. Petrum anno Incarnationis Dominicæ 1530. Pridie Idus Augusti, Pontificatus nostri anno septimo.

XXXVII.

Ex Brevi originali. Romæ in Archivio S. Chrysogoni n. 22. tit. Congregationis.

SUMMARIUM.
Confirmat omnia privilegia Congregationi Mantuanæ a Prædecessoribus concessa.

Hujus Constit. revocationem vide in alia mox subsequente.

CLEMENS PAPA VII.

Ad perpetuam rei memoriam.

Sacer Ordo in agro Dominico Divina dispositione plantatus, ac Gloriosissimæ Dei Genitricis, semperque Virginis Mariæ titulo specialiter insignitus, Apostolicis favoribus, & gratiis dignè meretur attolli. Quapropter Nos ea, quæ à Romanis Pontificibus Prædecessoribus nostris eidem Ordini ex benignitate Sedis Apostolicæ providè concessa fuisse comperimus, ut eò firmiùs inviolata, & inconcussa permaneant, quò fuerint sæpius apostolico stabilita præsidio, cum à Nobis petitur, prout ejusdem Sacræ Religionis statui convenire novimus, libenter frequentiori communis firmitate, aliaque ei eò modo concedimus, prout secundùm solicitudinis nostræ partes id in Domino conspicimus salubriter expedire.

1 Sanè pro parte Placiti de Albino decretorum professoris Vicarii, & Joannis Baptistæ Pallavicini in Romana Curia Procuratoris generalis, ac universorum modernorum Priorum, & fratrum dicti Ordinis ejusdem Beatæ Mariæ de Monte Carmelo Congregationis Mantuanæ regularis observantiæ nuncupatorum dilectorum

An. 1531.
31. Mar.

Appendix 4

Paul III

Birth name	Alessandro Farnese
Papacy began	October 13, 1534
Papacy ended	November 10, 1549
Predecessor	Clement VII
Successor	Julius III
Born	February 29, 1468 Canino, Lazio
Died	November 10, 1549 (age 81) Rome

Pope Paul III: Alessandro Farnese

Papacy: 1534 – 1549

Summary of Contents:

1).   The Bull: *Provisionis nostre*, dated November 3, 1534, found in the *Bullarium Carmelitanum Pars Secunda*.

This Bull of Pope Paul III, confirms and approves the authenticity of the Bull of his predecessor, Clement VII, in his Bull: *Ex Clementi Sedis* who ratified the Bulls of his predecessors John XXII and Alexander V containing the Sabbatine Privilege. The original text follows and is in Latin.

(Cited from The Irish Ecclesiastical Record, Vol. VIII, Dublin, 1887, p. 802)

B.ULLARIŲM
ÇARMELITANUM
PLURES CONTINENS SUMMORUM PONTIFICUM LITTERAS ET CONSTITUTIONES

Ad Ordinem Fratrum Beatiſſimæ , ſemperque Virginis Dei Genitricis MARIÆ de Monte Carmelo ſpectantes

Nunc primùm in lucem editum , duasque in partes diviſum

A FRATRE ELISEO MONSIGNANO
Ejuſdem Ordinis Procuratore Generali .

PARS SECUNDA
Duplici Indice inſtructa .

Præmittitur brevis Additio ad Primam Partem.

ROMÆ, MDCCXVIII.

Typis Georgii Plachi, Cælaturam Profitentis, & Characterum Fuſoriam, apud S. Marcum.
SVPERIORVM PERMISSV.

68   *Paulus Tertius.*

jubet, ssasque authoritate transcriptam munit.

Vid. infra ejuss. Pontif. Conss. 27. Incip. Dum a Nobis, &c.

PAULUS EPISCOPUS
Servus Servorum Dei.

Ad futuram rei memoriam.

An. 1534. 3. Nov.

1 PRovisionis nostræ provenire debet subsidio, ut suum jus cuilibet conservetur. Hinc est, quòd nos tenorem quarumdam litterarum sel. rec. Clementis Papæ VII. prædecessoris nostri in registro ipsius prædecessoris compertum, pro eo quòd, sicut exhibita nobis pro parte dilectorum filiorum Nicolai Audet Prioris Generalis, & Provincialium, ac Priorum Domorum Ordinis B. Mariæ Virginis de Monte Carmelo, nec non Confratrum utriusque sexus Confratérnitatum in Ecclesiis Domorum ejusdem Ordinis institutarum, petitio continebat, ipsi hujusmodi tenore certis de causis dignoscuntur indigere, de Registro ipso de verbo ad verbum transcribi, & ad ipsorum Generalis, Provincialium, Priorum & Confratrum supplicantium instantiam præsentibus annotari fecimus, qui talis est.

Clemens Episcopus Servus Servorum Dei; ad perpetuam rei memoriam. Ex Clementi &c. prout supra pag. 47.

2 Ceterùm ut earumdem tenor litterarum hic insertus omnimodam rei seu facti certitudinem faciat, authoritate nostra decernimus ut illud idem robur, eamdemque vim, eumdemque vigorem dictus tenor habeat, quæ haberent originales litteræ supradictæ; ac eadem prorsùs eidem tenori fides adhibeatur quandocumque, & ubicumque, sive in judicio, sive alibi, ubi fuerit exhibitus seu ostensus, & eidem tenori firmiter servetur in omnibus, sicut eisdem originalibus literis daretur, si forent exhibitæ, vel ostensæ. Per hoc autem, jus cuiquam de novo acquiri nolumus, sed antiqua tantummodo conservari.

Nulli ergo omnino hominum liceat hanc paginam nostræ voluntatis, Constitutionis, & Decreti infringere, vel ei ausu temerario contraire. Si quis autem &c.

Datum Romæ apud S. Petrum anno Incarnat. Dominicæ 1534. III. Nonas Novemb. Pontificatus nostri anno primo.

II.

Ex transs. auth. Romæ in Arch. Ord.

SUMMARIUM.
Ut omnibus proventibus Conventus Florentini fideliter collectis, & assumpta congrua portione pro Fratrum sustentatione, convertant residuum in debitorum solutionem.

PAULUS EPISCOPUS
Servus Servorum Dei.

Dilectis Filiis Subdecano, & Vannio de Oricellariis Canonico Ecclesiæ Florentinæ Salutem &c.

An. 1535. 13. Mar.

AD audientiam nostram noveritis pervenisse, quòd dilecti filii Prior, & Fratres Domus Beatæ Mariæ de Monte Carmelo Florentin. Ordinis ejusdem Beatæ, & gloriosæ, ac semper Virginis Mariæ de Monte Carmelo, tanto premuntur onere debitorum, quòd nisi per Sedem Apostolicam eis celeriter succurratur, vix effici poterit, ut resurgant: eorumque bona adeò, usurarum præsertim voragine, consumúntur, quòd necessario sumptu deducto pro substentatione Prioris, & Fratrum ipsius Domus, & aliorum habitantium in eadem, vix totum residuum ad solutionem sufficit usurarum.

1 Nos igitur volentes super hoc eidem domui paterna solicitudine providere, ac de vestra circumspectione plenam in Domino fiduciam obtinentes, discretioni vestræ per Apostolica scripta mandamus: quatenus reductis in unam summam omnibus debitis supradictis per vos, vel alium seu alios, quos ad hoc duxeritis deputandos, universos redditus, & proventus ejusdem Domus fideliter colligatis, & assumpta ex ipsis redditibus, & proventibus, Priori, & Fratribus memoratis, ac Personis ejusdem Domus pro eorum substentatione congrua portione, convertatis residuum, usuris cessantibus, in solutionem hujusmodi debitorum, satis faciendo primitùs illis, qui in jure fuerint potiores, nec permittatis interim dd. Priorem & Fratres super alia solutione ab aliquibus molestari, molestatores hujusmodi per censuram ecclesiasticam appellatione remota compescendo; non obstantibus renunciationibus, confessionibus,

Po-

Paulus Tertius. 69

pœnarum addictionibus, juramentis, Inftrumentis, & litteris quibufcumque tempore contractuum interjectis: feu fi aliquibus à Sede Apoftolica fit indultum, quòd interdici, fufpendi, vel excommunicari non poffint per litteras Apoftolicas non facientes plenam, & expreffam, ac de verbo ad verbum de indulto hujufmodi mentionem, & qualibet alia dictæ Sedis indulgentia generali, vel fpeciali, cujufcumque tenoris exiftat, per quam præfentibus non expreffam, vel totaliter non infertam, veftræ Jurifdictionis explicatio valeat in hac parte quomodolibet impediri, quæ quòad hoc nolumus eis aliquatenus fuffragari, univerfas excommunicationis, fufpenfionis, & interdicti fententias Apoftolica, feu alia quavis auctoritate occafione prædicta in eofdem Priorem, & Fratres, feu in perfonas alias ejufdem Domus communiter, vel divifim promulgatas juxta formam Ecclefiæ confuetam fine difficultate relaxando; quòd fi non ambo iis exequendis potueritis intereffe, alter veftrum ea nihilominus exequatur.

Datum Romæ apud Sanctum Petrum Anno Incarnat. Dominicæ 1534. III. Idus Martii, Pontificatus noftri anno primo.

III.

Ex tranf. auth. Romæ in Arch. S.Chryfogoni n.11. tit. Vic. gener.

SUMMARIUM.

Ut libros, & fcripturas Martini Lutheri, ejufque fectatorum perquirat, accipiat, & comburat.

Dilecto Filio moderno Vicario Generali Congregationis Mantuanæ Ordinis Fratrum Carmelitarum Regularis Obfervantiæ.

PAULUS PAPA III.

Dilecte Fili, Salutem &c.

1535. April. UT in Congregatione Mantuana Ordinis fratrum Carmelitarum regularis obfervantiæ, cui præes, fides catholica, & mores optimi, ficut femper viguerunt, vigeant, & omnis occafio mali tollatur: tibi in virtute Sanctæ obedientiæ, & fub noftræ indignationis pœna

committimus, & mandamus, quatenus quofcumque libros, & quafcumque Scripturas per filium perditionis Martinum Lutherum, & quofcumque ejus complices, hactenus editos, & editas, apud quofcumque fratres dictæ Congregationis exiftentes, omni diligentia perquiras, & quùm primùm poteris, accipias, & comburas, nec permittas, quòd aliquis frater dictæ Congregationis librum aliquem ex prædictis, vel aliis aliquid contra determinationes S.R.E. continentibus deinceps teneat. Contradictores quoslibet, & rebelles per privationes quorumcumque actuum legitimorum, incarcerationis etiàm perpetuæ, & alias quafcumquè de quibus tibi placebit, cenfuras, & pœnas appellatione poftpofita compefcendo, invocato etiam ad hoc, fi opus fuerit, auxilio brachii fecularis. Non obftantibus apoftolicis, ac Provincialibus, & fynodalibus Conftitutionibus, & ordinationibus, ac ftatutis, & confuetudinibus etiam juramento, confirmatione apoftolica, vel quavis firmitate alia roboratis, privilegiis quoque, & Indultis, ac litteris apoftolicis etiam in forma Brevis per quofcumque Romanos Pontifices Prædeceffores noftros, & Nos, ac Sedem prædictam cum quibufvis efficaciffimis, & infolitis claufulis quomodolibet, etiam pluries conceffis, confirmatis, & innovatis, quibus, etiamfi pro illorum fufficienti derogatione, de illis, eorumque totis tenoribus fpecialis, & individua, ac de verbo ad verbum, non autem per claufulas generales idem importantes mentio, feu quævis alia expreffio habenda aut certa exquifita forma fervanda foret, etiam fi in eis caveatur expreffè, quòd illis nullatenus derogari poffit, illorum omnium tenores præfentibus pro fufficienter expreffis, ac de verbo ad verbum infertis, nec non modos, & formas ad id fervandos pro individuo fervatis habentes, hac vice dumtaxat, illis aliàs in fuo robore permanfuris, harum, ferie fpecialiter derogamus, cæterifque contrariis quibufcumque.

Datum Romæ apud Sanctum Petrum fub anulo Pifcatoris die quintadecima menfis Aprilis 1535. Pontificatus noftri anno primo.

Ex

Pius V

Birth name	Antonio Ghislieri
Papacy began	January 7, 1566
Papacy ended	May 1, 1572
Predecessor	Pius IV
Successor	Gregory XIII
Born	January 17, 1504 Bosco, Italy
Died	May 1, 1572 Rome, Italy

Pope St. Pius V: Antonio Ghislieri

Papacy: 1566 – 1572

Summary of Contents:

1). The Bull: *Superna dispositione*, dated February 18, 1566, found in the *Bullarium Carmelitanum, Pars Secunda*.

In the Bull, *Superna dispositione* St. Pius V confirms the concessions of his predecessors, amongst whom he expressly mentions the name of John XXII regarding the Sabbatine Bull. He grants, amongst other things, to the Church of St. Mary of Transpontina, built at Rome, to replace the one that was destroyed, all the privileges, Indulgences, etc; and amongst the rest, the privileges of the Sabbatine Bull of John XXII, etc., and this without being requested to do so; but of his own free will, as is said, "motu proprio."The original text is on the following page and is in Latin.

(Taken from Section II, Chapter 2: The Chronology of Events; The Irish Ecclesiastical Record, Volume VIII, Dublin, 1887, p. 803); (The Carmelites and the Brown Scapular, A. E. Farrington, D.D.O.C.C., Dublin, 1891, p. 131)

BULLARIUM
CARMELITANUM

**PLURES CONTINENS SUMMORUM PONTIFICUM
LITTERAS ET CONSTITUTIONES**

*Ad Ordinem Fratrum Beatiſſimæ, ſemperque
Virginis Dei Genitricis MARIÆ
de Monte Carmelo ſpectantes*

Nunc primùm in lucem editum, duasque
in partes diviſum

A FRATRE ELISEO MONSIGNANO

Ejuſdem Ordinis Procuratore Generali.

PARS SECUNDA
Duplici Indice inſtructa.

Præmittitur brevis Additio ad Primam Partem.

ROMÆ, MDCCXVIII.

Typis Georgii Plachi, Cælaturam Profitentis, & Characterum
Fuſoriam, apud S. Marcum.
SVPERIORVM PERMISSV.

tio feu quævis alia expreffio habenda, aut aliqua alia exquifita forma adhoc fervanda foret, tenores hujufmodi ac fi de verbo ad verbum infererentur, præfentibus pro fufficienter infertis, & expreffis habentes, illis aliàs in fuo robore permanfuris, hac vice dumtaxat fpecialiter, & exprefsè pari motu derogamus, cæterifq; contrariis quibufcumque. Nulli ergo &c.

Datum Romæ apud S. Marcum Anno Incarnationis Dominicæ. 1565. X. Kal. Septembris. Pontificatus noftri anno fexto.

PIUS V.

Ex Oppido Bofchi Diœc. Alexandrinæ, antea Michael Ghislerius ex Ordine Prædicatorum, die 7. Januarii 1566. Summus Pontifex Romæ creatur. Ibidem ad Cœlos evolavit. 1. Maii. 1572. A Clemente XI. Sanctorum cathalogo adfcriptus 1712.

CONSTITUTIO I.

Ex originali. Romę in Arch. Ord.

SVMMARIVM.

Concedit facultatem conftruendi novam Ecclefiam, & Conventum in Burgo S.Petri, eifque attribuit omnia privilegia, & jura, quæ fpectabant ad antiquam Ecclefiam, & Domum S.Mariæ Tranfpontinæ.

Vid. in Pio IV. Conft. 21.

PIUS EPISCOPUS
Servus Servorum Dei.

Ad perpetuam rei memoriam.

An.1566.
18. Febr. Uperna difpofitione, cujus infcrutabili providentia ordinationem fufcipiunt univerfa, in fupereminenti Apoftolicæ Dignitatis fpecula, meritis licèt imparibus, conftituti, inter cæteras curas humeris noftris incumbentes, illam libentèr amplectimur, per quam noftræ provifionis ope, fingula Ecclefiæ, Conventus, & alia religiofa loca ob reipublicæ commodum ruinis obnoxia, minori, quoad ejus fieri queat, rerum fuarum difpendio, ad alia opportuna loca transferantur, &

inftaurentur, ipfique Chrifti Fideles ad translatarum Ecclefiarum hujufmodi vifitationem donis cœleftibus in peccatorum fuorum remiffionem invitentur, aliifque in his difponimus, prout perfonarum, locorumque neceffitate penfata, falubriter in Domino confpicimus expedire.

1 Cum itaque fel. rec. Pius Papa IV. Prædeceffor nofter Ecclefiam DomusBeatæ Mariæ Tranfpontinæ nuncupatę in Burgo S.Petri de Urbe prope arcem S.Angeli, Ordinis ejufdem Beatæ Mariæ de Monte Carmelo pro ipfius Arcis fortificatione, aut aliàs dirui, ac in recompenfam demolitionis hujufmodi bifinille fcuta dilecto filio Joanni Baptiftæ Rubeo moderno, & pro tempore exiftenti Generali, feu Procuratori Ordinis, vel Domus prædictorum Priori, pro Conftructione unius novæ Ecclefiæ in ipfo Burgo facienda, dari mandaverit, ex quibus mille, & quingenta fcuta folùm dicto Procuratori, feù Priori tradita, ac ducentæ Cannæ fundi, feu terreni, in Civitate Pia nuncupata propè Curritorium à Palatio Apoftolico ad eamdem Arcem directum, ad ipfius novæ Ecclefiæ Conventufque conftructionem affignatę fuerunt.

2 Nos ne in eventum totalis ipfius Ecclefiæ demolitionis, Prior, & dilecti filii fratres dictæ Domus, ipfaque Religio abfque Ecclefia, & Conventu in eadem Urbe remaneant, opportunè providere volentes, ac Priorem, & fingulares perfonas Conventus hujufmodi à quibufvis excommunicationis, fufpenfionis, & interdicti, aliifque ecclefiafticis fententiis, cenfuris, & pœnis à jure vel ab homine quavis occafione vel caufa latis, fi quibus quomodolibet innodati exiftunt, ad effectum præfentium dumtaxat confequendum, harum ferie abfolventes, & abfolutos fore cenfentes:nec non omnium, & fingulorum privilegiorum, Indulgentiarum, & aliarum gratiarum *etiam Sabbatinorum*, & aliàs nuncupatorum eidem antiquæ Ecclefiæ per piæ mem. Joannem XXII. Innocentium VIII., & Clementem VII. ac forfan alios Romanos Pontifices prædeceffores noftros, quomodolibet concefforum, & approbatorum, ac quarumcumque litterarum defuper confectarum tenores, nec non Areæ infrafcriptæ Confines præfentibus pro fufficienter expreffis habentes; motu proprio, non ad ipforum Prioris, & Conventus, vel alte-

alterius pro eis Nobis super hoc oblatæ petitionis instantiam, sed nostra mera deliberatione, omnia, & singula Privilegia indulgentias, & alias gratias prædictas, quoad ea, quę sunt in usu, & decretis Concilii Tridentini non repugnant, auctoritate apostolica, tenore præsentium approbamus; nec non ipsam Ecclesiam Beatæ Mariæ Transpontinæ cum illius Cappellis, Altaribus, Reliquiis, Gratiis, Indulgentiis, ac Conventu, nec non redditibus parochialibus, & aliis Juribus, bonis, oneribus, sepulturis, lapidibus, lignis, cœmentis, omnibusque aliis, quæ Prior, & Fratres Conventus hujusmodi in d. Ecclesia ante illius demolitionem habebant, & hodie habent; nec non Domo, & suppellectili sua, omnibusque, & singulis privilegiis, Indulgentiis, & aliis gratiis prędictis ad locum, vel aream juxtà rectam ipsius Burgi viam in Insula priori post Transpontinam antiquam, quę tendit ad viam Sixtinam., ubi aliàs seu nuper quędam domuncula pro d. Ecclesia construenda, empta vel aliàs acquisita fuit, juxtà suos confines consistentem, eisdem auctoritate, & tenore transferimus, & inibi unam aliam Ecclesiam sub eadem Invocatione cum eisdem Cappellis, Altaribus, ac omnibus aliis, quę in d. Ecclesia antiqua erant, nec non domo, seu Conventu, & aliis necessariis, sine tamen alicujus præjudicio, auctoritate, & tenore prædictis perpetuò erigimus, & instituimus, ac eidem Procuratori Generali novam Ecclesiam, prout sibi videbitur in loco, vel Area hujusmodi construendi, & ampliandi facultatem, ac tam illi, quàm Priori, & Fratribus pręfatis, quòd ab antiquis suis Domo, & Ecclesia, in quibus adhuc existunt, amoveri seu expelli non possint, nec ad ulteriorem d. antiquę Ecclesię demolitionem procedi queat, quousque ipsa nova Ecclesia cum illius Domo, & aliis divino Cultui necessariis totaliter ędificata, & postquàm antiqua Ecclesia ab eisdem Fratribus, & de eorum voluntate solo ęquata fuerit, ipsi in ejus situ fodere, fundamenta illius eruere, & quidquid fodiendo invenerint, in Ecclesiæ novæ, & illius Conventus utilitatem convertere; & nihilominus, quòd illi etiam, postquàm actu translata fuerit, ut præfertur, omnibus, & singulis privilegiis, gratiis, facultatibus, exemptionibus, & Indultis

antiquæ Ecclesiæ, & illius Domui, fratribusque prædictis concessis, uti, frui, & potiri liberè, & licitè valeant, eisdem auctoritate, & tenore concedimus.

3   Et insuper: ut Christi fideles ad ipsam novam Ecclesiam visitandam illiusque constructioni subveniendum spiritualibus alliciantur muneribus: de Omnipotentis Dei misericordia, ac Beatorum Petri, & Pauli Apostolorum ejus auctoritate confisi, omnibus, & singulis utriusq; sexus Christi fidelibus verè pœnitentibus, & confessis, seu statutis à jure temporibus firmum propositum confitendi habentibus, qui infra decennium proximè futurum ipsam novam Ecclesiam in Festo Nativitatis Ipsius Gloriosæ Virginis Mariæ à primis Vesperis, usque ad secundas Vesperas ipsius festi per se, ac senes, & valetudinarii, mulieres prægnantes, vel aliàs impediti, qui per alios devotè visitaverint, & ter Orationem Dominicam, ac toties Salutationem Angelicam pro fidei Christianæ exaltatione recitaverint, centum annos de injunctis ejs pœnitentiis misericorditer in Domino relaxamus; ac præsentes litteras sub quibusvis revocationibus, suspensionibus, limitationibus, derogationibus, & aliis contrariis dispositionibus etiam in favorem Basilicæ S. Petri, & Hospitalis S. Spiritus de ipsa Urbe, aliorumque ejusdem Urbis piorum locorum, & Ecclesiarum factis, & faciendis nullatenùs comprehensas, sed semper ab illis exceptas esse, volumus, decernimus, & declaramus. Non obstantibus præmissis, & quibusvis constitutionibus, & ordinationibus apostolicis, ac Cancellariæ apostolicæ regulis editis, & edendis; privilegiis quoque indultis, & litteris apostolicis, etiam à d. Pio Prædecessore super translatione dictæ Ecclesiæ ad Civitatem Piam, aut aliàs sub quibuscumque tenoribus, & formis, ac cum quibusvis, etiam derogatoriis, aliisque efficacioribus, efficacissimis, & insolitis clausulis, irritantibusque, & aliis decretis in genere, vel in specie, ac aliàs quomodolibet concessis, ac etiam iteratis vicibus approbatis, & innovatis, quibus omnibus, & singulis, etiamsi pro illorum sufficienti derogatione de illis eorumque totis tenoribus specialis, specifica, expressa, & individua, non autem per clausulas generales idem importantes mentio, seu quævis alia expressio habenda,

da,

da, aut aliqua alia exquiſita forma ad hoc ſervanda foret, illorum tenores, ac ſi de verbo ad verbum inſererentur, præſentibus pro ſufficienter expreſſis habentes, illis aliàs in ſuo robore permanſuris, hac vice dumtaxat ſpecialiter, & expreſsè motu ſimili derogamus, cæteriſque contrariis quibuſcumque.

Nulli ergo &c. Si quis autem &c.

Datum Romæ apud Sanctum Petrum, Anno Incarnationis Dominicę.1565. XII. Kalend. Martii. Pontificatus noſtri anno primo.

II.

Ex originali. Romę in Arch. Ord.

SVMMARIVM.

Facultas imponendi taxam quinque ducatorum pro quolibet centenario ad conſtructionem novæ Ecclesiæ S.Mariæ Tranſpontinæ.

Dilecto Filio Joanni Baptiſtæ Rubeo Ordinis glorioſæ Virginis Mariæ de Monte Carmelo Priori Generali.

PIUS PAPA V.

Dilecte Fili, Salutem &c.

An.1566. 22. Febr.

Cum ob Ecclesiæ Domus tui Ordinis ſub invocatione Beatæ Mariæ Tranſpontinæ in Burgo Sancti Petri de Urbe ſitæ, de mandato fel. record. Pii Papæ IV. Prædeceſſoris noſtri pro Arcis Sancti Angeli etiam de Urbe fortificatione, demolitionem ferè jam factam, aliam novam Ecclesiam in ipſo Burgo ſub eadem invocatione juxta voluntatem noſtram de proximo conſtrui facere velis: ad idque faciendum tibi per dilectos filios ipſius tui Ordinis Priores, & Conventus, juxta Domorum facultates, ſubveniri cupias, ſi tibi per Nos deſuper licentia concedatur; Nos in præmiſſis tuo deſiderio annuere volentes, Tibi, ut in ſingulis ejuſdem tui Ordinis Domibus Provinciarum, & Congregationum, tam ultra, quàm citra montes, in Hiſpaniarum, Portugalliæ, & Siciliæ, Franciæ, ac totius Italiæ, & aliis Mundi Partibus conſiſtentibus, taxam ad rationem quinque Ducatorum pro quolibet centenario reddituum certorum cujuslibet Domorum hujuſmodi;

& ſi alicujusDomús redditus certi ad centum Ducatos non aſcendant: in ea pro ipſo pauco redditu duorum Ducatorum cum dimidio taxam ad dictam ædificationem faciendam, quæ ſingulis duobus annis per cujuslibet Domus hujuſmodi Priorem, & Conventum tibi, vel à te ad id deputando, ſeu deputandis uſque ad ipſam totalem ædificationem ſolvi debeat, imponere, & exigere, ac in ipſam ædificationem convertere liberè, & licitè valeas, authoritate apoſtolica, tenore præſentium concedimus, ac licentiam, & facultatem impartimur. Mandantes in virtute Sanctę obedientiæ, & ſub indignationis noſtræ, & aliis tibi viſis pœnis, ſingulis Prioribus, & Conventibus prædictis: ut ratam eos juxtà dictam taxam tangentem, ut præfertur, tradant, & ſolvant, omni mora, & dilatione, ac excuſatione poſtpoſitis.

Datum Romæ apud Sanctum Petrum ſub anulo Piſcatoris, die 22. Februarii 1566. Pontificatus noſtri anno primo.

III.

Ex Arch. Vatic. In minut. regiſtrat. anni 1566.

SVMMARIVM.

Prior Generalis deputatur Viſitator, & Commiſſarius Apoſtolicus in toto Ordine.

Dilecto Filio Joanni Baptiſtę Rubeo Priori Generali Ordinis Glorioſæ Virginis Mariæ de Monte Carmelo, Noſtro, & Apoſtolicæ Sedis Commiſſario.

PIUS PAPA V.

Dilecte Fili, Salutem &c.

An.1566. 24. Febr.

1 Cum ad cunctorum fidelium, præſertim Religioni deditorum, in quorum proſperitate reficimur, ſalubrem ſtatum noſtra jugiter aſpiret intentio, & Ordo Glorioſiſſimæ Dei Genitricis, ſemperque Virginis Mariæ de Monte Carmelo antiquiſſimus fore noſcatur, & ſicut accepimus, antiquis temporibus præ cæteris fulgeret; Nos, qui cura ſuſcepti Regiminis paſtoralis Officii Religioſis perſonis aſtringimur, & quorum eſt, quæ ad Religionis perſeverantiam profutura ſint, effectui ſalubriter demandare, cupientes

Or-

Gregory XIII

Birth name	Ugo Boncompagni
Papacy began	May 13, 1572
Papacy ended	April 10, 1585
Predecessor	Pius V
Successor	Sixtus V
Born	January 7, 1502 Bologna, Italy
Died	April 10, 1585 (aged 83) Rome, Italy

Pope Gregory XIII: Ugo Boncompagni

Papacy: 1572 – 1585

Summary of Contents:

1). The Bull, *Ut laudes*, date September 18, 1577, found in the *Bullarium Carmelitanum, Pars Secunda*.

In this Bull, *Ut laudes*, Gregory XIII, confirms the concessions and renewed and confirmed all the privileges, etc. of his predecessors, to the Confraternity; amongst the rest, the privilege of the Bull of John XXII, and inserted, as was said, the words, the "Saturday after their death," as in the Bull of John XXII, and declares that the force of these Bulls mentioned is sufficient, notwithstanding the contrary, and he expressly mentions the names of John XXII and Alexander V. The original text is on the following page and is in Latin.

(Cf. The Irish Ecclesiastical Record, Vol. VIII, Dublin, 1887, p. 803); (The Carmelites and the Brown Scapular, A. E. Farrington, D.D.O.C.C., Dublin, 1891, p. 131)

BULLARIUM
CARMELITANUM

PLURES CONTINENS SUMMORUM PONTIFICUM LITTERAS ET CONSTITUTIONES

Ad Ordinem Fratrum Beatiſſimæ, ſemperque Virginis Dei Genitricis MARIÆ de Monte Carmelo ſpeƐantes

Nunc primùm in lucem editum, duasque in partes diviſum

A FRATRE ELISEO MONSIGNANO

Ejuſdem Ordinis Procuratore Generali.

PARS SECUNDA
Duplici Indice inſtruƐa.

Præmittitur brevis Additio ad Primam Partem.

ROMÆ, MDCCXVIII.

Typis Georgii Plachi, Cælaturam Profitentis, & CharaƐerum Fuſoriam, apud S. Marcum.

SVPERIORVM PERMISSV.

614

XIX.

Ex originali . Romæ in Arch. Ord.

SVMMARIVM.

*Confirmatio Indulgentiarum Ordini con-
ceſſarum, dempta clauſula porrigendi ele-
moſynas, aut manus adjutrices, cujus loco
alia pia opera ſubſtituuntur .*

*Ad hæc vid. in Alexand.IV. pag.7. In Joan.XXII.61.
Vrban. VI. 141. In Alexand.V. 166. In Sixt.IV.
327.336.346. In Innoc.VIII 391. In Alex.VI. 412.
In Julio II. 428. In Leone X.506. In Clem.VII.47.
In Paulo III. 68. 98. 99. In Paulo IV. 107. In
Pio V. 141.*

*Vid. infra in Sixto V. 11.Julii.1587. In Paulo V. 31.
Aug. 1609. & 19. Julii. 1614 In Greg. XV. 19.
Septemb. 1622. In Vrban. VIII. 10. Maii. 1624.
In Clem.X. 11. Aug. 1670. 2. Januarii. 1672. 14.
Maii . 1672. 8. Maii. 1673. 27. Junii. 1673. in
Summ. Indulgent. & 26. Septembris. 1674.*

GREGORIUS PAPA XIII.

Ad perpetuam rei memoriam .

*An.1577.
die 18.Se-
ptembris.* 1 UT laudes glorioſiſſimæ Virginis
Mariæ referre, quæ ſalutis no-
ſtræ protulit Auctorem, lingua nunquam
ceſſet humana, ſed ejus Sanctiſſimum Nomen pia devotione celebretur, ac veneretur, Sacrum Ordinem ſub invocatione ejuſdem Beatæ Mariæ de Monte Carmelo, quem eadem Virgo venuſtiſſima,
& omnium virtutum floribus inſignita edi-
dit, propriique Nominis Titulo inſigni-
vit, à pluribus Romanis Pontificibus Præ-
deceſſoribus noſtris probatum, variiſque
Privilegiis, & facultatibus jam pridem de-
coratum, ex quo in agro Domini uberes
fructus manarunt, & in dies non medio-
cres producuntur, gratia noſtra ſpeciali
complectendum eſſe cenſemus, quò, &
antiqua privilegia illi Ordini, noſtra ad id
accedente auctoritate,ſublatis quibuſcumque impedimentis præſerventur, ac Fideles ſinguli ad Eccleſias ejus Ordinis ſtatu-
tis diebus confluentes, eò libentiùs ibidem
conveniant, ac orationi incumbant, aliaque infraſcripta pia opera exerceant, quò
exindè dono Cœleſtis gratiæ conſpexerint
uberiùs ſe eſſe refectos .

2 Dudùm ſi quidem plerique Romani Pontifices Prædeceſſores noſtri, & inter alios fel. rec. Sixtus PP. Quartus Ordinem prædictum illiuſque Domos, & Eccleſias in quibuſvis locis conſiſtentes variis exemptionibus, immunitatibus, privilegiis, libertatibus, & gratiis tam ſpi-

ritualibus, quàm temporalibus, nec non
indulgentiis, etiam plenariis, & peccatorum relaxationibus, vel remiſſionibus
decorarunt, & ornarunt ac etiam locupletarunt, illaq; anteà conceſſa confirmarunt,
& approbarunt, & aliàs, prout in ſingulis dictorum Prædeceſſorum litteris pleniùs continetur. Cum autem ea firmiùs
ſubſiſtere, ac majorem vim, & robur obtinere noſcantur, quò ſæpiùs fuerint Apoſtolica auctoritate communita : proptereà
dilectus filius Joannes Baptiſta Rubeus,
Theologiæ Profeſſor, & ejus Ordinis Generalis Magiſter Nobis humiliter ſuppli-
cari fecit : ut præmiſſa omnia confirmare,
& approbare, ac Indulgentias, & peccatorum remiſſiones, & relaxationes Chriſti Fidelibus propoſitas, in quibus clauſula (porrigendi manus adjutrices,& elar-
giendi eleemoſynas) continerentur, pridè
revocatas (citrà eam clauſulam) Chriſti
Fidelibus, alia forma eaſdem conſequen-
di præſcripta, revalidare de benignitate
Apoſtolica dignaremur.

3 Nos igitur Ordinem ipſum, illiuſque Perſonas inter cæteros Regularium
Ordinum Profeſſores in Catholica Eccleſia militantes tamquam Religionis exemplar ſpeciali charitate fulgentes, Sancto-
rumque Prophetarum Heliæ, Heliſei, &
Enoch, nec non & aliorum Sanctorum
Patrum, qui Montem Sanctum Carmeli
juxtà Heliæ Fontem inhabitarunt, ſucceſ-
ſionem hæreditariam tenentes, ſpecialibus favoribus, & gratiis proſequentes,
eumdemque Joannem Baptiſtam Magiſtrum, & dicti Ordinis ſingulares perſonas à quibuſvis excommunicationis, ſuſpenſionis, & interdicti aliiſque Eccleſiaſticis ſententiis, cenſuris, & pœnis à jure, vel ab homine quavis occaſione vel
cauſa latis, ſi quibus quomodolibet innodati exiſtunt, ad effectum præſentium
dumtaxàt conſequendum, harum ſerie
abſolventes, & abſolutos fore cenſentes,
ac exemptionum, privilegiorum, indulgentiarum, & gratiarum quarumcumque
eidem Ordini conceſſarum tenores præſentibus pro expreſſis, ac de verbo ad
verbum inſertis habentes, hujuſmodi ſupplicationibus inclinati : omnia, & ſingu-
gula privilegia, facultates, gratias, exemptiones, immunitates, libertates dicto
Ordini, illiuſque Eccleſiis, ac Domibus,
ac ab illo dependentibus locis conceſſa,
quatenùs ſint in uſu, & Concilio Tridentino

Gregorius Decimustertius. 195

tino non contraria, Apostolica auctoritate tenore præsentium confirmamus, & approbamus, illisque perpetuæ & inviolabilis firmitatis robur adjicimus, ac præsentis scripti patrocinio communimus. Indulgentias verò per infrascriptos Romanos Pontifices cum dicta clausula(porrigendi eleemosynas, aut manus adjutrices) concessas,& per fel. rec.Pium PP. V. etiam Prædecessorem nostrum revocatas, dempta ea clausula, ita tamen quòd hi Christi fideles, qui illas consequi voluerint, Ecclesias visitando sint contriti, & confessi ac loco eleemosynæ prædictæ juxta Prædecessorum prædictorum voluntatem erogandę, septies Orationem Dominicam, itidemque Salutationem Angelicam recitent, vel habitum dicti Ordinis, sicut in litteris Apostolicis piæ me.Joannis PP. XXII., ac Alexandri V. nec non Pii V. Prædecessorum nostrorum continetur, gestent, vel Vesperas pro defunctis recitent, aut antè Sanctissimum Domini Nostri Jesu Christi Corpus terram exosculentur, ac pro hæresum extirpatione, Sanctæque Matris Ecclesiæ tranquillitate, Christianorumque Principum pace, & unione pias ad Deum preces effundant, & aliàs juxta dictorum Prædecessorum nostrorum litterarum seriem orent, aliaque peragant,in pristinum, & eum in quem ante revocationem hujusmodi erant, statum restituimus, ac revalidamus. Summarium autem Indulgentiarum concessarum sequitur, & est hujusmodi, videlicet.

4 Leo Papa Quartus omnibus Christi fidelibus, qui Ecclesias Beatæ Mariæ de Monte Carmeli hujusmodi in festis Nativitatis Dominicæ, Paschæ, Apostolorum Petri & Pauli, Pentecostes, Assumptionis, Nativitatis, Annunciationis, Purificationis ejusdem Beatæ Dei Genitricis Mariæ, Sancti Michaelis Archangeli, omnium Sanctorum, in duobus festis S.Crucis, Nativitatis S.Joannis Baptistæ, Sanctorum Martyrum Fabiani,&Sebastiani, & in die Parasceves, & per Octavas prædictorum festivitatum, & vocabulis omnium Ecclesiarum dicti Ordinis devotè visitarent, septem annos, & totidem quadragenas. Et Adrianus Secundus, Stephanus Quintus, Sergius Tertius, Joannes Decimus,& Joannes Undecimus, Sergius Quartus, & Innocentius Quartus, qui dictum Ordinem confirmavit, omnibus Christi Fidelibus verè pœni-

tentibus, contritis, & confessis, qui prædictas Ecclesias piè visitarent in prædictis festivitatibus, & earum Octavis, vel Confratriam dicti Ordinis assumerent, & eam intrarent, tertiam partem omnium peccatorum in Domino relaxarunt. Item Clemens Tertius, Alexander Secundus, Gregorius Quintus, & Gregorius Septimus in prædictis festis, & in quolibet eorumdem similem gratiam largiti sunt. Item Clemens Quartus eisdem Christi fidelibus, qui prædictas Ecclesias quater in anno visitarent, videlicet in quatuor festivitatibus ejusdem Dei Genitricis Mariæ, triginta annos, & totidem quadragenas piè concessit. Item in Privilegio generali Lucii PP. III. remittuntur ab eodem peccata levia, offensæ Parentum, negligentiæ Votorum fractorum, dùm tamen fractor ad Vota rediret, & malè acquisita, si nescitur cui restitui debeant, prædictis Locis, seu illorum Domibus assignentur. Demum Innocentius Quartus, & Gregorius Octavus concesserunt qualibet die cuilibet dicenti Pater noster,& Ave Maria in dd. Ecclesiis, semel pro vivis, & defunctis quadraginta dies indulgentiarum. Rursus Honorius Tertius, & Nicolaus Quartus Romani Pontifices omnibus verè pœnitentibus omnium peccatorum suorum veniam polliciti sunt. Insuper Honorius Quartus omnibus verè pœnitentibus, & confessis dicti Ordinis Ecclesias visitantibus quadraginta annos, & totidem quadragenas de injunctis eis pœnitentiis, videlicet in festo vocabulorum ipsarum Ecclesiarum, & in die Sancto Parasceves, nec non in die S.Crucis, ac in festivitatibus Nativitatis, Annunciationis, Purificationis, & Assumptionis Dei Genitricis Mariæ misericorditer in Domino relaxavit, & concessit. Ukeriùs Benedictus Undecimus omnibus verè pœnitentibus, & confessis, qui ter in hebdomada, videlicet quadragesimali tempore, secunda, & quarta, & sexta feriis, & etiam in festis vocabulorum omnium Ecclesiarum dicti Ordinis, nec non diebus Sabbati ad Beatæ Mariæ Dei Genitricis prædictæ reverentiam, & in diebus Dominicis easdem Ecclesias piè visitarent, quadraginta annos, & totidem quadragenas, & omnium peccatorum septimę partis remissionem in Domino relaxavit, omnes indulgentias, & peccatorum remissiones à suis Prædecessoribus Romanis

Pontificibus dictoOrdini concessas in diebus, & in festis prædictis duplicando. Item Joannes Vigesimussecundus omnes indulgentias, & peccatorum remissiones à Romanis Pontificibus Prædecessoribus suis dicto Ordini concessas confirmavit, ac quadraginta annos, & totidem quadragenas de injunctis pœnitentiis, universis Christi fidelibus dicti Ordinis Ecclesias in qualibet solemnitate quatuor festivitatum Beatæ Dei Genitricis Mariæ videlicet Nativitatis, Annunciationis, Purificationis,&Assumptionis, contritis, & confessis in Domino piè concessit. *Idemque Joannes Vigesimussecundus, pro animabus, quæ in purgatorio existunt, & habitum bujus Religionis gestarunt vel eorum Confraternitatem ingressi fuerint, vel Confratrum numero ascripti in honorem ejusdem Beatæ Mariæ Matris Dei, die Sabbati post earum transitum, intercessionibus continuis piis suffragiis, & meritis ac speciali protectione adjuvandis publicavit, corroboravit, & confirmavit.* Item Urbanus Sextus perpetuò concessit eis, qui Ordinem Carmelitarum, & Fratres ejusdem Ordinis, Ordinem, seu Fratres Ordinis Gloriosissimæ Dei Genitricis Mariæ, semperque Virginis Mariæ de Monte Carmeli vocaverint, nominaverint, & appellaverint, si in gratia extiterint, tres annos, & totidem quadragenas indulgentiarum. Nicolaus Quintus omnes indulgentias, & peccatorum remissiones, ac omnia privilegia dicto Ordini à supradictis Romanis Pontificibus Prædecessoribus suis in prædictis diebus, & festis concessa, Motu proprio duplicando confirmavit, atque annos septem, & totidem quadragenas in Domino relaxavit. Tandem Sixtus Papa Quartus omnes indulgentias Ordini prædicto, & illius Domibus, Ecclesiis, ac personis utriusque sexus in genere, vel in specie quomodolibet concessas in suo robore, suaque firmitate confirmavit, approbavit, innovavit, & denuò concessis, ac omnium Mendicantium indulgentias ad Carmelitas, & alias personas extendit, ac si nominatim illis concessæ fuissent. Idem Summus Pontifex in Conceptionis, Præsentationis, Nativitatis, Annunciationis, Visitationis, Purificationis, & Assumptionis Beatissimæ Dei Genitricis Mariæ festivitatibus, & per septem dies sequentes, & in diebus vocabulorum Ecclesiarum visitantibus Eccle-

sias, triginta annos, & totidem quadragenas de injunctis pœnitentiis misericorditer in Domino relaxavit. Denique Clemens Septimus post JoannemVigesimumsecundum, & Alexandrum Quintum eorum litteras approbando, Habitum gloriosissimæ, & Beatissimæ Virginis Mariæ Matris Dei gestantibus, seu Confraternitatem ingredientibus, & alia servantibus, ut in eisdem litteris continetur, indulgentias, peccatorum remissiones, & gratias singulis utriusque sexus concessas perpetuæ firmitatis robur addidit, & innovavit, ipsisque & aliis participationem omnium bonorum spiritualium totius Ordinis Carmelitarum, & universalis Ecclesiæ, nec non Indulgentias Stationum in Ecclesiis Almæ Urbis tam intùs, quàm foris, temporibus, quibus eædem indictæ sunt, indulsit, & concessit. Quas etiam idem Pius V. immediatè Prædecessor noster approbavit, & confirmavit.

5 Decernentes præsentes litteras, sub quibusvis similium, vel dissimilium gratiarum revocationibus, limitationibus, suspensionibus, aut derogationibus similium, seu dissimilium privilegiorum, gratiarum, indulgentiarum, & aliarum quarumcumque concessionum nullatenùs comprehendi, sed semper ab illis exceptas esse, censerique debere, ac de subreptionis, vel obreptionis vitio, aut intentionis nostræ defectu notari, aut impugnari non posse: sed præsentes validas semper, & efficaces existere, ac perpetuò suffragari; sicque, & non aliter in præmissis omnibus, & singulis per quoscumque Judices Ordinarios, & Delegatos, quavis auctoritate fungentes, etiam Causarum Palatii Apostolici Auditores, & Sanctæ Romanæ Ecclesiæ Cardinales, sublata eis, & eorum cuilibet quavis aliter judicandi, & interpretandi facultate, & auctoritate, judicari, & diffiniri debere, irritumque, & inane quicquid secùs super his à quoquam, quavis auctoritate scienter, vel ignoranter contigerit attentari.

6 Quocircà Venerabilibus Fratribus Maceratensi, & Amerino Episcopis, ac dilecto filio Causarum Curiæ Cameræ Apostolicæ Generali Auditori per Apostolica scripta mandamus: quatenùs ipsi, vel duo, aut unus eorum per se, vel alium, seu alios præsentes litteras, & in eis contenta quæcumque, ubi, & quando opus fuerit, ac quoties pro parte dicti Joannis

Ba-

Gregorius Decimustertius. 197

Baptiſtæ Generalis Magiſtri, vel Fratrum d.Ordinis fuerint requiſiti,ſolemniter publicantes, illisque in præmiſſis efficacis defenſionis præſidio aſſiſtentes, faciant auctoritate noſtra, Joannem Baptiſtam Generalem Magiſtrum, Ordinemque prædictum, & alios quos dictæ noſtræ litteræ reſpiciunt, confirmatione, approbatione, revalidatione, aliiſque præmiſſis juxtà præſentium continentiam, & tenorem pacificè frui, & gaudere; non permittentes eumdem Joannem Baptiſtam Generalem Magiſtrum, aut alios quoſcumque indebitè moleſtari, perturbari, & inquietari; contradictores quoslibet, & rebelles, ac præmiſſis ſe opponentes vel non parentes, per ſententias, cenſuras, & pœnas Eccleſiaſticas, appellatione poſtpoſita compeſcendo, invocato etiàm ad hoc, ſi opus fuerit, auxilio brachii ſecularis. Non obſtan. ſimilis mem. Bonifacii Papæ VIII. de una, & Concilii Generalis de duabus dietis, dummodò ultrà tres aliquis vigore præſentium ad judicium non trahatur, ac quibuſvis Apoſtolicis in Provincialibus, & Synodalibus Conciliis editis generalibus, vel ſpecialibus Conſtitutionibus, & Ordinationibus, Privilegiis quoque & Indultis quibuſvis in contrarium conceſſis, confirmatis, & innovatis; quibus omnibus, etiamſi de illis eorumque totis tenoribus ſpecialis, ſpecifica & expreſſa, non autem per clauſulas generales idem importantes mentio, aut quævis alia expreſſio habenda eſſet,illorum tenores præſentibus pro expreſſis habentes, illis aliàs in ſuo robore permanſuris, hac vice dumtaxat ſpecialitèr, & expreſſè derogamus, contrariis quibuſcumque. Aut ſi aliquibus communiter, vel diviſim ab Apoſtolica ſit Sede Indultum, quòd interdici, ſuſpendi, & excommunicari non poſſint per litteras Apoſtolicas non facientes plenam, & expreſſam, & de verbo ad verbum de Indulto hujuſmodi mentionem.

Cæterùm quia difficile foret præſentes litteras circumferri: volumus præſentium exemplis, etiàm impreſſis, manu Notarii publici ſubſcriptis, & dicti Ordinis Generalis Magiſtri,vel Ordinis ſigillo obſignatis, eamdem prorsùs fidem in judicio, & extrà haberi, quæ præſentibus exhibitis ubique gentium, & locorum adhiberetur.

Datum Romæ apud S.Petrum ſub anulo Piſcatoris. Die 18.Septembris. 1577. Pontificatus noſtri anno ſexto.

XX.

Ex originali, Romæ in Arch. Ord.

SVMMARIVM.
Conventui S. Mariæ Tranſpontinæ condonantur quindennia eatenus decurſa, & tria alia deinceps decurrenda, in recompenſam damnorum &c.

Dilectis Filiis Priori, & Fratribus Domus B. Mariæ Tranſpontinæ Ordinis ejuſdem Beatæ Mariæ de Monte Carmelo de Urbe,

GREGORIUS PAPA XIII.

Dilecti Filii, Salutem &c.

1 EXponi Nobis nuper feciſtis, à multis retroactis annis pro quibuſdam viis publicis faciendis è conſpectu Arcis Sancti Angeli, & ut ſpatium debitum pro dicta Arce Sancti Angeli versùs Eccleſiam ipſius B. Mariæ Tranſpontinæ haberetur, in quadam fornace cum area, & domibus, aliiſque bonis ſtabilibus ad ipſam Eccleſiam ſpectantibus diverſa damna, atque ruinas à Camera Apoſtolica ſuſtinueritis; quæ bona cum Eccleſia & redditibus à fel.rec.Innocentio Papa VIII. Prædeceſſore noſtro liberè tradita fuerunt Fratribus Carmelitis in perpetuum,neque de ejuſmodi damnis ullam adhuc recompenſam ab eadem Camera acceperitis. Nos indemnitati veſtræ in præmiſſis,quantùm poſſumus, paterno affectu conſulere volentes, voſque à quibuſvis excommunicationis, ſuſpenſionis, & interdicti, aliiſque Eccleſiaſticis ſententiis, cenſuris, & & pœnis à jure, vel ab homine quavis occaſione, vel cauſa latis, ſi quibus quomodolibet innodati exiſtitis, ad effectum præſentium dumtaxat conſequendum, harum ſerie abſolventes, & abſolutos fore cenſentes, veſtris hac in parte ſupplicationibus inclinati: vobis quæcumque quindennia per vos occaſione unionis, annexionis, & incorporationis ejuſdem Eccleſiæ Ordini prædicto à dicto Innocentio Prædeceſſore, ut præfertur, factæ, hactenùs decurſa, & per vos nondùm ſoluta, ac alia tria quindennia inpoſterùm decurrenda, dummodo tria quindennia futura prædicta, videlicet ſumma omnis inde proveniens in fabricam novæ Eccleſiæ omninò
con-

An.1578.
27. Febr.

Paul V

Papacy began	16 May 1605
Papacy ended	28 January 1621
Predecessor	Leo XI
Successor	Gregory XV

Orders

Consecration	27 May 1597 by Pope Clement VIII
Created Cardinal	5 June 1596

Personal details

Birth name	Camillo Borghese
Born	17 September 1552 Rome, Papal State
Died	28 January 1621 (aged 68) Rome, Papal State

Mosaic depicting the arms of Pope
Paulus V (Camillo Borghese)

Pope Paul V: Camillo Borghese

Papacy: 1605 – 1621

Summary of Contents

---

1). *A Summary of Indulgences, favors, and graces conceded by many Solemn Pontiffs to the Religious and Confraternity members of Our Lady of Mount Carmel, and to all the faithful who visit the Carmelite Churches*, dated June 24, 1673, found in the *Bullarium Carmelitanum, Pars Secunda.* The Text of the *Sabbatine Privilege*, granted by the Holy Office of the Inquisition under Pope Paul V, on February 15, 1613, is found in Latin and in Italian, on page 601 of the following Document, and is also found in English under Section II, Chapter One of this book. This Document is confirmative of the privileges of the Sabbatine Bull.

2). In the *Elenchus*, 1860, following the *Summary of Indulgences*, is found the "Sabbatine Privilege," of Pope Paul V, in Latin, on page 322, granted by the Church to the Faithful who wear the Scapular and fulfill the conditions to receive the *Privilege.* This Decree of the *Sabbatine Privilege* confirms the privileges of the *Sabbatine Bull.*

Four of the most learned Doctors at the University of Salamanca in Spain, as well as many other Doctors at other Universities around the world, examined the Sabbatine Bull and the Bulls of other Sovereign Pontiffs relating to it. They declared the Bulls to be authentic, and that the Carmelites could enjoy the privileges contained in them.

A Portuguese Bishop prohibited the Carmelites, in 1609, to speak in their sermons on the privilege of the Sabbatine Bull. The matter was referred to Rome, and the Congregation of the Holy Office, having examined the matter with the greatest care for three years, issued a Decree, approved by Paul V, 1613, declaring in express terms, that the substance of the Sabbatine Bull of John XXII, can be devoutly believed by the faithful, and may be preached by the Carmelite Fathers as worthy of all confidence.

(The Irish Ecclesiastical Record, Vol. VIII, Dublin, 1887, p. 803); (The Carmelites and the Brown Scapular, A. E. Farrington, D.D.O.C.C., Dublin, 1891, p. 131)

B.ULLARIUM
CARMELITANUM
PLURES CONTINENS SUMMORUM PONTIFICUM LITTERAS ET CONSTITUTIONES

Ad Ordinem Fratrum Beatiſſimæ, ſemperque Virginis Dei Genitricis MARIÆ de Monte Carmelo ſpeſtantes

Nunc primùm in lucem editum, duasque in partes diviſum

A FRATRE ELISEO MONSIGNANO

Ejuſdem Ordinis Procuratore Generali.

PARS SECUNDA
Duplici Indice inſtructa.

Præmittitur brevis Additio ad Primam Partem.

ROMÆ, MDCCXVIII.

Typis Georgii Plachi, Cælaturam Profitentis, & Characterum Fuſoriam, apud S. Marcum.
SVPERIORVM PERMISSV.

621

600   *Clemens Decimus:*

sonę in dignitate Ecclefiaftica conftitutę munitis, eadem prorfus fides ubique habeatur, quę haberetur ipfis preſentibus, fi forent exhibitę vel oftenſę.

Datum Romę apud Sanĉtam Mariam Majorem ſub anulo Piſcatoris. Die 8. Maji. 1673. Pontificatus noftri anno tertio.

XXXI.

Ex orig. in Arch. Ord.

Sommario dell'indulgenze, favori e grazie conceſſe da molti Sommi Pontefici sì a' Religiofi, e Confratelli della Madonna del Carmine, come anco à tutti i Fedeli, che viſitaranno le Chieſe dell'iſteſſ'Ordine.

Vid. Conflit. quæ mox præcedit.

AVVERTENZA AL LETTORE.

An. 1673. 27. Jun.

Perche l'Indulgenze conceſſe da Pontefici ſono in due modi, cioè Perſonali, e Locali. Le Perſonali, chiamiamo quelle, che immediatamente ſono così conceſſe a gli huomini, che pare le pertino ſeco, e ſiano affiſſe alle proprie perſone, poiche ovunque vadino le ponno conſeguire, e guadagnare. E le Locali chiamiamo quelle altre, che non a gli huomini immediatamente, ma alle Chieſe ſono conceſſe, accioche g'iſteſſi huomini le poſſano conſeguire, e guadagnare viſtandole, orandovi, e facendovi qualſivogl'altro eſercitio ſpirituale: Perciò compendioſa e diſtantemente deſcriveremo le une, e le altre, con ſuoi oblighi in queſto foglio; acciòche i Fedeli ſi rendino capaci di eſſe, e più facilmente le poſſano con la gratia del Signore conſeguire, e non confondere gl'oblighi delle Indulgenze, che ſi guadagnano in quella vita, con quelli, con che ſi guadagna il privilegio Sabbatino, come han fatto, e fanno molti per ignoranza.

INDULGENZE PERSONALI.

La Santità di Paolo Quinto di fel. rec. doppo haver revocate tutte l'Indulgenze per l'addietro conceſſe alla Compagnia, e Confrati della Madonna del Carmine (come a tutte le altre Confraternità) hà conceſſo nella Bolla, che comincia *Cum certas.* iſpedita ſotto li 30. Ottobre. 1606.

1 A tutti i Fedeli dell'uno, e l'altro ſeſſo, i quali entraranno nella Compagnia della Madonna del Carmine, e riceveranno l'habito d'eſſa, Indulgenza plenaria nel primo giorno dell'ingreſſo, ſe pentiti, e confeſſati ſi communicaranno.

2 Di più hà conceſſo Indulgenza plenaria a i deſeriti, ò à quelli, che ſi deſcriveranno nella detta Compagnia, ò Confraternità ſe pentiti, confeſſati, e communicati nella Feſta principale della Commemoratione della Beatiſſima Vergine, che viene alli 16. di Luglio (ò che ſecondo il rito d'alcuni luoghi, ſi celebra nella Domenica immediata ſeguente) pregaranno per la concordia de' Prencipi Chriſtiani, per l'eſtirpatione dell'hereſie, e per l'eſaltatione di S. Madre Chieſa.

3 Di più hà conceſſo Indulgenza plenaria à i Confratelli dell'uno, e l'altro ſeſſo, ſe pentiti, confeſſati, e communicati, invocaranno divotamente *in articulo mortis*, il nome di Gieſù con la bocca, ſe potranno; overo non potendo, con il cuore.

4 Di più hà conceſſo à tutti i Confratelli, ſe pentiti, confeſſati, e communicati, interveranno alla Proceſſione, che farà la Compagnia, con licenza dell'Ordinario, in una Domenica di ciaſchedun meſe, & ivi pregaranno come ſopra, Indulgenza di ſette anni, & altrettante quarantene.

5 Di più à quelli, che ſi aſterranno di mangiar carne in quei giorni, ne' quali i Confratelli per inſtituto della Compagnia non ſogliono mangiarla, hà conceſſo trecento giorni d'Indulgenza, e quaranta à quelli, che in qualſivoglia giorno recitaranno ſette volte il *Pater noſter*, e l'*Ave Maria* ad honore delle ſette allegrezze dell'iſteſſa Beata Vergine, e cento giorni, ſe recitarà divotamente l'Offizio della medema Vergine.

6 Di più hà conceſſo à quelli, i quali con l'Habito della Confraternità, pentiti e confeſſati una volta il meſe riceveranno il Santiſſimo Sacramento, e pregaranno come di ſopra, cinque anni, & altretante quarantene.

7 Di più à i Confratelli, i quali pentiti, e confeſſati in qualſivoglia Feſtività della Vergine, divotamente riceveranno il Santiſſimo Sacramento dell'Euchariſtia nella Chieſa, ò Capella d'eſſa Compagnia, e pregaranno come di ſopra, tre anni, & altretante quarantene.

8 Di più à quelli, che con il lume accompagnaranno il Santiſſimo Sacramento, quando ſi porta à gl'Infermi, e per eſſi pregaranno Iddio, cinque anni, & altrettante quarantene.

9 Di più à quelli, che accompagnaranno i corpi de i defonti, non ſolo de'Confratelli, e Conforelle, ma anco d'altri alla ſepoltura, e pregaranno Iddio per loro, cento giorni.

10 Di più à quelli, che interveranno alle Meſſe, ò ad altri Divini Officii, che ſi celebraranno nella Chieſa, ò Cappella, ò Oratorio della Compagnia, overo ſaranno preſenti alle Congregationi publiche, ò private dell'iſteſſa Compagnia in qualſivoglia luogo, che ſi faranno, overo daranno albergo a' poveri, ò li ſovveniranno nelle loro neceſſità, ò porgeranno ajuto à quelli, che ſi trovano in pericolo di peccare, ò li daranno elemoſine temporali, ò ſpirituali, ò procureranno, che ſi componghi pace con i proprj nemici, ò con altri, ò che ridurranno alcun iſviato alla via della ſalute, & inſegnaranno a gl'ignoranti i precetti di Dio, e quelle coſe, che appartengono alla ſalute, overo s'eſercitaranno in qualſivoglia opera di pietà, ò carità, ogni volta, che faranno una delle ſudette opere pie, cento giorni delle penitenze ingionte, ò in qualſivoglia modo douute, ſecondo la forma conſueta della Chieſa.

11 Per altre due Bolle iſpedite ſotto li 31. Agoſto. 1609. e 19. di Luglio. 1614. in vece dell'Indulgenza delli 7. anni, & altrettante quarantene, à quelli, ch'aſſiſtono alla Proceſſione mentovata ſopra nell'articolo quarto, hà conceſſo Indulgenza plenaria.

12. E la Santità di N. S. Clemente X. per Breve iſpedito ſotto li 2. Gennaro. 1672. hà conceſſo, che tutte le Indulgenze Indulgenze ſi poſſano applicare all'anime del Purgatorio *per modum ſuffragii*.

13 E per altro Breve ſpedito ſotto li 8. Maggio. 1673. hà conceſſo, che li Confratelli, e Conſorelle, li quali non potranno commodamente intervenire alla Proceſſione mentovata ſopra nell'articolo quarto, e confeſſati e communicati viſitaranno divotamente la Cappella della Confraternità, e pregaranno per la concordia de'Preucipi Chriſtiani, per l'eſtirpatione dell'hereſie, e per l'eſaltatione della Santa Madre Chieſa, conſeguiranno l'Indulgenza plenaria conceſſa da Paolo V. à quelli, che interveranno alla detta Proceſſione.

14 Di più, che gli ammalati, e quelli che ſtanno in cattività, e viandanti, li quali non potranno in eſſa Domenica viſitare detta Cappella, poſſano acquiſtare la medeſima Indulgenza, ſe però recitaranno l'Officio piccolo della Madonna, ò cinquanta *Pater noſter*, & altretante *Ave Maria*, & almeno ſaranno contriti, con proponimento di quanto prima confeſſarſi, e communicarſi; il che ſaranno obligati onninamente di fare.

15 Et ancora li Frati, e le Monache di detto Ordine, nelli cui Conventi non è inſtituita la Confraternità, ò non ſi fà la detta Proceſſione, recitando

do

do divotamente nel Choro le Litanie di tutti li Santi, ò privatamente, se qualcheduno legitimamente impedito non potesse intervenire al Choro, esacendo l'altre cose ordinate da Paolo V. guadagnino la detta Indulgenza plenaria.

16 Di più, che la Festa principale dell'istessa Confraternità, che si celebra alli 16. di Luglio, ò la Domenica immediatamente seguente, per la maggiore divotione, ò commodità de' Fedeli, ò quando concorre qualch'altra solennità, si possa trasferire in un'altra Domenica di detto mese.

17 Finalmente Sua Santità dichiara, che li suoi Superiori Generali di dett'Ordine possono fuori di Roma, istituire la detta Confraternità in ciascheduna Chiesa dell'Ordine, & in tutte l'altre col consenso dell'Ordinario (osservando però quanto viene ordinato nelle lettere di Paolo V.) e nessun'altro, sotto pena di nullità.

E di più molto tempo prima Clemente VII. concesse à detti Confratelli la participatione di tutti li beni spirituali, che si fanno, non solo nell'Ordine Carmelitano, ma anco in tutta la Chiesa universale.

Obblighi generali, che hanno i Confratelli della Compagnia della Madonna del Carmine, per guadagnare le sudette Indulgenze.

Degl'obblighi particolari, che hanno i Confratelli per conseguire, e guadagnare l'Indulgenze sudette concesse dalla Santità di Paolo V. già s'è detto di sopra, descrivendo esse Indulgenze. Hora si dice degl'obblighi generali d'essi Confratelli, e Consorelle della detta Compagnia.

E primeramente devono i divoti entrare in qualche Compagnia canonicamente eretta, & acciò il loro ingresso sia legitimo, bisogna per primo, che ricevino lo Scapulare benedetto dal Superiore della Religione, ò da altro Sacerdote, che dal Superiore habbia autorità di benedirlo; però se doppo si perde, ò consuma, ponno ripigliarne un'altro, che non sia benedetto.

Per secondo, devono portarlo del continuo, non nella saccoccia, nè alla cinta, ma al collo.

Di più è necessario, che siano descritti nel libro de' Confratelli della Compagnia, perche questo è uso antico d'essa Compagnia, e lo suppone la Santità di Paolo V. mentre concede la seconda Indulgenza à i Confratelli descritti, ò à quelli, che si descriveranno, come si è detto di sopra.

Per guadagnare le sudette Indulgenze, non sono obligati quelli che sanno leggere, à recitare ogni giorno l'Officio della Madonna, e quelli, che non sanno leggere à recitare sette volte l'Oratione Domenicale, e la Salutatione Angelica, nè meno ad astenersi dal mangiar carne il Mercordì, ma basta che recitino quell'orationi, e faccino quell'opere pie, che prescrive il Pontefice nella concessione di esse Indulgenze.

E però vero, che chi recita l'Officio della Madonna conseguisce cento giorni d'Indulgenza, e quaranta giorni chi recita sette Pater noster, e sette Ave Maria: e trecento giorni chi s'astiene dalla carne il Mercordì, come di sopra si è detto al numero quinto.

Si riferisce, e si esplica l'aiuto particolare della Beata Vergine, che hà promesso à i Frati, e Confratelli dello Scapulare del Carmine doppo la lor morte, nel Purgatorio.

Oltre le sudette Indulgenze, che guadagnano in questa vita i nostri Religiosi, e Confrati dello sacro Scapulare del Carmine, nell'altra ancora godono d'un particolare privilegio, e beneficio singolare, che volgarmente si chiama *Privilegio Sabbatino*; perche si crede, che la Beatissima, e Purissima Vergine Maria Padrona singolare dell'Ordine à' Fedeli tutti, che porteranno l'habito, ò scapulare della sudetta Confraternità, & haveranno osservato quel tanto, che si dirà à basso, per conseguire il sudetto privilegio, l'aiutarà con le sue efficacissime orationi per uscire, e particolarmente nel giorno del Sabbato, dall'acerbissime pene del Purgatorio, & andar à godere la gloria eterna nella Patria Celeste insieme con lei.

E questo privilegio concesso dalla Beatissima Vergin. l'hanno confermato ancora molti Sommi Pontefici, e particolarmente Giovanni XXII. Alessandro V. Clemente VII. Pio V. con un Motu proprio nella Bolla, che comincia, Superna dispositione, alli 12. delle Kal. di Marzo. 1566. e Gregorio XIII. nella Bolla, Ut lauder, sotto li 18. di Settembre. 1577. & ultimamente la Sacra Congregatione de' Riti, secondo consta dalle Lettioni del secondo Notturno dell'Officio della Commemoratione solenne della Beatissima Vergine, che si celebra da noi altri Carmelitani li 16. Luglio, approvate dall'istessa Congregatione.

Et anco quella del S. Officio dell'Inquisitione sotto Paolo V. nell'anno 1613. hà confermato il sudetto privilegio con suo decreto del tenor seguente.

Patribus Carmelitanis permittatur praedicare, quòd populus Christianus possit piè credere de adjutorio animarum Fratrum & Confratrum Sodalitatis Beatissimae Virginis Mariae de Monte Carmelo, videlicet, Beatissimam Virginem animas Fratrum & Confratrum in charitate decedentium, qui in vita habitum gestaverint, & castitatem pro suo statu coluerint, Officiumque parvum recitaverint, vel si recitare nesciverint, Ecclesiae jejunia observaverint, & feria quarta, & Sabbato à carnibus abstinuerint, nisi ubi in sit diebus Nativitatis Domini festum inciderit, suis intercessionibus continuis, suisque suffragiis & meritis, & speciali protectione post eorum transitum, praecipuè in die Sabbati (qui dies ab Ecclesia eidem B. V. dicatus est) adjuturam. Quod Decretum fuit publicatum die 15. Februarii. 1613. in Palatio S. Officii à D. Marcello Filonardo Assessore ejusdem S.Officii.

Il tenore del quale Decreto volgarizato, è il seguente.

Al Padri Carmelitani si permetta predicare, che il popolo Christiano possa piamente credere dell'aiuto dell'anime de' Frati, e Confratelli della Compagnia della Beatissima Vergine MARIA del Monte Carmelo, cioè, che la Beatissima Vergine con le sue continue intercessioni, e con i suoi suffragii, e meriti, e particolar protettione, aiutarà doppo il loro transito, particolarmente nel giorno del Sabbato (dedicato dalla Chiesa à essa Beatissima Vergine) l'anime di i Frati, e Confratelli, che moriranno in gratia, se in questa vita haveranno portato l'habito, servato castità nel loro stato, e recitato l'Officio piccolo della Madonna, quelli che sapevano leggere, e se non sapevano recitarlo, haveranno osservati i digiuni della Chiesa, e si saranno astenuti dalla carne il Mercordì, & il Sabbato, eccetto se in tali giorni accadesse il Natale del Signore. Il qual Decreto fù publicato li 15. Febbraro. 1613. nel Palazzo del Sant'Officio dal Signor Marcello Filonardo Assessore dell'istesso Sant'Officio.

L'obblighi ch'hanno i detti Frati, e Confratelli per conseguire il sudetto aiuto, e privilegio Sabbatino, si cava dall'istesso Decreto, cioè per primo.

1 Che portino l'habito, ò scapulare benedetto, secondo che si è detto di sopra.

2 Che servino castità nel loro stato.

3 Che quelli, che sanno leggere, recitino l'Officio piccolo della Madonna: e gl'altri, che non sanno recitarlo, osservino i digiuni con mandati dalla Chiesa, e s'astenghino dalla carne il Mercordì, & il Sabbato, eccetto se in tal giorno accadesse la Festa di Natale del Signore, perche in tal caso non sono tenuti alla detta astinenza dalla carne; ma potranno lecitamente mangiarla, e conseguentemen-

Pars II. G g g g

demente guadagnate, e godere il detto ajuto, e privilegio Sabbatino.

Altre Indulgenze per tutti li Fedeli concesse ad istanza de' Carmelitani.

LA Santità di Sisto V. nella Bolla *Redditturi* spedita sotto li 11. di Luglio 1587. hà concesso à tutti i Fedeli, che si saluteranno, dicendo in latino, ò in lor lingua volgare: *Lodato sia Giesù Christo*, & à quelli, che risponderanno *In secula*, ò *Amen*, ò pure *Sempre*, dovunque ciò si faccia, cinquanta giorni d'Indulgenza.

Di più à quelli, che nominaranno riverentemente il nome di GIESU, ò quello di MARIA concesse Indulgenza di 25. giorni.

Et à quelli, che in articolo di morte, con la bocca, e con il cuore (non potendo con la bocca) invocaranno il detto nome, purche prima habbiano havuto usanza di salutare, ò nominare il detto nome di GIESU, concesse Indulgenza plenaria, e remissione di tutti i peccati.

Di più à quelli, che reciteranno le Litanie dello stesso nome (purche siano approvate) concesse Indulgenza di 300. giorni, & à quelli, che reciteranno le Litanie della Madonna 200. giorni. Et i Predicatori, quali nelle loro Prediche esorteranno i Fedeli à salutarsi nella sopradetta maniera, ad invocare, recitare, ò nominare i nomi di GIESU, e MARIA, e tutti quelli, che procureranno, che vi sia uso di questa salutatione, otterranno le stesse Indulgenze.

Indulgenze locali concesse da diversi Sommi Pontefici à tutti quelli, che visiteranno le Chiese dell'Ordine Carmelitano, riferite, rinovate e confermate dalla Santità di Sisto IV. li 24. Marzo. 1477. nella Bolla, Dum attenta meditatione, e parimente riferite nella Bolla di Gregorio XIII. Ut laudes, spedita sotto li 18. Settembre 1577. il quale rivalidò quelle, ch'erano state annullate da Pio V. per haver la clausula Porrigendi manus adjutrices, havendola cangiata in quella, ò di recitare sette Pater noster, e sette Ave Maria, ò il Vespro per li Morti, ò di baciar la terra avanti il Santissimo SAGRAMENTO, e pregare per l'estirpatione dell'heresie &c. ò di portar l'habitino dell'Ordine Carmelitano, come si contiene nelle Bolle de' Pontefici.

1 LEone Papa IV. hà concesso sette anni, & altrettante quarantene d'Indulgenza à tutti i Fedeli, che divotamente visiteranno le Chiese della Madonna del Carmine nella Festività di Natale del Signore, della Pasqua, delli Santi Apostoli Pietro e Paolo, della Pentecoste, dell'Assonta, della Natività, dell'Annunciatione, della Purificatione dell'Istessa Madonna, di S. Michel'Arcangelo, di tutti i Santi, e nelle due Festività di Santa Croce, della Natività di S. Gio: Battista, e de' Santi Martiri Fabiano e Sebastiano, & il Venerdì Santo, e nell'Ottave di dette Festività, e titoli delle Chiese dell'Ordine.

2 Adriano II. Stefano V. Sergio III. Giovanni X. Giovanni XI. Sergio IV. & Innocenzo IV. hanno rilasciato la terza parte de' peccati à tutti i Fedeli, che contriti e confessati, piamente visitaranno le dette Chiese nelle Festività sudette.

3 Clemente III. Alessandro II. Gregorio V. e Gregorio VIII. hanno concesso l'istessa grazia nelle Festività sudette.

4 Clemente IV. hà concesso agl'istessi Fedeli, che visiteranno quattro volte l'anno, cioè nelle quattro Festività della Madonna le sudette Chiese del Carmine 30. anni, & altrettante quarantene, e le Feste sono la Natività, Annunciatione, Purificatione, & Assunta.

5 Innocenzo IV. e Gregorio VIII. hanno concesso ogni giorno à qualsivoglia Fedele, che reciterà nelle sudette Chiese il *Pater noster*, e l'*Ave Ma-*

ria una volta per li vivi, e defonti, quaranta giorni d'Indulgenza.

6 Honorio III. e Nicolò IV. hanno concesso à tutti li Fedeli veramente pentiti la remissione di tutt'i loro peccati.

7 Honorio IV. hà concesso à tutt'i Fedeli veramente pentiti e confessati, quarant'anni, & altrettante quarantene delle penitenze loro ingionte, se visiteranno le sudette Chiese ne' giorni delle Festività de' loro titoli, nel Venerdì Santo, ne' giorni della Croce, e nelle Festività della Natività, Annunciatione, Purificatione, Assuntione della Madonna.

8 Benedetto XI. à tutt'i Fedeli veramente pentiti e confessati, i quali visiteranno le Chiese dell'Ordine trè volte la settimana, cioè le ferie seconda, quarta e sesta della Quaresima, e nella Festività del Titolo di esse, & ad honore della Gloriosissima Vergine, i Sabbati, & ancora le Domeniche, hà concesso quarant'anni, & altrettante quarantene d'Indulgenza, con la remissione della settima parte de' peccati, & anco tutte l'Indulgenze, e remissioni de' peccati concesse da' suoi Predecessori al dett'Ordine Carmelitano, con duplicarle ne' giorni, e Feste sudette.

9 Giovanni XXII. hà confirmato tutte l'Indulgenze, e remissione de' peccati concesse da' Romani Pontefici suoi Predecessori al dett'Ordine, e di nuovo hà concesso à gl'istessi Fedeli contriti, e confessati, quarant'anni, & altrettante quarantene d'Indulgenza delle penitenze ingionte, nelle quattro Festività della Beatissima Vergine, cioè nella Natività, Annunciatione, Purificatione & Assunta di essa Santissima Vergine MARIA.

10 Urbano VI. hà concesso perpetuamente trè anni, & altrettante quarantene d'Indulgenza à quelli, che, se staranno in grazia, chiamaranno, nominaranno, ò diranno all'Ordine de' Carmelitani, & alli Frati dell'istesso Ordine: *L'Ordine, e Frati della Gloriosissima Madre di Dio, sempre Vergine Maria del Monte Carmelo.*

11 Nicolò V. con un *Motu proprio* hà confirmato, duplicando tutte l'Indulgenze, e remissioni de' peccati, e tutt'i Privilegi concessi al dett'Ordine del Carmine da' sopradetti Romani Pontefici suoi Predecessori ne' sopradetti giorni, e Festività, e di nuovo hà concesso sett'anni, & altrettante quarantene d'Indulgenza.

12 Sisto Papa IV. hà confirmato & approvato, e di nuovo concesso tutte l'Indulgenze di qualsivoglia modo concesse à dett'Ordine, nelle sue Case, Chiese, e persone, *utriusque sexus in genere*, *vel in specie*, e di nuovo hà concesso trent'anni, & altrettante quarantene d'Indulgenza di penitenze ingionte à quelli, che visiteranno le sudette Chiese nella Festività della Concettione, Presentatione, Purificatione, Natività, Annunciatione, Visitatione, & Assunta della Beatissima Vergine MARIA, & anco nelli sette giorni seguenti, e Titolo dell'istesse Chiese.

Le diligenze, che hanno da fare i Fedeli per guadagnare le sudette Indulgenze &c.

1 HAnno da visitare qualche Chiesa dell'Ordine Carmelitano, & esser contriti e confessati.

2 Recitare ò sette *Pater noster*, ò sette *Ave Maria*, ò il Vespro per li Defonti, ò baciar la terra avanti il Santissimo SAGRAMENTO, ò se saranno Confratelli, portare l'habito nostro del Carmine, secondo che si preserive nelle Bolle Pontificie.

3 Devono pregare Iddio per l'estirpatione dell'heresie, per la pace, e tranquillità della Santa Madre Chiesa, e per l'unione de' Principi Christiani.

4 Mettere in esecutione quel tanto, che dicono i Sommi Pontefici nella concessione di dette Indulgenze, come si è detto di sopra.

Queste diligenze però ordinate da Gregorio Decimoterzo per commutare l'obligo *porrigendi manus adjutrices*, non sono necessarie per conseguire l'In-

Elenchus

facultatum et gratiarum spiritualium

quibus potitur

Congregatio SS. Redemptoris

ex

Sedis Apostolicae concessionibus

et

aliorum Ordinum communicationibus.

———

In usum Presbyterorum ejusdem Congregationis.

Monachii, 1860.
Ex Typographia Academica
J. G. Weiss.

Elenchus facultatum et gratiarum spiritualium quibus potitur Congregatio SS. Redemptoris ex Sedis Apostolicae conecessionibus et aliorum Ordinum communicationibus in usum Presbyterorum ejusdem Congregationis (Monachii, 1860).

List of the faculties and spiritual graces obtained by the Congregation of the Most Holy Redeemer [the Redemptorists] by concessions of the Apostolic See and notifications of other Orders in use by the Priests of its Congregation (Munich, 1860).

(p. 318). IV On the Scapular of the Blessed Virgin Mary of Mount Carmel

48. Clement X by the Brief, *Commissae nobis* of May 8, 1673 in part confirmed and in part newly granted to the Confraternity of the Scapular the following indulgences applicable to the deceased, which later the Sacred Congregation of Indulgences multiple times recognized and most recently by the Decree of July 13, 1818, and which is shown and explained most abundantly in the new edition of the work of Fr. Simone Grassi written under this title: *"Compendious narration of the indulgences, privileges, and graces granted to the Order, confraternity and churches of the glorious Mother of God, the Virgin Mary of Carmel, with clear instruction for the confraternity members of the Sacred Scapular* (Rome, 1853)."

(pp. 321-322) V. On the Sabbatine Privilege

50. Only to the Scapular of the Carmelites are connected two special privileges. The first is that confraternity members wearing the Scapular and departing from this life in the state of grace enjoy the promise. For indeed the Most Blessed Virgin, on July 16, 1251, appearing to St. Simon Stock, and holding out the Scapular to him, said: "This will be the privilege to you and all Carmelites; in wearing this, the dying will not suffer fire." This is henceforth declared the privilege of a good death. The other is the privilege of prompt delivery from purgatory, or the Sabbatine privilege, whose origin is explained in the Bull of John XXII: *Sacrotissimo uti culmine* of March 3, 1322 published in the sixth year of his pontificate in Avignon. The Most Blessed Virgin certainly appeared to the same Supreme Pontiff and manifested to him the special grace that she had obtained from her divine Son for all the religious and confraternity members wearing the Carmelite scapular and fulfilling certain conditions: namely they will be freed from the pains of purgatory the first Saturday after their death, and "on this day," as is read in the same Bull, "those who depart from this world and hasten promptly to the state of purgatory, I, the Mother, will descend to on the Saturday after their death, and those I find in purgatory, I will free and lead to the holy Mountain of eternal life." And the same Most Blessed Virgin prescribed to the Supreme Pontiff that this privilege be openly granted, promoted, and, as it were, confirmed by the Vicar of Christ on earth. Therefore, the Pontiff complying with this mandate says in his Bull: "This holy indulgence, I therefore accept, establish, and confirm on the earth, just as through the merits of the Virgin it is granted in heaven."

318

Augusti ejusdem anni hoc votum approbavit. V. Ferraris V. *Altare privilegiatum* 29.

IV. De Scapulari B. M. V. de monte Carmelo.

48. Clemens X. Brevi: *Commissae nobis* de die 8. Maji 1673 Sodalibus hujus Scapularis sequentes indulgentias, Defunctis applicabiles, partim confirmavit, partim de novo concessit, quas deinceps S. C. Ind. pluries et novissime Decreto de die 13. Julii 1818 recognavit, et quae exhibentur et uberius explicantur in novissima editione Operis a P. Simone Grassi conscripti, cujus titulus: „*Compendiosa narrazione delle indulgenze, privilegii e grazie concesse all' Ordine, confraternite e chiese della gloriosa Madre di Dio Maria Vergine del Carmine, coll' istruzione distinta per i confratelli del Sacro Scapolare. Roma* 1853.“

Indulgentia plenaria.

Festo principali B. M. V. de Carmelo die 16. Julii, vel etiam subsequenti, aliave Dominica Julii, qua secundum locorum consuetudinem hoc Festum celebratur, confessis, S. Communione refectis, et preces consuetas fundentibus.

Indulgentiae partiales.

Ind. 5 annorum et totidem quad. Sodalibus semel in mense communicantibus; nec non SS. Sacramentum ad infirmos cum lumine comitantibus et pro ipsis orantibus. Ind. 3 annorum et totidem quad. confitentibus et communicantibus quacunque Festivitate B. M. V. Ind. 300 dierum abstinentibus a carnibus feria quarta et sexta. Ind. 100 dierum quodcunque opus pietatis vel misericordiae peragentibus. Ind. 40 dierum 7 Pater et Ave in honorem septem · gaudiorum B. M. V. recitantibus. Aliquas minoris momenti praetermittimus.

Rescripto de die 15. Junii 1855 indulsit, ut Sodales in iis locis, ubi Ecclesia Ordinis Carmeli non adest, omnes indulgentias Ecclesiis ejusdem Ordinis concessas lucrari possint, dummodo propriam Ecclesiam parochialem visitent, et cetera opera injuncta rite adimpleant. Jam antea anno 1825 Leo XII. Sodalibus propter infirmitatem aliamve causam impeditis, quominus ad lucrandas indulgentias Ecclesiam Ordinis visitent, indulserat, ut aliud opus pium a Confessario ipsis injunctum substituere possint. Sed hoc Indultum, ut ex ejus verbis patet, ad illas tantum indulgentias referendum est, quae Sodalibus Scapularis proprie et specifice concessae sunt, ut sunt indulgentiae Stationum et aliquae particulares minoris momenti, quibus conditio visitationis Ecclesiae Carmelitanae adnexa est.

49. Commendatur in citato Opere Patris Grassi omnibus Sodalibus, ut quotidie 7 Pater et Ave in honorem septem gaudiorum B. M. V. recitent, quippe quod haec devotio, quam S. Thomas Cantuariensis ab ipsa B. M. V. edoctus instituerat, in eadem Sodalitate usitata, et a Paulo V. pro omnibus Sodalibus toties quoties recitantibus indulgentia 40 dierum ditata sit. Subjungitur autem, manifestum errorem esse, si qui putant, ipsos ad hanc quotidianam recitationem teneri, et secus indulgentiarum et gratiarum spiritualium Sodalitatis participes non fieri.

V. De privilegio sabbatino.

50. Soli Scapulari Carmelitarum adnexa sunt duo privilegia specialia. Primum est, quod Sodales Scapulare gestantes et in articulo mortis habentes promissione gaudent, ipsos in statu gratiae ex hac vita esse decessuros. Sic enim Beatissima Virgo, die 16. Julii 1251 S. Simoni Stock apparens, et Scapulare ipsi porrigens, locuta est: „Hoc tibi erit et cunctis Carmelitis privilegium; in hoc moriens aeternum non patietur incendium." Unde etiam

21

322

privilegium bonae mortis dicitur. Alterum est privilegium promptae deliberationis ex purgatorio, seu sabbatinum, cujus origo in Bulla Joannis XXII: *Sacratissimo uti culmine* die 3. Martii 1322 anno Pontificatus sexto Avenione edita exponitur. Apparuit quippe Beatissima Virgo eidem Summo Pontifici, et ipsi manifestavit specialem gratiam, quam a Filio suo divino obtinuerat pro omnibus Religiosis et Sodalibus habitum Carmelitanum portantibus et certas conditiones adimplentibus: videlicet ipsas primo Sabbato post eorum obitum a purgatorii poenis liberandos fore. „Et a die,"˜ sic legitur in dicta Bulla, „quo isti recedunt ab hoc saeculo, et properato gradu accelerant ad purgatorium, ego Mater descendam Sabbato post eorum obitum, et quos in purgatorio invenero, liberabo, et ad Montem sanctum vitae aeternae perducam." Simulque Beatissima Virgo Summo Pontifici praecepit, ut hoc privilegium palam faceret, foveret, et tamquam Vicarius Christi in terris confirmaret. Quapropter Pontifex huic mandato obtemperans in Bulla sua dicit: „Hanc ergo sanctam indulgentiam accepto, roboro et confirmo in terris, sicut per merita Virginis concessit in coelis."

51. Cum postmodum controversiae de veritate hujus Bullae exortae essent, et nonnulli assererent, ipsam supposititiam esse, primo Alexander V. die 7. Decembris 1409, et deinceps plures alii Pontifices praedictum privilegium confirmaverunt. Paulus V. autem litibus denuo recrudescentibus speciali Declaratione finem imposuit. Cum enim anno 1609 Petrus de Castillio, Episcopus et Inquisitor in regno Lusitaniae, Carmelitis prohibuisset, ne in concionibus suis privilegii sabbatini mentionem facerent; causa hac Romam delata, S. Officium Decreto de die 15. Februarii 1613 a Paulo V. approbato definivit: „Patribus Carmelitanis permittatur praedicare, quod populus christianus possit pie credere de adjutorio animarum Fratrum

et Confratrum Sodalitatis Beatissimae Virginis Mariae de Monte Carmelo: videlicet Beatissimam Virginem animas Fratrum et Confratrum in charitate decedentium, qui in vita habitum gestaverint, et castitatem pro suo statu coluerint, Officiumque parvum recitaverint, vel si recitare nesciverint, Ecclesiae jejunia observaverint, et feria quarta et sabbato a carnibus abstinuerint, nisi ubi in iis diebus Nativitatis Domini Festum inciderit, suis intercessionibus continuis suisque suffragiis et meritis et speciali protectione post eorum transitum, praecipue in die Sabbati, qui dies ab Ecclesia eidem Beatissimae Virgini dicatus est, adjuturam." Jam antea, videlicet die 20. Junii 1609 et denuo die 15. Julii 1612, Lectiones secundi Nocturni ad Festum B. M. V. de monte Carmelo a Summo Pontifice secundum votum Cardinalis Bellarmini approbatae fuerunt. Postea vero Clemens X. in Brevi supra allegato de die 8. Maji 1673, Bullam sabbatinam Joannis XXII. authenticam esse, de novo sequentibus verbis confirmavit: „Idem Joannes XXII. pro animabus, quae in purgatorio existunt, et habitum hujus Religionis gestarunt, vel eorum, qui Confraternitatem ingressi fuerint, vel Confratrum numero adscripti, in honorem ejusdem B. Mariae Matris Dei die Sabbati post eorum transitum intercessionibus ejusdem continuis, ipsius suffragiis et meritis ac speciali protectione adjuvandis, privilegium publicavit, corroboravit et confirmavit."

Declarationi authenticae Pauli V., ut etiam Benedictus XIV. monet, omnino standum est, nec ulli Catholico eam impugnare licet. Ipsa gratia, de qua agitur, in hac Declaratione ita comprobata et confirmata reperitur, ut sententiae oppositae locus non relinquatur. In quantum vero liberatio non absolute in primo sabbato post obitum reponitur, sed tantummodo dicitur: *praecipue in die Sabbati*, hanc explicationem propter duplicem rationem datam

21*

324

fuisse putamus: primo quia certitudo haberi nequit, an quilibet conditiones injunctas tanta perfectione adimpleverit, ut promptissimum liberationem meruerit; et secundo quia ipsa Beatissima Virgo voluit, ut haec indulgentia, licet in coelis concessa, tamen a Vicariis Filii sui in terris confirmetur et executioni mandetur, et ideo eamdem conditionem induat, quam habent aliae indulgentiae a Summis Pontificibus in suffragium Defunctorum concessae.

52. Conditiones, quas Sodales rite aggregati et Scapulare gestantes adimplere debent, ut privilegii sabbatini participes fiant, jam in Decreto Pauli V. habentur, ita ut pauca tantum ad uberiorem explicationem addenda sint. Qui horas canonicas recitant, omnimode satisfaciunt, et nec ad Officium B. M. V. nec ad alia opera praestanda tenentur, etiamsi alioquin, ut omnes Sacerdotes, ad Horas canonicas obligati sint. Qui Officium B. M. V. recitare nequeunt, et ideo ad abstinentiam feria quarta et sabbato tenentur, non satisfaciunt, si in iis regionibus, ubi generaliter sabbatis carnibus vesci licet, hac licentia utuntur. Si quis ad tempus conditionibus praescriptis non satisfacit, ideo non in perpetuum privilegio sabbatino privatur; si enim de delicto, in quantum de violata castitate agitur, vel de negligentia quoad reliquas conditiones debitam poenitentiam agit, specialis Beatissimae Virginis protectio et gratiae spirituales ipsi adnexae reviviscunt.

53. Sed quaestio majoris prae ceteris momenti est: Utrum illi Sodales, qui neutrum praestare, i. e. saltem sine notabili incommodo nec Officium B. M. V. recitare, nec abstinentiam praescriptam et jejunia ecclesiastica servare possunt, alia pia opera a Confessariis suis in commutationem ipsis injuncta persolvere possint et debeant, ut privilegii sabbatini participes fiant vel maneant. P. Grassi affirmat: quia, ut ait, omnino credendum est, Beatissimam Virginem in hisce casibus bona voluntate contentam fore;

et quia etiam in Jubilaeo Confessarii facultatem habent, legitime impeditis visitationes Ecclesiae, eleemosynas vel jejunia praescripta in alia pia opera commutandi. Idem sentiunt alii Auctores ex Ordine Carmelitarum eamdem materiam tractantes.

Verum in hac re attendendae sunt novissimae Declarationes S. Congregationis Ind. de die 12. Augusti et 7. Septembris 1840, et speciatim de die 22. Junii 1842. Cum enim a Vicario Generali in Gallia dubium proponeretur: An Sacerdos, qui facultatem Scapularia B. M. V. de Carmelo benedicendi et Fidelibus imponendi obtinuit, eo ipso facultatem habeat commutandi obligationes commutabiles Confratrum, quando opus est? et secundo loco supplicaretur, ut in casu negativo omnibus Sacerdotibus in Gallia, qui absque facultatibus opportunis commutaverint, sanatoria in radice indulgeatur, et pro futuro unicuique specialis facultas commutandi, si opus sit, concedatur; S. C. rescripsit:

„Ad primum negative. Vigore enim obtentae facultatis benedicendi et imponendi Scapularia non sequitur, quod Sacerdos ea quoque gaudeat potestate commutandi obligationes injunctas, nisi expresse enuntietur in Rescripto concessionis pro benedictione et impositione Scapularium; atvero in una Bisuntina sub die 12. Augusti 1840 ab hac S. Congregatione responsum fuit: Accedente gravi impedimento non teneri Confratres neque ad jejunia, neque ad recitationem Horarum canonicarum, aut Officii B. M. V., neque ad abstinentiam die Mercurii et Sabbati. Consulendi tamen Fideles, ut in hoc casu se subjiciant judicio docti et prudentis Confessarii pro aliqua commutatione impetranda.“

„Ad secundum jam provisum fuit in primo: et quatenus opus sit SSmus D. N. Gregorius Papa XVI. sanavit quemcunque defectum hucusque incursum circa obliga-

326

tionum commutationem, modo tamen Sacerdotes bona se
gesserint fide."

Post haec Decreta Prior Generalis Carmelitarum Literis
circularibus de die 26. Julii 1841, et deinde ejus Successor P. Leopoldus a S. Hieronymo aliis de die 15. Decembris 1844 declaraverunt, omnes Confessarios, qui ab
ipsis vel a Praedecessoribus suis facultatem Scapularia
benedicendi et imponendi obtinuerunt, dummodo ipsi Sodalitati Scapularis aggregati sint, facultatem quoque pos-
sidere, obligationes ratione privilegii sabbatini praescriptas
ex justis causis in alia pia opera commutandi: pro futuro
autem hanc facultatem non subintelligi, sed expressam
concessionem requiri juxta Declarationem S. Congregationis Indulgentiarum.

Ex his omnibus duo Corollaria colligenda sunt. Confessarii nostri obligationes praedictas commutare possunt,
quandocunque grave impedimentum adest; quia in hujusmodi casibus commutatio non stricte obligatoria, sed tantum de consilio est. Si vero justae quidem causae adsunt,
verumtamen de gravitate impedimenti dubitatur, ea ratione commutare possunt, quia Congregatio nostra facultatem Scapularia benedicendi et imponendi jam ante annum 1841 in perpetuum obtinuerat.

(1) P. Maurel hanc indulgentiam praetermittit, at aliam indulgentiam plenariam omnibus feriis quartis lucrandam commemorat, quae, ut testatur, in diplomatibus a Generali Carmelitarum
Calceatorum traditis reperitur, et ibidem sequentibus verbis re-
censetur: „Et tandem omnibus totius anni feriis quartis, sicut
de novo eruitur ex Reg. Archivii Ordinis exhibito et approbato
a Visitatione Apostolica anno Jubilaei 1825." P. Maurel subjun-
git, se nullam rationem videre, cur huic indulgentiae fides non
sit adhibenda. Verum P. Grassi, ceteroquin accuratissimus in
singulis concessionibus citandis, aliam relationem de hac indulgentia habet. Dicit nempe C. XVI. Della divozione del
mercoldì, Benedictum XIII. habita ratione, quod in Ecclesiis

Carmelitarum singulis feriis quartis SS. Sacramentum exponi soleat, die 4. Martii 1727 omnibus Fidelibus hisce expositionibus intervenientibus indulgentiam plenariam concessisse una ex feriis quartis cujusvis mensis ab Ordinario assignanda, dummodo eadem die vere poenitentes et confessi S. Communionem suscipiant. Sed forsitan Carmelitae Calceati postmodum ampliorem illam concessionem specialiter obtinuerunt.

Caput IX.

De Indulgentiis ceterarum Sodalitatum.

54. Omnia quae L. II. C. XIV. et supra C. VIII. quoad Scapularia de Sodalium receptione et de conditionibus ad lucrandas indulgentias exposuimus, valent etiam pro illis Sodalitatibus, de quibus modo tractaturi sumus. Duae indulgentiae plenariae similiter ipsis communes sunt: scilicet die receptionis et in articulo mortis. Porro excepta Sodalitate Militiae Angelicae ceterarum Sodales indulgentias Stationum Urbis lucrari possunt, si diebus statutis Ecclesiam Religionis vel Sodalitatis visitant, ibique certas orationes recitant. Indulgentias autem cuilibet Sodalitati proprias in sequentibus recensebimus.

I. De Sodalitate Cinguli B. M. V. de Consolatione, S. Augustini et S. Monicae.

55. Indulgentiae hujus Sodalitatis, omnes Defunctis applicabiles, a Clementi X. Brevi: *Ex injuncto* de die 27. Martii 1675 confirmatae, deinceps a pluribus Pontificibus adauctae, et novissime Decreto S. C. Ind. de die 5. Maji 1821 ut authenticae recognitae, exhibentur in Opusculo: „*Sommario delle indulgense concesse alla Compagnia della Cintura della Beata Vergine Maria di Consolazione e di S. Agostino e S. Monaca. Roma* 1858,“ et sunt sequentes.

Benedict XIV[1]

Papacy began	17 August 1740
Papacy ended	3 May 1758
	(17 years, 259 days)
Predecessor	Clement XII
Successor	Clement XIII

Orders

Consecration	16 July, 1724
	by Pope Benedict XIII
Created Cardinal	30 April, 1728

Personal details

Birth name	Prospero Lorenzo Lambertini
Born	31 March 1675
	Bologna, Papal State
Died	3 May 1758 (aged 83)
	Rome, Papal State

Reference style	His Holiness
Spoken style	Your Holiness
Religious style	Holy Father
Posthumous style	None

Pope Benedict XIV: Prospero Lorenzo Lambertini

Papacy: 1740 – 1758

Summary of Contents:

---

1). The Treatise of Benedict XIV: *De Festis Domini Nostri Jesu Christi et Beatae Mariae Virginis*, published around 1766, is written in Latin. A concise English translation from an Italian text, of points 4, 6, 8, and 10, pp. 406-411 of the Latin Document is found on the following page. In this Treatise, His Holiness confirms the Visions of Our Lady to St. Simon Stock and to Pope John XXII granting the Sabbatine Privilege, stating : *"We believe the vision to be true, and as truth, should be retained by everyone."*

2). The Treatise of Benedict XIV: *De Servorum Dei Beatificatione et Beatorum Canonizatione*, published around 1840, written in Latin, follows *De Festis*. St. Simon Stock is found in the *Sanctorum, Pars Prima*, p. 203, acknowledging the vision of Our Blessed Mother to St. Simon, in which he accepted the Holy Scapular from Our Lady with the pledge of the "great privilege."

Pope Benedict XIV, as a private Doctor, examined the vision, and having put it through the ordeal of the most severe criticism, declared that he believed it himself, and that he considered nobody ought to question its truth. He clearly teaches and defends the authenticity of the Sabbatine Bull in both of the above works. In the first one, he stated reasons in favor of the Bull in Chapter 78, he says: *"All the difficulties that could be brought against both the vision of St. Simon Stock and the Sabbatine Bull have been removed, both by the wise disquisitions of learned men and by the decree of the Sovereign Pontiff."* In the second, he writes also in favor of the Scapular. It is clearly evident, therefore, that Benedict XIV was a strenuous defender of the Sabbatine Bull ...

Benedict XIV was the first to grant an indulgence of 100 days to the wearers of the Scapular, who would kiss the Scapular and repeat certain prayers....On the occasion of the fifth centenary of the Vision of St. Simon Stock, the Holy Father extended the Plenary Indulgence that formerly was only for the day of the Feast (July 16) to every day within the Octave. There is no doubting the reason of Benedict XIV for this concession regarding the Scapular, it was asked in *memoriam tanti beneficii*, in memory of the great gift of the Scapular.

(The Irish Ecclesiastical Record, Vol. VIII, Dublin, 1887, p. 807; The Sabbatine Privilege of the Scapular, 1322-1922, P. E. Magennis, New York, 1923, p. 57, paraphrased) ; (The Carmelites and the Brown Scapular, A. E. Farrington, D.D.O.C.C., Dublin, 1891, p. 132)

Pope Benedict XIV

Prospero Lambertini, was born in Bologna, Italy, on March 31, 1675. He was Pope from August 17, 1740, to May 3, 1758.

"In the course of the 13th century, Simon Stock, General of the Carmelite Order died, he was a man of eminent holiness, at which time, many years before his death, appeared to him the Blessed Virgin Mary, and she gave him the Scapular as a sign of recognition of the Carmelite Order with a particular guarantee of her special protection; therefore after 50 years, the Blessed Virgin appeared also to the Holy Pontiff, John XXII, notifying him of the great indulgence that she had acquired from Jesus Christ, her Son, for the Brothers and Sisters of the Carmelite Order, an indulgence that the same Pontiff promulgated then on March 3, 1322. This is what is known as the Sabbatine Privilege for the reason that follow. The same, it is said, has been confirmed successively by many Holy Pontiffs such as Clement VII, Pius V, and Gregory XIII ... It is said that the Blessed Virgin, having given to the Scapular to Blessed Simon Stock, said: "This is for you and for all Carmelites, a privilege; he who dies with this will not suffer eternal fire.........And we believe the vision to be true, and as truth, should be retained by everyone. This vision is mentioned in the Roman Breviary."

" Consistent with this Decree (The Decree: "Sapientissimo" of Paul V,) much is found in the Second Lessons of the Office of the Roman Breviary. In fact, in them it is read that the souls of the faithful, having been enrolled in the Society (Confraternity) of the Scapular, and having practiced the pious works that are therein prescribed, having fallen into the flames of Purgatory, will be aided by the Blessed Virgin, so that having been liberated from there first, they may be taken up in flight to Heaven; to all this, however, we add this phrase: "as is piously believed."

"Therefore, since they (the Visions) have been exceeded by knowledgeable arguments of scholarly men, by Decrees of the Roman Pontiffs, all those things that could have created much difficulty regarding the Vision of St. Simon Stock, as to the Sabbatine Bull; while the controversies were being further ignited, no one has dared to try to disapprove of the Cult towards the Blessed Virgin of Mount Carmel, which the Roman Pontiffs have enriched with many such singular indulgences; and finally, since God has completed, through the intercession of the Blessed Virgin, many miracles in favor of those who practice this pious Devotion;

He must be held in error, who denies this practice of wearing, with devotion, the Marian Scapular and who says that it has not been enriched by many graces from the Roman Pontiffs and proven also by many divine benefits.

(Translated and paraphrased from *"Lo Scapolare,"* 2, A Cura Del Comitato Italiano VII Centenario Dello Scapolare, Roma, Via Della Conciliazione, 14b, p. 65 which was taken directly from: *De festis D. N. I. C. et B. Mariae Virg.*, lib. II, cap. VI, nn. 4, 6, 8, and 10. This Document of Pope Benedict XIV can be found in the following pages, in Latin.

Prospero Lambertini, nato a Bologna il 31 marzo 1675; Papa dal 17 agosto 1740 al 3 maggio 1758.

« Nel corso del secolo XIII morì Simone Stock, generale dell'ordine dei carmelitani, uomo di eminente santità, al quale molto tempo prima della morte era apparsa la beata Vergine, e gli aveva dato lo Scapolare come segno di riconoscimento dell'ordine carmelitano, in peculiare garanzia di sua speciale protezione; quindi dopo cinquant'anni la beata Vergine apparve pure al sommo pontefice Giovanni XXII, e gli notificò molte indulgenze, che essa aveva impetrate da Gesù Cristo suo Figlio per i fratelli e le sorelle dell'ordine carmelitano, indulgenze che lo stesso Pontefice promulgò poi il giorno 3 marzo dell'anno 1322. E questo è quello che si chiama Privilegio Sabatino, per la ragione che porteremo in seguito; e lo stesso si dice sia stato confermato successivamente dai sommi pontefici Clemente VII, Pio V e Gregorio XIII... Si dice che la beata Vergine, dando al beato Simone lo Scapolare, abbia detto: Questo sarà per te, e per tutti i carmelitani, un privilegio: chi morrà con questo non patirà il fuoco eterno... E crediamo che la visione sia vera, e che come vera si debba ritenere da tutti... Di questa visione si fa menzione nel breviario romano... ».

« È consono con questo decreto (il decreto « Sapientissimo di Paolo V) quanto si trova nelle seconde lezioni dell'uffizio nel breviario romano. Infatti in esse si legge che le anime dei fedeli, che siano stati iscritti nella società dello Scapolare, ed abbiano praticate le pie opere, che in essa sono prescritte, cadute nelle fiamme del purgatorio, saranno aiutate dalla beata Vergine perchè liberate di lì quanto prima, possano volare al cielo: a tutte queste cose tuttavia si aggiunge questa frase: « come si crede piamente ». Quindi poichè son state superate, sia con sapienti argomenti di uomini dotti, sia per decreto del romano Pontefice, tutte quelle cose che potevano creare difficoltà tanto riguardo alla visione di S. Simone Stock, come alla Bolla Sabatina; inoltre mentre erano più accese le controversie, nessuno ha mai osato riprovare il culto verso la beata Vergine del Monte Carmelo, che i romani Pontefici hanno arricchito di tante e così singolari indulgenze; ed infine poichè Dio ha compiuto, per intercessione della beata Vergine, molti miracoli in favore di quelli che praticano questa pia devozione; deve stimarsi in errore chi nega che questa pratica di portare devotamente lo scapolare mariano non sia stata arricchita di molte grazie dai romani Pontefici, e comprovata pure da molti divini benefizi » (De festis D. N. I. C. et B. Mariae Virg., lib. II, cap. VI, nn. 4, 6, 8 e 10).

PIO VI

Giovan Angelo Braschi, nato a Cesena il 27 dicembre 1717; Papa dal 15 febbraio 1775 al 29 agosto 1799.

« ... Noi siamo stati insigniti dell'onore del sommo pontificato in un mercoledì dello scorso mese di febbraio, giorno che è dedicato con culto speciale alla sacratissima Vergine del Carmelo, così che attribuiamo al suo patrocinio la suprema autorità, che portiamo... » (Allocuzione del 3 giugno 1775 ai Gremiali del Capitolo generale. A. C. G. II, 434-437).

BENEDICTI XIV.

PONT. OPT. MAX.

O L I M

PROSPERI CARD. DE LAMBERTINIS

PRIMUM ANCONITANÆ ECCLESIÆ EPISCOPI,
DEINDE BONONIENSIS ARCHIEPISCOPI

D E F E S T I S

DOMINI NOSTRI JESU CHRISTI,

E T

BEATÆ MARIÆ VIRGINIS

L I B R I D U O.

EDITIO TERTIA LATINA POST PLURIMAS ITALAS
AUCTIOR, ET CASTIGATIOR.

PATAVII, Typis Seminarii. MDCCLVIII.
Apud Joannem Manfrè.
SUPERIORUM PERMISSU, ET PRIVILEGIO.

DE FESTIS
DOMINI NOSTRI
JESU CHRISTI.
LIBER PRIMUS.
CAPUT PRIMUM.

De Festo Circumcisionis Domini Nostri Jesu Christi , & de Octava Nativitatis ejusdem , quæ Kal. Januarii celebrantur.

Estum Circumcisionis & Octavæ Nativitatis Domini Nostri Jesu Christi Kalendis Januarii celebratur . Ut ad hoc argumentum paratiores aliquando accedamus , primo de Institutione Circumcisionis; secundo de illius effectibus ; tertio de Circumcisione Christi Domini verba faciemus : tum de Festo ipso dicere aggrediemur , quo fit Circumcisionis commemoratio , & Circumcisum Dominum adoramus .

Quatuor proponuntur examinanda.

. 2. Quod ad primum attinet , Circumcisionis ritum a Deo institutum esse constat in Cap. 17. Geneseos , ubi legimus , Deum Abrahamo apparuisse , multaque illi pollicitum , Circumcisionem imperasse ; quo quidem præcepto quinque continentur . Primum ad sexum pertinet , ut soli masculi circumciderentur : *Circumcidetur ex vobis omne masculinum* . Secundum masculorum circumcidendorum conditionem statuit : Deus enim jubet , ut Abraham se , suosque filios , atque etiam servos circumcidat: *Omne masculinum*

Deus fuit Circumcisionis auctor.

A

Appendix 4

406 *De Feſtis B. Mariæ Virginis Lib. II.*

proventurum pollicerentur. In eo monte Traditio eſt, adhuc vivæ B. Virgini Ædiculam eſſe extructam a piis quibuſdam viris, qui eam noverant, quique Joannis Baptiſtæ prædicatione Chriſti Adventum ſatis cognitum habentes, Euangelium amplexati quotidie illuc convenire conſueverant; ex quo nomen illis inditum Fratrum Montis Carmeli. Immo ſi fides habenda Joſepho Antiocheno, Joanni Hieroſolymitano, & Cyrillo, & recentioribus Ordinis Carmelitarum Scriptoribus, eadem illa fuit Ædicula, quo Veſpaſianus ſe contulit. Tacitus vero & Suetonius diverſa ſcripſere, quod Ethnici eſſent, & Religionis noſtræ auguſtiora quæque ad falſam, quam præceperant animo, Religionem traherent. Videatur Arnaldus Borſtius in Breviloquio Tripartito par. 2. cap. 2. P. Daniel a Virgine Maria in Vinea Carmeli cap. 13. & in Speculo Carmelitano tom. 1. part. 2. in Miſcell. Hiſtor. Theolog. pag. 924. & ſequen.

Papebrochius eam Traditioni, aliaſque ſimiles impugnavit.

2. Quidam vero in his non conquieſcunt, nec animum poſſunt inducere ut ea credant, quæ ſuper hac re tradunt Carmelitani Scriptores. Joſephi Antiocheni, Joannis Hieroſolymitani, & Cyrilli *Opera* ſuppoſititia eſſe contendit magni Bollandiani Operis Continuator *Papebrochius.* Addit, ſatis firmo carere fundamento, quod de extructa a primis *illis Chriſtianis* in monte Carmelo Ædicula traditur; Baſilidem a Veſpaſiano conſultum Sacerdotem fuiſſe Chriſtianum; & ea, quæ ſatis perſpicue ſcribunt de Oraculo & ritu Ethnicorum Tacitus & Suetonius, ad noſtræ Religionis ritus trahenda eſſe & explicanda, id vero abſurdum ſibi videri libere fatetur. Nec accuſationibus commovetur, quas adverſus illum apud Innoc. XI. intentavit Sebaſtianus a S. Paulo, ediditque typis Francofurdienſibus, ut apparet in part. 2. Reſp. Papebrochii Antuerpiæ edit. ann. 1697. Reſponſ. ad 9. accuſat.

Ad neutram partem accedit Auctor. In Lectionibus Officii de illa ædicula apponitur clauſula, ut fertur.

3. Ad neutram harum partium ſententiam noſtram adjicimus; nec ſuſcipimus probandum, Suetonium & Tacitum, ubi ſcribunt Veſpaſianum Carmeli oraculum adiiſſe, ita explicandos, ut Veſpaſianus Chriſtianos Sacerdotes, qui ædiculæ illi in honorem B. Virginis extructæ inſervirent, conſuluerit. Nam illam ædiculam in monte Carmelo tunc temporis eſſe excitatam, pie tantum creditum eſt. Quapropter in ſecundis Officii lectionibus, quæ habentur in Romano Breviario, ubi mentio fit illius ædiculæ, addita eſt cauta illa formula, *ut fertur,* cujus quæ, quantaque vis eſſe debeat, fuſe diſſeruimus tom. 4. par. 2. de Canonizat. Sanctorum, ubi quæ fides, qui honor & veneratio, & quatenus debeantur Hiſtoriis Breviario Romano contentis demonſtravimus.

Simonis Stokii & Joannis XXII. viſiones. Bulla ejus Pontificis, ſeu Privilegium Sabbathinū, qua dicitur

4. Ut autem ad hujus, de qua agimus, Feſtivitatis redeamus hiſtoriam; ſeculo 13. ineunte, mortuus eſt ſpectatæ Sanctimoniæ vir Simon Stockius Ordinis Carmelitarum Generalis; cui multo ante ejus obitum B. Virgo apparuit, deditque tanquam Ordinis teſſeram Scapulare, in præcipuæ protectionis ſuæ peculiare ſignum; deinde quinquaginta poſt annis B. Virgo itidem Joanni XXII. Summo Pontifici apparuit, eumque mo-

641

Cap. VI. De Festo B.V. De Monte Carmelo. 407

monuit de pluribus Indulgentiis, quas a Jesu Christo Filio suo Fratribus & Sororibus Carmelitani Ordinis impetrasset; quas Indulgentias deinde 3. Martii die ann. 1322. idem Pontifex promulgavit. Atque illud est, quod dicitur Sabbathinum privilegium ob eam, quam mox afferemus, rationem; idque confirmatum postea dicitur a Summis Pontificibus Clemente VII. Pio V. & Gregorio XIII. Ea autem Joannis XXII. Constitutio, etsi non extat in Bullario Romano, in pluribus tamen libris typis impressis edita est, & nuperrime in Bullario Carmelitarum per P. Eliseum Monsignanum Ordinis Generalem Procuratorem collecto par. 1. pag. 61. & sequen.

ab aliis Pontificibus confirmata, non habetur in Bullario Romano.

5. Sed hæc Simonis visio, & Joannis XXII. Bulla, si non majorem, certe æqualem habet difficultatem, atque ea, quæ in Monte Carmelo extructa ædicula dicitur. Adversus utramque quasi quodam, qui satis verbis explicari non potest, furore invehitur Launojus in Dissertationibus suis tom. 2. par. 2. postremæ edit. anni 1731. Præter P. Danielem Carmelitam in *Vinea Carmeli*, & in *Speculo Carmelitano*, & P. Paulum ab omnibus Sanctis in *Clavi aurea*, tum visionem, tum Joannis Bullam tuendam suscepit Theophilus Raynaudus tom. VII. suorum Operum. Papebrochius in continuatione Bollandiani Operis tom. 3. mensis Maji ad diem 16. de B. Simone loquutus est, & conquestus, communicatam secum non fuisse ejus vitam ab Auctore synchrono scriptam, ut eam posset expendere. Id vero graviter tulit Sebastianus a S. Paulo Carmelita, qui ex ea querela accusationem adversus Papebrochium procudit. Quamobrem temperare sibi non potuit Papebrochius, quin omnes in 3. par. suarum Responsionum proferret, quæ inter se & Carmelitas intercesserant, contentiones, ut quanta æquitate sese gessisset, omnibus palam faceret. Atque in eo, quod ad B. Simonis visionem attinet, se dixisse monet, suspectam eam esse Launojo; negat vero se umquam declarasse sibi Launoji sententiam probari; ut videre est par. 1. suarum Responsionum ad accusationem secundam, tertiam, & quartam; in eo tamen se Launojum sequi fatetur, quod Joannis Bulla sit supposititia. *Bullam Sabbathinam, Bullam fictitiam videri, nec a Joanne XXII. editam Launojo assentior.* Idque rursus inculcat in ead. part. 1. Responf. ad art. 3. §. 15. ubi num. 144. quædam documenta profert, quibus demonstrare nititur Theophilum Raynaudum numquam *Scapulare Marianum*, quod supra memoravimus, tamquam ingenii sui foetum agnovisse.

Launojus eam Bullam supposititiã existimas, & Papebrochius. Hujus contentiones cum Carmelitis Theophilo Raynaudo falso tribui opus, quod inscribitur, Scapulare Marianum, putas idem Papebrochius.

6. Ad has difficultates ex historia petitas accedunt eæ, quæ e sacra Theologia depromuntur. Nam B. Virgo, cum B. Simoni tradidit Scapulare, fertur hæc dixisse: *Hoc erit tibi, & cunctis Carmelitis privilegium: in hoc moriens æternum non patietur incendium:* quod juxta Sacræ Theologiæ principia quidam contendunt probari non posse. Joannes Episcopus Castoriensis tract. 1. de Cultu Sanctorum & B. Virginis §. 55. ostendit, nullam Scapulari, aut Rosario, aut Cingulis, aut imaginibus B. Virginis fieri injuriam, *si quis dicat hæc nihil profutura* (meritum intelligens de con-

Difficultates adversus eam Bullam e Theologia petitæ.

con-

condigno) *si desit charitas , si Christum non felicius corde , quam hæc symä bola carne gestemus :* & §. 56. omnia hæc symbola multum juvare dicit , si ea qui gestet , B. Virginis studeat innocentissimos mores imitari : his symbolis signisque B. Virgini colendæ comparatis ostendit §. 57. nimis multos abuti : ac §. 58. & sequen. malum eorum usum in eo esse, quod quidam ab illis æternæ salutis securitatem nimis fidenter sibi polliceantur . Inde Rivetus hæreticus eam adversus Catholicos confinxit calumniam : *Notandum est, cum omnibus sceleribus consistere posse in Papatu devotionem circa Deiparam* . Verum Castoriensis Episcopus tract. 3. §. 55. Rivetum ad incitas redigit . Ostendit enim ab ea, quam nobis hæreticus ille doctrinam affingit , quantum Catholica Religio abhorreat . Bailletus, seu quis alius Auctor Tractatus *de Devotione & Cultu erga Deiparam* , Lutetiæ Parisiorum editi anno 1696. cap. 9. explicat , quo sensu B. Virgo dicatur *Refugium peccatorum :* nam de iis peccatoribus id intelligendum , quibus est animus emendandi suos mores , quique de redeundo in Dei gratiam sedulo cogitant .

7. Provocat autem Rivetum , ex Catholicis , qui doctrina præstent , (nam imperitos, aut obscuri nominis nihil moratur Auctores) Scriptorem ut aliquem proferat, qui umquam dixerit , æternam salutem sola exteriorum Symbolorum devotione posse comparari , & devotionem erga Deiparam cum peccatis posse consistere. Porro vicissim Calvinianam doctrinam reprehendit . Nam in Calvinistarum Synodis definitur, qui semel Baptismo regenerati sint, & gratiam sanctificantem susceperint , eos neque regenerationis fructum ullo umquam tempore amittere posse , neque *Fidem,* quæ salvos facit , neque charitatem , neque securitatem illam , in qua de retinenda Dei gratia certi conquiescunt . Si enim gratia & justitia non amplius amittuntur, inde consequitur , teterrima posse homines scelera perpetrare , quin & filii Dei , & de æterna salute securi esse desinant . Ne quis tamen obtrectandi cupidus nostra hæc aliorsum accipiat , quasi cultum erga Beatam Virginem deferendum peccatori esse doceamus, nihilque prodesse ejus preces , aliosve pios actus , si de sua conversione non cogitet , advertendum id ex superioribus propositionibus minime consequi : peccatoris enim oratio impetratoria est ex mera Dei misericordia , modo *pro se petat necessaria ad salutem pie & perseveranter* , ut docet D. Thomas 2. 2. quæst. 83. art. 6. Fieri enim potest , ut infinita Dei misericordia peccatoris oratio exaudiatur, etiam sine proposito emendandæ vitæ ; dummodo non tam obstinato sit animo , ut omne pœnitentiæ consilium perpetuo abjecerit , piaque devotione & firma fide in oratione perseveret , a Deo petens auxilia, quæ sibi opus sunt ad æternam salutem consequendam . Vid. Suarez de Relig. tom. 2. lib. 1. cap. 25. Bulla Joannis XXII. eamdem B. Virginem tradit dixisse Pontifici , se Carmelitarum & Fratrum & Sororum animas in Purgatorium delapsas primo post eorum mortem Sabbatho ab illius loci pœnis ereptas in Paradisum adducturam . *Ego mater gloriosa descen-*

stendam Sabbatho post eorum mortem, & quos invenero in Purgatorio, libe-rabo, & eos in Montem Sanctum vitæ æternæ reducam . Quæ verba mul-tum negotii sane facessunt, quod ex iis dominatus quidam in animas Pur-gatorii inferri posse videatur . Quapropter sacra Parisiensis Facultas anno 1624. Carmelitanum quemdam religiosum virum ad eam propositionem re-jiciendam adegit, quam ex Joannis Bulla depromserat: *Hanc propositionem , quatenus dicit B. Virginem imperium spirituale in animas demonstrasse , cum pollicita est morientibus in Habitu Carmelitarum e Purgatorii flammis ere-ptionem, revoco :* ut videre licet apud Thiers Tract. de Superstitione tom. 2. cap. 16. pag. 253. & sequen. qui plura refert acta in Sorbona ad hanc rem pertinentia .

· 8. Duo itaque sunt, de quibus disputant viri docti ; alterum est B. Si-monis visio ; alterum ipsa Joannis XXII. Constitutio . Ac visionem qui-dem veram credimus, veramque habendam ab omnibus arbitramur . Eam enim accurate refert Suvaningron, qui B. Simonis Socius fuit & Secreta-rius , eamque se ab illius ore ait accepisse : *Hanc ego immeritus , homine Dei dictante , scribebam .* Ejus autographum in Burdigalensi quondam Ar-chivo delituit , cujus e tenebris erutum , cum hæ ferverent controversiæ, Typis fuit impressum a P. Joanne Cheron Burdigalensis Domus Priore in Vindiciis Scapularis pag. 157. & seq. De hac Visione fit mentio in Bre-viario Romano ; & quamvis illud tantummodo narretur in Lectionibus , B. Virginem Simoni Scapulare tradidisse: *Insigne sacri Scapularis B. Simo-ni Anglico præbuit, ut cœlesti hac veste Ordo ille Sacer dignosceretur, & a malis ingruentibus protegeretur :* nec quidquam de eo, quod supra retuli-mus , Privilegio memoretur : *Hoc erit tibi, & cunctis Carmelitis Privile-gium : in hoc moriens æternum non patietur incendium :* id tamen silentium visioni nihil detrahit ; nam juxta Scripturæ modum loquendi æterna vita promittitur propter quædam , quæ ad eam quidem conducunt, sed tamen, nisi alia quædam accedant, satis esse non possunt ad eam assequendam, ut ad Rom. cap. 3. v. 28. *Arbitramur enim justificari hominem per fidem,* & cap. 8. v. 24. *Spe enim salvi facti sumus :* & Tob. 12. v. 9. *Eleemosyna a morte liberat , & ipsa est , quæ purgat peccata .* Et apposite ad hanc rem scripsit Bellarminus Controversiar. tom. 4. lib. 2. de Pœnitentia cap. 7. *Sæ-penumero Scriptura divina tribuit vim justificandi, aut etiam salvandi diver-sis rebus , non quod sola illæ justificare, aut salvare possint , sed quod illæ vim suam habeant ad justificationem aut salutem , & ad eum finem perducant , si tamen cætera non desint .* Huc accedit, quod in ea visione non legimus, eum inferni pœnas vitaturum , qui nihil aliud præstiterit , quam ut Sca-pulare gestaret; alia enim bona opera præcipiuntur , in quibus perseverare necessarium est . *Fratres* (sunt verba Visionis) *conservando verbum istud in cordibus vestris satagite electionem vestram certam facere per bona opera , & nunquam deficere. Vigilate in gratiarum actione pro tanta misericordia, o-rantes sine intermissione, ut sermo mihi factus glorificetur ad laudem Sanctis-*

F f f *simæ*

Visio B. Si-monis pro-batur testi-monio Au-ctoris syn-chroni . Di-luuntur dif-ficultates Theologicæ adversus il-lam visioné.

simæ Trinitatis, & *Virginis Mariæ semper benedictæ*. Daniel a Virgine Maria in Speculo Carmelitano tom. 1. part. 2. pag. 433. accurate rem hanc expendit. Sibi enim ipse objicit pag. 531. etiam qui Dei servet præcepta & Ecclesiæ, puramque a peccatis vitam agat, licet Scapulare non gestet, Infernum evitare. Cui objectioni respondet, B. Virginem pollicitam esse, qui devote Scapulare gestaverit, devoteque Scapulare gestando injuncta opera, ut æquum est, impleverit, eum ab Inferno liberum fore. *Quantum est ex parte sua ; ex capite gratiæ illius copiosæ, quam eidem apud Filium suum impetrabit intuitu Scapularis jam olim collati in signum salutis, fœdus pacis, & pacti sempiterni, nisi scilicet ex alio capite impingat in petram scandali, & lapidem offensionis per temeriam divinæ legis transgressionem.* Iisdem principiis utitur Paulus ab omnibus Sanctis *in Clavi Aurea* par. 1. cap. 12. Sane Papebrochius in Responsionibus ad P. Sebastianum a S. Paulo par. 2. Responsione ad art. 20. num. 18. pro eo quo fuit animi candore declaravit, nihil quod improbaret, se in ea Visione reperisse, postquam legerat, quæ scripsit Suvaningron ; numero autem 28. de explicationibus, quas PP. Carmelitæ tribuunt illis verbis : *In quo moriens æternum non patietur incendium*, ita ait : *Ego in illis nullam video difficultatem. Ea enim Patres Carmelitæ tam commode exponunt, ut facile evadant omnem justam reprehensionem ; neque nata sint (sicut calumniantur nonnulli) stolidam fiduciam ingerere peccantibus adipiscendæ salutis, quomodocumque ducatur vita.*

Bulla Joannis non probatur genuina. Prudens Pauli V. Decretum.

9. Nunc vero post visionis examen expendenda esset Bulla Joannis XXII. quæ ideo Sabbathina appellatur, quod B. Virgo pollicita sit, se quotquot Carmelitano Mariæ cultui addicti fuerint, primo post eorum obitum Sabbatho a Purgatorii igne erepturam. Nonnihil de ea superius attigimus. Multo tamen plura essent afferenda, si nobis videretur conducibile, ad ejus auctoritatem convellendam, omnia ea, quæ ex quibusdam rebus omni verisimilitudine carentibus prodeunt, huc conferre argumenta : cujusmodi sunt illa, quod nunquam ejus repertum sit autographum ; & nunquam *in forma specifica*, nec nisi, ut vulgo dicitur *in forma communi* a Romanis Pontificibus ea Bulla approbata sit. Satis fuerit illud admonere, coortas in Lusitania de ea Bulla contentiones, & inde ad totum Christianum Orbem diffusas, quarum historiam tradidit Paulus ab omnibus Sanctis *in Clavi aurea* par. 2. cap. 15. sapientissimo Decreto tandem diremisse Paulum V. Pontificem ; quod vel ipse probavit, collaudavitque Launojus. Decretum autem habetur in Bullario Carmelitano tom. 1. pag. 62. & tom. 2. pag. 601. *Patribus Carmelitanis permittatur prædicare, quod populus Christianus posset pie credere de adjutorio animarum Fratrum, & Confratrum in charitate decedentium, qui in vita habitum gestaverint, & castitatem pro suo statu coluerint, Officiumque parvum recitaverint, vel si recitare nesciverint, Ecclesiæ jejunia observaverint, & feria quarta, & Sabbatho a carnibus abstinuerint, nisi ubi in iis diebus Nativitatis Domini Festum inciderit, suis intercessionibus continuis, suisque suffragiis & meritis, & speciali protectione*

post

Cap. VI. De Festo B. V. De Monte Carmelo. **411**

post eorum transitum, præcipue. in die Sabbathi (qui dies ab Ecclesia eidem Beatæ Virgini dicatus est) adjuturam. Videatur etiam Bailletus ad diem 15. Augusti §. 6. num. 34.

10. Congruunt cum hoc Decreto secundæ Officii Lectiones in Breviario Romano. Habetur enim in illis, animas Fidelium, qui in Scapularis Societatem adscripti fuerint; & pia opera, quæ in ea præscribuntur, servaverint, in Purgatorium ignem delapsas a B. Virgine adjuvari, ut inde quam celerrime liberatæ in Cœlum convolent; quibus tamen omnibus illud additur, *ut pie creditur*. Quapropter cum ea omnia, quæ tum in B. Stockii visione, tum in Sabbathina Bulla difficultatem creare poterant, & sapientibus doctorum virorum animadversionibus, & Romani Pontificis decreto sublata sint; cumque gliscentibus maxime contentionibus, nemo umquam cultum erga B. Virginem de Monte Carmelo ausus sit improbare, quem Romani Pontifices tot tantisque indulgentiis locupletarunt; cum denique, B. Virgine intercedente, plura Deus miracula ediderit in eorum utilitatem, qui huic devoto cultui sunt addicti (*Improbus porro sit qui neget, multis Romanorum Pontificum gratiis & privilegiis ornatam, multis etiam divinis beneficiis comprobatam fuisse istam Scapularis Mariani devote gestandi religionem ;* ut ait Papebrochius par. 2. Responsion. suarum art. 20. num. 28.) quisque fateatur necesse est, Festivitatem B. Mariæ de Monte Carmelo non sine gravi institutam esse judicio, & in universali Ecclesia cum Officio & Missa propria celebrari. Eam pro Carmelitarum Ordine ann. 1587. approbavit Sixtus V. ejusque Officium pro eodem Ordine Paulus V. ex Decreto S. Rituum Congregationis novis auxit lectionibus a Venerabili Cardinali Bellarmino recognitis, ut videre est apud Petrum Paulum ab omnibus Sanctis *in Clavi aurea* pag. 180. Eamdem Festivitatem temporibus ab ætate nostra haud ita remotis una cum Officio ad aliquot Civitates, Provincias, & Regna, ut Populorum, Episcoporum, & Principum. devotioni gratificarentur, Romani Pontifices extenderunt, quod ex S. Rituum Congregationis Actis colligitur. Eam denique cum Officio & Missa nunc Universa celebrat Catholica Ecclesia ex Decreto Benedicti XIII. quod etiam monuimus par. 2. tom. 4. de Canonizatione Sanctorum.

Illo decreto sublata contentiones. Defenditur institutio hujus Festivitatis & Officii.

CAPUT VII.

De Festo. Dedicationis Ecclesiæ Sanctæ Mariæ ad Nives, die 5. Augusti.

1. NOnis Augusti Solemnitas peragitur Dedicationis Ecclesiæ B. Mariæ ad Nives. Variis insignem hanc Basilicam nominibus in Ecclesiasticis monumentis appellatam novimus: nam interdum *Sancta Maria*; modo *Sancta Maria ad Nives*, ex miraculo, de quo paullo post ser-

Multiplex Basilicæ Liberianæ nomen.

F f f 2   mo-

1-

SS. D. N.
BENEDICTI
DECIMIQUARTI
PONTIFICIS OPTIMI MAXIMI

D E

SERVORUM DEI
BEATIFICATIONE

E T

BEATORUM
CANONIZATIONE

LIBER QUARTUS, ET ULTIMUS.
PARS PRIMA.

EDITIO NOVISSIMA ANTEACTIS OMNIBUS EMENDATIOR ET AUCTIOR.

Additis vel suo loco, vel in fine cujusque voluminis iis omnibus, quæ postea prodierunt, quæque ad complementum argumenti propositi spectare videntur.

V E N E T I I S
CIƆIƆCCLXIV.

EXCUDEBAT ANTONIUS FOGLIERINI
SUPERIORUM PERMISSU.

D E
SERVORUM DEI
BEATIFICATIONE
E T
BEATORUM
CANONIZATIONE
Liber Quartus, & Ultimus.
PARS SECUNDA

In qua agitur de Concessione Officiorum, & Missarum in honorem Beatorum,
& Sanctorum, Electionibus Sanctorum in Patronos, Descriptionibus
Nominum in Martyrologio Romano,

Et aliis hujusmodi rebus, de quibus tractatur in Sacrorum
Rituum Congregatione Ordinaria.

pugnationem ab eo fundata, cultuque eidem S. præstito. *Ibid.*
Ejus nomen juffu Clementis VIII. in Martyrologio Romano descriptum est. *l.* 4 *p.* 2 *c.* 18. *n.* 16.

S. *Silvester* Nonantulanus Officio proprio, ac Missa celebratur. *l.* 4 *p.* 2. *c.* 28. *n.* 27.

S. *Silvester* Papa nullam Synodum celebravit, ut Notarii
res gestas Martyrum conscriberent. *l.* 1. *c.* 3. *n.* 2. Non ante quartum seculum in Summum Pontificatum affumptus
fuit. *n.* 3. *n.* 3. Ab ejus tempore initium habuit cultus Ecclesiasticus præstandus Sanctis Christi Confessoribus. *n.* 8.
Beatus fuit appellatus a Summis Pontificibus. *c.* 37. *n.* 7.
Laudatur a Gregorio IX. *c.* 38. *n.* 12. De ejusdem pictura in
Patriarchio Lateranensi. *l.* 1. *n.* 19. & *n.* 32. Ejus historia
in Urbe & extra Urbem legebatur, teste S. Gelasio. *l.* 3. *c.* 9.
n. 2. Instituit Festum Translationis S. Pauli. *l.* 4 *p.* 2 *c.* 9.
n. 14. An Constantinum Magnum baptizaverit. *c.* 13. *n.* 8.
Festo de præcepto celebrabatur, quod extinxit Eugenius IV.
c. 16. al. 17. Ejufmodi festum innovatum fuit postea. *n.* 27.
An a Gallis acceptum fuerit. *n.* 31. & 33.

S. *Simeon* Episcopus martyrio occubuit, cum Christianus
esset. *l.* 3. 4. 14. *n.* 6. In Perside occisus fuit cum pluribus
aliis Sociis. *c.* 20. *n.* 11.

S. *Simeon* Monachus Solitarius asperrime corpus suum
afflixerat. *l.* 2. *c.* 28. *n.* 14.

S. *Simeon* Padolironensis Eremita a Benedicto VIII. in
Sanctorum numerum relatus est. *l.* 1. *c.* 8. *n.* 3. In Bulla Canonizationis definitur a Summo Pontifice, cultum ipsi præstandum esse. *c.* 39. *n.* 10. Canonizationis Diploma particularibus personis inscriptum fuit. *n.* 11. Quomodo ei cultus
a prædicto Summo Pontifice concessus fuerit. *c.* 44. *n.* 10.
& 11. A Benedicto VIII. merito beatificatus dicitur.
n. 12. Canonizatus fuit juxta præsentem Ecclesiæ Ritum.
l. 3. *c.* 35. *n.* 1.

S. *Simeon* senex inter SS. novi Testamenti recensendus est.
l. 4 *p.* 2. *c.* 29. *n.* 2. Colitur in Ecclesia Orientali. *n.* 9.

S. *Simeon* Stylita Junior affidue, ac devote Orationi va-
cabat. *l.* 3. *c.* 25. *n.* 14.

S. *Simeon* Stylita Senior cum adhuc vivens Antiochenum
Mercatorem miraculose sanaret, ejus Imaginem ad vesti-
bulum ædium suarum iste apposuit, eamdemque nonnulli
infideles a dicto loco deturbantes severe a Deo puniti fuerunt. *l.* 2. *c.* 11. *n.* 15. Ejusdem viventis adhuc Imaginem in
porticibus, & vestibulis Officinarum collocabant Romæ Ar-
tifices, unde tutelam, & incolumitatem sibi sperabant. *Ibid.*
Quomodo puerum a gravi periculo submersionis in aquam
liberaverit, ipsiusque S. cultus auctus fuerit. *Ibid.* Admoni-
tus a Joanne Monacho, ut a maceratione corporis asperri-
ma tantisper desisteret, id nunquam effecit. *l.* 3. *c.* 29. *n.* 8.
Fulgore percussus subito, jam pie mortuus est. *c.* 28. *n.* 24. An
ille sit, cujus meminit Theodoretus. *Ibid.* Ejus animam in
cælos ascendere, vidit Julianus Stylites. *Ibid.* Inspiratione
Divina permotus vitam in columna transegit. *c.* 41. *n.* 20.
Per 40. dies sæpe jejunavit, & die Paschatis, sumpta prius
S. Eucharistia, tantillum cibi accipiebat. *l.* 4. *p.* 1. *c.* 27.
n. 5. De ejus elogio. *l.* 4 *p.* 2. *c.* 29. *n.* 2.

S. *Simeon* Syracusanus a Benedicto IX. canonizatus est.
l. 1. *c.* 10. *n.* 2. In Bulla Canonizationis ratio habetur miraculorum, quæ ibm vixerat, patraverat. *c.* 33. *n.* 16. Ei cultum præstandum esse, decernitur a Summo Pontifice. *c.* 39.
num. 10.

S. *Simeon* Tridentinus, seu Trevirensis puer a Judæis in
odium Christi occisus est. *l.* 1. 4. 14. *n.* 4. Ejus martyrium
examinari præcepit Sixtus IV. idemque approbavit Gregorius XIII. *n.* 4. Eumdem, instante Cardinali Madrutio Episcopo Tridentino, Sixtus V. pro Ecclesia Tridentina celebrari jussit. *Ibid.* In eadem Ecclesia corpus ejus servatur cum
Passionis instrumentis, idque visitantibus Indulgentia plenaria concessa est. *Ibid.* De ipsius obitu extat in Urbe processus authenticus. *l.* 3. *c.* 15. *n.* 5. Canonizatus est ad nor-
mam præsentis Ecclesiæ consuetudinis. *c.* 35. *n.* 1. Ejusdem
nomen in Martyrologio Romano descriptum fuit jussu Gregorii XIII. *l.* 4. *p.* 2. *c.* 18. *n.* 16.

S. *Simon* Apostolus celebrari præcipitur. *l.* 4. *p.* 2. *c.* 16.
n. 27. Una, & eadem die cum S. Juda Apostolo colitur. *n.*
42. Ubi pro Christo occisus fuerit. *n.* 45.

Servus Dei Simon de Collazzono Ordini Minorum donum
dedit, & pro ejus processu literas Remissoriales expedivit
Innocentius IV. *l.* 2. *c.* 46. *n.* 3. Concessit Pontifex Judicibus subdelegatis facultatem alios subdelegandi. *n.* 20.

Servus Dei Simon de Lipnica, probato cultu immemora-
bili, ab Innocentio XI. beatificatus est. *l.* 1. *c.* 31. *n.* 12. Quid
circa ejusdem cultum ab Innocentio VIII. concessum fuerit,
quod non parum profuit in ipsius causa ad probandum casum
exceptum. *l.* 2. *c.* 20. *n.* 9. De ejus cultu. *c.* 24. *n.* 53. & 54.
In ipsius causa adhibiti fuerunt Adjuncti pro validitate processus Ordinarii juxta præscripta in Epistola Circulari. *c.* 43.
n. 13. Missa, & Officio celebratur, probato casu excepto,
& quia de ejus virtutibus examen præcesserit. *l.* 4 *p.* 2.
c. 4. *n.* 3.
Judæi.

Servus Dei Simon de Roxas virtutibus clarus fuit, ejusque
processus confectus auctoritate Julii Sacchetti Hispaniarum
Nuntii, sed nullus reputatus est ob defectum jurisdictionis.
l. 2. *c.* 2. *n.* 11. Cur in Hispaniarum Regnis judicatum fuerit ad ejus sepulcrum apponi posse tabellas votivas. *c.* 11.
n. 16. De Signatura Commissionis. *c.* 38. *n.* 8. Pro ipsius processu expedire sunt Literæ Remissoriales Episcopo Suffraga-
neo Præsidenti Bullæ Cruciatæ, & tribus Protonotariis Judicibus Ordinariis in Civitate Matritensi. *c.* 45. *n.* 17. De
ejusdem vita, & moribus testimonium exhibuerant etiam
Reges. *c.* 49. *n.* 19. Concessa fuit Cardinali Portocarrero
Archiepiscopo Toletano facultas processum ejus conficiendi
in Sacello Palatii sui Matritensis. *n.* 22.

S. *Simon* Stock visione B. Virginis Mariæ recreatus sit,
& ab ea pro Carmelitis accepit Sacrum Scapulare in pignus magni privilegii. *l.* 4 *p.* 2. *c.* 9. *n.* 10.

S. *Simphorianus* Martyr in odium Fidei occisus est. *l.* 3.
c. 14. *n.* 2. Cultum Dianæ, ac Apollinis contempsit, & Ty-
rannum acriter objurgavit. *c.* 17. *n.* 3. Ipsi Tyranno dixit,
se idola esse fracturum, si id sibi permitteretur. *Ibid.*

S. *Simplicius* Papa, & Confessor Leoni Imperatori pro-
pugnanti privilegia Ecclesiæ Constantinopolitanæ restitit,
misso ad eum Probo Episcopo Canusino Legato, damnavit
Timotheum Erulum, Petrum Fullonem, Joannem Apame-
num, & Paulum Episcopum Ephesinum, Zenonique Episcopo Hispalensi vices suas commisit pro conservanda Ecclesiastica
Disciplina. *l.* 3. *c.* 32. *n.* 13.

S. *Sisinnius* Martyr, & Diaconus pro Fide Catholica san-
guinem effudit, ejusque passio narratur in literis encycli-
cis. *l.* 1. *c.* 4. *n.* 2. & *c.* 7. *n.* 2.

S. *Sixtus* Martyr cum in Angliæ Regno coleretur, ejus
Reliquiæ quomodo probatæ fuerint, sic decernente S. Gregorio Magno. *l.* 3. *c.* 19. *n.* 9. & *l.* 4. *p.* 2. *c.* 24. *n.* 9.

S. *Sixtus* I. Papa sub Hadriano Imperatore martyrio co-
ronatus est. *l.* 4 *p.* 2. *c.* 27. *n.* 11. Ipsius corpus dono datum
ab Anacleto II. Rainulfo Comiti Aliphano, an in Civitatem Aliphanam translatum fuerit. *Ibid.* Ejusdem festum
cum choreis olim celebrabatur, quæ mox vetitæ fuerunt.
c. 31. *n.* 34.

Sophonias Propheta in Sanctorum numerum relatus est.
l. 4. *p.* 2. *c.* 20. *n.* 11. In Ecclesia Hierosolymitana celebratur. *c.* 29. *n.* 10.

Sophronia Romana in manibus Maxentii Tyranni dereli-
cta, ne ab eo corrumperetur, se ipsam occidit, & laudatur
a Cardinali Baronio, quamvis non sit canonizata; cum id ex
impulsu Spiritus Sancti effecisse non constet. *l.* 3. *c.* 11. *n.* 12.

B. *Sosteneus* in Martyrologio Romano celebratur. *l.* 4.
p. 2. *c.* 18. *n.* 15.

S. *Separatus* Martyr in odium Fidei occisus est. *l.* 3. *c.* 14.
num. 2.

S. *Stanislaus* Episcopus, & Martyr dum canonizatur,
hæreticis confusio suboritur. *l.* 1. *c.* 13. *n.* 3. Dum ab Innocentio IV. canonizandus esset, auditis prius aliis de more suffragiis, ejus causæ indagatio commissa est Joanni Cajetano
Ursino Cardinali, qui ad Summum Pontificatum electus dictus
fuit Nicolaus III. *c.* 15. *n.* 15. Pro virtutum approbatione
habitum est coram dicto Pontifice Consistorium Cardinalium, & Episcoporum. *n.* 16. Prædicta causa non fuit examinata a Raynaldo Cardinali Hostiensi ex delegatione. Innocentii IV. ut inquit Galesinius, sed a Cardinali Cajetano,
& Sancti ejusdem cultui se opposuit Reginaldus Cardinalis
Hostiensis, sed ab oppositione destitit, cum in ægrotanti ipse
S. appareret eumdem increpans, quod Canonizationem suam
vellet impedire. *c.* 20. *n.* 11. Ejusdem Acta iterum examinata sunt a Jacobo Velletrensi misso in Poloniam ab Innocentio IV. *n.* 12. In Bulla Canonizationis dicitur signa effecisse, idest miracula. *c.* 22. *n.* 14. Ejus martyrium, causa
martyrii, & conversatio dum in vivis erat, a Jacobo Velletrensi examinata fuerit. *c.* 29. *n.* 2. Canonizatus fuit ab Innocentio IV. sed examinatis prius accuratissime ejusdem miraculis. *n.* 3. Ipsius Canonizatio Assisii celebrata fuit. *c.* 36.
n. 2. In eadem civitate Pontifex Decretum Canonizationis
publicavit inter Missæ solemnia, & Ambonem conscendens.
n. 3. In Processione pro hujusmodi solemnitate distributæ
sunt candelæ omnibus, qui eidem interfuerunt. *n.* 10. Tunc
apparuit miraculosum vexillum, ex quo initium habuit consuetudo deferendi vexilla. *n.* 11. In Canonizationibus novorum Sanctorum. *n.* 10. Antequam canonizaretur, jussu Pontificis
publicata sunt ejus gesta, & miracula probata a Cardinali
Cajetano. *n.* 15. In Canonizationis Diplomate nihil de Officio
decernitur. *c.* 38. *n.* 5. & *c.* 39. *n.* 10. Electus fuit in Patronum Regni Poloniæ. *n.* 8. Bulla Canonizationis particularibus personis inscripta fuit. *n.* 11. Ut ipsum canoni-
zaret, Innocentius IV. rogatus fuit a Clero, & Capitu-
lo Cracoviensi per duos Nuntios. *l.* 2. *c.* 36. *n.* 9. Cur
Pontifex pro eadem causa Remissoriales inscripserit. *c.* 45.
n. 11. In ipsius processu supplevit Vicarius generalis Episcopi pro uno ex iis, qui ei interesse debebant.
n. 16. Pro eo a Summo Pontifice concessa est facultas
Judici-

C c 2

falem , uti defumitur ex decreto , edito die 3. Octobris 1716. quod eft vigefimum quintum inter decreta Congregationis facrorum rituum in Bullario fan. mem. Clementis XL pag. 574. ubi pius ille Pontifex ex circumftantiis in decreto expofitis retulit ad interceffionem B. Mariæ Virginis infignem victoriam de innumeris Turcarum copiis in Hungaria relatam , & civitatem arcemque Corcyrenfem ab eorumdem Turcarum oppugnatione feliciter liberatam ; cum hæc contigerint eo prorfus tempore , quo Confratres Sodalitatis Rofarii publicam Proceffionem magno populi concurfu , & fingulari devotione in Urbe peragebant , & dum Chriftifideles Rofarium precibus quotidie recitare pergebant : quorum beneficiorum caufa idem Pontifex extendit ad univerfam Eccleſiam Officium & Miffam fanctiffimi Rofarii , quæ antea in aliquibus tantum locis recitabatur .

6 Sanctiffima Virgo Maria ferena fronte apparens fe confpiciendam exhibuit S. Petro Nolafco , S. Raymundo de Pennafort , & Jacobo Aragoniæ Regi , dicens , fubi & Filio acceptiffimum fore , fi fuum in honorem inftitueretur Ordo Religioforum , quibus cura incumberet captivos e Turcarum manibus liberandi; hinc , collatis inter fe confiliis , & confentientibus animis , Regularem Ordinem inftituere aggreffi funt fub invocatione S. Mariæ de Mercede Redemptionis Captivorum , in quo tribus votis Religionis quartum additum eft , manendi fcilicet in pignus apud Infideles , fi id neceffe fuerit pro redemptione Chriftianorum . Scribentes de hoc infigni Ordine Regulari docent , quartum hoc votum ad effentiam & conftitutionem pertinere Religionis B. Mariæ de Mercede Redemptionis Captivorum , per quod contrahitur ratio communis Religionis in genere , & conftituitur talis Religio Redemptorum a ceteris Ecclefiæ Religionibus diftincta ; veluti late probant Zumel in fcholiis Conftit. hujus Ordinis dift. 1. cap. 25. §. Excellentia fol. 118. & §. Quod fratres fol. 119. Pellizar. in manual. Regular. tom. 1. tract. 4. de votis Regularium cap. 5. fect. 2. num. 27. Joannes Perez de Munebrega in fuo quæftione apologetica typis impreffo Cæfarauguftæ anno 1656. præfertim pag. 19.

7 Hiftoriam Apparitionis Beatiffimæ Virginis tum hujus Ordinis Hiftorici , tum ceteri referunt & approbant , Zumel in opufculo de initio & fundatione facri Ordinis B. Mariæ de Mercede Redemptionis Captivorum , Bernardus de Vargas in chronicis ejufdem Ordinis tom. 1. lib. 1. cap. 3. Alphonfus Remon in chronicis Ordinis tom. 1. lib. 1. cap. 6. Ignatius Vidondus in fpeculo charitatis cap. 3. Marcus Salmeron fec. 1. monum. 2. Spondanus ad annum 1218. num. 10. Hieronymus Romanus lib. 2. de republica Chriftiana cap. 22. Zurita in annal. Aragoniæ lib. 2. cap. 71. Ferdinandus de Caftillo lib. 2. chronicar. Ordin. Prædicat. cap. 17. Illefcas in Pontif. hiftor. lib. 5. cap. ult. Penia in vita S. Raymundi de Pennafort lib. 1. pag. 81.

7 Potiora vero hujufce apparitionis fundamenta ex tribus aliis monumentis defumi poffunt : quorum primum funt Acta authentica S. Petri Nolafci inferta in noftrum primum librum cap. 41. Secundum eft epiftola S. Raymundi de Pennafort eidem S. Petro Nolafco fcripta , in qua prædictam commemorat apparitionem . Epiftola hæc integra refertur a Stephano de Corbera in vita B. Mariæ de Socos cap. 28. a Sálmeron

in monumentis hiftor. facul. I. monum. 8. §. 3. atque a Ferdinando de Orio in lib. Tertulliani de patientia tom. 1. difcurf. 1. §. 1. ejufdemque epiftolæ meminit Nicolaus Antonius in ver. Bibliothec. lib. 8. cap. 4. num. 141. Et quamvis Pater Echardus in Biblioth. Dominicana eamdem epiftolam rejecerit , tamquam apocrypham , affumpto tamen juridico examine ipfius anno 1721. coram Ordinario Barcinonenfi , prolataque per iftum fententia de epiftolæ veritate , quælibet controverfia ceffare dicenda eft ; uti , vifis authenticis Actis , fatetur ingenuus & doctus vir Pater Antoninus Bremond in fuo Bullario Ordinis Prædicatorum tom. 1. in notis ad Conftit. 36. Gregorii X. Tertium denique fundamentum deducitur ex bulla Canonizationis S. Raymundi de Pennafort , in qua fic legitur : *Beatiffima Virgo Dei Mater eidem Petro (fermo eft de S. Petro Nolafco) qui fanctis meditationibus & orationi vacans cogitabat , qua ratione calamitatibus Chriftianorum in captivitate degentium fuccurri poffet , ferena fronte fe confpiciendam dedit , & acceptiffimum fibi ac unigenito fuo Filio fore dixit , fi fuum in honorem inftitueretur Ordo Religioforum , quibus cura incumberet captivos e tyrannide Turcarum liberandi : ac illa ipfa nocte eadem Virgo Sanctiffima Beato Raymundo & Jacobo I. Aragoniæ Regi apparuit , id ipfum de Religiofis admonens .*

9 Ut igitur tanti beneficii & inftitutionis debitæ Deo & Virgini Matri gratiæ redderentur , indultum primo fuit Religioni B. Mariæ de Mercede Redemptionis Captivorum , ut Officium recitaret , ficut in fefto B. Mariæ ad Nives ; poftea tempore fummi Pontificis Pauli V. facta eft conceffio propriarum lectionum , in quibus fæpe memorata exponitur apparitio : tempore autem Innocentii XI. extenfio facta eft ad univerfa Regna Hifpaniarum , & fub eodem Pontifice facta eft defcriptio in Martyrologio Romano ita prorfus : *In Hifpania Apparitio Beatæ Mariæ Virginis , quæ Sanctis Petro Nolafco, & Raymundo de Pennafort , & Jacobo I. Aragoniæ Regi fe confpiciendam dedit , ut fundaretur Ordo Beatæ Mariæ de Mercede Redemptionis Captivorum .* Sub Alexandro VIII. nova indulta eft extenfio ad Regna Galliarum ; & tandem fub Innocentio XII. ftatutum eft , ut in univerfa Ecclefia idem Officium recitaretur die 17. Septembris cum Oratione propria , propriifque lectionibus iterum recenfitis , examinatis , & correctis . Apoftolica harum rerum Indulta edita funt in Bullario Ordinis B. Mariæ de Mercede Redemptionis Captivorum pag. 224. pag. 373. pag. 399. pag. 415. & pag. 424. & feqq.

10 Demum nota eft apparitio Beatiffimæ Virginis Beato Simoni Stok : narratur enim , ab ea huic Beato exhibitum fuiffe facrum Scapulare , ut ea cælefti vefte facer Ordo Carmelitarum dignofceretur & a malis ingruentibus protegeretur . Fertur etiam , Beatiffimam Virginem Mariam promififfe Filiis in Scapularis Societatem relatis , dum igne Purgatorii expiabuntur , fe folamen effe præftituram , & celerem in cæleftem patriam adventum impetraturam , fi abftinentiam & certas quafdam preces frequentaffent , ac pro fui ftatus ratione caftitatem coluiffent . Francifcus de Mendoza in viridario facra & profana eruditionis lib. 2. problemat. 5. num. 75. difputandum proponit , an Beatiffimæ Virgini conceffum fuerit privilegium extrahendi damnatos ab Inferis ; & afferere quidem videtur , probabile effe,

id ei

id ei fuisse concessum, cum de Fide sit, pœnam Inferni esse æternam juxta legem ordinariam, sed de Fide non sit, nunquam ab ea lege fuisse dispensatum, neque dispensandum . At eum strenue redarguit Cardinalis Capisucchius *controv.* 8. *quæst. unic.* ubi late demonstrat, Beatissimam Virginem precibus juvare utique posse, ne quis in peccato mortali decedat, & Deus ei gratiam conferat ad pœnitentiam peragendam ante mortem ; illi vero indultum non fuisse, ut anima æternis cruciatibus addicta ejus intercessione liberetur . De virtutibus porro, miraculis, & beatitate prædicti Simonis plura habentur apud Bollandianos *ad diem* 16. *Maji*. Joannes autem Launojus per integram dissertationem, & Pater Papebrochius in responsione ad exhibitionem errorum sibi oppositorum a Patre Sebastiano a Sancto Paulo *art.* 3. §. 15. & *art.* 10. §. 2. & *duobus seqq.* & *art.* 20. §. 2. & §. 3. multa adduxerunt adversus prædictam *Scapularis* traditionem. Sed bullæ Sabatinæ veritas, & multa pro dictarum rerum vindicatione legi possunt apud Theophilum Raynaudum in opusculo, cui titulus, *Scapulare Marianum illustratum*, inter ejus opera *tom.* 7. Præcesserant concessiones Officii B. Mariæ Virginis de Carmelo cum lectionibus propriis prædictam apparitionem referentibus factæ pluribus Regnis & provinciis orbis Catholici ; quarum concessionum decreta extant *tom.* 2. *Bullarii Carmelitarum pag.* 614. *pag.* 627. *pag.* 632. & *pag.* 636. Porro dum munere fungebar Fidei Promotoris, actum est de Officii extensione ad universam Ecclesiam ad petitionem Christianissimi Galliarum Regis : tunc vero sacra Congregatio ipsam Officii extensionem tantum ampliavit ad dominium Regis Christianissimi, quæ postea facta est ad universam Ecclesiam, insertis tamen in secundas lectiones nonnullis verbis, quæ infra a Nobis referentur.

11 In capite antecedenti egimus de Stigmatibus S. Catharinæ Senensis, & de Officii concessione in memoriam eorum Impressionis pro particularibus quibusdam locis : nunc autem aliqua afferemus de Stigmatibus S. Francisci, & de eorum Officii concessione pro universa Ecclesia . Notissimum prodigium Stigmatum S. Francisci a S. Bonaventura refertur, qui etiam narrat, Gregorium IX. summum Pontificem, qui eumviventem familiari conversatione cognoverat, mortuumque post paucos menses in Sanctorum album retulit, dubitantem de vulnere laterali, quod oculis non viderat, fuisse cælesti visione de vulneris veritate edoctum . Tiburtius Navarrus ex annalibus Lucæ Wadingi vitam S. Francisci Institutoris Ordinis Minorum fideliter desumpsit, recitatisque S. Bonaventuræ & aliorum testimoniis, suo modo dicta sunt, amplissime confirmavit ; quemadmodum videri potest *lib.* 4. *cap.* 3. necnon *cap.* 17. In nova collectione & compilatione privilegiorum Apostolicorum edita ab Emmanuele Roderico multæ reperiuntur summorum Pontificum Constitutiones, Gregorii videlicet IX. Alexandri IV. & Nicolai III. de veritate Stigmatum Sancti Francisci, & de eorum mirifica impressione. In Constitutionibus quippe octava & nona prædicti Gregorii nonnulli increpantur contrarium asserentes; ipseque in iisdem testatur, se sacrorum Stigmatum rationem habuisse in Canonizatione ejusdem Sancti. Memoratus autem Alexander in bulla inscripta ad omnes Prælatos testatur, se fuisse S. Francisci familiarem dum in

minoribus esset, certamque habuisse notitiam prædictorum Stigmatum, imposita pœna adversus eos, qui contrarium docerent, aut Stigmata a picturis S. Francisci abradere auderent. Nicolaus demum summus Pontifex supra citatus *in allata collectione* bullam Gregorii IX. confirmavit . Itaque quamvis in lectionibus Officii, quod recitatur die festo S. Francisci in Ecclesia universali, mentio haberetur sacrorum Stigmatum, Benedictus tamen Papa XI. ut cælestis hujus charismatis memoria peculiariter coleretur, festum sacrorum Stigmatum S. Francisci instituit ; veluti referunt Cardinalis Baronius *in notis ad Martyrol. Rom. ad diem* 17. *Septembris*, & Pagi *in brev. Romm. Pontif. in Alexandro IV. num.* 12. Sixtus Papa V. elogium composuit, quod habetur in Martyrologio Romano *ad dictam diem* 17. *Septembris*, teste Tiburtio Navarro *in vita* S. *Francisci cit. lib. cap.* 5. & particulare tandem Officium eadem die recitandum primo indultum est Religiosis S. Francisci, extensum deinde ad alios locos & diœceses, postremo sub Paulo V. ad Ecclesiam universalem propagatum.

12 Alia subsequuntur exempla Officiorum, quæ in honorem Sanctorum in Ecclesia universali recitantur, præter Officium quod in eorumdem honorem in eadem universali Ecclesia aliis certis diebus recitatur, ob quædam peculiaria fundamenta seu peculiares quasdam circumstantias, quæ novi Officii additionem poscere visæ sunt . In Ecclesia itaque universali non solum Officium recitatur & Missa celebratur die mortis seu decollationis S. Joannis Baptistæ, sed etiam die nativitatis ejusdem, & apud Græcos die 23. *Septembris* colitur conceptio ejusdem S. Joannis Baptistæ; ut est in Menologio Græcorum edito jussu Basilii Imperatoris, alibi memorato, & Urbini formis impresso anno 1728. *ad dictam diem*, de quo festo apud Græcos loquitur etiam Cardinalis Bellarminus *tom.* 1. *controv. de cultu Sanctorum lib.* 3. *cap.* 16. *de festis Sanctorum*. Colitur autem in Ecclesia universali, saltem Occidentali, dies nativitatis ejusdem, cum præter morem sanctificatus fuerit in utero matris suæ, & facta sint in ejus ortu multa miracula, quæ legi possunt in Euangelio S. Lucæ. Quocirca S. Augustinus *ser.* 287. *alias de diversis* 40. *cap.* 1. *n.* 1. ait: *Attendat charitas vestra, quam magni hominis nativitas facta sit. Natalem diem caruit nulli Prophetarum, nulli Patriarcharum, nemini Apostolorum celebravit Ecclesia . Solos duos natales, hujus* (scilicet S. Joannis Baptistæ) & *Christi:* & *ser.* 288. *alias* 23. *ex Sirmondianis : Diei hodierna festivitas anniversario reditu memoriam revocat, tantum esse Domini Præcursorem ante mirabiliter, cujus nativitatem considerare nos & laudare maxime hodie convenit. Ad hoc enim & dies anniversarius huic miraculo dedicatus est, ut beneficia Dei, & Excelsi magnalia non deleat oblivio de cordibus nostris:* & *ser.* 289. *alias* 3. *ex Vignerianis: Celebramus natalem Joannis, sicut Christi, quoniam ipsa nativitas plena est mysteriis:* & *ser.* 290. *alias* 44. inter homilias 50. *c.* 2. *Quia in magno sacramento natus est Joannes, ipsius solius justi natalem diem celebrat Ecclesia . Et natalis Domini celebratur, sed tamquam Domini. Date mihi alium servum præter Joannem inter Patriarchas, inter Prophetas, inter Apostolos, cujus natalem diem celebramus: nativitatis diem nemini, nisi Joanni :* & *serm.* 293. *alias* 5. *ex Vignerianis: Nativitatem Joannis quodammodo consecratam observat Ec-* cle-

Pius IX

Birth name	Giovanni Maria Mastai-Ferretti
Papacy began	June 16, 1846
Papacy ended	February 7, 1878
Predecessor	Gregory XVI
Successor	Leo XIII
Born	May 13, 1792 Senigallia, Italy
Died	February 7, 1878 (aged 85) Apostolic Palace, Rome

Coat of Arms of Pope Pius IX

Blessed Pope Pius IX: Giovanni Maria Mastai-Ferretti

Papacy: 1846 – 1878

Summary of Contents:

1). A *Brief* or *Breve* written by His Holiness Blessed Pope Pius IX on October 23, 1869, to author Alfred Monbrum, in recognition of his book: *The Life of Saint Simon Stock*, 1884, in which the Pope, affirmed the sanctity and admirable virtues of this great Saint. The text, on the following page is in French.

2). Summarium of Indulgencences granted to the Confraternity members of the Blessed Virgin of Mount Carmel, which includes the Decree of the Holy Roman and Universal Inquisition under Pope Paul V, 1613, (The Decree of the Sabbatine Privilege), can be found on p. 15. The Decree of the Sabbatine, is prefaced not only by the name of Pope John XXII, but by the words of the beginning of the Sabbatine Bull itself *(Sic mihi)*. It is also prefaced by the successors of Pope John XXII who confirmed and ratified the contents of the Sabbatine Bull. The Decree of the Sabbatine Privilege, published in the *Summarium of Indulgences* was issued on December 1, 1866, under the Pontificate of Pope Pius IX. The official Document is in Latin, and follows the *Breve* of Pope Pius IX.

(translated and paraphrased from the French Letter)

653

BREF DE S. S. PIE IX

à A. Monbrun

A NOTRE BIEN-AIME FILS ALFRED MONBRUN.

PIE IX, Papa.

Bien-aimé fils. Salut et Bénédiction Apostolique.

La Vie de saint Simon de Stock, dont vous êtes l'auteur, Nous a été d'autant plus agréable que les admirables vertus de ce grand saint, son zèle et les grandes et innombrables fatigues qu'il endura pour progager en Europe l'Ordre insigne du Carmel, ne sont pas seulement capables d'arracher à l'indifférence et presque à l'oubli où l'ont plongé les vicissitudes des temps, le culte d'un si grand saint ; mais encore d'entretenir et d'augmenter le nombre des fidèles pour la Bienheureuse Vierge Marie, soit par les admirables exemples de cette piété qui se reflète dans la vie tout entière de saint Simon, soit par les merveilleux témoignages d'affection qu'il a reçus de la Mère de Dieu, affection qui s'est surtout manifestée par le magnifique bienfait du Saint-Scapulaire. Ce Scapulaire ne lui a pas été donné seulement pour l'utilité de l'Ordre du Carmel, mais aussi pour le bien des autres fidèles qui, conjointement avec cet ordre religieux, voudraient honorer Marie d'un culte spécial. C'est pourquoi Nous patronnons de tout Notre cœur votre ouvrage, que Nous avons reçu avec le plus grand plaisir pour qu'il excite les fidèles à honorer davantage la divine Mère du Christ ; et comme gage de ce succès que nous prédisons à votre livre, recevez Notre Bénédiction Apostolique que Nous vous adressons bien affectueusement en témoignage de Notre gratitude et de Notre paternelle bienveillance.

Donné à Rome, près Saint-Pierre, le 25ᵐᵉ jour d'octobre 1869, de notre Pontificat le XXIVᵉ.

PIE IX, Pape.

Appendix 4

Letter of His Holiness Pius IX To A. Monbrun

To our beloved son Alfred Monbrun

The Life of St. Simon Stock, of which you are the author, was so much more pleasing to Us in that the admirable virtues of this great saint, his zeal, and the great and innumerable hardships that he endured for spreading the Carmelite Order in Europe not only are able to be rescued from the indifference and the near oblivion that the vicissitudes of time have plunged the cult of this great saint but also to support and increase the number of faithful for the Blessed Virgin Mary—both by the admirable examples of this piety reflected by the entire life of St. Simon and by the marvelous testimonies of affection that he received from the Mother of God—affection manifested above all by the magnificent favor of the Holy Scapular. The Scapular was not given to him only for the use of the Carmelite Order but also for the benefit of other members of the faithful who conjointly with this religious order would wish to honor Mary with a special devotion. This is why We endorse with our whole heart this work, which We received with the greatest pleasure, so that it may move the faithful to honor ever more the divine Mother of Christ; and as an indication of this success that we predict for your book, please receive Our Apostolic Blessing that We direct with great affection in testimony of Our gratitude and Our paternal benevolence.

Given in Rome, by St. Peter, the 23rd day of October, 1869, the 24th year of our Pontificate.

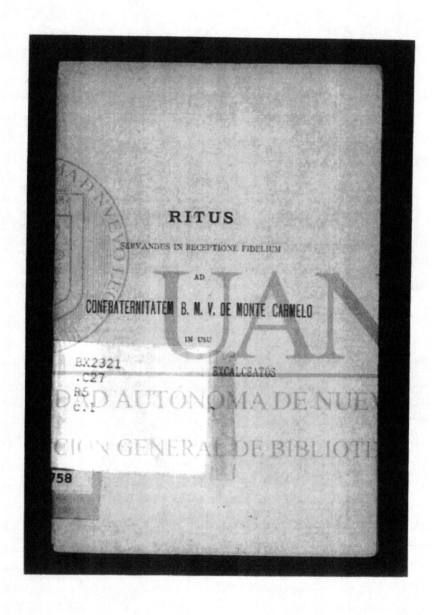

RITUS

SERVANDUS IN RECEPTIONE FIDELIUM

AD

CONFRATERNITATEM B. M. V. DE MONTE CARMELO

IN USU

EXCALCEATOS

— 12 —

piissimam misericordiam recipiat confessionem tuam, et restituat tibi stolam primam, quam in baptismate recepisti; et ego facultate mihi ab Apostolica Sede tributa, indulgentiam plenariam, et remissionem omnium peccatorum tibi concedo. In nomine Patris ✠ et Filii et Spiritus Sancti.

Per sacrosancta humanae reparationis mysteria, remittat tibi omnipotens Deus omnes praesentis et futurae vitae poenas, paradisi portas aperiat, et ad gaudia sempiterna perducat. Amen.

Benedicat te omnipotens Deus, Pater, et Filius ✠ et Spiritus Sanctus. Amen.

Si vero infirmus sit adeo morti proximus, ut neque confessionis generalis faciendae, neque praemissarum precum recitandarum tempus suppetat, statim Sacerdos Benedictionem ei impertiatur, dicens: Indulgentiam Plenariam et remissionem omnium peccatorum tibi concedo, in nomine Patris, et Filii ✠ et Spiritus Sancti. Amen.

SUMMARIUM

INDULGENTIARUM ET GRATIARUM

CONFRATRIBUS

B. VIRG. MARIAE DE MONTE CARMELO

A SUMMIS PONTIFICIBUS CONCESSARUM

Indulgentia plenaria sub conditione sacramentaliter confitendi, SS. Eucharistiam sumendi, et preces fundendi pro christianorum principum concordia, haeresum extirpatione, sanctaeque matris Ecclesiae exaltatione.

1. Die illa, qua quis recipiendo habitum, confraternitatem ingreditur. Paul. V. *Cum certas*, 30 Oct. 1606.

2. In festo principali COMMEMORAT. B. V. MARIAE DE MONTE CARMELO, 16 Iulii, vel Dominica immediate sequenti, aut alia eiusdem mensis, iuxta locorum consuetudinem. Ibid.

3. In mortis articulo, Poenitentiae et Eucharistiae Sacramentis susceptis, ad devotam SS. Nominis Iesu invocationem ore, si fieri potest, sin autem corde. Ibid.

4. In una Dominica cuiusvis mensis, interessendo processioni per confraternitatem de Ordinarii loci licentia faciendae. Idem. *Piorum hominum*, 3 Aug. 1609, et *Alias volentes*, 19 Iul. 1614.

5. Iis, qui praedictae processioni commode assistere non valent, si capellam respectivae confraternitatis devote visitaverint. Clem. X. *Commissae nobis*, 8 Maii 1673.

6. Infirmis, captivis et peregrinis, qui huiusmodi capellam dicta Dominica visitare nequiverint, si Officium parvum B. M. V. aut quinquagies *Pater et Ave* recitaverint, et saltem contriti fuerint cum proposito confitendi, et sacram Communionem recipiendi quam-

primum potuerint, quod adimplere omnino tenentur.
Clem. X. Bulla nuper citata.

INDULGENTIAE PARTIALES

1. *Indulg. 5 annor. et totidem quadragenar.* Semel
in mense, si poenitentes et confessi SS. Eucharistiae
Sacramentum sumpserint, et pro christianorum principum concordia, haeresum extirpatione, et sanctae
matris Ecclesiae exaltatione oraverint. Paul. V. *Cum
certas,* supra cit.

2. *Item comitando SS. Sacramentum* dum ad infirmos defertur, cum candela accensa, et pro iisdem
pias ad Deum preces fundendo. Ibid.

3. *Indulg. 3 annor. et 3 quadrag.* In qualibet ex
festivitatibus B. M. V. quae celebrantur ab universa
Ecclesia, confitendo et SS. Eucharistiam sumendo in
ecclesia, vel capella confraternitatis, et ut supra orando. Ibid.

4. *Indulg. 100 dier.* Corpora defunctorum tam confratrum et consororum, quam aliorum ad sepulturam
associando, ac pro eorum animabus Deum exorando.
Officium parvum B. M. V. devote recitando. Assistendo Missis aliisque divinis officiis in ecclesia vel capella
confraternitatis. Pauperes hospitio recipiendo, aut eis
in eorum necessitatibus vel periculo peccandi existentibus auxilium ferendo. Pacem cum inimicis propriis,
vel alienis, componendo. Ignorantes Dei praecepta et
ea, quae sunt ad salutem, edocendo, aut aliud quodcumque pietatis vel charitatis opus exercendo. Ibid.

Omnes et singulae indulgentiae praedictae per Paulum V. concessae, animabus Purgatorii per modum
suffragii possunt applicari. Clem. X. *Cum sicut accepimus* 2 ian. 1672.

— 15 —

GRATIAE NUPER CONCESSAE (1)

1. Omnes confratres et consorores, si in locis versantur ubi nulla Carmelitani Ordinis reperiatur ecclesia, omnes indulgentias ab Apostolica Sede eiusdem Ordinis ecclesiis concessas lucrari possunt, si vere poenitentes et confessi, ac sacra Communione refecti, respectivam parochialem ecclesiam statis diebus devote visitaverint, ac reliqua iniuncta pietatis opera rite in Domino praestiterint. Pii IX. Brev. 15 Ian. 1855.

2. Omnes et singulae Missae, quae in suffragium celebrantur confratrum et consororum, eodem gaudent privilegio ac si in altari privilegiato celebratae fuissent. S. Cong. Indulg. 22 Iunii 1865.

ALIAE GRATIAE

 Privilegium, vulgo dictum *Sabbatinum*, a Summis Pontificibus Ioan. XXII, Bulla *Sic mihi*, 3 Mart. 1322; Clem. VII, *Ex Clementi*, 12 Aug. 1530; S. Pii V, *Superna dispositione*, 18 Febr. 1566; Gregor. XIII, *Ut laudes*, 18 Septemb. 1577; aliisque approbatum et confirmatum, nec non a S. Romana et Universali Inquisitione sub Paulo V, die 20 Ian. 1613, Decreto tenoris sequentis:

« Patribus Carmelitanis permittitur praedicare quod populus christianus possit pie credere de adiutorio animarum fratrum et confratrum sodalitatis Beatissimae Virginis de Monte Carmelo, videlicet Beatissimam Virginem animas fratrum et confratrum in charitate decedentium, *qui in vita habitum gestaverint et castitatem pro suo statu coluerint, Officiumque parvum reci-*

(1) Gratiae olim concessae, praeter promissiones B. Simoni Stok a SS. Virgine factas, sunt: 1. Indulgentiae personales praedictae. 2. Participatio omnium bonorum spiritualium nostri Ordinis ex Bulla Clem. VII, *Ex Clementi*, 12 Augusti 1530. 3. Facultas in articulo mortis recipiendi Absolutionem generalem cum plenaria indulgentia, etc. ut supra.

— 16 —

*taverint, vel si recitare nesciant, Ecclesiae ieiunia ob-
servaverint, et feria quarta et Sabbato a carnibus abstinuerint (nisi in iis diebus Nativitatis Domini festum
inciderit)* suis intercessionibus continuis piisque suffragiis et meritis ac speciali protectione, post eorum
transitum, praecipue in die Sabbati, qui dies ab Ecclesia eidem Beatissimae Virgini dicatus est, adiuturam ».

Aliae multae Indulgentiae, quae brevitatis causa
omittuntur, in Summario Indulgentiarum Bullarii Ordinis, part. 2, pag. 600 continentur.

DECRETUM

Hoc Summarium rite recognitum, et authenticis
documentis, revisorum iudicio, conforme repertum,
imprimi posse, et ubique promulgari permittitur.

Datum Romae ex Secretaria S. Congregationis Indulgentiarum, 1 Decembris 1866.

L. ✠ S.

ANTONIUS M. CARD. PANEBIANCO Praef.

Philippus Can. Cossa Subst.

— 17 —

INDULGENTIAE PLENARIAE

ECCLESIIS ORDINIS CARMELITARUM

IN ALIQUIBUS ANNI FESTIVITATIBUS CONCESSAE.

Die 2 Febr., et 4 S. Andr. Cors. ep. et conf. 19 et 25 Martii. — Fer. V. in Coena Domini. Domin. Paschatis. In festo Patrocinii S. Ioseph, vel infra octavam. In Ascensione Domini. — 5 Maii S. Angeli Martyr. 16 S. Simonis Stok conf. et 25 S. Mariae Magdalenae de Pazzis virginis. — 2 Iulii Visitationis B. M. V. 16 B. M. V. de Monte Carmelo, vel infra octavam. 20 S. P. N. Eliae Prophetae. 26 S. Annae — 7 Augusti S. Alberti conf. 15 et Dom. infr. octav. Assumptionis. S. Ioachim. 27 Transverberat. Cordis S. M. N. Teresiae. — 8 Septembris. — 15 Octob. S. M. N. Teresiae virg. vel infr. octav. — 15 Nov. Commemorat. Defunctorum Ordinis, et occurrente in Dominica, die 16, 21 Praesentationis B. M. V., 24 S. P. N. Ioannis a Cruce Conf. vel infr. octav. — 8 Decembris, et die Nativitatis Domini ad 3 Missam. Una die in expositione XL horar. Passim ex Bullario Ordinis.

Lucrantur dictis diebus indulgentiam plenariam qui rite sacramentaliter confessi sint et sacra Communione refecti, atque ecclesiam Ordinis Carmelitani visitaverint, vel respectivam parochialem ecclesiam, si confratres in locis versantur ubi nulla Carmelitani Ordinis reperiatur ecclesia. Vid. supra *Gratiae nuper concessae n. 1.*

NOTANDUM quod, iuxta decretum Urbis et Orbis Pii Pp. IX 18 Septembris 1862 per S. C. Indulg. emanatum, si confratres habitualiter sint infirmi, chronici, ob physicum permanens aliquod impedimentum e domo egredi impotentes (exceptis tamen illis, qui in communitate morantur) acquirere possunt praedictas indulgentias plenarias, dummodo vere poenitentes et confessi loco sacrae Communionis et visitationis, alia pia opera a respectivo Confessario iniungenda, fideliter adimpleam.

Obligationes Confratrum ad supradicta consequenda.

I. Ut quis sacrum Scapulare a Sacerdote deputato cum solitis coeremoniis recipiat.

II. Ut eius nomen inscribatur in Album Confraternitatis in quavis Ecclesia Ordinis, vel in alia in qua sit canonice erecta.

III. Ut illud semper super humeros portet; et si fuerit attritum, aliud sive benedictum, sive non benedictum, absque alia nova coeremonia assumendum est.

Obligationes particulares pro consequendo privilegio Bullae Sabbatinae.

I. Ut servetur castitas secundum proprium statum.

II. Ut scientes legere, quotidie recitent Officium parvum B. M. V. in Breviario Romano appositum; nescientes vero legere, Ecclesiae ieiunia observent, ac diebus Mercurii et Sabbati abstineant ab esu carnium, excepto die Natalis Domini. Ob iustam tamen causam Confessarius, habens specialem facultatem, in aliud pium opus commutare potest.

RESOLUTIONES

1. An ad lucrandas indulgentias sacri Scapularis necesse sit, ut una pars ab humeris, altera a pectore dependeat, an vero sit sufficiens ipsum deferre absque distinctione circa modum? S. C. Indulg. respondit: *Affirmative* quoad primam partem, *Negative* quoad secundam. 12 Febr. 1840.

2. An color *taneus* semper requiratur in Scapularibus ad indulgentias lucrandas? S. C. Indulg. respondit: *Negative*, dummodo colori vulgo *tanè* subrogetur alter consimilis, seu niger. 12 Febr. 1840.

3. Utrum Sacerdos habens facultatem imponendi

scapulare B. M. V. de Monte Carmelo, sibimet illud possit imponere? S. C. Indulg. respondit: *Affirmative*, quatenus haec facultas habeatur indiscriminatim, minime vero si taxative, ex. gr. pro aliqua monialium communitate tantum etc. 17 Martii 1840.

4. An rata sit fidelium adscriptio non servata forma Ritualis et Breviarii Ordinis Carmelitarum? S. C. Indulg. respondit: *Affirmative*, dummodo Sacerdotes facultates habentes non deficiant in substantialibus, nempe benedictione et impositione habitus, ac in receptione ad Confraternitatem. 24 Augusti 1844.

5. Sacerdotes qui nequeunt transmittere nomina fidelium in scapularis Societatem receptorum, vel ad proximam eius Sodalitatem, vel ad monasteria religiosorum, quaerunt utrum fideles sic recepti indulgentias lucrari possint? S. C. Indulg. per decretum sub die 27 Aprilis 1887 respondit: inscriptionem in Album Confraternitatis esse necessariam ad lucrandas indulgentias.

6. An qui rite semel adscripti in Sodalitatem postea habitum dimiserunt, teneantur ad novam receptionem? S. C. Indulg. respondit: *Negative*, et sufficit ut habitum sacrum ipsi denuo resumant simpliciter. 27 Maii 1857.

7. Utrum ad scapularia conficienda necessario et exclusive adhibenda sit materia ex lana, vel utrum sumi etiam possit xylinum (cotone), aliave similis materia? S. C. Indulg. respondit: *Affirmative*, ad primam partem, *Negative* ad secundam. 18 Augusti 1868.

8. Utrum vox *panniculus* sumi debeat sensu stricto, idest de sola lanea textura proprie dicta vulgo *tessuto*, *tissu*, vel utrum etiam intelligi possit de lanea textura reticulata vulgo *maglia*, *tricotage*, et de quocumque laneo opere acu picto vulgo *ricamo*, *broderie*? S. C. Indulg. respondit: *Affirmative*, ad primam partem, *Negative* ad secundam. 18 Augusti 1868.

9. An Scapularia confecta non ex lana contexta sed subcoacta (*feutre*, *feltro*), Christi fidelibus imponi possint, quin ipsi amittant Indulgentias, gestantibus scapularia concessas?

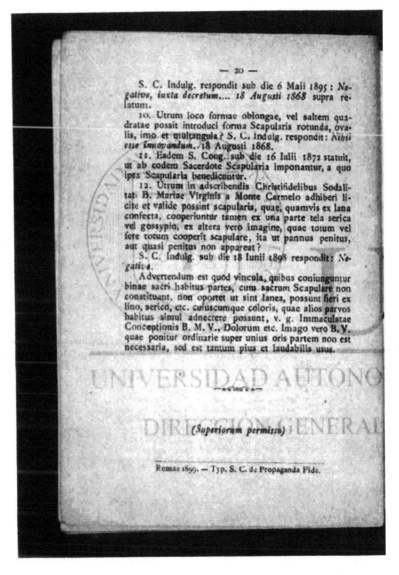

— 20 —

S. C. Indulg. respondit sub die 6 Maii 1895 : *Negative, iuxta decretum.... 18 Augusti 1868* supra relatum.

10. Utrum loco formae oblongae, vel saltem quadratae possit introduci forma Scapularis rotunda, ovalis, imo et multangula? S. C. Indulg. respondit: *Nihil esse innovandum*. 18 Augusti 1868.

11. Eadem S. Cong. sub die 16 Iulii 1872 statuit, ut ab eodem Sacerdote Scapularia imponantur, a quo ipsa Scapularia benedicuntur.

12. Utrum in adscribendis Christifidelibus Sodalitati B. Mariae Virginis a Monte Carmelo adhiberi licite et valide possint scapularia, quae, quamvis ex lana confecta, cooperiuntur tamen ex una parte tela serica vel gossypio, ex altera vero imagine, quae totum vel fere totum cooperit scapulare, ita ut pannus penitus, aut quasi penitus non appareat?

S. C. Indulg. sub die 18 Iunii 1898 respondit: *Negative*.

Advertendum est quod vincula, quibus coniunguntur binae sacri habitus partes, cum sacrum Scapulare non constituant, non oportet ut sint lanea, possunt fieri ex lino, serico, etc. cuiuscumque coloris, quae alios parvos habitus simul adnectere possunt, v. g. Immaculatae Conceptionis B. M. V., Dolorum etc. Imago vero B. V. quae ponitur ordinarie super unius oris partem non est necessaria, sed est tantum pius et laudabilis usus.

(Superiorum permissu)

Romae 1899. — Typ. S. C. de Propaganda Fide.

Leo XIII

Birth name	Vincenzo Gioacchino Raffaelle Luigi Pecci
Papacy began	February 20, 1878
Papacy ended	July 20, 1903
Predecessor	Pius IX
Successor	Pius X
Born	March 2, 1810 Carpineto Romano, Italy
Died	July 20, 1903 (aged 93) Apostolic Palace, Rome, Italy

Coat of arms for Pope Leo XII

Pope Leo XIII: Vincenzo Gioacchino Raffaelle Luigi Pecci

Papacy: 1878 – 1903

Summary of Contents:

1). Apostolic Brief *Ad Perpetuam Rei Memoriam, Toties Quoties*, May 16, 1892, enriching the Carmelite Churches with a special privilege for all those who devoutly visit a Church or Public Oratory of the Carmelite Community on July 16 of each year, the day in which is celebrated the Feast of Our Lady of Mount Carmel, from morning until sunset etc.......will receive a Plenary Indulgence......

2). From the Acta Sanctae Sedis: The Sacred Congregation of Indulgences, A Decree of the Order of Carmelites of the Ancient Observance, date April 27, 1887: His Holiness, Pope Leo XII speaks of the Virgin Mary and the special favors, graces, and privileges granted to those who devotedly wear the Scapular, the sign of Our Lady's predilection and affection...

3). Encyclical of Pope Leo XIII, *Fidentem Piumque*, dated September 20, 1896, in which His Holiness refers to the Blessed Virgin as *"Mediatrix to the Mediator."*

4). From the Acta Sanctae Sedis: Ex S. Congreg. Indulgentarium, dated June 14, 1901, p. 120: It is a Decree on behalf of the pious works of the Confraternity of the Blessed Virgin Mary of Mount Carmel of Guatemala for obtaining the Sabbatine Privilege. Those who can recite the Little Office of the Blessed Virgin (to gain the Sabbatine Privilege) are bound to do so, but the fulfilling of the obligation is rendered easy by the permission given by the Sacred Congregation, namely that the Little Office may be recited in the vernacular, that is in the spoken language of the member of the Scapular Confraternity. An exception is made in the case of those languages peculiar to the rites approved by the Holy See; the wearer of the Scapular can obtain the Sabbatine Privilege by the recital of the Office in such languages. (1)   The official Documents: 1 and 2, are in Latin and are found in the pages following; 3 is in English. This is a Decree issued from the Sacred Congregation of Indulgences regarding the third condition of the Sabbatine Privilege, and it is approved and confirmed by His Holiness Pope LeoXII.

(1). S. Cong. Indulg. 14 June, 1901. Acta Sanctrae Sedis (1901-1902), p. 120 found in <u>The Ecclesiastical Review,</u> Vol. LVI, Philadelphia, 1917, p. 166; (This is a 20ᵗʰ century mention of the Sabbatine Privilege by the Church)

(excerpts translated and paraphrased from <u>Lo Scapolare,</u> 2, A Cura Del Comitato Italiano, VII Centenario Dello Scapolare, Roma, 1950, p. 66)

ACTA
SANCTAE SEDIS

II COMPENDIUM OPPORTUNE REDACTA ET ILLUSTRATA

STUDIO ET CURA

VICTORII PIAZZESI

IURIS   UTRIUSQUE   DOCTORIS

Acta iuridica et solemniora ex Supremo Romano Pontifice immediate dimanantia: acta
inter ea quae publici fieri possunt iuris, sive sint Decreta, sive Instructiones, sive Responsa
et alia huiusmodi; praesertim vero Causarum expositiones et resolutiones ex variis
EE. Cardinalium Sacris Congregationibus, ad ecclesiastici iuris accuratam intelligentiam
et observantiam conferentes, in compendium diligenti studio redactae: alia denique iuridica,
quibus opportune illustrantur quae in expositis actis vel difficultatem parere possint, vel
ad vigentis iuris notitiam ulterius conducant: in utilitatem eorum qui in Ecclesiae legibus
studiose dignoscendis, et in regimine christiani gregis, vel in colenda Domini vinea
sedulo adlaborant.

Volumen XXIV.

ROMAE

EX TYPOGRAPHIA   POLYGLOTTA

S. CONGR. DE PROPAGANDA FIDE

1891-92.

clesiam Beatae Mariae Virginis ad Montem Bericum ingredi cum stola?

3. Et quatenus Negative ad 1. et 2, supplicibus et communibus votis expetitur, ut exposita consuetudo servari possit.

Sacra porro eadem Congregatio ad relationem infrascripti Secretarii, exquisitoque voto alterius ex Apostolicarum Caeremoniarum Magistris, re mature perpensa, ita propositis Dubiis censuit rescribendum, videlicet : *Expositam eonsuetudinem servan posse.* Atque ita rescripsit die 20 Maii 1892.

CAL CARD. ALOISI MASELLA, S. R. C. *Praef.*

L. * S.

VINC Nussi, S. R. C. *Secretarius.*

EX SECRETARIA BREVIUM

BREVE quo conceditur Indulgentia toties quoties Ordini carmelitano pro die festi B. V. M. de Monte Carmelo.

LEO PP. XIII.

Ad perpetuam rei memoriam.

Quo magis fidelium erga Bmam Virginem Karmelitidem devotio augescat et pietas, unde eorum animis uberrimi et salutiferi fructus derivare possunt, piae postulationi Dilecti Filii Aloisii Mariae Galli, summi Moderatoris Ordinis B. M. V. de Monte Carmelo veteris Observantiae benigne inclinati, peculiari privilegio Carmelitanas Ecclesias locupletare statuimus. Quapropter de Omnipotentis Dei misericordia ac BB. Petri et Pauli App. Eius auctoritate confisi, omnibus et singulis utriusque sexus christifidelibus vere poenitentibus et confessis ac S. Communione refectis, qui quamlibet ex Ecclesiis vel quodlibet ex publicis Oratoriis sive Fratrum sive Monialium universi Ordinis Karmelitidis, tum Calceatorum, tum Excalceatorum ubique locorum existentibus die decimasexta mensis Iulii cuiusque anni, qua festivitas Deiparae Virginis de Monte Carmelo celebratur, a primis vesperis usque ad occasum solis diei huiusmodi devote visitaverint, ibique pro Christianorum Principum concordia, haeresum

669

extirpatione, peccatorum conversione, ac S. Matris Ecclesiae exaltatione pias ad Deum preces effuderint, quoties id egerint,, toties Plenariam omnium peccatorum suorum Indulgentiam et remissionem, quam etiam animabus christifidelium, quae Deo in charitate coniunctae ab hac luce migraverint, per modum suffragii applicare possint, misericorditer in Domino concedimus. Non obstantibus Nostra et Cancellariae Apostolicae regula de non concedendis indulgentiis ad instar, aliisque Constitutionibus et Ordinationibus Apostolicis, ceterisque contrariis quibuscumque. Praesentibus perpetuis futuris temporibus valituris. Volumus autem, ut praesentium Litterarum transumptis seu exemplis etiam impressis manu alicuius Notarii publici subscriptis, et sigillo personae in ecclesiastica dignitate constitutae munitis eadem prorsus fides adhibeatur, quae adhiberetur ipsis praesentibus, si forent exhibitae vel ostensae.

Datum Romae apud S. Petrum, sub annulo Piscatoris die xvi Maii anno MDGGGXGII. Pontificatus Nostri anno decimo quinto.

L.   S.

S. CARD. VANNUTELLI.

EX S. CONGR. INDULGENTIARUM

SODALITATES sub titulo B. V. Mariae in coelum assumptae ad iuvandas animas igne Purgatorii detentas, ubique locorum erectae, nequeunt gaudere indulgentiis et privilegiis, quibus gaudet Archisodalitas eiusdem nominis in urbe erecta, nisi! fuerint eidem Archisodalitati aggregatae.

Beatissime Pater,

Hermes Martinelli Congregationis SSmi Redemptoris Procurator Generalis ad pedes S. V. provolutus demisse exponit olim in Ecclesia S. M. vulgo in Monterone nuncupata, in hac alma Urbe existente, erectam fuisse Archisodalitatem sub titulo B. M. Virg. in Coelum Assumptae, ad iuvandas animas purgatorii igne detentas, eiusdemque Sodalitatis ceu moderatorem constitutum fuisse Procuratorem generalem pro tempore existentem Congregationis SSmi Redemptoris.

Appendix 4

ACTA

SANCTAE SEDIS

IN COMPENDIUM OPPORTUNE REDACTA ET ILLUSTRATA

STUDIO ET CURA.

IOSEPHI PENNACCHI ET VICTORII PIAZZESI

℞

Acta iuridica et solemniora ex Supremo Romano Pontifice immediate dimanantia: acta inter ea quae publici fieri possunt iuris, sive sint Decreta, sive Instructiones, sive Responsa, et alia huiusmodi; praesertim vero Causarum expositiones et resolutiones ex variis EE. Cardinalium Sacris Congregationibus, ad ecclesiastici iuris accuratam intelligentiam et observantiam conferentes, in compendium diligenti studio redactae: alia denique iuridica, quibus opportune illustrantur quae in expositis actis vel difficultatem parere possint, vel ad vigentis iuris notitiam ulterius conducant: in utilitatem eorum qui in Ecclesiae legibus studiose dignoscendis, et in regimine christiani gregis, vel in colenda Domini vinea sedulo adlaborant.

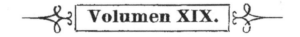

Volumen XIX.

ROMAE

TYPIS POLYGLOTTAE OFFICINAE

S. C. DE PROPAGANDA FIDE

MDCCCLXXXVI.

Reprinted with the permission of Libreria Editrice Vaticana

JOHNSCN REPRINT CORPORATION
111 Fifth Avenue, New York, N. Y. 10003

JOHNSON REPRINT COMPANY LTD.
Berkeley Square House, London, W. 1

Dubium

An et quomodo sit locus provisionibus a Confratribus petitis in casu.

RESOLUTIO. Sacra Congr. Concilii, re discussa, sub die **5.** Martii, censuit respondere : « *Negative in omnibus et amplius.* »

Ex QUIBUS COLLIGES. I. Liquidum in iure esse quod liceat confratribus suas facere congregationes pro lubitu et iuxta peculiaria statuta, absque interventu aliorum in propriis ecclesiis.

II. Sodalitium in themate haud haberi quoad Ecclesiam s. Augustini ceu patronum in propria ecclesia, sed veluti hospitem in ecclesia aliena, cui precario indultum fuit ibi proprias explere posse functiones, donec pax turbaretur cum rectore Ecclesiae, a qua depelli posset ; et ideo expetita a confratribus denegata fuerunt.

———— = ^ = > ^ e « 0 ^ c r =————

EX S. CONGREG. INDULGENTIARUM

DECRETUM. Ordinis Carmelitarum antiquae Observantiae de scapulari B. M. Y. de Monte Carmelo a simultanea plurium scapularium traditione excipiendo.

Die 27 Aprilis 1887,

Ab initio huius saeculi in usu esse coepit quatuor Scapularium simultanea et compendiosa traditio, nempe SS. Trinitatis, B. M. V. de Monte Carmelo, Immaculatae Conceptionis, septem Dolorum, quibus nuperrime additum est quintum, scilicet Scapulare rubrum Passionis D. N. I. C. Haec facultas benedicendi imponendique simul praedicta Scapularia collata primitus alicui religioso Instituto, tempore praesertim ss. Missionum, breviori adhibita formula a S. R. C. approbata, deinde Sacerdotibus quoque saecularibus indulta est, qua etiam extra tempus ss. Missionum peragendarum ipsi utuntur. Quamvis autem haec agendi ratio fortasse contulerit ad istorum Scapularium receptionem facilius propagandam, ea ta-

men occasio fuit cur praecipuus ille honor, quo christifideles Scapulare carmeliticum quavis aetate celebrarunt, imminueretur, et
fervens erga illud devotio aliquantulum tepesceret. Porro Scapulare Carmelitarum, quod nobilitas ipsa originis, veneranda anti-
quitas, latissima eiusdem in christiano populo pluribus abhinc sae-
culis propagatio, nec non salutares per Illud habiti pietatis effectus,
et insignia quae perhibentur patrata miracula mirabiliter commen-
dant, omnino postulare videtur distinctionem honoris in ipso receptionis ritu, ut non quidem cum aliis commixtim, quasi unum ex
pluribus, sed prouti in sua primitiva institutione illud beatissima
Virgo uti tesseram propriam sui Ordinis tradidisse fertur B. Simoni
Stokio, fidelibus quoque distinctim tradatur, nec cum aliis simul
Scapularibus connumeretur. Ex quo procul dubio fiet ut illa singularis omnino, universalis et constans totius catholici Orbis religio integra servetur erga hoc sacrum Scapulare marianum, quod
veluti antonomastice Scapulare audit, iure meritoque orta ex eo
quod, uti traditur, pientissima Virgo speciales favores, gratias et
privilegia conferre spoponderit devote gestantibus hoc suum prae-
dictionis signum.

Haec sedulo perpendens hodiernus Vicarius carmelitici Ordinis
antiquae observantiae Rmus P. Angelus Savini honori simul con-
sulere exoptans et devotioni sacri Scapularis B. M. V. de Monte
Carmelo, instantibus quoque sui Ordinis Fratribus, huic s. Congregationi Indulg. et ss. Reliq. sequens dubium discutiendum pro-
posuit :

« Utrum conveniens sit Scapulare B. V. M. de Monte Carmelo,
honoris et devotionis causa, separatim potius et distincte, quam
cumulative et commixtim cum aliis quatuor vel pluribus Scapularibus benedicere et imponere? »

Emi ac Rmi Patres in generali Congregatione apud Vaticanum
habita die 26 Martii 1887, re mature perpensa, rescripserunt: « *Affirmative:* et consulendum SSmo, ut Indultum huc usque in perpetuum concessum, etiam Regularibus Ordinibus et Congregationibus induendi christifideles Scapulari carmelitico commixtim cum
aliis Scapularibus revocetur, et ad determinatum tempus coarcte-
tur, neque in posterum amplius concedatur.

Facta vero de his relatione in audientia habita die 27 Aprilis 1887 ab infrascripto Secretario, Sanctissimus D. N. Leo Papa XIII
Patrum Cardinalium responsionem approbavit, decrevitque ut praefatum Indultum in posterum non amplius concedatur, ac illi omnes,

S56   EX S. G. INDULGENTIARUM

-etiam Regulares Ordines vel Congregationes, quibus Indultum ipsum, quocumque nomine vel forma ab Apostolica Sede est concessum eo tantummodo *ad decennium* perfruantur ab hac die computandum.

Datum Romae ex Secretaria eiusdem S. Congregationis die 27 Aprilis 1887.

Fr. THOMAS M. CARD. ZIGLIARA *Praefectus.*

jig ALEXANDER Episcopus Oensis *Secretarius.*

DECRETUM. Ordinis fratrum minorum excalceatorum et recollectorum de inscribendis nominibus christifidelium qui sacra scapularia recipiunt.

Die 27 Aprilis 1887.

Iam inde ab anno 1838 sub die 30 Aprilis s. m. Gregorius XVI •ex speciali Indulto exemit ab onere inscribendi in albo Confraternitatis nomina Christifidelium, qui Scapulare B. Mariae Virginis de Monte Carmelo recipiunt. Iam vero Procurator generalis Fratrum Minorum excalceatorum et recollectorum preces humiliter porrexit Sanctissimo Domino Nostro Leoni Papae XIII, ut ad Confraternitates aliorum Scapularium idem omnino Indultum benigne extendere dignaretur. Ad id postulandum haec potissimum eum permovebant rationum momenta, defeotus nimirum vicinarum Confraternitatum ad quas forent nomina Confratrum et Consororum inscriptarum transmittenda, nec non maxima difficultas colligendi nomina plurimorum adscribi petentium sacris Scapularibus tempore Missionum.

Alias egit de hac quaestione haec S. Congregatio Indulgentiis sacrisque Reliquiis praeposita, mentemque suam pandidit in una Cameracensi sub die 18 Augusti 1868, in qua expresse denegavit praefatum gregorianum Indultum aliis Scapularium Confraternitatibus esse applicandum.

Modo vero occasione exhibiti supplicis libelli supramemorati P. Procuratoris, huic S. Congregationi opportunum visum est praesentem quaestionem de inscribendis nominibus, qui sacra Scapularia recipiunt, denuo perpendere, eamque, audito alterius ex Consultoribus voto, dirimere sequenti proposito dubio :

PAPAL TEACHINGS

OUR LADY

Selected and Arranged

by

THE BENEDICTINE MONKS OF SOLESMES

Translated by

THE DAUGHTERS OF ST. PAUL

ST. PAUL EDITIONS

their authority, privileges of wide extent were granted to
the Order of Preachers in favor of this Project. The hoped-
for results were forthcoming thanks to the energetic activity
of the brethren of that Order, results to which many a
bright record bear witness, although time and adversity
have since raised great obstacles in the way of further
progress.

*(Present devotion of the East shown by erection of a
basilica of the Rosary at Patrasso.)*

"Monstra te esse Matrem"

186
(34,
169,
178)
And now, Venerable Brethren, our exhortation returns
to the point from which it began. Well may all, shepherds
and flocks alike, fly with fullest confidence to the protection of the Blessed Virgin, especially next month, let them
not fail to call upon her name with one voice beseeching
her as God's Mother, publicly and in private by praise, by
prayer, by the ardor of their desire: "Show thyself our
Mother" (a). May her motherly compassion keep her whole
family safe from every danger, lead them in the path of
genuine prosperity, above all establish them in holy unity.
She looks upon Catholics of every nation with a kindly eye.
Where the bond of charity joins them together she makes
them more ready, more and more determined, to uphold
the honor of religion which, at the same time, brings upon
the state the greatest blessings.

187
(161,
171)
May she look with utmost compassion upon those great
and illustrious nations which are cut off from the Church
and upon the noble souls who have not forgotten their
Christian duty. May she inspire in them most salutary desires, foster their holy aspirations and bring them to happy
completion. In the East, may that widespread devotion to
her, which the dissident nations profess, as well as the

186a *Ave Maris Stella.*

Appendix 4

countless glorious acts of their ancestors in her honor, effectively aid them. In the West, may the memory of her beneficent patronage stand its dissidents in good stead; with surpassing kindness she has, through many ages, manifested her approval of, and has rewarded, the admirable devotion shown her among every class.

May the peoples of the East and the West, and all the others wherever they may be, profit by the suppliant voice of Catholics united in prayer, and by Our voice which will cry to Our last breath: "Show thyself a Mother."

CLOSE TO THE MEDIATOR

Encycl. *Fidentem Piumque*, September 20, 1896.

We have already had the opportunity on several occasions during Our pontificate of bearing testimony to that confidence and devotion toward the Blessed Virgin which we sustained in Our tenderest years, and have endeavored to cherish and develop all our life long. For, having come upon times of calamity for Christendom and of peril for nations, We have realized how prudent it is warmly to recommend this means of safeguarding happiness and peace which God has most mercifully granted to men through His august Mother, and which has always been celebrated in the annals of the Church. The manifold zeal of Christian people has responded to Our desires and exhortations, most particularly by showing a devotion to the Rosary, and a plentiful harvest of excellent fruits has not been wanting. *188 (120, 134, 146)*

Still We can never do enough in honoring the Mother of God, who is in truth worthy of all praise, and with urging love and affection toward her, who is also the Mother of mankind, who is full of mercy, full of grace. Yea, Our soul, wearied with the cares of the apostolate, the nearer it feels the time of Our departure to be at hand, *189 (136, 143, 175)* the more earnestly and confidently do We look up to her from whom, as from a blessed dawn, rises the day of happiness which has no sunset.

It is happiness for Us to remember, Venerable Brethren, that We have in other Letters, issued from time to time, extolled the devotion of the Rosary, for it is in many ways most pleasing to her in whose honor it is employed, and most advantageous to those who properly use it. But it is equally a happiness to be able now to insist upon and confirm the same fact. Herein We have an excellent opportunity paternally to exhort men's minds and hearts to an increase of religion, and to stimulate within them the hope of eternal reward.

*The Rosary is endowed with the qualities
of a true prayer*

190
(143)
The form of prayer We refer to has obtained the special name of "Rosary," as though it represented by its arrangement the sweetness of roses and the charm of a garland. This is a most fitting way to venerate the Blessed Virgin, who is rightly styled the "Mystical Rose" of Paradise (a), and who as Queen of the Universe shines therein with a crown of stars. By its very name it appears to foreshadow and be an augury of the joys and garlands of heaven offered by her to those who are devoted to her.

(*Nature and necessity of prayer in a general way,—
Unanimity and assiduousness.*)

191
(145,
149)
Both of these qualities are conspicuous in the Rosary. For, to be brief, by repeating the same prayers we strenuously implore from Our Heavenly Father the kingdom of His grace and glory; we again and again beseech the Virgin Mother to aid us sinners by her prayers, both during our whole life and especially at that last moment which is the steppingstone to eternity. The formula of the Rosary

190a Litany of Our Lady.

Appendix 4

too, is excellently adapted to prayer in common, so that it has been styled, not without reason, "The Psalter of Mary."

The old custom of our forefathers ought to be preserved or restored, whereby Christian families, whether in town or country, used to gather piously at the close of the day, when their labors were at an end, before an image of our Lady, and alternately recite the Rosary. She, delighted at this faithful and unanimous homage, was ever near them like a loving mother surrounded by her children, distributing to them the blessings of domestic peace, the foretaste of the peace of heaven.

Considering the efficacy of public prayer, We, among other decrees which We have from time to time issued concerning the Rosary, have spoken thus: "It is our wish that in the principal church of each diocese it should be recited daily, and that in parish churches it should be said on every feast day" (a). Let this be constantly and devoutly carried out. We also see with the joy the custom extended to other solemn occasions of public devotion and to pilgrimages to venerated shrines, the growing frequency of which is to be commended. **192** *(152)*

This association of prayer and praise to Mary is a source at once of joy and of salvation for souls. We ourselves have most strongly experienced this—and Our heart rejoices to recall it—when at certain times in Our pontificate We have been present in the Vatican Basilica, surrounded by great crowds of all classes who, united with us in mind, voice and hope, all earnestly invoked, by the mysteries and prayers of the Rosary, her who is the most powerful Patroness of the Catholic name. **193** *(135, 178)*

Mediatrix with the Mediator

Who could think or say that the confidence so strongly felt in the patronage of the Blessed Virgin is excessive. **194** *(28,*

192a Apost. Letter *Salutaris Ille*, December 24, 1883.

43
39.
42)

Undoubtedly the name and attributes of the absolute Mediator belong to no other than Christ; for being one Person and yet both Man and God He restored the human race to the favor of the Heavenly Father. "One Mediator of God and men, the Man Jesus Christ, Who gave Himself a redemption for all" (a).

And yet, as the Angelic Doctor teaches: "there is no reason why certain others should not be called in a certain way mediators between God and Man, that is to say in so far as they cooperate by predisposing and ministering in the union of man with God" (b). Such are the angels and saints, the prophets and priests of both Testaments, but especially has the Blessed Virgin a claim to the glory of this title. For no single individual can even be imagined who has ever contributed or ever will contribute so much toward reconciling man with God. To mankind heading for eternal ruin, she offered a Savior when she received the announcement of the mystery brought to this earth by the Angel, and in giving her consent gave it "in the name of the whole human race" (c). She is from whom Jesus is born; she is therefore truly His Mother and for this reason a worthy and acceptable "Mediatrix to the Mediator" (d).

195
(42)

As the various mysteries present themselves one after the other in the formula of the Rosary for the meditation and contemplation of men's minds, they also elucidate what we owe to Mary for our reconciliation and salvation. No one can fail to be sweetly affected when considering who appeared in the house of Elizabeth as the minister of the

194a Tim. 2:5-6.
194b *Summa Theologica.* III q. 26. a. i.
194c *Summa Theologica.* III q. 30. a. i.
194d *Nemo etenim unus cogitari quidem potest qui reconci liandis Deo hominibus parem atque illa operam vel um quam contulerit vel aliquando sit collaturus. Ipsa est "de qua natus est Jesus," vera scilicet eius Mater, ob eamdem que causam digna ac peraccepta "ad Mediatorem Media trix"*

Appendix 4

divine gifts, who presented her Son to the shepherds, to the kings and to Simeon. Moreover one must remember that the blood of Christ shed for our sake, and those members in which He offers to His Father the wounds He received "as the price of our liberty," are no other than the flesh and blood of the Virgin: "The flesh of Jesus is the flesh of Mary, and however much it was exalted in the Glory of His Resurrection, nevertheless the nature of His flesh derived from Mary remained and still remains the same" (a).

(*Meditation on the Mysteries of the Rosary nourishes faith.—Everyone can recite the Rosary.—Pray for unity.*)

...For that earnest desire which We have learned from the Divine Heart of Jesus, of fostering the work of reconciliation among those who are separated from us, daily urges us more pressingly to action, and We are convinced that this reunion cannot be better prepared and strengthened than by the power of prayer.

The example of Christ is before us, for in order that His disciples might be one in faith and charity, He poured forth prayer and supplication to His Father. And concerning the efficacious prayer of His most holy Mother for the same end, there is a striking testimony in the Acts of the Apostles. Therein is described the first assembly of the disciples, expecting with earnest hope and prayer, the promised fullness of the Holy Spirit. And the presence of Mary, united to them in prayer, is specially indicated: "All these were persevering with one mind in prayer with Mary the Mother of Jesus" (a).

Wherefore, as the nascent Church rightly joined itself in prayer with her as the patroness and most excellent custodian of unity, so in these times it is most opportune to do

196
(81,
121)

197
(171)

195a St. Augustine, *De Assumpt.* B.M.V., c. 5.
196a Acts 1:14.

156   SPOUSE OF THE HOLY SPIRIT

the same all over the Catholic World, particularly during
the whole month of October, which we long ago decreed to
be dedicated and consecrated, by the solemn devotion of
the Rosary, to the Mother of God, in order to implore her
help for the afflicted Church.

198
(122,
171)
Let, then, zeal for this prayer everywhere be rekindled,
particularly for the end of holy unity. Nothing will be more
agreeable and acceptable to Mary; for as she is most closely
united with Christ, she especially wishes and desires that
they who have received the same Baptism with Him may
be united with Him and with one another in the same Faith
and perfect Charity. So may the sublime mysteries of this
same Faith be more deeply impressed in men's minds by
means of the Rosary devotion, with the happy result that
"we may imitate what they contain and obtain what they
promise."

SPOUSE OF THE HOLY SPIRIT

Encycl. *Divinum illud*, May 9, 1897.

(Mission and Worship of the Holy Spirit.)

199
(57,
81)
Our mind and heart turn back to those hopes with
which We began, and for the accomplishment of which
We earnestly pray, and will continue to pray to the
Holy Spirit. Unite, then, Venerable Brethren, your prayers
with Ours, and at your exhortation let all Christian peoples
add their prayers also, invoking the powerful and ever-
acceptable intercession of the Blessed Virgin. You know
well the intimate and wonderful relations existing between
her and the Holy Spirit, so that she is justly called His
Spouse. Her intercession was of great avail both in the mystery of the Incarnation and in the coming of the Holy Spirit
upon the Apostles. May she continue to strengthen our
prayers with her suffrages, that in the midst of all the stress
and troubles of the nations, those divine prodigies may be

Appendix 4

happily revived in the Holy Spirit, which were foretold in the words of David: "Send forth Thy Spirit and they shall be created, and Thou shalt renew the face of the earth" (a).

MARY'S IMPLORING OMNIPOTENCE

Encycl. *Augustissimæ*, September 12, 1897.

Whoever considers the height of dignity to which God has raised the most august Virgin Mary will easily perceive how important it is, both for the public and private good, that devotion to her should be assiduously practiced and daily promoted more and more.
    God chose her from all eternity to be the Mother of the Incarnate Word, and for that reason so eminently distinguished her among all His most beautiful works in the triple order of nature, grace and glory, that the Church justly applies to her these words:—"I came out of the Mouth of the Most High, the firstborn before all creatures" (a).

200
(21,
126)

And when in the beginning of the human race, the parents of mankind fell into sin, involving their descendants in the same ruin, she was set up as the pledge of the restoration of peace and salvation.

201
(34)

The only-begotten Son of God at all times paid to His most holy Mother most evident marks of honor. During His private life on earth, He associated her with Himself in each of His first two miracles—the miracle of grace when, at the salutation of Mary, the infant leaped in the womb of Elizabeth; the miracle of nature when He turned water into wine at the marriage feast of Cana. And at the supreme moment of His public life, when sealing the New Testament in His precious blood, He committed her to

202
(27)

199a Ps. 103:30.
200a Eccl. 24:5.

ACTA
SANCTAE SEDIS

IN COMPENDIUM OPPORTUNE REDACTA ET ILLUSTRATA

STUDIO ET CURA

VICTOR» PIAZZESI

IURIS   UTRIUSQUE   DOCTORIS

SEU

Acta iuridica et solemniora ex Supremo Romano Pontifice immediate dimanantia: acta inter ea quae publici fieri possunt iuris, sive sint Decreta, sive Instructiones, sive Responsa, et alia huiusmodi ; praesertim vero Causarum expositiones et resolutiones ex variis EE. Cardinalium Sacris Congregationibus, ad ecclesiastici iuris accuratam intelligentiam et observantiam conferentes, in compendium diligenti studio redactae: alia denique iuridica, quibus opportune illustrantur quae in expositis actis vel difficultatem parere possint, vel ad vigentis iuris notitiam ulterius conducant: in utilitatem eorum, qui in Ecclesiae legibus studiose dignoscendis, et in regimine christiani gregis, vel in colenda Domini vinea. sedulo adlaborant.

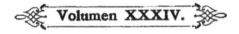

Volumen XXXIV.

ROMAE

EX TYPOGRAPHIA POLYGLOTTA

S. CONGR. DE PROPAGANDA FIDE

1901-902.

•120

EX S. CONGREG. INDULGENTIARUM

DECRETUM, de Guatemala de piis operibus sodalibus confr. Beatae Mariae Virginis a Monte Carmelo ad assequendum privilegium sabbatinum iniunctis.

Archiepiscopus de Guatemala huic S. Congregationi Indulgentiarum sequentia dubia dirimenda proponit, quae ad pia quaedam opera referuntur a Confratribus B. Mariae Virginis a Monte Carmelo praestanda, in eum finem ut privilegio, quod nuncupatur *Sabbatinum,* perficiantur :

I. *Estne necessarium ut Confratres B. Mariae Virginis a Monte Carmelo recitent parvum officium prouti extat in Breviario romano, etsi maior pars populi linguam latinam penitus ignoret ?*

II. *Ii Confratres qui legere nesciunt, et ideo loco recitandi parvum officium B. Mariae Virginis servare tenentur abstinentiam feria IV et die Sabbati, tenentur quoque eam servare feria VI, uti reapse tenentur fideles non americani latini?*

III. *Tenenturne pariter servare omnia ieiunia Ecclesiae universalis, quin gaudere valeant amplissima dispensatione nuper data degentibus in America latina ex decreto S. Congregationis Neg. EE. EE. die 6 Iulii 1900?*

Et Emi Patres in Palatio Vaticano coadunati propositis dubiis die 11 Iunii 1901 respondendum mandarunt :

Ad I·· *Affirmative, nisi quis pertineat ad ritum a S. Sede approbatum, qui alia lingua utatur, iuxta Decretum huius S. C. diei 18 Augusti 1868, sed supplicandum SSmo, ut in privata recitatione vulgari lingua uti liceat.*

Ad II™ *Negative, ad effectum fruendi privilegio Sabbatino.*

Ad III·· *Supplicandum SSmo, ut Confratres B. Mariae Virginis a Monte Carmelo, quod attinet ad ieiunia, uti valeant indulto dioecesano, facta Confessariis facultate commutandi singulis petentibus abstinentiam feriae IV et Sabbati in alia opera: atque utrumque valere pro omni regione declarare dignetur. Contrariis quibuscumque, ac praesertim Capuana 3 Decembris 1892, minime obstantibus.*

De quibus facta relatione SSmo Dno Nostro Leoni Pp. XIII in audientia habita ab infrascripto Cardinali Praefecto die 14 Iu-

iiii 1901, Sanctitas Sua Emorum Patrum resolutiones ratas habuit et confirmavit, et benigne annuere precibus in dubio I et III expressis dignata est.

Datum Romae ex Secretaria eiusdem S. Congregationis die 14 Iunii 1901.

S. **CARD**. CRETONI, *Praefectus*.

L. * S.

f **FRANCISCUS SOGARO** Archiep. Amiden., *Secretarius*.

URBIS et ORBIS. Decretum quo Sodalitates *Viae crucis viventis* approbantur.

Pietati Christifidelium fovendae nihil est tam aptum, nihil tam efficax, quam frequens Dominicae Passionis meditatio, in qua dum ipsi recolunt quanta Verbum Dei Caro factum pro nobis pati dignatum est, eorum corda ad poenitentiam excitantur, et ad redamandum Christum Iesum vehementer infiammantur.

Iam vero inter plura quae id praestant pia exercitia, illud procul dubio prae ceteris eminet, quod a *Via Crucis* nuncupatur, a S. Leonardo e Portu Mauritio primitus invectum, et in universa catholica Ecclesia tam salubriter propagatum.

Quoniam vero plures vel occupationibus distenti, vel valetudine laborantes, prohibentur quominus integro huiusmodi pio Exercitio vacent, nonnulli pietatis zelo praestantes viri, ne spiritualium fructum ex eodem Exercitio manantium copia deperdatur, Sodalitates quasdam instituere excogitarunt ex quatuordecim sociis constantes, qui singuli unam quotidie sibi attributum ex quatuordecim stationibus meditando peragant, ad instar Sodalitatum *Rosarii   Viventis*.

Hinc Ssmo Dno Nostro Leoni PP. XIII preces humiliter sunt delatae, ut praedictas Sodalitates, earumque leges approbare, et nonnullas sociis indulgentias tribuere dignaretur.

Has porro preces, relatas in audientia habita die 16 Augusti 1901 ab infrascripto Cardinali Praefecto S. Congregationis Indulgentiis Sacrisque Reliquiis praepositae, Eadem Sanctitas Sua peramanter excepit, Sodalitatesque Viae Crucis *Viventis* summopere commendans approbavit, earumdemque leges, prout

Appendix 4

Translation of pg. 120
from the Sacred Congregation of Indulgences,
confirmed by His Holiness Pope Leo XII,
on the Third condition of the Sabbatine Privilege
June 14, 1901

DECREE: *on behalf of the pious works of the Confraternity of the Blessed Virgin Mary of Mount Carmel of Guatemala for obtaining the Sabbatine Privilege.*

The Archbishop of Guatemala presents to this Sacred Congregation of Indulgences the following questions, which refer to the prescribed pious works directed to the attainment of the privilege called the "Sabbatine."

I. Is it necessary that the members of the Confraternity of the Blessed Virgin Mary of Mount Carmel recite the Little Office as it appears in the Roman Breviary even if the majority of the people do not know well the Latin language?

II. Are the members of the Confraternity who do not know how to read and are, therefore, bound to abstain on Wednesdays and Saturdays also bound to abstain on Fridays, as indeed all the faithful are bound who are not Latin American?

III. Are they likewise bound to observe all the fast days of the universal Church, or do they enjoy the full dispensation recently given to the people of Latin America by the Sacred Congregation on July 6, 1900?

The Eminent Fathers meeting in the Apostolic Palace on June 11, 1901 ordered the following responses to be given:

To the first: *Affirmative, unless it pertains to an approved rite allowing for another language by the Holy See according to the Decree of this Sacred Congregation given on December 18, 1868, that only by an appeal to the Sacred Congregation may the private recitation in the vernacular language be permitted.*

To the second: *Negative, with regard to the purpose of obtaining the Sabbatine privilege.*

To the third: *By an appeal to the Holy See, as pertains to fasting, confessors who have received the faculty by diocesan indult may, for the members of the Confraternity of the Blessed Virgin of Mount Carmel, commute the Wednesday and Saturday abstinence into other works: and this is said to be effective for any other region: notwithstanding anything to the contrary, especially what was given at Capua on December 3, 1892.*

In an audience given to the Cardinal Prefect of this Congregation by our most holy Lord, Leo XIII, His Holiness considered and confirmed the resolutions of the Fathers and graciously granted his explicit assent to petitions I and III.

Given in Rome by the Secretary of this Sacred Congregation on June 14, 1901.

Pius X

Birth name	Giuseppe Melchiorre Sarto
Papacy began	August 4, 1903
Papacy ended	August 20, 1914
Predecessor	Leo XIII
Successor	Benedict XV
Born	June 2, 1835 Riese, Italy
Died	August 20, 1914, age 79

Coat of Arms of Pope Pius X

Pope St. Pius X: Giuseppe Melchiorre Sarto

Papacy: 1903 – 1914

Summary of Contents:

1). Acta Apostolicae Sedis of Pius X: By a Decree of the Holy Office of December 16, 1910, granted by Pius X, the substitution of the medal for the Scapular was granted. According to this Decree, "in wearing the medal one participates, as with the Scapular proper, in all the Indulgences and in all the privileges, not excepting that called the Sabbatine Privilege of the Scapular of Mount Carmel." But the same Decree begins with the following words: "As the holy Scapular contributes efficaciously to the progress of the spiritual life among the faithful and is in great favor amongst them, the Holy Father desires that the habitual form (cloth) be maintained." (Act. Ap. Sedis, III, p. 22-23) The official Document, taken from the A.A.S., is in Latin and is found on the following page.

(Information taken from: "Catholic Monitor,": Saint Dominic's Prophecy, Fatima and the Scapular)

ACTA

APOSTOLICAE SEDIS

COMMENTARIUM OFFICIALE

ANNUS III. - VOLUMEN III.

ROMAE

TYPIS POLYGLOTTIS VATICANIS

MDGCCGXI

rum, apostolicam benedictionem vobis omnibus, Venerabilis Frater et dilecti filii, amantissime impertimus.

Datum Romae apud S. Petrum, die VII mensis Ianuarii anno MCMXI, Pontificatus Nostri octavo.

PTUS PP. X.

S. CONGREGATIO S. OFFICII
(SECTIO DE INDULGENTIIS)

I.

DE ABSOLUTIONE SEU BENEDICTIONE PAPALI TERTIARIIS ACCIPIENDA.

DECRETUM

Die 15 Decembris 1910.

SSmus N. D. Pius divina Providentia PP. X, in Audientia R. P. D. Adsessori S. Officii impertita, preces a nonnullis Tertiariorum Sodalitatum Moderatoribus pluries porrecta, benigne excipiens, quo facilius Tertiarii ex utroque sexu, cuiuscumque Ordinis, iis non exceptis, qui vitam communem agunt, diebus statutis generalem Absolutionem seu Papalem Benedictionem recipere valeant, clementer indulsit, ut, quoties ipsi ad hunc finem una simul convenerint, et Sacerdos, cuius est illam impertiri, quacumque ex causa, abfuerit, eamdem Absolutionem seu Benedictionem accipere possint a quolibet Sacerdote, sive saeculari, sive regulari, -qui ad sacramentales confessiones audiendas sit approbatus. Praesenti in perpetuum valituro. Contrariis quibuscumque non obstantibus.

Aloisius Giambene,
Substitutus pro Indulgentiis.

L $ S.

II.

DE METALLICO NUMISMATE PRO LUBITU FIDELIUM
SACRIS SCAPULARIBUS EX PANNO SUFFICIENDO.

DECRETUM

Cum sacra, quae vocant, scapularia ad fidelium devotionem fovendam sanctiorisque vitae proposita in eis excitanda maxime conferre compertum sit, ut pius eis nomen dandi mos in dies magis invalescat,

The Brown Scapular of Our Lady of Mount Carmel

SSmus D. N. D. Pius divina providentia PP. X, etsi vehementer exoptet ut eadem, quo hucusque modo consueverunt, fideles deferre prosequantur, plurium tamen ad Se delatis votis ex animo obsecundans, praehabito Emorum Patrum Cardinalium Inquisitorum Generalium suffragio, in Audientia R. P. D. Adsessori huius Supremae Sacrae Congregationis Sancti Officii, die 16 Decembris anni currentis, impertita, benigne decernere dignatus est:

Omnibus fidelibus, tam uni quam pluribus veri nominis atque a Sancta Sede probatis scapularibus (exceptis quae Tertiorum Ordinum sunt propria), per regularem, ut aiunt, impositionem iam adscriptis aut in posterum adscribendis, licere posthac pro ipsis, sive uno sive pluribus, scapularibus ex panno, unicum numisma ex metallo seu ad collum seu aliter, decenter tamen super propriam personam, deferre, quo, servatis propriis cuiusque eorum legibus, favores omnes spirituales *(Sabbatino,* quod dicunt, scapularis B. M. V. de Monte Carmelo *privilegio* non excepto) omnesque indulgentias singulis adnexas participare ac lucrari possint ac valeant;

Huius numismatis partem rectam, SSmi D. N. I. C. suum sacratissimum Cor ostendentis, aversam, Bmae Virginis Mariae effigiem referre debere;

Idem benedictum esse oportere tot distinctis benedictionibus quot sunt scapularia regulariter imposita, queis, pro lubitu petentium, sufiici velit;

Singulas has, demum, benedictiones impertiri posse *unico crucis signo,* vel in ipso adscriptionis actu, statim post absolutam regularem scapularis impositionem, vel etiam serius, pro petentium opportunitate, non interest an servato vel non diversarum adscriptionum ordine, nec quanto post temporis ab ipsis, a quovis Sacerdote, etiam ab adscribere distincto, qui respectiva scapularia benedicendi sive ordinaria sive delegata facultate polleat, firmis ceteroquin primitivae facultatis limitibus, clausulis et conditionibus.

Contrariis quibuscumque, etiam specialissima mentione dignis, non obstantibus.

Datum Romae, ex Aedibus S. Officii, die 16 Decembris 1910.

ALOISIUS GIAMBENB,
Substitutus pro Indulgentiis.

L.)Sj S.

692

Appendix 4

Benedict XV

Birth name	Giacomo della Chiesa
Papacy began	September 3, 1914
Papacy ended	January 22, 1922
Predecessor	Pius X
Successor	Pius XI
Born	November 21, 1854 Genoa, Italy
Died	January 22, 1922, (age 67) Apostolic Palace, Rome, Italy

Arms of Pope Benedict
XV

Pope Benedict XV: Giacomo Della Chiesa

Papacy: 1914 – 1922

Summary of Contents:

---

1). *Letter* of Pope Benedict XV: Il 27 Aprile, 1915, to Cardinal P. Gasparri, May 5, 1917: *"The Pope's efforts to stop the War."* This Letter, in English is found on the following page. It was written to the Cardinal, in which the Holy Father recalled his repeated pleas for peace from the beginning of World War I; he authorized the title of "Queen of Peace," to be inserted in the Litany of the Blessed Virgin, and made his ultimate appeal to the Mother of God for an end to the War. It is interesting to note, that after Benedict XV made his ultimate plea to the Mother of God, she answered him by appearing eight days later at Fatima, Portugal, on May 13, 1917, telling the children, Lucia, Jacinta, and Francisco, to pray the Rosary every day to obtain peace for the world <u>and the end of the war.</u> It was at her final appearance at Fatima, October 13, 1917, that she appeared during the Miracle of the Sun, dressed in the habit of Carmel, holding down to the world, the Scapular in her hand. (This Letter is taken from <u>Papal Teachings, Our Lady,</u> Daughters of St. Paul, Boston, 1961, p. 192)

2). The *Osservatore Romano* Newspaper, dated July 18, 1917, citing the *Allocution* of Benedict XV to the Pupils of the Pontifical Seminary in Rome, in which His Holiness exhorted the Seminarians to *"arm themselves with Scapular of Our Lady of Mount Carmel, for the protection of the Virgin, which continues even after death."* The article is found at the top of the page of the *Osservatore Romano*, under the main title of *"La Cronaca Di Roma,"* *Il Pontif. Seminario Maggiore e Minore dal Santo Padre.* It is written in Italian.

3). The *Osservatore Romano* Newspaper, dated July 28, 1917, citing the *Allocution* of Pope Benedict XV to the Third Order Carmelites, in which he refers to taking the words of the Prophet Isaiah: "clothe me with the garments of salvation," remembering especially, the powerful aid the Virgin bestows beyond the tomb, to the "incarceration"of Purgatory, for all those, who in life, wore her heavenly badge with the proper disposition. The article is found in the *Osserevatore Romano*, under the title: *Cronaca di Roma; I Terziari Carmelitani della Traspontina ricevuti in udienza dal Santo Padre."* It is written in Italian.

(Translated and paraphrased from <u>Lo Scapolare</u> 2, p. 67; Soul Magazine, "Why the Blessed Virgin Mary came to Fatima," Warren H. Carroll, Ph.D, May-June, 1995, pp. 4,5)

When man has hardened his heart and hate has over-run the earth, when fire and sword convulse the world and make it resound with clash of arms and of wailing, when human plans have proved misleading, and when all social well-being is upset, faith and history point to Mary as the only refuge, the all powerful intercessor, the Mediatrix of all grace . . . therefore, let us say with sure trust: Queen of Peace, pray for us!

(*Conclusion.*)

QUEEN OF PEACE

Letter *Il 27 Aprile* 1915, to Cardinal P. Gasparri, May 5, 1917.

(*The Pope's efforts to stop the War.*)

263
(37,
46,
169)
. . . And since all the graces which God deigns to be-stow in pity upon men are dispensed through the most holy Virgin, We urge that more than ever in this terrible hour, the trusting petitions of her most afflicted children be directed to the august Mother of God.

Hence we direct Your Eminence to make known to all the bishops of the world that it is our fervent desire that mankind turn to the Sacred Heart of Jesus—the Throne of Grace—and that recourse to this Throne be made through Mary. Accordingly We ordain that beginning with the first day of June this year, there be placed in the Litany of the Blessed Virgin the invocation: *Queen of Peace* pray for us. . . . We have so authorized the Ordinaries to add it temporarily by the decree of the Sacred Congregation of Extraordinary Ecclesiastical Affairs by date of November 16, 1915.

264
(169)
From every corner of the earth—from the majestic churches and the humble chapels; from the mansions of the rich as well as from the huts of the poor; from wherever dwells a faithful soul; from the bloodstained battlefields and war swept seas, may this pious and ardent

Appendix 4

invocation arise to Mary, the Mother of Mercy who is all-powerful in grace! To Mary may be brought each anguished cry of mothers and wives, each tear of innocent children, each longing of generous hearts! May her loving and most merciful solicitude be moved to obtain for this convulsed world the peace so greatly desired! And may the ages yet to come remember the efficacy of Mary's intercession and the greatness of her blessings to her suppliants!

(*Blessing.*)

PATRON OF A HAPPY DEATH

Letter *Inter sodalicia*, to the Association for a Happy Death, May 22, 1918.

Among the associations that promote devotion to the **265** Blessed Virgin Mary and at the same time contribute to the *(173)* spiritual interests of the faithful the association which bears the title of "Our Lady of a Happy Death," recently founded· by the Fathers of Saint Mary of Tinchebray, certainly occupies a most honorable place if one considers the purpose which animates it and its already large diffusion throughout the world with abundance of fruit.

Those who take part in it, as the principles and rules **266** of this society show, have the following aims: to venerate *(173)* the Virgin of Sorrows and to do all in their power to have her honored by everyone; to offer God the merits of the prayers and sufferings of the same Virgin who stood at the foot of the cross of Jesus; trusting in these merits to obtain for themselves and for others the grace to persevere in faith and in the Christian life or at least to return to these; and, above all, to obtain the grace of a happy death in the love of Christ on whom eternal happiness depends.

The choosing and invoking of Our Lady of Sorrows **267** as patroness of a happy death is in full conformity with *(22,* Catholic Doctrine and with the pious sentiment of the *Al-*

7. *Our Lady*

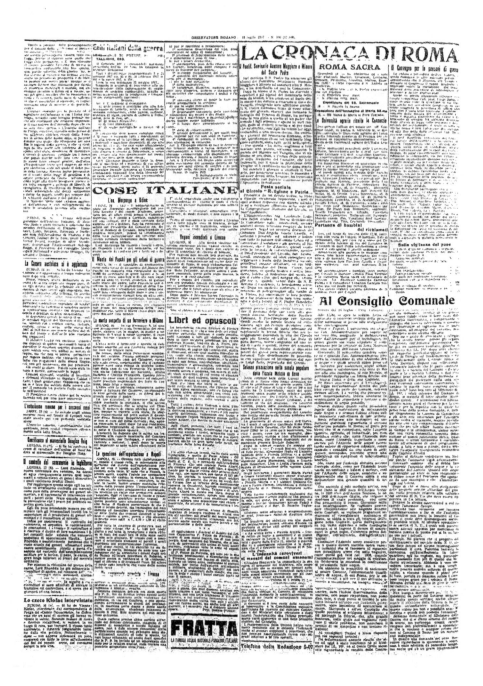

OSSERVATORE ROMANO — 28 luglio 1917 - N. 156 (17.218)

Cronaca di Roma

ROMA SACRA

Informazioni e ultimi dispacci

Nostre Informazioni

Piccola cronaca

Le ultime della guerra

Il conflitto italo-austriaco

Teatri ed Arte

Olio puro d'Oliva

FUGASSA OTTAVIO (Produttore)
ALASSIO (Liguria)
Si cercano Rappresentanti

Grand Café

E' il ritrovo più elegante di Parigi

LA FOSFATINA FALIÈRES

Pius XI

Birth name	Ambrogio Damiano Achille Ratti
Papacy began	February 6, 1922
Papacy ended	February 10, 1939
Predecessor	Benedict XV
Successor	Pius XII
Born	May 31, 1857 Desio, Italy
Died	February 10, 1939, age 81 Apostolic Palace, Vatican City

Coat of Arms of Pope Pius XI

700

Pope Pius XI: Ambrogio Damiano Achille Ratti

Papacy: 1922 – 1939

Summary of Contents:

1). *Acta Apostolicae Sedis* of Pope Pius XI, *Letter, Petis tu quidem*, to Father Elias Magennis, Superior General of the Carmelites, dated March 18, 1922. (*Sixth centenary of the Sabbatine Privilege – The Confraternities of Our Lady of Mt. Carmel.*) This *Letter* of His Holiness commemorates, at the closing of the sixth centennial, the universal diffusion in the Church of the "Sabbatine Privilege – to the faithful throughout the Catholic world, the Devotion to Our Lady of Mt. Carmel... confirming, by the authority of the Holy Father, the authenticity of the Sabbatine Privilege.

The *Acta Apostolicae Sedis* contains the *Letter* of Pius XI in Latin. Following the official Document in Latin, is the English translation of the *Letter*, taken from the book: "Papal Teachings, Our Lady," translated by the Daughters of St. Paul.

(Taken from Papal Teachings, Our Lady, Daughters of St. Paul, Boston, Mass, 1961, p. 204)

ACTA

APOSTOLICAE SEDIS

COMMENTARIUM OFFICIALE

ANNUS XIV— VOLUMEN XIV

ROMAE

TYPIS POLYGLOTTIS VATICANIS

MCMXXII

EPISTOLAE

I

AD R. P. ELIAM MAGEN NIS, MODERATOREM GENERALEM ORDINIS CARMELITARUM, LABENTE SAECULO SEXTO EX QUO « PRIVILEGIUM SABBATINUM » VULGATUM EST, RELIGIONEM IN B. M. V. DE MONTE CARMELO IMPENSE INCULCAT.

Dilecte fili, salutem et apostolicam benedictionem. — Petis tu quidem a Nobis ut, labente saeculo sexto ex quo *Sabbatinum Privilegium* vulgari coepit in Ecclesia, religionem in Virginem Mariam a Monte Carmelo et laicorum sodalitates quae a Virgine eadem nuncupantur, omnibus quotquot sunt per orbem catholicis commendemus. Hisce iisdem litteris ac libenter admodum id facimus. Almam enim Dei Matrem, quam a pueris amamus impense, placet hoc etiam demereri pietatis testimonio atque ea auspice initia ordiri Pontificatus Nostri. Nec diu commorandum Nobis est in commendandis sodalitatibus, quas et Virgo ipsa commendat liberalitate sua, et Praedecessores Nostri plurimis cumularunt gratiis, et actuosa caritas Religiosorum Carmelitarum tam late per orbem tamque ubere cum fructu propagavit. Satius ducimus eos hortari qui sodalitatibus iisdem nomen dederunt, ut perseveranti studio haereant iis omnibus quae praescripta sunt ad lucrandas concessas Indulgentias in primisque maximas illas quae Sabbatinae dicuntur. Diligentes enim se diligit Virgo, nec quisquam sperare iure potest se eam habiturum adiutricem in morte, nisi in vita eius inierit gratiam .tum abstinendo a culpa, tum quidpiam praestando quod cedat in eiusdem honorem.

De delatis officiis memorem tibi profitemur animum, ac caelestium conciliatricem munerum Nostraeque testem benevolentiae, apostolicam benedictionem tibi, dilecte fili, religiosis viris quibus praees iisque omnibus qui sunt ex sodalitatibus quas supra memoravimus, peramanter in Domino impertimus.

Datum Romae apud Sanctum Petrum, die xvm martii anno MCMXXII, Pontificatus Nostri primo.

PIUS PP. XI

Appendix 4

SABBATINE PRIVILEGE

Letter *Petis tu quidem*, to Father Elias Magennis, Superior General of the Carmelites, March 18, 1922.

(*Sixth centenary of the Sabbatine Privilege.—The Confraternities of Our Lady of Mt. Carmel.*)

281
(128.
136,
173)
You ask Us to recommend—at the closing of the sixth centennial commemorating the universal diffusion in the Church of the "Sabbatine Privilege"—to the faithful throughout the Catholic world the devotion to Our Lady of Mount Carmel, and the sodalities for lay people, which take their name from the Virgin herself. We willingly do so with this Letter. In fact, with this attestation of devotion We wish to draw down upon us the good will of the great Mother of God, whom We have greatly loved since our infancy, and thus place under her care the beginning of Our Pontificate.

We do not deem it necessary to be lengthy in recommending the sodalities which the Virgin herself recommends with her liberality, and which Our Predecessors enriched with many favors, and which the zealous devotion of the Carmelite Fathers have diffused everywhere with such copious fruits. Instead We believe it more opportune to exhort those enrolled in these sodalities to observe, with persevering fervor, the conditions required to gain the various indulgences granted and above all those most important indulgences which are called "sabbatine." The Virgin, in fact, has a predilection for those who love her, nor can anyone rightfully hope to have her assistance at the point of death if, during life, he did not merit this assistance both by avoiding sin, as well as by doing that which would honor her (a).

(*Blessing.*)

281a *Diligentes enim se diligit Virgo, nec quisquam sperare iure potest se eam habiturum adjutricem in morte, nisi in vita eius inierit gratiam tum abstinendo a culpa, tum quid piam præstando quod cedat in eiusdem honorem*

705

Pius XII

Birth name	Eugenio Maria Giuseppe Giovanni Pacelli
Papacy began	March 2, 1939
Papacy ended	October 9, 1958
Predecessor	Pius XI
Successor	John XXIII
Born	March 2, 1876 Rome, Italy
Died	October 9, 1958 (aged 82) Castel Gandolfo, Italy

Pope Pius' Coat of Arms
featured a dove, a symbol
of peace

Venerable Pope Pius XII: Eugenio Maria Giuseppe Giovanni Pacelli
Papacy: 1939 – 1958

Summary of Contents:

---

1). The *Letter* of Pope Pius XII, *Neminem profecto*, to the Superior General of the Carmelites, February 11, 1950. *The Scapular of Our Lady of Mount Carmel*. This *Letter* of His Holiness commemorates the anticipated anniversary of the Seventh Centenary of the institution of the Scapular of Our Lady of Mt. Carmel. He states that *"the Sacred Scapular is certainly a sign and guarantee of the protection of the Mother of God."* His Holiness is also very quick to warn against those who wear it and think they can *"in sloth and indolence of spirit attain eternal life..."* Pius XII, again, has recognized and confirmed the authenticity of the Sabbatine Privilege in the closing paragraph of this *Letter.* (This *translation* is taken from Papal Teachings, Our Lady, Daughters of St. Paul, Boston, Mass, 1961, p. 288)

2). *Acta Apostolicae Sedis*, Pope Pius XII, *Letter, Neminem profecto*, dated February 11, 1950. The text of this official Document is in Latin. The English translation is in the above Document.

3). *Acta Apostolicae Sedis*, Pope Pius XII, *Letter*, dated June 30, 1951, *"The Manifold Manifestations,"* a *Letter from the Holy Father, (written in English), on the occasion of the transference of the remains of Saint Simon Stock from France to Aylesford, England in July, 1951*; (during the seventh centenary of the institution of the Scapular of Our Lady of Mount Carmel). In this *Letter*, Pius XII both confirmed and acknowledged the tradition of the Scapular Vision in these words: *Seven hundred years have passed since according to the sacred traditions of the Carmelite family, Simon Stock was vouchsafed the vision of Our Lady of Mount Carmel....*

4). *Acta Apostolicae Sedis*, Pope Pius XII, *Letter: "Septimo Expleto Saeculo,"* dated July 6, 1951, is a letter which the Holy Father wrote approving the national Marian Congress in Brazil. The Congress was held in July, 1951 on the occasion of the seventh centenary of the institution of the Scapular of Our Lady of Mount Carmel. The "pilgrimage of Mary" mentioned in the document is a statue of Our Lady of Mount Carmel which was flown all over Brazil by the Carmelites. Below is an excerpt from this *Letter* is in English. The Latin text follows:

....now it is Our firm hope that by reason of your presence and that of the other bishops, by reason of the fervent participation of the people under the leadership of the civil authorities, the coming centenary celebration will happily prove to be a magnificent triumph for the Virgin of Carmel and also be a powerful influence for the perfection of souls by means of the Scapular Devotion.". (Taken from a translation found in Mary, Vol. 20, No. 4, July, August, 1959, p. 56)

Venerable Pope Pius XII (cont.)

5). *Acta Apostolicae Sedis, Pope Pius XII, Letter,* dated October 29, 1951, *naming Our Lady of Mount Carmel patroness of the city of Purchena in Spain.* The official Document of this *Letter* found in the A.A.S., is on the following pages in its entirety, in Latin. Below is an excerpt, translated in English, taken from the *Letter* of Pius XII:

"Through the ages the devotion of the Spanish race toward the Blessed Virgin, a devotion warm, fervent, and active has shown itself in many ways. In this devotion the Order that honors the Virgin Mary under the title "Ornament of Carmel" or "of Mount Carmel" occupies a special place, because of its great antiquity, but even more because of the special privileges promised by Our Lady to the souls suffering in the fire in Purgatory."

The official Document of this *Letter* found in the A.A.S., is on the following pages in its entirety, in Latin. (The above translation is taken from <u>Mary,</u> Vol. 20, No. 4, July, August, 1959, p.58)

6). *Acta Apostolicae Sedis,* Pope Pius XII, *Letter to Third Order of Discalced Carmelites at Malabar, India,* dated October 30, 1955. This *Letter* is found in its entirety, in Latin, in the following pages under the A.A.S. Below is an excerpt, translated in English, from this *Letter* of Pius XII:

"And from heaven, may the Blessed Virgin Mary, the ornament of Carmel, whom you cherish so much and love so exceedingly, be your support. Turn not your eyes away from the light of this star, turn not away your mind and heart. Look to Mary. In dangers, in difficulties, in doubts, think of Mary. Call on Mary. May she not be absent from your lips, may she not be absent from your heart. At all times keep before your minds the words of Saint Bernard: "Following after her, you wander not; beseeching her, you lose not hope; thinking of her, you go not astray. With her support, you do not fall; with her favor, you attain the goal." In the apostolic labors and the difficulties of your sacred ministry have recourse to her most powerful protection; by her intercession with her divine Son, you will certainly have the experience that there is never anything which with the help of divine grace you are not able to bring to a happy conclusion."

(The above translation is taken from <u>Mary,</u> Vol. 20, No. 4, July, August, 1959, p. 58)

7). *Message,* Pope Pius XII, *To the Carmelite Pilgrims at Lourdes, July 2, 1958, the Feast of Our Lady of Mt. Carmel, on the occasion of the centenary of the last apparition of Our Lady of Lourdes, July 16, 1858.* The final apparition of Our Blessed Mother to Bernadette of Lourdes, was on the Feast of Our Lady of Mount Carmel, July 16, 1858. The text of the *Letter* is in English. The Pope's *Message,* written in French, was read by Bishop Theas of Lourdes during the Solemn Pontifical Mass in the Basilica of St. Pius X, July 16, 1958.

(Taken from <u>Mary,</u> Vol. 19, No. 6, November, December, 1958, p. 36)

PAPAL TEACHINGS

OUR LADY

Selected and Arranged

by

THE BENEDICTINE MONKS OF SOLESMES

Translated by

THE DAUGHTERS OF ST. PAUL

ST. PAUL EDITIONS

est need surrounding us a just solution may be found for disputes, and that a firm and free peace will finally dawn resplendent for the Church and for all nations.

451
(37,
132)
Some years ago, as all will remember, while the late war was still raging, when human means showed themselves to be uncertain and inadequate to that terrible conflagration, We addressed our fervent prayers to the all-merciful Redeemer, invoking the powerful patronage of the Immaculate Heart of Mary.

And even as Our Predecessor of immortal memory, Leo XIII, at the dawn of the twentieth century saw fit to consecrate the whole human race to the Most Sacred Heart of Jesus, so We have likewise, as the representative of the whole human family which He redeemed (a), desired to dedicate it in turn to the Immaculate Heart of the Virgin Mary.

It is Our wish, consequently, that wherever the opportunity suggests itself, this consecration be made in the various dioceses, as well as in each of the parishes and families. And we are confident that abundant blessings and favors from heaven will surge forth from this private and public consecration.

THE SCAPULAR OF MOUNT CARMEL

Letter *Neminem profecto,* to the Superior General of the Carmelites, February 11, 1950.

452
(136)
No one is ignorant how much love of the Virgin Mother of God helps to quicken Catholic faith and improve morals, more especially through those forms of devotion which enlighten men's minds with heavenly doctrine, and incite their wills to practice Christian virtues. Among such forms of devotion the one first to be

451a Cf. above, no. 373 ff.

recorded is that of the Sacred Scapular of the Carmelites, which, adapting itself through its simplicity to the character of every one, is largely diffused among the faithful and produces many good fruits.

For this reason We have been glad to hear that as the Seventh Centenary of the institution of this scapular of the divine Mother of Mount Carmel approaches, the Carmelite brethren (calced and discalced) have decided to hold solemn celebrations in honor of the Blessed Virgin Mary. We, who have always nourished an ardent love toward the Holy Mother of God and since our early childhood have been admitted into the Confraternity of the said Scapular, do heartily recommend this devout project, and We confidently hope that, with God's favor, it will produce abundant spiritual fruits. Indeed, this is not a small matter; it is a question of the attainment of eternal life in virtue of the most Blessed Virgin's promise; therefore, it is an extremely important project, on which it behooves all concerned to proceed with prudence.   453 *(150, 158)*

As a Marian vestment, the Sacred Scapular is certainly a sign and guarantee of the protection of the Mother of God. However, let not those who wear it think that they can in sloth and indolence of spirit attain eternal life, for the Apostle thus openly admonishes: "Work out your salvation in fear and trembling" (a). Therefore, all Carmelites—(whether in cloisters of the first or second order, in the regular or secular third order, or in the confraternities) who belong, by a special particular bond of love, to the family that honors itself with the name of the most Blessed Virgin should recognize in this badge of the said Virgin a pattern of humility and chastity; in the very form of the vestment itself they should recognize an epitome of modesty and simplicity; above all they should see in the vestment itself, which they wear day and night, an eloquent expression of the prayers with which they ask for   454 *(50, 131, 150)*

454a Phil. 2:12.

10. *Our Lady*

divine assistance; finally they should recognize in it an invitation to that consecration to the Immaculate Heart of the Virgin Mary which We recently earnestly recommended.

On her part, the most holy Mother will not fail to intercede with God that her children who in purgatory are expiating their sins may, at the earliest possible moment, reach the Eternal Fatherland in accordance with the so-called Sabattine Privilege (b).

A MARIAN CENTURY

Letter *Cum audiverimus Romam,* to the Superior General of the Jesuits, April 15, 1950.

(History of Marian congregations; their object, sanctity, deep formation ...)

455
(131,   ... Finally must be given a total and constant obedi-
154)   ence and homage to Christ our Lord and His Church, under the leadership and example of the most Blessed Virgin Mary. In that we recognize the happiest omen of our century, a century which may well be called "Marian," because it has experienced the effective protection and powerful patronage of the Mother of God.

(Invitation to expand Marian sodalities.—One should be particularly watchful about inner formation.)

456
(125)   This sound spiritual formation and its consequent Apostolic activity must be of an outstandingly Marian character; for this inclination of the mind to honor and love the most Blessed Virgin, which has ever been professed by your sodalities, must be always and everywhere the distinctive and obvious feature of true faith and doctrine.

(Sodalities should be established in every quarter.)

454b See above, no. 281 ff.

Appendix 4

MARIAN HERITAGE

All. on the canonization of St. Joan of France, May 457
28, 1950.   (125)

*(The great number of French pilgrims testify to the
faith of this nation.—It is necessary to imitate St. Joan.)*

... The deep penetration of Joan of France into the
life of the Blessed Mother of God, her total consecration
to Mary, the resplendent reflection of Marian sentiments
and virtues in her life and in her Order of. the Annunciation give in our days to her example and rules the appearance of a new message to France. In the difficult spiritual
struggles of our times wherein believers in Christ and
those who deny Him are confused in the multitude, devotion to the Mother of God is an infallible touchstone for
distinguishing the one from the other.

Catholics of France, your history so entirely interwo- 458
ven with Mary's graces and favors compels you, in a very *(123,*
special way, to watch over the integrity and purity of *159)*
your Marian inheritance. Defend it against those who
have broken the bonds with your ancient and glorious traditions, by your courageous perseverance in the pursuit of
your most sacred interests and the example of your respect for just laws and the legitimate order of the State.

You are about to leave these scenes where you witnessed the triumph of your Saint; you are about to return
to your country which, so many times, has felt the effects
of the Blessed Virgin Mary's powerful intercession and
protection. Let the desire of your hearts, then, the ardent
prayer of your souls ascend to the blue and luminous
heavens: "Holy Mary, make us strong in the struggle
against thy enemies." *Virgo, Sacrata, da mihi virtutem
contra hostes tuos* (a).

*(Part which women took in the story of France; their
mission at the present time.)*

458a Office of Our Lady.

ACTA

APOSTOLICAE SEDIS

COMMENTARIUM OFFICIALE

ANNUS XXXXII - SERIES II - VOL. XVII

TYPIS POLYGLOTTIS VATICANIS

M · DCCCC · L

Appendix 4

II

AD REVMOS P. KILIANUM LYNCH, PRIOREM GENERALEM ORDINIS FRATRUM BEA-
TAE MARIAE VIRGINIS DE MONTE CARMELO ET P. SILVERIUM A SANCTA THE-
RESIA, PRAEPOSITUM GENERALEM FRATRUM DI SC ALCE ATORUM BEATAE MA-
RIAE VIRGINIS DE MONTE CARMELO : SEPTIMO EXEUNTE SAECULO AB INSTI-
TUTIONE SACRI SCAPULARI S CARMELITARUM.

PIUS PP. XII

Dilecti filii, salutem et Apostolicam Benedictionem. — Neminem profecto latet, quantum ad excitandam catholicam fidem moresque emendan-
dos conferat amor erga Beatissimam Virginem Dei Matrem, iis praesertim devotionis significationibus, quibus prae ceteris et mentes caelesti
doctrina illustrari et animi in christiana vita excolenda exacui videntur. Hisce est in primis accensenda Sacri Scapularis Carmelitarum devotio, quae, sua ipsius simplicitate omnium ingenio accommodata, inter
Christi fideles cum salutarium fructuum incremento quam latissime per-
vulgata est. Quapropter laeto admodum animo intelleximus, septimo vergente saeculo ab institutione istius Scapularis Deiparae de Monte Carmelo, fratres Carmelitas, quum Calceatos tum Excalceatos, consilium
iniisse, ut sacra sollemnia in honorem ipsius Beatae Mariae Virginis
summo studio concelebrentur. Quae quidem pia incepta, pro constanti
Nostro erga almam Dei Matrem amore proque etiam Nostra in Confraternitatem ipsius Scapularis a puero cooptatione, perlibenter commen-
damus, iisque uberem bonorum copiam a Deo ominamur. Neque enim agitur de re parvi momenti, sed de vita aeterna capessenda ex ea, quae traditur, promissione Beatissimae Virginis : agitur videlicet de summo omnium negotio deque modo ipsum tute peragendi. Est quidem Sacrum
Scapulare, veluti habitus Marianus, protectionis Deiparae signum et pignus ; sed ne putaverint hac veste induti pigritia vel socordia spirituali
se esse salutem aeternam adepturos, monente Apostolo : « cum metu et
tremore vestram salutem operamini » (Phil., II, **12**). Omnes igitur Carmelitae, qui, sive in claustris primi et secundi Ordinis, sive in tertio Ordine regulari vel saeculari, sive in confraternitatibus, ad unam Beatissimae Matris familiam peculiari amoris vinculo pertinent, sibi habeant
in memoriali ipsius Virginis speculum humilitatis et castitatis ; habeant
modestiae et simplicitatis breviarium in ipsa vestis ingenua structura ;
habeant potissimum in eadem veste, quam die noctuque induunt, elo-
quenti symbolo significatas preces, quibus divinum implorant auxilium ;

715

habeant denique illam consecrationem sacratissimo Cordi Virginis Immaculatae, quam nuper quoque impense commendavimus. Nec desinet profecto piissima Mater, ut filii sui, in Purgatorio admissa expiantes, quam primum, ipsa quidem apud Deum intercedente, iuxta traditum illud, quod vocant, Privilegium Sabbatinum, aeternam patriam consequantur. Superni interea praesidii auxiliique in auspicium, inque peculiaris Nostrae caritatis pignus, Apostolicam Benedictionem vobis, dilecti filii, universoque Carmelitarum Ordini amantissime in Domino impertimus.

Datum Romae apud Sanctum Petrum, die xi mensis Februarii, in Apparitione Beatae Mariae Virginis Immaculatae, anno MDCCCCL, Pontificatus Nostri undecimo.

PIUS PP. XII

III

AD. REVV. PATRES SODALES SOCIETATIS IESU, QUI IN COMMENTARIOS CONSCRIBENDOS ((LA CIVILTÀ CATTOLICA)) INCUMBUNT : SAECULO EXEUNTE AB IPSO COMMENTARIO INITO.

PIUS PP. XII

Dilecti filii, salutem et Apostolicam Benedictionem. — Vix undecimus elapsus est annus, ex quo in ipso limine Nostri Pontificatus litteras vobis olim amplissimas et benevolentissime dedimus, quibus nonagesimi anni cursum a commentariis vestris feliciter inchoatum gratulabamur ; ac iam nova Nobis causa occurrit, qua vos hisce litteris alioqui quodammodo iubemur, tanto gravior tantoque sollemnior quanto rei ipsius natura facile demonstratur.

Considerantibus enim Nobis quam raro factum sit ut commentariorum vita in hac humanarum rerum vicissitudine plenum aevi centenarii curriculum emetiatur, ut prope unicum potius quam singulare munus omnipotentis et benignissimi Dei huc provecti celebrare possitis, peropportunum visum est ut, plurimis undequaque vobis gratulantibus ac faustissima quaeque adprecantibus, apostolica vox ipsa accedat, quo magis magisque manifestum omnibus pateat, quam intento animo quantoque studio haec Apostolica Sedes operam vestram prosequatur.

Neque propositum Nobis est ea omnia hic commemorare quae passim his diebus a plurimis viris, nec tantum catholicis, sunt de vobis merito praedicata; qua integritate et constantia commentarii vestri sinceram sui naturam primaevamque formam hactenus servaverint ; quo studio, qua

716

APOSTOLICAE SEDIS

COMMENTARIUM OFFICIALE

ANNUS XXXXIII - SERIES II - VOL. XVIII

TYPIS POLYGLOTTIS VATICANIS

M · DCCCC · LI

The Brown Scapular of Our Lady of Mount Carmel

rum Mariae Caelestem Patronam aeque principalem cum Sancta Agnete, constituimus et declaramus, omnibus adiectis honoribus ac privilegiis liturgicis, quae praecipuis coetuum Patronis rite competunt. Contrariis quibusvis nihil obstantibus. Haec edicimus, statuimus, decernentes praesentes litteras firmas, validas atque efficaces iugiter exstare ac permanere ; suosque plenos atque integros effectus sortiri et obtinere ; illisque ad quos spectant, seu spectare poterunt, nunc et in posterum plenissime suffragari ; sicque rite iudicandum esse ac definiendum ; irritumque ex nunc et inane fieri, si quidquam secus, super his, a quovis, auctoritate qualibet, scienter sive ignoranter attentari contigerit.

Datum Romae, apud Sanctum Petrum, sub anulo Piscatoris, die XXV mensis Novembris, anno MCML, Pontificatus Nostri duodecimo.

De speciali mandato Sanctissimi
Pro Domino Cardinali a publicis Ecclesiae negotiis

GILDO BRTIGNOLA
Officium Regens
Pontificiis Diplomatibus expediendis.

EPISTULAE

I

AD REVMUM P. KILIANUM LYNCH, PRIOREM GENERALEM ORDINIS FRATRUM B. MARIAE V. DE MONTE CARMELO : SEPTIMO IMPLETO SAECULO AB INSTITUTIONE SACRI SCAPULARIS CARMELITARUM

The manifold manifestations of sincere Catholic piety which have characterized the célébration throughout the world of the seventh centenary of the institution of the Scapular of Our Lady of Mount Carmel have afforded Us much joy and consolation of spirit. It is with especial affection, therefore, that We extend to you, beloved son, and to all Our dearly-beloved children of the Carmélite family Our paternal félicitations, as the hymn of prayerful praise and joyful thanks evoked by the centenary célébrations is swelling to its grand finale.

Wafted out over the waves which lap the shores of Kent, this hymn will be taken up in divers tongues by the faithful of the various nations of the earth who have donned the Scapular that, under the inspiration of the Mother of God, they may grow in the likeness of her divine Son, Jesus Christ. But, in the storied halls and hallowed grounds of the hermitage of Aylesford, this paean of praise of the Blessed Virgin will resound with a distinctive quality as, sweetened by haunting harmonies of former générations and enriched by dulcet overtones from a historie past, it recaptnres a melody suspended for nigh four centuries.

By a benign dispensation of Divine Providence which reaches from end to end mightily and Orders all things sweetly *(Wisd.* VIII, 1), it is your happy privilège, belo ved son, to close the cycle of thèse centenary célébrations with a function of historie import, namely, the transfer of the mortai remains of Saint Simon Stock from their sheltered exile on the hospitable shores of France to their rightful place in the Dowry of Mary, to the home of his earthly sojourn at Aylesford. For you as for all Our dearly-loved children of England this event must be a source of untold joy in this year of national festival.

Seven hundred years have passed since, according to the sacred traditions of the Carmélite family, Simon Stock was vouchsafed the vision of Our Lady of Mount Carmel, yet, in the light of that vision, countless thousands throughout the world sustain the warf are of life and walk through the darkness and shadow of death to the mount of God. What more fitting close, therefore, could there be to the Sept-centenary célébrations of the Scapular than that the hallowed remains of him who sang the praises of the Flower of Carmel should have come to rest again in Aylesford for the festival of promise which he opened to the world-the feast of Our Lady of Mount Carmel. May she who is the Mother of Fair Love, and of knowledge, and of holy hope strengthen the bonds of faith, hope and charity which link those who participate in thèse festive célébrations.

With this prayer in Our heart, We cordially impart to you, beloved son, and to ail those associated with you in thèse cérémonies of prayer - ful thanksgiving Our paternal Apostolic Blessing.

From the Vatican, June 30th 1951.

PIUS PP. XII

APOSTOLICAE SEDIS

COMMENTARIUM OFFICIALE

ANNUS XXXXIII - SERIES II - VOL. XVIII

TYPIS POLYGLOTTIS VATICANIS

M · DCCCC · LI

Appendix 4

III

AD EMUM P. D. CAROLUM CARMELUM TIT. SANCTI PANCRATII S. R. E. PRESB. CARDINALEM DE VASCONCELLOS MOTA, ARCHIEPISCOPUM SANCTI PAULI IN BRASILIA, PRAESIDEM CONVENTUS NATIONALIS IN RECIPENSI URBE HABENDI OB VII IMPLETUM SAECULUM AB INSTITUTIONE SACRI SCAPULARIS SARMELITARUM.

PIUS PP. XII

Dilecte Fili Noster, salutem et Apostolicam Benedictionem. — Septimo expleto saeculo ad instituto sacro Scapulari Deiparae de Monte Carmelo, consilium istic initum est, ut libenter didicimus, celebrandi, medio hoc mense, Marialem ex tota natione Congressum, cui quidem tu, Dilecte Fili Noster, clarissimae sedis istius moderator, sollemniter praesidens. Scimus praeterea bonos Brasilienses fideles in ea, quae « Peregrinatio Mariae » appellatur, splendidas iam dedisse erga caelestem Reginam pietatis amorisque significationes. Certa autem tenet spes, proxima saecularia sollemnia, pro tua aliorumque sacrorum Antistitum praesentia, pro populi ipsius frequentia ac fervido studio praeeuntibus quidem publicis magistratibus, in magnificum triumphum Virginis de Monte Carmelo, simulque per sacri Scapularis devotionem in animarum profectum feliciter esse evasura. Quapropter Nosmet Ipsi non modo pia ac salutaria incepta merita laude exornamus secundisque votis prosequimur, sed tibi ultro potestatem largimur, ut, constituta die, Sacro pontificali ritu peracto, adstantibus fidelibus nomine Nostro Nostraque auctoritate benedicas, plenariam indulgentiam iisdem proponens, ad Ecclesiae praescripta lucrandam. Superni interea auxilii in auspicium, inque praecipuae caritatis Nostrae pignus, Apostolicam Benedictionem tibi, Dilecte Fili Noster, iisque universis, qui Marialibus sollemnibus intererunt, peramanter in Domino impertimus.

Datum Romae apud Sanctum Petrum, die vi mensis Iulii, anno MDCCCCLI, Pontificatus Nostri tertio decimo.

PIUS PP. XII

ACTA

APOSTOLICAE SEDIS

COMMENTARIUM OFFICIALE

ANNUS X X X X I V - SERIES II - VOL. X I X

722

III

BEATA MARIA V. ((DE MONTE CARMELO)) PRAECIPUA CAELESTIS PATRONA CON-STITUITUR OPPIDI ET PAROECIAE VULGO « PURCHENA)) NUNCUPATAE. IN-TER FINES ALMERIENSIS DIOECESIS.

PIUS PP. XII

Ad perpetuam rei memoriam. — Hispanorum erga Deiparam Vir-ginem Mariam pietas multifariam multisque modis per saecula pate-facta est eademque fervens, aestuans, actuosa fuit. Peculiarem sane locum illa tenet religio quae Mariam Virginem sub invocatione « Decor Oarmeli » seu « de Monte Carmelo » praecipue colit, tum quia anti-quissima, tum praesertim, permultis confirmantibus Diplomatibus Pon-tificiis, ob specialissima pro animabus igne purgatorio expiandis ab Tpsa promissa privilegia. Exstat quidem in Hispania, intra Almeriensis dioecesis fines, pagus quidam, « Purchena » vulgo nuncupatus, in quo cives in Deiparam Virginem de Monte Carmelo ab antiquis iam tempo-ribus maximum ostenderunt obsequium hodieque ostendunt, adeo ut Eam in privatis publicosque necessitatibus atque in rebus adversis ha-buerint Patronam. Ut vero tanta fidelium Marialis pietas Apostolico beneplacito atque praemio coronetur, Venerabilis Frater Alfonsus R   o   - denas Garcia, Episcopus Almeriensis, enixa Cleri, Optimatum omnium-que memorati oppidi civium vota depromens, a Nobis expostulavit ut Beatam Virginem Mariam Carmelitidem oppidi <(Purchena » caelestem Patronam benigne confirmare et renuntiare dignaremur. Nos autem, qui ob peculiarem Nostram in Virginem Carmelitidem, cuius Sacrum Scapulare a puero gessimus, observantiam permulta edidimus, septimo ab institutione Sacri huius Insignis vertente saeculo, documenta, huius-modi preces excipere libentissime statuimus. Audito igitur Venerabili Fratre Nostro Clemente Sanctae Romanae Ecclesiae Cardinali Micara, Episcopo Veliterno atque Sacrae Rituum Congregationis Pro-Praefecto, omnibusque rei momentis attente perpensis, certa scientia ac matura deliberatione Nostra, deque Apostolicae {potestatis plenitudine, prae-sentium Litterarum tenore perpetuumque in modum, Beatissimam Vir-ginem Mariam « de Monte Carmelo » praecipuam paroeciae, vulgo « Pur-chena » nuncupatae et intra Almeriensis dioeceseos fines positae, apud Deum *Patronam* confirmamus seu declaramus et constituimus, omnibus et singulis honoribus et privilegiis liturgicis adiectis, quae locorum Pa-

723

The Brown Scapular of Our Lady of Mount Carmel

tronis rite competunt. Contrariis quibuslibet minime obstantibus. Haec edicimus, statuimus, decernentes praesentes Litteras firmas, validas atque efficaces iugiter exstare ac permanere ; suosque plenos atque integros effectus sortiri et obtinere; illisque ad quos spectant seu spectare poterunt, nunc et in posterum, plenissime suffragari; sicque rite iudicandum esse ac definiendum ; irritumque ex nunc et inane fieri, si quidquam secus snper his, a quovis, auctoritate qualibet, scienter sive ignoranter contigerit attentari.

Datum ex Arce Gandulphi sub anulo Piscatoris, die xxix mensis Octobris, anno MCMLT, Pontificatus Nostri tertio decimo.

De speciali mandato Sanctissimi
Pro Domino Cardinali a publicis Ecclesiae negotiis

GILDO PRUGNOLA
Officium   Regens
Pontificiis   Diplomatibus   expediendis

IV

SANCTA BARBARA, V, ET M., IN PRAECIPUAM PATRONAM CAELESTEM ELIGITUR PRO ITALIS MILITIBUS P YROB ALLI STARI IS, NAUTIS, MACHIN ARIIS ET EX- TINGUENDIS INCENDIIS ADDICTIS.

PIUS PP. XII

Ad perpetuam rei memoriam. — Consueverant Romani Pontifices, ad fovendam pietatem et pericula arcenda, quibusdam ordinibus apud Deum Patronos constituere, quorum praesidio fideles uterentur et a quibus ducerent exemplum. Haud raro tamen accidit ut iidem antea, superno quodam acti afflatu, caelestes Patronos sponte sibi eligerent, quos postea suprema confirmavit Potestas. Nec aliter evenit in Virgine illa Nicomediensi, Barbara, cuius « passio » a pristinis Ecclesiae temporibus fidelium mentes, cum in Oriente tum in Occidente, adeo commovit, ut Ea et mirabilis animi fortitudinis exemplum et signum haberetur Christianae victoriae. Quae quidem, prout pia eaque vetus ferebat opinio, cum in turri, e caelo repente fulmine concussa, esset inclusa, gloriosum subiit martyrium. Hoc mortis genere insignem milites pyroballistarii haud perperam Patronam sibi adoptaverunt. In Alma quoque Urbe milites ipsi Sancti Angeli Arci tutandae praepositi in validam Sanctae Barbarae tutelam se commiserunt, atque, nonnullis spiritualibus muneribus et privilegiis

ACTA
APOSTOLICAE SEDIS

COMMENTARIUM OFFICIALE

ANNUS XXXXVIII - SERIES II - VOL. XXIII

TYPIS POLYGLOTTIS VATICANIS
M·DCCCC·LVI

siderate e meditate da quanti credono di poter fare tutto da sè. L'umanità di oggi colta, potente, dinamica, ha forse un maggior titolo alla terrena felicità nella sicurezza e nella pace ; ma essa non varrà a tramutarla in realtà, fino a quando nei suoi calcoli, nei suoi disegni e nelle sue discussioni non inserirà il più alto e risolutivo fattore : Dio e il suo Cristo. Ritorni il Dio-Uomo tra gli uomini, Re riconosciuto e obbedito, come spiritualmente torna ogni Natale ad adagiarsi nella culla per offrirsi a tutti. Ecco l'augurio che Noi oggi esprimiamo alla grande famiglia umana, certi d'indicarle il cammino della sua salvezza e della sua felicità.

Si degni il divino Infante di accogliere la Nostra fervida preghiera, affinchè la sua presenza sia avvertita quasi sensibilmente, come nei giorni della sua terrena dimora, nel mondo di oggi. Vivo in mezzo agli uomini, illumini le menti e corrobori le volontà di coloro che reggono i popoli, a questi assicuri la giustizia e la pace, incoraggi i volonterosi apostoli del suo eterno messaggio, sostenga i buoni, tragga a sè gli sbandati, conforti coloro che soffrono persecuzioni per il suo Nome e per la sua Chiesa, soccorra i poveri e gli oppressi, lenisca le pene ai malati, ai prigionieri, ai profughi, dia a tutti una scintilla del suo amore divino, affinchè trionfi in ogni luogo sulla terra il suo pacifico regno. Così sia.

EPISTULA

AD REVMUM P. MAURUM A PERDOLENTE V. MARIA, TERTII ORDINIS CARMELITARUM DI SCALCEATORUM MALABARENSIUM MODERATOREM GENERALEM, OB SAECULUM ELAPSUM AB EODEM ORDINE CONDITO.

PIUS PP. XII

Dilecte fili, salutem et Apostolicam Benedictionem. Quidquid Malabarensi christianorum communitati laetum accidit, Nobis quoque iucundum contingit, cum erga eos omnes paternum amantissimumque geramus animum. Quamobrem cum Nobis perlatum fuerit Tertium Ordinem Carmelitarum discalceatorum Malabarensium, cui tu digne praees, plenum saeculum proxime esse commemoraturum, ex quo idem conditus fuit, volumus per has litteras celebrationes vestras participare, vobisque et de praeclare gestis gratulari, et majora usque ominari incrementa. Novimus siquidem vos omni ope allaborare ut catholica veritas Indorum populis

Appendix 4

affulgeat : scriptis nempe prelo editis non paucis ; litterarum ludis iuven-
tuti instituendae, atque altiorum etiam disciplinarum domiciliis ; sacris
Missionibus quam latissime vobis licet provehendis ; atque institutis christianae pietati, religioni caritatique fovendis.

Praeterea Nos non latet vos Ordinis vestri disciplinam studiose ada-
mare ac contendere pro viribus ut cotidie magis effecta detur ac vigeat ;
idque non modo ad umbratilem et contemplativam vitam quod attinet,
sed ad activam etiam; hoc est sive precando pieque meditando, sive ad
ministeria sacra et ad cetera religionis auxilia et adiumenta laudabili
incumbendo alacritate. Vobis procul dubio illa Jacobi Apostoli sententia
perspecta est : « Omne datum optimum et omne donum perfectum desur-
sum est, descendens a Patre luminum *yy.'* Quapropter, non aspirante
iuvanteque Deo, inania opera hominum, cum non « sufficientes simus
cogitare aliquid a nobis, quasi ex nobis : sed sufficientia nostra ex Deo
est)).' Nihilo secius non precationi solum ad Deum admovendae, non
contemplationi tantum caelestium rerum vacare oportet, sed actuosae
etiam navitati, secundum sapientissimum illud divi Thomae Aquinatis
effatum : « Sicut... majus est illuminare, quam lucere solum, ita m a jus
est contemplata aliis tradere, quam solum contemplari ».' Pergite igitur,
ut facitis, in ejusmodi pietatis studium in omneque rerum genus incum-
bere, quod ad catholicam veritatem ceteris collustrandam valeat, itemque
possit quam plurimos ex vestratibus ad christiana praecepta christia-
naeque vitae mores feliciter adducere. Ac vobis adsit a caelo Beata Virgo
Maria, Carmeli decus, quam vos tam impense colitis, tam studiose ada-
matis. Ne oculos, ne mentem, ne animum avertatis a fulgore hujus sideris.
Respicite ad Mariam ; in periculis, in angustiis, in rebus dubiis Mariam
cogitate, Mariam invocate. Non recedat ab ore, non recedat a corde.' Illa
menti vestrae nullo non tempore praesens esto Doctoris Melliflui sententia : ((Ipsam sequens, non devias ; ipsam rogans, non desperas ; ipsam
cogitans, non erras. Ipsa tenente, non corruis ; ipsa propitia, pervenis ».'
In apostolicis igitur laboribus et in sacri ministerii vestri difficultatibus
ad ejus confugite tutelam potentissimam ; ipsa divinum Filium suum
rogante, pro certo experiemini nihil esse umquam quod vos, caelesti
suffulti gratia, non possitis ad felicem exitum perducere.]

· JAO. **I,** 17.
' *II Cor.* **III,** 5.
' IP-IP-*, *q.* 188, a. 6, 3.
' Cfr. S. BERN., super « Missus est », homil. II, n. 17; Migne, P. L. 183, eol. 70-c, D.
' Ibid.; Migne P. L. 183, col. 71-A.

727

The Brown Scapular of Our Lady of Mount Carmel

Qua suavi spe freti, cum tibi, dilecte fili, tum cunctis tui Ordinis sodalibus Apostolicam Benedictionem libenter impertimus, quae vobis omnibus et supernorum munerum et amantissimae voluntatis Nostrae sit pignus et auspex.

Datum Romae, apud S. Petrum, die xxx mensis Octobris, anno **MDCCCCLV,** Pontificatus Nostri septimo decimo.

PIUS PP. XII

ALLOCUTIONES

I

Sociis Sodalitatis Italicae elementara ludi Magistrorum Catholicorum, oo decennium a Sodalitate ipsa condita coadunatis. *

L'intima letizia, che a Noi proviene nel mirarvi, diletti figli e figlie, in così gran numero convenuti alla Nostra presenza, per celebrare il primo decennio della vostra Associazione di Maestri cattolici, è la medesima di chi, dopo aver seminato nel tardo autunno e coltivato con alacre fiducia per lunga stagione, contempla la distesa ondeggiante della messe e nelle turgide spighe ravvisa la certezza di un migliore avvenire.

giusto che al Nostro conforto si unisca la vostra esultanza, così ardentemente espressa e quasi riecheggiata dalla maestà di questo massimo Tempio, come inno di ringraziamento a Dio, da cui ogni opera buona e feconda trae inizio e incremento.

Dieci anni di assidue fatiche, di lotte superate, di conquiste ottenute nell'arduo e delicato campo della educazione: ecco il prezioso dono, che oggi volete offrire al Vicario di Cristo, cui ben sapete quanto sta a cuore la fanciullezza e, per essa, la futura sorte della Chiesa e della vostra Patria.

E veramente, da chi altri mai sulla terra, dopo i genitori, principalmente dipende il destino religioso e civile della Nazione, se non dai Maestri delle scuole elementari, per le cui mani, in virtù della legge, deve passare l'intiera fanciullezza? A voi dunque va la gratitudine Nostra e della società civile per gli stessi e buoni risultati conseguiti nel decorso decennio, mentre su di voi si posa ansioso lo sguardo Nostro e delle

Habita die 4 Novembris mensis a. 1955.

To the Carmelite Pilgrims at Lourdes, July 16, 1958, the Feast of Our Lady of Mt. Carmel, on the occasion of the centenary of the last apparition of Our Lady of Lourdes, July 16, 1858.

PIUS XII

"On the Feast of Our Lady of Mount Carmel, We wish to salute the pilgrim of Lourdes, and, in the first place, the representatives of the Order of Carmel who are preparing to commemorate the centenary of the 18th and last apparition of the Immaculate Virgin to Bernadette. In the very same places, they shall call to mind with emotion the simple scene which unfolded itself on the banks of the Gave. Silent and unobtrusive like that of the 11th of February, this last vision ravished the soul of the child by its immaterial beauty: 'Never,' she said, 'I have seen her so beautiful.' Already within five months, the manifestations of the piety of the people, but also, alas! the contentions of men, had made the Pyrennean grotto well known. Nevertheless, on the evening of July 16th, 1858, the apparitions of Lourdes terminated almost without witnesses in the recollection (recueillement) and admiration of the virginal beauty of the Mother of God. 'Tota pulchra es, O Maria!' You also, dear sons, know how to keep silence in your souls and to open yourselves up to the contemplation of the divine splendours realised in Mary. Does not this paternal exhortation which We address to you on this anniversary day, fall in with the spiritual lesson of the ancient and venerable tradition of Carmel, which saw flourish throughout the long ages admirable contemplative vocations?

In this age, agitated by so many passions and fascinated by so many vain mirages, raise up your eyes to God, and then they shall be only all the more clear and serene to judge the things of earth. And while a dire servitude oppresses the spirit of millions of men, uproots from their hearts the knowledge and love of God and bends them to the service of worldly ambitions alone, receive with faith the last message of the Marian apparitions, that of the silent prayer of a soul docile to grace, and enlightened by the brightness of the things of Heaven. Pray all the more, beloved sons, for the spiritual needs of the world are great. Combat in yourselves and around you the enterprises of the enemy of good. Pray all the more, for the apostolic labours of the Church are immense; and offer for Her sacrifices proportionate to the vastness of Her task. In this effort of prayer and action to which We invite you, may Our Lady of Lourdes help you! Undoubtedly, She has not shown Herself on the rock of Massabielle since She bade Her last farewell to Bernadette, but the water of the fountain continues to flow on, a symbol of the innumerable graces poured out on this privileged place. To the Mother of God rise up the hopes of the crowds gathered at the grotto, who borrow, so to speak, from the liturgical invocations of July 16th their filial and confident prayer: 'Be mindful, O Virgin Mother, to speak good things before God's face in our behalf, so that He may turn away His anger from us. Most worthy Queen of the world, Mary, ever virgin, pray for our peace and safety.'

Blend your voices, beloved sons, pilgrims of the Jubilee Year, with this collective supplication which for a century has never ceased. Meditate anew the profound lesson of the apparitions of Lourdes at the moment when you close their cycle. Listen to the appeal of your Mother; follow Her counsels, proclaim Her benefits!

We invoke on you the grace of a Marian holiness ever more radiant and more generous, and We grant you as a pledge Our Paternal and Apostolic Blessing.

P. Pius XII
The Vatican, July 2, 1958

The Pope's Message, written in French, was read by Bishop Theas of Lourdes during the Solemn Pontifical Mass in the Basilica of St. Pius X, July 16, 1958.

John XXIII

Birth name	Angelo Giuseppe Roncalli
Papacy began	October 28, 1958
Papacy ended	June 3, 1963
Predecessor	Pius XII
Successor	Paul VI
Born	November 25, 1881 Sotto il Monte, Italy
Died	June 3, 1963 (age 81) Vatican City

Pope John's Coat of
Arms.

Pope St. John XXIII: Angelo Giuseppe Roncalli
Papacy: 1958 – 1963
Summary of Contents:

---

1). *"The Voice of the Pope,"* An excerpt from the *Allocution* of Pope John XXIII preached on February 18, 1959, at the Church of St. Louis of France, in Rome, Italy. Referring to the day of his election and how Cardinal Tisserant of France came to ask him what name he would take, he reflected on the name of John. Then speaking of his predecessor, Pope John XXII, he said: *"to him also is assigned "the paternity of the "Saturday Privilege,"* (known as the Sabbatine Privilege), *so precious and so dear to those who wear the Scapular of Our Lady of Mount Carmel. "* (This excerpt of the Sermon of Pope John XXIII was taken from Mary, Vol. 22, No. 1, January, February, 1961, p. 64)

2). *Acta Apostolicae Sedis,* Official Document of Pope John XXIII, of the *Allocution of Pope John XXIII, at the Church of S. Luigi dei Francesi, (the Church of St. Louis of France, Rome,)* given February 18, 1959 for the closing of the Lourdes centenary year It is in this *Allocution* that His Holiness speaks of his predecessor, Pope John XXII as the Father of the Sabbatine Privilege. The official text is in French.

3). *Osservatore Romano Newspaper: "Il Sommo Pontefice Giovanni XXIII visita la chiesa e le istituzioni di S. Luigi dei Francesi"* (The Solemn Pontiff, John XXIII, visits the Church and the Institutions of St. Louis of France) This issue of the *Osservatore Romano*, dated February 20, 1959, contains the entire *Allocution* of the Holy Father, given in French; it is the same content as the above Document from the A.A.S., also speaking of Pope John XXII, as the Father of the Sabbatine Privilege.

4). *Osservatore Romano Newspaper: "La Chiesa sempre presente a tutte le necessita` della famiglia umana.* ("The Church is always present for all of the necessities of the human family"). This issue, is dated July 16, 1961. In this article, His Holiness, Pope John XXIII, in a *General Audience*, reminded the people of the Commemoration of Our Lady of Mount Carmel, on July 16th. He also stated it was recorded that it was his predecessor, Pope John XXII, in the 14th century, who promoted the devotion to Mary under the title of "Our Lady of Mount Carmel."

732

In France there is little reason for men to bother with social convention, because they despise that society. At bottom we have much in common; their present plight, their psychological and physical environment is different, that's all.

Elliott Egan, O.Carm.

THE VOICE OF THE POPE

Referring to the day of his election and how Cardinal Tisserant of France came to ask him what name he would take, the Holy Father reflects on the name of John, saying:

The name of John, so sacred and apostolic a name, unites Us to the person of Jesus, the Divine Founder and Head of the Holy Church. John was a name that was not strange to Our thoughts; it was very agreeable to feel Ourselves united across six centuries of history to the last of the Popes who bore this name, John XXII, James Duèse of Cahors, Bishop of Avignon, who governed the Church for eighteen years and died past the age of ninety in 1334. Here was a great Pontiff. His life was full of troubles, but rich in deeds and merits in every respect: a true servant of the servants of the Lord. He had among other things, the honor of canonizing St. Thomas Aquinas. But especially he was very devoted to Mary. It is to him that history attributes the happy idea of having the Our Father and the Hail Mary said at the sound of the evening bell; to him also is assigned the paternity of the "Saturday Privilege" so precious and so dear to those who wear the Scapular of Our Lady of Mount Carmel.

> *From a sermon of Pope John XXIII (opening words: "La voix du pape") preached at St. Louis of France Church, Rome, February 18, 1959, for the closing of the Lourdes centenary year.*

POPE JOHN XXIII
see opposite page

Carmelite

**SECTION FOR THE SCAPULAR
CONFRATERNITY AND THIRD ORDER**

ACTA

APOSTOLICAE SEDIS

COMMENTARIUM OFFICIALE

ANNUS LI - SERIES III - VOL. I

TYPIS POLYGLOTTIS VATICANIS

M -DCCCC-LIX

The Brown Scapular of Our Lady of Mount Carmel

II

Quam habuit in Ecclesia 8. Ludovici, Francorum Regis, cum primum eam invisit, adstantibus Emis Patribus Cardinalibus, Praelatis prdeclarisque Viris e Gallica Natione*

Vénérables Frères, Chers Fils,

La voix du Pape, humble serviteur des serviteurs de Dieu, s'est fait entendre ce matin dans toute la France et aussi en tous lieux de la terre. C'était un remerciement au Seigneur pour le don immense des grâces célestes accordées au monde pendant l'année centenaire des Apparitions de Lourdes.

A Eome, cette voix résonna déjà par avance dimanche dernier sous les voûtes de la Basilique Libérienne consacrée à la Mère du Seigneur qui y est invoquée sous le double titre de « Salut du Peuple Romain » et — par l'initiative de Benoît XV de sainte mémoire — de « Reine de la Paix ».

Au soir de ce jour, où les motifs liturgiques du temps de Carême ont fait transférer la célébration officielle de ce glorieux anniversaire en France et dans toutes les églises du monde catholique, Nous voici donc en personne au milieu de vous, heureux d'avoir accueilli votre aimable invitation. Et Nous vous redisons, comme en écho, les mêmes paroles d'action de grâces pour la joie particulière des fils de France qui perpétuent avec bonheur la présence à Rome de leur noble Nation au cours des siècles.

Siècles de foi religieuse et catholique sans défaillance: depuis le temps où se dressa en ces lieux la première église consacrée à la Sainte Vierge — que les Bénédictins de Farfa remplissaient de leurs chants mélodieux et pacifiques — jusqu'aux progressives transformations artistiques et décoratives dont le sommet fut la construction de cett« église dédiée à Saint Louis IX : témoignage de la ferveur et de la générosité des Français du temps de Sixte IV et de Sixte Quint. Et depuis lors, que de manifestations diverses de piété, de culture et d'art, qui continuent la belle tradition des ancêtres et qui sont pour les Romains un objet d'admiration respectueuse et cordiale!

Cette visite que Nous faisons à votre église nationale, et qui évoque également à Notre cœur les doux et chers souvenirs des huit années de

* Die 18 Februarii mensis a. 1959.

Notre séjour à Paris au service du Saint-Siège, est pour vous, Nous le savons, un motif de joie.

Mais ce fut un bien plus grand motif d'allégresse pour le monde entier que la visite, dix-huit fois répétée, de Marie, la Mère de Jésus et la nôtre, à ses enfants sur cette terre qui est un jardin de délices naturelles pour les yeux, mais pour tout le monde d'ailleurs la vallée de larmes des pauvres mortels *gementes et fientes* à toutes les époques de l'histoire humaine.

Ces Apparitions si remarquables de Marie, au milieu du XIX^{ime} siècle, demeurent un titre particulier d'honneur pour la France, patrie bénie de saints et de héros, où l'histoire du christianisme a inscrit des pages glorieuses et inoubliables.

Dans l'ordre de la Providence, chaque nation a une mission, et il suffit parfois d'une devise pour la qualifier. Or quand on dit : « *Regnum Galliae, regnum Mariae))*, on énonce de façon parfaite Te témoignage d'honneur et d'amour des fils et des nombreux descendants de Clovis.

Certes le mouvement spirituel vers la Grotte de Lourdes en terre de France, déterminé par les Apparitions de l'Immaculée — et qui, bien loin de s'affaiblir, semble devoir grandir encore en un édifiant crescendo, — est une manifestation de ferveur religieuse; il est en même temps pour le monde entier un doux et insistant rappel adressé aux consciences profondément chrétiennes comme aussi aux moins ferventes : c'est le rappel d'un mystérieux dessein de la Providence ; qui devrait réveiller les responsabilités individuelles et collectives en face des grands problèmes de la vie et de la mort, chez tous et chacun, dans le présent et à l'avenir.

Permettez que sur ce point Nous reprenions quelques pensées de Notre Radio-message de ce matin, lancé de Rome au monde entier.

L'année centenaire des Apparitions de Lourdes se termine sur cette date du 18 février, que la liturgie d'aujourd'hui consacre au culte de la voyante de Massabielle, Sainte Marie Bernard, la fille du meunier Soubirous. Elle, et elle seule, a entendu les confidences de Marie, et elle les a transmises au monde. Et le monde — c'est là le grand miracle d'Ordre moral — le monde y a cru, et continue d'y croire.

Combien admirable, chez Bernadette, la parfaite conformité à la doctrine dont la céleste Dame l'avait rendue dépositaire! Et combien lumineux l'exemple de cette sainteté qui ouvrit à une enfant si petite et si humble la voie des cieux, dans l'au-delà, et lui assura pour toujours sur la terre, la gloire des autels et la vénération de tout le peuple chrétien ! Quelle doctrine ! Quel exemple ! Quel encouragement pour nous !

« Ce qu'il y a de faible dans le monde, dit Saint Paul, voilà ce que Dieu a choisi pour confondre la force; ce qui dans le monde est sans naissance et qu'on méprise, voilà ce que Dieu a choisi ».*

« Modèle de la prière à Marie, disions-Nous dans Notre message de ce matin, exemple de force humble et souriante, éloquente par le silence même dans lequel elle s'est enveloppée une fois remplie sa mission, Sainte Bernadette nous reporte comme irrésistiblement vers ce vrai centre spirituel de Lourdes, la grotte des apparitions, où les paroles de la Mère de Dieu ne cessent de retentir au cœur de ses enfants. Et en même temps la voyante qui eut le courage de quitter pour toujours ce lieu de l'ineffable recontre nous rapelle que Lourdes n'est qu'un point de départ : la grâce qu'on y reçoit est un trésor que, loin d'enfouir stérilement, on doit faire fructifier pour la gloire de Dieu et le service de l'Eglise.

« Très chers fils, ajoutions-Nous, notre siècle, vous le savez, voit se réaliser d'admirables progrès scientifiques, et l'humanité est comme saisie d'un frémissement d'orgueil devant les possibilités insoupçonnées qui s'offrent à elle. Et voici — en contraste — que, de Lourdes, un appel à l'humilité et à la prière nous est transmis par Bernadette : sans crainte, Nous l'adressons Nous-même avec force à tous ceux qui courent aujourd'hui le risque grave d'être aveuglés par cette puissance de l'homme au point de perdre le sens des vraies valeurs religieuses. De Lourdes, c'est encore un appel à la pénitence et à la charité qui nous parvient, pour nous détacher des richesses et nous apprendre à les partager avec plus pauvres que nous : et Nous le reprenons également à Notre compte, en ce temps où des millions l'hommes prennent conscience — parfois hélas dans la révolte — du scandaleux contraste entre le bien-être des uns et l'insuffisance vitale des autres ».

Chers fils, Nous aimons conclure cet entretien simple et bref, — en une circonstance si solennelle destinée à marquer une date dans l'histoire de l'église de Saint Louis des Français, — par le rappel d'un souvenir qui, Nous le pensons, ne vous déplaira pas.

Lors de la récente élection de Notre humble personne aux graves responsabilités du Souverain Pontificat, P Eminentissime Cardinal Doyen du Sacré Collège, Notre très cher Frère Eugène Tisserant, illustre

---

' *1 Cor.* 1, 27-28.

Appendix 4

représentant et gloire insigne de la France chrétienne, nous demanda quel nom Nous voulions prendre dans la succession des Pontifes Romains. Nous répondîmes : Jean, ajoutant quelques paroles pour donner le sens de ce choix.

Le nom de Jean, éminemment sacré et apostolique, Nous unissait à la personne de Jésus, le divin Fondateur et le Chef de la Sainte Eglise. Mais il n'était pas étranger à Notre pensée; il lui était même agréable, de Nous sentir unis, à travers six siècles d'histoire, au dernier des nombreux Pontifes de ce nom, Jean XXII, Jacques Duèse de Cahors, évêque d'Avignon, qui gouverna 18 ans l'Eglise et mourut plus que nonagénaire en 1334. Ce fut un grand Pontife. Sa vie fut pleine de tribulations, mais riche d'oeuvres et de mérites à tous égards : un vrai Serviteur des Serviteurs du Seigneur. Il eut, entre autres, l'honneur de canoniser Saint Thomas d'Aquin. Surtout il était très dévot à Marie. C'est à lui que l'histoire attribue l'heureuse idée de faire réciter un *Pater* et un *Ave* au tintement de la cloche du soir ; à lui aussi la paternité du « privilège du samedi », si précieux et si cher à ceux qui portent le scapulaire de Notre Dame du Mont Carmel.

Chers fils ! tout ce qui Nous rappelle la France Nous touche au vif. Les fils savent lire dans le cœur de ceux qui les aiment, sans rien enlever pour autant à celui qui, comme père dans le Christ et pasteur, appartient à l'Eglise universelle, mère de toutes les Nations.

Et Nous voulons ajouter encore ceci : le Pape Jean XXII accompagnait son nom de sa devise personnelle : *Dominus mihi adjutor*, le Seigneur est mon secours.

Chers fils ! Ces premiers mois du grand service, que le ministère pontifical Nous imposa, ont ouvert devant Nos yeux une grande vision : vision de bon travail pastoral au bénéfice du diocèse de Rome, dont le Pape est P Evêque comme successeur de Saint Pierre, Prince des Apôtres, et au bénéfice de l'Eglise universelle, dont son autorité est le fondement. Veuillez intercéder par votre prière auprès de la Mère de Jésus, notre Mère, pour que ce secours du Seigneur ne Nous manque pas le long du chemin.

Dans Notre jeunesse, Nous avions sous les yeux l'exemple de l'activité pastorale d'un grand Cardinal qui avait placé dans ses armes le rappel de Marie Immaculée avec les paroles : *Tu fortitudo mea.*

Rien n'est plus souhaitable pour Nos humbles efforts. O Jésus, *Tu mihi adjutor*, comme vous invoquait Notre lointain Prédécesseur Jean. O Marie Immaculée, *Tu fortitudo mea*. Amen.

L'OSSERVATORE ROMANO

GIORNALE QUOTIDIANO POLITICO RELIGIOSO

UNICUIQUE SUUM NON PRAEVALEBUNT

CITTA DEL VATICANO

Il Sommo Pontefice Giovanni XXIII visita la chiesa e le istituzioni di S. Luigi dei Francesi

Intorno al Vicario di Gesù Cristo la rappresentanza di un grande popolo

L'Udienza General

L'OSSERVATORE ROMANO

LIRE 40

GIORNALE QUOTIDIANO  POLITICO RELIGIOSO

UNICUIQUE SUUM — NON PRAEVALEBUNT

CITTA DEL VATICANO

Ai rilievi storici e attuali del Sommo Pontefice

sulla Enciclica "Mater et Magistra"

risponde il fervido consenso della stampa e il plauso del mondo

La Chiesa sempre presente

a tutte le necessità della famiglia umana

La Enciclica "costruisce, convince ed ama"

Al centro la persona umana

Qualificazione del problemi in termini mondiali

Manifestazioni dei lavoratori cristiani

Occorre superare il materialismo

Le trasmissioni all'estero

Una dichiarazione del Ministro Gonella

Paul VI

Birth name	Giovanni Battista Enrico Antonio Maria Montini
Papacy began	June 21, 1963
Papacy ended	August 6, 1978
Predecessor	John XXIII
Successor	John Paul I
Born	September 26, 1897 Concesio, Italy
Died	August 6, 1978, age 80 Castel Gandolfo, Italy

Coat of arms of Pope
Paul VI in fleur de lys

Blessed Pope Paul VI
Giovanni Battista Enrico Antonio Maria Montini
Papacy: 1963 – 1978
Summary of Contents

1). *"Pope Paul VI speaks about the Scapular and the Rosary."* Pope Paul VI, in his *Letter, "In Dominica Republicana,"* dated February 2, 1965, appointing Cardinal Silva of Santiago, Chile, papal legate to the Mariological and Marian Congresses held in Santo Domingo, March 1965, below is an excerpt:

"Let the faithful hold in high esteem the practices and devotions to the Blessed Virgin approved by the teaching authority of the Church in the course of the centuries.....it is Our conviction that the Rosary of Mary and the Scapular of Carmel are among these recommended practices.....
(Taken from Mary, Vol. 26, No. 3, July, August, September, 1965, pp. 10, 11)

2). *Osservatore Romano Newspaper: "Voti augurali di Paolo VI per il Congresso Mariologico e Mariano in Santo Domingo,"* dated March 22 – 23, 1965. Under this title, is the entire text of the *Letter* of Pope Paul VI to Cardinal Raul Silva Henriquez, his Legate, in which his words are repeated regarding the Rosary and the Scapular of Our Lady of Mount Carmel. The entire text is in Latin.

3). "Dogmatic Constitution on the Church," *Lumen Gentium,"* Solemnly promulgated by His Holiness Pope Paul VI, on November 21, 1964, Chapter VIII: *The Blessed Virgin Mary, Mother of God in the Mystery of Christ and the Church."* Following is an excerpt from Chapter VIII: The Cult of the Blessed Virgin in the Church, #67:

"This most Holy Synod deliberately teaches this Catholic doctrine and at the same time admonishes all the sons of the Church that the cult, especially the liturgical cult, of the Blessed Virgin, be generously fostered, and the practices and exercises of piety, recommended by the Magisterium of the Church, toward her in the course of the centuries be made of great moment..."

4). *Apostolic Exhortation: Signum Magnum,* Pope Paul VI, dated May 13, 1967. *Signum Magnum* was presented during Paul VI's visit to Fatima to commemorate the 50th anniversary of the Fatima apparitions. This Exhortation called for and repeated the consecration of the world to the Immaculate Heart of Mary, and gives the theological basis for Mary's spiritual maternity. It was at Fatima, on October 13, 1917, that our Blessed Mother appeared to the three children, Lucia, Francisco and Jacinta, during the Miracle of the Sun, dressed in the habit of Carmel, holding down the Scapular in her hand to the world. Below, is an excerpt of this Document:

"The great sign which the Apostle John saw in heaven, "a woman clothed with the sun," is interpreted by the Sacred Liturgy, not without foundation, as referring to the most Blessed Mary, the mother of all men by the grace of Christ the Redeemer....Oh, glorious Lady, grant that through you we may deserve to ascend to Jesus, your Son, who through you deigned to descend among us..." (Some information was cited from http://campus.udayton.edu/mary/resources/documents.SM.html)

Pope Paul VI Speaks
about the Scapular and the Rosary

As the bearer of Our Words to all who have come as pilgrims to Santo Domingo, especially the faithful from Latin America and the Dominican Republic, you are expressing warmly and eloquently Our hopes and exhortations which We make known in the suitable phrases of the dogmatic constitution of the Second Vatican Council: "Let the faithful hold in high esteem the practices and devotions to the Blessed Virgin approved by the teaching authority of the Church in the course of the centuries" (no. 67—from the constitution "on the Church," published November 21, 1964). It is Our conviction that the Rosary of Mary and the Scapular of Carmel are among these recommended practices. This Scapular was worn by the heroes of Latin America. The Scapular is a practice of piety, "which by its very simplicity is suited to everyone, and has spread widely among the faithful to their spiritual profit" (Pius XII, the letter, *Neminem profecto*, February 11, 1950, for the Scapular centenary year, 1950-51). In instructing the Christian people let it be pointed out repeatedly and emphatically that when the Mother is honored, then the Son is rightly known, loved and praised—the Son through whom all things have their being (Colossians 1, 15-16) and in whom it has pleased the Eternal Father that all fulness should dwell (Col. 1, 19). Then his commandments are kept (no. 66 of the constitution "on the Church"). Let it be stressed also that devotion to the Mother of God consists not in sterile and superficial sentiment, not in empty credulity, but proceeds from true faith, which leads us to recognize the excellence of the Mother of God, and inspires us to love her as our mother and to imitate her virtues.

From the letter, In Dominica Republicana, *dated February 2, 1965, appointing Cardinal Silva of Santiago, Chile, papal legate to the Mariological and Marian Congresses held in Santo Domingo, March, 1965.*

—translated by Rev. Eamon Carroll, O.Carm.

MARY JULY-AUGUST-SEPTEMBER, 1965

L'OSSERVATORE ROMANO — 22-23 Marzo 1966 — N. 67 (31.642) — pag. 2

Voti augurali di Paolo VI per il Congresso Mariologico e Mariano in Santo Domingo

Come Mosca inten il «dialogo» coi catto

Visita del Papa alla parrocchia di San Luca al quartiere romano Prenestino

The Brown Scapular of Our Lady of Mount Carmel

Second Vatican Council

DOGMATIC CONSTITUTION ON THE CHURCH
LUMEN GENTIUM
SOLEMNLY PROMULGATED BY HOLINESS
POPE PAUL VI
ON NOVEMBER 21, 1964

CHAPTER VIII

THE BLESSED VIRGIN MARY, MOTHER OF GOD IN THE MYSTERY OF CHRIST AND THE CHURCH

I. Introduction

52. Wishing in His supreme goodness and wisdom to effect the redemption of the world, "when the fullness of time came, God sent His Son, born of a woman, ..that we might receive the adoption of sons".(283) "He for us men, and for our salvation, came down from heaven, and was incarnate by the Holy Spirit from the Virgin Mary."(1*) This divine mystery of salvation is revealed to us and continued in the Church, which the Lord established as His body. Joined to Christ the Head and in the unity of fellowship with all His saints, the faithful must in the first place reverence the memory "of the glorious ever Virgin Mary, Mother of our God and Lord Jesus Christ".(2*)

53. The Virgin Mary, who at the message of the angel received the Word of God in her heart and in her body and gave Life to the world, is acknowledged and honored as being truly the Mother of God and Mother of the Redeemer. Redeemed by reason of the merits of her Son and united to Him by a close and indissoluble tie, she is endowed with the high office and dignity of being the Mother of the Son of God, by which account she is also the beloved daughter of the Father and the temple of the Holy Spirit. Because of this gift of sublime grace she far surpasses all creatures, both in heaven and on earth. At the same time, however, because she belongs to the offspring of Adam she is one with all those who are to be saved. She is "the mother of the members of Christ . . . having cooperated by charity that faithful might be born in the Church, who are members of that Head."(3*) Wherefore she is hailed as a pre-eminent and singular member of the Church, and as its type and excellent exemplar in faith and charity. The Catholic Church, taught by the Holy Spirit, honors her with filial affection and piety as a most beloved mother.

746

Appendix 4

54. Wherefore this Holy Synod, in expounding the doctrine on the Church, in which the divine Redeemer works salvation, intends to describe with diligence both the role of the Blessed Virgin in the mystery of the Incarnate Word and the Mystical Body, and the duties of redeemed mankind toward the Mother of God, who is mother of Christ and mother of men, particularly of the faithful. It does not, however, have it in mind to give a complete doctrine on Mary, nor does it wish to decide those questions which the work of theologians has not yet fully clarified. Those opinions therefore may be lawfully retained which are propounded in Catholic schools concerning her, who occupies a place in the Church which is the highest after Christ and yet very close to us.(4*)

II. The Role of the Blessed Mother in the Economy of Salvation

55. The Sacred Scriptures of both the Old and the New Testament, as well as ancient Tradition show the role of the Mother of the Saviour in the economy of salvation in an ever clearer light and draw attention to it. The books of the Old Testament describe the history of salvation, by which the coming of Christ into the world was slowly prepared. These earliest documents, as they are read in the Church and are understood in the light of a further and full revelation, bring the figure of the woman, Mother of the Redeemer, into a gradually clearer light. When it is looked at in this way, she is already prophetically foreshadowed in the promise of victory over the serpent which was given to our first parents after their fall into sin.(284) Likewise she is the Virgin who shall conceive and bear a son, whose name will be called Emmanuel.(285) She stands out among the poor and humble of the Lord, who confidently hope for and receive salvation from Him. With her the exalted Daughter of Sion, and after a long expectation of the promise, the times are fulfilled and the new Economy established, when the Son of God took a human nature from her, that He might in the mysteries of His flesh free man from sin.

56. The Father of mercies willed that the incarnation should be preceded by the acceptance of her who was predestined to be the mother of His Son, so that just as a woman contributed to death, so also a woman should contribute to life. That is true in outstanding fashion of the mother of Jesus, who gave to the world Him who is Life itself and who renews all things, and who was enriched by God with the gifts which befit such a role. It is no wonder therefore that the usage prevailed among the Fathers whereby they called the mother of God entirely holy and free from all stain of sin, as though fashioned by the Holy Spirit and formed as a new creature.(5*) Adorned from the first instant of her conception with the radiance of an entirely unique holiness, the Virgin of Nazareth is greeted, on God's command, by an angel messenger as "full of grace",(286) and to the heavenly messenger she replies: "Behold the handmaid of the Lord, be it done unto me according to thy word".(287) Thus Mary, a daughter of Adam, consenting to the divine Word, became the mother of Jesus, the one and only Mediator. Embracing God's salvific will with a full heart and impeded by no sin, she devoted herself totally as a handmaid of the Lord to the person and work of her Son, under Him and with Him, by the grace of almighty God, serving the mystery of redemption. Rightly therefore the holy Fathers see her as used by God not merely in a passive way, but as freely cooperating in the work of human salvation through faith and obedience. For, as St. Irenaeus says, she "being obedient, became the cause of salvation for herself and for the whole human race."(6*) Hence not a few of the early Fathers gladly assert in their preaching, "The knot of Eve's disobedience was untied by Mary's obedience; what the virgin Eve bound through her unbelief, the Virgin Mary loosened by her faith."(7*) Comparing Mary with Eve, they call her "the Mother of the living,"(8*) and still more often they say: "death through Eve, life through

The Brown Scapular of Our Lady of Mount Carmel

Mary."(9*)

57. This union of the Mother with the Son in the work of salvation is made manifest from the time of Christ's virginal conception up to His death it is shown first of all when Mary, arising in haste to go to visit Elizabeth, is greeted by her as blessed because of her belief in the promise of salvation and the precursor leaped with joy in the womb of his mother.(288) This union is manifest also at the birth of Our Lord, who did not diminish His mother's virginal integrity but sanctified it,(10*) when the Mother of God joyfully showed her firstborn Son to the shepherds and Magi. When she presented Him to the Lord in the temple, making the offering of the poor, she heard Simeon foretelling at the same time that her Son would be a sign of contradiction and that a sword would pierce the mother's soul, that out of many hearts thoughts might be revealed.(289) When the Child Jesus was lost and they had sought Him sorrowing, His parents found Him in the temple, taken up with the things that were His Father's business; and they did not understand the word of their Son. His Mother indeed kept these things to be pondered over in her heart.(290)

58. In the public life of Jesus, Mary makes significant appearances. This is so even at the very beginning, when at the marriage feast of Cana, moved with pity, she brought about by her intercession the beginning of miracles of Jesus the Messiah.(291) In the course of her Son's preaching she received the words whereby in extolling a kingdom beyond the calculations and bonds of flesh and blood, He declared blessed(292) those who heard and kept the word of God, as she was faithfully doing.(293) After this manner the Blessed Virgin advanced in her pilgrimage of faith, and faithfully persevered in her union with her Son unto the cross, where she stood, in keeping with the divine plan,(294) grieving exceedingly with her only begotten Son, uniting herself with a maternal heart with His sacrifice, and lovingly consenting to the immolation of this Victim which she herself had brought forth. Finally, she was given by the same Christ Jesus dying on the cross as a mother to His disciple with these words: "Woman, behold thy son".(295) (11*)

59. But since it has pleased God not to manifest solemnly the mystery of the salvation of the human race before He would pour forth the Spirit promised by Christ, we see the apostles before the day of Pentecost "persevering with one mind in prayer with the women and Mary the Mother of Jesus, and with His brethren",(296) and Mary by her prayers imploring the gift of the Spirit, who had already overshadowed her in the Annunciation. Finally, the Immaculate Virgin, preserved free from all guilt of original sin,(12*) on the completion of her earthly sojourn, was taken up body and soul into heavenly glory,(13*) and exalted by the Lord as Queen of the universe, that she might be the more fully confimed to her Son, the Lord of lords(297) and the conqueror of sin and death.(14*)

III. On the Blessed Virgin and the Church

60. There is but one Mediator as we know from the words of the apostle, "for there is one God and one mediator of God and men, the man Christ Jesus, who gave himself a redemption for all".(298) The maternal duty of Mary toward men in no wise obscures or diminishes this unique mediation of Christ, but rather shows His power. For all the salvific influence of the Blessed Virgin on men originates, not from some inner necessity, but from the divine pleasure. It flows forth from the superabundance of the merits of Christ, rests on His mediation, depends entirely on it and draws all its power from it. In no way does it impede, but rather does it foster the

Appendix 4

immediate union of the faithful with Christ.

61. Predestined from eternity by that decree of divine providence which determined the incarnation of the Word to be the Mother of God, the Blessed Virgin was in this earth the virgin Mother of the Redeemer, and above all others and in a singular way the generous associate and humble handmaid of the Lord. She conceived, brought forth and nourished Christ. she presented Him to the Father in the temple, and was united with Him by compassion as He died on the Cross. In this singular way she cooperated by her obedience, faith, hope and burning charity in the work of the Saviour in giving back supernatural life to souls. Wherefore she is our mother in the order of grace.

62. This maternity of Mary in the order of grace began with the consent which she gave in faith at the Annunciation and which she sustained without wavering beneath the cross, and lasts until The eternal fulfillment of all the elect. Taken up to heaven she did not lay aside this salvific duty, but by her constant intercession continued to bring us the gifts of eternal salvation.(15*) By her maternal charity, she cares for the brethren of her Son, who still journey on earth surrounded by dangers and difficulties, until they are led into the happiness of their true home. Therefore the Blessed Virgin is invoked by the Church under the titles of Advocate, Auxiliatrix, Adjutrix, and Mediatrix.(16*) This, however, is to be so understood that it neither takes away from nor adds anything to the dignity and efficaciousness of Christ the one Mediator.(17*)

For no creature could ever be counted as equal with the Incarnate Word and Redeemer. Just as the priesthood of Christ is shared in various ways both by the ministers and by the faithful, and as the one goodness of God is really communicated in different ways to His creatures, so also the unique mediation of the Redeemer does not exclude but rather gives rise to a manifold cooperation which is but a sharing in this one source.

The Church does not hesitate to profess this subordinate role of Mary. It knows it through unfailing experience of it and commends it to the hearts of the faithful, so that encouraged by this maternal help they may the more intimately adhere to the Mediator and Redeemer.

63. By reason of the gift and role of divine maternity, by which she is united with her Son, the Redeemer, and with His singular graces and functions, the Blessed Virgin is also intimately united with the Church. As St. Ambrose taught, the Mother of God is a type of the Church in the order of faith, charity and perfect union with Christ.(18*) For in the mystery of the Church, which is itself rightly called mother and virgin, the Blessed Virgin stands out in eminent and singular fashion as exemplar both of virgin and mother. (19*) By her belief and obedience, not knowing man but overshadowed by the Holy Spirit, as the new Eve she brought forth on earth the very Son of the Father, showing an undefiled faith, not in the word of the ancient serpent, but in that of God's messenger. The Son whom she brought forth is He whom God placed as the first-born among many brethren,(299) namely the faithful, in whose birth and education she cooperates with a maternal love.

64. The Church indeed, contemplating her hidden sanctity, imitating her charity and faithfully fulfilling the Father's will, by receiving the word of God in faith becomes herself a mother. By her preaching she brings forth to a new and immortal life the sons who are born to her in baptism, conceived of the Holy Spirit and born of God. She herself is a virgin, who keeps the faith given to her by her Spouse whole and entire. Imitating the mother of her Lord, and by the

power of the Holy Spirit, she keeps with virginal purity an entire faith, a firm hope and a sincere charity.(20*)

65. But while in the most holy Virgin the Church has already reached that perfection whereby she is without spot or wrinkle, the followers of Christ still strive to increase in holiness by conquering sin.(300) And so they turn their eyes to Mary who shines forth to the whole community of the elect as the model of virtues. Piously meditating on her and contemplating her in the light of the Word made man, the Church with reverence enters more intimately into the great mystery of the Incarnation and becomes more and more like her Spouse. For Mary, who since her entry into salvation history unites in herself and re-echoes the greatest teachings of the faith as she is proclaimed and venerated, calls the faithful to her Son and His sacrifice and to the love of the Father. Seeking after the glory of Christ, the Church becomes more like her exalted Type, and continually progresses in faith, hope and charity, seeking and doing the will of God in all things. Hence the Church, in her apostolic work also, justly looks to her, who, conceived of the Holy Spirit, brought forth Christ, who was born of the Virgin that through the Church He may be born and may increase in the hearts of the faithful also. The Virgin in her own life lived an example of that maternal love, by which it behooves that all should be animated who cooperate in the apostolic mission of the Church for the regeneration of men.

IV. The Cult of the Blessed Virgin in the Church

66. Placed by the grace of God, as God's Mother, next to her Son, and exalted above all angels and men, Mary intervened in the mysteries of Christ and is justly honored by a special cult in the Church. Clearly from earliest times the Blessed Virgin is honored under the title of Mother of God, under whose protection the faithful took refuge in all their dangers and necessities.(21*) Hence after the Synod of Ephesus the cult of the people of God toward Mary wonderfully increased in veneration and love, in invocation and imitation, according to her own prophetic words: "All generations shall call me blessed, because He that is mighty hath done great things to me".(301) This cult, as it always existed, although it is altogether singular, differs essentially from the cult of adoration which is offered to the Incarnate Word, as well to the Father and the Holy Spirit, and it is most favorable to it. The various forms of piety toward the Mother of God, which the Church within the limits of sound and orthodox doctrine, according to the conditions of time and place, and the nature and ingenuity of the faithful has approved, bring it about that while the Mother is honored, the Son, through whom all things have their being (302) and in whom it has pleased the Father that all fullness should dwell,(303) is rightly known, loved and glorified and that all His commands are observed.

67. This most Holy Synod deliberately teaches this Catholic doctrine and at the same time admonishes all the sons of the Church that the cult, especially the liturgical cult, of the Blessed Virgin, be generously fostered, and the practices and exercises of piety, recommended by the magisterium of the Church toward her in the course of centuries be made of great moment, and those decrees, which have been given in the early days regarding the cult of images of Christ, the Blessed Virgin and the saints, be religiously observed.(22*) But it exhorts theologians and preachers of the divine word to abstain zealously both from all gross exaggerations as well as from petty narrow-mindedness in considering the singular dignity of the Mother of God.(23*) Following the study of Sacred Scripture, the Holy Fathers, the doctors and liturgy of the Church, and under the guidance of the Church's magisterium, let them rightly illustrate the duties and privileges of the Blessed Virgin which always look to Christ, the

Appendix 4

source of all truth, sanctity and piety. Let them assiduously keep away from whatever, either by word or deed, could lead separated brethren or any other into error regarding the true doctrine of the Church. Let the faithful remember moreover that true devotion consists neither in sterile or transitory affection, nor in a certain vain credulity, but proceeds from true faith, by which we are led to know the excellence of the Mother of God, and we are moved to a filial love toward our mother and to the imitation of her virtues.

V. Mary the sign of created hope and solace to the wandering people of God

68. In the interim just as the Mother of Jesus, glorified in body and soul in heaven, is the image and beginning of the Church as it is to be perfected is the world to come, so too does she shine forth on earth, until the day of the Lord shall come,(304) as a sign of sure hope and solace to the people of God during its sojourn on earth.

69. It gives great joy and comfort to this holy and general Synod that even among the separated brethren there are some who give due honor to the Mother of our Lord and Saviour, especially among the Orientals, who with devout mind and fervent impulse give honor to the Mother of God, ever virgin.(24*) The entire body of the faithful pours forth instant supplications to the Mother of God and Mother of men that she, who aided the beginnings of the Church by her prayers, may now, exalted as she is above all the angels and saints, intercede before her Son in the fellowship of all the saints, until all families of people, whether they are honored with the title of Christian or whether they still do not know the Saviour, may be happily gathered together in peace and harmony into one people of God, for the glory of the Most Holy and Undivided Trinity.

Each and all these items which are set forth in this dogmatic Constitution have met with the approval of the Council Fathers. And We by the apostolic power given Us by Christ together with the Venerable Fathers in the Holy Spirit, approve, decree and establish it and command that what has thus been decided in the Council be promulgated for the glory of God.

751

APOSTOLIC EXHORTATION
OF HIS HOLINESS PAUL VI

SIGNUM MAGNUM

TO THE CATHOLIC BISHOPS OF THE WORLD

May 13, 1967

Venerable brothers, health and apostolic blessings

INTRODUCTION

The great sign which the Apostle John saw in heaven, "a woman clothed with the sun,"(1) is interpreted by the sacred Liturgy,(2) not without foundation, as referring to the most blessed Mary, the mother of all men by the grace of Christ the Redeemer.

The memory, venerable brothers, is still vivid in our mind of the great emotion we felt in proclaiming the august Mother of God as the spiritual Mother of the Church, that is to say, of all the faithful and of the sacred pastors, as the crowning of the third session of the Second Vatican Council, after having solemnly promulgated the Dogmatic Constitution on the Church.(3) Great also was the happiness of numerous Council Fathers, as well as of the faithful, who were present at the sacred rite in St. Peter's basilica and of the entire Christian people scattered throughout the world:

The memory came spontaneously to many minds of the first grandiose triumph achieved by the humble "handmaid of the Lord"(4) when the Fathers from East and West, gathered in an ecumenical council at Ephesus in the year 431, greeted Mary as "Theotokos" - genitrix of God. The Christian population of the illustrious city associated themselves with a jubilant impulse of faith with the exultance of the Fathers and accompanied them with torchlights to their dwelling.

Oh! with how much maternal satisfaction the Virgin Mary must have looked on the pastors and the faithful in that glorious hour of the history of the Church, recognizing in the hymns of praise, raised in honor principally of the Son and then in her own, the echo of the prophetic canticle which she herself on the impulse of the Holy Spirit had raised to the Most High;

"My soul magnifies the Lord,
and my spirit rejoices in God my Savior,
because He has regarded the lowliness of His handmaid; for,
behold, henceforth all generations shall call me blessed,
because He who is mighty has done great things for me

and holy is His name."(5)

On the occasion of the religious ceremonies which are taking place at this time in honor of the Virgin Mother of God in Fatima, Portugal, where she is venerated by countless numbers of the faithful for her motherly and compassionate heart,(6) we wish to call the attention of all sons of the Church once more to the indissoluble link between the spiritual motherhood of Mary, so amply illustrated in the (council's) Dogmatic Constitution on the Church(7) and the duties of redeemed men toward her, the Mother of the Church.

Once it is acknowledged, by virtue of the numerous testimonies offered by the sacred texts and by the holy Fathers and remembered in the constitution mentioned above, that "Mary, the Mother of God and Mother of the Redeemer"(8) has been "united to Him by a close and indissoluble tie"(9) and that she has a most singular role in "the mystery of the Incarnate Word and of the Mystical Body,"(10) that is to say, in "the economy of salvation,"(11) it appears evident that the Virgin is "rightly honored by the Church with a special veneration,(12) particularly liturgical,"(13) not only as "the most holy Mother of God, who took part in the mysteries of Christ,"(14) but also "as the Mother of the Church."(15)

Nor is it to be feared that liturgical reform, if put into practice according to the formula "the law of faith must establish the law of prayer"(16) may be detrimental to the "wholly singular" veneration(17) due to the Virgin Mary for her prerogatives, first among these being the dignity of the Mother of God. Nor is it to be feared that the greater veneration, liturgical as well as private, given to her may obscure or diminish "the adoration which is offered to the Incarnate Word, as well as the Father and to the Holy Spirit."(18)

Accordingly, without wishing to restate here, venerable brothers, the traditional doctrine of the Church regarding the function of the Mother of God on the plane of salvation and her relations with the Church, we believe that, if we dwell on the consideration of two truths which are very important for the renewal of Christian life, we would be doing something of great utility for the souls of the faithful.

PART I

The first truth is this: Mary is the Mother of the Church not only because she is the Mother of Christ and His most intimate associate in "the new economy when the Son of God took a human nature from her, that He might in the mysteries of His flesh free man from sin,"(19) but also because "she shines forth to the whole community of the elect as a model of the virtues."(20) Indeed, just as no human mother can limit her task to the generation of a new man but must extend it to the function of nourishing and educating her offspring, thus the blessed Virgin Mary, after participating in the redeeming sacrifice of the Son, and in such an intimate way as to deserve to be proclaimed by Him the Mother not only of His disciple John but - may we be allowed to affirm it - of mankind which he in some way represents,(21) now continues to fulfill from heaven her maternal function as the cooperator in the birth and development of divine life in the individual souls of redeemed men. This is a most consoling truth which, by the free consent of God the All-Wise, is an integrating part of the mystery of human salvation; therefore it must be held as faith by all Christians.

But in what way does Mary cooperate in the growth of the members of the Mystical Body in the life of grace? First of all, by her unceasing prayers inspired by a most ardent charity. The

Holy Virgin, in fact, though rejoicing in the union of the august Trinity, does not forget her Son's advancing, as she herself did in the "pilgrimage of the faith".(22) Indeed, contemplating them in God and clearly seeing their necessities, in communion with Jesus Christ, "who continues forever and is therefore able at all times to intercede for them,"(23) she makes herself their Advocate, Auxiliatrix, Adjutrix and Mediatrix.(24) Of this intercession of hers for the People of God with the Son, the Church has been persuaded, ever since the first centuries, as testified to by this most ancient antiphon which, with some slight difference, forms part of the liturgical prayer in the East as well as in the West: "We seek refuge under the protection of your mercies, Oh Mother of God; do not reject our supplication in need but save us from perdition, O you who alone are blessed."(25) Nor should anyone believe that the maternal intervention of Mary would prejudice the predominant and irreplaceable efficacy of Christ, our Savior. On the contrary, it draws its strength from the mediation of Christ of which it is the luminous proof.(26)

But the cooperation of the Mother of the Church in the development of the divine life of the souls does not come to an end with the appeal to the Son. She exercises on redeemed men another influence: that of example. An influence which is indeed most important, according to the well-known axiom: "Verba movent, exempla trahunt" (Words move, examples attract). In fact, just as the teachings of the parents become far more efficacious if they are strengthened by the example of a life conforming with the norms of human and Christian prudence, so the sweetness and the enchantment emanating from the sublime virtues of the immaculate Mother of God attract souls in an irresistible way to imitation of the divine model, Jesus Christ, of whom she was the most faithful image. Therefore the council declared: "The Church, devotedly meditating on her and contemplating her in the light of the Word made man, enters more intimately into the supreme mystery of the Incarnation and becomes ever increasingly like her Spouse"(27).

Furthermore, it is well to bear in mind that Mary's eminent sanctity was not only a singular gift of divine liberality. It was also the fruit of the continuous and generous cooperation of her free will in the inner motions of the Holy Spirit. It is because of the perfect harmony between divine grace and the activity of her human nature that the Virgin rendered supreme glory to the Most Holy Trinity and became the illustrious ornament of the Church, which thus greets her in sacred Liturgy: "You are the glory of Jerusalem, the joy of Israel, the honor of our people"(28).

Let us then admire in the pages of the Gospel the testimonies of such sublime harmony. Mary, as soon as she was reassured by the voice of the Angel Gabriel that God had chosen her as the unblemished mother of His only-begotten Son, unhesitatingly gave her consent to a work which would have engaged all the energies of her fragile nature and declared: "Behold the handmaid of the Lord; be it done to me according to thy word"(29). From that moment, she consecrated all of herself to the service not only of the heavenly Father and of the Word Incarnate, who had become her Son, but also to all mankind, having clearly understood that Jesus, in addition to saving his people from the slavery of sin, would become the King of a messianic Kingdom, universal and eternal(30).

Therefore, the life of Joseph's pure spouse, who remained a virgin "during childbirth and after childbirth" - as the Catholic Church has always believed and professed (31) and as was fitting for her who was raised to the incomparable dignity of divine motherhood(32) - was a life of such perfect union with the Son that she shared in His joys, sorrows and triumphs. And even after Christ had ascended to heaven she remained united to Him by a most ardent love while she faithfully fulfilled the new mission of spiritual Mother of the most beloved of the disciples and of the nascent Church. It can be asserted that the whole life of the humble handmaid of the Lord, from the moment when she was greeted by the Angel, until her assumption in body and soul to heavenly glory, was a life of loving service.

We, therefore, associating ourselves with the Evangelists, with the Fathers and the Doctors of the Church, recalled in the dogmatic constitution "Lumen gentium" (Chap. VIII), full of admiration, contemplate Mary, firm in her faith, ready in her obedience, simple in humility, exulting in praising the Lord, ardent in charity, strong and constant in the fulfillment of her mission to the point of sacrificing herself, in full communion of sentiments with her Son who immolated Himself on the Cross to give men a new life.

Before such splendor of virtue, the first duty of all those who recognize in the Mother of Christ the model of the Church, is to unite themselves to her in giving thanks to the Most High for working great things in Mary for the benefit of all mankind. But this is not enough. It is also the duty of all the faithful to pay as tribute to the most faithful handmaid of the Lord, a veneration of praise, of gratitude and of love because, by a wise and mild divine provision, her free consent and her generous cooperation in the designs of God had, and still have, a great influence in the attainment of human salvation(33). Therefore every Christian must make St. Anselm's prayer his own: "Oh, glorious Lady, grant that through you we may deserve to ascend to Jesus, your Son, who through you deigned to descend among us".(34)

PART II:
DEVOUT IMITATION OF THE VIRTUES
OF THE MOST HOLY MARY

1. True devotion to the Most Holy Mary reflects her virtues.

Neither the grace of the divine Redeemer, nor the powerful intercession of His Mother and our spiritual Mother, nor yet her sublime sanctity, could lead us to the port of salvation if we did not respond to them by our persevering will to honor Jesus Christ and the Holy Virgin with our devout imitation of their sublime virtue.

It is therefore the duty of all Christians to imitate in a reverent spirit the examples of goodness left to them by their heavenly Mother. This, venerable brothers, is the other truth to which we are pleased to call your attention and the attention of the faithful entrusted to your pastoral care, that they may second with docility the exhortation of the Fathers of the Second Vatican Council: "Let the faithful remember that true devotion consists neither in fruitless and passing emotion, nor in a certain vain credulity. Rather, it proceeds from true faith, by which we are led to know the excellence of the Mother of God, and are moved to a filial love toward our mother and to the imitation of her virtues."(35)

Imitation of Jesus Christ is undoubtedly the regal way to be followed to attain sanctity and reproduce in ourselves, according to our forces, the absolute perfection of the heavenly Father. But while the Catholic Church has always proclaimed a truth so sacrosanct, it has also affirmed that imitation of the Virgin Mary, far from distracting the souls from the faithful following of Christ, makes it more pleasant and easier for them. For, since she had always done the will of God, she was the first to deserve the praise which Christ addressed to His disciples: "Whoever does the will of my Father in heaven, he is my brother and sister and mother."(36)

2. "Through Mary to Jesus."

The general norm "Through Mary to Jesus" is therefore valid also for the imitation of Christ. Nevertheless, let our faith not be perturbed, as if the intervention of a creature in every way similar to us, except as regards sin, offended our personal dignity and prevented the intimacy and immediacy of our relationships of adoration and friendship with the Son of God. Let us rather recognize the "goodness and the love of God the Savior,"(37) who, condescending to our misery, so remote from His infinite sanctity, wished to make it easier for us to imitate it by giving us as a model the human person of His Mother. She, in fact, among human beings, offers the most shining example and the closest to us, of that perfect obedience whereby we lovingly and readily conform with the will of the eternal Father. Christ Himself, as we well know, made this full closeness to the approval of the Father, the supreme ideal of His human behavior, declaring: "I do always the things that are pleasing to Him."(38)

3. Mary, the new Eve, the dawn of the New Testament.

If we then contemplate the Virgin of Nazareth in the halo of her prerogative and of her virtues, we will see her shine before our eyes as the "New Eve,"(39) the exalted daughter of Sion, the summit of the Old Testament and the dawn of the New, in which "the fullness of time"(40) was realized, which was preordained by God for the mission in the world of His only-begotten Son. In truth, the Virgin Mary, more than all the patriarchs and prophets, more than the "just" and "pious" Simeon awaited and implored "the consolation of Israel...the Christ of the Lord"(41) and then greeted His advent with the hymn of "Magnificat" when He descended into her most chaste womb to take on our flesh.

It is in Mary, therefore, that the Church of Christ indicates the example of the worthiest way of receiving in our spirits the Word of God, in accordance with the luminous sentence of St. Augustine: "Mary was therefore more blessed in receiving the faith in Christ than in conceiving the flesh of Christ. Accordingly, maternal consanguinity would not have benefited Mary if she had not felt more fortunate in having Christ in her heart then in her womb."(42) And it is still in her that Christians can admire the example of how to fulfill, with humility and at the same time with magnanimity, the mission which God entrusts to each one in this world, in relation to his own salvation and that of his fellow beings.

"Therefore, I beg you, be imitators of me as I am of Christ."(43) These words, and with greater reason than the Apostle Paul to the Christians of Corinth, can be addressed by the Mother of the Church to the multitudes of the faithful, who, in a symphony of faith and love with the generations of past centuries, acclaim her as blessed.(44) It is an invitation which it is a duty to heed docilely.

4. Marian message of invitation to prayer, penance and the fear of God.

And then a message of supreme utility seems today to reach the faithful from her who is the Immaculate, the holy, the cooperator of the Son in the work of restoration of supernatural life in souls.(45) In fact, in devoutly contemplating Mary they draw from her a stimulus for trusting prayer, a spur to the practice of penance and to the holy fear of God. Likewise, it is in this Marian elevation that they more often hear echoing the words with which Jesus Christ announced the advent of the Kingdom of heaven: "Repent and believe in the Gospel"(46); and His severe admonition: "Unless you repent you will all perish in the same manner."(47)

Therefore, impelled by love and by the wish to placate God for the offenses against His sanctity and His justice and, at the same time, moved by trust in His infinite mercy, we must bear the sufferings of the spirit and of the body that we may expiate our sins and those of our fellow beings and so avoid the twofold penalty or "harm" and of "sense," that is to say, the loss of God--the supreme good--and eternal fire.(48)

5. Christ Himself indicates the Mother as the model of the Church.

What must stimulate the faithful even more to follow the examples of the most holy Virgin is the fact that Jesus Himself, by giving her to us as our Mother, has tacitly indicated her as the model to be followed. It is, in fact, a natural thing that the children should have the same sentiments of their mothers and should reflect their merits and virtues. Therefore, as each one of us can repeat with St. Paul: "The Son of God loved me and gave Himself up for me,"(49) so in all trust he can believe that the divine Savior has left to him also, in spiritual heritage, His Mother, with all the treasures of grace and virtues with which He had endowed her, that she may pour them over us through the influence of her powerful intercession and our willing imitation. This is why St. Bernard rightly affirms: "Coming to her the Holy Spirit filled her with grace for herself; when the same Spirit pervaded her again she became superabundant and redounding in grace for us also."(50)

6. The history of the Church is always illumined by the edifying presence of Mary.

From what we have been illustrating in the light of the holy Gospel and of Catholic tradition, it appears evident that the spiritual motherhood of Mary transcends space and time and belongs to the universal history of the Church, since she has always been present in the Church with her maternal assistance. Likewise the meaning of the affirmation appears clear, which is so often repeated: our era may well be called the Marian era. In fact, if it is true that, by an exalted grace of the Lord, the providential role of the most holy Mary in the history of salvation has been more deeply understood by the vast strata of the Christian people, this, however, should not lead us to believe that in past ages we had no intuition whatever of this truth or that future ones will ignore it. In truth, all periods of the Church's history have benefited and will benefit from the maternal presence of the Mother of God because she will remain always indissolubly joined to the mystery of the Mystical Body, of whose Head it was written: "Jesus Christ is the same, yesterday and today, yes, and forever."(51)

7. The Mother of the Church, banner of unity, stimulus for perfect Brotherhood among all Christians.

Venerable brothers, the persuasion that the thought of the Church regarding the veneration of praise, gratitude and love due to the most blessed Virgin is in full accord with the doctrine of the holy Gospel, as it was more precisely understood and explained by the tradition of the East as well as of the West, stirs in our spirit the hope that this pastoral exhortation of ours for an ever more fervid and more fruitful Marian piety will be received with generous acceptance not only by the faithful entrusted to your care, but also by those who, while not enjoying full communion with the Catholic Church, nevertheless, together with us, admire and venerate the handmaid of the Lord, the Virgin Mary, Mother of the Son of God.

May the Immaculate Heart of Mary shine before the eyes of all Christians as the model of perfect love toward God and toward our fellow beings; may it lead them toward the Holy Sacraments by virtue of which souls are cleansed from the stains of sin and are preserved from it. May it also stimulate them to make reparation for the innumerable offenses against the Divine Majesty. Lastly, may it shine like a banner of unity and a spur to perfect the bonds of brotherhood among all Christians in the bosom of the one Church of Jesus Christ, which "taught by the Holy Spirit, honors her with filial affection and piety as a most beloved mother."(52)

8. Invitation to renew personal consecration to the Immaculate Heart of Mary.

Since the 25th anniversary is recalled this year of the solemn consecration of the Church and of mankind to Mary, the Mother of God, and to her Immaculate Heart, by our predecessor of venerated memory, Pius XII, on Oct. 31, 1942, on the occasion of the broadcast message to the Portuguese nation(53)—a consecration which we ourself have renewed on Nov. 21, 1964 (54)—we exhort all the sons of the Church to renew personally their consecration to the Immaculate Heart of the Mother of the Church and to bring alive this most noble act of veneration through a life ever more consonant with the divine will (55) and in a spirit of filial service and of devout imitation of their heavenly Queen.

Lastly, venerable brothers, we express the trust that, thanks to your encouragement, the clergy and the Christian people entrusted to your pastoral ministry will respond in a generous spirit to this exhortation of ours so as to demonstrate toward the Virgin Mother of God a more ardent piety and a firmer confidence. Meanwhile while we are comforted by the certainty that the glorious Queen of Heaven and our most sweet Mother will never cease to assist all and each one of her sons and will never withdraw from the entire Church of Christ her heavenly patronage, to you yourselves and to your faithful, as a pledge of divine favors and as a sign of our benevolence, we wholeheartedly impart the apostolic blessing.

Given in Rome, at St. Peter, on the 13th day of the month of May in the year 1967, the fourth of our pontificate.

PAULUS PP. VI

NOTES

1. Cf. Apocalypse 12,1.

2. Cf. Epistle of Mass for the feast of the Apparition of Mary Immaculate, Feb. 11.

3. Cf. Acta Apostolica Sedis 57, 1965, pp. 1-67.

4. Cf. Luke 1:38

5. Ibid., 1:46 and 48-49

6. Radio message of Pius XII, May 13, 1946, given for the Christians of Portugal, Acta Apostolicae Sedis 38, 1946, p. 264.

7. Cf. chapter VIII, paragraph III, on the Blessed Virgin and the Church, Acta Apostolicae Sedis, 57, 1965, pp. 62-65.

8. Cf. ibid. n. 53, p. 58.

9. Cf. ibid.

10. Ibid. n. 54, p. 59.

11. Ibid. n. 55. p. 59.

12. Ibid. n. 66, p. 65.

13. Allocution to the Council Fathers in the Vatican Basilica on the feast of the Presentation, third session of the Council, Acta Apostolicae Sedis, 56, 1964, p. 1016.

14. Cf. dogmatic constitution Lumen Gentium, n. 66: Acta Apostolicae Sedis, 57, 1965, p. 65.

15. Cf. ibid., n. 67, p. 65.

16. Pius XII, encyclical letter Mediator Dei: Acta Apostolicae Sedis, 38, 1947, p. 541.

17. Cf. dogmatic constitution Lumen Gentium, n. 66: Acta Apostolicae Sedis, 57, 1965, p. 65.

18. Ibid. n. 66, p. 65.

19. Ibid. n. 55, p. 60.

20. Ibid. n. 65, p. 64, also n. 63.

21. Cf. ibid. n. 58, p. 61; Leo XIII encyclical letter Adiutricem populi, Acts of Leo XIII, 15, 1896, p. 302.

22. Dogmatic constitution Lumen Gentium, n. 58; Acta Apostolicae Sedis, 57, 1967, p. 61.

23. Heb. 7, 25.

24. Cf. dogmatic constitution Lumen Gentium, n. 62: Acta Apostolicae Sedis, 57, 1965, p. 61.

25. Cf. Dom F. Mercenier, L'Antienne Mariale grecque la plus ancienne in Le Museon 52, 1939, pp. 229-233.

26. Cf. dogmatic constitution Lumen Gentium, n. 62: Acta Apostolicae Sedis, 57, 1965, p. 63.

27. Ibid. n. 65, p. 64.

28. Second Antiphon of lauds, feast of the Immaculate Conception

29. Luke 1, 38.

30. Cf. Matt. 1, 21; Luke 1, 33.

31. Cf. St. Leo, martyr, letter, Lectis dilectionis tuae to Flavianum; PL 54, 759; idem, letter, Licet per nostros to Julian, Ep. Coensem: p. 54, 803; St. Hormisdas, Ep. Inter ea quae to Justinian, emperor, PL 63, 407; Lateran Council, October, 609, under Martin I, canon 3: Caspar, ZKG, 51, 1932, p. 88; Conc. Tolet. XVI, Symbol. article 22: J. Madoz El Simbolo del Concilio XVI de Toledo in Estudios Onienses, ser. I, volume 3, 1946; dogmatic constitution Lumen Gentium, nn. 52, 55, 57, 59, 63; Acta Apostolicae Sedis, 57, 1965, pp. 58-64.

32. Cf. St. Thomas, Summa Theologica, Part I, q. 25, a. 6, ad. 4.

33. Cf. dogmatic constitution Lumen Gentium, n. 56; Acta Apostolicae Sedis, 57, 1965, p. 60.

34. Orat. 54, PL 158, 961.

35. Dogmatic constitution Lumen Gentium, n. 67; Acta Apostolicae Sedis, 57, 1965, p. 66; confer St. Thomas, Summa Theologica, Part II-II, q. 81, a. 1, ad. 1; Part III, q. 25, aa. 1, 5.

36. Matt. 12, 50.

37. Cf. Titus 3, 4.

38. St. John 8, 29.

39. Cf. St. Irenaeus, Adv. Haer. III, 22, 4: PG 959; St. Epiphanius, Haer. 78, 18: PG 42, 728-729; St. John Damascene, first homily on the birth of Mary: PG 96, 671 ss; dogmatic constitution Lumen Gentium, n. 56; Acta Apostolicae Sedis, 57, 1965, pp.

60-61.

40. Galatians 4, 4.

41. St. Luke 2, 25-26.

42. Serm. 215, 1: PL 38, 1074.

43. 1 Cor., 4, 16.

44. Cf. St. Luke. 1, 48.

45. Cf. dogmatic constitution Lumen Gentium, n. 61; Acta Apostolicae Sedis 57, 1965, p. 63.

46. St. Mark 1, 15; cf. St. Matthew 3, 2; 4, 17.

47. St. Luke 13, 5.

48. Cf. St. Matthew 25, 41; dogmatic constitution Lumen Gentium, n. 48: Acta Apostolicae Sedis, 57, 1965, p. 54.

Appendix 4

49. Galatians 2, 20; cf. Eph. 5, 2.

50. Second homily super Missus est, n. 2: PL 183, 64.

51. Heb. 13, 8.

52. Dogmatic constitution Lumen Gentium, nn. 53: Acta Apostolicae Sedis, n. 53, 57, 1965, p. 59.

53. Cf. discourses and radio messages of Pius XII, volume IV, pp. 260-262; cf. Acta Apostolicae Sedis, 34, 1942, pp. 345-346.

54. cit. Apostolicae Sedis, 56, 1964, p. 1017.

55. Cf. oration for feast of the Immaculate Heart of Mary, Aug. 22.

John Paul II

Birth name	Karol Józef Wojtyła
Papacy began	October 16, 1978
Papacy ended	April 2, 2005
Predecessor	John Paul I
Successor	Benedict XVI
Born	May 18, 1920 Wadowice, Poland ▬
Died	April 2, 2005 (aged 84) Apostolic Palace, Vatican City

Coat of Arms of Pope
John Paul II. The Letter M
is for Mary, the mother of
Jesus, to whom he held
strong devotion

Pope St. John Paul II: Karol Jozef Wojtyla

Papacy: 1978 – 2005

Summary of Contents:

1). *Angelus*, Pope John Paul II, Sunday, July 16, 2000; Below is an excerpt from the *Angelus*, commemorating the Feast of Our Lady of Mount Carmel:

".....my thoughts turn today to Mount Carmel, praised in the Bible for its beauty. We are, in fact, celebrating the feast of Our Lady of Mount Carmel. On that mountain, located in Israel near Haifa, the holy prophet Elijah strenuously defended the integrity and purity of the chosen people's faith in the living God. On that same mountain some hermits gathered in the 12th century after Christ and dedicated themselves to contemplation and penance. The Carmelite Order arose from their spiritual experience."

2).. *Message of John Paul II to the Carmelite Family*, Pope John Paul II, March 25, 2001; This message of the Holy Father to the Carmelite Community commemorates the 750th anniversary of the bestowal of the Scapular. This *Message* to the Carmelites, commemorating the anniversary, implies an affirmation and acknowledgement of the venerable tradition in the Church, confirmed by many Predecessors of His Holiness, as well as numerous Carmelite Historians, Prior Generals themselves, of the authenticity of the vision of Our Blessed Mother to St. Simon Stock, taking place on July 16, 1251. Below is the excerpt:

"I cannot fail to stress a happy coincidence: the celebration of this Marian year for the whole of Carmel is taking place...on the 750th anniversary of the bestowal of the Scapular." "Over time, this rich Marian heritage of Carmel has become, through the spread of the Holy Scapular Devotion, a treasure for the whole Church. By its simplicity, its anthropological value and its relationship to Mary's role in regard to the Church and humanity, this devotion was so deeply and widely accepted by the People of God that it came to be expressed in the memorial of 16 July on the liturgical calendar of the universal Church...I too have worn the Scapular of Carmel over my heart for a long time!

3). *Message of John Paul II to the Order of the Brothers of the Blessed Virgin Mary of Mt. Carmel*, Pope John Paul II, September 8, 2001. In this *Message*, the Holy Father, again, implies the authenticity of the vision of Our Lady to St. Simon Stock, on July 16, 1251, by his acknowledgement of the 750th anniversary. Below is an excerpt:

"I want to underline the fact that the General Chapter is held during the year celebrating the 750th anniversary of the gift of the Scapular....Your reference to human experience of a journey belongs to Carmelite spirituality. From the first hermits established on Mount Carmel who had

arrived in the Land of the Lord Jesus as pilgrims, life is represented as an ascetical ascent towards the holy mountain, that is Christ Jesus our Lord (cf. Roman Missal Collect of the Mass in Honor of the B.V. Mary of Carmel, 16, July).

4). *Message of John Paul II for the 550th Anniversary of the Addition of the Cloistered Nuns and the Third Order of the Laity to the Carmelite Order,* October 7, 2002.   This *Message* of Bl. Pope John Paul II, commemorates the establishment of the Third Order of Carmelites consisting of lay people desirous of living Carmelite Spirituality in the world, and the entrance into the Order of the cloistered nuns. His Holiness mentions that it was Bl. John Soreth, Prior General of the Carmelite Order at the time, who approached his venerable predecessor, Pope Nicholas V and obtained canonical status for the Third Order, which was granted by Pope Nicholas V with his *Bull: Cum Nulla,* October 7, 1452.

(It was also Blessed John Soreth, as is recalled in Chapter 8 of this book and bears repeating, who, carried out what Blessed Joan of Toulouse had begun. She had received the habit of the Tertiary from St. Simon Stock and had persuaded thousands to be enrolled in the Brown Scapular. Animated by her zeal, Blessed John (Soreth) preached and taught love for the Scapular and led thousands to follow the footsteps of Blessed Joan of Toulouse.)

Below is an excerpt of this *Message* of Bl. John Paul II:

"Bl. John Soreth, Prior General at the time, perceived that the life of sacrifice, solitude and prayer of the nuns would be beneficial for the friars recalling them to the primitive and genuine spirit; and also that it would be useful to offer lay people, as was the case with the Mendicant Orders, the possibility of drawing life from the common spiritual source....So on 7 October, 1452, the Order asked my venerable predecessor, Pope Nicholas V for the faculty to set up in the Order the enclosed nuns of contemplative life and an association of lay persons living in the world, the Carmelite Third Order. The Pope granted this with the Bull Cum nulla that is now being commemorated." May these brothers and sisters whom the Scapular joins to the other members of the Carmelite Order, be grateful for the gift received and in every circumstance be faithful to the duties that derive from this charismatic belonging..."

5). *Osservatore Romano Newspaper, Angelus,* Pope John Paul II, dated 25-26 July, 1988, article entitled: *La Vergine Madre di Dio "Flos Carmeli" possiede la bellezza di tutte le virtu'" (The Virgin Mother of God, Flower of Carmel, possesses the beauty of all the virtues)* The Holy Father, during the *Angelus* speaks of Marian piety, Our Lady of Mount Carmel and the gift of the Scapular to the world. Below is an excerpt of the *Angelus,* translated from Italian into English:

"This month of July we celebrate the memory of Our Lady of Mt. Carmel, very dear to the piety of the Christian people of all the world and tied in a special way to the religious family of the Carmelites..."

Appendix 4

"Our thoughts go to the sacred mountain, which in the biblical world is always considered as a symbol of grace, of blessings, and of beauty. On this mountain (Mt. Carmel), the Carmelites dedicated to the Virgin Mother of God, Flower of Carmel, who possesses the beauty of all the virtues, their first Church ... ...

"A particular grace from Our Lady to the Carmelites, recorded in a venerable tradition bound to St. Simon Stock, has radiated among the Christian people with much spiritual fruit. It is the Scapular of Carmel, the sign of affiliation to the Carmelite Order for participation in the spiritual benefits, and is a vehicle of tender and filial Marian devotion..."

6). *Osservatore Romano Newspaper,* dated Monday-Tuesday, November 7, 8, 2005: The article is entitled: " *La prima session del Tribunale del processo rogatorio per la Causa di beatificazione e canonizzazione del servo di Dio Giovanni Paolo II"* (The first session of the Tribunal in the process for the Cause of Beatification and Canonization of the Servant of God, John Paul II). Below is an English translation of a paragraph taken from the article which is published in Italian:

"Some of the practices of piety, in which the Servant of God, expressed his love for Christ and His Mother, are numbered among Popular Piety. (John Paul II) a man of great intellect and ardor, was not ashamed of the Scapular of Our Lady of Mount Carmel and of these simple forms of piety."

7). *"A Brown Scapular of the Servant of God, John Paul II"* "The Scapular of Pope John Paul II was sent as a gift to Father Lucio Maria Zappatore, O. Carm,, Parish Priest of S. Maria Regina Mundi, (Rome), a Scapular of Our Lady of Mount Carmel worn by the Servant of God, John Paul II. It was given to him with the authority of His Eminence the Most Reverend Cardinal Stanislao Dziwisz, Metropolitan Archbishop of Cracow, himself, secretary of Pope John Paul II. The declaration of authenticity of the Scapular of John Paul II was signed by the Cardinal himself, on October 6, 2007. (http://carmelown38.blogspot.com/2008/01/pope-john-paul-ii-scapular.html)

765

The Brown Scapular of Our Lady of Mount Carmel

JOHN PAUL II

ANGELUS

Sunday, 16 July 2000

1. I thank the Lord who this year has again offered me the opportunity to spend a period of rest in this stupendous mountain setting, which calls to mind the majestic presence of God. I thank the Bishop of Aosta, the President of the Council and Board of Valle d'Aosta and all the people of this region, which is dear to me, for their invitation and their welcome, as cordial as it is every year. I express my special gratitude to the Salesians, who always show me great hospitality, as well as to those who each day ensure that my collaborators and I will have a peaceful stay. Here, among the pleasant woods and valleys, the body is restored and the spirit can be more devoted to reflection and contemplation.

From this peaceful place, I would like to send a cordial greeting to those who are on holiday in these valleys and elsewhere, in the mountains or by the sea. I invite everyone to make these days of well-deserved summer rest a time of inner enrichment and worthwhile family relaxation. I am also thinking of those who cannot allow themselves a vacation and have stayed at home. I extend my affectionate greeting especially to the sick, the elderly, prisoners and those who are alone. I assure each one of a daily remembrance in my prayer.

2. As I look at these mountains, my thoughts turn today to Mount Carmel, praised in the Bible for its beauty. We are, in fact, celebrating the feast of Our Lady of Mount Carmel. On that mountain, located in Israel near Haifa, the holy prophet Elijah strenuously defended the integrity and purity of the chosen people's faith in the living God. On that same mountain some hermits gathered in the 12th century after Christ and dedicated themselves to contemplation and penance. The Carmelite Order arose from their spiritual experience.

Walking with the Blessed Virgin, the model of complete fidelity to the Lord, we will fear no obstacles or difficulties. Supported by her motherly intercession, like Elijah we will be able to fulfil our vocation as authentic "prophets" of the Gospel in our time.

3. Today's liturgy for the 15th Sunday in Ordinary Time urges us to make this ascetic and apostolic effort. It invites us to follow the example of the prophet Amos and the Apostles, who were chosen by the Lord to cooperate in his work of salvation.

May Our Lady of Mount Carmel, whom we call upon today with special devotion, help us tirelessly climb towards the summit of the mountain of holiness; may she help us love nothing more than Christ, who reveals to the world the mystery of divine love and true human dignity (cf *Opening Prayer*).

Appendix 4

After leading the recitation of the Angelus, the Holy Father greeted the faithful present in Italian, French and Spanish.

Today, the memorial of Our Lady of Mount Carmel, the presence of a group of Carmelite Sisters of St Teresa from Turin, who are holding their General Chapter, is particularly significant. In greeting you affectionately, dear sisters, I would also like to extend a cordial wish to all Carmelite men and women, as well as to the associations inspired by this charism. I invoke constant divine assistance on the entire Carmelite family, as I urge all its members to seek and love God, who first loved us, above all things and to strive in every circumstance to foster the values of the contemplative life, from which love of neighbour flows and is urged on for the salvation of the world and the building up of the Church.

I also greet the Swiss Benedictine monks who have wished to pay me a visit. Dear friends, may St Benedict, whose feast we celebrated a few days ago, help you and the entire Benedictine family to be faithful to the teaching he set down in the Book of the Rule.

I next greet the Alpine guides of Courmayeur, the Mountain Milk Producers' Associations of the Arco Alpino regions who are celebrating their Jubilee, the faithful from the parish of Giussano, the group of sculptors who have carved this artistic cross, the artist who created the work depicting St Laurence, which I will shortly bless, and "Les Enfants du Paradis" Children's Choir.

Dear French-speaking pilgrims who have joined the Marian prayer of the Angelus, I cordially greet you. In particular, I extend my greetings and thanks to you, the authorities and inhabitants of the Valle d'Aosta, who welcome me to your beautiful region where contemplation of the mountain peaks invites us to lift our eyes to the Lord, Creator of heaven and earth. On this first day of the week, I ask the Holy Spirit to fill your hearts with the gift of wonder at the beauties of creation, which lead us to discover the divine mysteries. May God bless you and keep you!

On this Sunday when we also recall Our Lady of Mount Carmel, I am pleased to greet the Spanish-speaking pilgrims who are taking part in this Marian prayer. I cordially bless you all and your families. Thank you very much for coming.

Dear brothers and sisters, I thank you all for your heartfelt participation and cordially bless you.

MESSAGE OF JOHN PAUL II
TO THE CARMELITE FAMILY

To the Most Reverend Fathers
Joseph Chalmers
Prior General of the Order of Brothers of the Blessed Virgin Mary of Mount Carmel
(O.Carm.)
and
Camilo Maccise
Superior General of the Order of Discalced Brothers of the Blessed Virgin Mary of Mount Carmel (O.C.D.)

1. The providential event of grace, which the Jubilee Year has been for the Church, prompts her to look with trust and hope to the journey we have just begun in the new millennium. *"At the beginning of this new century"*, I wrote in the Apostolic Letter *Novo millennio ineunte*, "our steps must quicken.... On this journey we are accompanied by the Blessed Virgin Mary, to whom ... I entrusted the third millennium" (n. 58).

I therefore learned with deep joy that the two branches of the Order of Carmel, the ancient and the reformed, intend to express their filial love for their Patroness by dedicating the year 2001 to her, invoked as the Flower of Carmel, Mother and Guide on the way of holiness. In this regard, I cannot fail to stress a happy coincidence: the celebration of this Marian year for the whole of Carmel is taking place, according to a venerable tradition of the Order itself, on the 750th anniversary of the bestowal of the Scapular. This celebration is therefore a marvellous occasion for the entire Carmelite Family to deepen not only its Marian spirituality, but to live it more and more in the light of the place which the Virgin Mother of God and of mankind holds in the mystery of Christ and the Church, and therefore to follow her who is the "Star of Evangelization" (cf. *Novo millennio ineunte*, n. 58).

2. In their journey towards the "mountain of God, Christ the Lord" (*Roman Missal*, Opening Prayer of the Mass in honour of Our Lady of Mount Carmel, 16 July), the various generations of Carmel, from the beginning until today, have sought to model their lives on Mary's example.
In Carmel therefore and in every soul moved by tender affection for the Blessed Virgin and Mother, there has thrived a contemplation of her, who from the beginning knew how to open herself to hearing God's Word and to obeying his will (Lk 2: 19, 51). For Mary, taught and formed by the Spirit (cf. Lk 2: 44-50), was able by faith to understand her own history (cf. Lk 1: 46-55) and, docile to the divine promptings, "advanced in her pilgrimage of faith, and faithfully persevered in her union with her Son unto the cross, where she stood, in keeping with the divine plan (cf. Jn 19: 25), enduring with her Only-begotten Son the intensity of his suffering and associating herself with his sacrifice in her mother's heart" (*Lumen gentium*, n. 58).

3. Contemplation of the Virgin presents her to us as a loving Mother who sees her Son growing up in Nazareth (cf. Lk 2: 40, 52), follows him on the roads of Palestine, helps him at the wedding at Cana (cf. Jn 2: 5) and, at the foot of the Cross, becomes the Mother associated with his offering and given to all people when Jesus himself entrusts her to his beloved disciple (cf. Jn 19: 26). As Mother of the Church, the Blessed Virgin is one with the disciples in "constant prayer" (Acts 1: 14); as the new Woman who anticipates in herself what will one day come to pass for us all in the full enjoyment of Trinitarian life, she is taken up into heaven from where she spreads the protective mantle of her mercy over her children on their pilgrimage to the holy mountain of glory.

Such a contemplative attitude of mind and heart prompts admiration for the Virgin's experience of faith and love; she already lives in herself all that every believer desires and hopes to attain in the mystery of Christ and the Church (cf. *Sacrosanctum Concilium*, n. 103; *Lumen gentium*, n. 53).

Therefore, Carmelites have chosen Mary as their Patroness and spiritual Mother and always keep before the eyes of their heart the Most Pure Virgin who guides everyone to the perfect knowledge and imitation of Christ.

Thus an intimacy of spiritual relations has blossomed, leading to an ever increasing communion with Christ and Mary. For the members of the Carmelite Family, Mary, the Virgin Mother of God and mankind, is not only a model to imitate but also the sweet presence of a Mother and Sister in whom to confide. St Teresa of Jesus rightly urged her sisters: "Imitate Our Lady and consider how great she must be and what a good thing it is that we have her for our Patroness" (*Interior Castle*, III, 1, 3).

4. This intense Marian life, which is expressed in trusting prayer, enthusiastic praise and diligent imitation, enables us to understand how the most genuine form of devotion to the Blessed Virgin, expressed by the humble sign of the Scapular, is consecration to her Immaculate Heart (cf. Pius XII, Letter *Neminem profecto latet* [11 February 1950: *AAS* 42, 1950, pp. 390-391]; Dogmatic Constitution on the Church *Lumen gentium*, n. 67). In this way, the heart grows in communion and familiarity with the Blessed Virgin, "as a new way of living for God and of continuing here on earth the love of Jesus the Son for his Mother Mary" (cf. *Angelus Address*, in *Insegnamenti* XI/3, 1988, p. 173). Thus, as the blessed Carmelite martyr Titus Brandsma expressed it, we are put in profound harmony with Mary the *Theotokos* and become, like her, transmitters of divine life: "The Lord also sends his angel to us ... we too must accept God in our hearts, carry him in our hearts, nourish him and make him grow in us so that he is born of us and lives with us as the God-with-us, Emmanuel" (*From the report of Bl. Titus Brandsma to the Mariological Congress of Tongerloo*, August 1936).

Over time this rich Marian heritage of Carmel has become, through the spread of the Holy Scapular devotion, a treasure for the whole Church. By its simplicity, its anthropological value and its relationship to Mary's role in regard to the Church and humanity, this devotion was so deeply and widely accepted by the People of God that it came to be expressed in the memorial of 16 July on the liturgical calendar of the universal Church.

5. The sign of the Scapular points to an effective synthesis of Marian spirituality, which nourishes the devotion of believers and makes them sensitive to the Virgin Mother's loving presence in their lives. The Scapular is essentially a "habit". Those who receive it are associated more or less closely with the Order of Carmel and dedicate themselves to the service of Our Lady for the good of the whole Church (cf. "Formula of Enrolment in the Scapular", in the *Rite of Blessing of and Enrolment in the Scapular,* approved by the Congregation for Divine Worship and the Discipline of the Sacraments, 5 January 1996). Those who wear the Scapular are thus brought into the land of Carmel, so that they may "eat its fruits and its good things" (cf. Jer 2: 7), and experience the loving and motherly presence of Mary in their daily commitment to be clothed in Jesus Christ and to manifest him in their life for the good of the Church and the whole of humanity (cf. "Formula of Enrolment in the Scapular", cit.).

Therefore two truths are evoked by the sign of the Scapular: on the one hand, the constant protection of the Blessed Virgin, not only on life's journey, but also at the moment of passing into the fullness of eternal glory; on the other, the awareness that devotion to her cannot be limited to prayers and tributes in her honour on certain occasions, but must become a "habit", that is, a permanent orientation of one's own Christian conduct, woven of prayer and interior life, through frequent reception of the sacraments and the concrete practice of the spiritual and corporal works of mercy. In this way the Scapular becomes a sign of the "covenant" and reciprocal communion between Mary and the faithful: indeed, it concretely translates the gift of his Mother, which Jesus gave on the Cross to John and, through him, to all of us, and the entrustment of the beloved Apostle and of us to her, who became our spiritual Mother.

6. A splendid example of this Marian spirituality, which inwardly moulds individuals and conforms them to Christ, the firstborn of many brethren, is the witness to holiness and wisdom given by so many Carmelite saints, all of whom grew up in the shadow and under the protection of their Mother.

I too have worn the Scapular of Carmel over my heart for a long time! Out of my love for our common heavenly Mother, whose protection I constantly experience, I hope that this Marian year will help all the men and women religious of Carmel and the devout faithful who venerate her with filial affection to grow in her love and to radiate to the world the presence of this Woman of silence and prayer, invoked as Mother of Mercy, Mother of Hope and Grace.

With these wishes, I gladly impart my Apostolic Blessing to all the friars, nuns, sisters and lay people of the Carmelite Family, who work so hard to spread among the people of God true devotion to Mary, Star of the Sea and Flower of Carmel!

From the Vatican, 25 March 2001.

Appendix 4

MESSAGE OF JOHN PAUL II
TO THE ORDER OF THE BROTHERS
OF THE BLESSED VIRGIN MARY OF MT CARMEL

To the Most Reverend Father Joseph Chalmers,
Prior General of the Order of the Brothers
of the Blessed Virgin Mary of Mount Carmel

1. I am delighted to know that the centuries old Order of the Brothers of the Blessed Virgin Mary of Mount Carmel is celebrating its General Chapter, moved by the desire to continue serving Christ and the Church in total fidelity to its charism and to the directives of the Papal Magisterium.

This resolve is most important at the beginning of the new millennium, in which the Church confidently goes toward the future fixing her eyes on Christ - "the Alpha and the Omega, the first and the last, the beginning and the end" (Apoc 22,13) - striving to fulfil faithfully the mission He entrusted to her.

I want to underline the fact that the General Chapter is held during the year celebrating the 750th anniversary of the gift of the Scapular. For this special jubilee I did send, 25 March, a special message to the whole Family of Carmel. Further, this year also marks the 7th centenary of the birth of the great Carmelite bishop, St Andrew Corsini, rightly remembered as an example for pastors and a model of consecrated life for all religious.

While uniting myself spiritually to your Chapter to invoke the Spirit of the Lord upon its work, I greet you, Most Reverend Father, and I thank you for the service rendered to the Order of Carmel and to the Church during the past six years. With you I greet the participants in the General Chapter coming from various nations, and through them, I extend my warm best wishes to the whole Carmelite Order.

2. The theme of the chapter is: *The journey continues*. Your reference to human experience of a journey belongs to Carmelite spirituality. From the first hermits established on Mount Carmel, who had arrived in the Land of the Lord Jesus as *pilgrims*, life is represented as an ascetical ascent towards the holy mountain, that is Christ Jesus our Lord (cf. Roman Missal *Collect of the Mass in honour of the B.V. Mary of Carmel*, 16 July). Two Biblical icons, precious to the Carmelite tradition, inspire this interior pilgrimage: that of the prophet Elijah and that of the Virgin Mary.

The prophet Elijah burns with zeal for the Lord (cf. I Kgs 19,10); he sets off toward Mount Horeb and, although tired, he continues walking until he reaches the goal. It is only at the end of his difficult journey that he meets the Lord in the still small voice (cf. I Kgs 19,1-18).

771

Looking at his example, the Brothers of the Blessed Virgin Mary of Mount Carmel understand more deeply that only those who train themselves to listen to God and to interpret the signs of the times are able to meet the Lord and recognize Him in daily events. The Lord speaks in many ways, even through realities that at times can seem insignificant.

The other icon is that of the Virgin Mary, whom you venerate under the title of *Sister* and *Beauty of Carmel*. Our Lady sets out to visit an elderly cousin, St Elizabeth. As soon as she received the announcement of the angel (cf. Lk 1,26-28), she generously departs, running along mountain paths (cf. Song 2,8; Is 52,7), to visit Elizabeth when she learned that she needed her help. In the meeting with her cousin, from within her rich spirit she pours forth her hymn of joy, the Magnificat (cf. Lk 1,39-56). It is a hymn of praise to the Lord and a witness of humble readiness to serve her neighbour. In the mystery of the Visitation, every Christian can discern the shape of his own vocation. Let it be so for you, gathered together in your Chapter, to give to your Order a fresh ascetical and missionary impulse. With a heart full of praise to the Lord in the contemplation of his mystery, go forward joyfully on the paths of charity, opening yourselves with fraternal readiness in order to be credible witnesses of the merciful love of the Word of God become man to redeem the world.

3. *"The journey continues"*. Yes, brothers, your spiritual journey continues in the world of today. You are called to reread your rich spiritual inheritance in the light of the current challenges so that "the joys and hopes, the sorrows and anguish of the people of today, of the poor and of all those who suffer may be the joys and hopes, sorrows and anguish of the disciples of Christ (*Gaudium et Spes*, n. 1) and especially, of every Carmelite.

This year, when you commemorate the 750th Anniversary of the gift of the Scapular, you need to make more vigorous and decisive your will to allow yourselves to be clothed with Christ (cf. Rom 13,14). Ask Mary, who was so caring and so gentle towards the Child Jesus (cf. Lk 2,7b), to clothe each of us with the wisdom and love of her divine Son. While you are fully aware of the mission that God has entrusted to your beloved Order, offer to the world the witness of your fidelity so that Christ may be known and accepted by all as the only Saviour of mankind, yesterday, today and forever (cf. Heb 13,8).

For this end, I invoke the abundance of divine grace on you. May the Holy Spirit, in a renewed Pentecost, descend on you and enlighten you so that you can discern the will of your merciful and heavenly Father so as to be able to speak to the men and women of today in a way that is effective and appropriate (cf. Acts 2,1-13).

With these sentiments I impart my Apostolic Blessing to you, to the members of the Chapter, and to the entire Family of Carmel, imploring on each of you the maternal protection of Our Lady of Mt Carmel along with the intercession of the prophet Elijah and of the numberless Saints of your Order.

Castel Gandolfo, 8 September 2001

IOANNES PAULUS II

772

MESSAGE OF JOHN PAUL II
FOR THE 550th ANNIVERSARY OF THE ADDITION
OF THE CLOISTERED NUNS AND THE THIRD ORDER
OF THE LAITY TO THE CARMELITE ORDER

To Reverend Fr Joseph Chalmers
Prior General of the Order of Carmelites (O.Carm.)

1. I learned with joy that this year, this religious family observes the 550th anniversary of the entrance into the Order of the cloistered nuns and of the establishment of the Third Order, consisting of lay people desirous of living Carmelite spirituality in the world.

With the spread of the Order in Europe, some women asked to be united with it by the same ties as the men religious. Many lay faithful also desired to live the same spirituality while staying in their homes. Bl. John Soreth, Prior General at the time, perceived that the life of sacrifice, solitude and prayer of the nuns would be beneficial for the friars recalling them to the primitive and genuine spirit; and also that it would be useful to offer lay people, as was the case with the Mendicant Orders, the possibility of drawing life from the common spiritual source.

So, on 7 October 1452, the Order asked my venerable predecessor, Pope Nicholas V, for the faculty to set up in the Order the enclosed nuns of contemplative life, and an association of lay persons living in the world, the Carmelite Third Order. The Pope granted this with the Bull *Cum nulla* that is now being commemorated.

I am sure that to recall this authoritative papal intervention is a motive for intimate satisfaction for the cloistered sisters of contemplative life in papal enclosure, while it is an incentive to the Third Order to an ever more courageous spiritual dedication to serve the new evangelization.

2. The Carmelite nuns, immersed in silence and prayer, recall to all believers, and especially their brothers dedicated to the active apostolate, the absolute primacy of God. Consecrated totally to the quest for God, they witness that he is the source of the full realization of the human person and of every spiritual activity. When they open their hearts to him, he comes to meet his children to introduce them into intimacy with him, achieving with them an ever more perfect communion of love. For the Carmelites, the choice of living in solitude, separated from the world, responds to this special call from the Lord. Carmel for this reason enriches the entire Christian community.

From the beginning, this form of cloistered life bore fruit; over the centuries it was enriched with the bright witness of exemplary women, some of whom are officially recognized as blesseds or saints and are even pointed out today as models to imitate. I would like to mention Bl. Frances d'Amboise, considered the foundress of the Carmelite nuns in France, because she worked in close unity and friendship with Bl. Soreth; Bl. Giovanna Scopelli, one of the outstanding exponents of this experience in Italy and Bl. Girlani, who chose the name "Archangel" because she wanted to dedicate herself completely to the praise of God like the angels in heaven. In Florence, St Mary Magdalene de' Pazzi was an eminent example of apostolic and ecclesial zeal and a mirror of the unceasing quest for God and his glory.

In this furrow of holiness, in Spain, we find St Teresa of Jesus, the most illustrious member of the enclosed Carmelite congregation, by whom the nuns of every era have been inspired. Teresa re-elaborated and renewed the Carmelite tradition, fostering the desire to live more perfectly in solitude with God, imitating the first Fathers, hermits of Mount Carmel. Following her example, Carmelite nuns are called, as it is written in their Constitutions, "*to prayer and contemplation, for in these are our origins; we are the offspring of those holy fathers of Mount Carmel, who in deep solitude and total disregard of the world, sought this treasure and precious pearl*" (*Constitutions of the Carmelite Nuns*, n. 61).

3. I gladly join in the thanksgiving of the Carmelite family for the countless miracles worked by God in the course of the centuries through this established form of consecrated life which, as we read in the Rule of St Albert of Jerusalem, "is holy and good" (n. 20). In the silence of Carmel, in so many parts of the world, they continue to bring forth perfumed flowers of holiness, souls in love with Heaven, who with their evangelical heroism have sustained and effectively sustain the mission of the Church.

People are reminded by Carmel, though they are busy with so many concerns, that they must give absolute priority to seeking "*the kingdom of God and his justice*" (Mt 6,33). Looking to Carmel, where prayer becomes life and life flourishes with prayer, the Christian community can more easily understand, as I wrote in my Apostolic Letter *Novo Millennio ineunte*, how they can become "genuine "schools' of prayer" (n. 33). I ask the beloved Carmelite Sisters, who are so completely given over to the praise of the Lord, to help the Christians of our time to achieve this demanding ascetical and apostolic task. May their monasteries become beacons of holiness, especially for the parishes and dioceses which have the good fortune to have them.

4. The 550th anniversary of the Bull *Cum nulla* also recalls the incorporation of lay people into the Carmelite family, by establishing the Third Order. They are men and women called to live the Carmelite charism in the world, sanctifying their daily activity by their fidelity to their Baptismal promises. For them to fulfil this vocation fully, they must learn to sanctify the day with prayer, especially with the celebration of the Eucharist and the Liturgy of the Hours. They follow the example of Elijah, whose prophetic mission arose out of an uninterrupted experience of God; above all, let them imitate Mary, who listened to the word of the Lord and, keeping it in her heart, put it into practice.

May these brothers and sisters whom the Scapular joins to the other members of the Carmelite Order, be grateful for the gift received and in every circumstance be faithful to the duties that derive from this charismatic belonging. May they not be satisfied with a superficial Christian life, but respond to the radical appeal of Christ, who calls his disciples to be perfect as the heavenly Father is perfect (cf. Mt 5,48)

Appendix 4

With these sentiments, I invoke upon the entire Carmelite family a renewed outpouring of the gifts of the Holy Spirit, so that they may live in fidelity to their vocation and communicate the merciful love of God to the men and women of our time. To this end I implore the motherly protection of the Blessed Virgin Mary, Mother and Beauty of Carmel, and I cordially impart my Apostolic Blessing to the men religious, to the cloistered nuns, to the members of the Third Order, encouraging them all to make their own contribution to the sanctification of the world.

From the Vatican, 7 October 2002, Memorial of Our Lady of the Rosary.

JOHN PAUL II

PAGINA **7** · L'OSSERVATORE ROMANO · Lunedì-Martedì 7-8 Novembre 2005

La cerimonia si è svolta nella Cattedrale di Wawel a Cracovia nel giorno della festa di san Carlo Borromeo

La prima sessione del Tribunale del processo rogatorio per la Causa di beatificazione e canonizzazione del servo di Dio Giovanni Paolo II

CZESŁAW DRAŻEK

I lavori della prima sessione nella Cattedrale di Wawel a Cracovia

CARMELITE NEWS

No. 36 - JULY-DECEMBER 2007

A BROWN SCAPULAR OF
THE SERVANT OF GOD JOHN PAUL II

His Eminence the Most Reverend Cardinal Stanislao Dziwisz, Metropolitan Archbishop of Cracow, who was secretary of the Servant of God Pope John Paul II, has sent as a gift to Father Lucio Maria Zappatore, O.Carm., Parish Priest of S. Maria Regina Mundi (Rome), a Scapular of Our Lady of Mount Carmel worn by the Servant of God John Paul II.

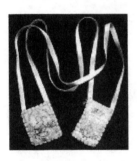

This scapular reminds us of the great devotion of the Pope to Our Lady of Mount Carmel through this sign (cf. article and letter to the Carmelites of the 25-3-2001 in which the Pope affirmed: "For a very long time I too have worn the Carmelite Scapular!"). Father Lucio received the brown scapular together with the declaration of authenticity signed by the Cardinal himself, on 6th October 2007 directly from Sister Tobiana Sobotka, "the guardian angel of the Pope".

Father Lucio, several times and insistently had asked the Cardinal of Cracow for this remembrance, very precious for the Carmelite Order, but had always received a vague and negative response. Finally, during the Congress of the International Federation of the *Pueri Cantores* which took place in Cracow (Father Lucio is the National Ecclesiastic Assistant of the Italian Federation), Cardinal Stanislao promised that he would do everything possible to satisfy him.

Benedict XVI

Birth name	Joseph Alois Ratzinger
Papacy began	April 19, 2005
Papacy ended	*Incumbent*
Predecessor	John Paul II
Successor	*Incumbent*
Born	April 16, 1927 (age 80) Marktl am Inn, Bavaria, Germany

Papal Arms of Pope Benedict XVI. The papal tiara was replaced with a bishop's mitre, and pallium of the Pope was added beneath the coat of arms.

Pope Benedict XVI: Joseph Alois Ratzinger

Papacy: 2005 – 2013

Summary of Contents:

1). *Angelus*, Pope Benedict XVI, Sunday May 29, 2005. *Pastoral Visit of His Holiness Benedict XVI to Bari for the closing of the 24th Italian National Eucharistic Congress.* The Holy Father, in his *Angelus*, refers to Mary as the "Woman of the Eucharist," repeating the words of his predecessor, Bl. Pope John Paul II…

2) *Osservatore Romano*, Monday-Tuesday, May 30-31, 2005, "*Accogliamo Gesu` alla scuola di Maria, "Donna Eucaristica."* ("Receive Jesus at the School of Mary, Woman of the Eucharist.") The article on the Holy Father, commemorates the closing of the 14th Eucharist Congress of the Church in Italy. Before the final blessing, he recited the Angelus, repeating the words of his predecessor, Bl. John Paul II: *"At the School of Mary, Woman of the Eucharist, as she was lovingly invoked by Pope John Paul II, let us ourselves receive the presence of the living Jesus bringing Him to others, in loving service."*

3). *Address, His Holiness Benedict XVI, during the Prayer Meeting in the Vatican Gardens for the conclusion of the Marian Month of May,* Grotto of Our Lady of Lourdes in the Vatican Gardens, Tuesday, May 31, 2005: At the conclusion of the Rosary, His Holiness, emphasizes in the Year of the Eucharist that Mary's journey, in the Mystery of the Visitation to her cousin Elizabeth was the first *"Eucharist Procession"* in history, exhorting us to "follow and imitate" Mary, a deeply Eucharistic Soul, so that we can bring Christ to others.

4). *Angelus*, Pope Benedict XVI, "On Our Lady of Mount Carmel," July 16, 2006; Recalling the Feast of Our Lady of Mount Carmel on that day, the Pope spoke of the great Prophet Elijah, the Defender of the Faith, through whose inspiration the contemplative Order of Carmelites arose, recalling also that the Carmelites have spread among the Christian people, devotion to Our Lady of Mount Carmel….He then entrusted all contemplative life communities, "scattered throughout the world," to the Queen of Mount Carmel.

5). *Osservatore Romano, Angelus,* "Queen of Carmel, Queen of Peace," published on Sunday July 19, 2006, reflects the words of His Holiness, Benedict XVI, in the above listed Document, #4, commemorating the Feast of Our Lady of Mount Carmel, and reiterating the words of the Holy Father, entrusting contemplative life communities to the Queen of Carmel.

6). *Letter of His Holiness Benedict XVI to the Prior Generals of the Order of the Friars of the Blessed Virgin of Mount Carmel on the occasion of the Eighth Centenary of the "Formula Vitae,"* August 14, 2007: His Holiness spoke of the preparation for the eighth centenary of the presentation of the formula vitae. *"This was the first recognition by the Church of this group of men who left everything to live worshipping Jesus Christ, imitating the Blessed Virgin and the Prophet Elijah. The Order is also celebrating the seventh centenary of the death of St. Albert of Trapani, known as the Pater Ordinis..."*

7). Catholic News Agency: *"Benedict XVI to send Our Lady of Mt. Carmel statue to earthquake-stricken Chile,"* March 22, 2010, His Holiness blessed and presented a statue of Our Lady of Mt. Carmel as a gift to the Church and people of Chile, to "bring consolation to those suffering from the devastating February 27 earthquake."

8). *Address,* Pope Benedict XVI, Castel Gandolfo, Italy, July 17, 2011: After the Angelus, the Holy Father greeted the people in various languages; Speaking on the Scapular in Polish he said:

"I welcome the Poles who have come to Castel Gandolfo. I also greet your countrymen in Poland and around the world. Yesterday, we celebrated the memorial of Mary, Mother of God of the Scapular (Our Lady of Mount Carmel.) The Scapular is a particular sign of union with Jesus and Mary. For those who wear it, it is a sign of filial abandonment to the protection of the Immaculate Virgin. In our battle against evil, may Mary our Mother, wrap us in her mantle...."

9). *Osservatore Romano, General Audience,* Pope Benedict XVI: "Catechesis:" *"Without Mary the Church does not exist."* Wednesday, March 14, 2012: His Holiness exhorted that "It is impossible to talk about the Church unless Mary, Mother of the Lord is present..." *"There is no Pentecost without the Mother of Jesus, because she experienced uniquely what the Church experiences every day under the action of the Holy Spirit."*

10). *Message of His Holiness Benedict XVI to the Bishop of Avila (Spain) on the occasion of the 450th Anniversary of the Monastery of San Jose` in Avila and the Beginning of the Reform of Carmel.,* July 16, 2012, Commemorating the upcoming anniversary of the Reform of Carmel, in this *Message,* His Holiness writes: *"St. Teresa proposed a new way of being a "Carmelite" in a world that was also new. The "times were dangerous" and in these times, as this spiritual teacher said, "The friends of God should be strong in order that they may support the weak." He also writes: "St. Teresa knew how to honor with deep devotion, the Most Holy Virgin, whom she invoked with the sweet name of Carmel....."*

11). *Letter of the Prior General of the Carmelite Order, to His Holiness Benedict XVI., February 12, 2013.* In this Letter, the Prior General of the Carmelites bestows a letter of gratitude and of farewell to His Holiness thanking him for his gracious service and support of the Carmelite Community and for all of the beatifications of Carmelite Religious and martyrs.

PASTORAL VISIT
OF HIS HOLINESS BENEDICT XVI
TO BARI FOR THE CLOSING OF THE
24th ITALIAN NATIONAL EUCHARISTIC CONGRESS

ANGELUS

Esplanade of Marisabella
Sunday, 29 May 2005

Dear Brothers and Sisters,

This solemn liturgical celebration marks the end of the 24th Eucharistic Congress of the Church in Italy. I wanted to be present at this great witness of faith in the divine Eucharist. I am delighted to tell you now that I was truly impressed by your fervent participation.

With deep devotion you have all gathered closely to the Eucharistic Jesus, at the end of an intense week of prayer, reflection and adoration. Our hearts are filled with gratitude to God and to all who have worked to bring about such an extraordinary ecclesial event, an event especially meaningful as it takes place during the Eucharistic Year, which had its prominent moment in the Congress.

Before the final blessing, we now recite the *Angelus Domini*, contemplating the mystery of the Incarnation, to which the mystery of the Eucharist is intimately connected. At the school of Mary, "Woman of the Eucharist", as the late Pope John Paul II loved to call her, we welcome Jesus' living presence in ourselves to bring him to everyone by loving service.

Let us learn to always live in communion with the Crucified and Risen Christ, allowing ourselves to be led by his and our heavenly Mother. In this way, nourished by the Word and Bread of Life, our existence will become entirely Eucharistic and thanks will be given to the Father through Christ in the Holy Spirit.

La preghiera dell'Angelus guidata dal Santo Padre al termine della Santa

Accogliamo Gesù alla scuola

Al termine della Concelebrazione Eucaristica, prima di impartire la Benedizione Apostolica conclusiva, il Papa ha guidato la preghiera mariana dell'Angelus. Queste le sue parole:

Cari fratelli e sorelle,
con questa solenne *celebrazione liturgica si conclude il XXIV Congresso Eucaristico della Chiesa che è in Italia. Ho desiderato essere presente a questa grande testimonianza di fede nella divina Eucaristia. Sono lieto di dirvi ora che mi ha realmente molto colpito la vostra fervida partecipazione. Con profonda devozione vi siete tutti stretti attorno a Gesù Eucaristico, al termine di un'intensa settimana di preghiera, di riflessione e di adorazione. I nostri cuori sono colmi di gratitudine, verso Dio e verso quanti hanno lavorato per la realizzazione di un così straordinario evento ecclesiale, un evento particolarmente significativo perché si svolge nel contesto dell'An-*

di Maria, «donna eucaristica»

Messa

no dell'Eucaristico, che ha avuto nel Congresso un suo momento saliente.

Prima della benedizione finale, recitiamo ora l'Angelus Domini, contemplando il mistero dell'Incarnazione, al quale il mistero dell'Eucaristia è intimamente connesso. Alla scuola di Maria, «donna eucaristica», come amava invocarla il compianto Papa Giovanni Paolo II, accogliamo in noi stessi, la presenza viva di Gesù, per portarlo a tutti nell'amore servizievole. Impariamo a vivere sempre in comunione con Cristo crocifisso e risorto, facendoci in questo guidare dalla sua e nostra celeste Madre. Così, nutrita dalla Parola e dal Pane di vita, la nostra esistenza diventerà interamente eucaristica, e si farà rendimento di grazie al Padre per Cristo nello Spirito Santo.

Pope Benedict XVI

Osservatore Romano

Lunedì - Martedì - 30-31 Maggio 2005

ADDRESS OF HIS HOLINESS BENEDICT XVI
DURING THE PRAYER MEETING IN THE VATICAN GARDENS
FOR THE CONCLUSION OF THE MARIAN MONTH OF MAY

Grotto of Our Lady of Lourdes in the Vatican Gardens
Tuesday, 31 May 2005

Dear Brothers and Sisters,

I join you with great joy at the end of this prayer meeting organized by the Vicariate of Vatican City. I note with pleasure that a large number of you have gathered in the Vatican Gardens for the conclusion of the month of May.

Among you, in particular, are many people who live or work in the Vatican, with their families. I offer a warm greeting to you all; in a special way the Cardinals and Bishops, beginning with Archbishop Angelo Comastri who has led this prayer meeting. I then greet the priests and the men and women religious present, with a thought also for the contemplative Sisters of *Mater Ecclesiae* Monastery who are spiritually united to us.

Dear friends, you have wound your way up to the Grotto of Lourdes reciting the holy Rosary, as if to respond to the Virgin's invitation to raise your spirit towards Heaven. Our Lady accompanies us every day in our prayers. During this special Year of the Eucharist in which we are living, Mary helps us above all to discover ever better the great sacrament of the Eucharist.

In his last Encyclical, *Ecclesia de Eucharistia*, our beloved Pope John Paul II presented her to us as "Woman of the Eucharist" throughout her life (cf. n. 53). "Woman of the Eucharist" through and through, beginning with her inner disposition: from the Annunciation, when she offered herself for the Incarnation of the Word of God, to the Cross and to the Resurrection; "Woman of the Eucharist" in the period subsequent to Pentecost, when she received in the Sacrament that Body which she had conceived and carried in her womb.

Today, in particular, we pause to meditate on the mystery of the Visitation of the Virgin to St Elizabeth. Mary went to see her elderly cousin Elizabeth, whom everyone said was sterile but who instead had reached the sixth month of a pregnancy given to her by God (cf. Lk 1: 36), carrying in her womb the recently conceived Jesus. She was a young girl but she was not afraid, for God was with her, within her.

In a certain way we can say that her journey was - we like to emphasize in this Year of the Eucharist - the first "Eucharistic procession" in history. Mary, living Tabernacle of God made flesh, is the Ark of the Covenant in whom the Lord visited and redeemed his people. Jesus' presence filled her with the Holy Spirit.

When she entered Elizabeth's house, her greeting was overflowing with grace: John leapt in his mother's womb, as if he were aware of the coming of the One whom he would one day proclaim to Israel. The children exulted, the mothers exulted. This meeting, imbued with the joy of the Holy Spirit, is expressed in the Canticle of the *Magnificat*.

Is this not also the joy of the Church, which ceaselessly welcomes Christ in the holy Eucharist and brings him into the world with the testimony of active charity, steeped in faith and hope? Yes, welcoming Jesus and bringing him to others is the true joy of Christians!

Dear Brothers and Sisters, let us follow and imitate Mary, a deeply Eucharistic soul, and our whole life can become a *Magnificat* (cf. *Ecclesia de Eucharistia*, n. 58), praise of God. May this be the grace that we ask from the Virgin Most Holy this evening at the end of the month of May. My Blessing to you all.

Appendix 4

Angelus Message
On Our Lady of Mount Carmel
H.H. Benedict XVI
July 16, 2006
www.zenit.org

Dear Brothers and Sisters,

I again have the joy this year of spending a period of rest here in the Aosta Valley, in the house that so often welcomed beloved John Paul II and in which I feel perfectly at home, truly on holiday, in a place where the Creator gives us this fresh air, beauty and restfulness and the joy of being alive.

I have immersed myself immediately in this magnificent Alpine scenery that helps reinvigorate body and spirit, and today I am happy to have this family meeting, for as the Bishop has said, it is not a crowd but a gathering, indeed, it is a family of the faithful. A cordial greeting to each one of you, residents and vacationers!

I would first like to greet and thank Aosta's Bishop Giuseppe Anfossi, Pastor of the Church that resides in this valley, whom I thank for his words and his hospitality. And I also very cordially greet the Metropolitan present here, Cardinal Poletto, Archbishop of Turin - welcome, your Eminence!

I greet the priests, Religious and lay people of the diocesan community. I assure each one of my remembrance in prayer, and I am grateful for your prayers of which the Bishop of Aosta has assured me and which I carry in my work; and a special remembrance in prayer is always for the sick and the suffering.

My grateful thoughts then go to the Salesians, who have put their most beautiful house at the Pope's disposal.

I address a respectful greeting to the Authorities of the State and the Region, the Municipal Administration of Introd, the Forces of Order and all who in various ways are collaborating to ensure that my stay is peaceful, and there are very many of them. May the Lord reward you!

Through a happy coincidence, this Sunday falls on 16 July, the day when the liturgy commemorates Our Lady of Mount Carmel. The slopes of Carmel, a high ridge that runs down the eastern coast of the Mediterranean Sea at the altitude of Galilee, are dotted with numerous natural caves, beloved by hermits.

The most famous of these men of God was the great Prophet Elijah, who in the ninth century before Christ strenuously defended the purity of faith in the one true God from contamination by idolatrous cults. Inspired by the figure of Elijah, the contemplative order of Carmelites arose. It is a religious family that counts among its members great saints such as Teresa of Avila, John of the Cross, Thérèse of the Child Jesus and Teresa Benedicta of the Cross (in the world: Edith Stein).

The Carmelites have spread among the Christian people devotion to Our Lady of Mount Carmel, holding her up as a model of prayer, contemplation and dedication to God. Indeed, Mary was the first, in a way which can never be equalled, to believe and experience that

787

The Brown Scapular of Our Lady of Mount Carmel

Jesus, the Incarnate Word, is the summit, the peak of man's encounter with God. By fully accepting the Word, she "was blessedly brought to the holy Mountain" (cf. *Opening Prayer of the Memorial*), and lives for ever with the Lord in body and soul.

Today, I would like to entrust to the Queen of Mount Carmel all contemplative life communities scattered throughout the world, especially those of the Carmelite Order, among which I recall the Monastery of Quart, not far from here, that I have had the opportunity to visit in these days. May Mary help every Christian to find God in the silence of prayer.

After the Angelus:

Dear Friends,

In recent days news from the Holy Land has been a cause of serious alarm to everyone, particularly because of the extension of aggressive actions also to Lebanon and the many victims among the civil population. At the root of these merciless contrasts, unfortunately, are objective situations of the violation of law and justice. But in no way can terrorist acts or reprisals be justified, especially when they have tragic consequences for the civilian population. These are not paths - as bitter experience shows - to positive results.

Today, as I said, is dedicated to Our Lady of Carmel, a Mountain in the Holy Land only a few kilometres from Lebanon that dominates the Israeli city of Haifa, which has also recently been hit. Let us pray to Mary, Queen of Peace, to implore from God the fundamental gift of harmony, redirecting political leaders to the path of reason and opening up new possibilities for dialogue and understanding. With this in view, I invite the local Churches to raise special prayers for peace in the Holy Land and throughout the Middle East.

I am pleased to greet the English-speaking visitors here today. I pray that all who are on holiday at this time will find refreshment in body and spirit and an opportunity to draw closer to the Lord in prayer and thanksgiving. May God bestow his Blessings of joy and peace upon all of you, your families and loved ones at home.

I wish you all a good Sunday!

Return to main page
www.piercedhearts.org

L'OSSERVATORE ROMANO

EDITORIAL AND MANAGEMENT OFFICES VATICAN CITY

WEEKLY EDITION  **IN ENGLISH**

THIRTY-NINTH YEAR
N. 29 (1953) - 19 July 2006

UNICUIQUE SUUM   NON PRAEVALEBUNT

€$2.50

Editorial Office: Via del Pellegrino, 00120 Vatican City, Europe - Telephone 39/06.698.99.390 - Telefax 39/06.698.83675 INTERNET: www.vatican.va/news_services/or/home_eng.html E-MAIL: ornet@ossrom.va

ANGELUS AND HOLY LAND APPEAL: SUNDAY, 16 JULY

Queen of Carmel, Queen of Peace

On Sunday, 16 July, before praying the Angelus with the locals and tourists in the Italian Alpine village of Les Combes, Introd, the Holy Father gave the following Reflection, translated from Italian.

Dear Brothers and Sisters,

I again have the joy this year of spending a period of rest here in the Aosta Valley, in the house that so often welcomed beloved John Paul II and in which I feel perfectly at home, truly on holiday, in a place where the Creator gives us this fresh air, beauty and restfulness and the joy of being alive.

I have immersed myself immediately in this magnificent Alpine scenery that helps reinvigorate body and spirit, and today I am happy to have this family meeting, for as the Bishop has said, it is not a crowd but a gathering, indeed, it is a family of the faithful. A cordial greeting to each one of you, residents and vacationers!

I would first like to greet and thank Aosta's Bishop Giuseppe Anfossi, Pastor of the Church that resides in this valley, whom I thank for his words and his hospitality. And I also very cordially greet the Metropolitan present here, Cardinal Poletto, Archbishop of Turin — welcome, your Eminence!

I greet the priests, Religious and lay people of the diocesan community. I assure each one of my remembrance in prayer, and I am grateful for your prayers of which the Bishop of Aosta has assured me and which I carry in my work; and a special remembrance in prayer is always for the sick and the suffering.

My grateful thoughts then go to the Salesians, who have put their most beautiful house at the Pope's disposal.

I address a respectful greeting to the Authorities of the State and the Region, the Municipal Administration of Introd, the Forces of Order and all who in various ways are collaborating to ensure that my stay is peaceful, and there are very many of them. May the Lord reward you!

Our Lady of Mount Carmel

Through a happy coincidence, this Sunday falls on 16 July, the day when the liturgy commemorates Our Lady of Mount Carmel. The slopes of Carmel, a high ridge that runs down the eastern coast of the Mediterranean Sea at the altitude of Galilee, are dotted with numerous natural caves, beloved by hermits.

The most famous of these men of God was the great Prophet Elijah, who in the ninth century before Christ strenuously defended the purity of faith in the one true God from contamination by idolatrous cults. Inspired by the figure of Elijah, the contemplative order of Carmelites arose.

It is a religious family that counts among its members great saints such as Teresa of Avila, John of the Cross, Thérèse of the Child Jesus and Teresa Benedicta of the Cross (in the world: Edith Stein).

The Carmelites have spread among the Christian people devotion to Our Lady of Mount Carmel, holding her up as a model of prayer, contemplation and dedication to God.

Indeed, Mary was the first, in a way which can never be equalled, to believe and experience that Jesus, the Incarnate Word, is the summit, the peak of man's encounter with God. By fully accepting the Word, she "was blessedly brought to the holy Mountain" (cf. Opening Prayer of the Memorial), and lives for ever with the Lord in body and soul.

Today, I would like to entrust to the Queen of Mount Carmel all contemplative life communities scattered throughout the world, especially those of the Carmelite Order, among which I recall the Monastery of Quart, not far from here, that I have had the opportunity to visit in these days. May Mary help every Christian to find God in the silence of prayer.

After the Angelus, the Pope said:

Dear Friends,

In recent days news from the Holy Land has been a cause of serious alarm to everyone, particularly because of the extension of aggressive actions also to Lebanon and the many victims among the civil population. At the root of these merciless contrasts, unfortunately, are objective situations of the violation of law and justice. But in no way can terrorist acts or reprisals be justified, especially when they have tragic consequences for the civilian population. These are not paths — as bitter experience shows — to positive results.

Today, as I said, is dedicated to Our Lady of Carmel, a Mountain in the Holy Land only a few kilometres from Lebanon that dominates the Israeli city of Haifa, which has also recently been hit. Let us pray to Mary, Queen of Peace, to implore from God the fundamental gift of harmony, redirecting political leaders to the path of reason and opening up new possibilities for dialogue and understanding. With this in view, I invite the local Churches to raise special prayers for peace in the Holy Land and throughout the Middle East.

I am pleased to greet the English-speaking visitors here today. I pray that all who are on holiday at this time will find refreshment in body and spirit and an opportunity to draw closer to the Lord in prayer and thanksgiving. May God bestow his Blessings of joy and peace upon all of you, your families and loved ones at home.

I wish you all a good Sunday!

*LETTER OF HIS HOLINESS BENEDICT XVI
TO THE PRIOR GENERAL OF THE ORDER
OF THE FRIARS OF THE BLESSED VIRGIN
OF MOUNT CARMEL ON THE OCCASION
OF THE EIGHTH CENTENARY OF THE "FORMULA VITÆ"*

*To the Very Reverend
Father Joseph Chalmers
Prior General
of the Order of Carmelite*

Fathers and Brothers I am pleased to learn that this ancient and illustrious Order is preparing to celebrate its General Chapter this September, on the occasion of the eighth centenary of the presentation by St Albert, Patriarch of Jerusalem (1205-1214), of the formula vitae which inspired the Latin-rite hermits who settled "near the spring on Mount Carmel" (Carmelite Rule, 1). This was the first recognition by the Church of this group of men who left everything to live worshipping Jesus Christ, imitating the sublime examples of the Blessed Virgin Mary and the Prophet Elijah. The canonical process ended with several amendments, followed in 1247 by the approval of the Rule by my Predecessor, Pope Innocent IV.

This year, through a happy coincidence, the Order of Carmel is also celebrating other events perceived as moments of grace, such as the seventh centenary of the devout death of St Albert of Trapani, known as the *Pater Ordinis*, and the fourth centenary of the entry into eternal life of St Mary Magdalene de' Pazzi, the Seraph of Carmel. It is therefore a cause of deep joy for me to be able to express my participation in the intense spiritual experience which the Carmelite Family will be living on the occasion of the Chapter.

The first Carmelites went to Mount Carmel because they believed in the love of God, who so loved the world that he gave his Only-Begotten Son (cf. *Jn* 3: 16). Welcoming into their lives the Lordship of Christ, they made themselves available to being transformed by his love. This is the basic choice that faces every Christian. I pointed it out in my first Encyclical: "Being Christian is not the result of an ethical choice or a lofty idea, but the encounter with an event, a person, which gives life a new horizon and a decisive direction" (*Deus Caritas Est*, n. 1). If this concern challenges the Christian, how much more must the Carmel-ite feel challenged by it, since his vocation is to scale the mountain of perfection!

We know well, however, that it is far from easy to live this call faithfully In a certain sense, we need to wear armour to guard ourselves from the snares of the world. This is also specified in the Carmelite Rule "Your loins are to be girt with chastity, your breast fortified by holy meditations, for, as Scripture has it, "holy meditation will save you"". Justice must be "your breastplate and it will enable you to love the Lord your God with all your heart and soul and strength, and your neighbour as yourself. Faith must be your shield on all occasions, and with it you will be able to quench all the flaming missiles of the wicked one" (n. 19). And, further: "The sword of the Spirit, the Word of God, must abound in your mouths and hearts. Do all that you have to do in the Name of the Lord" (ibid.). Many women and men have attained holiness by living with creative fidelity the values of the Carmelite Rule. Looking to them, as to all the other disciples who have faithfully followed Christ, "we are seeking with a new reason the city which is to come..., while at the same time we are taught to know a most safe path by which, despite the vicissitudes of the world, and in keeping with the state of life and condition proper to each of us, we will be able to arrive at perfect union with Christ, that is, holiness" (cf. *Lumen Gentium*, n. 50).

The theme of your Chapter Meeting - Worshipping Jesus Christ: A praying, prophetic community in a changing world - clearly highlights the special style in which the Order of Carmel seeks to respond to God's love by means of a life steeped in prayer, brotherhood and a prophetic spirit. At the heart of your Rule is the precept of coming together every morning to celebrate the Eucharist. In fact, "The Eucharist reveals the loving plan that guides all of salvation history.... God's whole life encounters us and is sacramentally shared with us" (Apostolic Exhortation *Sacramentum Caritatis*, n. 8). Daily Mass: God is all in all The first Carmelites, who pursued their personal sanctification through daily participation in the Eucharistic Banquet, were already fully aware of this: in fact, the daily celebration of the Eucharist introduces "a change meant to set off a process which transforms reality, a process leading ultimately to the transfiguration of the entire world, to the point where God will be all in all (cf. I *Cor* 15: 28)" (ibid., n. 11).

With his gaze fixed on Christ and trusting in the help of the Saints who in the course of these eight centuries have embodied the dictates of the Carmelite Rule, each member of the Order of Carmelite Fathers and Brothers should feel called to be a credible witness of the spiritual dimension proper to every human being. The lay faithful will thus be able to discover that Carmelite communities are "genuine "schools' of prayer, where the meeting with Christ is expressed not just in imploring help but also in thanksgiving, praise, adoration, contemplation, listening and ardent devotion, until the heart truly "falls in love'" (Apostolic Letter *Novo Millennio Ineunte*, n. 33). May the Blessed Virgin Mary, Mother and ornament of Carmel, help Carmelite men and women, the members of the Third Order and all who in various capacities participate in the Great Family of Carmel, and teach them to obey the Word of God, cherishing it in their hearts and meditating upon it daily. May the Prophet Elijah make them assiduous heralds of the Living God and guide them to the holy mountain where they were granted to perceive the light breeze of the Divine Presence.

With these sentiments, as I invoke upon the entire Carmelite Family an abundance of gifts of a renewed Pentecost that will increase zeal for the Lord, I cordially impart my Apostolic Blessing to all, with a special thought for the Capitulars.

Castel Gandolfo, 14 August 2007

BENEDICTUS PP. XVI

www.catholicnewsagency.com

Benedict XVI to send Our Lady of Mt. Carmel statue to earthquake-stricken Chile

Santiago, Chile, Mar 22, 2010 / 02:11 pm (CNA).- Pope Benedict XVI will present a new statue of Our Lady of Mt. Carmel to Chile during this week's Wednesday General Audience. The statue will travel throughout the country bringing consolation to those suffering from the devastating February 27 earthquake.

Related articles:

- Special message of Pope Benedict XVI in English to the peoples of Israel, Jordan and the Palestinian Territories, at the end of the General Audience May 6th, 2009
- Statue of Our Lady of Fatima
- Our Lady of Mount Carmel
- Wednesday of Holy Week

According to a press release, Cardinal Francisco Javier Errazuriz of Santiago, Bishop Alejandro Goic Karmelic of Rancagua and Auxiliary Bishop Santiago Silva Retamales of Valparaiso will be at the audience, where the Pope will bless the statue and present it as a gift to the Church and people of Chile on the occasion of the country's bicentennial.

The statue will be official delivered to the Chilean prelates by Vatican Secretary of State, Cardinal Tarcisio Bertone, during a Mass concelebrated with all the country's bishops during the first week of April.

Appendix 4

ZE11071701 - 2011-07-17
Permalink: http://www.zenit.org/article-33087?l=english

ON OUR GOOD AND GREAT FATHER

"Where He Is Not, There Can Be No Good"

CASTEL GANDOLFO, Italy, JULY 17, 2011 (Zenit.org).- Here is a translation of the address Benedict XVI gave today before and after praying the midday Angelus with those who had gathered at the papal summer residence in Castel Gandolfo.

* * *

Dear Brothers and Sisters!

The Gospel parables are brief narratives that Jesus uses to proclaim the mysteries of the Kingdom of Heaven. Using images and situations of daily life, the Lord "wishes to indicate the true foundation of everything. He shows us ... the God who acts, who enters our life and wants to take us by the hand" (Gesu di Nazaret, I, Milan, 2007, 229).

With these reflections, the divine Teacher invites us to recognize first of all the primacy of God the Father: Where he is not, there can be no good. He is a decisive priority for everything. Kingdom of Heaven means, in fact, lordship of God, and that means that his will must be assumed as the guiding criterion of our existence.

The subject contained in this Sunday's Gospel is precisely the Kingdom of Heaven. "Heaven" should not be understood only in the sense of some height that is above us, because this infinite space also has the form of man's interiority. Jesus compares the Kingdom of Heaven to a field of wheat, to make us understand that within us is sown something small and hidden, which, nevertheless, has an unrestrainable vital force. Despite all the obstacles, the seed will develop and the fruit will mature. This fruit will only be good if the terrain of life has been cultivated according to the divine will. Because of this, in the parable of the good seed and the weeds (Matthew 13:24-30,) Jesus warns us that, after the owner planted the seed, "while all were sleeping," "his enemy" came and sowed weeds. This means that we must be ready to guard the grace received on the day of our baptism, continuing to nourish faith in the Lord, which prevents evil from taking root. Commenting on this parable, St. Augustine observed that "many at first are weeds and then become good seed" and he added: "if the former, when they were evil, were not endured with patience, they would not have attained the praiseworthy change" (Quaest. septend. in Ev. sec. Matth., 12, 4:PL 35, 1371).

Dear friends, the Book of Wisdom -- from which today's first reading draws, emphasizes this dimension of the divine being and states: "There is no god besides you who have the care of all ... For your might is the source of justice; your mastery over all things makes you lenient to all." (Wisdom 12:13,16). And Psalm 85 [86] confirms it: "You, O Lord, are good and forgiving, abounding in kindness to all who call upon you" (verse 5).

Hence, if we are children of such a great and good Father, we must seek to resemble him! This was the aim that Jesus set himself with his preaching; he said, in fact, to those who listened to him: "Be perfect as your heavenly Father is perfect" (Matthew 5:48). Let us turn with confidence to Mary, whom we invoked yesterday with the title of Most Holy Virgin of Mount Carmel, so that she will help us to follow Jesus faithfully, and thus live as true children of God.

[After the Angelus, the Holy Father greeted the people in various languages. In Italian, he said:]

I am following with profound concern the news from the region of the Horn of Africa and in particular of Somalia, stricken by a severe drought and afterward, in some areas, by intense rain, which is causing a humanitarian catastrophe. Innumerable people are fleeing from that tremendous famine in search of food and help. I hope that international mobilization will increase to send help in time to these brothers and sisters of ours, already sorely tried, among whom are so many children. May our solidarity, and the concrete support of all people of good will, not be lacking to these suffering populations.

[In French, he said:]

Dear French-speaking pilgrims, the time of vacations is certainly propitious for cultural and spiritual enrichment. Through the innumerable places and monuments that you visit, you can discover the beauty of that universal patrimony that refers us to our roots! Be attentive in allowing yourselves to be swept up by the beautiful ideal that inspired the builders of cathedrals and abbeys, when they built these striking signs of the presence of God on our earth. May that ideal become yours and may the Holy Spirit, who sees the depth of hearts, inspire you to pray in these places, rendering thanks and interceding for humanity of the third millennium! I bless you from my heart, particularly the families here present!

[In Spanish, he said:]

I greet affectionately the Spanish-speaking pilgrims present at this Marian prayer, as well as those who join it through radio and television. Today's liturgy presents to us a God, kind and rich in clemency, who governs the world with wisdom and whose patience has no limit, giving the sinner the necessary time to open his heart to the divine Word, to learn how he behaves, he who can do all, and to reflect in our lives the greatness of his love and mercy. May we be helped in this by the Most Holy Virgin Mary. Happy Sunday.

[In Polish, he said:]

Appendix 4

I welcome the Poles who have come to Castel Gandolfo. I also greet your countrymen in Poland and around the world. Yesterday, we celebrated the memorial of Mary, Mother of God of the Scapular (Our Lady of Mount Carmel). The scapular is a particular sign of union with Jesus and Mary. For those who wear it, it is a sign of filial abandonment to the protection of the Immaculate Virgin. In our battle against evil, may Mary our Mother wrap us in her mantle. I commend you to her protection and I bless you from my heart.

[Translation by ZENIT]

[In English, he said:]

I offer a warm welcome to the English-speaking visitors gathered for this Angelus prayer, including the pilgrims from Meath, Ireland, and from Nazareth, the home of Jesus. Today's Gospel encourages us to let the good seed of God's word bear fruit in our lives and to trust in his mysterious plan for the growth of the Kingdom. Let us work for an abundant harvest of holiness in the Church and ask to be found among Christ's righteous ones on the Day of Judgment. Upon all of you I invoke the Lord's abundant blessings of joy and peace!

At the General Audience the Pope talks about the Blessed Virgin's prayer

Without Mary the Church does not exist

"It is impossible to talk about the Church unless Mary, Mother of the Lord is present". This comment of Cromatius of Aquileia on the Acts of the Apostles was taken up by the Pope in his *Catechesis* at the General Audience of Wednesday, 14 March, in St Peter's Square.

Speaking of the "Virgin's prayerful presence" in the earthly life of Jesus and at the moments when "the Church

was taking her first steps", the Pontiff pointed out that the stages on this journey – from the house of Nazareth to that of Jerusalem, passing through the experience of the Cross – "were marked by her capacity for preserving a persevering atmosphere of recollection in order to meditate on every event before God in the silence of her heart".

In the Upper Room in particular where she gathered with the Eleven after the Ascension, Mary shares the gift of the Spirit with the Apostles. "If there is no Church without Pentecost", Benedict XVI noted in this regard, "there is no Pentecost without the Mother of Jesus, because she experienced uniquely what the Church experiences every day under the action of the Holy Spirit".

This bond, more specifically emphasized by the Second Vatican Council, testifies that "the privileged place of Mary is the Church". Venerating her, therefore, means "learning from her to be a prayerful community": not only in situations of hardship or need", the Pope explained, "but always "in a unanimous, persevering and faithful manner", with "one heart and soul".

"Let us entrust to her", was Benedict XVI's final invitation, "every phase we pass through in our personal and ecclesial existence, and not the last that of our final transit. Mary teaches us the need for prayer and points out to us that it is only through a constant, intimate and loving bond with her Son that we can come out of ourselves to reach the the the frontiers of the world and proclaim the Lord everywhere".

March 15, 2012

Appendix 4

MESSAGE OF HIS HOLINESS BENEDICT XVI
TO THE BISHOP OF AVILA (SPAIN)
ON THE OCCASION OF THE 450TH ANNIVERSARY OF
THE MONASTERY OF SAN JOSÉ IN AVILA AND
THE BEGINNING OF THE REFORM OF CARMEL

To my Venerable Brother
Bishop Jesús García Burillo of Avila

1. *Resplendens stella*: "a star shining in great splendour" (*Libro de la Vida*, [The Book of My Life] 32, 11). With these words the Lord encouraged St Teresa of Jesús to found the Monastery of San José in Avila. This was the beginning of the Reform of Carmel which will be celebrating its 450th anniversary next 24 August. On this happy occasion I would like to join in the rejoicing of the beloved Diocese of Avila, of the Order of Discalced Carmelites and of the People of God on pilgrimage in Spain, as well as of all those in the universal Church who have found in Teresian spirituality a sure light for men and women to attain a true renewal of their life through Christ. In love with the Lord, this illustrious woman did not want anything other than to please him in all things. Indeed, it is not those who do great things based on the excellence of their human qualities who are holy; on the contrary, holy people are those who humbly let Christ penetrate their soul and act through them, who truly allow him to play the lead in all their actions and aspirations, inspiring every project and sustaining every silence.

2. Only those who have an intense prayer life are able to let Christ lead them in this manner. The Saint of Avila says that a life of prayer consists in "being on terms of friendship with God, frequently conversing in secret with him who, we know, loves us" (*Libro de la Vida* 8, 5). The reform of Carmel whose anniversary fills us with inner joy was born from prayer and is inclined to prayer. By distancing herself from the Mitigated Rule in order to further a radical return to the primitive Rule, St Teresa de Jesús wished to encourage a form of life that would favour the personal encounter with the Lord, for which "we have only to find a place where we can be alone and look upon him present within us. Nor need we feel strange in the presence of so kind a Guest" (*Camino de perfección* [the Way of Perfection] 28, 2). The Monastery of San José came into being precisely in order that all its daughters might have the best possible conditions for speaking to God and establishing a profound and intimate relationship with him.

3. St Teresa proposed a new way of being a Carmelite in a world that was also new. The "times were dangerous" (*Libro de la Vida* 33, 5) and in these times, as this spiritual teacher said, "the friends of God should be strong, in order that they may support the weak" (*ibid.*, 15, 5). And she eloquently insists: "the world is on fire. Men try to condemn Christ once again, as it were, for they bring a thousand false witnesses against him. They would raze his Church to the ground.... No, my sisters, this is no time to treat with God for things of little importance" (*Camino de perfección*, 1, 5). Does not this most luminous and challenging reflection made by the holy mystic more than four centuries ago seem familiar to us in the situation in which we are living?

The ultimate aim of the Teresian Reform and of the creation of new monasteries in the midst of a world devoid of spiritual values was to strengthen apostolic work with prayer; and to propose an evangelical lifestyle that might serve as a model to those in quest of a way of perfection, based on the conviction that every authentic personal and ecclesial reform passes through reproducing, ever more faithfully, the "form" of Christ (cf. Gal 4:19) within us. The Saint and her daughters strove to do exactly this and this was the exact commitment of her

797

Church to the ground.... No, my sisters, this is no time to treat with God for things of little importance" (*Camino de perfección*, 1, 5). Does not this most luminous and challenging reflection made by the holy mystic more than four centuries ago seem familiar to us in the situation in which we are living?

The ultimate aim of the Teresian Reform and of the creation of new monasteries in the midst of a world devoid of spiritual values was to strengthen apostolic work with prayer; and to propose an evangelical lifestyle that might serve as a model to those in quest of a way of perfection, based on the conviction that every authentic personal and ecclesial reform passes through reproducing, ever more faithfully, the "form" of Christ (cf. Gal 4:19) within us. The Saint and her daughters strove to do exactly this and this was the exact commitment of her Carmelite sons who endeavoured solely to "advance in virtue" (*Libro de la vida*, 31, 18). In this regard Teresa writes: "He [Our Lord] prizes one soul which of his mercy we have gained for him by our prayer and labour more than all the service we may render him" (*Libro de las Fundaciones* [The Book of the Foundations] 1, 7). In the face of forgetfulness of God the Holy Doctor encourages prayerful communities that protect with their fervour those who proclaim Christ's name everywhere, so that they may pray for the Church's needs and bring the cry of all the peoples to the Saviour's heart.

4. Today too, as in the 16th century and also among rapid changes, trusting prayer must be the soul of the apostolate so that the redemptive message of Jesus Christ rings out with deep clarity and vigorous dynamism. It is urgently necessary that the Word of life be harmoniously vibrant in souls, with resonant and attractive tones.

Teresa of Avila's example is a great help to us in this exciting task. We can say that in her time the Saint evangelized without mincing her words, with unfailing ardour, with methods foreign to inertia and with expressions haloed with light. Her example keeps all its freshness at the crossroads of our time. It is here that we feel the urgent need for the baptized to renew their hearts through personal prayer which, in accordance with the dictates of the Mystic of Avila, is also centred on contemplation of the Most Holy Humanity of Christ as the only way on which to find God's glory (cf. *Libro de la Vida*, 22, 1; *Las Moradas* [Interior Castle] 6, 7). Thus they will be able to form authentic families which discover in the Gospel the fire of their hearths; lively and united Christian communities, cemented on Christ as their corner-stone and which thirst after a life of generous and brotherly service. It should also be hoped that ceaseless prayer will foster priority attention to the vocations ministry, emphasizing in particular the beauty of the consecrated life which, as a treasure of the Church and an outpouring of graces, must be duly accompanied in both its active and contemplative dimensions.

The power of Christ will likewise lead to the multiplication of projects to enable the People of God to recover its strength in the only possible way: by making room within us for the sentiments of the Lord Jesus (cf. Phil 2:5), seeking in every circumstance a radical experience of his Gospel. This means, first of all, allowing the Holy Spirit to make us friends of the Teacher and to conform us to him. It also means accepting his mandates in all things and adopting such criteria as humility in behaviour, the renunciation of the superfluous and giving no offence to others or proceeding with simplicity and a docile heart. Those who surround us will thus perceive the joy that is born from our adherence to the Lord and see that we put nothing before his love, being ever ready to account for our hope (cf. 1 Pet 3:15) and, like Teresa of Jesus, living in filial obedience to our Holy Mother, the Church.

5. Today, this most illustrious daughter of the Diocese of Avila invites us to this radicalism and faithfulness. Accepting her beautiful legacy at this moment in history, the Pope asks all the members of this particular Church, and especially youth, to take seriously the common

vocation to holiness. Following in the footsteps of Teresa of Jesus, allow me to say to all who have their future before them: may you too, aspire to belong totally to Jesus, only to Jesus and always to Jesus. Do not be afraid to say to Our Lord, as she did, "I am yours; I was born for you, what do you want to do with me?" (*Poem* 2). And I ask him to obtain that you may also be able to respond to his call, illuminated by divine grace with "determined resolve" in order to offer "that little" which is in you, trusting in the fact that God never abandons those who leave everything for his glory (cf. *Camino di perfección* 21, 2; 1, 2).

6. St Teresa knew how to honour with deep devotion the Most Holy Virgin, whom she invoked with the sweet name of Carmel. I place under her motherly protection the apostolic aspiration of the Church of Avila so that rejuvenated by the Holy Spirit she may find appropriate ways for proclaiming the Gospel with enthusiasm and courage. May Mary, Star of Evangelization, and her chaste spouse, St Joseph, intercede so that this "star" which the Lord set alight in the universe of the Church with the Teresian Reform, may continue to shine with the great splendour of the love and truth of Christ for all humankind. With this wish, Venerable Brother in the Episcopate, I send you this message. I ask you to make it known to the flock entrusted to your pastoral care and, especially, to the beloved Discalced Carmelites of the Convent of San José in Avila so that they may perpetuate in time the spirit of their Foundress. I am ever grateful to them for their fervent prayers for the Successor of Peter. To them, to you and to all the faithful of Avila I impart the Apostolic Blessing as a pledge of abundant heavenly favours.

From the Vatican, 16 July 2012

BENEDICTUS PP. XVI

Letter of the Prior General to His Holiness Benedict XVI

- CITOC News [1]

Rome, 12 February 2013
Prot. 21/2013

Your Holiness Pope Benedict XVI

Most Holy Father,

We were very surprised and moved by the announcement today of your decision to step down from the ministry of Peter. On my own behalf and on behalf of the

[2]

whole Carmelite Order, I wish to express to you, at this moment in your life and in the history of the Church, our deepest affection and gratitude for the service that devotedly and unselfishly you have given to the community of believers in Christ. I welcome with the greatest of respect the reasons that you have revealed and I see them as a further sign of your great love for the Church and of the thoughtfulness with which you have carried out and continue to carry out your service as Universal and Roman Pastor.

I will always cherish the memory of those moments when I met you personally. I remember your expressions of close interest and support on more than one occasion, not just for me but for our Order and for its life, going back to the first public audience which I attended soon after my election as Prior General, in 2007. What joy my confreres and I and all the members of the Carmelite Family felt when on the 26th of April, 2009, we heard your voice in St. Peter's Basilica declaring that the name of Nuno de Santa Maria was being inscribed among the saints. I was deeply moved by the interest you showed in the work that we do with young people when we came to meet you in Castelgandolfo with young people from Europe who were taking part in the "Pilgrimage of Hope" in 2010. On that occasion you said to me that the Carmelites are the people "who teach us how to pray". I can assure you that those words have remained in each one's heart ever since. A year later a number of those young people along with myself and a number of Carmelite friars and sisters, took part in the World Youth Day in Madrid, where once again we were able to hear your strong message encouraging everyone to follow Jesus Christ and to bring him to the world. More recently I had the opportunity to offer you my good wishes during the general audience of the 19th of September, 2012, on the occasion of the International Congress for Lay Carmelites.

I thank you for the beatifications which you approved and celebrated during your pontificate, some of which were in the time of my predecessor, Fr. Joseph Chalmers: Bl. Maria Crocifissa Curcio, Bl. Maria Teresa Scrilli, Blesseds Angel Prat and companions, carmelite martyrs, Bl. Candelaria de San José and Bl. Angelo Paoli. Two further groups of martyrs in Spain in the 20th century are due to be beatified this coming October. Similarly, the heroic virtue of a number of important figures, known for their holiness, has been recognised. To all of them and the Saints of Carmel I entrust you so that they may help you and protect you always.

We are indeed well aware of your love for the Mother and Sister of Carmel and on many occasions, we have rejoiced at your references to her. We have also appreciated that you have not forgotten that for many years you lived within the boundaries of the parish of Santa Maria in Traspontina and you visited the Church on many occasions as a Cardinal, especially during a novena in preparation for the feast of Our Lady of Mount Carmel, and to lead a lectio divina.

We thank you for the courage and the hope with which you spoke of your resignation, hope and courage which you always saw as essential to Christian life. We feel that we are close to you Holy Father in this important moment in your own life and in our life as Catholics. As we have done in the past and now more than ever, we assure you of our prayer and affection, certain as we are that your decision is a sign of the presence and action of the Holy Spirit, for the good of the Church.

Together with my brother and sister Carmelites I once again offer my filial devotion to the Church, to you Holy Father and to whomsoever the Holy Spirit and the Cardinals will give us as the next successor of Peter.

P. Fernando Millán Romeral, O.Carm.
Priore Generale

www.ocarm.org
Source URL: http://ocarm.org/en/content/citoc/letter-prior-general-his-holiness-benedict-xvi

BIBLIOGRAPHY

* Indicates extended publications in defense of the authenticity of the visions of Our Blessed Mother to St. Simon Stock and to Pope John XXII and the traditional teachings of the Church on the Brown Scapular (n-signifies neutral)

* Aquinas, Thomas of St. Joseph, O.C.D., *Pro Sodalitio Sacri Scapularis Adversus Duplicem Dissertationem I. Launoy,* Tutelae, 1648

* Ancelle, J.J.L., *Instruction sur L'Adoration Perpetuelle,* du Tres-Saint Sacrement de l'autel, Evreux, 1810

* Bartley, John E., *The Irish Ecclesiastical Record,* Third Series,Volume VIII, 1887

* Benedictine Monks of Solesmes, *Papal Teachings; Our Lady,* Boston, 1961

* Besalduch, P. Simon M., Carmelita Calzado, *Enciclopedia del Escapulario Del Carmen*, Barcelona, 1931

* Biroat, J. Dr., *Histoire des Miracles du Saint Scapulaire,* Bruges 1 mai, 1963

* Bishop of Salford, now Cardinal Archbishop of Westminster, *The Meaning and Use of The Scapular of Our Lady of Mt. Carmel* Salford, 1893

Boaga, Emanuele, O. Carm. *Our Lady of the Place,* Roma, 2001

* Bracchi, Remo, *Vicarius Amoris,* Alcune fra le pagine sacaerdotali piu significativi del Ven. Giuseppe Quadrio, Rome, 2011

* Brancadoro, Giuseppe, *Notizia Istorica Dell'Origine. Della Ven Archiconfraternita Del Sacro Scapolare Di Maria SSMA Del Carmine,* Roma, 1843

* Calciuri, Nicola, O.C., *Vita Fractrum Del Sancto Monte Carmelo.* (+1466,) A Cura di P. Graziano di Santa Teresa O.C.D., Ephemerides Carmeliticae, Collegium Internationale O.C.D. de Urbe -1955

* Carmelites, *Mount Carmel, Abridgement of Carmel: Its' History and Spirit,* Burns, Oates, and Washbourne, London, 1923

* Carmelite Fathers and Tertiaries, *Take This Scapular*, The Carmelite Third Order Press, Chicago, 1949

* Ceroke, Rev. Christian P., O. Carm., *The Credibility of the Scapular Promises,* A Dissertation submitted to the Faculty of Sacred Theology of the Pontifical Athenaeum Angelicum in partial Fulfillment of the Requirements for the Degree of Doctor of Sacred Theology, Rome, 1950

* Cheron, John, O. Carm., *Privilegiati Scapularis et Visionis S. Simonis Stockii Vindiciae,* Bordeaux, 1642

Clarke, Father Hugh, O.Carm, *Mary and the Brown Scapular,* The Carmelite Charitable Trust, Faversham, Kent, 1994, 2002

Copsey, Richard, O. Carm., *Simon Stock and the Scapular Vision.* The Carmelite Scapular Today, *Journal of Ecclsiastical History,* Vol. 50, No. 4 October, 1999

* Cura Del Comitato Italiano, VII Centenario Dello Scapolario, Lo Scapolare. Roma, 195

* Di Liguori, St. Alphonsus, *The Glories of Mary,* Illinois, 1977

* Esteve, Henricus M., O. Carm., *De Valore Spirituali Devotionis S. Scapularis,* Romae, 1953

* Farrington, A.E., D.D., O.CC, *The Carmelites and the Brown Scapular,* Dublin, 1891

* Fesysus, Philibertus O. Carm., *Duplex Privilegium Sacri Scapularis Ordinis et Confraternitatis Gloriosae Virginis Mariae de Monte Carmelo Seu Responsio Ad Joannis Launoy Dissertationes,* Aix, 1645

* Fielding, Edwina, *Courage to Build Anew*, taken from the Newsletters of Fr. Malachi Lynch, Westminster, 1968 and 1989

* Forcadell, Augustinus M., O. Carm., *Commemoratio Solemnis Beatae Mariae Virginis De Monte Carmelo,* Roma: Cura Generalizia O. Carm, 1951

* Fox, Fr. Robert Francis J., *Rediscovering Fatima,* Indiana, 1982

* Gallo, Monsignor Francesco, Vescovo di Avellino, Brevi Notizie sulla Bolla Detta Sabbatina, Avelino, 1887

Gerusalemme, Maria Anastasia, O. Carm., *La Vesta Piu Bella.,* Roma, 2001

* Grassi, Simone P., Carmelitano, *Miracoli E Grazie Della Santissima Vergine Maria Del Carmine,* Firenze, MDCCXXVII (1727)

* Gray, Tim, *The Luminous Mysteries, Biblical Reflections on the Life of Christ,* Ohio, 2004

* Haffert, John M., *Mary in Her Scapular Promise,* The Scapular Press, New Jersey, 1942

* Haffert, John M. *Her Glorious Title; Our Lady of Mount Carmel, Star of the Sea,* Asbury, New Jersey, 1993

* Hunerman, Peter; Fastiggi, Robert; Nash, Anne Englund: *Heinrich Denzinger-Enchiridion symbolorum difinitionum et declarationum de rebus fidei et morum, (Compendium of Creeds, Definitions, and Declarations on Matters of Faith and Morals),* Latin-English, 43rd Edition, Ignatius Press, San Francisco, 2012

Bibliography

* I Carmelitani di Palermo, *Spighe Del Carmelo* Ricordo del VI Centenario del Privilegio Sabatino, Palermo, Carmine Maggiore, 1923

* Improta, Raffaele dello Scapolare del Carmine, *Alla Madre di Dio, Regina dell'Universo Gloria Letizia.*, 1956, Napoli

* Johnston, Francis, *Fatima: The Great Sign,* Rockford, Illinois, 1980

* Kaczmarek, Louis, *The Wonders She Performs,*Virginia, 1986

Launoy, John De, *Dissertatio Duplex, Una De Origine Et Confirmatione Privilegiati Scapularis Carmelitarum Altera De Visione Simonis Stochii,* Dissertatione Paris, 1642

Launoy, John De, *De Simonis Stocchi Viso, de Sabbatinae Bullae Privilegio et de Scapularis Carmelitarum Sodalitate Dissertationes V,* Paris, 1653

* Liguori, St. Alphonsus, *The Glories of Mary,* Illinois, 1868 (reprinted in 1977, Tan Books)

* Lynch, Killian, O. Carm., *Our Lady of Fatima and the Brown Scapular,* St. Albert's Press, Aylesford, England, 1956

* Lynch, E. K., O. Carm., *Your Brown Scapular,* Westminster, MD, 1950

* Magennis, P. E., Ord. Carm., *Scapulare B.M.V. de Monte Carmelo; Joannes Cheron Et Fragmentum Petri Swanyngtoni,* Roma, 1915

* Magennis, P. E. Ord. Carm., *The Sabbatine Privilege of the Scapular, 1322 - 1922 AD,* C.F. Connolly, New York, 1923.

* Magennis, P. E. Ord. Carm., *The Scapular and Some Critics,* Istituto Pio IX, Rome, 1914

* Magennis, P. E. Ord. Carm., *The Scapular Devotion, Origin. Legislation and Indulgences Attached to the Scapular,* Dublin, 1923

* Magennis, P. E., Ord. Carm., *The Scapular of Our Ladv of Mt. Carmel, Its History and Privileges,* Dublin, 1928

* Marini, Emilio, *Il Cuore Che Si Dona A Tutti,* Ave Maria Institute, New Jersey, 1972

* Mattei, P. S., *Ristretto Della Vita Di S. Simone Stock; Aggiunta L'Apologia Delle* Lettere Apostoliche di Giovanni XXII Dette Volgarmente La Bolla Sabatina, Roma, 1873

* McCaffrey, Rev. P. R., Ord. Carm., *The White Friars,* M. H. Gill and Son Ltd., Dublin, 192

* Miravalle, Dr. Mark, S.T.D., *Introduction to Mary,* Santa Barbara, California, 1993

Molinari, Giampiero, O.Carm, Antologia dello Scapolare, Roma, 2000

* Mombrum, Alfredo, *Vita di San Simone Stock,* Sienna, 1884

* Monk of St. Joseph Abbey, *The Scapular of Mount Carmel,* Traditions Monastique, France, 1998

* Monsignano, Eliseo Rev., *Bullarium Carmelitanum,* Volume I, 1715 and Volume II, 1718, Rome

* Most, Fr. William G., *Vatican II On the Church, Vatican II Marian Council,* St. Paul Publication, Ireland, 1972

* Most. Fr. William G., *Mary in Our Life,* P. J. Kennedy and Sons, First Edition, 1954

* North American Provincials of the Carmelite Orders, *The Scapular of Our Lady of Mount Carmel, Catechesis and Ritual,* Washington, DC, October 30, 2000

* P. Elisee De La Nativite, O.C.D., *Le Scapulaire du Carmel Etude Historique,* Editions Du Carmel, Paris, 1958

* P. Enrico Maria Del SS. Sacramento, Carmelitano Scalzo, *La Divozione Illustrata Dello Scapolare Della B.V Maria Del Carmine,* Oneglia, 1876

* P. Marie-Joseph du Sacre-Coeur, *Le Scapulaire de Notre-Dame du Mont Carmel est Authentique,* Avignon, 1928

* P. Teofano di S. Teresa Del Bambino Gesu O.C.D., *Rosario E Scapolare, La Madonna Li Vuole Uniti,* Roma, 1955

* Provincia Italiana dei Carmelitani, *Nella Famiglia di Maria,* I Papi e lo Scapolare del Carmine, Roma, 1996

* Raynaud, Theophilus, S. J. *Scapulare Parthenico Marianum Illustratum et Defensum,* Paris, 1654

* R. P. Archange de la Reine du Carmel, O.C.D., *Miracles du S. Scapulaire au XVIIme siècle,* Bruges, 1964

* R. P. Brocardo de Sta. Teresa, *Coleccion de Instrucciones,* Escapulario de N.S. Del Carmen, Vitoria, 1895

* R. P. F. Gabrielle Ferri da Bologna, *Sacre Instruttioni Per Beneficio de Divoti Del S. Scapolare Della Gloriosissima sempre Vergine Maria, Nostra Signora del Carmine,* Bologna, 1656

* Rushe, P. James, O. D. C., *Irish Ecclesiastical Record,* Fourth Series, Vol. XXIX, Dublin, 1911

Saggi, Ludovico, O. Carm., La Bolla Sabbatina. Roma, Institutum Carmelitanum, 1967

* Shouppe, Fr. F. X. S. J., *Purgatory,* Tan Books and Publishers, Rockford, Illinois, Oct. 11, 1893, reprinted, 1973

* Trochu, Abbe Francois, *Saint Bernadette Soubirous*, Tan Books, Rockford, Illinois, 1844-1879

* Valabek, Rev. Redemptus Maria, O. Carm., *Isidore Bakanja, Africa's Scapular Martyr,* Washington, New Jersey, 1990

* Ventimiglia, F. Mariano, *Historia Chronologica,* Neapli MDCCLXXIII (1773)

* Xiberta, Bartholomaeus F.M., O. Carm., *De Visione Sancti Simonis Stock,* Roma, 1950

* Ximenez, Rev. Josepho Alberto, *Bullarium Carmelitanum,* Volume III, Rome, 1768

* Indicates extended publications in defense of the authenticity of the visions of Our Blessed Mother to St. Simon Stock and to Pope John XXII and the traditional teachings of the Church on the Brown Scapular (n-signifies neutral)

ADDITIONAL REFERENCES

* Carmelite Fathers, Province of the Most Pure Heart of Mary, *A Little Manual for the Scapular Confraternity,* 1922

* Gunasekera, Friar Gabriel, O.C.D., *The Excellence and the Power of the Scapular of Our Blessed Mother of Carmel,* Belgium, 1989

* Huguet, R. P. Mariste, *La Devotion à Marie En Exemples ou Excellence Des Prieres Et Des Pratiques En L'Honneur De La Tres-Sainte Vierge,* Paris-Lyons, 1861

* Lynch, Most Rev. E. K., O. Carm., *Mary's Gift to Carmel,* Aylesford, Kent, 1955

* Lynch, P. Kiliano, Priore Generale Dei Carmelitani, *Fatima e lo Scapolare del Carmine,* Edizione L'Abitino Del Carmine, 1958

* Magennis, Most Rev. P. E., *The Life of St. Simon Stock,* New York City, 1920

* Magennis, Most Rev. P. E., Ord. Carm. Prior General, *Life of Saint Albert (Carmelite),* Dublin, 1929

* Mould, D.D.C. Pochin, B. Sc., Ph.D., *The Resurrection of Aylesford,* St. Albert's Press, Aylesford, 1957

* Serra, R. P. Fr. Joan Angel, *Libre de Miracles de Nostra Senyora del Carme,* 1701

The following *MARY* books may be used for additional reference and are edited by Fr. Howard Rafferty and published with Episcopal approbation by the Carmelite Fathers, Province of the most Pure Heart of Mary, Chicago, Illinois:

* *MARY, Sign of Consecration,* Fr. Howard Rafferty, O. Carm., Volume 17, No. 5, 1956, pp. 48-53

* *MARY, Scapulars,* Eamon Carroll, O. Carm, Volume Four, Number One, Summer, 1957 found in Volume 18, 1957, p. 1

* *MARY, The Scapular Question,* Fr. Bartholomew F. M. Xiberta, O. Carm., Volume 19, No. 4, 1958, p. 39

* *MARY, The First Monastery,* Elias of the Queen of Carmel, O.C.D., Volume 20, No. 1, 1959, pp. 51-56 *Pius XII and His Heritage to Carmel,* compiled by Brendan Hill, O. Carm., Volume 20, No. 4, 1959, pp. 51-64

* *MARY, Chasing Clouds,* Angela Hall, Volume 21, No. 1, 1960, pp. 55-58

* *MARY, Devotion of Humility and Hope,* Bartholomew M. Xiberta, Volume 22, Nos. 3 & 4, 1961, pp. 89-91

* *MARY, In the Spirit of Mary and Elias,* Bruno Borchert, O. Carm., Volume 23, No. 4, 1962, pp. 5-23

* *MARY, Sabbatine Privilege,* Gabriel N. Pausback, Volume 23, No. 3, 1962, pp. 61-63

* *MARY, Scapular Feastday,* Earmon Carroll, O. Carm., Volume 24, No. 3, 1963, pp. 45-51

* *MARY, My Scapular,* Ambrose F. Casey, O. Carm., Volume 25, No. 1, 1964, pp. 5-13

* *MARY, Brothers of our Lady,* Titus Brandsma, O. Carm., Volume 26, No. 2, 1965, pp. 17-22

PERIODICALS

* *Consecration,* (a pamphlet) Fr. Howard Rafferty, O. Carm., Chicago, 1953 *Mary,* Vol. 20, No. 2, March–April, England, 1959, *Mary's Garment,* p. 71

* *The Voice of the Pope,* Pope John XXIII, Referring to the day of his election…(taken from a Sermon of Pope John XXIII preached at St. Louis of France Church, Rome, February 18, 1959, for the closing of the Lourdes centenary year. *Mary,* Vol. 22, No. 1, Jan., Feb., 1961, p. 64

* *Pope Paul VI Speaks about the Scapular and the Rosary, Mary,* Vol. 26, No. 3, July, August, September, 1965, pp. 10, 11 n-National Geographic, October, 1983

* *Don't forget Mary* - Cardinal Ratzinger (Pope Benedict XVI) The Ratzinger Report, Ignatius Press, 1985

* Our Sunday Visitor, *Unearthing a Buried Treasure of the Church,* Fr. Charles M Mangan, February 24, 1991

* Our Sunday Visitor, *Descended into Hell?* Monsignor M. Francis Mannion, October 30, 2011

* *New Saint Gives Joy to the Pope,* VOICE of the Sacred Hearts, John Haffert, July - August 1994

* *Blessed Isidore Bakanja,* The Annals of St. Anne de Beaupre/ Peter Dwan , July - August 1998 pp. 205, 206

St. Simon Stock: *The Scapular Vision and the Brown Scapular Devotion,* Bede Edwards, an article from the Carmelite Digest, Vol. 16, No. 3, Summer, 2001

* *Cries from a Suffering Soul, The Housetops,* A Quarterly Magazine, St. Benedict Center, 2005

* *Don Orione - Oggi,* n. 8 Settembre, 2006

*The Scapular, Re-appropriating an ancient symbol for a modern world-*a talk given at Ayelsford, Patrick Thomas McMahon, O. Carm, June 3, 1999

Garment of Grace; A Historical Appreciation of the Carmelite Scapular, Patrick Thomas McMahon, O. Carm., Carmel in the World, Vol. XLIII, N. 3, Roma, 2004

* *Scapular Testimonial,* SOUL Magazine, July-August, 2001

* *La Repubblica,* Silvano Mazzochi, 15 maggio, 1981

* Catholic Voice, *On Devotion to Our Lady of Mount Carmel, July 16,* Dr. William A. Thomas, Ph.D., Issue 112, Ireland, July 7, 2013

ONLINE PERIODICALS

* *The Rambler,* A Catholic Journal and Review, New Series, Vol. V, London, 1856

* *The Month,* "The Catholic Dictionary and the Brown Scapular," The Month, A Catholic Magazine and Review, Vol. LVIII, Sept. - Dec, 1886, London, No. 269 -November

* *Irish Ecclesiastical Record,* Vol. VIII, Third Series, John E. Bartley, O.C.C., Dublin, January, 1887

Irish Ecclesiastical Record, Vol. XV, January to June, Fourth Series, Dublin, 1904

Irish Ecclesiastical Record, Vol. XVI, July to December, Fourth Series, Dublin, 1904

* *Irish Ecclesiastical Record,* Vol. XXIX, Fourth Series, James P. Rushe, O.D.C., January-June, Dublin, 1911

* *The Ecclesiastical Review;* A Monthly Publication for the Clergy, Vol. LVI, Philadelphia, 1917

* *The American Ecclesiastical Review,* "The Sabbatine Privilege," Fr. Gabriel Pausback, Vol. CIX, July, 1943

The Carmelite Scapular Today, Carmelites.org; based on an article written by Richard Copsey, O.Carm, in the "Journal of Ecclesiastical History," Vol. 50, No. 4, October, 1999

* Mother of All Peoples: *Mary, Spiritual Mother and Mediatrix,* Saturday, January 28, 2006

* *A Brown Scapular of the Servant of God, John Paul II,* Carmel's Own: Pope John Paul II Scapular, the Declaration of Authenticity was signed on October 6, 2007

* *Did St. Mary Magdelene come to Provence,* Brother Thomas of Our Lady of Perpetual Help," #81, June, 2009

* *Benedict XVI to send Our Lady of Mt. Carmel statue to earthquake-stricken Chile,* Catholic News Agency, March 22, 2010

* Rome Reports, T.V. News Agency: *Who was St. Thomas Aquinas?* Benedict XVI Explains, 1/28/2011

* *On Our Good and Great Father,* (after the Angelus), Zenit, July 17, 2011

* Catholic Caucus: Sunday Mass Readings 07-01-12; Thirteenth Sunday

* Fr. William Most, *The Brown Scapular*

A Catechisis on the Brown Scapular, *Carmelitana Collection,* A Specialized Library in Carmelite Studies, A private Library belonging to the Carmelite Province of the Most Pure Heart of Mary, Whitefriars Hall, Washington, D.C.

n-Garments of Grace; A Garment of Innocence; *In the Light of the Cross*

* *The Miracle Hunter*: Marian Apparitions – Our Lady of Mount Carmel

* Father Callan's Commentary on Romans 13: 11-14, for the First Sunday of Advent

* *Most Theological Collection,* , Fr. William G. Most, A Basic Catholic Catechism, Part XVII, Prayer: Prayer in General: The Our Father and the Hail Mary

* *The Carmelite Review,* Vol. II, N. 7, July, 1894

* *The Carmelite Review,* Vol. X, N. 5, May, 1901

* *The Carmelite Review,* Vol. X, N. 3, March, 1902

* *The Carmelite Review,* Vol. X, N. 5, May, 1902

* *The Carmelite Review,* Vol. X, N. 6, June, 1902

* *The Carmelite Review,* Vol. X, N. 8, August, 1902

* *The Carmelite Review,* Vol. X, N. 10, October, 1902

CITOC News – Order of the Brothers of the Most Blessed Virgin Mary of Mount Carmel: St. Simon Stock, Religious (M), Thursday, May 16, 2013

CITOC News, No. 4, October-December 2003, Closure of the Diocesan Process of Canonization of Fr. Bartolome Fanti M. Xiberta, O. Carm.

CITOC No. 3, July-September 2007, Carmelite Presence at the Second Vatican Council

The British Province of Carmelite Friars-Heritage and Archive, Origins of the Carmelite Order, 2013

The Carmelitana Collection, A Catechesis on the Brown Scapular, 2008

The Catholic Herald.co.uk: ST. SIMON STOCK-a newspaper article written by Fr. Joachim Smet, O. Carm., published in the Catholic Herald on September 29, 1950

Carmelite Digest, Vol. 16, No. 8, Summer, 2001

The Carmelite Scapular: History and Devotion, Fr. Paul D'Souza, O.C.D., Institute of Philosophy, Vijayanagar, Bangalore, India

National Catholic Register, "The Brown Scapular Still Sanctifies Souls," Joseph Pronechen, July 13-19, 2008 Issue

* *The Sacramentals of the Catholic Church*, Rev. A. A. Lambing, L.L.D., Benzinger Brothers, Printers to the Holy Apostolic See, New York, Cincinnati, Chicago, 1892

DICTIONARIES

The Catholic Dictionary, William E. Addis and Thomas Arnold, M. A, New York, 1887, 1898, Scapular

Our Sunday Visitors Catholic Dictionary, Reverend Peter M. J. Stravinskas, PhD., S. T. L., 1994

ENCYCLOPEDIAS

Britannica Online Encyclopedia – Blessed (Pope) Gregory X

OSV's Encyclopedia of Catholic History, Matthew Bunson, D. Min., Indiana, 1995, 2004

New Catholic Encyclopedia/Highbeam Research – Jean de Launoy

Catholic Encyclopedia, new advent.org

The Catholic Encyclopedia, McGraw-Hill, 1965

Our Sunday Visitor's Catholic Encyclopedia, Reverend Peter M. J. Sstravinskas, Ph.D., S.T.L, Our Sunday Visitor, 1994

Enciclopedia Cattolica, Citta del Vaticano, Volume 10, Firenze, Italia, 1953

Nation Master Encyclopedia

OSSERVATORE ROMANO

* 18, luglio, 1917, Papa Benedetto XV, *Il Pontificio Seminario Romano Maggiore e Minore dal Santo Padre*

* 28 luglio, 1917, Papa Benedetto XV, *I Terziani Carmelitani della Traspontina ricevuti in audienza del Santo Padre*

* venerdi, 20, febbraio, 1959, Papa Giovanni XXIII, *Il Sommo Pontefice Giovanni XXIII visita la chiesa e le istituzioni di S. Luigi dei Francesi*

* domenica 16 luglio, 1961, Papa Giovanni XXIII, La Chiesa sempre presente a tutte le necessita`della famiglia umana

* 22-23 marzo, 1965, Papa Paolo VI, *Voti augurali di Paolo VI per il Congresso Mariologico e Mariano in Santo Domingo*

* lunedi-martedi 25-26 luglio 1988, Papa Giovanni Paolo II, *La Vergine Madre di Dio Flos Carmeli possiede la bellezza di tutte le virtù*

* lunedi - martedi, 30-31 maggio, 2005: Papa Benedetto XVI, *Accogliamo Gesu alla Scuola di Maria, Donna Eucaristica*

* lunedi-martedi 7-8 Novembre, 2005, *La prima session del Tribunale del processo rogatorio per la Causa di beatificazione e canonizzazione del servo di Dio Giovanni Paolo II*

* 16, July 2006, Pope Benedict XVI, *Queen of Carmel, Queen of Peace*

* 15, March, 2012, Pope Benedict XVI, General Audience, *Without Mary the Church does not exist*

*PAPAL DOCUMENTS

Bull of Pope John XXII: *Sacritissimo uti culmine,* March 3, 1322 (The Sabbatine Bull)

Bull of Pope Alexander V: *Tenorem cujusdam privilegii,* (Bull contains and confirms the Sabbatine Bull of Pope John XXII), December 7, 1409)

Bull of Pope Clement VII: *Ex Clementi Sedis Apostolicae,* August 12, 1530 in which (Clement VII confirms the Bull of John XXII)

Bull of Paul III: *Provisionis nostre,* dated November 3, 1534

Bull of Pope Pius V: *Superna dispositione,* dated February 18, 1566

Bull of Pope Gregory XIII, *Ut laudes,* dated September 18, 1577

Decree of the Sabbatine Privilege, Pope Paul V, of the Holy Roman

Bibliography

and Universal Inquisition, "Privilegium Bullae Sabbitinae," January 20, 1613; February 15, 1613

Sommario dell'indulgenze, favori e grazie concesse da molti Sommi Pontifici si à Religiosi, e Confratelli della Madonna del Carmine, come` à tutti i Fedeli, che visitaranno le Chiese dell'istess'Ordine, June 27, 1673

Apost. Const., Pope Benedict XIV, *Nuper ad Nos,* March 16, 1743

Apost. Const., Pope Pius VIII, *Praesentissimum sane,* March 3, 1830

Treatise, Pope Benedict XIV, *De Servorum Dei Beatificatione,* Prato: (Collection) printed in 1841

Pope Benedict XIV, De Festis Domini Jesu Christi et Beatae Mariae Virginis, Prato, printed in 1843

Encyclical, Pope Pius IX, *Ubi Primum,* February 2, 1849

Encyclical, Pope Pius IX: *Ineffabillis Deus,* December 8, 1854

Elenchus facultatum et gratiarum spiritualium quibus potitor Congregatio SS. Redemptoris, Sedis Apostolicae concessionibus et aliorum Ordinum communicationibus, 1860

Encyclical, Pope Pius IX, *Quanta Cura,* December 8, 1864

Syllabus of Pius IX: A Collection of Errors Proscribed in Diverse Documents of Pius IX, Published December 8, 1864, "Propositions of the Syllabus," 2922, #22

Ritus ad Confraternitatem B.M.V. de Monte Carmelo, "Privilegium, vulgo dictum *Sabbatinum*...December 1, 1866

Brief, Pope Pius IX, *Bref de S. S. Pie IX a A. Monbrun,* October 23rd, 1869

Decretum, Pope Leo XIII, EX S. CONGREG. INDULGENTIARUM: *Ordinis Carmelitarum antiquae,* 27, April, 1887

Encyclical, Pope Leo XIII, *Vi è ben noto,* On the Rosary and Public Life, September 20, 1887

Encyclical, Pope Leo XIII, *Octobri Mense,* September 22, 1891

Apostolic Letter, Pope Leo XIII: *Ad Perpetuam Rei Memoriam,* May 16, 1892

Encyclical, Pope Leo XIII, *Magnae Dei Matris,* September 8, 1892

Encyclical, Pope Leo XIII: *Jucunda semper,* September 8, 1894

Encyclical, Pope Leo XIII: *Fidentem Piumque,* September 20, 1896 (Close to the Mediator)

Encyclical, Pope Leo XIII: *Diuturni temporis spatium,* September 5, 1898, *ASS* 31, 1898, 146

Apostolic Letter, Pope Leo XIII, *Parta humano generi,* September 8, 1901, *ASS* 34, 1901, 195

CARMELITARUM ANTIQUAE OBSERVANTIAE: DECRETUM, quo consuetude Carmelitarum Missam de B Virgine canendi in Sabbatis confimatur, A. S. S., Volume XXXV, December 13, 1902

Encyclical, Pope Pius X: *Ad diem illum laetissimum,* February 2, 1904

Encyclical, Pope Pius X: *Pascendi Dominici Gregis,* July, 1907

Decree of the Holy Office, Pope St. Pius X: *A.A.S., III* p. 23, December 16, 1910 (Scapular Medal)

Declaration, Pope St. Pius X: Motu-Propio *Sacrorum Antistitum,* December 17, 1910

Epistle, Pope Benedict XV, *Decessorem nostrum,* April 19, 1915 (Mediatrix of Peace)

Allocution: Pope Benedict XV, *To the Consistory,* December 24, 1915

Letter, 27 Aprile, 1915, Pope Benedict XV: to Cardinal P. Gasparri, May 5, 1917 *Queen of Peace* (The Pope's efforts to stop the War)

Allocution, Pope Benedict XV: *To the Seminarians of Rome,* (On the Scapular of the Virgin of Carmel), July 17, 1917

Allocution, Pope Benedict XV: *To the Third Order Carmelites,* July 28, 1917

Letter, Pope Pius XI: *Petis tu quidem,* March 18, 1922, (Sixth Centenary of the Sabbatine Privilege)

Letter, Pope Pius XI, *Cum valde,* to Cardinal Esteban, February 20, 1929

Allocution, Pope Pius XI: *To pilgrims from Vicenza,* November 30, 1933 ("The Coredemptrix")

R.M., Pope Pius XII: *On the Occasion of the Coronation of the statue of Our Lady of Fatima,* May 13, 1946

R.M., Pope Pius XII, *to the National Marian Congress of Columbia,* (The Safety of Society), July 19, 1946

Letter, Pope Pius XII: *Neminem profecto* February 11, 1950, The Scapular of Mt. Carmel: "To the Superior General of the Carmelites"

Apostolic Constitution of Pope Pius XII: *Munificentissimus Deus,* Defining the Dogma of the Assumption, November 1, 1950

Pope Pius XII, "Discourses and Radio Broadcasts," Vol. 12 (1950-51)

Epistulae, Pope Pius XII, to Fr. Killian Lynch, Superior General of the Orders of the Friars of the Blessed Virgin Mary of Mt. Carmel *On the Seventh Centenary of the Institution of the Sacred Carmelite Scapular,*

Bibliography

June 30, 1951, *A.A.S.*, 43, Series II, Vol. 18

Letter, Pope Pius XII, *Septimo Expleto Saeculo,* July 6, 1951

Encyclical, Pope Pius XII, *Ingruentium Malorum,* September 15, 1951

Letter, Pope Pius XII, Naming Our Lady of Mount Carmel patroness of the city of Purchena in Spain, October 29, 1951

Apostolic Letter, Pope Pius XII, *Sacro vergente anno,* to the People of Russia, July 7, 1952

Pope Pius XII: Encycl.: *Ad coeli Reginam,* October 11, 1954

Pope Pius XII: R.M. "To the International Mariological Congress," October 24, 1954

Letter, Pope Pius XII, to the Third Order of Discalced Carmelites at Malabar, India, October 30, 1955 Letter, Pope Pius XII, *Ex obsequentissimis litteris,* On the occasion of the International Third Order Congress held at Fatima in August 1957, and in congratulations on the opening of the new retreat house there, April 3, 1957

Pope Pius XII: "To the Carmelite Pilgrims at Lourdes, July 16, 1958, the Feast of Our Lady of Mt. Carmel, on the occasion of the centenary of the last apparition of Our Lady of Lourdes, July 16, 1858. " (July 2, 1958)

Bl. Pope John XXIII: Allocution: at St. Mary Major, February 15, 1959, *Rome and Lourdes*

Pope John XXIII, A.A.S., 51, Series III, Vol. I: Commentarium Officiale: "Quam habuit in Ecclesia S. Ludovici, Francorum Regis, cum primum eam invisit, adstantibus Emis Patribus Cardinalibus, Praelatis praeclarisque Viris e Gallica Natione." Spoke of Lourdes, and John XXII, as the Father of the Sabbatine Privilege, Feb. 18, 1959

Pope Paul VI, Dogmatic Constitution on the Church: *Lumen Gentium,* November 21, 1964

Pope Paul VI, Letter: *In Dominica Republicana,* February 2, 1965, (appointing Cardinal Silva of Santiago, Chile, papal legate to the Mariological and Marian Congresses held in Santo Domingo, March, 1965.)

Apostolic Exhortation, Pope Paul VI, *Signum Magnum,* May 13, 1967

Pope Paul VI: Apostolic Exhortation: *Marialus Cultis* - of His Holiness Paul PP VI to all the Bishops having peace and communion with the Apostolic See, February 2, 1974.

Pope John Paul II, Homily on the Anniversary of the Apparitions at Fatima, Portugal, May 13, 1982, cf. *L'Osservatore Romano,* July 17, 1982

Pope John Paul II, Encyclical Letter: *Redemptoris Mater,* March 25, 1987

Pope John Paul II, General Audience: *Mary has a Universal Spiritual Motherhood,* Wednesday, 24 September, 1997

Pope John Paul II, General Audience: *We can count on Mary's Intercession,* Wednesday, 5, November, 1997

Pope John Paul II, Angelus: *Feast of Our Lady of Mount Carmel,* Sunday, July 16, 2000

Pope John Paul II, Letter: "On the occasion of the 750th anniversary of the Bestowal of the Scapular of Mount Carmel," March 25, 2001. Pope John Paul II, Message, "To the Order of the Brothers of the Blessed Virgin Mary of Mt. Carmel," September 8, 2001

Pope John Paul II, Message: "For the 550th Anniversary of the Addition of the Cloistered Nuns and the Third Order of the Laity to the Carmelite Order," October 7, 2002

Pope John Paul II: Apostolic Letter: *Rosarium Virginis Mariae* of the Supreme Pontiff John Paul II to the Bishops, Clergy and Faithful, on the Most Holy Rosary, October 16, 2002

Pope Benedict XVI, Angelus, Esplanade of Marisabella, Sunday, May 29, 2005, (At the School of Mary, Woman of the Eucharist)

Pope Benedict XVI, Address of His Holiness Benedict XVI During The Prayer Meeting in the Vatican Gardens for the conclusion of the Marian Month of May, Tuesday, May 31, 2005 (In the Mystery of the Visitation, Mary was the first Eucharistic Procession)

Pope Benedict XVI: *Angelus, "Feast of Our Lady of Mt. Carmel,"* Les Combes Aosta Valley, Sunday, July 16, 2006

Homily, Pope Benedict XVI, *Canonization Mass of Fr. Antonio de Sant'Ana Galvao, O.F.M.,* Brazil, May 11, 2007

Pope Benedict XVI, *Letter*: To The Prior General of the Order of the Friars of the Blessed Virgin Of Mount Carmel on the Occasion of the Eighth Centenary of the "Formula Vitae," August 14, 2007

Pope Benedict XVI, Homily, "Pastoral Visit to the Pontifical Shrine of Pompeii," October 19, 2008

Pope Benedict XVI, *Angelus*, to the Polish Speaking pilgrims, Castel Gondolfo, July 17, 2011, *Pope Benedict XVI Praises Wearing the Scapular*

Pope Benedict XVI: General Audience, March 14, 2012, Vatican Radio

Pope Benedict XVI: *Message* of His Holiness Benedict XVI to the Bishop of Avila (Spain) *on the Occasion of the 450th Anniversary of the Monastery of San Jose in Avila and the Beginning of the Reform of Carmel,* July 16, 2012

Pope Benedict XVI: *Epistula Data Sigismundo Zimowski Nominato*

Misso Extraordinario Ad Celebrationes XXI Diei Mundialis Infirmorum, (*Letter* of Pope Benedict XVI designating Archbishop Zygmunt Simowski, President of the Pontifical Council for Health Pastoral Care), Rome, January 10, 2013 [in which His Holiness invokes Mary as the "Mediatrix of All Graces."]

Pope Benedict XVI: *Letter of the (Carmelite) Prior General to His Holiness Benedict XVI,* Rome, 12 February, 2013

Congregation for Divine Worship and the Discipline of Sacraments; Magisterial Documents

* *The Decree of the Sabbatine Privilege,* Pope Paul V, January 20, 1613 (1)

* La Santa Messa Della Madonna Del Carmine, *La S. Messa Del 16 Luglio e La Messa Sabatina.* Collana VII Centenario dello Scapolare, N. 2, Biblioteca Carmelitana, Collegio di Sant'Alberto, Roma

* *Dogmatic Constitution* on the Church, *Lumen Gentium,* Solemnly Promulgated by His Holiness, Pope Paul VI, November 21, 1964

* *Apostolic Constitution* of Pope Paul VI, *Indulgentiarum Doctrina,* Whereby the Revision of Sacred Indulgences is Promulgated, January 1, 1967

* National Conference of Catholic Bishops, *Behold Your Mother,* Woman of Faith, United States Catholic Conference, 1973

* *Directory on Popular Piety and the Liturgy, Principles and Guidelines*; (Veneration of the Holy Mother of God) Vatican City, December, 2001

* See "Papal Documents" on the preceding pages of this section.

1   The case of the Privilege was presented to the Holy Office under Pope Paul V, decided on January 20, 1613, and confirmed by the Supreme Pontiff in February, 1613. This decision really gives the last official judgment of Holy Church in the matter and is still quoted today, after more than (four) hundred years, as the surely solid foundation for our belief in the Sabbatine Privilege. Succeeding Popes also, in decrees and statements have fostered the Sabbatine Privilege. (*MARY, Sabbatine Privilege,* Vol. 23, No. 3, 1962, pp. 61-63)

See also Chapter 2, The Sabbatine Bull / Sabbatine Privilege in this book

ONLINE BOOKS

The Romish Doctrine of the Immaculate Conception. Dr. Edward Preuss, Edinburgh, 1867

* *History of the Catholic Church from the Renaissance to the French Revolution,* Rev. James MacCaffrey, Dublin, 1914

n-*The Christian Remembrancer,* Volume 23, January to June, William Scott, Francis Garden, James Bowling Mozley, London, 1852

n-*Studies in Hiberno-Latin Literature* - google books, Mario Esposito, Michael M. Gorman, Ashgate Pub. Ltd., 2006, p. 138, index p. 8 - Jean de Launoy

* *The Life of Joan of Arc,* Anatole France, London, New York, 1909

* *The Sacramentals of the Holy Catholic Church,* or Flowers from the Garden of the Liturgy, Rev. William J. Barry, London, 1879

n-*Curiosities of Literature; First Series,* Isaac D'Israeli, New York, 1766-1848, "Secret History of Authors Who Have Ruined their Booksellers"

n-*Irish Historical Studies:* Vol. 10, "The Patrician Problem, and a Possible Solution," Mario Esposito, 1956-1957

* *A Short Treatise on the Antiquity, Institution, Excellency, Indulgences, privileges, etc., of the ancient Confraternity of Our Blessed Lady of Mount Carmel, called the Scapular,* The Very Rev. R. J. Colgan, D.D., S.M.T., Perpetual Procurator-General of the Grand Carmelite Order, Philadelphia, the 1850s

* *Our Lady of Fatima's Peace Plan from Heaven,* 1950, Abbey Press

ONLINE NEWS AGENCIES

Zenit, Benedict XVI, *Angelus,* Message on Our Lady of Mount Carmel, July 16, 2006

EWTN News, "Pope Blesses a Statue of St. Luigi Orione," June 25, 2008

Zenit, "Brown Scapular: A Silent Devotion," Disc. Carm., Fr. Kieran Kavanaugh July 16, 2008

Catholic News Agency, "Benedict XVI to send Our Lady of Mt. Carmel Statue to Earthquake-stricken Chile," March 22, 2010

Zenit, Benedict XVI, "Pontiff Praises wearing the Scapular," July 17, 2011, Castel Gandolfo, Italy

Catholic News Service: "Vatican II's call for renewal did not break with tradition, Pope says," Pope Benedict XVI, October 12, 2012

Catholic News Service: Misreading of Vatican II led to "collapse in

Bibliography

Mariana Devotion, Studies," Fr. James Phalen, President of the Mariological Society of America, September 7, 2012;

(* indicates in defense, n signifies neutral)

WEBSITES

* www.ewtn.com/saintsholy/saints/Q/queenshipofmary.asp

www.agapebiblestudy.com/documents/Church_History_Menu. php The Virgin Mary's Role in Salvation History

* www.ourladyswarriors.org/articles/mother.htm

n-http://www.newworldencyclopedia.org/entry/Pope_ Telesphorus

n-http://www.highbeam.com/doc/1G2-3407706500.html

* www.zenit.org/article-33087?l=english "On Our Good and Great Father"

www.vatican.va/holy_father/benedict_xvi/angelus/2006/ documents/hf_ben-xvi_ang_20060716_en. html

* www.catholicnewsagency.com/news/benedict_xvi_to_send_our_ lady_of_mt._carmel_statue _ to_earthquake-stricken_chile/

nwww.britannica.com/EBchecked/topic/640848/Western-Schism

www.infoplease.com/cc6/society/A0820065.html

* http: //catholicity. el core. net/MacCaffrey/HCCRFR_TOC. html

* http://www.catholicnewsagency.com/resource.php?n=977

* http://catholicity.elcore.net/MacCaffrey/HCCRFRl_Chapter07a. html

* http://www.crc-internet.org/CCR/2009/82-Mary-Magdelene php

www.carmelites.org/review/march2001/marchapril2001_9.pdf

* www.catholictradition.org/mary/scapular-text.htm

* www.saintisidore.org/religious-info/brown-scapular.htm

www.scribd.com/doc/23480406/apparitions-of-st-bernadette-soubirous

* http://fountainofelias.blogspot.com/2009/08/god-france-and-marguerite.html

* www, ourgardenofcarmel. org/carmspecial.html

* http://www.freebrownscapular.com/brown_scapular_miracles. html

* http://onbehalfofall.Org/2009/11/17/st-constantine-and-the-triumph-of-iconography

* http://www.zenit.org/article-33093? l=english

* http://traditionalromancatholicism.org/TheBrownScapular.html (research)

http://carmelitanacollection.com/catechisis.php

n-http://www.bing.com/Dictionary/search?q=define+perception&qpvt=m

n-http://ecoggins.hubpages.com/hub/Perception-is-an-Individuals-Self-Deception

n-http://thinkexist.com/quotes/gustave_flaubert

* http://www.indefenseofthecross.com/Lourdes.htm

n-http://www.seekingtruth.co.uk/truth.htm

* http://www.vatican.va/roman_curia/congregations/ccdds/documents/re_con_ccds_doc_2002

* http://biblecommenter.com/1_samuel/18-4.htm

* http://www.agapebiblestudy.com/genesis/LESSON_16.htm

* catholicity@elcore.net

* http://www.thesacredpages.com/2008/12/christmas-star.html

* www.drbo.org/chapter/01003.htm

* www.oecumene.radiovaticana.org/EN1/articolo.asp?c=571235

* www.osv.com/tabid/7621/itemid/8567/Msgr-M-Francis-Mannion

* http://www.evangelicaloutreach.org/official.htm

* http://www.therealpresence.org/archives/Mariology/Mariology_030.htm

* http://www.catholicreference.net/index.cfm

* http://catholicharboroffaithandmorals.com.baptism.html

* http://www.marypages.com/DonBoscoEng.htm

 http://ocarm.org/en/content/ocarm/shield

* www.thetruthcoded.org/au/Ignatius-of-Antioch.php

* http://www.ewtn.com/library/MARY/SIMONSTO.HTM

* www.catholictradition.org/mary/scapular7.htm

* www.saintisidore.org/religious-info/brown-scapular.htm

* www.roman-catholic-saints.com/blessed-gregory-x.html

* www.ewtn.com/library/scriptur/scapular.txt

* http://traditionalromancatholicism.org/TheBrownScapular.html (under reconstruction)

* http://www.catholicdoors.com/courses/baptism.htm

* http://www.opusangelorum.org/English/Sacramentals.html

* http://www.fisheaters.com/sacramentalsintro.html

Bibliography

* http://www.30giorni.it/articoli_ed_8513_l3.htm

* www.ourladyswarriors.org/abtmary.htm

n www.thefriars.org.uk/history.htm

* www.catholictradition.org/Mary/purgatory3.htm

* www.twoheartsdesign.com/jmh_obit.html

* www.freerepublic.com/focus/f-religion/2997871/posts

* http://www.catholicnews.com/data/stories/cns/1203755.htm

* http://www.catholicnews.com/data/stories/cns/1204312.htm

* http://www.evangelicaloutreach.org/official.htm

* www.unitypublishing.com/Apparitions/NunoCanon.htm

* http://www.marypages.com/DonBoscoEng.htm

* www.britannica.com/.../Saint-John-Bosco

* www.ewtn.com/expert/answers/apparitions.htm

* onbehalfofall.org/2013/02/06constantine-and-the-triumph-of-iconography

* www.carmelites.org/review/march2001/marchapril2001_9.pdf p. 2

* www.veritasbible.com/drb/compare/haydock/Genesis_3

* www.oocities.org/timothyc1/peace_plan.html

Search Engines: Bing, Google

EPILOGUE

A very dear friend and Spiritual Director for "A Study of the Scapular Devotion of Our Lady of Mount Carmel," Archbishop Emeritus, Dom Vitorio` Pavanello, former Metropolitan Archbishop of the Diocese of Campo Grande, Brazil, recently recounted to the author the beautiful story of the "Bells and the Drums." "When he hears the Bells," he said, "it raises his heart and mind to the Heavenly Court, and he is drawn to the lovely contemplation of the Mother of God, reciting the Angelus with love and devotion to the Queen of Heaven. Then there are the drums; the drums are empty, they only make noise, they draw your mind and heart, not to God, but to others, and to the things of this world."

****

"When the promises of the Virgin Mary are removed from the scapular, the bells no longer ring, it is no longer celestial, the bells are gone, it becomes terrestrial and the heart is drawn to the attractions of the world, and only the drums remain."

About the Author

For over 750 years, the Brown Scapular of Our Lady of Mt. Carmel has been one of the most treasured and ancient sacramentals in the history of the Church. Beginning with the Prophet Elias on Mt. Carmel in Palestine, its origins are Divine, its message is clear and its promise is everlasting.

As a young child at the age of four, I was introduced to Our Lady through "Our Mother of Perpetual Help" devotions at our parish. I learned to love Our Heavenly Mother through the example of great devotion my own beloved earthly mother accorded the Blessed Virgin Mary. An immigrant from the Island of Sicily, she survived the atrocities of World War II and courageously crossed the ocean into an unknown world wrapped in the loving arms of Our Lady's Scapular for protection, clutching her precious Rosary in her hands and with a confidence in Our Lord and His Holy Mother, that she would be guided safely to a new land to begin a new life for her family. The Rosary became a part of my daily life and at the age of seven, I was enrolled in the Brown Scapular on the eve of my First Holy Communion, understanding that when worn with faith, it would be my protection against the fires of Hell at the moment of death.

Now, as an adult and a consecrated Marian Catechist, a mother of six children and a grandmother of twenty beautiful grandchildren, the Brown Scapular has taken on a new and greater meaning, with a clearer and deeper understanding. First and foremost, the Brown Scapular is an external sign of Consecration to the Immaculate Heart of Mary, my Queen and my Mother. It is a symbol of the bond of love between a Mother and her child, a sign of Mary's protection against the perils of this world. It was through this inspiring research on the Scapular of Carmel, that I grew deeper in love with Our Blessed Mother. In 2015, under the guidance of my Spiritual Director, I became founder of the Association of the Faithful entitled: "A Call to Mary" – a lay organization dedicated to spreading the Message of Fatima: The Rosary and the Brown Scapular, including Devotion to Mary's Immaculate Heart and educating the faithful on the teachings of the Church in imitation of Our Lady of Fatima.

The Brown Scapular of Our Lady of Mount Carmel is an invitation from Our Lady to gather under her "Special Mantle," given the knowledge that as I wear her Scapular, I am always in her mind and heart. She loves me as her child and I love her as my dearest Mother.

Finally it is a visible, tangible sign of her constant, invisible, never-ending mediation for us. It is a powerful means of grace, as the prayers of Mary, "Mediatrix of All Graces," are always interceding for our eternal salvation.

The Scapular has taken on a greater meaning for me now, through a deeper understanding of this beautiful Devotion. Through the Scapular and the Rosary, I have obtained a greater love for Our Blessed Mother.

How privileged we are, not only to be called sons and daughters of Mary, Queen of the Most High, but to become her "special children" by adoption, by gathering under the "mantle of her protection" and wearing the visible sign of her love and mediation, the Brown Scapular.

She has given us as a true and loving mother, the means for peace in our life, peace in our heart and the gift of her loving protection of body and soul, with the promise of eternal salvation. We need only respond to her gracious invitation.

Rosalia Vitale Kehrig,
A Call to Mary